Marketing Today

FOURTH EDITION

Gordon Oliver
University of Portsmouth

PRENTICE HALL
LONDON • NEW YORK • TORONTO • SYDNEY • TOKYO • SINGAPORE
MADRID • MEXICO CITY • MUNICH

First published 1980
This edition published 1995 by
Prentice Hall
A Pearson Education Company
Edinburgh Gate,
Harlow,
Essex, CM20 2JE, England

Typeset in 10½ on 12 pt Garamond by
Mathematical Composition Setters Ltd, Salisbury

Printed and bound in Great Britain by
T. J. International Ltd.

Library of Congress Cataloguing in Publication Data

Oliver, Gordon, 1941–
    Marketing today / Gordon Oliver – 4th ed.
        p.   cm.
    Includes bibliographical references and index.
    ISBN 0-13-203001-2
        1. Marketing.   I. Title
HF5415.05544   1995
    658.8–dc20   94-45430
                                                        CIP

British Library Cataloguing in Publication Data

A catalogue record for this book is available from the British Library

ISBN 0-13-203001-2

---

    5   6   7   01   00   99

Contents

Preface

This introductory text is designed particularly for undergraduate and diploma students. It offers a broad, contemporary foundation in the concepts and techniques required for an understanding of marketing processes. It differs from other texts in terms of both the balance and presentation of the material, as well as in the assumptions made about the reader's background knowledge.

More emphasis than normal is given to the behavioural bases of consumer choice decisions. There are two reasons for this. First, it reflects the fact that research into buyer behaviour has been one of the most dynamic areas in marketing thought in recent years. Second, it stems from the belief that a sound grasp of this background is fundamental for the appreciation of the problems in the development of marketing strategy. None the less, the bulk of the book concerns the planning of the organisation's marketing activity.

All textbooks necessarily make assumptions about the academic background of their readers. Here it is assumed that the student is following a course which is not restricted just to marketing. Previous and parallel courses in economics accounting, quantitative methods and behavioural studies are typically taken. Since marketing draws heavily from these disciplines the problem is one of how much to assume about knowledge from these areas. The premise in this book is that the reader is acquainted with basic economics and accounting, and has some elementary statistical skills. However, with behavioural studies the position is more complicated because marketing makes special demands. It has attached great significance to some theories and little to others. Moreover, the application of behavioural theories in marketing is slanted towards choice behaviour. Thus there is some reiteration of concepts with which the reader may already be familiar, although the marketing context directs and refines them. The criterion for the inclusion of material from the basic disciplines has been whether or not there is likely to be a different treatment of that material in a marketing course. Wherever possible, straight recapitulation has been avoided.

The book's framework can be gauged from the contents pages, but this structure need not be followed dogmatically. Courses differ in their ordering of the major marketing topics, and to accommodate this the ordering of the chapters can be altered without interfering with the flow. It might be useful to consider the chapter on developing marketing strategy (Chapter 9) immediately after the opening chapter. Segmentation and positioning, marketing research and forecasting could be studied earlier or later than they appear. Pricing could be introduced after product planning, as could the chapters on marketing channels.

At the end of each chapter there are a number of questions which can form the basis for reviewing the ideas presented and for extending the discussion of some controversial issues. A glossary of key terms is included at the end of the text and it stands as a ready reference to check comprehension.

Features of the fourth edition

This edition carries forward the same basic framework as previous editions, but there have been major revisions to many chapters to reflect important developments in both marketing theory and practice.

A new chapter deals with marketing in newly deregulated industries in the public sector and in other settings which have extended the scope of application. The opening chapter has been rewritten to take account of current ideas about the role of marketing. Much greater attention is now given by companies to customer service and customer care, and this is dealt with explicitly in a section of that chapter. Relationship marketing is introduced in that chapter and developed in several other chapters.

Positioning strategy has now become a central aspect of marketing activity and its importance is recognised with a new section in a chapter which concentrates on segmentation and positioning. New material on psychographics and business profiling has also been added to that chapter.

Developments in the application of new technology in marketing are shown in several contexts from database marketing to scanning stores and applications in marketing research. The chapter on product planning has been extended with a treatment of product differentiation and the augmented product. And the proliferation of brand extensions has led to a more detailed consideration of that topic.

Ideas and applications concerning the formulation of marketing strategy have been particularly dynamic and they are incorporated into the chapter on developing marketing strategy.

Trends and new issues in the channels of distribution are recorded, and the continuing growth in sales promotion and direct marketing is acknowledged with more attention to the issues in the planning of these activities. The much enhanced concern with environmental matters and the emergence of 'green' marketing are discussed in the concluding chapter. Additionally, many new, short, case studies and company illustrations are included throughout the text.

I wish to acknowledge gratefully the contributions of two of my colleagues. As in the third edition Joe Penn has written the chapter on international marketing; and Richard Christy has written the new chapter on marketing in deregulated industries.

GORDON OLIVER

Chapter 1 ══════════════

The role of marketing

What do the following have in common?

> Coca-Cola, Marks & Spencer, Kellogg,
> Gillette, Guinness, Mars, Pepsico,
> Sainsbury, McDonalds and Cadbury Schweppes

The answer is that they are all very good indeed at marketing, according to a survey of British marketing executives [1]. What makes them so good? First, you, and most other people, have probably heard of them all – you may even be able to bring to mind all of their logos. Second, you probably have a very good understanding of what they offer, and you can probably recall at least some of their advertising. Third, you know where to go if you want to buy from them. Fourth, it is likely that you have bought something from many of them. Finally, you liked what you bought, considered it to be relevant to your needs, to be of the right quality and good value, and you have continued buying. Just like millions of other people.

Seven of the ten have been developing their businesses for over a century and the others for fifty years or more. They nurture and build their markets and their relationship with their customers, and have established and retained enviable reputations. They are referred to as exemplars of business practice and not only as leaders in marketing. All are well-balanced organisations with distinction in areas such as employee relations, quality management and the use of information technology and other modern technology. In addition, they have been careful in balancing the claims of, and in satisfying, all their principal stakeholders over a very long period of time, whether these be their owners, customers, employees or suppliers. In short, they are successful businesses, and effective marketing has been at the heart of that success.

Developing effective marketing requires an understanding of the role of marketing. That gives the purpose of this chapter, which starts with a discussion of marketing and the exchange process and the activities required to facilitate the exchange. It considers the prime areas in which marketing managers make decisions and shows several conceptions of the role ascribed to marketing. Customer care and customer service are highlighted as central to today's approaches to delivering

1

customer satisfaction. Finally, there is some consideration of the complexities with which marketing managers need to deal.

Marketing and exchange

Marketing concerns voluntary, mutually satisfying exchange relationships, and marketing activities are designed to enable these exchanges. Traditionally, the exchanges considered were confined to goods and services and consumers paid producers. The considerable application of marketing techniques outside this traditional domain has extended its scope to include other exchanges where there is a limited supply and where there is a market. It has therefore broadened to include non-business exchanges involving not-for-profit organisations and many public sector organisations.

Despite the difficulties in defining the edge of marketing, the central focus is on the exchange. An exchange is precipitated when people recognise that someone else has something which they would like to have. Both sides assign values to that which they currently have and to that which they would like to have. If they both value what the other has more than they value that which they have themselves, then an exchange will be mutually satisfying.

Marketing activities by organisations facilitate such exchange through:

- Understanding what it is that buyers value.
- Designing a product or service offering so that it has those values.
- Ensuring that those values are communicated effectively.
- Making the product or service offering conveniently available.
- Arriving at a price beneficial to both buyer and seller.

Understanding what buyers value

A key way in which firms learn about what buyers value is by finding out what they have bought in the past, what they currently buy and the degree to which their needs are satisfied. Much of all market research has this as its aim and in this it attempts to describe the pattern of consumer purchasing. An established firm will also learn from its own past experience and from the direct and indirect contacts it has had with buyers. In addition, it will learn from observing the relative success or failure of its competitors. The rigour of this search for information, the thoroughness of the learning and how well its implications permeate throughout the organisation are the roots of the marketing concept.

Gleaning market intelligence of this kind is not always straightforward and it is not always accurate. If a survey is involved, interpretations and judgements are required and the results are often indicative rather than conclusive. It is also dependent on what is asked of respondents and how well they are able to respond. If the interest concerns what they might need in the future, the position is even more complicated because consumers may have no way of anticipating their future needs and no knowledge of the potential ways in which their needs might be best served in the future.

A major block is the extent to which this information on buyer needs is disseminated and acted on company-wide. It is insufficient if information is collected, but which does not shape the response of the whole organisation, because delivering customer satisfaction depends on the activities of the entire enterprise.

Designing attractive offerings

Decisions about the kinds of product or service that will be offered could be based on what the organisation knows it can do well. Perhaps the organisation has a special expertise or special plant, which allows the provision at lower cost than others. Superficially, that might be a good basis for the decision, but equally well it could result in a complete mismatch with the market requirements. Supply does not motivate demand.

Consumers buy what they require to satisfy their needs and there is no in-built mechanism to ensure that these needs are the same as an individual firm's production capability. The firm could trust to luck and proceed with production and wait to discern any mismatch between its market offering and the market requirement. If there were a mismatch, it could learn not to make the same mistake again – but it could make similar ones. Clearly, it is sensible to start with the market requirement: to attempt to match capabilities with requirements. Such a prescription usually holds, but there may be situations where the organisation specifically does not wish to follow the market, as in some parts of the music business, or it is unable to respond or to change except in the very long term.

Communicating valued benefits

To accomplish the exchange, consumers have to be aware of what is available and persuaded that it meets their needs. They have to be convinced that it possesses benefits they value. Communicating with consumers requires decisions about the volume of communication required to stimulate the desired level of awareness and persuasion, about the communication means to be employed and about the kind of messages to be transmitted.

In the distant past, and in some circumstances today, small-scale production for local consumption meant that there was intimate contact between producers and consumers. Perhaps consumers lived within a short distance of the production point. Producers therefore talked to their consumers and they could give immediate news about what was available, keyed to the particular interests of individuals. To achieve similar objectives today producers make recourse to far more complicated and less effective means. Mass media advertising aims at generating awareness and favourable attitudes, and direct mail campaigns try to induce trial with coupons and offers. But they can hardly carry the same conviction as the small producer in friendly conversation with customers.

On another level the producer has one other difficult promotional problem: communicating with intermediaries. The firm has no guarantee that retailers will stock the product and there is as much competition for retail shelf space as for the consumer's patronage. Strategies need to be evolved to encourage retailers to handle the product.

Pricing the exchange

Agreement is required between the producer and consumer about the price of the exchange. While the market mechanism operates, its working in an advanced economy is sometimes made cumbersome by the sophisticated institutional arrangements. Producers cannot react minute by minute to market circumstances, and they cannot adjust their prices and output levels continuously. Instead, they adopt a pricing policy that is relatively fixed in the short term. The determination of that policy is another key part of marketing activity.

Managing marketing

Marketing managers make decisions about a wide range of activities in order to accomplish the market exchange. They make choices between various types and levels of effort and expenditure in respect of the product, its price, how it will be promoted and how it will be made available to the consumer. These choices result in a particular *mix* of marketing efforts and this has become known as the marketing mix. Although the mix can contain numerous marketing decision variables (sometimes referred to as 'tools' or 'instruments'), a common shorthand is to cluster them into the 4Ps of:

- product,
- price,
- promotion,
- place (subsuming distribution decisions).

In their discussion of the marketing mix Christopher, Payne and Ballantyne [2] argue for the inclusion of two additional Ps:

- people (to emphasise the personal care needed in performing services for customers); and
- processes (because people cannot perform without structured processes in product and service delivery).

This listing should not be interpreted as a comprehensive picture of marketing decisions, because it omits important strategic considerations. It also gives no explicit recognition to the emergence of relationship marketing. Increasingly, the trend is not to emphasise the individual exchange transaction but to consider the development of long-term customer relationships, with some accent on customer service. This point is examined further in the customer care and customer service section of this chapter.

Decisions about the marketing mix are informed by careful research and analysis and require a great deal of marketing information. This information concerns descriptions of customers and their requirements, perceptions, preferences and behaviour in respect of the product and its competitors. It also concerns studies into the effectiveness of past marketing activity by the firm so that there will be an accumulation of knowledge and experience. These studies may be useful because they could show something of the relative responsiveness of the market to the various marketing instruments, and thus be helpful in deciding on the balance between the tools. The capture and analysis of data on these factors form an important bedrock of marketing decision-making.

It was implied above that marketing managers do not only make decisions about the marketing mix. The mix needs strategic direction in terms of what is to be accomplished in what target markets, and a crucial aspect of this is the decision about the kind of positioning that should be achieved in target market segments. For example, this might be the attempt to be perceived by consumers who buy heavily in a given product class as the brand which offers excellent value relative to rivals and the one which is best fitted to a particular type of usage. These decisions help to focus the marketing efforts into a concerted, synchronised plan, which then needs to be implemented and controlled.

There are other strategic dimensions to marketing decisions. Marketing managers need to be involved in the fundamental decisions required in determining how the organisation will gain and sustain competitive advantage in the long term. Will it aim to become the low-cost supplier, or will it try to differentiate its offering with high quality and distinctive products and services? Related to this are decisions about how it will match its particular set of capabilities to the market opportunities and how it will fend off competitive threats. In searching for viable strategies managers take account of a wealth of information on environmental influences including data on the present position and prospects in the industry and its competitive structure, trends in the technology, the economy, demographic and social trends and developments in the regulatory and political framework.

Conceptions of the role of marketing

There are three main conceptions of the role that marketing could take in the organisation. They have been termed the production concept, the sales concept and the marketing concept. Additionally, increasing attention is being given to societal dimensions of the operation of the marketing system.

Production concept

In this view marketing is equated with distribution, and the central problem is seen as one of ensuring that factory output is available in widely dispersed markets. Business is conceived to be about producing things and it is hoped that insatiable demand will provide ready markets. Business success flows from efficient production with competitive advantage being secured by low-cost manufacturing.

This introspective approach has a passive marketing contribution. Decisions about products, prices and distribution are shaped mainly by production considerations. Markets are assumed to exist and firms offer what they can make well, but this may not necessarily be what the market wants.

However, there may be limited situations in which production orientation is the appropriate marketing role [3]. For some organisations their basic rationale and needs may be defined partly in terms of sustaining certain product standards. Their goal may not be profit-maximisation. The traditional craftworker, the artist, some fashion designers and musicians may value adherence to their standards more than they do those of the market. This may or may not lead to commercial success.

Sales concept

This concept asserts the need for the firm to sell its output. Marketing is seen to be about selling. Factory output needs to be sold and if there is insufficient effective demand, then it should be created by hard selling. Production considerations dominate decisions on the product range, but it is acknowledged that products do not sell themselves. Advertising, sales promotion, branding and product differentiation are important. In some industries great attention is given to special product features which may be formulated into 'unique selling propositions'.

Effectively customer requirements are only taken into account during the selling process, and then simply to find a means of overcoming objections. In organisational terms there would be a sales department but an absence of a marketing department. A variation has the trappings of a marketing department carrying out ill-defined functions (perhaps compiling competitive sales information or co-ordinating sales promotions), but this is subservient to a strong sales department.

Marketing concept

Three terms are used synonymously: consumer orientation, market orientation and the marketing concept. They espouse the importance of the consumer and suggest the need to define properly what customers require and then deliver it. Consumer satisfaction is seen to be the means to the achievement of corporate goals. This approach advocates that firms should make what consumers require rather than persuading them to buy what the firm can make. An essential ingredient is the need to define customer requirements and that emphasises the role of market research.

Some zealots have gone further: marketing, they said, is the proper business of business. Firms cannot survive without customers and the marketer has unique access to customers' needs and aspirations. Market research gives a direct channel in the quest for definition of these needs and aspirations and so the marketer has a strong power base. Marketing can dominate companies which assume that the delivery of customer satisfaction is the sole preserve of the marketing department. Such an imbalance is criticised by Levitt when he says [4]:

> Marketing undoubtedly must have a say. But to suggest that, simply because it knows the market, it should have the most authoritative say about the company's reactions to the market – this is to go too far.

Acceptance of consumer orientation spurs a great change in the outlook of companies, even to the extent of changing the definition of the product. From a producer's viewpoint the product might be defined in terms of its physical properties. However, consumers buy these properties as but one element in a bundle of psychological satisfactions. For example, cars are bought for what they are and for what they can do, but what they can do is not just related to transportation because they can confer status and support self-images. Packaged baby foods are bought for convenience and as an expression of maternal caring. Drinks may be props in role playing. If consumer satisfaction is psychological in nature, then the means of communication between producer and consumer also needs review. Advertising does not just make crude claims because it can project images suggesting and enhancing the psychological satisfaction.

One way to summarise the viewpoint of the marketing concept is to consider the firm and its customers as being joined in a system. Both have their reasons for wishing to be associated: the firm remains as long as its profit and sales goals are met and the consumers as long as they gain satisfaction. The two are tied by two types of flow: a physical flow of money for goods and an information flow. The latter flow from the firm to the consumer includes promotional activity and information on prices and availability. The reverse flow could contain sales information and, perhaps more pertinently, market research data.

To underline the significance of the acceptance of the marketing concept it is worth quoting from a study of British companies by Goldsmith and Clutterbuck [5]. They found it to be a central characteristic of most successful businesses and comment:

> Successful companies understand and inter-react with their market. The brand image is important to them, especially if it ties closely to the company identity, as is St Michael to Marks & Spencer, or Clarks to shoes. That the 'customer is king' is axiomatic in their operations. Every function of the company has as its prime objective the satisfaction of customer requirement, they go to great lengths to gather detailed market information. Quality is intrinsic in everything they do.

The marketing concept has been linked with success, in terms of sales and profit, and empirical studies have found that it is an important determinant of performance [6]. Its implementation requires that top management recognise its significance. It also requires recognition and acceptance throughout the organisation in order to prevent the isolation of the marketing function as the sole market-orientated part of the organisation.

Societal dimensions

Concern has been expressed about the possible consequences for society if consumers, and consumption, are paramount. Consumer orientation emphasises the interests of the individual consumer, but it is argued that this need not always be in the interest of society. For example, the individual consumer may have no interest in the environmental impact of the production and marketing activities needed to satisfy wants. Indeed, the consumer may have no knowledge of how consumption decisions indirectly affect the environment. On another level individual consumers may take only a short-term view of personal gratification and choose to consume potentially harmful products such as tobacco and alcohol, not worry about emissions from their car, and choose to consume a totally unbalanced diet without care for the long-term effects on their health.

Taking a societal orientation the company would assess the environmental impact and would look to the consumers' long-term interests. An increasing number of firms declare an ethical stance in their business mission, report on aspects of environmental concern to their shareholders and their societal orientation is evident in some of their activities. But other firms appear to see this orientation as requiring government initiative: they will work within whatever legal framework is established.

Company attitudes

Doyle has studied the corporate philosophies of firms in the *Times 1000*, and their own perceptions of their orientation revealed [7]:

	%	Doyle's definition of the orientation
Production-oriented	10	Success is achieved through producing goods of optimum quality and cost. Therefore, the major task of management is to pursue improved production and distribution efficiency.
Sales-oriented	21	Effective selling and promotion are the key to success.
Marketing-oriented	50	Success primarily depends on identifying changing customer wants and developing products and services which match these better than competitors.

Financially-oriented	19	Success is about using assets and resources to optimise profit and return on capital employed.

As can be seen, only half the companies considered themselves to be marketing-oriented. Commenting on this, Doyle says:

> For most companies the focus is on raising returns through cost reduction rather than building long-term market position through innovation and better marketing. . . . Marketing and strategic planning are very weak in most companies because the prominent focus of the board is on budgets and financial returns. . . . This long-term lack of concentration on external opportunities and change has resulted in three-quarters of our sample companies finding themselves trapped in increasingly competitive, mature or declining markets with very little opportunity for growth.

Customer care and customer service

Satisfying customers is central to all marketing activities, and in this drive for customer satisfaction focus is placed not only on the product, but also on the care and the service received. The pivotal position of customer service and customer care means that they are playing an increasingly important role in organisations' plans in three ways:

1. They can assist in establishing and maintaining a differentiated position in the market.
2. They can be important in attempts to encourage existing customers to stay loyal.
3. They can cement the long-term relationship between an organisation and its customers.

In reviewing the literature in this area, Stewart comments on the meaning of customer service and customer care as follows [8]:

> The increased scope of customer service means that it is now much more proactive than its physical distribution/logistics predecessor. While there is no universally accepted definition of customer service, those which are popular in the literature focus on customer-impinging activities, especially those relating to interaction.
>
> Customer care is seen as 'more' than customer service. The literature does not provide a definitive version of what customer care is. However, this may well be due to the qualitative nature of customer care. It is variously described as an approach, an attitude, and a concept which embraces company/customer relationships and their derivatives, with customer satisfaction as its aim.

Interactions between customers and company staff can signify much about the quality of customer care, and because of this many firms have explicit staff training programmes to foster positive staff attitudes in dealing with customers. In situations where employees have frequent customer contact, some organisations 'empower' service staff to put things right immediately if there is a complaint. Many retailers adopt this approach, and exchange or money refunds are common. Car manufacturers have joined this trend with 'exchange or return' schemes. But the full implications of these practices need to be thought through because on occasion they can lead to difficulties. A recent example is the major off-licence drinks retailer which gave its shop assistants authority to give customers who complained two free bottles with no questions asked. The scheme was withdrawn within a few weeks as the (sometimes trivial) complaints became mountainous.

Effective staff are the lynchpin of good customer care. People like to be cared for by other people. This is highlighted by Gavaghan, who says [9]:

> . . . the only way to meet the fast evolving needs of more discerning customers is to ensure that the person in the green overalls in the DIY store, the teller in the bank, the woman on the lingerie counter, the car salesman and the rest have the knowledge, the customer skills and personal confidence to give information and advice that is honest, reliable and appropriate.

Retaining customers

Better customer care can help to win new customers, but perhaps of more significance is that it can also help to retain existing customers. Customer retention is important because:

- Retaining customers who have bought before can be far less expensive than locating and cultivating entirely new prospects.
- Keeping existing customers satisfied has additional benefits in that they may provide positive word-of-mouth recommendations to others.

In some situations this positive word-of-mouth can be a source of new customers. For example, many new bank customers make their decisions to open accounts on the basis of the personal recommendation of friends. In the industrial market satisfied customers are sometimes willing to allow prospective customers to visit their premises to inspect the product in operation and in the process they may offer favourable comments and give helpful demonstrations. Satisfied customers can become advocates of the product and may therefore be valuable not only because they buy themselves, but because they might also assist in generating further customers to be satisfied. Such a virtuous circle is well worth developing.

Loyalty schemes

Firms seek to retain customers in a variety of ways, which include a range of loyalty schemes. Purchase volume bonuses are common and may involve a price reduction for customers who exceed a specified level of purchases in a period. Purchase frequency inducements include schemes which reward frequent usage, as exemplified by the airlines and hotels which offer additional services or some special

---

Handling complaints at British Airways

The way an organisation handles complaints reflects its stance on customer care. Does a complaint irritate the organisation and put it on the defensive?

British Airways have overhauled their approach with the introduction of a comprehensive, computer-based system for dealing with the four hundred letters received daily. The system aims to give swift response and a proper answer so that complainants feel that they have been listened to. It links in with other systems throughout the organisation for thorough investigation and communication to the departments accused of a service shortfall. Customer satisfaction with the system is measured by the fact that two-thirds of complainants fly again with BA, with much positive word-of-mouth replacing what might otherwise have been grim stories of an unfeeling, careless organisation.

Complaint handling can be part of the positive dialogue the organisation has with its customers.

Source: Various press reports.

---

treatment to those who purchase frequently. Sometimes both purchase volume and frequency are combined in loyalty schemes such as those operated in Stenna Sealink's Compass Points, the DIY chain Do It All's Bonus Card, Barclaycard's Profiles and the loyalty schemes introduced by Sainsbury and Tesco. In some cases these approaches are extended with the use of a type of 'club' or 'user group', in which members receive regular communications, perhaps a company magazine, news about product developments and special purchase offers.

Relationship marketing
There is an emerging change in emphasis from a focus on individual transactions to a focus on long-run relationships with customers. The essence of this change

---

Some European loyalty schemes

IBM operates its Helpware scheme across Europe for PC purchasers. It includes a free 24-hour telephone helpline and a regular magazine.

In France the Barbie Fan Club has 250,000 members who pay to belong. Monthly mailings include magazines, birthday messages and information about new dolls and accessories. The club receives 300 telephone calls a week from members.

Bolls Wessanen, the Dutch liqueur company, devised a scheme aimed at men with above-average income aged over 30. A database of 20,000, thought to represent a third of the market, was developed. Regular mailings include stories about products and the people who use them.

Source: Based on C. Murphy, 'A rewarding experience', *Marketing Week*, Supplement on Customer Loyalty, 25 March 1994, pp. 19–21.

is a stress on customer retention, high levels of customer service and customer contact and company-wide attention to quality.

Effective marketing builds long-term relationships with customers and customer care is a key part of this building process. In the business-to-business market highly valued customers can receive considerable attention, which is not confined to the kinds of purchase inducement noted above, nor is it confined just to meeting particular customer demands concerning product or service specification and delivery. The frequent interactions between numerous individuals in a selling organisation and its key customer organisations establish a web of relationships which may be furthered in organised or informal business, social and even sporting events. These relationships are not restricted to a vendor's marketing department and a buyer's purchasing department: they can be, and frequently are, company-wide.

Building relationships with customers establishes a part of what Kay refers to as an organisation's 'architecture'. He sees this as being one of the distinctive capabilities of the firm and one of the foundations of competitive advantage. Kay defines 'architecture' as [10]:

> a network of relational contracts within, or around, the firm. Firms may establish these relationships with and among their employees (internal architecture), with their suppliers or customers (external architecture), or among a group of firms engaged in related activities. . . . The value of architecture rests in the capacity of organizations which establish it to create organizational knowledge and routines, to respond flexibly to changing circumstances, and to achieve easy and open exchanges of information.

Building relationships at Lever Industrial International

Lever Industrial International (LII) is in the business of supplying cleaning and hygiene systems to industrial and institutional markets. Its customers include Heineken Breweries, the Coca-Cola Company, airline catering operations and many of Unilever's food companies. Its managers describe the company's approach to marketing as follows:

'LII sells much more than a basic commodity; it sells solutions to our customers' needs.'

'We are a service business offering customers consultancy, specialist products and equipment, all supported by comprehensive training packages and reliable technical support.'

'We have moved from simply selling products to developing long-term business partnerships. Our approach is based upon a recognition of customers' needs to maintain the highest standards of cleaning and hygiene at optimal cost. This requires us to help our customers to become better at what they do, whether this be operating a laundry, producing food hygienically, or running a clean and efficient hotel.'

Source: L. Conway, 'Partners in hygiene', *Unilever Magazine*, no. 90, 1993, pp. 4–8.

Each firm assembles its own unique set of relationships and in competition any one firm's architecture is in effect competing against the architecture of its rivals: one system of relationships competes with all the other systems. Failure in any part of the system can prejudice the working of the whole, and the firm's relative success will, in part, be a reflection of the strength and appropriateness of its system of relationships. Effective relationships replace suspicion and conflict by trust and co-operation. And customer care can play an important part in building and sustaining this architecture in one of the crucial relationships.

Customer expectations

According to Zeithaml, Parasuraman and Berry, customers use five criteria in evaluating the quality of the service which they receive. These are [11]:

Tangibles	The appearance of physical facilities, equipment, personnel and communications materials.
Reliability	Ability to perform the promised service dependably and accurately.
Responsiveness	Willingness to help customers and provide prompt service.
Assurance	Knowledge and courtesy of employees and their ability to convey trust and confidence.
Empathy	Caring, individualised attention.

Customer expectations about all these criteria provide the basis for them to make comparisons between the service expected and the service received, and so to make judgements on the quality. Zeithaml *et al.* suggest that these expectations are shaped by three factors: word-of-mouth communication, personal needs and any relevant past experiences. This underlines the importance of managers having real knowledge about what customers expect, but unfortunately that is not always evident. An example of this is that bank customers value confidentiality in their transactions, yet in their dealings with banks they are required to form queues at counters in public areas.

To what extent have companies accepted the priority to care about customer satisfaction and to implement the marketing concept effectively? Some companies have, but in others there may only be the trappings of marketing which are restricted to the creation of a marketing department, strengthened advertising function and increased marketing expenditure. A recent study by Wong, Saunders and Doyle into a number of traditional British manufacturing companies found [12]:

> The kind of transformation required in practising true marketing demands, first, a fundamental shift in thinking and attitude throughout the company resulting in every functional unit believing in responsiveness to customer or market needs as paramount to the firm's survival and success (our study suggests the British managers, in theory, largely advocate this) and, second, a deliberate strategy move to commit resources to enable every functional area of the firm to adopt key tasks in the process of satisfying customer wants (in practice, our British companies fail to achieve this criterion for successful marketing implementation).

In explaining this the authors considered that one of the blocks in the companies studied was the lack of professionalism among marketing staff, as perceived by their non-marketing colleagues, and that this retards the transformation into a truly marketing-oriented firm.

This lack of development of the marketing function is further illustrated in a report by management consultants Coopers & Lybrand of a survey they conducted among one hundred managing directors [13]. Confusion about the potential role of a marketing department is demonstrated in the conclusion that marketing departments in the companies surveyed undertake an ill-defined mix of activities, lacked responsibility and accountability and were seen by respondents to be quite separate and distinct from sales departments. Only a quarter of the marketing departments in the companies in the survey were said to have had any responsibility at all in the area of customer service.

In both these studies some part of the problem may be a deficiency in internal marketing. The lack of acceptance of market orientation and the confused role of marketing departments indicate a failure to understand and to appreciate the role of modern marketing.

Competition and complexity

Typically the marketing environment is a challenging one; it is both competitive and complex. Marketing managers make their plans in a context which demands sound analysis and critical judgements about their competitors and the complexities.

Competition

Marketing concerns consumers, but it also concerns competitors. Marketing plans are constructed to be competitive and they aim to win or to maintain customer patronage at the expense of rivals. Understanding competitors' activities, the form and intensity of the competition, and of the evolution of industry structure, are central to shaping an organisation's view of its environment. These factors constitute vital ingredients in the development of competitive strategies, and monitoring them needs to be continuous because the competitive environment is likely to be dynamic: change is endemic. That change might include new strategies being adopted by competitors, the arrival of new entrants to an industry, a technological innovation by a rival, developments in channels of distribution, or some change in customer preferences or circumstances.

As an example of these kinds of change reference can be made to the electronic video games industry; some developments in this industry are noted in the next box.

In another context monitoring the competition is now becoming of major importance for the first time. The privatisation and deregulation of large parts of

Video games

Electronic video games have a household penetration of 40 per cent in Japan and the United States and 15 per cent in the United Kingdom. Sales in the United Kingdom were just £20 million in 1989 but had reached £750 million by 1993. Two companies dominate: Nintendo, with Super Mario, and Sega, with Sonic the Hedgehog. Nintendo have held an 80 per cent share of the global market, but Sega increased their share sharply in the 1990s, especially in TV-based systems.

Both the market and the industry saw dramatic changes in the 1980s. Early in that decade Pac Man was the state-of-the-art product and the Atari Corporation was the leading company. A flood of me-too products from many small, unreliable suppliers all but killed the industry as consumers became disillusioned with the poor quality. At that time Nintendo was a maker of arcade games, but its launch of the Super Mario Brothers in 1984 led to a remarkable revival of the industry.

Today there are hand-held, 8-bit, 16-bit and CD-ROM systems. Sega has the larger share of the market for the more sophisticated systems. The battle between Nintendo and Sega has been fierce. In 1990 accusations were made in the United States that Nintendo had restricted supplies to retailers in order to maintain high prices. After investigation by the Federal Trade Commission the company agreed to give consumers 5 dollar redeemable coupons. The companies' promotional efforts centre on strenuous advertising campaigns, high visibility in retail outlets and sports sponsorship.

In 1994 the computer games industry was referred for investigation to the Monopolies and Mergers Commission in the United Kingdom.

Source: Based partly on G. Mead, 'Computer characters champing at the bit', *Financial Times*, 1 October 1992, and other press reports.

public services have forced organisations unused to competing into profound consideration of the bases of how to compete. It is just the kinds of issue discussed in this section which now pose problems for these organisations. This ranges from the determination of the best approach to securing competitive advantage, to matching resources and capabilities with market opportunities, and to framing strategies which are appropriate to customer requirements and which rival effectively those of competitors.

The complexity of marketing

Some of the most worrying problems faced by marketing managers are caused by the difficulty in predicting and controlling precisely the effects of marketing actions. Lilien, Kotler and Moorthy point to eight characteristics of the marketing environment which contribute to this complexity [14]:

1. *Sales response to a single marketing instrument*: the relationship between the market's response and the level of a given type of marketing instrument like advertising is typically unknown.
2. *Marketing mix interaction*: marketing effort, far from being a homogeneous

input, is a composite of many different types of activities. The market's response to variations in the level of any one marketing input is conditional on the level of the other activities. Furthermore, the variation of two or more marketing activities at the same time can have effects that are greater or less than the sum of the separate effects.

3. *Competitive effects*: the market's response to the marketer's actions is related to competitors' actions as well, and the firm rarely has good knowledge of, or control over, competitors' actions.

4. *Delayed response*: the market's response to current marketing (especially advertising) outlays is not immediate and in many instances may be delayed by weeks or months.

5. *Multiple territories*: the firm typically sells in several territories with different rates of response to additional marketing expenditure.

6. *Multiple products*: most companies market a number of products and need to allocate marketing funds among them.

7. *Functional interactions*: marketing decisions cannot be optimised without joint decision-making in the production and financial areas.

8. *Multiple goals*: a company tends to pursue multiple and often contradictory goals.

Balancing stakeholders' claims

A further complication is in the determination of suitable measures of overall performance. In this regard Doyle has written on the difficulties in characterising an excellent company [15]. Too often, he argues, this is seen in a unidimensional way, with stress put on earnings per share or shareholder value, from the perspective of just one interest group. But organisations have a range of other stakeholders, and Doyle suggests that managers should seek a balanced performance over time which gives all stakeholder groups a satisfactory level of achievement. This means identifying and evaluating the aspirations of key interest groups, such as owners, employees, customers, suppliers and the community more generally. Undue emphasis on any one of these groups is at the expense of the others. The judicious balancing of stakeholders' claims is a key measure of senior management competence.

Summary

The core of marketing concerns market exchange processes and organisations' marketing efforts are designed to facilitate these exchanges. A very apparent aspect of these efforts is the physical movement of goods, and considerable resources are devoted to the operation of the channels linking producer to consumer. But prior to distribution the manufacturer needs to make decisions about what products to offer. Such decisions could be conditioned solely by the firm's ability to produce, but there is no in-built mechanism that ensures that this ability matches a consumer's requirement. Some early warning and direction finding through market research could reduce the risk of a mismatch between what is offered and what the market requires.

For exchange to take place consumers have to be aware that products exist and persuaded that they meet their needs. In historical times relatively local production for local consumption meant that communication between the two was not a major problem. The increasing separation of producer from consumer has necessitated mass media advertising and this presents complicated issues in the determination of the volume of communication, the choice of communication medium and the messages to be transmitted.

A price has to be set for the exchange to be finalised. But while the market mechanism operates, its working in an advanced economy is made cumbersome by the (geographical and time) distances between producer and consumer. Firms set pricing policies in advance and decisions about these form another important marketing activity.

There are three main conceptions of the role of marketing. First, in the production-oriented view, marketing can be equated with distribution, and business is seen essentially to be about producing things. The firm's market offering is dictated by its production expertise. Second, with a sales orientation, marketing can be seen to be mainly about selling. Third, consumer orientation, operating what is referred to as the marketing concept, gives strong recognition to the importance of the consumer and to the need to base all marketing plans on the prior definition of buyer requirements. Today, organisations are asked to take a wider view of their social responsibilities with a societal orientation and not to measure their effectiveness only in profit terms.

Customer care and customer service are taking on much added significance as ways of supporting firms' attempts to differentiate their market offerings, in encouraging customer loyalty and in building long-term customer relationships.

Marketing managers operate in complex and competitive environments. The complexities limit the extent to which the effects of marketing actions are predictable and controllable.

Questions for review and discussion

1. Is consumer orientation only required in industries that have a high level of competition?

2. Brand names and mass media advertising are vitally important aspects of marketing today. Why? How do you explain the fact that groceries such as flour, rice, salt and soap are not sold, as they used to be, as unbranded, unpackaged commodities?

3. Charities make widespread use of marketing techniques. What is their apparent conception of the role of marketing?

4. As a consumer, what marketing activities would you be involved in if you were considering buying a new pair of shoes?

5. Is the notion of building long-term customer relationships only really relevant in industrial markets? How might this be reflected in consumer markets?

6. 'Explicit customer care policies should not be needed in a truly consumer orientated company.' Do you agree?

7. What blocks the complete acceptance by companies of a societal orientation in their approach to marketing?

8. Why is it sometimes difficult to understand customer requirements?

References

1. *Marketing Week*, 17 September 1993.
2. Christopher, M., Payne, A. and Ballantyne, D. 1991. *Relationship Marketing*. Oxford: Butterworth-Heinemann, p. 12.
3. See Houston, F., Gassenheimer, J. and Maskulka, J. 1992. *Marketing Exchange Transactions and Relationships*. Westport, Conn.: Quorum Books, ch. 3.
4. Levitt, T. 1969. *The Marketing Mode*. New York: McGraw-Hill, p. 11.
5. Goldsmith, W. and Clutterbuck, D. 1985. *The Winning Streak*. Harmondsworth: Penguin Books, p. 10.
6. Jaworski, B. and Kohli, A. 1993. 'Market orientation: antecedents and consequences', *Journal of Marketing*, vol. 57, July, pp. 53–70.
7. Doyle, P. 1987. 'Marketing and the British chief executive', *Journal of Marketing Management*, vol. 3, no. 2.
8. Stewart, K. 1992. 'A review of customer care and customer service', in Baker, M. *Perspectives on Marketing Management*, vol. 2. Chichester: John Wiley, p. 381.
9. Gavaghan, K. 1993. 'Honing the skill of the chase', *Marketing Week*, 25 June, p. 26.
10. Kay, J. 1993. *Foundations of Corporate Success*. Oxford: Oxford University Press, p. 66.
11. Zeithaml, V., Parasuraman, A. and Berry, L. 1990. *Delivering Quality Service*. New York: The Free Press, p. 26.
12. Wong, V., Saunders, J. and Doyle, P. 1992. 'The effectiveness of marketing implementation: functional managers' views of practices in their firm', in Baker, M. *Perspectives on Marketing Management*, vol. 2. Chichester: John Wiley, p. 194.
13. 'Report finds marketers wanting', *Marketing Week*, 17 December 1993, p. 8.
14. Lilien, G., Kotler, P. and Moorthy, K. 1992. *Marketing Models*. Englewood Cliffs, NJ: Prentice Hall International, p. 5.
15. Doyle, P. 1992. 'What are the excellent companies?', *Journal of Marketing Management*, vol. 8, pp. 101–16.

Chapter 2
Consumer psychology

A convincing market offering is one that the customer believes has valuable benefits at a reasonable price. Marketing decisions made by organisations make presumptions about these benefits and beliefs. Decisions are made about which benefits to build into the offer, about which benefits should be described and to whom, and how that description should be communicated.

Describing products to consumers may appear to be a simple, straightforward exercise and one not related to any complicated issues. However, consider the two cases in the following illustration. Quorn was first described as a protein-rich product for developing countries, but how should it be described to consumers in developed countries? It was decided that it should be positioned as a meat substitute, initially targeted at vegetarians and later at a wider group who wished to reduce red meat consumption. In each of these cases there was considerable scope for alternative descriptions variously emphasising different attributes, uses and kinds of people using the brand.

The way Babycham is described to consumers changed radically in 1993. The light, romantic, youthful tone, which had been employed for forty years, was not appreciated by today's confident, independent young women. Over the years the attitudes, values and behaviour of target groups had changed; old descriptions were out of keeping.

Presumptions are made about what to describe to which consumers. How apposite those presumptions are depends on how well the bases of consumer behaviour are understood. The purpose of this chapter is to review current understanding of consumer psychology before widening the discussion in Chapter 3 to include cultural and social influences.

Consumer problem-solving

Today a dominant approach taken in the study of consumer behaviour is that of information processing. This derives from cognitive psychology with a focus on

---

Explaining Quorn to consumers

Quorn is the first major branded meat substitute in the United Kingdom. It is a myco-protein invented in the 1960s by RHM and now owned by Zeneca. Originally, it was con-ceived as a protein-rich product for developing countries, but it was unsuccessful in that context.

Its low fat content led to another proposition – that it should be marketed as a meat substi-tute. For several years it has been a constituent in retailer own-label vegetarian pies, and in the last few years it has been introduced to the consumer market.

Two contrasting approaches have been employed in describing the product to consumers. At first heavy emphasis was put on a vegetarian positioning and the advertisements showed animals dancing with joy because Quorn was being used in place of meat. Subsequently it was thought that was too limiting a position with insufficient market potential. In moving from that positioning a subsequent campaign featured recipe ideas which demonstrated the brand's versat-ility. People who were trying to reduce red meat consumption became the target audience, rather than vegetarians.

Source: C. Murphy, 'Doubts mushroom over Quorn future', *Marketing Week*, 15 October 1993, p. 22.

Changing the description of Babycham

The Babycham brand goes back to the 1950s and from that time it held to its romantic, youthful positioning epitomised by its Bambi look-alike symbol. In 1993 it was relaunched with a changed image. A new approach was adopted for how the brand should be explained to consumers. Aimed as a fun brand for confident, independent women the advertise-ments had a much harder and unconventional edge and the product was repackaged in blue glass.

Source: *Marketing Week*, 15 October 1993, p. 11.

---

the internal processes engaged by the individual. An alternative view is that of the behaviourist school, which emphasises environmental factors and offers explanations in terms of classical conditioning [1].

In the information processing view the consumer is seen as a problem-solver. Purchase decisions are occasioned when the consumer perceives a problem. Infor-mation is acquired and used to help to solve the problem and a simple formula-tion would have just three elements: inputs, processing and outputs. The processing need not be specified so that the analysis concentrates on the inputs (informa-tion) and outputs (purchase behaviour). Only restricted understanding could come from this simplicity and the lack of systematic relationships between the two would undermine its usefulness. Researchers have been forced to open the 'black box' between input and output, and to delve into the nature of the processing. Unfor-tunately, this has uncovered a host of variables which might be more or less rele-vant. Our knowledge remains limited, although progress is reported throughout this chapter.

Levels of problem-solving

Relatively few purchase decisions are really important to most consumers. For groceries and other fast-moving consumer goods, the sheer number of regular decisions usually precludes undue attention being attached to any one. Consumers do not have the time or the inclination to think much, if at all, about which brand of toilet soap or toothpaste to buy every time a purchase is made. On the other hand, some purchases are very important and have powerful consequences. Decisions to install double glazing, to buy a new car or a fashionable pair of shoes present a range of risks and uncertainties which may prompt wide-ranging search and evaluation of alternatives. Purchase decisions therefore differ in their significance and in the type of problem-solving activity undertaken by the consumer.

A threefold classification is usually adopted to distinguish the level and type of consumer decision-making [2]:

Extensive problem-solving
Limited problem-solving
Routine problem-solving

Extensive problem-solving occurs when the consumer feels that the purchase has considerable implications. Initially, there may be little knowledge of the alternatives and little or no recent experience of buying in that product field. The basic points on which to make comparisons (the evaluative criteria) may not have been established, so that there is difficulty in discriminating options. At the same time, the potential purchase may have high levels of financial or social risk and have symbolic significance for the consumer. Such circumstances would trigger active search – positive attempts to collect information, pick up leaflets and brochures, to look at advertisements, to 'window shop', to seek advice from family, friends and salespeople, and to observe what other people do. This describes a high involvement purchasing decision.

Limited problem-solving concerns a more constrained situation. The purchase could still be important but the consumer would be more knowledgeable and experienced in the product field. Previous purchases may have been made, evaluative criteria formed and the options to be considered narrowed to just a few. But there would be some active search, to verify the points of difference, to take account of developments in the product field or to adjust judgements in the light of changes in the consumer's circumstances or perceptions (of the product and the problem).

Both extensive and limited problem-solving depict an active, involved consumer reaching solutions by gathering and evaluating information. They suggest a sequence of building awareness, increasing comprehension of the alternatives and how far they meet requirements, of developing a favourable attitude and choosing the most favoured brand. It is a time-consuming learning process.

Routine problem-solving applies to more prosaic situations. Each purchase made in everyday shopping, or in a weekly visit to a grocery superstore, cannot be characterised as a big problem. Any single purchase is fairly unimportant, does not have major financial or social implications, and the level of consumer involvement is low. Experience is accumulated in buying and using products in the category, and as much is known by the consumer as is needed. Through time, a small number of acceptable alternatives may be determined, a repertoire of brands is established: The consumer is relatively passive, undertaking no active search. Limited information is acquired in passing, perhaps just by observing what is available in the shop or from the incidental viewing of a television commercial. Fuller comprehension and the development of attitudes take place after rather than before the purchase and result from experience of using the product. Periodically, there may be some reason to revise the repertoire, possibly caused by a major new product launch, by some change in the consumer's circumstances or by shopping patterns being thrown into turbulence by changes in retailing. For a short time the consumer may be more active and buying behaviour takes on some of the features of more extensive problems. There will likely be pressure to settle to more habitual patterns, to return to routine and to overcome the inconvenience of the interruption. In another way, the repertoire could be changed occasionally just to add a little novelty or surprise.

Consumer perceptions and decisions

Very broadly consumer behaviour can be studied in terms of the perceptions that consumers hold about their problems and about products, and in terms of how they evaluate and decide the extent to which alternatives offer solutions. Consumer perceptions and decisions are intimately interrelated and feed each other. Perceptions can inform the decision, and the decision can lead to new knowledge about how well consumption of the product deals with the problem, which may subsequently alter the perception. The nature and the depth of perception vary with the level of problem-solving. Highly involving situations would stimulate rich perceptions with a complex set of connections and associations, sometimes touching reasonably profound beliefs and aspirations. More mundane situations may be accompanied by simple perceptions and few associations (Table 2.1).

Much of the remainder of this chapter concerns consumer perceptions and decisions. Consumer perceptions are considered under the section entitled consumer information processing because this deals with how information is picked

Table 2.1   *Consumer perceptions, decisions and involvement*

	Perceptions	Evaluations and decisions
High involvement	Rich perceptions with complex associations	Attitudes formed before purchase and they influence choice decision
Low involvement	Simple perceptions with many fewer associations	Attitudes formed after purchase from experience of using product; the first purchase is trial behaviour

up, manipulated and stored. The section on the consumer decision process is mainly about the role of attitudes.

Consumer information processing

Through our senses we become aware of 'what is out there'. We give more or less attention to the stream of stimuli reaching our senses and try to make some kind of meaning out of them by comparing the new information with the store held in memory. Key parts of this process are exposure to information, the amount of attention given, the comprehension that follows and the way memory is organised.

Exposure

To take up information from the environment the individual first has to be exposed to it. Information relevant to consumption comes from many sources of which the most obvious is advertising and the other elements of strategy over which the marketing manager has control. This might, or might not, be the most potent information. Alternative sources derive from the individual's immediate social setting – family and friends – and from the environment more generally (e.g. government agencies, consumer groups). Research in this area is dominated by measures of consumers' exposure to the various media, with the rationale that as much as possible should be known about that part of all the sources which is under the control of the firm. The size and composition of media audiences are therefore continuously monitored to determine how many and what type of people are exposed to which media. The viability of commercial media is directly related to their ability to attract audiences of interest to advertisers, and so media owners, advertising agencies and advertisers expend a great deal of effort in measuring audiences. A review of the methods employed is contained in Chapter 17 on advertising media decisions.

Major complications arise from the fact that people do not expose themselves indiscriminately to information; they are selective. The notion of selective exposure posits that individuals tend to expose themselves to information with which they are likely to agree and to avoid information with which they are likely to disagree. People of a given political persuasion, for example, will buy newspapers that carry editorials with which they know they will agree before they buy them. However, the basis of the selectivity is probably not that straightforward. Personal characteristics such as age, sex and education may partly determine it, as may interests and lifestyle. Additionally, it has been argued that people do not necessarily avoid opposing information. Novelty, surprises and controversies have their appeal. Fear might even draw attention. Whatever the bases for selective exposure, it is clear that there is selectivity, and so there is a need to investigate how it operates in specific cases.

The selective nature of exposure is underlined in the differences between extensive and routine problem-solving. In the former the individual will deliberately seek information, but will be highly selective in the sources to be consulted. In the latter, the exposure to new information may be extremely limited and restricted to casual viewing of some advertising and to cursory inspections of shelf displays at the shop normally used.

Attention

Even with selectivity in exposure a vast amount of information still reaches the individual: far too much to be handled or comprehended. Meaning is attached to stimuli received by the senses in a very discriminatory and individualistic way:

> of all the stimuli reaching our sense organs only a small fraction are acted upon and this 'acting upon' is very much a function of the perceiver's characteristics – attention, past experience and memory and social and cultural factors. The active role of the perceiver is also a very creative one . . . we create percepts from the information we have and this information is partly sensory, partly personal and partly social. We may even create a percept with no sensory input at all, as in the case of hallucinations. [3]

We do not react to all stimuli; we attend to just a few. Attention marks out some stimuli on which to concentrate and a conscious impression is made. There is a filtering process so that even those stimuli that are presented internally have only a slim chance of registering further. It will be useful here to bring in the concept of active memory, as distinct from long-term memory. Some stimuli will be presented to active memory and displayed for very short periods of time – seconds, or less. A fraction of these will be picked for further attention and will pass through the filtering device for further processing, bringing in long-term memory. Active memory is then cleared for the onrush of new stimuli. If there is considerable pressure of new stimuli it may be that even significant bits of information will be pushed out of active memory, and will not receive attention.

Determinants of stimulus selection have been summarised as the characteristics of the stimulus, our motives, expectancies and experiences [4]. Intensity, size, novelty, contrast and colour are all physical properties of stimuli which may mark them out for attention, and all are widely used in advertising [5]. Advertising messages also employ appeals related to motives in the attempt to get noticed. Much research is undertaken in the development of advertising campaigns to assess the likelihood of alternative messages receiving attention. This is investigated in Chapter 16 on advertising objectives and assessment.

Attention may also be a function of current needs. A person who is hungry will pick out a restaurant or pub sign from a mass of competing stimuli because of its relevance to present needs. Additionally, the consumer's persisting values could have some effect. Stimuli consistent with an individual's values will be more easily attended to and, alternatively, barriers may be established to prevent attention.

If a consumer holds foreign-made cars in low esteem there will be less likelihood of noticing their advertisement than those for domestic cars [6].

Another stream of thought considers whether active attention is a prerequisite for further information processing [7]. Television advertising for fairly mundane grocery items may receive only passive attention and yet the commercial may later have some effect in contributing to the purchase. Constant repetition produces familiarity, and if the brand is relatively risk-free and given some extra stimulus at the point of purchase, the individual may be prompted to buy because of the build-up of familiarity. There may not be active attention to the message, but something has been learned about the brand.

Comprehension and concept formation

The perceptual system filters and also interprets the stimuli. In this part of the process information is exchanged with memory. New messages are compared with the established store of meanings to lead to meaningful comprehension of the new information. Meanings are assigned to messages, but these meanings need not be what was intended by the transmitter of the message. They are likely to be entirely personal, and may or may not reflect a similar perception to those of others receiving the same message. This is influenced by what is termed the concept formation process.

Human memory is sometimes thought frail because it rarely reproduces exactly [8]. This very frailty is essential since we require abstraction of the general form of stimuli in everyday life. Events, indeed objects, are never the same from one moment to the next, and so we abstract the general form, otherwise we should never recognise even very familiar faces. In this process of abstraction we form concepts, that is classes that have common characteristics. Generally, the more abstract the concept, the more difficult it is to learn, and the more concrete, the easier to learn. 'Soap' is an easier concept than 'clean'. The reason for the development of concepts is put by Hansen as follows: 'In order to cope with an unlimited number of colours, shapes, sounds, tastes and the like, and all the possible combinations of these inputs, human beings have to systematise their sensory inputs' [9].

Concepts aroused by a particular perception may vary between people, or may vary for the same person over time, or in different situations. We all probably have quite enduring and similar concepts regarding very basic items such as tables and chairs, but some degree of variability is probable with many concepts of marketing interest. Take the concept 'soya': some people would think of this in terms of animal feedstuff; others may see it as a human food. In the second case it may be related to many other concepts. Some people may associate it with cheap inferior meat substitute with derogatory evaluations, and for still others the concept 'soya' may arouse concepts of exciting base ingredients for exotic dishes. In all these cases it is the same thing in the real world, but the consumer comprehension shows marked differences in interpretation. Situations can also affect comprehension. We might react differently to the same message in different situations, because it arouses different associations or because we vary the evaluation.

Consterdine and McDonald [10] have commented on this by saying:

> It is clear that people see the world (and the advertisements in it) through their own personal microscope (or blinkers). A great deal of filtering and selective perception takes place. Readers/viewers are active, not passive, elements in the relationship between a medium and its audience.

They illustrate this with some individuals' responses to advertisements:

> 'The name on the envelope was the same as ours' (paraffin heaters commercial).

> 'I looked at the picture (and the rain) because we had just returned from what should have been two weeks of summer sun' (Dunlop SP Radials press advertisement).

> 'If I get any thinner I won't need a bra at all' (Playtex bra commercial).

> 'It made me think that the electricity bill was due' (paraffin heaters commercial).

It can be seen that in these examples the meaning taken from the stimulus (the advertisement) was hardly that intended by the advertisers. The perception of the advertisements was, and could only be, entirely personal. Individuals interpret messages within their own frames of reference.

Advertisers benefit from understanding what concepts the consumer classifies as relevant to their product classes. Sometimes advertising deliberately aims at shifting the concept structure so that an old, established brand can be related to concepts in a modern lifestyle. Thus McGuire [11] has said:

> If your product doesn't sell it is presumably because the consumer categorizes it in a cognitive cubbyhole with a 'no-buy' tag. Increasing the probability that he will buy the product can be done most efficiently, not by convincing him that this category of products should be bought, but rather by changing his perception so that he categorizes it differently.

Message reception does not necessarily lead to the formation of concepts that are an accurate reproduction of the real world. The notion of perceptual distortion attempts to explain the potential for this inaccuracy. Kerby [12] classifies the types of distortion as follows:

1. *Distortion created by the source of the message*
   (a) Message overload: too large or too swift a stream of information.
   (b) Ambiguous symbols: lack of familiarity with the codes used, e.g. pictures or photographs may employ subtle symbolism which has great potential for misinterpretation. Even the familiar verbal code can be ambiguous, e.g. the word blend can be perceived as bland; friend as fiend.

(c) Naive assumptions by the source: an advertiser may have a completely different frame of reference from that of his target audience. He may associate a mountain stream with freshness; his audience may associate it with a polluted river.

2. *Distortion produced in the transmission process*
   (a) Conflicting stimuli: a men's fashion store tries to update its image and appeal to younger age groups, but retains rather elderly assistants.
   (b) Non-coincidence: an advertising campaign is designed for one segment of the population, but the media used exposes the message to other people.

3. *Distortion by the perceiver*
   (a) Inattentiveness: message in active memory read erroneously, e.g. a petrol price display casually noticed by a passing motorist who confuses 294p and 249p.
   (b) Stereotyping: we may have built up fairly rigid sets of expectations concerning certain types of people and objects, and assume new messages about them will conform to the stereotype.
   (c) Need for consistency: simplicity and order may be placed upon stimuli even if some have to be distorted to accomplish this, e.g. an individual may have a preconception that a certain hotel chain is expensive and will therefore be suspicious of its special offers; he may totally discount them as being inconsistent.

Concept formation is interwoven with the method of encoding used by the individual in storing information in memory [13]. Researchers have paid most attention to symbolic coding. Language is a symbolic code since it uses symbolic representation. Increasingly these days, research is exploring an alternative code – that of imagery. There is even the suggestion that long-term memory store may be differentiated between these two codes, with left-brain employing symbolic codes and right-brain employing image codes [14]. Additionally, there is speculation that people have differing propensities to use these two code forms. Some may respond easier to images (e.g. television) and others to symbolic codes (e.g. print). Ultimately it may be possible to include code use propensities along with other descriptions of target markets, but that is highly speculative.

Symbolic encoding may focus on the attributes of objects. This has led to a considerable preoccupation in marketing with brand or product class attributes. In these studies lists of attributes are generated and respondents are invited to scale their feelings about whether brands or product classes are associated with those attributes.

An extension is to develop a 'perceptual map' with the perceived positions of brands related to 'key' attributes, and perhaps with an added notion of an ideal

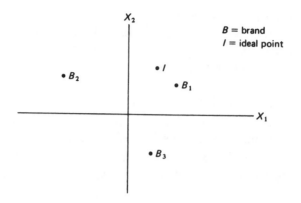

Figure 2.1 *Perceptual mapping*

brand. Figure 2.1 illustrates this. In the figure the three brands are located against the two dimensions with the consumers' ideal point. Data for such an exercise would come from a survey which sought scaled responses of consumer feelings about the brands, and the ideal levels, on important product attributes. Say the product class was restaurants and the X_1 dimension the type of service (self-service to silver service) and the X_2 dimension the breadth and type of menu (simple to sophisticated). In this case B_1 is seen to be best, but if there was another segment with an ideal in the bottom left quadrant there would be a market opportunity. Fuller treatments of perceptual mapping, or brand mapping as it is sometimes called, can be found in both Hughes [15] and in Assael [16]. An application to the UK cheese market is reported by Sowery [17].

Long-term memory

Marketing interest in memory has, until recently, been concerned mostly with forgetting. It is clear that how much, and for how long, an advertisement is remembered is of importance, as is the extent to which memory is affected by varying repetitions of the message.

Equally significant, as yet with little research in a marketing context, are the methods used for information storage. Psychologists are now investigating the structure of this storage [18]. Two types of store are of great potential interest in consumer behaviour. First, there is the most simple structure of all: a straightforward list. Simple concepts are associated with other concepts in a one-dimensional sequence. For example, bread may be associated with butter, butter associated with jam, and so on. For many fairly inconsequential items such simple structures may be realistic. A more complex alternative is to conceive of the storage as a hierarchy, that is to relate one concept to a wider concept of which it is a part. As Calder [19] says:

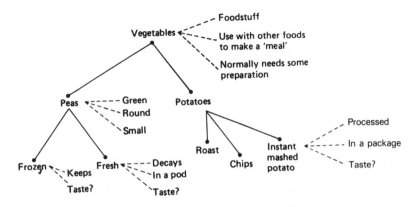

Figure 2.2 *Hierarchical memory organisation*

The resulting organization is a hierarchical structure of units which are successively redefined at higher levels of organization. Such a pattern is not a list but a list structure . . . . Thus, beliefs relevant to a given topic might be organized so that concepts of increasingly greater specificity are encountered as one moves down through the structure.

A hypothetical example of hierarchical relationships at several levels is shown in Figure 2.2. One consequence of these structures is that they might lead to stereotyping. For example, all brands of instant mashed potato might be thought of as possessing all the attributes of the general category. One individual might therefore dislike all such brands on the basis of very limited experience (frequently, of course, just hearsay).

For some products, memory organisation is probably quite simple, with few concepts and few ties between these concepts. But for some people some products can have enormous concept structures, with untold ties and associations. Interesting products, used in interesting situations, are bound to have a complicated web of relationships. An example is beer, where there is a very complex relationship between the brand of beer, the image of a particular pub and the corporate image of the brewery. A study by Pharoah [20] found that brands of beer were categorised by consumers into the following six groups:

1. Strong/real ales/pulled from a pump/been around for years/local breweries.

2. Big breweries' attempt at real ale.

3. All IPAs/not sure if real/not fizzy like kegs.

4. For afternoon drinking/not strong/acceptable to a real ale drinker.

5. Kegs with a bit of taste/not too gassy.

6. Typical kegs/weak and watery/gassy/rubbish/made by brewery X.

Commenting on these categories Pharoah made four generalisations:

(a) Positioning bore no relationship to the standard brewery classification of bitter (premium, classes 1 and 2) and quite disparate beers were often linked together.

(b) Corporate imagery was prominent at the two extremes – heritage real ale versus stereotyped kegs.

(c) Distinctions were made between acceptable kegs believed to be stronger and the widely rejected stereotyped kegs.

(d) There were other beers between the extremes thought to be 'a good pint', irrespective of whether they were 'real' or not.

Consumers also criticised the 'big six' national companies as breweries if they did not have a brand between the heritage real ales and keg bitters. As Pharoah says, 'ritualised criticism of at least one of the big six had become enshrined in the mythology'.

This example helps to underline the significance of the ways consumers perceive and organise messages about companies and their brands. Company perceptions about themselves as companies, about their brands, and about what they consider to be the prime attributes, are not very relevant. What is important is the way the company describes itself and its brands to the consumer and, over-whelmingly, the construction the consumer puts upon that description.

Another factor which might have some relevance is how product information is stored in memory. Do brands feature within a broader grouping of all brands in a product category? There is some evidence that for some products memory is predominantly brand-based [21]. This might imply that an important determinant of the beliefs about a given brand are beliefs about its competitors. Some firms, therefore, attempt to influence consumer views about their brands by influencing how they classify the competition. Product positioning strategies are as much about positioning the brand against competitors as positioning it in respect of product attributes. This is illustrated in the case of the extruded cracker. All major brands take a position against crackers and crispbread, but they also take a position against each other. Strategies for product positioning are considered in the product planning chapter later in this book.

Consumer decision process

The problem-solving approach suggests a rational decision sequence (Figure 2.3). This sequence would be most appropriate to extensive and limited problem-solving with an active, involved consumer. For routine buying behaviour the search activity

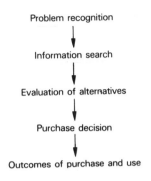

Problem recognition

Information search

Evaluation of alternatives

Purchase decision

Outcomes of purchase and use

Figure 2.3 *Decision sequence*

would be minimal with little or no evaluation before purchase – that would come from experience in using the product. There could also be situations where purchase is not preceded by a decision process [22]. This may be because in some cases the consumer does not consider there to be a choice, other than to buy or not to buy at all, or if there is a choice process it is very limited. Elliott and Hamilton comment [23]:

> that under conditions of low involvement, when a consumer does not consider a product particularly salient or central to his/her belief system, then a substantially different form of information processing will be operational. This low involvement decision process will be characterised by the assumption that as the level of involvement decreases, the amount of cognitive effort, information search and processing also decreases. It is assumed that in relatively unimportant decisions the goal is not to optimize choice but to make a satisfactory choice while minimizing cognitive effort.

They studied evening leisure activities and found that consumers used simple decision tactics, such as 'Do what I'm in the mood to do' or 'Do what my friends are doing' in order to minimise their decisional effort.

In this section of the chapter much of the material is, therefore, most relevant to higher involvement situations and in some cases to initial purchases. Key steps in the decision process sequence are problem recognition, evaluation of the alternatives and the outcomes of the purchase. Problem recognition will be considered later in the discussion of motives. Attention here will be on the evaluation of alternatives which focuses on the role of attitudes.

In making evaluations the main considerations are as shown in Figure 2.4. Evaluative criteria are the standards used in reaching judgements. They are the points that the consumer thinks important and which assist in discriminating between alternatives. Beliefs are the consumer's estimation of the extent to which a brand possesses the characteristics deemed significant in the evaluative criteria. They influence the predisposition towards the brand (the attitude) and so form the intention [24].

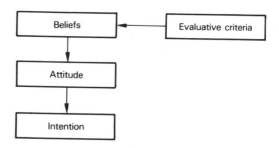

Figure 2.4 *Evaluating alternatives*

A complication is that the understanding of attitude is still evolving. It is generally agreed that it concerns predisposition to respond, and so a favourable predisposition might be thought to increase the probability of purchase. However, there are two views about the nature of the predisposition. Is it the predisposition to the object (brand) or to the act of buying? If the former, then the study would concentrate on the attributes of brands. If the latter, then other relevant factors that might influence the behaviour would need to be included, and particularly the influence of what other people think about the behaviour. The following discussion contrasts these approaches.

Attitude to object

This approach measures individuals' attitudes to brands. The measurement is made by determining which attributes of the product are significant to the consumer, and obtaining an evaluation of the brand on each of these attributes. Research employing this approach secures from a sample of consumers:

1. A list of product attributes that they consider significant.

2. A weighting for these attributes, e.g. each might be scored on a scale from 1 to 10, with 10 as the highest weight.

3. Assessments of the brand on each attribute, perhaps again on a 1 to 10 scale.

Sometimes the procedure is extended to include an ideal level for each attribute. On the rationale that 'more' is not necessarily 'better', it could well be that an optimum assessment for a product attribute would be below a maximum score. For instance, the optimum sweetness of a soft drink would be below some theoretical maximum sweetness. An illustration using this approach to attitudes is shown in Table 2.2.

In the example in the table, assume that the product category is sausages. Each attribute is evaluated on a 10-point scale, so that 'spicy flavour' might range from

Table 2.2 *Attribute profiles*

Attribute	P	I	Brand A			Brand B		
			E	d	(P × d)	E	d	(P × d)
Spicy flavour	10	6	5	1	10	8	2	20
Skin texture	5	2	3	1	5	4	2	10
Light colour	7	5	4	1	7	8	3	21
Even consistency	8	6	5	1	8	8	2	16
					30			67

Notes:

P = importance or relative weight for each attribute
I = ideal level for each attribute
E = evaluation of each brand on each attribute
d = deviation of the evaluation from the ideal
$(P \times d)$ = weighted deviation, i.e. importance weight multiplied by deviation

'not at all spicy', scoring 1, to 'very spicy', scoring 10. The sample of consumers puts the ideal on this attribute somewhere between the extremes, as shown by the score of 6. At the same time respondents are asked to give the relative weight of the four attributes, and it can be seen in the table that 'spicy flavour' carries most importance for them and 'skin texture' the least. The two columns dealing with importance weights and ideal levels determine the ideal sausage, as far as this sample of consumers is concerned. Brands A and B are now compared with that ideal.

Consumer evaluations of brand A show it to be fairly close to the ideal levels on the four attributes and so the deviations are comparatively small. The weighted deviations take into account the relative importance of the attributes and magnify the deviations. Brand B is clearly thought inferior, and this can be traced to particularly poor evaluations on flavour and colour. This technique would advocate that improvements on these two attributes would allow that brand to compete more effectively.

Beliefs about brands may reflect a degree of confusion or conflict. In these circumstances it would be beneficial to investigate the nature of any possible conflict that may be apparent in consumers' understanding of the product. For example, Eden Vale make 'cold cabinet' products and were perturbed to find that two conflicting beliefs were commonly held by consumers. Consumers simultaneously believed that 'manufacturing processes take some of the goodness out' and that cold cabinet products are 'natural, good things'. Consequently, a successful advertising campaign was conceived on the theme of 'Down at Eden Vale we do as little as possible. For your sake. We know nature only needs a little help' [25].

Research into the relative importance to consumers of different product attributes can be combined with investigations into an organisation's performance on those attributes. A simultaneous importance–performance grid could be derived, possibly for the several competitors in a market[26]. Both the importance and the performance can be depicted on a scale from high to low, as shown in Figure 2.5.

In the top left quadrant good performance on a highly important attribute indicates a favourable position: the firm is doing well in an important area. In the top right quadrant performance is poor on an important attribute. If other

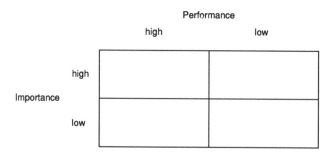

Figure 2.5   *Simultaneous importance-performance grid*

competitors are doing well in respect of that attribute, then there is a competitive disadvantage, and if all the others competitors are just as poor, then there is a neglected opportunity. Good performance on an unimportant attribute may not be the best use of resources.

Service organisations in both the public and private sectors have found this to be a useful diagnostic device. A recent British application in health care considered the attitudes of GPs in their decisions to refer patients to hospitals. The relative importance attached by GPs to a wide range of service attributes was informative, but comparative evaluations of the performance of several providers on the key attributes were surprising and challenged the opinions previously held by management. The organisation in question found that it was not as highly rated on some important attributes as some potential competitors. This led to a reappraisal of its priorities.

Some usefulness might also be derived from studying attribute importance along with brand satisfaction ratings. This would be a similar analysis to that noted above, but with brand satisfaction ratings replacing performance.

Attitude to behaviour

The essence of the first approach to attitudes was detailed investigation of product attributes. A more recent approach is to investigate the consumer's attitude to the *act* of buying a particular brand. This specifically attempts to predict the behavioural intention, and its proponents would argue that it thus moves nearer to predicting actual behaviour.

These studies use what is referred to as the intentions model. This suggests that the intention to buy is found from considering two elements:

1. The individual's attitude to the act of buying a specified brand.

2. The individual's 'subjective norm', i.e. the influence of other people who are significant to him.

Each of these elements has two sets of factors that might condition their strength

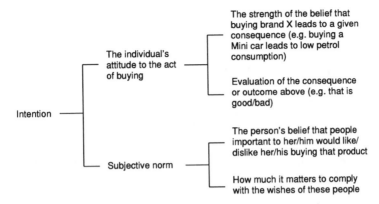

Figure 2.6   *The intentions model*

and direction. They are shown in Figure 2.6. There may be six or seven major beliefs associated with buying, say, a Mini car, and also several people whose views the individual takes into account. The intention to behave is the sum of all these elements for each belief.

One of the main contributions of this model is that it does explicitly acknowledge the social environment of the consumer, since it does allow the possibility that individual buying behaviour is strongly influenced by what other people might be expected to feel about that behaviour. But it should be noted that it is the individual's perception of these other people's views that counts – which may or may not be an accurate representation, and may or may not be taken as being important.

This model also allows for the possibility that such social influences could be more heavily weighted than the individual's own attitude to the act of buying. This might be expected with product categories that are socially conspicuous and with those with which the individual has little experience or knowledge.

Attitudes and situations

An essential factor not yet discussed is the situation in which the product is to be used, and the situation in which it is bought. The attitude about the product may well vary in different situations. Thus the choice of a restaurant, a holiday destination or clothes would be dependent on the situation.

Miller and Ginter have sought to assess how far evaluations of fast-food restaurants changed according to the situation [27]. They asked consumers to rate restaurants on attributes like speed of service, cleanliness and convenience in each of four situations. These situations were: lunch on a weekday, a snack while shopping, evening meal when rushed for time, and evening meal with the family when not rushed for time. As may be expected, the importance attached to the attributes varied in these situations. So too did the evaluations of the restaurants.

Equally well, the situation at the time of the purchase can alter the consumer's evaluation of the product. One aspect of this could be the extent of pre-planning.

Highly rigid shoppers who make detailed lists are less likely to be influenced by the situation at the time of purchase. More relaxed shoppers could be.

Attitude change

Much marketing activity is designed to stimulate consumers to change their attitudes. Most of this activity takes the form of presenting persuasive arguments and takes a particular view of the way information is processed, that is, a series of sequential steps that flow from exposure through attention and comprehension, yielding to the arguments and retention of the new belief [28]. We shall consider attitude change in the context of the intentions model.

Changing social environment
The individual's perception of the social norm is a major variable. There may be substantial changes evolving in society, but these will be differentially perceived by individuals. Some will be highly sensitive to, say, fashion changes; others will be very insensitive. A host of factors is likely to affect the norm; some are shown in Figure 2.7. Changes in any of these factors could contribute a change in the social environment. For example, the widespread adoption of tea bags in Britain in the 1970s represents a radical change in attitude to the act of buying tea bags. Previously tea bags were viewed by many as socially unacceptable and as used only by people with little discrimination. Developments in most of the variables in the diagram led to the eventual change in the social norm as perceived by perhaps half the population. Tea bags became acceptable and widely used.

Changing beliefs
The possibility of changes in the associations and consequences of the act is dependent on the concept structure and also the quality and quantity of information. The concept 'soya protein for human consumption' could be related to the concept 'meat' or to that of 'ingredients for exotic dishes' . The first relation could have unfortunate connotations of being a cheap substitute; the second could have highly favourable evaluations. A change in the concept structure from one to the other could result in different attitudes.

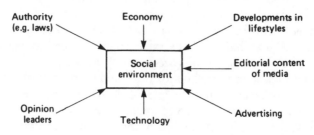

Figure 2.7   *Some influences on the social norm*

Evaluation of beliefs

Experience, or vicarious assimilation of experience by observing others, could alter the way in which beliefs are evaluated. In the tea bag case above, some people undoubtedly 'changed their mind' about buying tea bags as they realised their friends were using them without derogatory effect.

In an experiment, Lutz [29] compared three possible strategies:

1. Changing beliefs.

2. Changing evaluations of those beliefs.

3. Adding a new belief and evaluation.

He found that the potential for changing beliefs was much higher than that for changing evaluations. He did not test strategy 3. This research indicates that it might be easier to persuade people that buying a brand will lead to a given consequence than to persuade them that an established consequence is better than currently evaluated.

Sometimes beliefs about a product can be indistinct and confused. An instance is provided in the case of food processors, which took a considerable time to enter widespread usage. Moulinex found that people did not really know what a food processor was and that many confused such machines with blenders. In these circumstances the task would be to sharpen and to distinguish the concept, before surrounding a particular brand with favourable beliefs.

Attitude stability

High involvement usually implies extensive search and deliberate evaluations. The product is important to the individual and attitudes may not be formed lightly. With considerable expenditure of time and money the consumer is motivated to be careful in evaluating the alternatives. Therefore the attitude may be reasonably stable and enduring, at least until some major new piece of information becomes available. In low involvement the product is not as important and for some product fields attitudes may not be at all strong, enduring or stable. As noted earlier there may be quite slow learning and fast forgetting. Some evidence for such instability is given by Day. He monitored the attitudes of a sample of people towards a new convenience food over a period of five months. Table 2.3 shows some of his results arranged as a matrix of transition probabilities, that is the probabilities of moving between states over time. Entries in each of the cells in the table show the probability that those in a given state at time T_1 are in the same, or an alternative, state at time T_2. So in the top left cell we see a transition probability of 0.53. This can be interpreted as 53 per cent of those with a favourable attitude at T_1 remaining in that state at T_2. Reading across that row shows what happened to all those with favourable attitudes at T_1: 17 per cent moved to neutral or unfavourable attitudes, 16 per cent became 'aware only', and 14 per cent became 'unaware'. That last figure is, of course, interesting. It reflects the fact that in the intervening five months between T_1 and T_2 the respondents had probably made several thousand purchasing

Table 2.3 *Attitude stability and change for new convenience food*

T₁ \ T₂	Favourable	Neutral or unfavourable	Aware only	Not aware
Favourable	0.53	0.17	0.16	0.14
Neutral or unfavourable	0.20	0.44	0.24	0.12
Aware only	0.30	0.30	0.24	0.16
Not aware	0.20	0.25	0.23	0.32

Source: G.S. Day, 'Attitude change and the relative influence of media and word of mouth sources', in J. Sheth (ed.), *Models of Buyer Behavior*. New York: Harper & Row, 1974.

decisions. Most of these were fairly routine or inconsequential, as are most purchasing decisions. One flake of information that these respondents had five months ago, albeit with favourable evaluations, had been dislodged. They forgot that they had heard of one out of thousands of brands to which they were exposed.

Routes to persuasion

The elaboration likelihood model proposes two routes to attitude change: a central and a peripheral route [30]. If the product is highly relevant to the individual, then the purchase is likely to be one of high involvement. This will motivate the individual to devote effort to finding out about the product and to consider information carefully. Attitude change is through a learning process and could be relatively enduring. In contrast, the peripheral route relates to less involved consumers. The individual has less interest in the product and less motivation to learn about it. Shallow attention might be given to advertisements featuring a celebrity endorsement or usage situations. Repetition increases the chance of attitude change, although it is likely to be less enduring.

Outcomes of the process

The decision to purchase sets up expectations about how the product will perform. Experience in use may confirm or exceed these expectations, and so lead to satisfaction which would be remembered and fill out the understanding the consumer has of the product. This may result in favourable word-of-mouth communication and in consequence others may become aware and interested in the product. A reverse outcome may have unfortunate consequences for the product's manufacturer. The critical factor in this is the level of expectation. Consumers may have unrealistically low or high expectations, which may be based on a wealth of knowledge and experience or on hardly any. It would be in the company's interest to investigate these expectations, how consumers develop them and the dimensions they consider in establishing their expectations. The role of the firm's promotional activity may be relevant: descriptions may have been inadequate, confused or too exaggerated.

An interesting comparison might be between the evaluative choice criteria and the criteria used in post-purchase evaluations. Differences might appear as a result of the use experience, and could be carried forward to change subsequently the choice criteria for further purchases. If this were chronic, there might be a case for considering different types of communication to stimulate first buys and to establish brand loyalty. Different messages may be appropriate to new buyers and to those with experience. A particular situation in which this may be important relates to what is termed cognitive dissonance.

Cognitive dissonance

There is some potential for attitudes to change after the purchase has been made. Post-purchase evaluation by the buyer could result in a revision to what might originally have been a favourable attitude. The scope for such changes is increased if the buyer feels anxious about the decision because the buyer has received new information about the product. This information could include opinions from other people, press comment on the product and initial experience in using it. Doubts and anxieties might question the wisdom of the choice, and the buyer would be motivated to allay their impact – by reaffirming that the decision was correct or by admitting that a mistake had been made.

This phenomenon has been explained by the theory of *cognitive dissonance*. Literally, this means a lack of balance or harmony between cognitions, bits of knowledge or understanding. For example, a new cognition (e.g. a very stiff gear change in a car just purchased) may be inconsistent with an established cognition (e.g. from the sales appeals in the car showroom suggesting ease of operation). Dissonance is a post-decisional and, therefore, a post-purchase phenomenon. In reviewing the theory and empirical research associated with it Cummings and Venkatesan [31] say:

> Dissonance theory works according to a reality principle in that the cognition least anchored in reality will be the one most likely to change; since the purchase will be a strongly anchored behaviour, the cognitions most likely to change will be those concerning satisfaction with the purchased product relative to rejected products.

This means that, having purchased a product, the consumer may feel psychologically uncomfortable because in making the decision she or he has had to forgo the good, as well as the bad, attributes of the rejected product. The individual will be motivated to reduce the dissonance since it is uncomfortable and there will be a degree of self-commitment to the already purchased product. It is likely then that the individual will reinforce the wisdom of the choice by stressing the positive factors of that product bought and the negative factors of the rejected choice. In some cases s/he may admit s/he made a mistake and attempt to revoke the decision, and thus restore consistency.

An important determinant of the degree of dissonance is the significance of the purchase. High financial risk and ego-involvement, allied with numerous possible choices, appear ripe for both pre-purchase conflict and post-purchase dissonance. This is why a large number of the studies of this topic concern consumer durables and especially cars. It is also probable that such products have numerous associations and connections with other concepts, and so have a high probability of being inconsistent with at least some of them. On the other hand, basic grocery items have very restricted connections with other concepts and so have less chance of being inconsistent, and in any case are not intrinsically important enough for the individual to worry about.

An interesting case of cognitive dissonance has been reported by Moutinho, who studied British holidaymakers in Portugal [32]. Questionnaires before and after the holiday revealed some changes in evaluations. Before the trip, price consciousness was high; afterwards 'curiosity' and 'relaxation' became dominant explanations for the holiday. Attaching greater weight to these latter factors would seem to be the strategy for overcoming the anxiety about the price.

Personal variables

A wide range of personal factors can contribute to forming consumer behaviour. Demographic and socio-economic factors are considered in the next chapter. In this section two psychological factors are investigated: motivation and personality.

Problem recognition

The solution to a problem requires first that the individual recognises that there is a problem. This means awareness of a difference between some desired state and the actual state. Examples where an individual might discover a discrepancy could include [33]:

- A current problem that causes discomfort – thirst or hunger, or an ill-fitting pair of shoes.
- Anticipation of a problem – preventive maintenance (cars, clothes, health, personal grooming).
- Stock run down – routine consumer products.
- An interest opportunity – the individual becomes aware of something that might be fun to do or to have (sports, hobbies, holidays).
- A sensory opportunity – sensory pleasure from taste, smell, sound or sight (confectionery, perfume, music, flowers).

Taking a wider view of problem recognition brings in motivation theory. Motives impel behaviour and this relationship tantalised researchers in the 1950s. It was assumed by some that there was a direct causal link between the two, and it followed that if a motive could be pinpointed, then behaviour patterns could be predicted. This spawned many studies based on extended individual depth interviews. They were aimed at exploring the underlying, unconscious motivational patterns of purchase and consumption behaviour. They typically employed very small samples of participants and made gross generalisations. Tuck [34] has commented on motivation research as follows:

> Motivation research reports have the great advantage that clients feel they can understand them. There is no elaborate mathematics . . . you only have to be able to read. Also, the results tend to have the splendid quality of being neither counter-intuitional nor banal. The client feels 'Oh I had never thought of that. But it does sound likely.'

It seems, then, that depth research into motives can certainly furnish insights. The problem is that these insights are largely a function of the particular researcher employed. Different researchers can easily derive quite different explanations since the basic research methodology is so subjective, being dependent on indirect questioning. Added to which, it is naive to expect a direct causal relationship between motive and behaviour. No doubt there is some relationship, but its exact form is likely to be mediated by the processing between the two, so that the motive might be transmuted. In any case, any behavioural act could well have multiple motives and any single motive could lead different individuals into quite disparate behaviour.

There are many schemes for classifying motives. That originally proposed by Maslow in 1954 and restated in 1970 is the most widely known in marketing [35]. This has a fivefold classification as follows:

Physiological needs	–	hunger, thirst
Safety needs	–	security, stability
Belonging needs	–	affiliation, affection
Esteem needs	–	prestige, achievement
Self-actualisation	–	self-fulfilment, full use of talents

Satisfaction of basic needs permits the higher-level needs to emerge. Needs that dominate at any time are dependent on the level of satisfaction met for the more basic needs. So, given chronic hunger, the other needs might be sacrificed. In affluent societies needs for affiliation, esteem and self-actualisation tend to dominate behaviour. Given relative abundance, then, the more basic needs can be fulfilled and the problem is choosing which of many alternatives would be most suitable. That choice is likely to be heavily influenced by the higher-level needs. So people choose security in housing consistent with affiliation or prestige needs; they may also choose to fulfil physiological needs in accordance with these. Work is now proceeding in pursuit of adequate instruments to measure self-actualisation in consumer behaviour [36].

Schiffman and Kanuk [37] illustrate a possible use of the need hierarchy in the marketing of microwave ovens as follows:

> An appeal to physiological needs would show how quickly food can be prepared (i.e. satisfy hunger needs). A safety appeal would demonstrate how safe the

microwave oven is in comparison with other cooking appliances (e.g. no burned fingers). Social appeals can be invoked by illustrations of party and holiday dinners prepared in a microwave oven. Status is easily demonstrated through such standard appeals as 'impress your friends' or 'for a luxury kitchen, you need a microwave oven.' Finally, appeals to self-actualization may point out to career couples how easy it is to prepare last-minute dinners after a long and challenging workday.

Bettman [38] has suggested an alternative theory of motivation related to choice behaviour. He sees motivation as a mechanism governing the movement from one state to another (i.e. reaching a desired state), and so consumer choices are aimed at achieving those desired states. Bettman presents the notion of a 'goal hierarchy' in which consumers develop a collection of overall goals and subgoals relevant to purchasing behaviour. For example, in a given choice the individual may have three basic goals:

1. To determine which attributes are important.
2. To evaluate the alternatives on these attributes.
3. To obtain the best alternative.

Each of these may be subdivided into sets of subgoals required for their accomplishment. But it is not a hierarchy in the same sense as that of Maslow, since there is no necessary implied ordering of the motives.

One important consideration in the development of goal hierarchies is that consumers may use different approaches to their construction. They may have clear goals prior to a shopping trip or, alternatively, the goals may emerge during the shopping. Prior to shopping the goals might vary from being very general to quite specific. Bettman gives three illustrations descending from general to specific:

1. 'Get something for dessert'.
2. 'Get a frozen pie'.
3. 'Get a brand X apple pie'.

If the goal hierarchy is developed during the course of shopping, then there could be much more opportunity for in-store information to affect the criteria to be employed. The presentation of information in a supermarket, and particularly how easily it might be assimilated, could be significant in some choice processes. This may be as basic as whether or not unit pricing allows 'value-for-money' to be used as a criterion by the shopper.

Personality

Personality is unique, it is what makes each of us different from every other person. It is expressive in that it represents our individual adjustment to our environment;

that is, it is at the interface between the individual and 'what's out there'. Because of this it is likely to be affected by everything that goes on within the individual, and by everything outside the individual, which is perceived. It is, then, totally conditional on these other factors.

Consumer theorists have worried over this uniqueness for more than twenty years. Many studies have considered personality traits such as dominance, sociability, achievement and so on, in the hope of tracing correlation between these and purchase behaviour. Kerby [39] reviews some of these studies in detail. Most show, at best, weak correlations. It is thought that this is partly because of the test instruments used, which are often standard personality tests. Percy [40] contends it is also because of the range of intervening factors between personality and behaviour. He advocates that personality is more strongly associated with attitude than behaviour. Work continues in this area with the development of better techniques [41]. Foxall [42] believes the measures taken of personality have not been appropriate and that there is evidence of more useful results with alternative approaches. He quotes Allsopp's study of beer and cider consumption in support of this view [43]. But the position remains equivocal [44].

There have been moves towards research using more market-related instruments. It incorporates some questions on personality in more general studies of buying behaviour, media exposure and activities, interests and opinions. Lifestyle studies of this kind will be considered in Chapter 6 under 'market segmentation'.

A person's self-perception can also be an important influence on behaviour. Individuals may deliberately buy things that support an idealised self-image, with products having some symbolic value in portraying the kind of person they would like to appear to be. Purchasing decisions for some products may then be an attempt to seek consistency between self-images and product images.

Summary

The approach taken to understanding consumer psychology viewed the buyer as a problem-solver. Consumer decision-making was categorised on three levels from extensive problem-solving to routine problem-solving. Consumer perceptions and decisions are central concerns in the study of consumer behaviour. Exposure, attention and concept formation describe important facets of consumer information processing and lead to the development of perceptions. With higher levels of involvement, consumer decisions will be influenced by attitudes. Studies tend to focus on brand attitudes, and therefore on attributes, or take a wider view to encompass attitudes to behaviour, which may subsume the attitudes of others to the individual's behaviour.

Outcomes could be consumer satisfactions: the purchase solved the problem and met expectations. Alternatively, for some product categories, there may be some feeling of anxiety after the purchase because some good alternatives may have been forgone. This phenomenon is termed cognitive dissonance.

Many personal variables may have a bearing upon consumer behaviour. Motives and personality were considered.

Questions for review and discussion

1. Perception is by definition highly individualistic. A manufacturer might have millions of potential customers and so, potentially, millions of perceptions of the product. Does that make it an impractical notion for the marketing manager?

2. Derive new examples for each of the types of perceptual distortion quoted in this chapter.

3. What are the essential differences between the attitude to object and attitude to behaviour models?

4. Which of the two models in (3) above would you use in studying consumer attitudes to: breakfast cereals. fashion shoes, refrigerators, commercial banks? What kinds of information would be obtained from a study using either approach, which would not be obtained by using the alternative approach?

5. Define the term 'concept structure'. What is the importance of understanding the ties and associations between concepts? Suggest some concepts (products) that might have few ties and associations, and some that might have numerous connections. What are the implications in each case for the possible contribution of advertising?

6. In what circumstances might high levels of consumer search activity be anticipated? In what circumstances might very low levels be expected?

7. Find advertisements which exhibit alternative approaches to changing attitudes. Are there any common characteristics different among those that attempt to change beliefs and those that attempt to change evaluations?

References

1. Horton, R.L. 1984. *Buyer Behavior: A Decision-making Approach*. Columbus, Ohio: Merrill; Chapter 1 considers alternative approaches to the study of consumer behaviour. For a critique of the information processing approach, see Foxall, G. 1983. *Consumer Choice*. London: Macmillan.
2. Howard, J.A. 1977. *Consumer Behavior: Applications of Theory*. New York: McGraw-Hill.
3. Mussen, P. and Rosenzweig, M. 1973. *Psychology: An Introduction*. Lexington, Mass.: Heath.

4. Hilgard, E.G., Atkinson, R.C. and Atkinson, R.L. 1975. *Introduction to Psychology*. New York: Harcourt Brace Jovanovich, p. 148.

5. Examples can be found in Britt, S.H. 1978. *Psychological Principles of Marketing and Consumer Behavior*. New York: Lexington, ch. 10.

6. Block, C.E. and Roering, K.J. 1982. *Essentials of Consumer Behavior*. Hinsdale, Ill.: Dryden, p. 169.

7. Krugman, H.E. 1965. 'The impact of television advertising: learning without involvement', *Public Opinion Quarterly*, vol. 29, no. 3.

8. Posner, M. 1973. *Cognition: An Introduction*. Glenview, Ill.: Scott Foresman.

9. Hansen, F. 1972. *Consumer Choice Behavior*. New York: Free Press, p. 97.

10. Consterdine, G. and McDonald, C. 1976. 'Using linguistic coding to explore the way advertisements in press and TV communicate', in *Research that Works for Today's Marketing Problems*. Venice: ESOMAR Congress, pp. 789–806.

11. McGuire, W. 1971. 'The changing theories behind attitude change research', in King, C.W. and Tigert, D.J. (eds), *Attitude Research Reaches New Heights*. Chicago: American Marketing Association, p. 28.

12. Kerby, J.K. 1975. *Consumer Behavior*. Chicago: Dun-Donnelley, ch. 11.

13. Johnson, E.J. and Russo, J.E. 1978. 'The organization of product information in memory identified by recall times', in Hunt, H.K. (ed.), *Advances in Consumer Research*, vol. 5. Chicago: Association for Consumer Research.

14. Krugman, H.E. 1977. 'Memory without recall, exposure without perception', *Journal of Advertising Research*, vol. 17, no. 4.

15. Hughes, G.D. 1978. *Marketing Management*. Reading, Mass.: Addison-Wesley, ch. 7.

16. Assael, H. 1981. *Consumer Behavior and Marketing Action*. Boston: Kent, p. 456.

17. Sowery, T. 1987. *The Generation of Ideas for New Products*. London: Kogan Page.

18. Bettman, J.R. 1979. 'Memory factors in consumer choice: a review', *Journal of Marketing*, vol. 43, no. 2.

19. Calder, B.J. 1975. 'The cognitive foundation of attitudes: some implications for multi-attribute models', in Schlinger, M.J. (ed.), *Advances in Consumer Research*, vol. 2. Chicago: Association for Consumer Research, p. 242.

20. Pharoah, N. 1982. 'Corporate image research in the brewing industry, or, from red revolution to country goodness in ten years', *Journal of the Market Research Society*, vol. 24, no. 3.

21. Biehal, G. and Chakravarti, D. 1982. 'Information presentation format and learning goals as determinants of consumers' memory retrieval', *Journal of Consumer Research*, vol. 8, March.

22. Olshavsky, R.W. and Granbois, D.H. 1979. 'Consumer decision making – fact or fiction?', *Journal of Consumer Research*, vol. 6, September, pp. 93–100, reprinted in Kassarjian, H.H. and Robertson, T. S. 1991. *Perspectives in Consumer Behavior*, 4th edn. Engelwood Cliffs, NJ: Prentice Hall International, ch. 5.

23. Elliott, R. and Hamilton, E. 1991. 'Consumer choice tactics and leisure activities', *International Journal of Advertising*, vol. 10, pp. 325–32.

24. Engel, J.F., Blackwell, R.D. and Miniard, P.W. 1986. *Consumer Behavior*, 5th edn. Hinsdale, Ill.: Dryden, p. 92.

25. Reid, T. 1981. 'The key that can turn on buyers', *Marketing*, 4 November.

26. Burns, A.C. 1986. 'Generating marketing strategy priorities based on relative competitive position', *Journal of Consumer Marketing*, vol. 3, Fall.

27. Miller, K.E. and Ginter, J.C. 1979. 'An investigation of situational variation in brand choice behaviour and attitudes', *Journal of Marketing Research*, vol. 16, February.

28. Day, G.S. 1973. 'Theories of attitude structure and change', in Ward, S. and Robertson, T.W. (eds), *Consumer Behavior: Theoretical sources*. Englewood Cliffs, NJ: Prentice Hall Inc.

29. Lutz, R.H. 1975. 'Changing brand attitudes through modification of cognitive structure', *Journal of Consumer Research*, vol. 1, March.

30. Cacioppa, J., Petty, R., Kao, C. and Rodriguez, R. 1986. 'Central and peripheral routes to persuasion: an individual difference perspective', *Journal of Personality and Social Psychology*, vol. 51, no. 5, pp. 1032–43.

31. Cummings, W.H. and Venkatesan, M. 1975. 'Cognitive dissonance and consumer behavior: a review of the evidence', in Schlinger, M.J. (ed.), *Advances in Consumer Research*, vol. 2. Chicago: Association for Consumer Research, p. 22.

32. Moutinho, L. 1984. 'Vacation tourist decision process', *Quarterly Review of Marketing*, vol. 9, no. 3.

33. Fennell, G. 1978. 'Consumers' perceptions of the product use situation', *Journal of Marketing*, vol. 42, April.

34. Tuck, M. 1976. *How Do We Choose?* London: Methuen, p. 116.

35. Maslow, A.H. 1970. *Motivation and Personality*. New York: Harper & Row.

36. Brooker, G. 1975. 'An instrument to measure consumer self-actualization', in Schlinger, M.J. (ed.), *Advances in Consumer Research*, vol. 2. Chicago: Association for Consumer Research, p. 563.

37. Schiffman, L.G. and Kanuk, L.L. 1983. *Consumer Behavior*. Englewood Cliffs, NJ: Prentice Hall Inc., p. 72.

38. Bettman, J.R. 1979. *An Information Processing Theory of Consumer Choice*. Reading, Mass.: Addison-Wesley.

39. Kerby, op. cit., pp. 444–60.

40. Percy, L. 1976. 'A look at personality profiles and the personality–attitude–behavior link in predicting consumer behavior', in Anderson, P.B. (ed.), *Advances in Consumer Research*, vol. 3. Chicago: Association for Consumer Research, p. 114.

41. Schiffman and Kanuk, op. cit., pp. 93–4.

42. Foxall, G.R. 1987. 'Consumer behaviour', in Baker, M.J. (ed.), *The Marketing Book*. London: Heinemann.

43. Allsopp, J.F. 1986. 'The distribution of on-licence beer and cider consumption and its personality determinants among young men', *European Journal of Marketing*, vol. 20, no. 3/4.

44. Kassarjian, H.H. and Sheffet, M.J. 1991. 'Personality and consumer behavior: an update', in Kassarjian, H.H. and Robertson, T.S., *Perspectives in Consumer Behavior*, 4th edn. Englewood Cliffs, NJ: Prentice Hall Inc., pp. 281–303.

Chapter 3

Social influences on buyer behaviour

So far only a little has been implied of the impact of others on the individual; now a wider view of social influences on consumers is taken. From our earliest years we learn to live with others, and one part of this learning concerns what, and how, to buy and to consume. This consumer socialisation has been defined as 'processes by which young people acquire skills, knowledge and attitudes relevant to their functioning as consumers in the marketplace' [1]. The process proceeds in subtle social exchanges rather than training in families or schools, and observation and imitation are central methods by which material goods acquire social meaning.

Six of the main sets of social influences will be considered here: culture, group norms, reference influences, social class, lifecycle and family.

Culture

From the perspective of consumer behaviour, culture can be defined as 'the sum total of learned beliefs, values and customs which serve to regulate the consumer behaviour of members of a particular society' [2]. These beliefs, values and customs may influence behaviour in a general way, in so far as they provide standards which direct lifestyle. They can sometimes be very specific by encouraging or discouraging consumption of certain products.

In commenting on the importance of values in understanding behaviour Nelson and Cowling [3] have said:

> We know there is a strong relationship between personal values held and
> behaviour. Unlike attitudes, which may or may not have the significant effect
> upon behaviour, there are strong forces that compel the individual to act in
> accordance with his personal values.

Because of this importance there has been considerable interest in recent years in measuring and monitoring personal values and in drawing out possible marketing implications. Nelson and Cowling discern four core trends:

1. *The autonomy of the individual.* Greater emphasis on self-employment and risk-taking, creative leisure, participation in work decisions, demands for new reward systems at work, a demand for equal opportunity for female careerism and for continuing adult education.

2. *Tolerance, empathy and feelings.* In the workplace, meaningful relationships with workmates will be increasingly important. Rationality will be less important, understanding feelings, a desire for more leisure time will be more important. They also see a putting down of roots, greater home-centredness and identification with small communities.

3. *Diffusion of authority.* Society will become very complex. The blurring of the sexes, greater individual autonomy and expansion of role sharing, all argue against the traditional structures.

4. *Decline of materialism.* Anti-materialistic values will exacerbate the suspicion of marketing and advertising practices.

Values in convenience foods

An example of how understanding consumer value systems can assist in marketing decisions is provided by Arnold. He relates the developments in the competition between MenuMaster (Birds Eye) and Lean Cuisine (Nestlé).

Three characteristics were driving consumer demand: a new awareness of nutrition, a new concern for convenience and a new interest in exotic dishes. MenuMaster was a well-established brand, but sales were declining and new strategies were needed. An analysis using three groupings found in a social values survey was undertaken. The groups were: sustenance-driven (concerned with survival, tradition and security), outer-directed (draw values from society, materialistic, status-conscious) and inner-directed (concern for quality of life, self-fulfilment and individualism). MenuMaster tended to be associated with the sustenance-driven group and Lean Cuisine with the outer-directed. Initially, MenuMaster attempted a repositioning to be associated with the inner-directed group. This failed because it was too radical a shift from its heritage. Birds Eye decided to launch a new brand called Healthy Option, which was specifically aimed to appeal to the inner-directed group. And this brand has now become a successful competitor.

Source: D. Arnold, *The Handbook of Brand Management*. London: Century Business, 1992, pp. 89–93.

One approach to understanding consumer values considers the following nine items [4]:

Self-direction

1. *self-respect*

2. *self-fulfilment*

Achievement

3. *sense of accomplishment*

4. *being well respected*

Enjoyment

5. *fun and enjoyment*

6. *excitement*

Enjoyment/maturity

7. *warm relationships*

Maturity

8. *a sense of belonging*

9. *security*

Four distinctive segments were found in a study which used a ranking of these items, and the most important values in each segment are shown in order of importance below:

Segment A	*Segment B*	*Segment C*	*Segment D*
security	warm relations	accomplishment	warm relations
self-respect	self-respect	self-respect	fun and enjoyment
self-fulfilment	security	self-fulfilment	self-respect
fun and enjoyment	belonging	warm relations	self-fulfilment

Within an overall culture there may be distinct subcultures. Williams [5] has suggested four factors which could define subcultures in the United Kingdom. First, nationality groupings are apparent, including sections of the indigenous population such as the Welsh and Scots and more recent migrants. With a geographical concentration of these groupings, aspects of language, traditions, eating habits and lifestyles may be retained. If the retention is sufficiently strong, this will be expressed in different types of retailing and entertainment. Second, religious groupings exert influence on the values and lifestyle of their members. Third, there may be some cultural variation resulting from geographical location. There are some small variations even within this country. Finally, age might contribute to differences in values. Williams argues that older people brought up in the 1930s experienced frugal circumstances in their formative years and share a common attitude towards unnecessary waste. Opposed to this, a 'youth culture' may also be distinguished.

Group norms and role behaviour

Within any human group each member assumes a distinctive place in relation to all the other members. Reactions to events facing the group and to other group members are heavily constrained by the adopted role. Each becomes an actor and fulfils just those activities assigned to that role for the furtherance of the group's goals. The definition of the role and the degree of allowable individual initiative is dependent on the type and purpose of the group. A squad of soldiers would have much more tightly defined roles than members of the Women's Institute.

Role behaviour is related to the norms held by the group. Social norms regulate the relationship between individuals; they are guides to behaviour. Zaltman and Wallendorf [6] consider the characteristics of norms to be as follows:

1. Norms are collective: they are held by many members of a social system or group.
2. Norms are only guides or expectations about what behaviour should be; they are not necessarily followed.
3. Norms are enforced: people are either positively rewarded for complying or negatively rewarded (punished) for not complying.
4. Norms usually reflect the values of the social system or group.

In affluent societies the scope and number of roles that each individual might adopt are enormous and all will adopt a multiplicity. Increasingly, it seems that goods are important props to role enactment; hence the marketing interest in role theory.

Whether by accident or design certain products have become essential, or at least desirable, for the proper execution of some role behaviour. Golf clubs, cars, lawnmowers, furniture and clothing all feature in role playing. It might even become brand-specific. Some products are bought because they are required by a role relationship; some symbolise the existence of a role relationship; and some improve the quality of a relationship.

Because of the number of different roles taken by the individual it is possible for some to conflict and cause strain. Again, this gives a marketing interest. Take the example of the role of mother. An old-fashioned description of this role might be illustrated by a country kitchen and a matronly, aproned woman preparing fresh vegetables and pies for her family. A more modern description would remove the woman from the kitchen and picture her at a coffee morning, or taking her children to the zoo, or helping their creative play, and, probably, holding down at least a part-time job as well. For some women there would be no conflict because they would perceive only one possible role for themselves. But others could be far less definite and find difficulty in reconciling the pressures. Their own mothers might have very set views, as might their husbands and friends. Public authorities also have certain expectations of this role. Conflict needs to be resolved and much attention has been given to the mother's role by the manufacturers of convenience foods, in the hope that they could supply an answer to part of the problem.

Reference groups

One of the most pervasive of group influences is termed the 'reference group'. This could be one or more, real or imagined, persons with whom individuals compare their behaviour, or to whom they ascribe a set of standards and then model their behaviour accordingly. It could be as real as the person living next door, as ephemeral as the current top pop star, or as vague as being 'middle-class' or a member of the ' international jet-set'. Some of the most transparent acceptances of reference influences can be seen among teenagers.

Once more the marketing interest is that aspects of group standards could be associated with certain patterns of consumption. This might be product-specific or even brand-specific. If manufacturers were able to get their brands identified with a particular reference group, and that group could exert compliance from members and aspirants, then this might be a method of obtaining competitive advantage.

The extent to which this concept has operational significance is limited by how conspicuously the product is consumed: the more conspicuous, the more relevant to marketing. Choice of brand of car is open to more reference influence than brand of shoe polish. Another limitation is the proper identification of the reference. A toothpaste company launched a new brand in the United Kingdom aimed specifically at girls in their teens. The television advertisements hinted at the development of a friendship between a member of a band and a girl at a dance hall. Unfortunately, the band selected looked and played ten years out of date. The next campaign dropped that approach and returned to a safer yachting scene featuring a much older girl.

Apart from how conspicuous the product is, there are three other factors that could affect reference group influence [7]. First, the amount of information and experience individuals can draw on may be relevant. With limited information and personal experience of a product category, they may seek out the advice and copy the example of others. Second, perceived risk in purchasing may be significant. Group discussion can influence the amount of risk accepted in purchase decisions. An individual's acceptance of risk can be increased or reduced as a result of discussions with other respected individuals. Third, the credibility of the reference group as perceived by the individual can affect the degree of acceptance of its standards.

Recognition of the power of reference groups has led Baggaley and Duck [8] to speculate that the influence of television is due to its separation of the individual from primary social anchor points. The act of watching television presents a reduced social environment and, so they argue, encourages dependence as a major source of information. Such speculation is interesting, although it still requires empirical validation.

A classification of reference influences has been suggested by Bourne [9]. He was concerned to determine whether the influence was more related to product category choices or to brand choices. Building on this work, Bearden and Etzel empirically tested and supported a classification based on two dimensions [10]. The first was whether the product was a luxury or a necessity, and the second whether it was consumed privately or publicly. Table 3.1 uses these dimensions and gives examples of where the reference influence might be stronger or weaker for the brand or product category. As can be seen, public necessities are open to

Table 3.1   *Reference influence by product and brand*

Consumed in public

		Weak influence for product	Strong influence for product
Product is a necessity	Strong influence for brand	Public necessities: e.g. wristwatches, some cars, men's suits	Public luxuries e.g. some cars, restaurants, holiday resorts
	Weak influence for brand	Private necessities: e.g. roof insulation, beds, fruit squash	Private luxuries: television game, microwave oven, video recorder

Product is a luxury

Consumed in private

Changing markets for Doc Martens

When Klaus Maertens injured his foot in a skiing accident he resolved to make himself a pair of comfortable walking shoes, constructing the soles to trap air in order to provide a cushion. The product was patented and put on the market in Germany with elderly women as the target. In 1960 the British R. Griggs Group took out a manufacturing licence.

Initially its market in Britain was among boys, and the boots were taken up widely as a fashion item. In the early 1980s it became apparent that women were buying Doc Martens as well. That led to the introduction of a line especially for young women. High-heeled and colourful variants of the basic black boot are now part of the range, as well as a more conservative 'county' collection of brogues. Brand extensions into clothing aimed at men aged 25 to 40 followed.

Source: Based on M. O'Brian, 'Booty treatment', *Marketing Week*, 20 August 1993, pp. 44–5.

---

influence on the brand choice because they are publicly consumed; but because they are necessities there can be no reference influence on whether or not to buy in such a product field. Alternatively, private luxuries will have little reference influence for the brand since they are consumed privately, but much more reference influence on buying or not buying the product type because they are luxurious and probably exclusive.

Such a classification of products need not be enduring. Promotional schemes can be devised to shift the product from being seen to be privately consumed to being seen to be publicly consumed. Everyday shoes and clothing would be classed as private necessities. The simple device of displaying labels on the outside, rather than the inside, has turned many kinds of shoes and clothing into public necessities. Strong brand identification has stimulated a reference influence for the brand, where there was little influence before. Some private luxuries have been similarly treated. Better quality travelling bags and briefcases are a case in point. Visible labels, or particular design features, have been aimed at turning what was private into public. Changing private luxuries into public luxuries may also be possible. A drinks firm could attempt this by insisting that in restaurants its brand is only served in a distinctive container.

Social class

Martineau has asserted that a rich man is not just a poor man with money [11]. To some a class system is iniquitous because the heart of the concept is inequality. Others recognise class distinctions as inevitable because society values the relative contributions of individuals differentially. What is clear is that in all societies people do different jobs, receive different levels of reward, live in 'better' or 'worse' districts in 'better' or 'worse' housing, receive different education, mix differentially with other members of society and have different belief systems. If enough people have any given mix of these variables, then they can constitute a social class. Usually we simplify and accept that each is associated, and that a given job implies a level of reward, type of district and housing, sort of affiliations and sometimes even aspects of belief systems.

Attempts to measure social class can employ three categories of approaches, as shown in Table 3.2. Neither subjective nor reputational approaches are used in consumer studies, the former because too many individuals emerge as middle-class, and the latter because it is too cumbersome for large-scale commercial application. By way of contrast, the objective measures are relatively easy to obtain from the answers to a few factual questions. Of these the occupational and income factors are most widely used in marketing [12]. With regard to occupation, many studies

Table 3.2 *Measurement of social class*

Subjective measures	Individuals are asked to estimate their own social class positions
Reputational measures	Participants make judgements about the social class of others in their community
Objective measures	1. Occupation 2. Income 3. Education 4. Quality of neighbourhood 5. Value of residence 6. Inventory or quality of possessions

Source: L.G. Schiffman and L.L. Kanuk, *Consumer Behavior*. Englewood Cliffs, NJ: Prentice Hall, 1983, p. 297.

in the United Kingdom use the definitions of the advertising agencies' professional body (the Institute of Practitioners of Advertising), which are:

AB managerial and professional
C1 supervisory and clerical
C2 skilled manual
DE unskilled manual and unemployed

Widespread use is made of this classification. It is the standard approach taken in the United Kingdom, largely because it is a main method of classification used in media audience studies. The reliance it has on the occupation of the head of household has been a cause for great concern, and attempts are being made to broaden it to take into account level of education. High social class would be inferred from high occupation and high education, and low social class in the opposite case [13].

Market researchers have the most immediate operational problems with the method of defining social class since they need to collect such information from thousands of people daily. The professional associations of market researchers in all Western European countries are now trying to introduce a common classification across Europe [14]. This classification is based on a points score for various groupings of education and occupation. Consistency is a major concern, but problems abound in the measurement of social class, and they are very evident in any assessment of the extent to which purchasing behaviour is class-related. Coleman writing in 1971, thought social class more significant than just income level as a determinant of purchasing behaviour [15]. He says: 'if you take three families all earning [about the same annual income] but each from a different social class, a radical difference in their ways of spending money will be observed', although he also says that social class may be irrelevant for some product categories. Wasson finds class differences in both quantity and quality of consumption [16]. But there is now a growing body of research that finds income to be more significant than social class as a correlate of buying behaviour [17].

Social class and income do affect many aspects of consumer behaviour, although attempts to trace simple causal relationships often fail. As Felson [18] says, 'consumption is organized by the structure of opportunities available to consumers. Material resources are only one limitation upon opportunities.' Other factors that condition those opportunities are time, information, age, lifecycle and family composition. We now turn to one of those – lifecycle.

Lifecycle

Consumer needs and goals naturally reflect their circumstances. A major variable in these circumstances is the stage in the lifecycle from birth to death, because

Table 3.3 *Socio-economic/lifecycle grid*

Lifecycle stage	Socio-economic class				
	Lower %	Lower middle %	Upper middle %	Upper %	Lifecycle total %
Younger – no children	1.5	5.7	6.8	2.9	16.9
Younger – younger children	0.9	6.2	8.1	4.3	19.5
Younger – older children	1.4	8.7	10.8	4.8	25.7
Older	12.5	13.5	8.8	3.1	37.9
Class total	16.3	34.1	34.5	15.1	100.0

Source: R.B. Ellis, 'Composite population description: the socio-economic/life cycle grid', in M.J. Schlinger (ed.), *Advances in Consumer Research*, vol. 2, p. 490, Chicago: Association for Consumer Research, 1975. See also P.E. Murphy and W.A. Staples, 'A modernized family life cycle', *Journal of Consumer Research*, vol. 6, June 1979.

'we find that humans develop – they change in an orderly coherent pattern. The rate of development . . . varies from person to person, of course, but all persons follow virtually the same pattern' [19]. Ways of describing the stages in this development vary. Some of the characteristics included are age of the head of household, marriage, ages of children and income [20]. Appropriate descriptions are likely to vary with product type. For example, ages of children could be the most significant variable in the consumption of baby products.

The value of stage in lifecycle as a predictor of purchasing behaviour has been criticised in some specific applications. In a study of clothing purchases it was not found to be as sensitive as income, or income combined with demographic variables. On the other hand, combining lifecycle with another factor could be more meaningful. Table 3.3 shows lifecycle combined with social class. Research Services, a market research firm, have used family lifecycle and social grade in the development of a segmentation system they call Sagacity.

Family influence

Family is clearly relevant in consumer behaviour as one of the dominant contributors to socialisation. It is also relevant in a more direct fashion in that many consumer decisions may be an outcome of a family decision process. Scott [21] suggests such processes can be studied in two ways:

1.   Influence on the wife's decision by the husband can be measured by the more mechanical method of 'product-based' research. This involves a 'gross' measure which merely notes the incidence of influence by the husband in a particular product decision and the 'net' measure which breaks this influence down into significant stages of the decision.

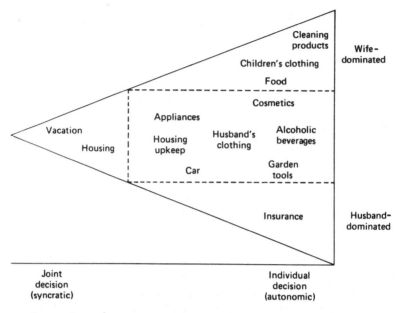

Source: Adapted from H.C. Davis and P.B. Rigaux, 'Perceptions of marital roles in decision processes', *Journal of Consumer Research*, vol. 1, June 1974. See also E.H. Bonfield, 'Perception of marital roles in decision processes: replication and extension', in H.K. Hunt (ed.), *Advances in Consumer Research*, vol. 5, Chicago: Association for Consumer Research, 1978, pp. 300–7.

Figure 3.1   *Husband and wife roles in purchasing decisions*

2.   Joint decisions between partners can be evaluated, particularly in the larger consumer durable purchase, by recourse to sex/power role measures. These attribute relative influence of the partners on the product decision to factors associated with balance of the sex roles and the power relationships that this reveals within the partnership.

Davis and Rigaux studied the roles played by husbands and wives in 73 Belgian households in 25 decisions. Figure 3.1 is taken from that study. The vertical axis is a measure of role specialisation. Towards the right the decisions are more individual (autonomic) and towards the left they are joint (syncratic). Purchasing decisions falling into each of the four broad areas in the diagram represent different situations for the marketing manager attempting to influence those decisions. Advertising in particular should vary both in message and media, and it is clear that many campaigns already recognise this. Additionally, Davis and Rigaux investigated the relative roles through the decision process and found that in 20 out of the 25 cases the wife's influence was greater at the problem recognition stage than in making the final decision. Thus, for many products, advertising directed

Table 3.4 *Schiffman and Kanuk's trends and impacts*

Trend	Impact
1. More leisure time	Increased emphasis upon family recreation and entertainment.
2. More formal education	More aware and demanding consumers; interest in products and services that satisfy the need for individualism.
3. More working married women	High family income; increased joint husband/wife decision making; greater sharing of domestic responsibilities; continued preference for smaller families.
4. Increased life expectancy	Demand for products and services that cater for the health, recreation and entertainment needs of older people.
5. Smaller-sized families	Parents will be able to spend more time and money on the development of each child's skills and capabilities; more discretionary income for parents to spend on their own interests.
6. Women's movement	Traditional sex stereotyping will continue to decline; some products that have been aimed at either males or females will increasingly be aimed are both sexes.

at wives may work most effectively if it assists in problem identification, whereas advertising directed at husbands may stress the favourable outcomes of decisions.

The term 'family finance officer' has been coined to describe the authority structure in households in consumption decision-making [22]. This term is given credence by a study of carpet buying, which found that the dominant authority figure in the house is generally apt to handle the family money and bills. This research suggested 'that husband-dominated families are generally high on mean annual income and general social status; wife-dominant families are generally low on these two variables' [23].

Schiffman and Kanuk [24] have isolated a number of trends that could affect the future of the family and they have drawn the implications for marketing. Their six trends and impacts are given in Table 3.4.

Summary

Culture was examined as a source of learned beliefs, values and customs which from a marketing viewpoint pervade consumer behaviour. Changes in personal values can have substantial effects on all aspects of marketing activity, and so it is important to monitor developments in society that interact with values held by individuals.

Individual behaviour is heavily constrained by other people. Part of this is a reflection of the roles adopted by individuals and by the groups to which they belong. Group membership defines roles and sometimes might have quite explicit associations with the consumption of particular products.

Reference groups set standards which the individual could adopt and subsequently contribute to the shaping of his or her behaviour. This influence, in marketing terms, is related to how conspicuous the product is, the amount of relevant information and experience the individual has, the degree of perceived risk and the credibility of the reference group.

Social class is widely used as a descriptor in commercial research, although there is dispute over its definition, measurement and relationship to consumption Lifecycle, family composition and family decision-making may be just as significant in explaining consumer behaviour.

Questions for review and discussion

1. List as many types of role relationship as possible (e.g. daughter/mother; sports club member/club captain). For each, determine whether there are products that: (a) are a requisite for that relationship, (b) help to symbolise it, and (c) add quality to it.

2. Do many of those relationships conflict and cause strain? Is there a marketing interest?

3. Go through the lists in Table 3.1 with advertisements cut from magazines as illustrations.

4. What are the problems in measuring social class?

5. Why is a study of family decision-making relevant? Draw out implications for advertising strategy from the research reported in Figure 3.1.

6. Assume that regular monitoring of personal values revealed much greater emphasis being placed on individual autonomy. How should product and service marketing reflect that? Can, and should, marketing activity be in the van or the rear of such changes in personal values?

References

1. Ward, S. 1975. 'Consumer socialization', *Journal of Consumer Research*, vol. 1, September.
2. Vison, D.E., Scott, J.E. and Lamont, L.M. 1977. 'The role of personal values in marketing and consumer behaviour', *Journal of Marketing*, vol. 41, April. See also Chisnall, P.M. 1985. *Marketing: A Behavioural Analysis*. Maidenhead: McGraw-Hill, ch. 6.

3. Nelson, E. and Cowling, T. 1982. 'The challenge of change', *Journal of the Market Research Society*, vol. 24, no. 3.

4. Kamakura, W. and Novak, T. 1992. 'Value-system segmentation: exploring the meaning of LOV', *Journal of Consumer Research*, vol. 19, June.

5. Williams, K.C. 1981. *Behavioural Aspects of Marketing*. London: Heinemann, p. 82.

6. Zaltman, G. and Wallendorf, M. 1979. *Consumer Behavior: Basic Findings and Managerial Implications*. New York: John Wiley, p. 114.

7. Schiffman, L.G. and Kanuk, L.L. 1983. *Consumer Behavior*. Englewood Cliffs, NJ: Prentice Hall Inc., p. 214.

8. Baggaley, J. and Duck, S. 1976. *Dynamics of Television*. Farnborough: Saxon House, p. 11.

9. Bourne, F.S. 1961. 'Group influences in marketing and public relations', in Likert, R. and Hayes, S.P. (eds), *Some Applications of Behavioural Research*. Paris: UNESCO.

10. Bearden, W.O. and Etzel, M.J. 1982. 'Reference group influence on product and brand purchase decisions', *Journal of Consumer Research*, vol. 9, September.

11. Martineau, P. 1957. *Motivation in Advertising*. New York: McGraw-Hill, p. 166.

12. Foxall, G. 1977. *Consumer Behaviour*. Corbridge: Retailing and Planning Associates. Chapter 8 gives fuller descriptions of social class.

13. Quinlan, F. 1981. 'The use of social grading in market research', *Quarterly Review of Marketing*, vol. 7, no. 1, gives a critique of the use of social class in marketing. The case for composite measures is made in Osborn, A.F. and Morris, T.C. 1979. 'The rationale for a composite index of social class and its evaluation', *British Journal of Sociology*, vol. 30, no. 1.

14. Rohme, N. and Veldman, T. 1983. 'Harmonization of demographics', *Journal of the Market Research Society*, vol. 25, no. 1.

15. Coleman, R.P. 1971. 'The significance of social stratification in selling', in Day, R.L. and Ness, T.E. (eds), *Marketing Models: Behavioral Science Applications*. Scranton, Pa.: International Textbook, p. 83.

16. Wasson, C.R. 1975. *Consumer Behavior: A Managerial Viewpoint*. Austin, Texas: Austin Press, p. 218.

17. Myers, J.H., Stanton, R.R. and Hang, A.F. 1971. 'Correlates of buying behaviour: social class vs. income', *Journal of Marketing*, vol. 35, October.
Rich, S.U. and Jain, S.C. 1968. 'Social class and life cycle as predictors of shopping behaviour', *Journal of Marketing Research*, vol. 5, February.
Myers, J.H. and Mount, J.E. 1973. 'More on social class vs. income as correlates of buying behaviour', *Journal of Marketing*, vol. 37, April.

18. Felson, M. 1975. 'A modern sociological approach to the stratification of material life styles', in Schlinger, M.J. (ed.), *Advances in Consumer Research*, vol. 2. Chicago: Association for Consumer Research, p. 33.

19. Reynolds, F.D. and Wells, W.D. 1977. *Consumer Behavior*. New York: McGraw-Hill, p. 40.

20. Jain, S.C. 1975. 'Life cycle revisited: applications in consumer research', in Schlinger, M.J. (ed.), *Advances in Consumer Research*, vol. 2. Chicago: Association for Consumer Research, p. 40.

21. Scott, R. 1976. *The Female Consumer*. London: Associated Business Programmes, p. 140.

22. Ferber, R.F. and Lee, L.C. 1974. 'Husband–wife influence in family purchasing behavior', *Journal of Consumer Research*, vol. 1, no. 1.

23. Christopher, M. 1977. 'Household decision making', in Midgley, D. and Wills, G. (eds), *European Insights in Marketing Management*. Bradford: MCB Books, p. 68.

24. Schiffman and Kanuk, op. cit., p. 342.

Chapter 4

Models of buyer behaviour

Previous chapters gave an indication of the wealth of variables thought to be important in shaping buyer behaviour. Parallel to the development of this thought has been a wide range of attempts to organise the variables into models of the buying process. Models of buyer behaviour are not new though. Marketing managers have always had models of consumer response. Usually they were verbal; frequently rather less than explicit. They might have taken the form of a statement about the relationship between sales to be expected following a price increase or a doubling of advertising expenditures or the recruitment of additional sales personnel. Deeper understanding of the maze of intervening variables has spurred attempts at more profound statements of the nature of the relationship between factors in the consumer purchasing decision.

But why model at all? The very complexity uncovered in the last two chapters really gives the answer. Models can abstract, simplify and display a huge number of ideas in a very economic manner. They can highlight weaknesses in the definitions of variables and indicate where new variables need to be considered. Because of this they might direct theoretical research and market experiments. They might demonstrate causal relationships, albeit at the moment in a crude fashion, and they do require the explicit statement of assumptions: implicit theories hide their assumptions [1]. This means that management discussion can be better directed and more fruitful. Long debates, which end merely in the realisation that participants had different premises, may be avoided. The clear exposition of the variables also allows them to be questioned and, it is hoped, better understood. There is also the spectre of simulation and refined prediction if models are sufficiently robust. And, finally, models are a convenient learning device – both in the classroom and in the company. If the model represents the distillation of current best views, then that knowledge can be passed along in a relatively easy manner. These and other uses of models are shown in Table 4.1.

Table 4.1 *Uses of management science models*

I   *Understanding problems – descriptive and predictive models*

A. Descriptive models:
    1. Transform data into more meaningful forms
    2. Indicate areas for search and experimentation
    3. Generate structural hypotheses for testing
    4. Provide a framework for measurement
    5. Aid in systematic thinking about problem
    6. Provide bases of discussion that will lead to common understanding of problem

B. Predictive models:
    1. Make forecasts of future events
    2. Validate descriptive models
    3. Determine sensitivity of predictions to model parameters

II   *Solving problems – normative models*
    1. Provide framework for structuring subjective feelings and determining their decision implications
    2. Provide a tool for the analysis of decisions
    3. Assess system implications of decisions
    4. Yield solutions to problems
    5. Determine sensitivity of decision to the model's characteristics
    6. Provide a basis for updating and controlling decisions

Source: D.B. Montgomery and G.L Urban. *Management Science in Marketing*. Englewood Cliffs, NJ: Prentice Hall Inc. 1969.

Essentials of a buyer behaviour model

A useful starting point for the subsequent discussion of models of buyer behaviour is shown in Figure 4.1. This suggests the basic ingredients in existing models. External stimuli cover a range of factors from advertisements, statements from family and friends to even the individual's observation that, for example, the coffee is running short. Internalised stimuli bring in memory and feelings about such things as what family or friends thought about the last brand of coffee bought. It could also include 'preferences due to the consumer's personality, how the person defines the roles he or she occupies, how the consumer responds to financial circumstances' [2]. The decision leads to an output, which may be to buy, or not to buy, or to search for more information.

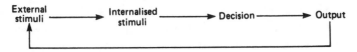

Source: G. Zaltman and M. Wallendorf, *Consumer Behavior: Basic Findings and Managerial Implications*. New York: John Wiley, 1979, p.540.

Figure 4.1 *Essentials of a consumer behaviour model*

The Howard and Sheth model

In the 1970s this became one of the classic and most widely discussed models of all. Lunn praises it because, 'It is distinguished by a richer specification of variables and their interrelationships, and it attempts a much deeper and more detailed integration of theoretical positions from several behavioural sciences' [3]. Four groups of elements are contained in the model:

1. *Inputs*. Advertising or social factors.

2. *Hypothetical constructs of internal processes.*
    (a) Perceptual – the gleaning and processing of information.
    (b) Learning – the development of concepts and response readiness.

3. *Exogenous influences*. Such environmental factors as social class, culture, financial status.

4. *Outputs*. Largely purchases, but also results of the development of concepts, e.g. attitudes.

Perceptual constructs in the model include, first, overt search – the intensity with which the buyer scans the environment for information relevant to the purchase. This is partly conditioned by stimulus ambiguity – for example, which of two brands best fits a given reference influence? Is the new higher quality claimed by a manufacturer really consistent with the new lower price? These two factors determine the amount of information taken in by the buyer's degree of attention to the problem. But that information would be filtered by the buyer's perceptual bias.

Of the learning constructs, 'motives' give the impetus to behaviour, and 'brand comprehension' shows the current state of the buyer's information. 'Choice criteria' offer the characteristics that will be used in making a selection between brands, and 'attitude' expresses preferences. 'Confidence' indicates the certainty with which the buyer judges a brand. 'Satisfaction' is feedback possibly to change evaluations after purchase.

However, the full set of variables need not be to the fore in every purchasing situation. Howard conceived of buying behaviour as being extensive or limited problem-solving, or routinised. Extensive problem-solving is where the buyer 'does not have a firmly established attitude structure on individual brands . . . in fact, he may not have the necessary attitude dimension for evaluating brands' [4]. It follows that extensive problem-solving is characterised by a great deal of searching and learning. If past exposure to information about the product category had generated attitude dimensions for evaluating the category, then the problem-solving is limited. In this case, information search would be to aid brand comprehension. For everyday grocery items the behaviour may be generally far more a matter of routine. The buyer could have accumulated much information through experience. He may have a favourite brand, or a set of preferred brands, for a long list of product categories. Again, Howard and Sheth provide a useful concept – that

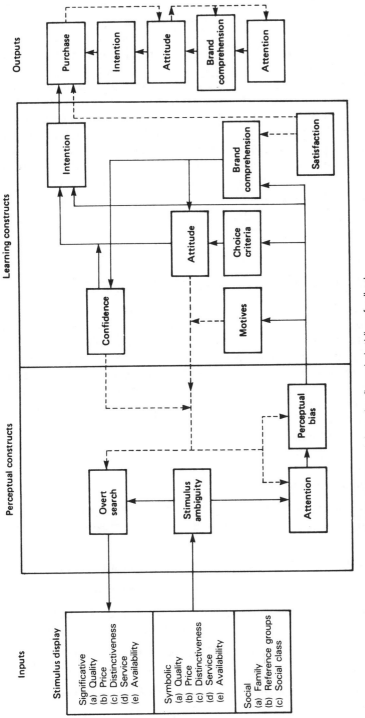

Solid lines indicate information flow; dashed lines feedback.

Source: J. A. Howard and J.N. Sheth, *The Theory of Buyer Behavior*, New York:
John Wiley, 1969, p. 30. Copyright © John Wiley & Sons, 1969.

Figure 4.2   *The Howard and Sheth model of buyer behaviour*

of *evoked set*. This refers to the fact that the consumer may not actively consider all the brands available at each purchase occasion. The consumer will have narrowed the choice down to just a few, or only one. So the routine decision requires not the recall and evaluation of all possible brands, but merely the almost automatic revival of just the evoked set.

The Howard and Sheth model emerged in outline in 1957, and the model just discussed in 1969. A revision in 1973 can be found in Howard and Ostlund [5] and empirical testing in Farley and Ring [6] and Lehman *et al.* [7]. Howard continues to contribute to marketing thought in this area and has elaborated his theories about routinised response behaviour, limited problem-solving and extensive problem-solving by constructing three models to correspond to each of these [8].

Can the marketing manager make use of comprehensive models in the current stage of their development? This question will be considered in terms of how far they might assist explanation and prediction.

Models as explanations

Explanation of behaviour implies statements about the factors that could potentially influence the strength and direction of responses to given stimuli. It requires that all the significant variables are properly identified and that the linkages between them are clearly understood. For example, assume a manager could depict buyers' behaviour as in the following listing (using Howard and Sheth terminology). It may go some way to explaining that behaviour, but is hardly a full explanation:

1. Relatively routinised behaviour.

2. Narrow evoked set.

3. Our brand in 50 per cent of such sets.

4. Movement in and out of these evoked sets is largely a function of slow changes in the ways consumers evaluate the product category (e.g. stressing a different attribute).

5. Current buyers of our brand value attribute A, others attribute B.

6. Price and retail availability critical to choice within evoked sets.

7. When required, overt search is principally through word-of-mouth and at point-of-purchase.

8. Most common forms of stimulus ambiguity stem from methods of preparation and serving (e.g. should the product be deep-fried or grilled?).

9. Perceptual distortion frequently attaches low nutritional value to the product class.

10. Higher socio-economic groups consume relatively small amounts of the product class, although our brand has more than a proportional penetration in these groups.

11. The product class is usually bought on shopping trips involving numerous other purchase decisions, therefore considerable time pressure.

With such knowledge the manager would be in a position to deal partially with a number of major problems. It has implications for the role of the salesforce, advertising and sales promotion, pricing and product planning. The market seems to be price-sensitive and so further investigation might indicate the extent of this sensitivity and suggest the acceptability of current price plans. Point-of-purchase promotional activity would also seem to be essential. Advertising may serve as a reminder and only gradually help to develop beliefs about the brand. It would appear that a long-term communication goal could be to rectify the distorted view about the nutritional value of the brand. Packaging should be distinctive and readily recognisable because of the time pressure on buyers.

These kinds of points could become significant elements in the development of marketing strategy and provide a framework for the analysis of competitive reaction. But sophisticated users would be worried by the adequacy of the definition of the variables in the model in operation terms. Farley and Ring met considerable difficulty in their empirical testing of the Howard and Sheth model because of this problem [9]. Tuck has criticised the model because of what she sees as its lack of specification [10]. But it cannot be written off in a cursory fashion. It has exerted great influence on marketing thought and, as Hunt says, 'the bogeyman of premature closure should deter no one from the formalization of theories, at least to the extent that formalization facilitates both theoretical analysis and empirical testing' [11].

Foxall [12] encourages new directions to be taken. He takes issue with the fundamental assumption of a highly involved consumer, able to detect important difference between brands and becoming committed to one because of its unique attributes. He says:

> Whether the reasons for the poor results are that the posited relationships do not hold or that the model is not sufficiently well-specified to enable better testing to take place is an open question. The development of alternative models based on different assumptions about the nature of consumer choice is indicated and has received a major impetus with the wider recognition that consumer behaviour should be depicted as uninvolving or, at least, as much less involving than the comprehensive modellers assumed.

Models as predictors

We shall consider one controversial type of predictive model to do with brand loyalty and brand switching. It employs a Markhov probability model with the idea of 'transition probabilities'. These refer to movements from one time period to another and the probabilities of subjects moving or staying constant between several states. In this context the states are buying different brands (Table 4.2). Assume that the brand choice behaviour of a sample of households has been monitored in two periods. We have the brand shares of the three brands in a product class and a record of the degree of switching between the brands from time T_1 to time T_2. This is displayed in the table as transition probabilities, so that it can be seen that 80 per cent of brand A's consumers in T_1 stay loyal in T_2 and 10 per cent switch to brand B and 10 per cent to C. Brand B has an 80 per cent loyalty and C 90 per cent. The rows show where consumers went and the columns where they came from. It can be observed that at end of T_2 the brand shares have therefore changed to C's advantage. Now, if the substantial assumption is made that the transition probabilities remain static, then it would be possible to project for T_3 and derive expected brand shares.

The Markhov model is one type of stochastic model, i.e. it views consumer choices as the outcome of a probabilistic process. Predictions using such models assume that knowledge of past brand choices is all that is needed. They do not describe or explain the reasons for consumer behaviour, relying on observation of the outcomes. They sweep away most of the complexities in behaviour; they take no account of new factors that might influence brand switching in the prediction period, and they imply homogeneity among consumers.

Ehrenberg's [13] criticisms suggest that these models are simplistic and naive, but Montgomery and Ryans argue that Markhov models can provide useful diagnostic information. The predictions are obviously conditional on circumstances remaining unchanged; none the less, ideas about where the market might go within this condition can be useful. 'Naturally, if a prognosis for a firm's brand looks bad, the firm will attempt to rectify the situation by positive market actions, which it hopes will alter the unfavourable situation' [14]. Economists have given us the *ceteris paribus* mode of analysis, and for purely analytical purposes it can be useful, even if, in the real world, nothing ever holds very steady.

A predictive model has been derived by Ehrenberg [15] from empirical studies in stationary markets, that is, markets such as soap, soap powders and toothpaste where there is little or no change in competitive circumstances in successive time periods. Two terms are central to this model:

1. Penetration: b = proportion of the population buying a brand in a time period.

2. Purchase frequency: w = average number of times these buyers buy in the period.

Ehrenberg suggests that the distribution of purchases across consumers in a time period can be expressed in a negative binomial distribution and he offers formulae for estimating the parameters of this distribution. Given that, he also provides expressions for estimating over two time periods the numbers of repeat buyers (buyers in periods 1 and 2), new buyers (buyers buying in period 2 but not in

Table 4.2 *Brand share predictions model*

Brand bought T_1	Brand bought T_2			Market share T_1 %	Market share T_2 %
	A	B	C		
A	0.8	0.1	0.1	50	45
B	0.1	0.8	0.1	30	29
C	0.1	0.0	0.9	20	26

period 1) and lapsed buyers (buyers buying in period 1 but not period 2). Certain regularities have emerged from this work, e.g. new buyers have an average purchase frequency of 1.4 units.

Applications of this approach included evaluations of promotional activity. If predictions are made of repeat buying and new buyers for a brand without changes in marketing activity, and then some aspect of strategy is changed, then the difference between the predicted and actual data can be attributed to the impact of that change in strategy.

Adoption process models

Much marketing activity concerns the planning and introduction of new products. Ultimately the success of this activity is dependent upon customer reactions, and so there has been considerable interest in learning about the process of consumer adoption of new products. The basic process is shown in Figure 4.3.

In this model the stages are defined as follows:

1. Problem perception – perception of a need or motive and search for relevant knowledge.
2. Awareness – a product's existence becomes known.
3. Comprehension – the consumer's conception of what the product is.
4. Attitude – disposition towards the product.
5. Legitimation – conviction that the right course of action would be to try the product.
6. Trial – may be commitment to adopt or evaluation.
7. Adoption – acceptance and continued purchase use.
8. Dissonance – may reinforce the legitimation stage, or result in abandonment of the product.

Note that it is not necessary to progress through all stages in strict sequence. Problem perception need not necessarily be the first step; awareness of an

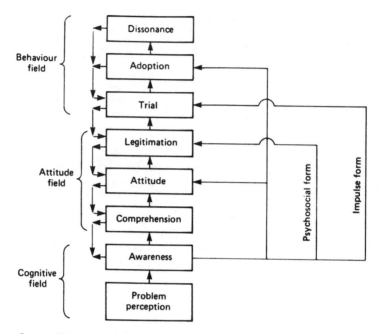

Source: T.S. Robertson, 'A critical examination of adoption process models of consumer behaviour', in J.N. Sheth, *Models of Buyer Behavior*. New York: Harper & Row, 1974. Copyright © Harper & Row, 1974.

Figure 4.3   *Summary adoption decision process model*

innovation could precede it. And downward movement is equally as possible as upward movement.

One of the central concerns in studying new product adoption relates to the reasons for the process to be frustrated. Table 4.3 sets out some causes for the potential adopter to reject the innovation. Many of these can be attributed to poor marketing. At the most basic level there may simply have been no marketing research, or the research was wrong. The benefits built into the product may not serve the consumer's needs. But even if there is a real need and the product seems to offer some of the right benefits, there are major problems in getting customer attention and full comprehension. People may not understand how the product fits their problem, and not be motivated to find out. Selective exposure, selective and possibly distorted perception and selective retention could all contribute to put consumers off. The communication may not be sufficiently persuasive to help the consumer form a favourable disposition to the new product. And at the legitimation stage conviction may stall because of uncertainty about the generalised image and reputation of the company: consumers may perceive high levels of risk in dealing with a little-known firm. Trial may be frustrated by lack of availability or customer confusion concerning how to go about buying, and in use the product may not live up to expectations.

Table 4.3 *Potential causes of uncompleted adoption process*

Adoption process stage	Marketing organisation causes	Consumer causes
Dissonance	Innovation attributes incorrectly communicated	Innovation fails to meet expectations
Adoption	Failure to develop new products and improve old ones	Replaced by another innovation
Trial	Behaviour response not specified in communications Poor distribution systems	Alternative equally as good Innovation not available
Legitimation	Poor source effect of communications	Peer-group pressure against adoption Laws regulating use of innovation
Attitude	Communication not persuasive	Complacency Suspended judgement
Comprehension	Communication difficult to understand	Selective retention
Awareness	Poorly used or too little communication	Selective exposure Selective perception
Problem perception	Poor marketing research	Lack of problem

Source: G. Zaltman and R. Stiff, 'Theories of diffusion', in S. Ward and T.S. Robertson (eds), *Consumer Behavior: Theoretical sources*. Englewood Cliffs, NJ: Prentice Hall Inc., 1973, p. 451.

Another area of interest in the diffusion process is the difference between consumers in their willingness to adopt innovations. Rogers [16] considers that all those who will eventually accept an innovation can be considered in five groups as depicted in Figure 4.4. Understanding the characteristics of each of these groups as they might apply to any given new product introduction holds out the possibility of the firm being able to devise more effective marketing strategies. If it could be shown that the innovators constituted a unique group with quite different

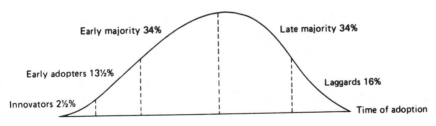

Source: E. M. Rogers, *Diffusion of Innovations*, New York: Free Press, 1962.

Figure 4.4 *Adopter categories by time of adoption*

motivations, attitudes, personality traits, socio-economic, demographic and media exposure profiles, then distinctive strategies aimed just at those people could speed the acceptance process. We shall consider first why the innovators are important, and then just how unique they are.

Since innovators are the first to buy and use the new products, their essential significance is in putting the innovation on public show. This social display can provide the initial impetus to word-of-mouth communication which is generally now seen to be one of the necessary prerequisites for successful product launches [17]. In an age of conspicuous consumption this display could also contribute points for emulation by others. Thus the importance of the innovator is not that he or she usually actively communicates with and persuades the bulk of the population, but that he or she supplies notions of what is fashionable or desirable. The importance attached to innovators has stimulated research into their characteristics. The types of characteristic considered have been:

1. Venturesomeness – willingness to take risks.
2. Social mobility – upward movement in social hierarchy.
3. Privilegedness – relatively high income level.
4. Social integration – degree of participation in community.
5. Interest range – innovators assumed to have wider range.
6. Status concern – need to be noticed and admired.
7. Cosmopolitanism – orientation beyond immediate community.

In a study of the adoption of a new household appliance it was found that venturesomeness and social mobility were the main factors discriminating the innovators [18]. Status concern and interest range were of minor importance and cosmopolitanism negatively related. But it should not be concluded that these are necessarily the same in all product classes. Many research studies give conflicting results [19], although Midgley [20] draws the following conclusion for first buyers of a radical innovation:

> The innovator is a competent self-assured person, intelligent and educated enough to set his/her own standards, and to evaluate innovations against these criteria. They can comprehend the abstract implications of adopting major innovations, and furthermore have the financial resources to experiment. Above all else the innovators favour changes and are willing to take risks.

Innovators are therefore still somewhat elusive, and it is probable that those for expensive durables are quite distinct from those for, say, baby food. Little consistency could thus be expected in terms of their media exposure. None the less their importance is undeniable, and it would be as well for the marketing manager to attempt to define the innovators in his product class, and to assess the ease with which they might be reached by various media.

The manager could also find advantage in discovering how the innovation is perceived by consumers. Zaltman and Stiff [21] comment that:

> A manufacturer may define the relevant aspects of an innovation in a totally dissimilar way than the consumer. The manufacturer may view a new product as a major labour-saving device and develop his marketing strategy accordingly. Consumers, however, may not perceive the time saved as significant and thus reject the new product; or they adopt it for other reasons, such as the desire for social approval, ease of operation, low cost and so on.

Ostlund [22] goes further by concluding that, in his study of six product classes, perceptual factors were more important than predispositional or socio-economic factors. The six elements of product perception which he researched were:

1. Relative advantage – Is the innovation perceived superior?

2. Compatibility – Is the innovation consistent with existing values, habit and experiences?

3. Perceived risk – What degree of risk is perceived to be associated with the product?

4. Divisibility – Can it be tried on a limited basis?

5. Complexity – Is it difficult to understand and use?

6. Communicability – Will results of an innovation be apparent and possible to communicate to others?

If the firm were able to determine current or probable product perceptions, then it might be able to revise its promotional planning if difficulties were uncovered. In a further study, Ostlund [23] suggests that these measures have another importance. They might be used as predictors of innovativeness, as a method, then, of pinpointing the innovators. If the research necessary for this type of study also included background demographic and media exposure data, then it could be a most powerful tool in product management.

Difficulties identifying the very small proportion of people thought to be innovators have increasingly led researchers to employ a wider definition, and to contrast 'earlier adopters' with the rest. For example, Wills has studied the fashion adoption process and finds the 'earlier adopters' there to be young, but, interestingly, of lower social class; 'the DE social grouping has more than its proportionate share of earlier adopters, while the AB group has less. Further, the majority (70 per cent) of earlier adopters belong to either the DE or C2 social grouping' [24].

Individuals are not the only source of influence in the adoption process. Groups may also affect the acceptance of innovations. Robertson [25] has recently studied the possible impact of groups on innovative behaviour. Significant relationships were found:

1. If the group norm was favourable to innovation, then there was a higher

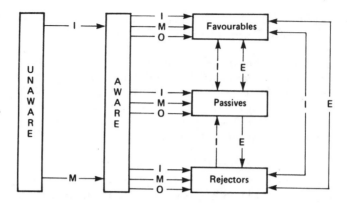

Transfer mechanisms: I = interpersonal communication; M = mass media communication; O = other marketing activities; E = individual experience.

Source: D. F. Midgely, *Innovation and New Product Marketing,* London: Croom Helm, 1977, p. 118.

Figure 4.5   *Innovative behaviour states*

tendency for innovative behaviour by group members as a whole. This was much more clearly demonstrated for clothing than for food.

2. Cosmopolitanism increased the likelihood of innovation acceptance. In this case cosmopolitanism was defined as extra-group communication; that is the degree of contact outside the small groups of three or four friends.

3. Greater perceived risk encouraged more intra-group communication.

4. Innovativeness was associated with lower levels of perceived risk.

Midgley's theory of innovative behaviour

In constructing his theory Midgley says that, in respect of an innovation, individuals may be in any of five states [26]. They may be favourable, having tried it and liked it. They may be unfavourable, having tried but not liked it. They may be passive, having tried it but not communicating anything about it to others. They may be only aware without having tried or, lastly, unaware of the existence of the innovation.

Understanding the movement between these states is crucial. Midgley offers four transfer mechanisms: individual experience, interpersonal communication, mass media communication and other marketing activities (e.g. samples, free offers, etc.). The possible relationship between these states and the movement between them is shown in Figure 4.5. Companies may uncover problems in any of the states

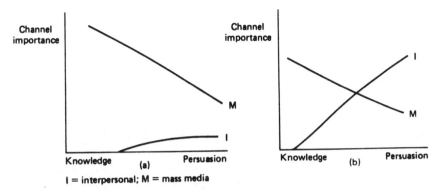

Source: D.F. Midgley, *Innovation and New Product Marketing,* London: Croom Helm, 1977, p. 92.

Figure 4.6   *Information sources in new product introductions.* (a) *Innovators.* (b) *Early adopters*

and in any of the transfer mechanisms. Market acceptance may be accelerated if something could be done to ease these problems.

Midgley also draws some conclusions about the relative importance of mass media and interpersonal sources of information in new product introductions. His views are that it is necessary to distinguish between innovators and early adopters, and between information acquisition to build up knowledge and persuasive information (Figure 4.6). It can be seen that entirely different roles are expected of the two sources in the case of innovators and early adopters. If the problem were one of attempting to persuade innovators, then both sources would be relevant. If it were one of giving more information to early adopters, then mass media should dominate. Generally, it can be seen that once there are some adopters of the new product then interpersonal influence becomes much more significant.

The discussion of adoption in this chapter has been restricted to consumer products For a wide review of the adoption and diffusion of new industrial products see the literature survey by Kennedy [27] and Chisnall [28] on innovative strategy.

Summary

Models of buyer behaviour simplify and organise the mass of variables relevant to purchasing decisions. In doing so they spur development in thought and research, but as yet are only partial explanations of behaviour. Among numerous models, the Howard and Sheth model is one of the best known. It has undergone several major modifications in recent years.

Predictive models such as the Markhov model are controversial, but may give some limited insight into the dynamics of a market.

A major class of models studied in this chapter concerns the adoption of new products and the diffusion of innovations. The difficulties in identifying the characteristics of the innovators were considered and Midgley's theory of innovative behaviour was investigated.

Questions for review and discussion

1. 'Companies can make profits whether or not they have a comprehensive market model.' Does it follow that the developments considered in this chapter have little operational significance?

2. 'It is one thing putting a label on a box in a chart and quite another to define that variable in such a way that survey data could be collected.' What are the consequences for model-building?

3. Assume the transition probabilities in Table 4.2 remain the same for the third period. Compute the brand shares in that period.

4. Only about 3 per cent of the British population wear contact lenses compared with 8 per cent in Holland and 12 per cent in the United States. Over 80 per cent of those using contact lenses are women aged 18 to 23, and there is a high rate of reversion to spectacles in the age range 25 to 30, with some further interest in lenses by those in their mid-forties. Use Table 4.3 to predict potential difficulties in the adoption of contact lenses.

5. The Association of Contact Lens Manufacturers promotes the use of contact lenses, but does not advertise specific brands. Use Midgley's theory to suggest target groups and 'transfer mechanisms' for a promotional campaign. How might the target groups be identified? Should they receive the same or different messages?

6. How might innovators for a new kind of consumer durable product be identified, and would they constitute a target group which could be easily reached?

7. Would the adoption process for a new service be more or less complicated than that for a consumer product? Contrast the adoption of a new bank service which combines investment advice with a savings plan with (a) new kitchen appliances, and (b) a new range of frozen food.

References

1. Lunn, J.A. 1977. 'Application of behavioral models to the study of individual consumers', in Nicosia, F.M. and Wind, Y., *Behavioral Models for Market Analysis*. Hinsdale, Ill: Dryden, p. 62. A wider discussion of models in marketing can be found in Lilien, G.L. and Kotler, P. 1983. *Marketing Decision Making*. New York: Harper & Row.

2. Zaltman, G. and Wallendorf, M. 1979. *Consumer Behavior: Basic findings and managerial implications*. New York: John Wiley.
3. Lunn, J.A. 1974. 'Consumer decision-process models', in Sheth, J. (ed.), *Models of Buyer Behavior*. New York: Harper & Row.
4. Howard, J.A. and Ostlund, E. 1973. *Buyer Behavior*. New York: Alfred A. Knopf, p. 23.
5. Ibid.
6. Farley, J.V. and Ring, L.W. 1974. 'Deriving an empirically testable version of the Howard–Sheth model of buyer behavior', in Sheth, J. (ed.), *Models of Buyer Behavior*. New York: Harper & Row.
7. Lehman, D.R., O'Brien, T.V., Farley, J.U. and Howard, J.A. 1974. 'Some empirical contributions to buyer behaviour theory', *Journal of Consumer Research*, vol. 1, December.
8. Howard, J.A. 1977. *Consumer Behavior: Application of Theory*. New York: McGraw-Hill.
9. Farley, J.V. and Ring, L.W. 1974. 'Deriving an empirically testable version of the Howard-Sheth model of buyer behavior', in Sheth, J. (ed.) *Models of Buyer Behavior*. New York: Harper & Row.
10. Tuck, M. 1976. *How Do We Choose?* London: Methuen, p. 31.
11. Hunt, S.H. 1976. *Marketing Theory*. New York: Grid, Inc., p. 117.
12. Foxall, G. R. 1987. 'Consumer behaviour', in Baker, M.J. (ed.), *The Marketing Book*. London: Heinemann, p. 128.
13. Ehrenberg, A.S.C. 1965. 'An appraisal of Markhov brand switching models', *Journal of Marketing Research*, vol. 2, no. 4.
14. Montgomery, D.B. and Ryans, A.B. 1973. 'Stochastic models of consumer choice behavior', in Ward, S. and Robertson, T., *Consumer Behavior: Theoretical Sources*. Englewood Cliffs, NJ: Prentice Hall Inc., p. 529.
15. Ehrenberg, A.S.C. 1972. *Repeat-buying, Theory and Application*. Amsterdam: North-Holland.
16. Rogers, E.M. 1962. *Diffusion of Innovations*. New York: Free Press.
17. See, for example, Day, G.S. 1974. 'Attitude change and the relative influence of media and word-of-mouth sources', in Sheth, J. (ed.), *Models of Buyer Behavior*. New York: Harper & Row.
18. Robertson, T.S. and Kennedy, J.N. 1966. 'Prediction of consumer innovators: application of multiple discriminant analysis', *Journal of Marketing Research*. vol. 5.
19. Ostund, L.E. 1973. 'Diffusion: a dynamic view of buyer behavior', in Howard, J.A. and Ostlund, E., *Buyer Behavior*. New York: Alfred A. Knopf.
20. Midgley, D.F. 1977. *Innovation and New Product Marketing*. London: Croom Helm, p. 60.
21. Zaltman, G. and Stiff, R. 1973. 'Theories of diffusion', in Ward, S. and Robertson, T.W., *Consumer Behavior: Theoretical Sources*. Englewood Cliffs, NJ: Prentice Hall Inc., p. 427.
22. Ostlund, L.E. 1973. 'Predictors of innovative behavior', in Howard, J.A. and Ostlund, E. (eds), *Buyer Behavior*. New York: Alfred A. Knopf.
23. Ostlund, L.E. 1974. 'Perceived innovation attributes as predictors of innovativeness', *Journal of Consumer Research*, vol. 1, September.
24. Wills, G. 1977. 'The management of fashion in marketing', *European Insights in Marketing*. Bradford: MCB Books, p. 13.
25. Robertson, T.S. 1974. 'Group characteristics and aggregate innovative behavior: preliminary report', in Sheth, J. (ed.), *Models of Buyer Behavior*. New York: Harper & Row.
26. Midgley, op. cit. p. 116.
27. Kennedy, A.M. 1983. 'The adoption and diffusion of new industrial products: a literature review', *European Journal of Marketing*, vol. 17, no. 3.
28. Chisnall, P.M. 1983. *Strategic Industrial Marketing*. Hemel Hempstead: Prentice Hall International, chapter 7.

Chapter 5

Organisational buying behaviour

The discussion now turns to some explicit consideration of marketing to industry and other organisations. Buying behaviour in the two situations is markedly different, with separate problems that require different responses from companies selling into them.

Size and frequency of purchase present a first difference. Grocery products are bought very frequently in small quantities: heavy machinery is bought infrequently and then the expenditure can be massive. Some radical consequences flow from this contrast. The small scale of each purchase in the consumer market means that consumers cannot be treated individually, and with self-service shopping they buy without face-to-face contact with the manufacturer or retailer. An obvious point, but perhaps it explains something of the scale of consumer advertising and the attention to sales promotional devices. On the other hand, machinery manufacturers can treat their customers more individually because, when they buy, each order could be worth tens or hundreds of thousands of pounds. Not only will direct face-to-face contact be made; but also the product itself may incorporate suggestions made by the customer. Specifications may be changed to suit the particular customer's requirements in specific applications of the machinery. The salesforce is the dominant part of marketing strategy.

Another difference is found in the numbers of potential customers. A breakfast cereal manufacturer may consider that there are ten million prospective consumers, and they will all expect to be able to buy the brand in an outlet within a few miles of their homes. Thus tens of thousands of shops need to be stocked regularly, which entails a huge, continuing operation physically moving millions of packets of cereal. The machinery manufacturer may have only a few hundred customers, or at most a few thousand. Within these, a small proportion will probably buy most of the output. If the manufacturer uses an independent marketing channel, then it is unlikely that high stocks will be carried in the channel. Most orders will probably be filled with direct delivery from the factory.

A further contrast is that the machinery firm is displaced from the origin of its demand [1], that is, its product is in derived demand. Its market prospects depend on the demand for the ultimate product made by its machinery. The accelerator principle makes for considerable demand variability, small changes in the demand for consumer goods being magnified into huge changes in the demand for capital goods. The very pronounced cyclical pattern in industrial markets imposes particular difficulties. If more attention is paid to the amplitude of the swings than to the secular trend, then long-term expansion plans can be seriously hampered. Assuming an average five-year cycle and a 3–4-year lead-time in bringing extra capacity into production, then some of the investment will be required during lean times. Cash flow problems may curtail the expansion. The cycle also affects marketing activity, e.g. in the continuity of salesforce effort and even the method of paying sales representatives. (They will not be too happy with great variation from one year to the next.) Thus economic forecasting is essential in industrial markets.

Most buying decisions in industry are of technical products which are evaluated technically by the buyer. Of necessity, much of the relationship between buyer and seller is therefore in a technical context. In the consumer market, technical products are not sold on the basis of the technology. The communication between buyer and seller is not in technical terms. Purchasers are not told the technicalities of washing machines or television sets.

Purchasing motives are also different [2]. Most buying decisions in industry are to fulfil organisational goals (e.g. to cut costs, increase output, etc.). Industry does not often buy to impress friends. But it would be wrong to suggest that motives are therefore less complex than in the consumer market. Organisations do not set goals, nor do they make decisions. People do. Individuals within the organisation determine the aims and decide what to do. Other people in the organisation translate these broad directions into operations. Perceptual factors naturally enter the process, and the earlier discussion of perception indicates what complexity might be added by that factor. An illustration of this can be seen in the seemingly trivial issue of company and brand names. In the industrial market different people may have different perceptions of the purchasing problem – the need to buy a product, the company's goals and the extent to which alternative suppliers might solve the problem. Superficially, it may be argued that purchasing problems in industry are obvious. However, consider the following example.

An engineering components factory is failing to meet production targets. Internal investigation blames an undue amount of rectification work caused by substandard machining. A natural response would be to evaluate the machine operators' performance. The production supervisor is sensitive to trade union reactions and therefore attributes poor work to some difficulties with the quality of materials. Perhaps the steel supplier is changed. Work quality does not improve, and from further discussion it becomes clear that the operatives are blaming the 20-year-old machine tools. The production manager had anticipated this, but in the plans for that year had proposed to the managing director that the only capital items should be some new type of finishing process.

He considered that the machine tools could gradually be replaced over the next five years. An engineering designer gets to hear of the disagreement and is excited by the unexpected suggestion that the plant replacement schedule should be brought forward. For some time he has been anxious to gain a machining facility that could offer the possibility of handling an improved range of components that

What's in a name?

Organisations do not make decisions: people do, and names matter to people
Shell market a premium diesel oil to commercial vehicle operators under the brand name Myrina.
Its advertising featured a shire-horse with dray, and this distinguished the campaign by giving
a sharp visual contrast to competitive advertising. But it was found that little awareness of the
brand name was achieved. A new approach was devised with more specific reference to brand
qualities.

The Myrina girl series was gradually shaped, but the agency ensured that these were
not seen as girlie ads. It was eye-catching, in publications packed with pictures of trucks
and containers; it was attractive to a tough audience; it was flexible, allowing many
versions; it capitalised on quality of product; and it could be carried through into point
of sale in a variety of ways. A year later unprompted recall was up from 3 per cent to 29
per cent.

Ozalid are an old, established and respected company supplying services to architects, engineering drawing specialists and printers. The company was acquired by Océ in the 1970s and
a new range of plan printers was to have been launched under the Océ brand name rather than
that of Ozalid. Preliminary research discovered enormous goodwill for the Ozalid name and
considerable reluctance amongst buyers to move to untried and untested products.

Océ, well known and admired internationally in other fields, had to be broken in
gradually in this professional and conservative sector.

Lovell Plant Hire is part of the Lovell Construction Group. In 1982 it was considering changing
its name to LPH and commissioned research to assess the consequences. One result was that
some construction companies who would not normally hire from Lovell would do so if equipment was branded as LPH, because it would not be seen as coming from a rival construction
company.

Source: J. Lovell, 'The key to an ad blindspot', *Campaign*, 15 July 1983.

he has been thinking of designing. He talks to the production manager and the
managing director and shows them a range of catalogues he had received some
time ago from several machine tool manufacturers.

Assume that the new machines are much more highly automated than the
existing ones. The engineering designer interests the sales manager in the new
components and the production manager gets his new finishing process. But a
committee is formed to investigate the feasibility of bringing forward the replacement dates for the machine tools, within the context of introducing the improved
range of components. Eventually a two-year programme is agreed with adequate
safeguards for redundancy. Thus significant orders will be placed with machine
tool firms.

Now it is debatable just how much of this process was obvious. Certainly the end-result did not necessarily follow from the original symptom. It is demonstrably more complex than the individual's selection of a brand of toothpaste. More people are involved, and those people could have entirely different perceptions of the nature of the problem. A longer time period is involved, and new variables enter over time. The whole process is adaptive to circumstances; pressures from interested parties wax and wane; the basic definition of the nature of the problem can change to appease one dominant individual or group. And none of this takes account of the incursions of suppliers into the process. Machine tool sales personnel might have been involved at any time, attempting to change the progress of events in their favour. If several competitors had become involved, their rival claims and assorted perceptions would have considerably increased the complexity.

While it is complex, it is not random. An outside observer with knowledge of the participants and their motives might have been able to assign rough probability statements to the various courses of action. That requires some understanding of the influences at work in the buying process, and therefore consideration of current thought in this area.

A general framework

Figure 5.1 shows some of the key factors to be considered in organisational buying behaviour. General environmental factors will be the backcloth to these influences. Webster and Wind point to ecological, technological, economic and political trends as particularly pertinent.

Ecological considerations

Business is not insulated from society. If, as has happened, society becomes more

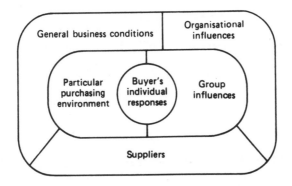

Source: F.E. Webster and Y. Wind, *Organizational Buyer Behavior,* Englewood Cliffs, NJ: Prentice Hall Inc., 1972.

Figure 5.1 *General framework for organisational buying behaviour*

concerned with the ecological impact of production, then industry's buying decisions will be affected. This might mean that new types of product will be bought (e.g. to recycle waste) or modifications of established products will be considered (e.g. a new type of closure for a soft drink can). These trivial examples give nothing of the universal impact that changing perceptions of the effect of industry on the environment can have in the whole of business operations. Such change would add a new set of evaluative criteria to almost any industrial purchase. The relative salience of such criteria would have to be established in any specific situation.

Technological development

Both the rate and direction of technical change can affect what is required and what is offered in industrial purchasing. It provides the most important factor in the dynamics of industrial markets. For supplying companies it gives major opportunities and major problems. Opportunities in that few industrial markets remain static for very long, and where there is change there is the hope that a particular firm's position can be improved. Problems because the firm's technical development effort may be out of step with the market. In all cases there will be the need to attempt to predict the way technology is moving, and so technological forecasting is a requisite. But that provides more problems because the firm will need to find a forecasting technique on which it can place some reliance. This may involve trend extrapolation by fitting curves to data on the historical rate of technical change. Alternatively, panels of experts may be consulted. Porter advocates the use of scenarios, which are composite descriptions of future technological events. Several different scenarios are projected under different assumptions about the technology, markets and competition. This is obviously imprecise, but as Porter [3] says,

> Having developed the scenarios . . . the firm is in a position to examine (and assess) which scenario it will bet on or how it will behave strategically if each scenario actually occurs. The firm may choose to try to cause the most advantageous scenario to occur if it has the resources; or it may be forced by limited resources or great uncertainty to maintain flexibility. In any case, the firm will benefit by identifying explicitly the key events which will signal whether one scenario or another is actually occurring, in order to create an agenda for its strategic planning and technological monitoring.

General business conditions

The business cycle is a well-established phenomenon. Cyclical variation is sometimes more important to the volume of industrial orders than the underlying secular trend. Cash flow is intimately related to the cycle, and every long-term capital project commitment can be seriously hampered by relatively short-term weak phases in the cycle. Industrial confidence swings with general business conditions. Optimism leads to new orders; pessimism to cancellation and postponement.

Companies selling to industry need, therefore, to predict the trend in business conditions. 'Leading indicators' such as unemployment rates, new engineering orders and new starts in construction need to be monitored, as well as the surveys of industrial confidence such as those of the CBI and the *Financial Times*, and the Department of Trade and Industry's investment intentions survey. Some firms carry out studies to relate such indicators to their own flow of new orders. Regression analysis has been widely applied in such studies.

Cyclical fluctuation can affect all aspects of a company's operations. For example, it can affect the salesforce. If the firm pays its representatives with part commission, then for perhaps 2 years in 5 they will earn very little, which would hardly be conducive to high morale. Additionally, many engineering companies employ a high proportion of skilled personnel in manufacturing, workers they do not want to lose. If they therefore attempt to maintain production through the weak phase of the cycle, there is the natural corollary of high finished stock levels. To overcome something of this problem, many schemes have been tried. For example, the machine tool industry has tried to persuade some major customers to spread their ordering across the cycle, with the inducement of substantial discounts for long-term contracts; alternatively, there is always the search for markets with out-of-phase business cycles. If, say, the Japanese business cycle was lagged in respect of the British, then it would be entering a rising trend as the British cycle was entering a declining trend. Since delivery time is a function of the cycle, and because demand in industrial markets is 'delivery-elastic', then just as Japanese delivery times for machinery might be increasing beyond six months, the British times might be falling below six months. In this connection it has been shown that a one-month increase in British delivery times for machine tools leads to a 1 per cent increase of German imports to the United Kingdom.

Organisational influences

The structure and style of an organisation condition much of what goes on within it. First, the degree of centralisation can shape the purchasing procedures. Highly centralised organisations might leave little discretion to operating branches. They might have fixed policies, which means that all purchases above a certain sum need central approval. They might also have some central list of approved suppliers and a highly systematic purchasing procedure. Quite small details might need to be documented on the authorised form. All this might be totally different in a decentralised structure.

A uniform, standardised marketing approach to organisations with differing degrees of centralisation is thus inappropriate. A sale could not be made to a branch of a centralised organisation if the head office was not in agreement. An axiom in marketing is 'first know your customer', and in this instance the 'customer' is probably several people at the branch and several people at the head office. And these people will usually abide by their organisation's rules and procedures. Successful sales representatives will hope to find out as much about the paperwork involved as members of the buying organisation.

Ideally, the selling company will know the buying organisation's structure, the relationships between divisions, key purchasing procedures and the important people involved.

Group influences

Throughout the discussion it has been implied that industrial buying decisions are frequently group, not individual, decisions. It is such a critical element that it has a special term, the *decision-making unit* (DMU), sometimes referred to as the 'buying centre'. The DMU may be large or small, formal or informal, constant or varying in membership, and the people involved may be aware or unaware of its very existence.

Buckner [4] gives information of the numbers of people that may have influence on the purchase. But these are generalisations, and the burden of the current argument is that DMUs are specific to particular company situations and so are likely to be highly variable between companies. There is no adequate replacement for hard information on the structure of DMUs in specific customer organisations. For small purchases it might be just one or two people; for large capital items it might be numerous layers of operatives, management and directors. Johnson and Bonoma report a study which attempts to trace the structure and interaction of DMU members [5].

Definition of DMU membership is problematic. It is not confined to those who actually place the order or just to those who make the final choice between alternative suppliers. It properly contains all those with some influence at any stage of the buying sequence. People who do not consciously recognise that they are significant in the buying process may give direction to the search for suppliers quite unwittingly. A leading manufacturer of earth-moving equipment changed its advertising media and message decisions after realising that the operatives were key influencers. Originally, they advertised in professional engineering journals with flat technical specifications. They switched to a construction industry weekly newspaper and used better illustrated copy when they concluded that the machine's driver was important in determining which piece of equipment to buy. Lorry manufacturers seem also to take this view: witness Ford's 'Custom Club' and the stress given to driver comfort.

Of course, DMU definition could be drawn very widely, taking in all members of the customer organisation. Rank Xerox used expensively made television commercials for the launch of their 9200 series. This could be interpreted as 'corporate advertising'; or it could be explained as an attempt to reach as many people as possible in potential customer organisations. Not that the majority would actively enter the purchasing process; but if it were possible to suggest to enough people that an organisation was behind the times unless it had the latest reprographic equipment, then this might create a generalised feeling of inadequacy with reprographic equipment currently being used. Just slight comments from numerous sources within the organisation might at least suggest the need for discussion of the topic and possibly the request for a visit from a representative. The same would be said of the widespread use of national newspaper advertising by Colt International for their industrial heating and ventilating systems, and for computing facilities.

There might also be more than one DMU with which to contend. In large construction projects architects, consultant engineers, contracting companies and the ultimate owners might all have some say in specifying suppliers. And each will have its own peculiar DMU. Sometimes, it is a matter of first determining which organisation to approach before any attempt is made at defining the DMU.

Another set of problems concerns the variable significance of DMU members and their motives. As suggested before, some will be more important than others, and this will not necessarily be a function of the formal authority structure of the organisation. Further, they could well have differing ideas about the product they are considering. A key element in this will be the resolution of conflict caused by different people having differing perceptions of the nature of the problem being faced. Something of this was implied in the illustration earlier in this chapter. Once more this suggests the need for specific information about the relative strengths of DMU members, their individual sets of evaluative criteria, their perceptions of the nature of the problem and some indication of the conflict resolution procedure employed [6].

Fisher [7] offers two variables that might dictate the functional areas that would be involved in a purchasing decision. These are product complexity – referring to the perceived complexity from the buyers' standpoint – and commercial uncertainty – referring to the degree of business risk in the purchase. High and low levels of each will have different implications for the emphasis given to different functional representatives in the DMU. Figure 5.2 shows the contrasts. Office stationery might be an example of cell 1, a clothing manufacturer's possible switch to a new synthetic fibre an example of cell 2, a brewer's consideration of new bottling machinery an example of cell 3, and the potential move to a new, completely automated plant an example of cell 4.

Webster and Wind consider the stage in the buying process as another variable affecting DMU membership at any one time (Table 5.1). Because this buying process may extend over a considerable time period, consideration of DMU membership at each stage leads to a secondary point: that is, from the supplier's viewpoint, the earlier the process is entered the better. If the supplier does not enter until being invited to do so at the overt search (determining alternatives) stage, then major decisions affecting the purchase would already have been made. The

Product complexity

		Low			High
Commercial uncertainty	Low	Buyer emphasis	①	③	Technologist emphasis
	High	Policy-maker emphasis	②	④	Total involvement

Source: L. Fisher, *Industrial Marketing,* 2nd edn, London: Business Books, 1976.

Figure 5.2 *Product complexity and commercial uncertainty and DMU membership*

Table 5.1 *DMU and stage in the buying process*

Stage in buying process	Users	Influencers	Buyers	Deciders	Gatekeepers
Identifying need	X	X			
Establishing specification	X	X	X	X	
Determining alternatives	X	X	X		X
Evaluating alternatives	X	X	X		
Selecting	X	X	X	X	

Notes:
X indicates that role active at that stage.
   Users: of the product.
   Influencers: especially technologists who might define many of the criteria.
   Buyers: those having formal authority for placing orders.
   Deciders: those having formal authority or informal power to select.
   Gatekeepers: those controlling the information flow concerning the purchase, i.e. controlling manufacturers' catalogues and the movement of sales representatives into the company.
Source: F.E. Webster and Y. Wind, *Organizational Buyer Behavior*. Englewood Cliffs, NJ: Prentice Hall Inc., 1972.

specification may have been drawn up in a manner not conducive to success. It may stress some characteristics not among the supplier's strengths and leave out other unique characteristics. This might be unavoidable, or it might be because the purchaser did not have full knowledge at the time specification was determined. It is very much in the supplier's interest to enter the process as early as possible. The best position is to assist the purchaser in identifying the problem, by making explicit a need that was previously only latent; as an example, a microfilm hardware sales representative pointing out to a prospect the deficiencies of storing and retrieving hard copy.

All this section on the DMU raises the difficulty of getting information. The firm may employ specialist market researchers to obtain some of it. But many firms see the gathering of such knowledge as an integral role of their sales personnel. After all, they are in continuing contact with customers, and they will need and use most of the information about DMUs. This is why industrial salespeople make comparatively few visits per day. On each visit they are expected to make as many contacts as possible within each customer organisation. They are expected to keep comprehensive records of DMU membership, motives and relationships, and to have knowledge of the organisation influences mentioned earlier. In addition, they should be monitoring their customers in terms of the stage reached in the buying process. The industrial sales representative can legitimately be considered as much a researcher as persuader.

However, that raises issues about the quality and reliability of research undertaken by the salesforce. Representatives may not see it as a central part of their role, and consequently not devote sufficient time or care to its completion. Grace and Pointon studied one company's use of sales personnel as researchers and recommend that their involvement needs to be explicitly rewarded if it is to be effective [8].

Just how many of these data stay with the salesforce and how many are passed back to management is an open question. In efficient organisations with effectively designed reporting procedures, a high proportion probably reaches management.

The purchasing executive

In some organisations the purchasing executive is a critical member of the DMU. In others she/he may be a very junior member of management. This relative status conditions some of her/his activities. There are instances where the function is reduced to that of 'gatekeeper', merely controlling the flow of information. Elsewhere she/he plays a much more dynamic part.

Much of the workflow of purchasing executives is laterally across the organisation, and this may create some difficulty. Because of this they may adopt several kinds of tactics. Strauss [9] nominates rule-oriented, rule-evading, personal–political, educational and organisational (i.e. change the rules and flows) types of tactic. The reception given to salespeople is likely to be affected by which tactic is being used. For instance, in one company the purchasing executive was very rule-oriented and concerned with his own relative status within the company. He decided to make the company more purchasing-minded by erecting large notices near the factory gates directing all sales representatives to his office. He took great delight in keeping them waiting, preferably two or three at a time.

The relative importance of various choice criteria employed by purchasing executives has been studied by Lehman and O'Shaughnessy [10]. They asked 220 executives to rate four kinds of criteria:

1. Performance criteria – how well will the product perform?

2. Economic criteria – costs of buying, using and maintaining.

3. Co-operative criteria – to what extent will suppliers co-operate and meet or exceed buyers' expectations?

4. Adaptive criteria – will the buyer have to adapt her/his plans because of uncertainty about the supplier's ability to meet the product and delivery specification?

It was found that as products became less standard, then economic factors decreased in importance and performance criteria became more important. Adaptive criteria were significant throughout, except in simple, standard products in standard applications. Co-operative criteria were less important.

While such surveys can yield useful insights they can be considerably enriched by more specific studies related to the particular circumstances faced by a selling company. Baker [11] gives several detailed case studies. One of these concerns TI Superform and the development of superplastic aluminium, which could potentially be used in place of other metals and plastics in the production of components. Market research uncovered specific barriers to the adoption of the new material:

1. The product design and specifications were controlled by a non-UK holding company.

2. Potential users employed a performance specification to which all materials must conform, e.g. a British standard.

3. Potential users' commitment to the known and existing technology, e.g. working in steel.

4. The costs of evaluating and testing the suitability of the new material.

5. Existing commitments to suppliers through forward orders.

6. Senior management unwilling to take risks.

These points added precision to the selling effort. They also demonstrate something of the complexity of industrial buying decisions.

Particular purchasing environment

Purchasing situations are likely to be highly variable. A key difference would be in the level of problem-solving triggered by the recognition that a problem exists. The decision to buy an expensive new computing system takes on a significance in the buying organisation of a quite different dimension from that caused by the observation that stationery supplies are running low. To distinguish alternative levels it has become conventional to refer to three generalised 'buyclasses' [12]:

1. New task – no previous experience with the product class and so an extensive problem requiring wide search activity and the development of choice criteria.

2. Modified rebuy – some prior experience with the product class, but perhaps changes in buyer circumstances or needs leading to changed

choice criteria, and maybe the need for the buyer to update knowledge of the technology and products available.

3. Straight rebuy – routine reordering; established choice criteria and wide experience of use; perhaps a list of approved suppliers already determined.

Similarities will be noted with the three levels of problem-solving typically discerned in consumer behaviour studies (extensive, limited and routine). Responses, however, are likely to be very different. An important implication of these buyclasses is in the role of the DMU. It will be active in the new task and dormant in straight rebuys.

Individual influences

As stated previously, people, not organisations, make decisions. Individual factors therefore present another set of influences on the buying decision. One element in this will be the acceptance and interpretation of information. The earlier study of perception showed how subjective this might be. Now another element will be added: the concept of source credibility.

The same information emanating from several sources may be ascribed 'differing credibility'. Levitt has investigated the relevance of source credibility in industrial purchasing [13]. He confirmed that who you are does affect how buyers react to what you say. High reputations ease the entry of sales representatives into prospective customer organisations and assist an initially favourable reception. Levitt also determined that the nature of the sales presentation had a marked effect. A 'bad presentation', with the representative emphasising her/his own company's problems in developing a new product, had a poor impact in comparison to a 'good presentation', with the emphasis on how the new product could overcome the customer's problems.

This research suggests that firms could improve in two ways. First, they could hope to enhance their generalised reputation through public relations (PR) and corporate advertising, and second, they could improve their representatives' performance through sales training.

Sheth's model of industrial buyer behaviour

A useful summary of the work done up to now in this chapter is given by Sheth's model shown in Figure 5.3. As a learning tool it is worth studying in detail. The serious student should be able to evoke much of the material considered here by

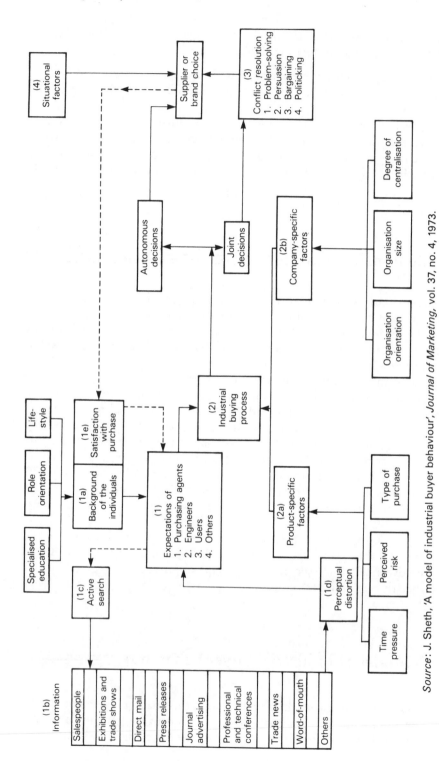

Source: J. Sheth, 'A model of industrial buyer behaviour', *Journal of Marketing*, vol. 37, no. 4, 1973.

Figure 5.3   *Sheth's model of industrial buyer behaviour*

referring to this model. Nearly all the variables have been studied, either in this chapter or in Chapter 4 when we introduced the Howard and Sheth classical model (Figure 4.2). One variable does need a little elaboration and that is 'situational factors'. Sheth proposes that some decisions may be heavily constrained by specific situations. Price controls, strikes and changes in customer budgets are examples that could divert or postpone the decision.

A more recent model of organisational buying behaviour is due to Choffray and Lilien [14]. This focuses on the adoption process and is designed to be empirically evaluated, but its specification is beyond the level of the present discussion.

Industrial buyer's information processing

Stiles [15] has reported a study of the variables that might affect an industrial buyer's information processing. He suggests it is a function of three factors:

1. Task complexity – the number of alternative courses of action and the number of attributes that differentiate the alternatives.

2. The individual buyer's conceptual complexity – the level of processing the individual can apply: a function of his experience with complex environment.

3. Workload and communication – the amount of workload and communication.

Use is made of the notion of 'level of information processing index'. This pictures information processing in choice situations as a hierarchy rising from numerous, detailed processing of each attribute through to more general, overall evaluations of 'value'. A small experiment by Stiles found a linear relationship between the three variables noted above and the level of information processing; that is, the more complex the task, the higher the level of conceptual complexity; and the higher the workload and communication, the more the processing moves away from detailed attribute investigations. This may be the beginning of a new stream of studies in industrial information processing. Its results should considerably improve our understanding and offer prescriptions for the development of marketing strategy.

Wilson suggests that the industrial buyer's information processing can be much more sophisticated with the use of 'a powerful external memory such as a computer' [16]. This clearly extends both information storage and search/retrieval ability. In the future it could lead to complex decision routines, with computer-based analytical procedures to sort and evaluate alternative vendor offerings against a large number of criteria. This therefore releases the severe constraint of information overload now thought to typify consumer information processing in some circumstances.

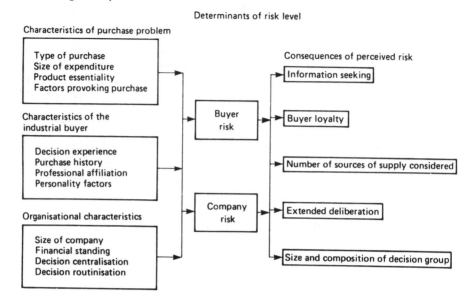

Source: J. Newell, 'Industrial buyer behaviour', *European Journal of Marketing,* vol. 11, no. 3, 1977. Copyright © 1977 by MCB Publications.

Figure 5.4   *Newell's perceived risk model*

Newell's perceived risk model

Perceived risk is recognised as an important variable in organisational buying. High risk is likely to stimulate different behaviour to low risk. Newell's model [17] is shown in Figure 5.4. In a study of office machinery purchasing it was found that type of purchase was the most important factor determining the level of perceived risk and that modified rebuys posed the highest risk and straight rebuys the lowest. Modified rebuys involving a change in product class considered for purchase, or a possible change in source of supply, showed significantly higher levels of risk. Some other important findings are as follows:

1. Among the purchase-provoking factors, dissatisfaction with equipment currently being used by the purchaser was associated with high risk.

2. Perceived risk has two dimensions: psycho-social risk and performance risk. Psycho-social risk is related to the extent to which the buyer feels he is held accountable for the consequences of the purchase. In large companies this was reduced via highly structured purchasing procedures.

3. DMU size (Newell uses the term 'buying group') does not appear to be a function of level of risk. It is more systematically related to the degree of decision centralisation and size of company.

4. High levels of perceived risk are associated with extended purchasing deliberation.

5. Source loyalty as a method of handling high risk is not substantiated.

The interaction model

This model, as explained by Turnbull, emphasises the processes and relationships in buying [18]. Long-term, active and complex links between buyers and sellers need to be sustained and nurtured. Much activity is therefore devoted to building and maintaining this web of linkages between organisations, and a good part of that will have little to do with a specific purchase. Four elements are thought influential: the interactive process, the atmosphere, the individual participants and the environment. The latter two have been considered earlier in this chapter; the first two are noted below.

The interactive process stresses the nature of the relationships and the role of communication. Modern communication theory views organisational communication as being associated with four kinds of exchange: that concerning goods, information, money or social relationships. Each may be present in the episodes of interaction between buying and selling organisations, and uncertainty in any of these could influence the nature of future communications. Through time, some exchanges may become routine and there could also be mutual adaptation of systems and procedures to improve the quality of the relationship.

Atmosphere refers to the tenor of the relationship – the degree of apparent conflict or co-operation. The stream of communication ties between organisations will have variously satisfactory results and contribute to expectations about future communications. Atmosphere will also be affected by other factors. In periods of transition, perhaps caused by technical change or changes in industry structure, tension may arise because the balance of power in the relationship is perceived to be changing.

Mapping communication ties between buying and selling organisations is a fruitful area for research. It also underscores the role of the sales representative or account manager in industrial marketing. That role could be interpreted as spearheading the communication flows, being involved crucially in all four kinds of communication exchange, frequently stimulating or co-ordinating the other flows and being a main contributor in establishing the atmosphere of the relationship. Substantial empirical support has been reported for this model [19].

Summary

Organisational buying behaviour differs from individual buying behaviour on a number of important accounts. Size and frequency of purchase, the numbers of potential customers, the importance of technical evaluations, the derived nature of the demand for industrial goods and differences in purchasing motives all provide sharp contrasts which could affect purchasing behaviour.

Webster and Wind's framework was used to investigate the major influences in organisational buying behaviour. Particular importance was attached to group influences and the particular purchasing environment. Identification of the DMU was seen as being fundamental, and Sheth's model provided a useful integration of much of the material in the chapter. Newell's perceived risk model offered an important empirical study. A wider view of the long-term relationships developed was given by the interaction model.

Questions for review and discussion

1. The early section of this chapter pointed out some differences between organisational and individual buying behaviour. What are the similarities?

2. Suggest how organisational influences might affect purchasing decisions for earth-moving equipment in the following kinds of organisation: local government, a large construction company, a small jobbing builder.

3. Draw out the implications for advertising media and message strategy of the concept of the DMU.

4. Devise new examples for each cell in Table 5.1.

5. How detailed should a selling company's records be about DMU members in customer and prospect companies? How personal should the information become and is there a difference in this respect between industrial and consumer markets?

6. What differences would you expect to find in the several stages in the buying process (Table 5.2) with different 'buyclasses'?

7. One of Newell's conclusions was that source loyalty was not substantiated as a method of handling high risk. What does that mean?

References

1. Haas, R.W. 1982. *Industrial Marketing Management*. Boston: Kent, ch. 2.
2. Hill, R.M., Alexander R.S. and Cross, J.S. 1975. *Industrial Marketing*, 4th edn. Homewood, Ill: Irwin, ch. 4.

3. Porter, M.E. 1980. *Competitive Strategy*. New York: Free Press, p. 235.

4. Buckner, H. 1967. *How British Industry Buys*. London: Hutchinson. An updated version conducted by the Cranfield School of Management was published by the *Financial Times* in 1984.

5. Johnson, W.J. and Bonoma, T.V. 1981. 'The buying centre: structure and interaction', *Journal of Marketing*, vol. 45, Summer.

6. Ryan, M.J. and Holbrook, M.B. 1982. 'Decision-specific conflict in organizational buying behavior', *Journal of Marketing*, vol. 46, Summer.

7. Fisher, L. 1976. *Industrial Marketing*, 2nd edn. London: Business Books.

8. Grace, D. and Pointon, T. 1980. 'Marketing research through the salesforce', *Industrial Marketing Management*, vol. 9, no. 1.

9. Strauss, G. 1962. 'Tactics of lateral relationship: the purchasing agent', *Administrative Science Quarterly*, vol. 7.

10. Lehman, D.R. and O'Shaughnessy, J. 1982. 'Decision criteria used in buying different categories of products', *Journal of Purchasing and Materials Management*, vol. 18, Spring. Quoted in Horton, R.L. 1984. *Buyer Behavior: A Decision-making Approach*. Columbus, Ohio: Merrill, p. 408.

11. Baker, M.J. 1983. *Market Development*. Harmondsworth: Penguin Books, p. 75.

12. Robinson, P.J., Faris, C.W. and Wind, Y. 1967. *Industrial Buying and Creative Marketing*. Boston: Allyn & Bacon.

13. Levitt, T. 1965. *Industrial Purchasing Behavior: A Study in Communications Effects*. Cambridge, Mass.: Harvard Business School Division of Research.

14. Lilien, G.L. and Kotler, P. 1983. *Marketing Decision Making*. New York: Harper & Row. Contains a modified version of the Choffray and Lilien model, pp. 273–85.

15. Stiles, G.W. 1974. 'Determinants of the industrial buyers level of information processing', in Hughes, G.D. and Ray, M.L., *Buyer/Consumer Information Processing*, Durham, NC: University of North Carolina Press.

16. Wilson, D.T. 1976. 'Organizational buying, a man and machine information processing approach', in Ray, M.L. and Ward, S. (eds), *Communicating with Consumers*, Beverly Hills: Sage.

17. Newell, J. 1977. 'Industrial buyer behaviour', *European Journal of Marketing*, vol. 11, no. 3.

18. Turnbull, P.W. 1987. 'Industrial marketing', in Baker, M., *The Marketing Book*. London: Heinemann. See also Turnbull, P.W. and Valla, J.-P. 1986. *Strategies for International Industrial Marketing*. Beckenham: Croom Helm, ch. 1.

19. Metcalf, L., Freer, C. and Krishnan, R. 1992. 'An application of the IMP Interaction Model', *European Journal of Marketing*, vol. 26, no. 2, pp. 27–46.

Chapter 6

Segmentation and positioning

Sellers have always used some of the ideas now formulated into the theory and practice of market segmentation. For a long time markets were divided geographically and on an income/social class basis. Mass production at first imposed some uniformity on consumers, as epitomised in Ford's early marketing strategy for the Model T ('You can have any colour as long as it's black'). But developments in production technology and the considerable increase in consumer affluence have given rise to the need for recognising and catering for disparities in consumer demand. So now there are not just broad generic classes of product, but a huge number of special subclasses. The household detergent and cleanser markets provide good examples of the trend over the past thirty years, with the plethora of special cleaning agents for any number of household chores.

Economists have dealt with one narrow type of market segmentation in price discrimination theory. A much richer literature has evolved in marketing since Smith [1] pioneered its sophisticated treatment in 1956. Today, segmentation is profoundly important in marketing thought, marketing research and marketing action. Some understanding of the concept and the difficulties in its application is necessary for all three, as well as for consumerist evaluations of the marketing process.

The rationale for segmentation

Market segmentation concerns the subdivision of markets. It is overt recognition that consumers are not homogeneous, and as Smith pointed out, several demand schedules may operate in the same market. Given the spur of competition firms may seek some advantage by designing products and appeals that more nearly match the differing requirements of distinct segments. To illustrate, consider the market for chocolate bars. A key product attribute might be the extent to which the chocolate was 'plain' or 'milk'. Assume research revealed consumer preferences for five formulations as follows:

Type of chocolate bar	% consumers preferring
Plain – no milk added to crushed cocoa	10
Brown chocolate-flavoured substitute	20
Milk – some milk added to cocoa	30
Full cream milk – high milk content	30
White chocolate-flavoured substitute	10

Now assume that hitherto only type 4 chocolate bars were available, although the research shows many people actually prefer any one of four other types. Indeed, only a third of the market has really been getting what it wanted in chocolate bars. Some probably did not buy because the type on offer was not appealing; others bought type 4 because it was the only one available. But let us assume rising affluence and a strong, positive income elasticity for chocolate bars. Furthermore, production engineers can now take advantage of new processing machinery with lower capital cost and a reduced labour requirement. Potentially, then, customer requirement can be more closely matched. At the very least, consideration should be given to bringing out additional types 2 and 3 chocolate bars.

So far the illustration is straightforward; but what if all the competitors already had brands on the market roughly equivalent to each type required? Research might now concentrate on the better identification of customer types in each segment, and the strategy could be to give very distinctive promotional treatments to these different groups of consumers. The 'plain' segment could be offered something like the Cadbury's Bourneville advertising which featured a rather bored man's appetite for confectionery being rekindled by the strong flavour of that brand. The 'white substitute' segment might be reached by something that would look remarkably like the 'Milky Bar Kid' campaign, with the fresh, young boy handing out that confection with the message 'The Milky Bars are on me'.

Segmentation – a theory or a strategy?

Market segmentation can be viewed as being both a theory and a strategy. As a theory it investigates markets to establish whether subsets exist, where each of these smaller groupings may react differently to marketing efforts. The main concern here would be the method used to describe and to distinguish the subsets. As a strategy market segmentation involves the creation of distinctive plans tailored to exploit the differences in the segments. Thus two segments might be given different marketing treatments with variations in any element of the marketing mix.

Viewing segmentation as a strategy, Frank et al. [2] have classified the alternatives by marketing tool variables and by method of targeting marketing effort (Table 6.1). Method of targeting marketing effort refers to the amount of control exercised by the firm. With customer self-selection there is little control: goods and services are made generally available. On the other hand controlled coverage may be possible if segments can be more or less isolated. This could mean the use of media targeted only at that segment, or distribution through channels only used by that segment.

Table 6.1 *Segmentation strategies*

Method of targeting marketing effort	Marketing tool variables	
	Product characteristics and appeals	Promotion, price and channels
Customer self-selection	(1)	(2)
Controlled coverage	(3)	(4)

Source: R.E. Frank, W.F. Massy and Y. Wind, *Market Segmentation.* Englewood Cliffs, NJ: Prentice Hall Inc., 1972.

The four alternatives in Table 6.1 can be illustrated as follows:

1. Some distinction has been made to the brand by changing some of its characteristics and consequently its appeal, but it is made widely available. An example is in breakfast cereals where each of the major companies has several brands on sale at most supermarkets. Each brand has a different appeal.

2. Promotional activity may be able to establish a unique image for the brand which appeals to particular segments. Cosmetics firms attempt this with only limited control over retail outlets.

3. Sometimes a distinctive product can be designed and the market coverage can be controlled. Financial products are an example. Insurance companies offer many product variants, but do not make them freely available. Prospective customers need to be 'qualified'.

4. Some package tours could provide the example here. There are operators that appeal only to particular age segments. They promote and price with those segments in mind, and might control the market coverage by recruiting prospects by direct mail.

A central issue in the implementation of a segmented strategy is, therefore, the degree of controlled coverage that is desirable and practical. Woodside and Motes [3] found it to be both desirable and practical in an application to tourist marketing. They established five segments, defined by different holiday lifestyles, and applied five alternative promotional campaigns. Each campaign used a distinctive creative approach and separate media schedules and promotional literature. The control was exercised by targeting the media schedules to the segments and through selective direct mailing of the promotional literature. But the efficacy of this approach to controlled coverage is dependent upon the degree of match between the segment and the available media. In the above example it would be easier to reach a segment interested in a fishing holiday than one interested in a beach holiday because there are specialist media dealing with fishing as a hobby. In such circumstances media planners look for tendencies rather than expecting an absolute match. With regard to direct mail to specific segments, it is becoming possible to operate with more precision as the classification of national mailing lists becomes more coherent.

Turning now to segmentation as a theory, Assael and Roscoe [4] suggest that two factors are important in determining the type of investigation undertaken. These are, first, whether the customer response is measured at one point in time, or whether the measures should concern demand elasticities over time. The second is whether the criteria employed should refer to just one factor, e.g. frequency of consumption, or to several, e.g. to identify several elements in predispositions to purchase. Most segmentation studies appear to concentrate on static, one-time measures, and relate consumption to demographic characteristics. Increasingly, however, these are being extended to multivariate analyses bringing in numerous additional descriptors of the segment. These could be a combination of many of the bases of segmentation described below. In the future there may be much more dynamic work aimed at classifying response elasticities of different groups over time.

Bases for market segmentation

Most debate about segmentation centres on the best way to distinguish the subclasses within the total market. Table 6.2 lists nine types which companies have used and subsequent sections of this chapter investigate these cases.

Operation of a segmentation strategy can offer considerable competitive advantage. It also has a remarkable capacity to generate disillusionment. Quite elegant studies on one or other of the descriptors already mentioned can frequently end inconclusively, with requests for further research, or with the ripe discovery of a new segment that could never be economically reached. Part of the problem is the range of bases that may be tried; part is the sometimes naive expectations of an absolute answer; and part is caused by the differing perspectives of the researcher and the manager. The nature of this problem will become clearer from a fuller discussion of the alternative bases and their application.

Geographic segments

The simplest approach to segmentation is to market variants of the product in different regions. Such an approach is dependent on there being regional disparities in taste or usage. Historically this was the case, and marked variations in commodities such as bread, cheese, beer and meats were very evident. Mass media, mass transportation and mass production have substantially eroded regional differences. But some remain, as can be seen in the regional differences in credit sources that people use (Table 6.3). Sharp differences in the share taken by bank loans in London and the South West, or the high penetration of credit cards in London and that of mail order in Scotland, present different competitive

Table 6.2 *Bases for segmenting consumer markets*

1. Geographic	National/regional differences in taste and product usage
2. Demographics: Age Lifecycle Education Sex Family composition	Can differences be distinguished between groups in each of these categories that reflect differences in propensity to purchase, or in product usage?
3. Socio-economic and income	Are consumption or media exposure related to social grade or income level?
4. Geodemographics	Does where we live condition how we live, and consequently relate to what we buy?
5. Benefits sought	Are there differences in the benefits sought by different people from the same product?
6. Usage rate and brand loyalty	Are those who consume a lot of the product different from those who consume a little? Can highly brand-loyal individuals be distinguished?
7. Psychographics	Is consumption better considered in the context of 'lifestyle' groups?
8. Situation	Does the situation in which consumption or purchase takes place vary? If so, can individuals be grouped according to these situations?
9. Responsiveness to marketing instruments	Do people respond differently to aspects of marketing activity? Are some more responsive to advertising or price? Do they use different distribution channels?

Table 6.3 *Regional sources of credit*

			% borrowings from		
	Credit card	Mail order	Indirect lending	Bank loans	Other direct loans	Other borrowing
Great Britain	21	10	11	31	21	6
London	30	11	8	23	22	6
South	23	10	8	30	19	10
East Anglia	22	10	13	20	26	8
Wales/West/ South-West	12	6	7	43	26	5
Lancashire	19	10	12	38	14	7
Yorkshire	13	13	15	29	25	5
Tyne Tees	17	12	14	33	17	7
Scotland	16	16	13	39	8	7

Source: AGB Index.

situations for companies in each of these markets. A uniform national marketing treatment would be expected to have quite different results in the several regions. An approach tailored to each region could be more effective.

More generally geographic segmentation is probably now used more for administrative ease than because consumers in the regions represent unique groups. Advertising planning can be broken down into regions, salesforces are often structured on a regional basis and new product launches are sometimes 'rolled-out' gradually across the regions. A regional breakdown of marketing plans is, therefore, often employed for these administrative purposes. Additionally, geographic descriptors may be incorporated into other kinds of segmentation study as supplementary background.

Demographic segments

For some products consumption is positively related to age. Clothing, holiday resorts, meals away from home and snack products provide examples. Similarly, product consumption can be related to sex, with some obvious, and some not so obvious, distinctions. Lifecycle may also be relevant to consumer durables, e.g. 'young marrieds' are heavy consumers of furniture. Family size may additionally yield different consumption patterns, as may length of education. The above factors are often present in attempts to build segmented strategies, if only as additional to other material. But sometimes no significant difference is discernible on these bases.

If a segmented strategy is to be based on demographic differences, then the segments need to be identified, isolated and reached. Separate marketing treatments, perhaps involving product variations, will have to be devised and implemented. Baby markets, for example, naturally demand specific products; disposable nappies are necessarily promoted to mothers with babies and expectant mothers. But that requires information on the attitudes and behaviour of mothers, prior to the design and direction of a promotional campaign. Such needs have led to the development of special kinds of market research: in this instance 'baby panels' composed of samples of mothers who regularly report their purchase and consumption of baby products. Analyses of their media exposure patterns can indicate whether a media schedule can be derived which would give controlled coverage. In many cases, though, sufficient controlled coverage may not be achieved: not enough of the segment may read specific magazines or newspapers, so the disposable nappies may have to be advertised on television, with the implication that the advertiser is paying for a lot of exposures of the advertisement to people not in the market.

Consideration of a company's relative appeal to various demographic segments can lead to strategies aimed at a realignment. Kentucky Fried Chicken undertook a large-scale promotion following research which showed that a third of its business came from young males after 10 o'clock at night. Outlets were therefore operating at well below capacity for most of the day. Advertising was targeted at families and groups of young adults to encourage daytime usage. Alongside this the product, packaging and staff uniforms were changed to support the development of a new image.

Socio-economic and income segments

The discussion of social class in previous chapters found some support for the view that income levels are a better predictor of consumption than social class. The balance between the two is probably related to the product: consumption of some may be more related to class than income and vice versa. Once more, it would be advisable to incorporate such variables along with others. Dogmatic statements which simply rest upon social class or income are not helpful. Generalisations can be dangerous. For example, occupation is usually taken as a surrogate for socio-economic class. A wife's class is thus inferred from her husband's job. In such segmentation analysis there is, therefore, the implication that brand choice and product class usage are related to the man's work. Comparisons between the highest and lowest groups may give a little justification to such an implication, but to apply it to middle groups may be completely wrong. Equally, to apply it to all product fields would probably be erroneous. On the other hand any study that ignored socio-economic factors would be incomplete. Income levels and social class do affect purchasing behaviour, along with a host of other variables. Thus some partial explanation of variations in consumption may sometimes be afforded by such study.

Despite the difficulties and uncertainties about the use of social class in segmentation, in practice a great deal of use is still made of the familiar AB/C1/C2/DE split. The prime reason for this is that many of the media data are presented in this way. The advertising industry was the first to collect systematically on a large scale, data which were relevant to segmentation, and it is that industry's classification that has become dominant. Marketing managers have been schooled in this classification and it has become part of the jargon. It may be used unwittingly because data classified on this basis are relatively easy to obtain. As media data change to incorporate other measures such as types of neighbourhood, then much less use may be made of social class in segmentation.

This would be favoured by Quinlan [5] who argues against the use of social grade in segmentation studies, and supports alternatives when he says:

> The marketing profession has a number of other practical ways of discriminating between groups of consumers without having to get bogged down in hybrid and probably archaic socio-economic constructs. If demographic discriminators are required with an economic bias, then income, age/marital status/family lifecycle, household size, number of earners/working wives, and residential district are available. If a strong culturally-related behaviour pattern is suspected, then terminal education age, media usage or residential district may be appropriate.

Geodemographic segments

Continuing doubt about the discriminating ability of demographics, including social grade, has spurred the development of alternatives or extensions. Geodemographics considers differences in the spatial distribution of key demographic variables. In the United Kingdom this has come to be associated particularly with an extra demographic factor – residential neighbourhood. One of the principal commercial services offering analyses by residential neighbourhood is Acorn: a classification of residential neighbourhoods. Pinpoint and Mosaic are competitive services. Use of these systems in market segmentation rests on the expectation that there is a connection between the kind of housing a person has and purchasing behaviour. This is likely to be more or less true depending on the product category, although advocates point out that where we live is intimately connected with how we live, and that subsumes what we consume.

A considerable advantage of this approach is its massive database. The analysis is derived from the census of population and all 125,000 districts in the census are assigned to a residential neighbourhood group. Table 6.4 shows a summary analysis with the main kinds of grouping used in the Acorn system, although much finer detail is available. For each district, full demographic information is generated, and a widening range of product usage data by district can be purchased, based upon the research undertaken in national surveys. More readership data for some newspapers and magazines analysed by Acorn group are becoming available.

Such data are being widely employed by retailers as a basis for estimating market size and trends within the marketing areas of stores. In a similar way it can be an ingredient in developing relative buying power indices for each small district, and can then be used in designing territories for sales representatives. Direct mailing can also be planned by Acorn groups, since the full electoral register for the entire country can be classified by Acorn groups and mailings made to any name on the register.

A special edition of the *Journal of the Market Research Society* has been devoted to applications of geodemographics (vol. 31, no. 1). Johnson outlines applications in retail store site selection and development and the uses made by firms such as Tesco, Woolworth, Boots and TSB [6]. Sleight comments on the growth in the application of geodemographics as follows [7]:

Table 6.4 *Acorn groups in Great Britain*

Group		%
A	Modern family housing with manual workers	9.6
B	Modern family housing, higher income	7.4
C	Older housing of intermediate status	10.4
D	Very poor quality, older, terraced housing	9.2
E	Rural areas	5.8
F	Urban local authority housing	20.6
G	Housing with most overcrowding	2.9
H	Low income areas with immigrants	4.2
I	Student and high status non-family areas	4.3
J	Traditional high status suburbia	19.1
K	Areas of elderly people, often resorts	6.4
Unclassified		0.2

Once you have identified the geodemographic categories that are of interest to you, it is easy to establish how many households there are in those categories, both nationally and in any small area of interest. By analysing your own data, either from a customer database (if you have one) or via syndicated research, you can establish your penetration in each of the neighbourhood types of relevance to you. And you can track your performance over time, by monitoring penetration or volume levels in these neighbourhood types. It is a far more sensitive measurement tool than standard demographics could possibly provide.

Geographical Information Systems (GIS) superimpose different sets of data on digitised maps and are also becoming important in marketing. As an example of their potential use in marketing consider the following example:

The scenario [is] a car manufacturer identifying potential market locations. Starting with a graphical illustration of comparative wealth in the United Kingdom the client could overlay market research to identify which part of the target market – for example, those with the money to afford a new car – has bought one in the past three years.

By adding data from a lifestyle database and creating a model of potential purchasing, GIS can show whether dealer sites are in the right place, carrying the right stock and, of course, where direct mail campaigns should be concentrated. [8]

Benefit segments

Haley [9] introduced this approach as a way of identifying causal rather than descriptive segments. He claims such studies can throw considerable fresh insight on to marketing problems. An example of the approach is given in Table 6.5.

It seems clear that quite different marketing strategies would be appropriate in these three segments. Different product variants and different promotional treatments would be warranted. There may also be the need to consider alternative distribution channels for each segment. The 'black box user' may be better reached in chain stores such as Boots; the 'timid photographer' may use more specialist chain stores such as Dixons, and the 'do-it-yourselfer' could be more attracted to smaller photographic shops.

Another illustration of the application of benefit segmentation is provided by the case of Cadbury Schweppes' dried milk powder sold under the brand name Marvel. This was devised to offer the following benefits [10]:

1. A standby for the housewife if she runs out of milk.

2. For those needing, for health reasons, a fat-free diet.

3. For slimmers and weightwatchers.

4. For single-person homes and elderly people, who might find it convenient because they would not consume a whole pint.

Table 6.5 *Benefit segments in the less expensive camera market*

The 'do-it-yourselfer' (25%)
Great pride in good pictures
Gratification from making settings and adjustments
Pride in a complex camera
Regards a good picture the result of expertise

The 'black box user' (40%)
Taking pictures considered a necessary evil
Little pride expressed if the picture is good
Desire for camera to be as simple as possible

The 'timid photographer' (38%)
Great pride in good pictures
High perceived risk that pictures will not be good
No confidence in ability to manipulate camera and
    settings
Desires camera to guarantee good picture without effort

Source: J.F. Engel, H.F. Fiorello and M.A. Cayley (eds), *Market
    Segmentation*. New York: Holt, Rinehart and Winston,
    1972, p. 18.

Demographic, and perhaps attitudinal, descriptions of these groups could lead to distinctive advertising appeals, using different media in each case. The choice of medium would depend on determining the media exposure profile for each segment, that is the typical reading (or listening or viewing) habits of the group. If all four groups were similar, then it would not be possible to employ a segmented media strategy. But, if there were tendencies for the groups to cluster their reading in different publications, then such a distinctive approach would be feasible.

An extension of this analysis would be to attempt to gauge the benefits wanted by consumers and to compare these to the benefits they perceive to have been received. Any resulting deficiency might offer a guide for product development or the introduction of a new product.

Usage segments

For most markets usage is not spread evenly across all consumers: the distribution is skewed. Analyses of volume of usage by several categories are commonly employed, and market research studies often report on heavy, moderate, light and non-users. As with many other variables discussed in this chapter, usage rate could be treated as a dominant factor or as one of several subsidiary factors in segmentation. It could be judged to be of major significance and be the essential approach to segmentation, or it may be viewed as a supplementary set of descriptive data where the main thrust was on other demographic, attitudinal or behavioural factors.

Usage could be a dominant factor where a skewed distribution was particularly marked. Heavy users of some consumer goods may be attracted by very large packages, perhaps only made available at certain outlets, at special prices. Heavy, regular users of some services might also be specially treated, maybe being enrolled in some 'club', or becoming eligible for added benefits by earning 'points' from extra purchases. In financial services, varying usage rates might 'qualify' for different treatments. Alternatively, light users may be targeted with product/ package variants, given the expectation that the relatively low level of sales in such a segment was satisfactory.

A complication is in the definition of usage. It could refer to volume used (consumed) in a recent, short time period such as a week or month. It could refer to some nominal, 'normal' period and it might be inferred from purchase frequency, rather than actual consumption. Usage data, therefore, require careful interpretation. An example in one market is given in the appendix to this chapter.

Attitude segments

Models of attitude to the brand, or to the act of buying the brand, can also provide a basis for segmentation. If several groups of consumers displayed markedly different attitudes, this could be used as a method of discriminating between them. With attitudes to the brand, it may be that different groups responded differently to several product attributes. A 'perceptual map' such as that described in the discussion about comprehension in Chapter 2 may help in this analysis. Studies of attitude to the act, using the Fishbein intentions model, might reveal differences caused by different social norms. Attitude to housework may be a case in point. Some women may comply to a more traditional norm, emphasising the work as rewarding in itself; others may take a more modern view and see it as necessary, but at times inconvenient and restricting. Buying behaviour for household cleaning products may conform to those different perceptions. Some brands may be associated with the traditional values and others with modern values.

The application of attitude research to segmentation can now be seen as part of a more general approach under the heading 'psychographics', which has become the generic term for attitude and lifestyle segmentation.

Psychographics

Research using profiles of personality, values and lifestyle has been employed to characterise consumers in new ways; this has come to be known as psychographics. Lifestyles are patterns of living and how people spend their time and money, and are related to the values they hold. Psychographic studies combine lifestyles along with personality traits. Psychographic segmentation attempts to partition consumers into groups on the basis of these two elements.

Lifestyles are inferred from questions put to consumers about their activities, interests and opinions (AIO). Respondents are given a series of general and specific statements to which they express their degree of agreement on Likert scales (five points from strongly agree to strongly disagree). An example of a

Table 6.6 *Topic areas in lifestyle studies*

Activities	Interests	Opinions	Demographics
Work	Family	Themselves	Age
Hobbies	Home	Social issues	Education
Social events	Job	Politics	Income
Vacation	Community	Business	Occupation
Entertainment	Recreation	Economics	Family size
Club membership	Fashion	Education	Dwelling
Community	Food	Products	Geography
Shopping	Media	Future	City size
Sports	Achievements	Culture	Stage in lifecycle

Source: J.T. Plummer, 'The concept and application of lifestyle segmentation', *Journal of Marketing*, vol. 38, January 1974.

general statement might be, 'these days I am more optimistic about the future' and a specific statement might be, 'I always eat eggs for breakfast'. The topic areas covered can be seen in Table 6.6.

Wells and Tigert [11] give illustrations of 'portraits' constructed from lifestyle research. For example, the heavy user of eye make-up is as follows:

Young, well educated, urban.
Uses a lot of other cosmetics.
Reads fashion magazines.
Watches television movies.
Agrees with statements such as:
    'I try the latest hairstyles.'
    'I usually have one or two outfits in the latest styles.'
    'I comb my hair and put on lipstick first thing in the morning.'
    'I like travel.'
Does not like shopping, does not consider herself a 'homebody' and does not enjoy housework.

Another product-specific example is shown in Table 6.7, which deals with camera purchases. Nikkon buyers saw themselves as more broadminded, creative, dominating, efficient and intelligent and less conformist and persuasible than all camera buyers. A number of examples of the application of lifestyle research in Europe and in Asia can be found in De Mooij and Keegan [12].

In discussing general, as opposed to product-specific, psychographic profiling systems, Gunter and Furnham note that several typologies have been developed covering the consumer population and that [13]:

As studies are repeated over time it becomes possible to accumulate trend data that show how consumers are changing. Such data are particularly valuable in an era when every other observer is prepared to describe 'the changing consumer' and to make predictions about the effects of the changes upon markets for goods and

Table 6.7   *Psychographic profiles of camera purchases*

	All camera purchasers	More expensive cameras	Nikon cameras
Awkward	106	79	77
Broadminded	112	123	150
Creative	119	141	158
Dominating	120	157	154
Efficient	114	130	150
Intelligent	117	156	206
Refined	110	127	136
Reserved	100	103	71
Stubborn	114	107	93
Tense	103	100	84
Conformist	88	93	59
Economy-minded	100	96	77
Experimenter	96	91	74
Pursuasible	104	93	47
Style-conscious	114	92	67

Index: all adults = 100.

Note: These data were derived from self-ratings on groups of adjectives (e.g. dominating: authoritarian, demanding, aggressive), or phrases (e.g. conformist: 'I prefer to buy things my friends would approve of'). These ratings were on a five-point scale from 'agree a lot' to 'disagree a lot'.

Source: Target Group Index, quoted in G.D. Hughes, *Marketing Management*. Reading, Mass.: Addison-Wesley, 1978.

services. In monitoring trends the task of empirical psychographic analysis is to highlight the changes that are actually happening given the factors that are remaining stable.

Such systems include the VALS (values and lifestyle) system in the United States, and Taylor Nelson's Monitor in the United Kingdom. The latter has been operating regularly since the early 1970s and identifies the following seven social value groups:

1. *Self-explorer*: youthful, independent, tolerant, comfortably situated, often female.
2. *Social register*: older, resist change, high need for control.
3. *Experimentalist*: independent, unconventional, energetic, work-oriented, often men in their late twenties and early thirties.
4. *Conspicuous consumer*: conformist, materialistic, lacking self-confidence.
5. *Belonger*: mature, stable, settled.
6. *Survivor*: dependent on protection of authority but sceptical of its intentions, identify with country and family, tend to be male, unskilled or skilled manual workers.
7. *Aimless*: goal-less, uninvolved, alienated, unable to improve their position.

Situation segmentation

Attention has recently been given to the study of situations in buyer behaviour. The main claim for lifestyle studies is that they give a fuller appreciation of the consumer's way of life and the role taken by consumption. They are more eclectic than many other segmentation bases which focus on one narrow variable, and so it is hoped a more realistic picture emerges. But Dickson [14] argues that even this is incomplete since it misses a powerful determinant of consumption – the situation in which the consumption is to take place. Consider the following products in various situations; in each case a different form of the product would seem appropriate.

Product	Situation
Beds	in a main bedroom
	in a children's room
Television	in a family room
	elsewhere
Drinks	at home
	at a picnic
	with friends
	with family
Ice cream	in a restaurant
	at home
	out walking

The same person in different situations would have different needs. One important facet of this could be the differing role that the individual takes in alternative situations. The situation broadly defines the role, and the role behaviour may be supported by particular purchases. As the situation changes so does the role, and hence the appropriate purchase. Dickson would interpret this as a type of benefit segmentation (Figure 6.1): the kind of benefit sought by the individual varying with the situation.

A corollary is that if the benefit sought varies with the situation, then so would the perception of products. The evaluation of the attributes of brands would change: some would score highly in a given situation and be thought entirely inappropriate in other situations. The attributes brought into the evaluation could also change, as might their order of importance. To use Howard's terminology, the evoked set, or brands first brought to mind, would be dependent on the situation. All this would indicate that if the brand was in a product field that was sensitive to situations, then the perceptual mapping referred to in the consumer psychology chapter should be situation-specific. But this raises the issue of the definition of situations. Figure 6.1 refers to 'determinant characteristics of usage situation'. These characteristics could encompass time, place and role behaviour. In some cases, like the listing above, a quite easy classification might emerge, but in others it might be more tortuous. One difficulty is that the

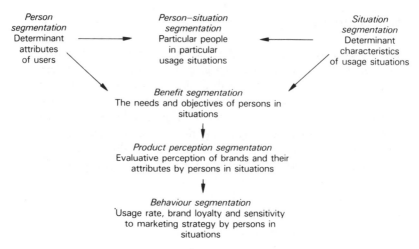

Source: P.R. Dixon, 'Person–situation: segmentation's missing link', *Journal of Marketing,* vol. 46, no. 4, p.60, 1982.

Figure 6.1   *Situation segmentation*

usage may not be all at one time in one place. Some services and products can be consumed over long periods. But this very difficulty for some products becomes an inherent part of their appeal. The sports bag which becomes an overnight bag, the family saloon car which becomes the light van, the flexible savings plan, and the students' hall of residence which becomes the holiday hotel are all examples of products being used in multiple situations.

If the benefits sought and the product perceptions change with the situation, then it would be expected that product usage would vary. It would be consistent if sensitivity to marketing strategy also varied with situations. That is, if groups could be isolated that sought different benefits in different situations, and if each of these groups responded differently to alternative marketing treatments. For example, hotel marketing offers a wealth of situations and diverse role behaviour. A large hotel would market to tourists, short-stay business clients, to conference business and to local markets in its bars and restaurants. The behaviour of customers in each group would be related to their situation; their dress, demeanour, activities and their expectations about the hotel services would follow their adopted roles. A standardised marketing approach to all groups would not be effective. Situation segmentation would be more appropriate.

The example of hotel marketing does uncover another problem in this form of segmentation. This refers to cases where several segments consume the product at the same time in the same place and are simultaneously seeking different benefits. Segment conflict can take on major significance if people in one role frustrate those in another. Illustrations are the conference delegates feeling out of place with informally dressed tourists in the dining room; the small family celebration taking place at the same time as a banquet for a rugby club or a large exhibition monopolising the public rooms. Such conflict can result in a discrepancy between the benefit desired and the benefit derived, and the implications can be severe for large hotel chains since the perceptions of one hotel may be generalised to the whole chain.

Attempts to deal with this conflict include segregating the segments by time, place or price. Time segregation can operate by only accepting certain segments at certain times – perhaps with a price inducement. This might be over different times of the year, so that the hotel determines which segments are compatible and aims to bring them in together at one time of the year. In doing so it might create a radically different atmosphere, and then target other segments at other times of the year. Its segment mix, and thus marketing strategy, changes according to the season. Time segregation could also operate during the day: certain segments being served at different times. Segregation by place includes offering several types of restaurant, with perhaps conference delegates being catered for in conference suites. It could also mean physically separating the segments, maybe in different wings. Some hotels even have different entrances for different segments. Price segregation aims to separate the segments by differential pricing, whether for accommodation or for food and beverages.

Segmenting by response to marketing strategy

An implication in all approaches to segmentation is that once the segments are identified, then a unique marketing treatment will be applied. Where the consumer response shows a very marked difference according to marketing treatment, the nature of the treatment can itself become the basis for distinguishing the segments. The most common form of this would be price elasticity, although the same concept could be applied to any part of the marketing mix. Just as in other bases the need would be to establish groups whose response displayed substantial differences. Thus there might be relatively inelastic segments and relatively elastic segments. This could include many aspects of promotion, and so segments might be considered in relation to their response to various promotional means. This has led to the notion of 'deal-prone' segments – the 'deal' being the kind of promotion. Investigations would attempt to discern if any demographic variables could additionally be used to describe these segments, mainly because that would be the key to media data. While media data give analyses by demographics they do not generally give analyses by, for example, 'deal-proneness'. Alternatively, if this form of segmentation were research-based, then it may be possible to collect data on the media habits of the sample of individuals being researched.

Another possibility is to consider the marketing channels used by consumers and to segment by type of channel. The bed manufacturers, Silentnight, adopt this strategy because bed retailers tend to concentrate on particular price/quality ranges and so attract consumers interested in the selected range. Silentnight markets four brands and each is distinctively placed in respect to retailers and price/quality range:

Sealy – luxury beds sold through department stores and top quality specialists.

Lay-E-Zee – middle-range beds sold through smaller independent retailers.

Silentnight – middle-range beds sold through department stores and retail chains.

Perfecto – bottom-range beds sold through small retailers and chains.

Segmenting service markets

Service operations often work with complex patterns of market segments. The complexity is caused by the very varied, and at the same time quite identifiable, groups of customers served. For example, in marketing its rooms a large hotel might consider three gross segments:

1. Rack – those paying the full rate (rack rate); individuals using a direct channel to the hotel or coming via a travel agent or referral or reservation system.
2. Commercial – organisational customers.
3. Travel trade – usually tour groups, either series or one-off.

The segmentation variable in these cases is a combination of customer characteristics and marketing channel used. To an extent it is also sensitivity to prices since rack customers pay the most and tour groups the least. Within each of these broad groups there could be a multiplicity of subgroups. The rack segment could be subdivided by marketing channel; the commercial segment by volume of usage and the travel trade by type of tour, its duration and 'package' contents. But, because the hotel offers numerous products, the segmentation could be even more complex with various additional groupings using its bars, restaurants, banqueting and conference facilities.

Given a fixed supply of guest rooms and dinner covers, the segmentation problem becomes one of determining and delivering a segment mix that will fulfil company sales or profit objectives. It is not an easy problem: it is most unlikely that all rooms can be sold at rack rate. Certain long-term contracts may be required by some segments, but these may be at relatively low rates. Therefore, does the hotel assure itself of high occupancy by making 'allocations' to tour operators for the next year, or does it deliberately restrict this business in order to have rooms available for other segments which buy in a much shorter time horizon?

A further complication in segmenting service markets is that the customers themselves contribute to the overall image of the service offered. Those in one segment may have requirements which conflict with, or reduce the satisfaction derived by, those in other segments. Managers in service companies thus have a complex balancing act in adjusting their segment mix.

Industrial market segmentation

All of the bases so far mentioned have referred to the consumer market, but the notion can be equally well applied to industrial markets. Table 6.8 gives some possible variables that could enter an industrial market segmentation study.

A typical application in industrial markets is to segment according to industry type, i.e. to classify customers to industry groups. This can sometimes be improved if there are diverse applications for the product. To illustrate, microfilm might be employed in administration, for engineering drawings or research. If a cross-classification of application type by industry type were made, then the result might be something like that revealed in Table 6.9. This hypothetical example shows the proportions of all users of microfilm by industry and application. The three applications may require different product types. They certainly present different situations in terms of system requirements, e.g. complexity of indexing of the film, the speed of access needed, and the degree and frequency of updating to material already on film. Even within each application the requirements could vary, for example, banks' use of microfilm could be very different from that of manufacturing companies. Promotional methods used certainly have to be varied by industry type.

Table 6.8 *Industrial segmentation variables*

Organisational characteristics	Organisation buyer's characteristics
Geography	Purchasing strategies used by buyers
End-use of the product purchased	Primary role of buyer
Type of business engaged in by customer	Buyer self-confidence
Type of supplier profiles developed by customer	Differences in buying information processes
Type of buying situation (new task, modified rebuy, straight rebuy)	Buyer risk tolerance and preference
Type of market served by customer	Perceptions of risks and problems by buyers
Value added by customer	Buyer evaluation style
Basis for competitive advantage (e.g. price, personal selling)	Buyer's working relationships with others
Customer profit margin	Buyer's workload
Customer innovativeness, purchasing profiles	Buyer decision-making style (normative and conservative)
Corporate name and address	Buyer personality traits

Source: D.W. Cravens, G.E. Hills and R.B. Woodruff, *Marketing Decision Making: Concepts and strategy*. Homewood, Ill.: Irwin, 1976, p. 267.

Table 6.9 *Microfilm usage by industry and application*

Industry	Administration	Main application % of all users Engineering documents	Research	Total
Manufacturing	20	15	1	36
Utilities	10	1	1	12
Banks	10	0	1	11
Professional services	20	3	5	28
Government	10	1	2	13
Total	70	20	10	100

This kind of segmentation is useful also for obtaining some measure of market trends. In many industrial markets it is possible to derive an estimate of the current stock of equipment classified in this manner. Sometimes this is by sample survey, although it is possible in some cases to obtain even a full census. With data for more than just one year it is possible to delineate stocks and flows to undercover trends in stock sizes by each industry/application type. Differences in the rate of stock change in each cell might be observed, and this might be compared with changes in company market share in each of those cells. The firm's current product range might then be found to be aligned to industries/applications with below-average growth rates. Alternatively, close monitoring might reveal major developing markets in new applications or industries.

Choffray and Lilien [15] advocate a two-stage approach to industrial market segmentation, first into macrosegments and subsequently into microsegments. The macrosegments could be distinguished by SIC code (Standard Industrial Classification), by company size or geographically. The microsegments are identified by DMU composition, and are clustered according to their purchasing decision processes. In an application for satellite copiers for the 3M company, two microsegments were detected. The first showed high involvement by purchasing executives, and was composed primarily of private sector firms. The second showed high involvement by product users and were public sector organisations. In terms of Table 6.8, macrosegments use organisational characteristics, and microsegments those of the organisational buyers.

Business profiling

Segmentation requires that some form of customer profile is developed – customers are described and divided into appropriate groups. As indicated above in the industrial market, a common descriptor is the type of business the customer is in, and for this purpose SIC codes are used. If all customers are assigned an SIC code, then it should be possible to analyse numbers of customers within each main SIC category by size of firm, probably using number of employees as the guide. This can be compared with estimates of the total number of firms in each of these categories to derive a measure of penetration.

For some in the business-to-business market, for example an office supplies company, an alternative or additional descriptor could be customer location. One such geographic segmentation system for the industrial market is Business Accumin, which classifies businesses by location [16]. This system uses thirty-one clusters of types of geographic area including 'financial districts', 'mixed office and retail centres' and 'heavy engineering and industrial parks'. A national database of about one million companies forms the base and users can compare their customer location profiles against this national profile. This might be instructive in uncovering areas of weak penetration and could be used in association with postcodes for direct mailing.

Choosing the segment base

Given the wide range of possibilities for segmenting a market, which segmentation variable should be chosen? An important factor in this choice will be the

Table 6.10 *Segmentation bases classified by purpose of study*

1. For general understanding of a market:
    Benefits sought (in industrial markets, the criterion used in purchase decision)
    Product purchase and usage patterns
    Needs
    Brand loyalty and switching pattern
    A hybrid of the above variables
2. For positioning studies:
    Product usage
    Product performance
    Benefits sought
    Hybrid of above
3. For new product concepts (and new product introductions):
    Reaction to new concepts (intentions to buy, preference over current brand, etc.)
    Benefits sought
4. For pricing decisions:
    Price sensitivity
    Deal-proneness
    Price sensitivity by purchase/usage patterns
5. For advertising decisions:
    Benefits sought
    Media usage
    Psychographic/lifestyle
    Hybrid of above and/or purchase/usage patterns
6. For distribution decisions:
    Store loyalty and patronage
    Benefits sought in store selection

Source: Y. Wind, 'Issues and advances in segmentation studies', *Journal of Marketing Research*, vol. 15, August 1978.

purpose of the exercise. Wind has declared his preference for classification by purpose of study, and this is shown in Table 6.10.

Use and limitation of market segmentation

Some of the reasons for considering segmentation have been commented on by Fitzroy [17]. He says it may be used to:

1. Achieve a better competitive position for existing brands.

2. More effectively position an existing brand by appealing to a limited market.

3. Separate two or more brands of the same company to minimise cannibalisation.

4. Identify gaps in the market which represent new product opportunities.

5. Identify potential new buyers for the product.

Kotler [18] warns that to be effective three major constraints need to be investigated. First the segments must be measurable. Very unusual bases for segmentation may lead to great difficulties in data collection for both planning and control. If segments are arranged in such a way that only specially collected data can be used, then the research costs must be properly incorporated in the costs of that strategy. Second, in markets where great use is made of advertising, there may be little match between segment population definition and media audience definition. For example, it is unlikely that all the audience for a particular national newspaper has similar attitudes to convenience foods. Thus mass advertising may be necessary to reach such segments, and the costs for reaching each member of that segment can be enormous. Third, each segment should be substantial enough in size to warrant particular attention. Most consumer goods companies would therefore use just a small number of segments. A major steel company could consider a much larger number.

Full implementation of a segmented strategy presupposes that there will be an adequate flow of accounting data for both planning and control purposes. To operate segmented strategies with only aggregate company accounting information is at least half-hearted and potentially dangerous. The relative worth of segmenting cannot be adequately defined without the proper costs and revenues being associated with segment activities. As Buzby and Heitger [19] say:

> Accounting reports which reflect the nature of a firm's market segments will provide the marketing manager with a valuable tool for improving his decision making with respect to the firm's profit objective . . . the firm's overall marketing mix can be viewed as an aggregation of the individual segment marketing mixes.

Each segment marketing mix can be translated into its cost and revenue implications by developing segment budgets. The segment budgets can then be aggregated to form the firm's overall marketing budget.

Dunne and Wolk [20] provide an example of how this might be done However, with some types of segment bases it might prove to be a difficult task. For example, problems may be met in allocating promotional costs to segments if media audiences are not concentrated in the same way as the segment. Mass television advertising may be particularly perplexing. Tracing revenues may also be difficult. If part of the strategy included some different product offering to different segments this problem would be eased. Similarly, if different distribution channels were employed to service each segment, then segment revenues could be calculated. Where neither of these differences exist, it will be impossible to accurately gauge segment revenues. Some impression may be derived from survey data, but that is likely to be far less rigorous than more normal accounting data. Certainly the methodology and the assumptions need to be made explicit.

Positioning

Segmentation helps to shape decisions about market targets. Just as important as this are the decisions about the factors which make the organisation and its products different: what will make it stand out as a preferred supplier and, most importantly, what do consumers perceive of these differences? Positioning is about these issues, and its importance is highlighted by Hooley and Saunders when they say:

> Positioning now has a central role within modern marketing, providing a bridge between the company and its target customers, describing to customers how the company differs from the current or potential competitors. Positioning therefore becomes the actual designing of the company's image so that the target customers understand and appreciate what the company stands for in relation to its competitors. [21]

Positioning concerns the perceptions and preferences consumers have in regard to the organisation and its products. It is a relative term describing customer perceptions of the firm's position in the market against rivals. It deals with customer assessments of the factors that they consider to be important in distinguishing the advantages and disadvantages of the various market offerings. Because of this it is related to the bases on which the firm wishes to build its differentiation, and thus related to the choice of platform on which to seek competitive advantage. Positioning therefore reaches deeply into the strategic decisions made by the organisation, and could reflect aspects of its basic mission.

Originally, the concept was applied to product positions, but it is now also used to describe corporate positions. In this respect it has been employed not just in commercial organisations: the notion has been adopted by public authorities, charities and hospitals.

Positioning is intimately connected with brand strategy. Indeed, it would be difficult, if not impossible, to develop effectively a positioning strategy without distinctive branding. In the absence of a brand name the volume of information the consumer would need to remember, in order to discriminate between products, would lead to much confusion and a considerable amount of forgetting.

There is strong connection between positioning and segmentation. In product positioning it is usual to consider this within a particular market segment. Wind suggests that this connection can be approached in two ways [22]:

1. Given a target market segment, which product positioning (and its associated marketing strategy) is likely to be most effective in reaching the firm's objectives? Or

2. Given a target product positioning, which market segment is most likely to be responsive to this positioning?

Whichever comes first, segmentation or positioning, it is necessarily an iterative process. An example is Grosvenor House, a grand hotel whose positioning can be inferred from the following:

> We try to be friendly and approachable. We are very English and want to create an understated country house feel. We are not glitzy; there is not a lot of gold leaf and marble floors here . . . . By using materials like polished limestone (instead of marble), English oak and slate, [we are] not trying to be too grand [23].

Located on Park Lane in London this hotel has developed two corporate packages. The Crown Club package equates to business class in airline marketing. The price per night (£215 for a single and £240 for a double) includes English breakfast, a room service lunch or dinner, valet pressing, a complimentary in-room bar, express check-in, use of a small boardroom for meetings and of a lounge where afternoon tea and cocktails are served. The Sovereign package equates to a first class airline ticket. Ten of the hotel's park-view suites, at £700 per night, offer private butler and maid service, a chauffeured limousine and a full crystal bar.

From the discussion so far it is clear that the positioning concept links three crucial factors:

1. The extent to which organisational marketing actions gain a distinctive market position.

2. Customer perceptions of the organisation and/or its product offerings.

3. The relative positioning of competitors and/or their products.

And it is well connected to the quite basic strategic issues of:

1. Differentiation and competitive advantage.
2. Brand strategy.
3. Segmentation strategy.

Determining product position

A first problem in fixing product position is the determination of a relevant set of products and brands. The criterion for inclusion in the set would be whether or not the alternatives were substitutes. It may be judged that the set is obvious and if not so then talking with consumers, perhaps in unstructured depth interviews, should draw out what they feel the substitutes to be. This could spread over several conventional product fields and only becomes a major problem if there is little consensus among consumers. That in itself could be turned into an opportunity, since numerous market segments may then be discerned which had not previously been fully recognised.

The next step is to define the attributes consumers use in making judgements about these products. These could be deduced from depth interviews or from the more structured repertory grid approach [24]. In the latter case, respondents are asked to express the ways in which products are similar or dissimilar. They are asked to make these statements among three products at a time; they say why two of the products are the same yet different from the third. The process continues by shuffling all the products with which the respondent is familiar until no new reasons are put forward for the similarities and differences. The result is a list of 'personal constructs' which, with editing, indicates 'determinant attributes' – those that satisfy needs and that discriminate among products [25].

With products and their attributes defined, the requirement is then for procedures to gather data on consumer perceptions and preferences. The aim is to locate product perceptions and product preferences in respect of the attributes. This could be one-dimensional in the (unlikely) event that consumers only considered a single attribute in making their judgements. It is difficult to conceive of any product in this category, but suppose it applied to shoelaces and that the attribute was durability. Assuming that respondents knew of several brands, they would be asked to rate them on this attribute, and they might be also asked to state their preferred level of durability. Normally such studies would be multi-dimensional, and if more than two-dimensional then computer analyses would be a requisite. To illustrate, assume a retail bank had elicited two key attributes: location and degree of service offered. Respondents had shown their feelings on scales for these two dimensions and had also indicated their ideal. This might have revealed the position in Figure 6.2 where several competitors are set against the two attributes.

It would be expected that the segment wanting relatively full service, in town centre locations, is well provided for by the banks which are perceived to offer a combination of these two attributes which is near to the ideal levels. It would also be expected that if these two attributes were established as determinant attributes, then there should be some correspondence between market share and relative distance from the ideal. For instance, this model would predict bank D to have the lowest market share in segment x. Additionally, it would seem that two segments are not being adequately catered for, and if they were of significant size, they could offer market opportunities. In this particular market it might be more useful to consider a more detailed analysis by, for example, benefit sought. Thus several maps may be envisaged with one for

---

Seiko: multi-brand positioning

Seiko has developed a strategy of distinctively positioning several brands of watches under the names Lassale, Seiko, Pulsar and Lorus in order to cover different market segments. The segmentation and positioning are:

Lassale

Target group:	Successful professional city-dwelling men and women aged 30–45.
Product:	An exclusive and limited collection of elegant watches whose main common characteristic is thinness and sophistication.
Price:	$300–900.
Positioning:	'The modern classic'.

Seiko

Target group:	All men and women (specific groups are targeted with separate collections within the Seiko brand).
Product:	The most complete watch collection, state-of-the-art technology, image most sharply focused on sports products and usages.
Price:	$100–600.
Positioning:	The world leader in technology.

Pulsar

Target group:	All adults, especially women aged 25–35.
Product:	Fashionable collection of dress watches.
Price:	$40–200.
Positioning:	'A statement in style'.

Lorus

Target group:	Teenagers and adults, especially men aged 15–30.
Product:	An accessibly priced collection of functional and sporty watches.
Price:	$20–100.
Positioning:	'Watches for winners'.

Source: R. Rijkens, 1992. *European Advertising Strategies*. London: Cassell, p. 191.

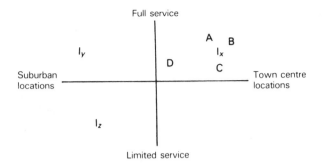

A, B, C, D are four banking companies; I_x I_y I_z are the ideal positions for three different market segments.

Figure 6.2 *Product positioning*

operating a current account in normal situations, one in abnormal situations, one for changing foreign currencies, one for arranging loans, and so on. In these cases the relevant dimensions would change, the ideal points would be different and perhaps the evaluations of the companies would also alter. An example of an application to the British car market can be found in Meade [26] and an application to the British cheese market in Douglas *et al.* [27].

Positioning strategy

To deliver the desired positioning in the market effectively the whole of the

---

Positioning Pampers

Procter & Gamble launched a range of disposable napkins under the brand name Pampers into most European markets in the early 1980s on the platform of keeping the baby drier and more comfortable. But market share soon peaked as a result of intense competition. P&G continued to develop the product, concentrating on the dryness and comfort attributes. It increased the product's absorbency through a manufacturing process which competitors found difficult to copy, because it was so expensive. It added to the comfort with boy and girl formats. The effect of these developments was very successful in all European countries, and several smaller competitors withdrew from the market.

From a market leading position in disposable napkins the emphasis shifted to attack traditional terry napkins. The dryness attribute was underlined in preventing soreness, and advertising campaigns centred on how well Pampers prevented 'nappy rash'. Continuing development of the product line led to the introduction of Pampers Phases, a range to correspond to different stages in a baby's development, and to Pampers Ultra Thin.

Sources: Various press reports and Market Research Europe (Euromonitor).

marketing mix needs to be synchronised. There must be consistent focus in all elements in order to provide mutual reinforcement of the basic positioning platform. Any one element not effectively supporting the position can undermine the strategy.

Products must be capable of occupying the position convincingly. It would be a nonsense to promote high quality positioning with patently inferior products. Most obviously that refers to the physical properties of the product, but it can also include its perceptual properties. An important aspect of this is the situation: consumer judgements of what is appropriate or appealing are conditioned by the situation in which it is purchased and consumed.

Services must be able to reinforce the position. Advertised same-day service must be just that. Claims to offer the fastest delivery, no-waiting-for-spares or friendly, competent and timely service engineers must be realistic.

Pricing needs to be appropriate to the position. A value-for-money position would not be supported by pricing which was among the highest. A prestige position would not be consistent with low prices, nor would it be assisted by the product being featured frequently in price promotions.

Distribution can help to sustain the positioning. This might refer to product availability: wide availability for a mass market product and selective availability for a product aiming for distinctive status. And it might not just refer to the numbers of outlets, but also to their quality. This could embrace their location, the quality of staff and their training, the services offered and the nature of the clientele. All these elements could contribute to how the consumer perceives the market offering.

Above all else positioning needs to be communicated: it requires expression. That expression can add considerable depth to the images conveyed, and for some positions it can be the vital ingredient. Product positions dependent on identification with certain types of people or lifestyles would be difficult, but not impossible, to cultivate without advertising. Products with unique applications need to spell out their claims to fame, and products with superior features need them to be known. For consumers to believe a positioning claim they must first know and understand.

Successful positioning strategies have several characteristics:

1. Factors on which the positioning is to concentrate must be relevant and important to consumers. They need to be based on some feature or benefit which is relevant to the target segment and which customers consider to be important enough to be the basis of ways by which they discriminate between brands.

2. The promoted image must be believable. If the positioning emphasises a reference influence, then that referent must be relevant and credible to the target segment. If the thrust of the positioning is on ease of operation, then it must be believed and demonstrated to be so. If a high quality image is sought by the firm, then all aspects of the product and its delivery to

Table 6.11 *Some bases of corporate and product positioning*

Corporate positioning	Product positioning
The organisation could strive to attain and to maintain leadership in terms of one or more of:	The product's position might emphasise:
market share	cost/economy/value
quality	product features
service	product range
technology	product quality
innovation	services/customer care
variety	customer types
integrity	customer problem solved
community service	use/application type
	disassociation

consumers must be believed to offer that quality. Incredible positioning is no positioning at all, and that could lead to lasting damage.

3. Positioning must be consistent. Effective positions need to be nurtured; they cannot be created instantly. Promises must be seen to be delivered by the users, whose subsequent supportive word-of-mouth can buttress the position. Trade customers should also be considered, because they would react badly to inconsistent suppliers who change strategy frequently.

4. Positioning must be reinforced by all aspects of the marketing mix, as noted above.

5. The whole exercise should be worthwhile.

Positioning problems

It was suggested earlier that the positioning concept is now applied to corporate as well as to product positions. That provides a complication in that the relationship between product and corporate positioning is not straightforward. There are organisations with a declared corporate positioning strategy which gives direction for the development of consistent product positioning strategies, and so there is a tight link between the two. There are, alternatively, organisations without an overt corporate positioning strategy and with a variable range of product positioning strategies. Some other organisations have consistency between product and corporate positioning for part of their business, and yet maintain deliberately a number of outliers, not integrated under the corporate umbrella. Car companies provide good examples of these alternatives.

Sometimes there is good reason for this diversity of approach: perhaps the same organisation is appealing to high quality segments with some products, while at the same time offering value-for-money products in the same or other sectors. It is interesting to read the annual reports of large corporations giving the reasons for their particular approach to this problem. History and inertia play a part. Large corporations have grown, at least in part, through acquisitions. They assemble a range of businesses each with a unique history. In some cases there may be several high-profile brands which have been built on decades of investment, and it may be imprudent to impose corporate uniformity on these brands because that might diffuse the intensity of their positioning.

Positioning intensity can give rise to other problems. Walker *et al.* point to the need to retain some flexibility over time when they say [28]:

> Although marketers should seek an intense position for their brands, they should also keep in mind that attaining such a position can impose constraints upon future strategies. If shifts in the market environment should cause customers to reduce the importance they attach to a current determinant attribute, marketers may have difficulty repositioning a brand with an intensely perceived position on that attribute.

Brand extensions, using a brand name established in one product class to enter another, have been widely employed. But they can be overexploited. If carried too far, there may be damage to an intensely positioned brand. This would be the case if the extensions do not fit the original positioning, if they weaken the associations, or are not of a sufficient quality.

Multinational positioning can also be problematical. Some brands can achieve similar positions in many countries simultaneously, but in many situations it would not be possible or appropriate. For example, Guinness has similar advertising in many European countries, along the 'Pure Genius' theme, but it needs an entirely different approach in Africa, where it stresses that it is 'powerful . . . exciting . . . deeply satisfying'.

Summary

Market segmentation is not new. Historically, some products were designed for particular social classes, or for particular regional or local markets. Mass production initially imposed homogeneity, but increasingly in the past thirty years the differences between consumers have been recognised and catered for by offering product variants or special products to subsections of markets. Segmentation is customer-oriented in that it attempts to match customer requirements more accurately.

Most segmentation studies have concentrated upon static, one-time measures and have related consumption to one or two demographic variables. Dynamic measures over time of many more variables have now become feasible, however, and will be more widely used in the future.

Much of the thought in segmentation studies has concerned the choice of segmentation variable. An extremely wide range of possibilities exists in both the consumer and industrial markets.

Positioning concerns the perceptions and preferences consumers may have in regard to the organisation and its products. It is connected strongly to the basic strategic issues of differentiation, competitive advantage, brand strategy and segmentation strategy. The determination of product positioning was considered, followed by an analysis of positioning strategy and potential problems in that strategy.

Questions for review and discussion

1. Does the economist's theory of price discrimination assist thought about market segmentation?

2. What is the connection between brand proliferation and market segmentation?

3. Can monopolists benefit from implementing a segmented strategy?

4. Give examples of products that are directed at specific segments. What is the segmentation variable used? Are there differences in product features, promotional, pricing or distribution strategies?

5. Is a strategy of market segmentation easier to operate in the industrial or consumer markets? What criteria would you use in making such a judgement?

6. If the only advertising media you could employ had mass audiences with little concentration in a particular segment being considered, then does that invalidate any thought of market segmentation?

7. In what kinds of market would you expect a fairly good match between media audience profiles and segment profiles? What is the segmentation variable in those instances?

8. How might the effectiveness of a positioning strategy be assessed?

References

1. Smith, W.R. 1956. 'Product differentiation and market segmentation as alternative marketing strategies', *Journal of Marketing*, vol. 21, July.
2. Frank, R.E., Massy, W.F and Wind, Y. 1972. *Market Segmentation*, Englewood Cliffs, NJ: Prentice Hall, Inc., p. 7.

3. Woodside, A.G. and Motes, W.H. 1981. 'Sensitivities of market segments to separate advertising strategies', *Journal of Marketing*, vol. 45, no. 1.
4. Assael, H. and Roscoe, A.M. 1976. 'Approaches to market segmentation analysis', *Journal of Marketing*, vol. 40, October.
5. Quinlan, F. 1981. 'The use of social grading in marketing', *Quarterly Review of Marketing*, vol. 7, no. 1.
6. Johnson, M. 1989. 'The application of geodemographics to retailing – meeting the needs of the catchment', *Journal of the Market Research Society*, vol. 31, no. 1.
7. Sleight, P. 1993. *Targeting Customers*. Henley-on-Thames: NTC Publications, p. 7.
8. Smith, D. 1993. 'Power tools of success', *Marketing Week*, 11 June, pp. 43–5.
9. Haley, R. 1968. 'Benefit segmentation: a decision-oriented research tool', *Journal of Marketing*, vol. 32, July. See also Haley, R. 1984. 'Benefit segmentation: backwards and forwards', *Journal of Advertising Research*, vol. 24, no. 1.
10. Reekie, W. 1979. *Advertising and Price*. London: Advertising Association, p. 13.
11. Wells, W. and Tigert, D. 1971. 'Activities, interests and opinions', *Journal of Advertising Research*, vol. 11, no. 4.
12. De Mooij, M. and Keegan, W. 1991. *Advertising Worldwide*. Hemel Hempstead: Prentice Hall, pp. 104–30.
13. Gunter, B. and Furnham, A. 1992. *Consumer Profiles: An Introduction to Psychographics*. London: Routledge, p. 100.
14. Dickson, P. 1982. 'Person-situation: segmentation's missing link', *Journal of Marketing*, vol. 46, no. 4.
15. Choffray, J-M. and Lilien, G. 1980. *Marketing Planning for New Industrial Products*. New York: John Wiley.
16. Gregory, G. and Humby, C. 1992. 'An examination of profiling techniques in the business-to-business sector', *Journal of Targeting, Measurement and Analysis for Marketing*, vol. 1, no. 1, pp. 61–76.
17. Fitzroy, P. 1976. *Analytical Methods for Marketing Management*. Maidenhead: McGraw-Hill, p. 18.
18. Kotler, P. 1994. *Marketing Management: Analysis, Planning and Control*, 8th edn. Englewood Cliffs NJ: Prentice Hall, p. 280.
19. Buzby, S. and Heitger, L. 1976. 'Profit-oriented reporting for marketing decision makers', *MSU Business Topics*, vol. 24, no. 3.
20. Dunne, P. and Wolk, H. 1977. 'Marketing cost analysis: a modular contribution approach', *Journal of Marketing*, vol. 41, no. 3.
21. Hooley, G.J. and Saunders, J. 1993. *Competitive Positioning*. Hemel Hempstead: Prentice Hall, p. 169.
22. Wind, Y. 1982. *Product Policy*. Reading, Mass.: Addison-Wesley, p. 94.
23. Barnard, L. 1993. 'English Renaissance', *Inside Hotels*, January, p. 18.
24. Crimp, M. 1985. *The Marketing Research Process*, 2nd edn. Hemel Hempstead: Prentice Hall International, p. 96.
25. Pessemier, E.A. 1977. *Product Management*. Santa Barbara, Calif.: John Wiley, p. 209.
26. Meade, N. 1987. 'Strategic positioning in the UK car market', *European Journal of Marketing*, vol. 21, no. 5.
27. Douglas, G., Kemp, P. and Cook, J. 1978. *Systematic New Product Development*. London: Halstead Press. Cited in Crawford, C.M. 1987. *New Products Management*, Homewood, Ill.: Irwin, p. 142.
28. Walker, O.T., Boyd, H.W. and Larréché, J.-C. 1992. *Marketing Strategy*. Homewood, Ill.: Irwin, p. 214.

Appendix
Demographics and segmentation

Frequently, consumer research makes use of a large range of demographic variables. Some syndicated services report routinely on product usage analysed by a host of such variables. An example is the Target Group Index and Table A.1 shows some data from a few years ago on Scotch whisky usage. This illustrates a fragment of the wealth of data available and can be used to indicate some of the problems and the possibilities in analysing demographics, and in developing demographic segmentation. It also underlines that categoric assertions cannot be made: judgements are needed.

About 44 per cent of all adults use scotch and 8 per cent of all adults are heavy users. That 44 per cent is about 19 million people. What kinds of people are they, and can this market be segmented on demographics?

A first split may be by sex, and it appears significant that more than a half of men are users but only a third of women. A very similar difference is apparent with age: a much higher proportion of those 35 and over are users. Social class does not discriminate anywhere near as well as age or sex. Taking age within social class adds little to understanding usage patterns. Regional figures and usage analysed by household income are not shown. but there are no major differences on these counts. Age and sex therefore seem to be the important demographic variables in this market.

Further analysis of age within sex reveals:

	Proportion of users	
	under 35	35 and over
Men	moderate	high
Women	low	moderate

From this we have a tentative approach to segmenting this market. Is it viable? Is it used by the companies involved? Analysis of usage data for leading brands may be instructive. Table A.2 takes leading brands and gives shares of the three-brand total users, by the four segments. Of all the users of these three leading brands, 46.6 per cent use Bells and 14.5 per cent use Haig; and of the men under 35 that use any of these three brands 47.6 per cent use Bells. However, inspection of use within the four segments does not point up any marked differences in brand shares from the overall position. That, together with observance of the promotional strategies for these brands, indicates that not much use is made of age within sex as a basis of a segmentation strategy. Alternatively, it could mean that all three brands use age/sex segmentation to equal effect – but there is little evidence of that in their promotion. The possibilities include one or more of the following:

(a) A potentially reasonable method of discriminating within this market is neglected.

(b) Other more sensitive bases are employed.

(c) Marketing without segmented strategies has been found to be effective.

Table A.1   *Demographics of Scotch whisky usage*

	Users 000s	% users	% heavy users
All adults	19,140	44.2	8.3
Men	11,867	57.0	11.9
Women	7,273	32.3	4.9
Age			
Aged 15–34	5,338	32.7	4.4
35–54	6,473	50.3	9.8
55+	7,330	51.7	11.3
Socio-economic group			
ABC1	8,212	49.1	10.3
C2DE	9,020	41.4	7.2
Age by socio-economic group			
ABC1 15–34	2,324	37.5	5.2
35–54	2,846	54.3	11.4
55+	3,042	57.6	15.0
C2DE 15–34	3,014	29.8	3.8
35–54	3,626	47.6	8.7
55+	4,288	48.2	9.1
Age by sex			
Men aged 15–34	3,051	36.8	6.4
35–54	4,233	58.3	12.2
55+	4,099	67.7	17.6
Women aged 15–34	1,649	20.6	2.2
35–54	2,395	37.4	5.9
55+	3,224	39.8	6.7

Notes: % users – whisky users as a percentage of total in row category, e.g. 57 per cent of all men are users, and that 57 per cent is 11,867,000 men. % heavy users – heavy whisky users as a percentage row category e.g. 4.9 per cent of all women are heavy users.

Heavy users defined as drinking three or more measures 'in last week', at the time of the survey.

Source: Based on tables in Target Group Index – BMRB.

Table A2   *Percentage share of the total of all users of the three brands in each of the four segments*

	Bells	Teachers	Haig
Men under 35	47.6	37.0	15.4
Men 35+	47.2	39.0	13.7
Women under 35	47.0	37.6	15.3
Women 35+	49.7	36.9	13.4

Questions

1. If (a) above, then what are the possibilities? Could or should these brands, or new variants, be marketed differentially within the four sex/age segments? If so, what would be the principal differences in strategy?

2. Is there any merit in developing a brand specifically for women? If so, what further research would be required? How might the product, the package, promotion and distribution be different?

3. Discuss the ethical issues in marketing whisky to younger people. What do you know of the regulations concerning the advertising of alcohol to young people?

4. If (b) above, what other segmentation base might it be useful to investigate? Would lifestyle, benefit sought or use situation be relevant? Explain.

5. If one of the variables in question 4 was employed would that make any demographic analysis redundant?

6. If (c) above, should brands nonetheless be positioned to appeal to heavier use segments in order to develop a 'core franchise', and then to take any other users that come along?

7. Would any of the above be different if the discussion were about malt whisky (such as Glenfiddich) rather than blended whisky?

Chapter 7

Marketing research

Decision-making in marketing concerns the evaluation of current positions, an interpretation of the established goals, the determination of alternative strategies to reach those goals and an assessment of the probabilities of the several outcomes of those strategies. Information relevant to this process therefore spans both current and future operations. It is the function of marketing research to gather and interpret this information to facilitate the decision-making process. Marketing research, then, is firmly related to marketing planning and control. It is an instrument that has worth only in so far as it contributes to decision-making [1].

First, the nomenclature needs attention. The terms 'market research' and 'marketing research' are frequently used synonymously. Strictly, marketing research subsumes market research, along with many other research activities. Market research describes market characteristics; marketing research covers any research relevant to marketing operations. It includes studies on advertising, packaging, distribution, salesforce activities, pricing and products, as well as market studies.

Research purpose

Essentially, research attempts to provide answers to questions. The preparation of marketing plans poses a legion of questions, and so marketing research potentially has a very significant role – all the more so if the organisation has adopted consumer orientation, since this espouses the fundamental importance of discovering consumer reactions to the present and planned marketing strategies. However, the effective fulfilment of this role is bounded by considerable problems, and none of these is more important than the very nature of the questions handed to the researcher.

Sometimes these are seemingly simple questions like 'Will the customer like it?' or, more balefully, 'Does the customer already like it?' Even more basic, 'How many currently buy it and what kinds of people are they?' Answers to such simple questions could use straightforward guesswork. This could prove to be right or wrong, but there would be no means of knowing which, no means of improving the guesswork and no means of passing the 'knack' on to others.

Sometimes the questions are more complex for example, 'How many will buy it if we drop our prices?' or 'What effect is our advertising having?' Many companies have, to some extent, to make judgements about the answers to these kinds of question. But, even then, research can play a part by giving a more logical, analytical framework within which the judgements are being made and by more properly identifying the real issues about which estimates are needed. This point is critical and will be examined by reference to the advertising question 'What effect is our advertising having?' That could be answered with vague statements such as 'a lot' or 'very little'. Perhaps the best answer is that which the researcher would give: 'What do you mean?' It can be seen that the question is probably implying a great deal. Does the questioner know what advertising is supposed to be doing? If so, is that supposition realistic – could it ever do what the questioner supposed? What is it supposed to be having an effect on? If the questioner and the researcher could agree a framework from these points, then the answer could become more manageable. Judgement would still play a part in specifying hypotheses that would need to be tested. For example, our advertising is aimed at increasing our sales, but for numerous reasons a direct relationship cannot be observed. Therefore we judge that attitudes affect behaviour (sales) and so investigate the effect of advertising on attitudes. As a result the researcher commissions a field study and obtains data on the change in attitudes. These data are by no means an unqualified answer to the original question; they are an answer that has been substantially shaped by the successive refining of the question into one that could be answered.

On the face of it, the research is merely answering its own questions, not the one originally put, and these might bear little similarity. But if the original question were seriously put, then it requires a rigorous answer. That rigour has the untidy habit of questioning the very assumption of the question, of translating it into a form amenable to data collection and of frequently supplying its own value judgements about the nature of the variables at issue – all of which sometimes surprises, and challenges, the questioner, but at the same time (hopefully) lays bare the central issues and assumptions. That exposure is often just as important as any data collected or hypothesis tested.

This serves as a further illustration of the need to appreciate the several viewpoints that different people will bring to the same problem. These several perceptions could lead to a gulf between the research user and the research provider. Users would inevitably be disillusioned if their crude questions were never 'correctly' answered. Providers could become cynical about the use to which their data are put and might look for appreciation of their work to professional associates outside their employing organisation. This could lead the providers to emphasise ever more sophisticated techniques, which could become quite sterile and divorced from the practicalities of feeding research into the decision-making process.

Research context

Research means many things to many people. This applies to the reasons for undertaking it, the processes involved and the interpretations of the results. Because it produces data, it might be thought that it produces facts – untarnished, pure replications of what actually is. But variations in the reasons, processes and interpretations cloud the connection between data and fact. Consider the following example.

An electronics manufacturer's research and development department had designed and built prototypes of a new product prior to any market research. The firm wanted to know what kinds of customer would be the best prospects and how many they should plan to make. Since it was a very sophisticated product they were optimistic and felt that an area of their factory should be cleared in preparation for its assembly. Time was of the essence because competitors were close on their heels. Because of this it was decided to restrict market investigations to only one of numerous possible applications of the product. The one chosen was that which could be most easily researched because it could be tightly defined to users of another product about which there was very full information. The result showed considerable interest in the novel technology, but resistance because the adoption of the new product would require large-scale changes in other systems used by potential customers. But with sufficient education in the technology and close monitoring to determine when prospects might be changing these other systems the outlook in this segment in the longer term (in this case 2–3 years) was encouraging. This outcome totally deflated the R&D department, which immediately abandoned the product to search for more exciting things. Other segments with other applications might well have been potentially far more important and might have been developed more rapidly. The 'disappointing' research led to the demise of the product; if it had been manufactured, it would have been a failure in any event because another firm brought out a product which totally changed this technology.

Research does not take place in a vacuum; it is embedded within and bounded by particular contexts. In the above context it came late and was called on by euphoric engineers in order to target prospects in an assumed market. One can argue that the parameters of the context should be changed, but research takes place in real time and involves real people. In 'solving' this case the prescriptions would have started by rearranging the organisational structure, replacing the sales office by a marketing department and appointing a marketing director and market research manager. Long-term (10–20 years) technological forecasting should also be introduced. But the company only wanted to know how many it should make.

This introduction to marketing research has served to establish three initial points:

1. The need to define the specific problem properly, which may mean the rigorous questioning of the original question posed.

2. The need to translate that problem into a form amenable to data collection, which usually means the construction of hypotheses.

3. The need to appreciate the context of the research since that supplies the motives for its use and influences the processes and interpretations.

It is as well to remember that research has no valid purpose of itself. It is an instrument, and as with all instruments its application and limitations should be understood by all interested parties. Haller [2] gives a welter of admonitions and advises that there are few axioms in this area:

> be skeptical of everything you first want to do. Examine every detail, in every step, in every project. Do not do anything just because it was done that way in the past, and neither should you do it because it sounds logical or correct. Every single project harbors some gaucherie, faux pas, or outrageous oversight. Most embody logic errors so momentous that, at first, you won't see them. Research isn't ever going to be perfect; new experiences will continually illuminate your procedures. But, by being skeptical and thorough in every matter, you will be able to improve your research quality immensely.

It is reassuring that, as an American practitioner, he admires the British market research profession for its high standards.

Approaches to research

Marketing problems come in many guises; research problems too. Three broad categories of research approaches have been identified: exploratory, descriptive and causal [3].

Exploratory work

Exploratory work is related to problem definition. It is ad hoc; no standardised procedures are used. It may involve study of internal records or have recourse to published information. It may even involve some rudimentary original research by, for example, holding informal group discussions with a handful of consumers. The aim is to obtain an insight into the problem by exploring symptoms, or indeed, by uncovering symptoms.

Example 1
A biscuit manufacturer may be unhappy about the failure to secure adequate 'listings' of a new product by retailers, i.e. they will not stock it. The

manufacturer wants to know why. The researcher may start by reviewing what was done in the attempt to secure the listings and then proceed by eliminating possible causes: salesforce call rates on retailers, advertising directed at retailers, the volume of consumer advertising, point of sale materials, packaging, and so on. The field may be narrowed down to the discount structure allowed to retailers, their perception of the quality of the consumer advertising and their view that there are too many comparable products. Each of these three could now be formulated into hypotheses.

Example 2

A soap company is concerned about the apparent failure of a recent coupon operation. It had distributed money-off coupons nationally, but sales had declined. Once more the researcher eliminates a welter of possible causes and focuses on two factors: (1) low coupon redemption rates, and (2) retailers redeeming coupons not against the brand of soap. There may also be regional disparities in redemption rates.

It can be seen that this first stage in research aims at crystallising the problem and suggests further avenues for investigation.

Descriptive research

Descriptive research is the attempt to depict market characteristics. It provides the important base data on such topics as market size, brand shares, consumer profiles, consumer evaluations of products and data relevant to marketing operations such as advertising media studies, salesforce effort and distribution research. The bulk of marketing research studies falls into this category.

In comparison with exploratory research, these types of study are distinguished by being altogether more prepared and structured. That is, the questions are more tangible and finite: 'How big is our market?' 'What kinds of people buy our brand?' But this research does not explain; associations between variables may be inferred, but descriptive research does not attempt to define cause–effect relationships.

Information sources for these descriptions span the major categories of official and unofficial published statistics, surveys and experiments.

Causal studies

Causal studies try to explain relationships: to determine which causes led to which effect. As such they are more dynamic than straightforward descriptions of what is and what has been, because they might offer guidelines to what might be. Much of the input to causal studies is derived from descriptive work, but such studies could also make use of experiments.

Data sources

Marketing research collects data to answer questions, and so the methods and sources of collecting these data are the substance of the research operation. Table 7.1 shows the major types of data category. Most attention here will be given to external data, but before that a short discussion of internal records is necessary.

It is surprising that even quite large companies sometimes have inadequate means of storing and retrieving internal data. It should be the easiest information to secure; sometimes the reverse is true, as the following examples show.

Example 1
Salesforce call reports are destroyed after one year when a simple analysis has been conducted. Perhaps the analysis has been to tabulate the number of calls against each customer and prospect. Later it is found that it would have been useful to pull out a calls-by-product analysis, but the information is lost for ever.

Example 2
A pricing study is to be conducted and some historical analysis is thought to be useful. Unfortunately, full information about past prices for all brands and all sizes, and for special deals, is not stored. Any attempt to gauge price elasticity in these circumstances would at best be highly partial and subjective.

Table 7.1   *Major data sources*

Internal	External
1. Sales records	*Primary*
2. Delivery and stock records	1. Surveys
3. Prices and quotations	2. Consumer panels
4. Sales promotion, e.g. price offers	3. Experiments
5. Advertising – media and messages; size of budget	4. Intelligence on competition
6. Salesforce's call reports and assessments of their effectiveness	*Secondary*
7. Past studies on marketing effectiveness	1. Government statistics, e.g. census data, family expenditure surveys, national income
	2. Trade association data
	3. International statistics – comparative data and trade statistics
	4. Surveys published by market research firms and official agencies
	5. Audits or retailers' stocks (usually thought of as secondary data, but if specially commissioned they could be classified as primary)

Note: Primary data are gathered for the company's own purposes and are therefore 'original'; secondary data are extant, they are published and so are widely available.

Example 3

An engineering company begins to think about segmentation. It is data-rich in that it has sales invoices going back fifty years. Customers have been assigned classificatory numbers, but the problem is that these numbers were allocated in strict chronological order, and the invoices are filed annually. This would be wonderful if the segment base were historical – but current thinking about segmentation seems to include all kinds of bases apart from history. Of course, it would be possible to go through all the invoices and reclassify them according to the type of industry the customer belonged to (Standard Industrial Classification [SIC] number), or they may be sampled. Whichever way is chosen it will be an elaborate task, which could have been avoided with prior analysis of information needs.

Example 4

This problem of data storage and retrieval is not confined to internal records. Sometimes expensive, specially commissioned survey work is lost. One food company finds it impossible to retrieve reports on test markets made more than a year ago. Numerous people in several departments have access to the same library and, when taken out, these test reports are seldom returned and are often misplaced.

These problems might appear trivial and easily rectified, but they are symptomatic of an attitude to data management. Unless the process is made systematic, then gathering external data is greatly hampered.

Secondary data

Secondary data are published data. Sources include government statistics, reports of government enquiries, trade association statistics, surveys undertaken by journal publishers or data from commercial research firms, which are subsequently published for general circulation. Studies of secondary data are sometimes referred to as desk or library research. Primary data are not published and are based on original fieldwork.

Government papers are the most comprehensive source of secondary data. The best and easiest way to appreciate the full scope of this source is to use it. This will also serve to indicate some of the frustrations in trying to assemble a long time-series. Changes in definitions, revisions to already published figures, variations in base dates for index numbers and alterations in base dates for constant price series are at best irksome. Go to any college library or large public library and you should be able to obtain the following data:

1. The total number of households in the country.

2. The proportion of married females in the 40–49-year-old population.

3. Average weekly expenditure by income group on jam, marmalade and other preserves.

4. Current population predictions from the Registrar General.

5. The value of refrigerators imported from Italy.

6. The value of orders-on-hand for engineering industries.

7. Total deliveries of textile machinery.

8. Number of starts in new house construction.

9. The retail price index.

10. Price indices by industry type and asset type.

Sources for these data include the Census of Population, the Family Expenditure Survey, reports from the Registrar General, the *Trade and Navigation Accounts*, *Monthly Digest of Statistics*, *Economic Trends*, *Social Trends* and various issues in the Business Monitor series. International statistics can be found in publications from the United Nations, the OECD and the European Union (formerly the EC), and by consulting sources quoted in the *Trade and Industry Review*.

Additionally, the National Economic Development Committee provides much useful information in the industry studies undertaken by its specialist committees. Trade journals are a fruitful source in industrial marketing research, and trade associations may supplement official statistics. Media publishers could also be worth consulting for both media and market studies.

Panel data

Some research companies have established panels of consumers who regularly report their buying behaviour, attitudes and intentions. These data are collected either by interview or by the panel member maintaining a diary of purchases. Sometimes they might be derived from a postal questionnaire. The essential characteristic of panels is that they are not 'one-shot'; they study the same people over several periods, or they may be 'continuous'. Most panel operations are syndicated rather than being for a single client. All the main rivals in a market may therefore be obtaining the same data.

Panels may be general-purpose, reporting on a wide range of markets; they may be specialised to a particular group of products (e.g. baby products); they may be limited to media use, such as monitoring television viewing; they may be established for finite periods, as in a test market, or be more enduring – some go back thirty years or more; they may be international, national, regional or restricted to just a few towns.

Some inducement is offered to participants. This could be gifts, shopping vouchers or free subscriptions to magazines. There may also be incentives for the prompt completion of diaries and questionnaires.

The composition of the sample may affect the validity of the exercise. The research firms strive to make it representative, but high refusal rates rule out random sampling. Membership is controlled against the economic and demographic characteristics of the population as a whole. This is probably reasonable enough for most general purposes, although the sampling error can never be calculated.

Despite these difficulties panel data are among the most useful that marketing managers can obtain. A continuous measure of market size may be made, and this could be analysed regionally. Brand shares may be monitored and sales trends by type of retail outlet discerned. Manufacturers could also discover the actual prices paid by consumers, rather than assume that their product is being sold at recommended prices. Because a great many supplementary personal data are collected it is also possible to analyse purchases against demographic, socio-economic and attitude variables. Panels can be used to assess the effects of changes in marketing strategy and afford a major instrument in the investigation of test markets.

Omnibus surveys

One further kind of regular, syndicated service is the omnibus survey. This is a survey operated by a market research firm, perhaps on a regular monthly basis, and the user can buy in a number of questions. Each omnibus can, therefore, cover topics put by several users, so that the cost is shared. There are general and more focused omnibuses. Some question parents, others retailers or doctors or financial analysts in the City. There is one confined to catering establishments, another on travel agents and several operating across Europe. Crouch [4] gives a listing of the suppliers.

The advantages are low cost and speed of response. They can be used for tracking general trends in awareness, for obtaining information on aspects of behaviour (e.g. how many reels of cotton does the consumer hold in stock) and for studies on confidence and intentions. (Are consumers more or less confident about their future circumstances? Do they intend to spend more or less on consumer durables or holidays?) Some include attitude studies with a few questions using attitude scales. The disadvantage is that the interview spans several product fields, often with no connection at all. This confines the amount of probing by the interviewer – it is less possible to put three or four supplementary probes after each question. (What else do you feel? Is there anything else? Anything more you like about it, or not?) It is this kind of probing that overcomes some of the difficulty inherent in highly structured questionnaires where respondents are forced to channel their answers into the researcher's preconceived notions about the possible replies.

Retail audit data

Another type of research service on a syndicated basis is the retail audit. This entails the recruitment of a sample of shops and a continuous (often bi-monthly) audit of their stocks in a number of product categories. The investigators determine stock levels at T_1 and at T_2 and consult delivery notes to the shop and thus estimate retail sales for the period. Nielsen is the major supplier of such data.

Table 7.2   *Spending on marketing research*

Market research agencies income 1991 by client's type of business

	£m	% change on 1990
Food and soft drinks	51.7	+2
Media	24.3	−1
Public services and utilities	21.6	+6
Alcoholic drinks	21.0	+9
Health and beauty aids	19.0	+7
Financial services	14.3	+1
Vehicle manufacturers	13.9	−13
Government	13.2	+21
Pharmaceuticals	12.4	−7
Business and industrial	11.4	−4
Advertising agencies	9.8	−8
Retailers	7.7	−12
Household products	7.7	+74
Travel and tourism	6.8	−9

Table 7.3   *Nature of market research agencies' fieldwork (%)*

Personal interview	55
Telephone interview	15
Self-completion survey	8
Hall test	12
Group discussion	10

Source: Association of Market Survey Organisations.

Table 7.4   *Some leading market research agencies*

	Turnover 1991 £m	Staff
AGB UK	38.8	578
AC Nielsen	38.4	850
MAI Research	31.3	380
Millward Brown International	23.3	315
Research International UK	21.3	240
British Market Research Bureau	17.8	257
Taylor Nelson	16.8	275
Research Services Limited (RSL)	10.1	150
The Research Business Group	9.4	90
MORI	9.0	117

Source: *Marketing*, 19 March 1992.

Reports can be used to gauge market size and shares, to check price levels, to assess proportions of retail outlets stocking various brands and to record movements in retail stock levels. Audits may be continuous and national, or specially arranged for test market operations.

Scanning databases

The widespread introduction of electronic scanners by retailers has enabled the development of new services, providing retail sales data on a weekly, or even daily, basis. The marketing director of Nielsen UK, the major supplier of these data, points up the advantages by saying:

> Scanning databases are fundamental to the changes we are witnessing. Not only do they offer much faster and more precise market measurement capabilities, they also provide the foundation for a host of diagnostic and analysis applications which shed new light on the workings of the marketing machine . . . . Scanning data is equipping manufacturers for a new pace of trading. Pricing moves, new marketing initiatives, even new product launches are now assessed in a few weeks, rather than over many months. And as the information helps the whole selling process to function more effectively, so decision making and implementation will become faster still. [5]

In-home scanners are also changing the operation of consumer panels. Traditionally, panel members completed diaries on their purchases, but some of this effort is relieved as in-home scanners read the bar codes on packages, although there is still the need for panel members to record the prices they paid. The integration of such household scanning databases with retail scanning databases offers the possibility of sophisticated monitoring and analyses, and it is anticipated that in the future these systems could be interlinked on a European or global level.

Survey data

To most people market research is probably synonymous with people carrying clipboards and stopping shoppers or calling at households. Certainly such activity is the most visible part of research; it is also one of the most important ways of gathering primary data.

Asking questions

Questions can be direct or indirect. They are direct if they are straightforward enquiries into behaviour or ownership: When did you last buy engine oil for your car? Where did you buy that oil? They are indirect if they ask about people in general, with the intention of drawing inferences about the individual respondent's attitudes: Today would you say people are more or less involved in their communities?

Answers can be closed or open-ended. If closed, they specify the choices. They are dichotomous if they are a simple yes/no, and they are multiple choice if there are more choices, such as several levels in the frequency or amount buying.

The four combinations of question and answer types determine the extent of structure in a questionnaire. Direct questions with closed responses give very structured questionnaires. Their great virtue is in the ease of administration and the scope for quantitative analysis, and that is why they dominate data collection procedures. But there are dangers arising from the very fact that they are direct questions with closed responses. Sometimes a direct question cannot obtain a reliable answer. If they rely on memory, they can often be flawed (How many pots of yogurt have you bought in the past year?). If they relate to sensitive issues they may ask more than respondents are prepared to tell (How much is currently outstanding on your credit card?). Closed answers can be notorious and occasionally antagonise respondents. This argues for the careful construction, and testing, of questions after a very critical appraisal of the nature of the information required.

Survey types

Surveys can use personal interviews with respondents; they may be conducted by mail questionnaire; or they can be carried out on the telephone.

Personal interviews

Personal interviews are the most flexible means and the most widely used – at least in consumer research. A major reason for their popularity is the high response rate they can elicit (although this may have to be achieved by using expensive call-back when desired respondents are not at home). With the sophisticated institutional arrangements they can also be quickly undertaken. Many of the larger research agencies maintain several hundred part-time interviewers and nationwide interviewing is quite easily arranged. Another advantage is that the interviewer can assist the respondent who may have difficulty understanding the question or offer some predetermined prompts in, for example, a study of advertising recall.

Survey fieldwork normally employs a highly structured questionnaire in the consumer market. Personal interviews in industrial marketing research are far less structured; there might not even be a questionnaire. Such interviews take the form of a dialogue, with the respondent asking as well as answering questions. This flexibility is necessary since the interviewer needs to be prepared for unexpected information and opinions. The respondent may even determine the issues that should be investigated in the interview. This does not imply that the interviewer is ignorant of the market, but that his or her knowledge may be restricted to particular applications, whereas the respondent may be better versed in novel uses for the product. The respondent could even supply the names of other people in other organisations that should be interviewed. Such a procedure is acceptable in industrial research; with new product studies it may be the only economical method of determining the sample in small markets.

Mail questionnaires

Mail questionnaires are less significant in consumer work, though they are important in industrial markets. One difficulty is the low response rate – less than 10 per cent is highly possible in the consumer market. Mailing several thousand questionnaires to receive back a couple of hundred clearly casts doubts on the sample's validity.

But mail can get to areas that interviewers cannot. Personal interviewing tends to be urban-biased; mail gets to the rural population just as easily as to those in the towns. Respondents can also work through the questionnaire at their own pace and any possible bias brought to bear by the presence of an interviewer is avoided.

Mail surveys are widely employed in the industrial market. Response rates may be higher, perhaps because respondents anticipate more tangible benefits from the research – for example, a copy of the report compiled from the study. The selection of individuals for personal interview can also be made from those that replied to a mail questionnaire, and the issues needing further clarification might also be determined [6].

Telephone surveys

There has been a very significant rise in the volume of telephone research now undertaken in the consumer market. Arnold [7] suggests that as much as 10 per cent of all market research revenue now derives from telephone interviewing. He attributes this increase to the greater domestic penetration of the telephone, technical developments in telephone research, the higher cost of personal interviewing and to the need for faster response in survey research.

Computer assisted telephone interviewing (CATI) is undertaken on a massive scale in the United States and its use is increasing in the United Kingdom. Interviewers work at computer terminals and feed responses straight into the computer. A typical application is in day-after-recall (DAR) of television commercials.

In industrial market research, telephone interviewing is undertaken frequently, often as one stage in a study. It has the advantage of offering a quick, if sketchy, view of the DMU because the interviewer can be switched to several of the key people by asking the right questions. Naturally the amount of information that can be obtained in this manner is limited, but it can form an essential first step in a wider survey which includes the other survey approaches.

Electronic interviewing

Cable television is in its infancy in the United Kingdom. Its widespread diffusion will introduce the prospect of electronic interviewing. Interactive viewdata systems might supplement, if not eventually supplant, personal interviewing. Monitoring consumer panels may be done via cable systems, or home computers might replace conventional diary completion of purchases. All this would have benefits in terms of the speed of surveying and the volume of data captured. Until the public becomes 'keyboard-literate', or until the technology allows voice recognition, the research might emphasise even more the direct question with the closed response. That might be necessary but it would not be sufficient; the open-ended question is invaluable in getting the respondent to articulate about the product field and is, after all, more consumer orientated.

More on the technology can be found in Connell [8]. Haller [9] dramatises the impact of technology on market research:

> The computer and its handmaidens at first started to influence the design of the questionnaires; and then, having won everyone's trust, they turned the research planners into pod people . . . it was infinitely better than the old way and its clumsy dependence on hand tabulation and card-sort equipment . . . after growing increasingly addicted to elaborate multivariate analyses instead of simpler forms of assessments, it was only natural that a whole new emphasis would emerge. The emphasis now was on the analysis itself.

In his view the emphasis on analysis takes over from the more profoundly important emphasis on the design of market research projects.

Survey errors

These occur in many ways. It is instructive to consider the scope for error because it could substantially improve understanding of the effectiveness of the instruments being employed.

Tull and Albaum [10] give three categories of sources of error: interpretative, reactive and interviewer-induced.

Interpretative error

Interpretative error arises mainly from ambiguity. The researcher or the respondent may use ambiguous words. Consider the following:

Q: How much breakfast cereal do you eat?
A: (scaled response from 'a great deal' to 'very little')

Problems: What is the time period? Should the answer be for one serving or for consumption over a month or a year? What is a 'great deal'? A consumer who eats small portions infrequently may perceive a quite modest amount as being enormous.

Q: How many books do you buy a month?
A: (multiple choice on number of books)

Problem: What is a 'book'? Some people think of a magazine as a book.

A day in the life of a pollster

It is a bright Thursday morning in leafy Beckenham. Sue Hugh patrols her manor like a cat burglar, eyes peeled for milk bottles left on doorsteps, an open upstairs window, a movement of the net curtains – any clue to habitation.

Her plastic folder and sensible shoes reveal her to be, not a cat burglar, but a market research fieldworker.

Over the next 2½ days, she will have to find 20 subjects of a given age, sex and social group, who are prepared to spend half an hour or so (at home) answering questions about their political opinions.

Mrs Hugh has a specific quota to meet. She must interview four males between the ages of 18 and 34; three between 36 and 54; and three over 55. Of the women in the sample, three must be between 18 and 34; three between 35 and 54; four over 55. Seven of the men must be in work; three working part-time or unemployed. She must find two working women and eight not working or doing part-time jobs. Four of her subjects have to fall into the AB social group, five into C1, six into C2 and five into the DE group.

Otherwise she is free to talk to whom she pleases. All the completed questionnaires must be packed up and in the first-class post before lunch on Saturday and for these 20 interviews Mrs Hugh will be paid £25. She went through the questionnaire with her husband the evening before and he collapsed with boredom halfway through. Still, the survey starts briskly enough. 'It's always like that,' Mrs Hugh says, 'at the beginning.'

Everybody interviewed on the first day fits into the quota somewhere. The required number of AB and C1 over 55 respondents are ticked off in a couple of hours, but the search for males, working, C2, aged 35 to 54, continues long into the evening, and into the next day when rain infects the soul of the suburb with a bleak reluctance to co-operate. By Friday evening 19 of the 20 interviews are completed.

Source: E. Dunn, 'A day in the life of a pollster', *Sunday Times*, 1 May 1983.

Reactive error

Reactive error occurs because of the measurement process. Respondents may feel that they are being singled out as 'special' because they are being asked questions. They could attempt to convey a good impression of themselves and to understate their attitudes and behaviour. They might be tempted to give what they perceive to be prestigious answers, or socially acceptable ones.

Interviewer-induced error

Interviewer-induced error flows from the fact that the interview is a social situation and the interaction between two people is unique. Bias could be presented by the background of the interviewer who is typically a middle-class woman in her thirties or forties. The respondents may impute a set of values to the interviewer and merely play these back, rather than give their own views. A lengthier discussion of these points can be seen in the book by Churchill [11]. This potential for error in surveys lends support to the following statement [12]:

The highly structured and completely standardised instrument is designed to be a uniform stimulus. Variations which appear in response can be attributed only to real differences in response and not to variations in the way the instrument works. There are several grounds for doubts as to whether such an aim can be achieved.

Knowing where errors might arise is the first step in trying to control them. Careful preparation and implementation of the research procedures are the next step. If a structured questionnaire is being used, then attention should be given to the question form and wording. A preliminary test of the instrument is advisable. Proper selection, training and field control of interviewers can also go some way towards reducing the impact of interviewer-induced error. But it must be recognised that some degree of error will almost inevitably remain. With tight budget constraints these could be quite large. Small non-probabilistic samples may be drawn; the instrument may not be tested; and unskilled or uncontrolled interviewers may be employed. Only a naive user would then be surprised that the research later proved incorrect.

A useful analogy is with photography. A survey tries to take a 'picture' of some market characteristics. Cheap 'cameras' in the hands of a novice may only give fuzzy, out-of-focus 'pictures'. They may even give photographs of subjects' feet instead of their heads. On the other hand, a high-quality 'camera' used by a professional can give excellent pictures with surprising clarity. Occasionally, however, the professionals may develop beautiful artistic compositions which are appreciated only by other professionals.

Holding the photographic analogy, it may help to reconsider the sources of error with some illustrations.

1. *Interpretative error.* Is that picture of gesticulating people meant to convey a happy event or an angry scene?

2. *Reactive error.* So we are told it is a wedding and shown more formal pictures of the people smiling. Are they smiling because that is what everyone does at a wedding or because they genuinely want to smile?

3. *Interviewer-induced error.* Some of the guests know the photographer to be artistic, or they infer that from his appearance, and then strike what they think to be 'artistic' poses.

Sampling

It is rare that surveys can cover the whole of a population, and so samples are drawn. A first task in this is to define the relevant population. A manufacturer of yacht fittings has a very particular target market; samples for the surveys must therefore be drawn from existing and potential yacht owners (as well as designers

Table 7.5 *Sample designs*

Probability samples	Purposive samples
Simple random	Quota
Systematic random	Judgement
Multi-stage	

Source: M. Crimp, *The Marketing Research Process*, 2nd edn. Hemel Hempstead: Prentice Hall International, 1985, p. 32.

and yacht builders). A baby food producer also has a restricted market and population from which to take a sample. But population definition is by no means always obvious.

Example 1

How should a large-scale house builder define the 'population'?
 All people?
 People who will buy a house in a given price range?
 People who already have a house or newcomers to the market?

Example 2

A restaurant wishes to determine its current image:
 Among all people in the area?
 Among tourists?
 Among people who regularly use it, or those that never have?

In both these cases the population needs further specification. Having specified the population, the job is then to design a sampling plan. Table 7.5 gives a summary of the main alternatives.

Purposive samples

These types of sampling plan are not randomly based: a degree of personal judgement is implied. In some cases this might be taken as being good enough, given time and cost constraints, but the user should appreciate that the degree of sampling error cannot be quantified.

Judgement samples

Judgement samples can be more meaningful, especially in industrial marketing; interviewing a sample of noted 'experts' about possible future developments in a technology can furnish considerable insights. As noted earlier, judgement samples can also employ a snowball technique, where the first respondent supplies the name of another. Again, this is really justified only in industrial markets although, with controls, it is used sometimes to top up specialised consumer panels.

Quota samples

Quota samples are the most widely used kind of non-probability sample. Krausz and Miller [13] describe the procedure thus:

> This is a method of sampling which is non-random in that the selection of the final unit of enquiry is left to the judgement of the interviewer. There is an attempt here to produce representativeness by means of 'quota controls' by stratifying the sample to be chosen in terms of certain basic population characteristics about which information is available from census and other well-established sources.

Quota controls are often specified in terms of age, sex, social class, with or without children, and wife working or not working. Reliable information can be consulted to determine the proportion of the population which falls within various classes for these variables. Thus we can determine the percentage of male and female, and that for several social classes and age groups. The sample drawn is then matched to these proportions. The interviewer is given these proportions and left to judge which people to select (often with great difficulty in obtaining the last few respondents to fill the quota).

Note that it would be difficult to impose some other types of quota control which might be far more relevant than demographics; for instance, heavy users of analgesics; people with unfavourable attitudes to keg beer; or those who plan a camping trip next year. All these examples present situations where it would be difficult to devise quota controls. But in practice it would be impossible to sample such groups randomly because no prior listing of the relevant population would be feasible. Thus a quota plan would be used, with the realisation that the quota controls were not absolutely reliable.

Probability samples

These are objectively determined and the sampling error can be computed.

Simple random samples

Simple random samples are the most widely known in marketing research, but are hardly ever used. They require an initial listing of the population and then the random drawing of subjects. The list-building can be highly restricting especially for nationwide surveys. With very large populations alternative probability sampling designs are sought.

Systematic samples

In this case from a listing of the population the first individual is chosen randomly and then a uniform, systematic interval is applied to draw the remainder, e.g. every tenth or hundredth after the first.

Multi-stage samples

With large, dispersed populations the sample will be drawn at several stages. A first cut may be by parliamentary constituencies, and then polling districts within the chosen constituencies. At the next stage individuals will be drawn from the electoral registers. The advantage of this kind of sampling is that it retains the virtue of being undertaken on a probability basis and is manageable. The interviewer does not have very widespread calls to make.

An alternative to using constituencies and polling districts is to consider the type of residential district. All 125,000 districts used in the census of population have been classified according to type of residence. Acorn is the acronym for 'a classification of residential neighbourhoods'.

The use of Acorn is spreading. It is being used increasingly in marketing planning for segmentation studies. The use of neighbourhood classification is also now used in some regular panel data and some media data are being presented on this basis. It is also being introduced in direct mailing with the targets being identified according to Acorn groups.

Psychological data

The increased emphasis now given to psychological variables in consumer behaviour has resulted in added attention being given to the collection of psychological data in market research studies. Attitudes, motivations and product perception have provided three areas for most research. Something of these has already been considered in Chapter 2. The discussion here will be restricted to just a few of the techniques [14].

Qualitative research

Most market research employs the techniques so far discussed in this chapter. They could be classified as quantitative in that they try to put quantities to marketing problems. For several decades it has been recognised that such work is necessary but not sufficient in illuminating the great variety of issues in marketing problems. As Robson [15] says:

> Quantitative research is hard put to provide ideas, to explain trends, to illustrate the colour and complexity of people's lives, or to identify the values and needs of the target audience, in a way that can be clearly communicated to the agency team.

To fill the gap, researchers have made recourse to qualitative research which tends to be unstructured and involves very small numbers of respondents. The aim is to listen to rather than to question respondents. In the 1950s it was called motivation research because the focus was on depth interviews which tried to explain consumer motivation. Gross generalisations derived from exceedingly small samples led to considerable disillusionment, and in the 1960s qualitative work was all but abandoned. It was revived in a less ambitious and more realistic guise in the 1970s. It dropped the pretence of psychoanalysis and became just another marketing research tool.

Individual depth interviews and small group discussions are the main methods used to listen to consumers. Typical applications are at the exploratory stage of a much larger study and in the early stages of creative development for an advertising campaign. In the first case the aim could be to highlight the issues to be investigated by a survey, or to generate ideas about the attributes that consumers use in evaluating products. In the second case the application can be more diffuse. It might be that preliminary advertising copy has been prepared. For a television commercial this could be an animatic – an animated video. This might be shown to several groups of people from the target audience and their reaction of its credibility, and how well the advertiser's point was made, is gauged. Alternatively, the research could be introduced earlier in creative development with the intention of conveying to the 'creative team' something of how the product, and its advertising, fit into people's lives. An important element of this will be recording the vocabulary people use in relation to the product and its usage.

Analysis of the tapes of these interviews and discussions provides the strength and the weakness of qualitative research – the strength because it can offer fresh insights about consumers, products and advertisements; the weakness because two different researchers, working on the same problem with the same people, could come to entirely different conclusions. Attempts are being made to make the process less intuitive, and Jones has proposed a procedure for the more formal coding and analysis of qualitative data [16]. The subjectivity remains and has led May to characterise the methods companies use in dealing with this uncertainty. He sees the client using the researcher for a flow of projects and buying 'the particular blend of empathy, insight and creativity that makes a good qualitative researcher' [17]. And he explains the popularity of qualitative techniques as being related to their pragmatic, action-oriented qualities.

Subjectivity and pragmatism are not favoured concepts by 'scientific' researchers, and so qualitative studies will always attract controversy. Despite this they do have utility and as with all marketing research techniques the only dogma can be that of the sceptic.

Attitudes

Attitudes have been examined by using self-report scaling procedures, physiological reactions and indirect techniques. We shall concentrate on scaling. There are numerous approaches to attitude scaling [18], some of which were referred to earlier in this book. Two methods will now be outlined: the Likert scale and the semantic differential.

Table 7.6   *A Likert-type rating scale*

	Has an attractive package	Is highly nutritional	Is good value for money
Strongly agree	—	—	—
Agree	—	—	—
Tend to agree	—	—	—
Tend to disagree	—	—	—
Disagree	—	—	—
Strongly disagree	—	—	—

Note: In this example a six-point scale is used, whereas a five-point scale is often employed: the difficulty with scales with an odd number of points is that too many respondents may use the middle point.

In the *Likert method of rating*, respondents are asked to indicate their degree of agreement or disagreement with a number of statements. The researcher proceeds by developing a long list of statements that may be thought to reflect something about the object of the study. A preliminary test on a small sample of respondents would purge the list of statements that do not discriminate between different people's attitudes. One way of doing this would be to score the several scale positions ('strongly disagree' to 'strongly agree', as in Table 7.6) from 1 to 6. If there were little difference in the scores across all respondents, then that item would not be sensitive enough to elicit attitudes. For example, in a study of public attitudes to robbery, it would hardly be helpful to discover that everybody strongly agreed with the statement, 'robbery is an anti-social activity': it would seem to be that by definition.

After this preliminary test the adjusted set of statements is administered to the full sample. Given a 10-item, 6-point scale, the maximum score for each individual will be 60. The mean score might be taken as the standard and individual scores compared with that. Assume we had seven other items in addition to the three in Table 7.6, e.g. 'has a pleasant taste', 'is convenient to use', etc. Further assume that the questionnaire was applied to 1,000 respondents and they were asked to rate our brand and three competitors. From this the mean score for all ten items for all four brands could be computed, and extra analyses could show averages for subgroups classified by demographic or usage variables.

Studies using the *semantic differential technique* ask respondents to describe the company's image, the brand's image, or whatever, on a series of bipolar adjectives (or phrases). Normally a 7-point scale is used. As an example a manufacturer may be rated by his retailers on, among other things, the following:

courteous service	_ _ _ _ _ _ _	discourteous service
fast delivery	_ _ _ _ _ _ _	slow delivery
good promotional back-up	_ _ _ _ _ _ _	poor promotional back-up

Subjects would indicate their feelings in one of the seven positions for each of the paired statements. Each of the positions could be given a score as in the Likert method. The positive poles might be scored 7 and the negatives 1. Every respondent's rating on each item would then be scored and an aggregate score for each item derived. For instance, in the example above the aggregate for the first item may be 500 for 100 retailers. The mean is 5, with the implication that the service is seen to be slightly towards 'courteous'. What exactly that implies is open to interpretation, without some benchmark or standard. Sometimes this problem is side-stepped by making it a comparative exercise against other companies or brands. Research reporting such exercises uses graphic 'attitude profiles' by drawing lines connecting the mean scores on each item.

Difficulty may be experienced if the items have not been screened – just as in the Likert method. But overall this technique has proved to be both useful and widely used. 'Perhaps it is the ease with which semantic differential scales can be developed, or the ease with which the findings can be communicated, or accumulated experience as to their value, that accounts for the semantic differential's great popularity in marketing' [19].

Marketing information systems

Marketing research supplies information for decision making. It is axiomatic that the information should be timely, relevant and as complete as possible. Furthermore, it helps if necessary analogies are drawn, significant relationships underlined and probability statements properly indicated to be such. More than that, the researcher should fully understand the user's requirements and the user should appreciate the problems and pitfalls in data collection. In sum, research should be effectively integrated into the decision-making system.

It is wasteful if potential users in an organisation do not know that a particular problem has received attention before. It is wasteful if research is completed and the reports mislaid, or stored at totally inconvenient locations. It is wasteful if research is undertaken and insufficient analysis takes place. For these reasons, information gathering, storage and retrieval should be systematic, and related to the decision-makers' needs. This is why Little refers to 'marketing decision support systems' rather than 'marketing information systems' [20].

Design considerations

A number of pertinent questions arise in discussing the type of system required.

How recent need the information be?
Do we need up-to-the-minute data or can several days, weeks or months elapse from when the event occurred to when it is recorded in the system? Clearly this

varies with the kind of data, their usefulness and their source. Data on stock levels at distribution centres for items in a market that is highly sensitive to delivery times could be among the most critical in the company. This kind of data should be as near to instantaneously available as cost constraints allow. The revolution in data processing technology makes this technically, if not economically, feasible. Many other types of data are less critical. Continuous research data on consumer panels and retail audits can be incorporated as they are received. The same can be said for government-generated data, which are often (unavoidably) years out of date before the company receives them.

Should information be stored in aggregate or disaggregate?

It may be possible to store data in their crude state, e.g. the actual sales invoices, despatch notes, and so on. But then every user would have to carry out an enormous amount of assembling of the data into a form amenable to analysis. Some data, therefore, are stored simply in aggregate, e.g. simple totals of sales of various items, perhaps on a regional basis. But then, if the originals are disposed of, it will never be possible to revert to disaggregate in order to aggregate in another way. Perhaps the first aggregation was product type by region, and the user now wants an analysis of order size by pack size. There is an argument to keep data in as disaggregated a form as possible with expected types of aggregation already made. This depends on the form in which the data are stored – hard copy, microfilm or computer. Computer-linked microfilm is costly, but extremely adaptable, and overcomes many of the problems in the level of aggregation in the data store.

How much analysis – as opposed to storage – should the system undertake?

It is possible to build into the system either an elementary or a very advanced analytical facility. Cross-tabulations can be easily generated. More complex systems may use statistical packages to search the data for relationships or conduct simulations. The questions here concern the hardware and software capabilities and, just as importantly, the level of managerial sophistication. It is pointless to produce elegant statistical explanations if managers find them incomprehensible.

Should the system take decisions?

Systems can be designed with varying degrees of autonomy for taking decisions. A good example of delegated decision making is in stock control, where routine reordering may be a normal function of the system. An example of a less autonomous system would be where it merely reported that current events were outside some predetermined control limits, as in sales or distribution costs analyses.

Establishing the system

There are two extremes in the approach to information management: ad hoc or fully integrated. In the first the system evolves through expedience. A new class of external data becomes available, or someone feels some new kind of monitoring would be useful, and so the new information is grafted onto the existing system. This ad hoc approach is typical of many companies. It suffers in that compromises are made. New data may not be amenable to storage in the same form as other data, and storage may then be in numerous forms at numerous locations. Furthermore, because the resulting system is not unified, a major drawback could be the mismatch between user requirements and data availability. Some users may be unaware that a new class of data is available; others may be regularly receiving mountainous print-outs which are irrelevant to their needs; others may not know that certain statistical operations could be routinely performed on their data prior to receipt. Additionally, the data flow around the organisation could lead to bottlenecks. For example, some accounting information may be used by several functional areas. These different users may require different analyses on the same data. In an ad hoc system compromise and expedience may not always give an optimum result.

It is because of these deficiencies that the quite opposite approach has been adopted by some companies. That is the rigorously planned and integrated system, which is embedded in the very design of the organisational structure. It should be clear that information management is intimately connected with organisational structure. Presumably the organisation has been designed to accomplish tasks – to take decisions. Information is central to decision-taking; and so information flows to decision-takers. It seems logical to fit the information system to the organisational structure. More profoundly, the rigorous information system may require that the organisational structure be designed in tandem with the information system, but such an ideal poses considerable problems. A prerequisite is for the systems analyst to audit information requirements, but a serious gap may emerge between the viewpoint of the user and the analyst. The unsympathetic user may not see the point of the analyst's questions and may unwittingly give a false impression of requirements because certain routine data are taken for granted. The user may forget to mention some periodic analyses that are undertaken, and may have little idea how these requirements relate to others in the organisation. The analyst may use huge checklists to delineate user needs, but will always have problems because she or he knows less about how the data are used than do the users, and because she or he will be attempting to systematise the disparate approaches of numerous users.

Designing a system that is appropriate, and one that will be used, is a complex and difficult task, about which Piercey [21] has said:

> This barrier is characterised by problems in defining marketing management information needs and meeting them in ways that do not sacrifice the essential intuition and creativity in using marketing information, for the sake of designing sophisticated, uniform systems. The common idea that simply providing marketing executives with more information faster, will improve effectiveness, is dangerously wrong.

Piercey advocates a planned, organised approach with involvement of top management and users as a way through this barrier.

Summary

The function of marketing research is to gather, interpret and report information relevant to marketing decision-making. It therefore includes market studies and any other research relevant to marketing operations. Three central considerations are: (1) the need to define the specific problem properly; (2) the need to translate it into a form amenable to data collection, and (3) to appreciate the context of the research.

Marketing research can be typified as being exploratory, descriptive or causal. Data sources may be either external or internal; in the former case they may be primary (original) or secondary (published). Survey research is one of the most important sources, and the survey methods are personal or telephone interviews or mail questionnaires. Response errors in surveys may be caused by difficulties in interpretation (of the question or answer), by the reaction of the respondent to being interviewed or by the fact that the interview is a social situation.

Surveys usually imply sampling, rather than a census. Probability samples are the only rigorous form of sampling and have the virtue of indicating the sample error. Two kinds of attitude scale method were discussed: the Likert scale and the semantic differential; and qualitative approaches were considered.

Research should be effectively integrated into the decision-making system. Consideration was given to some of the parameters in designing the marketing information system, and some problems in its implementation were investigated.

Questions for review and discussion

1. At the beginning of this chapter the question 'What effect is our advertising having?' was posed, and its implications for research traced through. Do the same for the question 'Are our prices too high?'

2. Devise some examples of exploratory research and work them through to the stage of specifying some hypotheses.

3. What kinds of information can be derived from continuous rather than 'one-shot' studies?

4. Compare the advantages and disadvantages of the three main approaches to survey research.

5. How might the several sources of response error in surveys be controlled?

6. 'Vox pop' interviews by media reporters aim at obtaining a cross-section of the population by stopping people at 'random'. Why is that not a random sample?

7. Assume you have attitude profiles for several brands based upon a study using the semantic differential. You are told that the profiles are based upon the mean averages. Why might you want to know the distributions about the means, and what might those distributions tell you?

References

1. For detailed consideration of market research techniques, see Worcester, R.M. and Downham, J. 1986. *Consumer Market Research Handbook*, 3rd edn. London: McGraw-Hill. See also Kent, R. 1989. *Continuous Market Measurement*. London: Edward Arnold.
2. Haller, T. 1983. *Danger: Marketing Researcher at Work*. Westport, Conn.: Quorum, p. 10.
3. Green, P.E. and Tull, D. 1975. *Research for Marketing Decisions,* 2nd edn. Englewood Cliffs, NJ: Prentice Hall Inc.
4. Crouch, S. 1983. *Marketing Research for Managers*. 2nd edn. Oxford: Butterworth-Heinemann.
5. Buckingham, C. 1992. 'New capabilities', *Admap*, October, pp. 32–5.
6. *Journal of the Market Research Society*, 1985, vol. 23, no. 1 is devoted to postal research.
7. Arnold, P. 1986. 'Telephone research', in Worcester, R.M. and Downham, J. (eds), *Consumer Market Research Handbook*, 3rd edn. London: McGraw-Hill, ch. 10.
8. Connell, S. 1982. 'The challenge of change', *Journal of the Market Research Society*, vol. 24, no. 3.
9. Haller, op. cit.
10. Tull, D. and Albaum, G.S. 1973. *Survey Research – A Decisional Approach*. Aylesbury: International Textbook.
11. Churchill, G.A. 1979. *Marketing Research*, 2nd edn. Hinsdale, Ill.: Dryden, ch. 11.
12. Krausz, E. and Miller, S.A. 1974. *Social Research Design*. London: Longman, p. 49.
13. Ibid., p. 36.
14. For a review of techniques, see Mostyn, B. 1978. *A Handbook of Motivational and Attitude Research Techniques*. Bradford: MCB.
15. Robson, S. 1983. 'Inside the soul of the consumer'. *Campaign*, 15 July, p. 44.
16. Jones, S. 1981. 'Listening to complexity – analysing qualitative marketing research data', *Journal of the Market Research Society*, vol. 23, no. 1.
17. May, J. 1978. 'Qualitative advertising research – a review of the role of the researcher', *Journal of the Market Research Society*, vol. 20, no. 4. See also Greenbaum, T.L. 1988. *The Practical Handbook and Guide to Focus Group Research*. Lexington, Mass.: Lexington.
18. See, for example Churchill, G.A. 1979. *Marketing Research*, 2nd edn. Hinsdale, Ill.: Dryden, ch. 11; and Foxall, G.R. 1977. *Consumer Behaviour*. Corbridge: Retailing and Planning Associates, ch. 5.
19. Churchill, G.A. 1979. *Marketing Research*, 2nd edn. Hinsdale, Ill.: Dryden.
20. Little, J.D.C. 1979. 'Decision support systems for marketing managers', *Journal of Marketing*, vol. 43, no. 3.
21. Piercey, N. 1981. 'Marketing information – bridging the quicksand between technology and decision-making', *Quarterly Review of Marketing*, vol. 7, no. 1. See also Piercey, N. 1987. 'Developing marketing information systems', in Baker, M.J. (ed.), *The Marketing Book*. London: Heinemann, ch. 11.

Chapter 8
Sales forecasting and market potential

A useful statement of the operational significance of forecasting is offered by Milne [1]:

> Business activity, and therefore managerial activity, is entirely based on expectations. Management is about the uncertain future. Formal forecasting has a modest place in that grand scheme of things, in so far as it can offer support for well founded, rather than badly founded expectations. Good forecasters aspire less to providing answers than to providing intelligent points of view . . . . Their end product is not facts but opinions: better thought out opinions than would exist in their absence.

Put another way, business decisions are entirely about the future; nobody knows with certainty what will happen in the future, but formal analysis may support the better opinions.

There are other good reasons for taking a formal approach to forecasting. Over time the experience gained may improve the forecasting procedures. Past failures are instructive and could show factors that were not taken properly into account. Additionally, a formal approach could aid understanding. The very process of explicitly attempting to derive a forecast forces attention on basic relationships in the marketplace. A firm may have implicitly assumed certain relationships, e.g. about income or price elasticities, which are seriously questioned only when a formal forecast is undertaken. By taking a formal approach, all the assumptions are laid out for inspection and critical appraisal.

The role of forecasting in the planning process

Two of the essential managerial activities are making and controlling plans. But at what point does the forecast enter the planning process? Some confusion is possible because managers may have different conceptions of the word 'forecast'. Compare the two following sequences:

Case 1 Forecast   →   Plan
Case 2 Plan   →   Forecast

It can be seen that in the first case some forecast is made and then a plan is based on it, whereas in the second the plan comes first. The two forecasts therefore represent entirely different entities, and so some further definition is required. It is useful to distinguish between these two by terming case 1 an unconditional forecast and case 2 a conditional forecast. In the second case the forecast is dependent on some statement of intended effort – the planned level of marketing activity.

In practice the role of forecasting in the planning process is never as neat and sequential as indicated above. Several series of unconditional and conditional forecasts may be combined with alternative plans in an iterative fashion. Take for example the case where an unconditional forecast of market (industry) demand leads to a given plan, and then to a conditional forecast of the firm's sales. The sales forecast may be judged unsatisfactory when compared with company goals, and so the plan is changed, leading to a new conditional forecast, by which time new information may be available which indicates a national economic growth rate higher than previously thought. And so the whole process begins again. Or then the manufacturing division adds, or reduces, a production constraint which will affect the plan and the conditional forecast.

These complexities reinforce the need for a formal approach to forecasting. An agreed and understood nomenclature within the organisation is quite basic, otherwise two managers might spend hours talking about forecasting without really communicating. Their differing use of the word may imply a different sequence in the planning process, and so the problems that they identify may be mutually incomprehensible.

Forecasting techniques

Support for the forecaster's opinions about the future comes from a wide range of techniques. They vary in their degree of sophistication, their use of statistical analysis and, sometimes, in the views they give. Therefore, just as in our discussion of marketing research, it is important to judge the tools employed. These tools may be more, or less, appropriate. Six criteria have been suggested as important to the selection of the forecasting methodology. These are: (1) the degree of accuracy desired, (2) the time horizon, (3) the value of the forecast, (4) the availability of data, (5) the type of data, and (6) the company's experience with forecasting [2].

There is a welter of forecasting techniques. The treatment here will be selective and rudimentary concentrating on the essence of the most important approaches. It considers something of the value of salesforce opinion, customer opinion, extrapolation, correlation and economic forecasting [3].

Salesforce opinion

Of all the people in the firm, salesforce personnel are in the most intimate and continuing contact with the market. Opinions that the salesforce may hold about the future are therefore very well worth considering. The simplest method is to aggregate the estimates that each salesperson makes for his or her territory. This could be supplemented by giving the salesforce some perspective (by supplying historical data) and some guide as to the firm's view of national economic prospects. That this approach to forecasting is widely used is demonstrated by a study carried out by Wotruba and Thurlow [4]. They found that 86 per cent of the companies they investigated asked their salespeople to submit forecasts. In more than a third of these cases the firms said that these forecasts were about right.

Objections to this process arise because it is difficult to assess how subjective the salesforce are being when making their territory forecast. They might feel that their forecasts will be used against them; that they will become their sales target. If a commission system is employed, they may adjust their figures to render a forecast that they feel would represent a sales level that could be achieved with only modest effort. It is also sometimes contended that the salesforce may over-react, becoming unduly optimistic, or pessimistic, with slight changes in the flow of new orders.

Despite these reservations it is still highly relevant to include some provision for salesforce views in the forecasting procedure. They do represent one set of influential opinions about the future, and many good sales personnel would be offended if they thought no attention was being paid to their views.

Surveys of buyer intentions

If salesforce opinion is relevant, then, potentially, the views of the people who will actually be buying the product are even more important. How far that potential is realised is a function of the validity of the means used to gather such opinions and of whether or not customers are able to supply any meaningful information about their future behaviour.

Considerable doubt has been cast on the use of surveys of buyer intentions in the consumer market. The US government has stopped publishing its surveys of customer expectations because they were found to be too unreliable. The difficulty is that too many things can intervene between a customer's statement of intent about, say, buying a washing machine next year and the actual purchase (or lack of it). If this were to be taken down to the brand-specific level, then the scope for even wider variance is considerable.

Both product category and brand-specific intentions may be obtained more reliably in the industrial market. It may be in the interests of the customers to inform their suppliers of their intentions to ensure they have sufficient stock. The validity of this information will be related to the connections that the buyer and seller have. Data concerning assessments of past intentions will assist, but it should always be borne in mind that over-capacity in a supplier industry is not the customer's responsibility.

More general surveys of industrial buyer intentions can be broadly useful. In the United Kingdom the survey produced by the Confederation of British Industry is often consulted by forecasters. This reports the opinions of a large sample of companies on whether they expect their investment, employment, production and exports to change or remain stable in the next four-month period [5]. The *Financial Times* also undertakes regular surveys of industrial and consumer confidence. While no absolute correlation would be expected between such surveys and any particular firm's sales, it would be worth investigating in case some kind of systematic relationship could be found. Added to this, the results of such work do influence economists making aggregate forecasts for the economy.

Extrapolation

These techniques project time-series data. Simple models may take last month's sales as the forecast for the next month's sales, or they may use the proportionate increase in sales at time $t - 1$ over $t - 2$ as the increase of sales in $t + 1$ over $t - 1$, with adjustments if necessary for seasonal variation.

Moving averages are an extension of the basic technique. Given sales figures for each of the last twelve months, the mean is calculated and becomes the forecast for the next month. When the actual for that month is available it is used in place of the figure for what is now thirteen months ago. Exponential smoothing is a sophistication that weights each of the observations so that more recent months are given greater emphasis than more distant months in the calculations.

Fuller analysis of time-series data seeks to describe the total variation in terms of four components: trend, cycle, season and irregular variations. Figure 8.1 illustrates how a composite time-series may be subject to these four influences.

The underlying trend – referred to as the secular trend – is a long-run variation. Such patterns are rooted in fundamental factors such as growth in gross domestic product (GDP), technological developments and taste changes. Trend extrapolation can be carried out with moving averages or regression analysis. In the latter case the process fits linear, or non-linear, regression lines to the sales data, the sales regressed against time.

Time-series that display a marked cyclical pattern can be troublesome. The cycles may be reasonably predictable for long periods – at least, that often seems to be the case with hindsight. Many engineering industries experienced, until

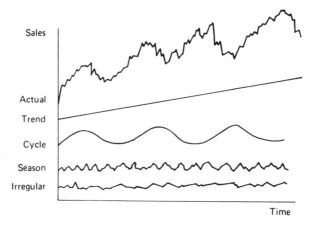

Figure 8.1 *Time-series components*

recently, three or four cycles each of about four to five years' duration. However, the analyst in the middle of a forecasting exercise is only too aware of the implied assumption that past basic relationships in the economy will endure for the forecast period. It is always too easy to give recent government initiatives powerful importance, and to suggest that some change in tax rates or investment incentives has radically disturbed any enduring relationships. Predictions of turning points in the cycle may therefore over-emphasise current circumstances.

Correlation

Some analysts believe they can obtain sufficient knowledge of a firm's market that they can postulate a model relating the forecast variable to other independent variables. It is assumed that part associations between the variables can be projected into the future, and that, given a forecast of the independent variable, then a forecast of the dependent variable emerges automatically. Clearly, this refers to correlation analysis.

To bring out the principle of this approach a simple example will be used, and the regression line will be fitted without employing the mathematical formula.

A carpet manufacturer believes his sales are correlated with GDP – that they are responsive to changes in the overall economic climate. He therefore plots the data comparing sales with GDP, overcoming the difficulty of dealing with entirely different orders of magnitude by comparing annual percentage changes. He also ensures that the data are reduced to a constant, rather than current, price basis. Each observation is for a given year, and relates the proportional changes for each variable over the previous year (Figure 8.2).

Without calculating the correlation coefficient and the standard error, it will

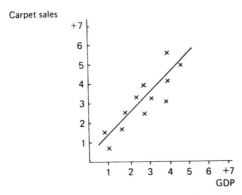

(hypothetical data; annual percentage changes)

Figure 8.2 *Proportional changes in GDP and carpet sales*

be assumed that there is a reasonable relationship between these two variables. Thus the fitted regression line is assumed to be a fair summary of the past association between changes in GDP and changes in carpet sales. If that association is assumed to hold in the future, then a forecast of the change in GDP can be used to derive the implied forecast change in carpet sales. Sometimes there may be good reason to suppose that the past association will not hold in the forecast period. A major technical innovation may be anticipated, or tax may be expected to change in a novel way. In these cases, arbitrary adjustments may be made to the forecast, or more informed judgements made.

If there had been a weak correlation, it might have been improved by lagging the data, for instance by correlating one year's carpet sales with the previous year's GDP, rather than with that of the same year. Or a multiple regression, bringing in more independent variables, might have explained more of the variation in carpet sales. The level of new house building, or the rate of new family formations or income levels could have a bearing upon carpet sales. However, apart from being complex, multiple regression has the handicap as a forecasting device of requiring forecasts of each independent variable. So a convincing model may have been derived by using the extra independent variables, but it would then need a forecast for each of these before the effect on carpet sales could be deduced. If some of the added independent variables had been aspects of the firm's marketing mix, for example advertising spending, then the problem is a little more contained because these can be taken from the marketing plan [6].

To appreciate more fully the use of multiple regression in forecasting, reference can be made to Figure 8.3. This considers three variables: our sales, our advertising volume and our competitors' advertising volume. Such a model therefore seeks to explain past variations in our sales by variations in our, and our competitors', advertising. This is a simplistic example, although the two independent variables could have been differently specified.

Some understanding of the relationship between these variables may come

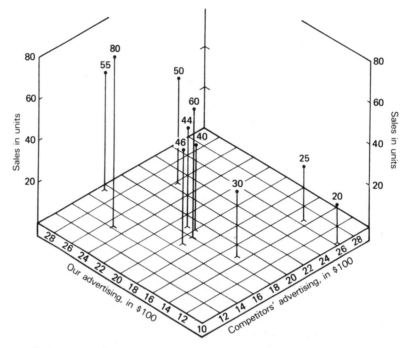

Source: N.E. Enrick, *Market and Sales Forecasting,* San Francisco: Chandler, 1969, p. 52.

Figure 8.3   *Sales related to two independent variables*

from visualising a plate of glass being placed into the box in such a way that the distances of the observations above it were equal to those below. That is, it would cut the 80, 60, 55 and 50 verticals below the top, and be suspended at or above the top of the others. (It would be a flat plane on a linear assumption.) The plane would tilt from top left to bottom right. From this visualisation, guess what our sales might be if our advertising were 22,000 and competitors' 24,000. Note, however, that any estimate made for quantities well outside past observations would be dubious – as would any estimate if the correlation were weak. (What would be the implication of high or low correlation for the distances above and below the fitted regression plane?)

To use this model in forecasting it would have to be assumed that the future relationship between the variables will follow the past, and there would still be the need for a forecast of competitors' advertising. One approach to this would be to employ probability statements. Each feasible level of competitive advertising could be assigned a probability, and the expectation for our sales deduced for each of these levels. Then each sales level would be multiplied by the corresponding probability to derive the overall implication for our sales, given those opinions about competitive advertising.

A by-product of such analyses might be improved understanding of the impact of our advertising. We could assume a given level of competitive advertising, and then assess the implication for our sales on every level of our advertising budget. Remember, though, that massive assumptions are being made about the uniform quality of advertising, the constancy of our and our competitors' product offerings, pricing and the remainder of the marketing mix – as well as all the external variables. This is a fundamental point: just because you are manipulating a lot of numbers does not necessarily make the forecast any better.

Test marketing

All the methods discussed in this chapter rely on some analysis of historical data, but for new products these do not exist. One of the purposes of test marketing may be to generate data that can be analysed for forecasting, but treatment of this will be left until Chapter 14.

Economic forecasting

In the above example we saw the need for a forecast of GDP. The firm need not go to the trouble of devising its own econometric model of the national economy because there are several regularly published forecasts. In the United Kingdom the most widely quoted is that of the National Institute for Economic and Social Research (NIESR) [7]. It is an interesting exercise to monitor the *Financial Times* index as these forecasts are published: it can move 10–20 points with a prediction at variance with the current wisdom. The Bank of England, the London Business School, the Henley Centre and various stockbrokers also issue influential forecasts.

Because there are several sources of economic forecasts the firm will need to 'feel' for the consensus. It could carry out a study of the past reliability of the various sources, and perhaps give each a differential weight. A composite could then be derived, which itself could be tested with historical data.

Firms may also make their own studies of leading indicators. These may support the consensus derived above. Regular monitoring of steel output, engineering orders on hand, unemployment rates, interest rates or even the stock of bricks for new houses is a common occupation of forecasters. The firm could compose its own index through trial and error by combining these and other indicators that are found to be more sympathetic to its particular business. Such investigations would also study the degree of lag between these indicators and company sales. It is probable that many managers within the firm have their own informal methods of monitoring leading indicators. A systematic monitoring scheme could share these diverse insights and, hopefully, improve the overall forecasting procedure.

Market potential

So far, the exact nature of the statistic for which we are attempting to derive a forecast value has not been defined. The discussion has been loosely of 'sales'. In fact, we have been dealing with direct forecasts of sales. There is an alternative – the derived forecast of sales. This requires the prior determination of market potential to which a forecast company market share is applied [8].

Market potential refers to the maximum amount of a product that could be bought in a time period from all suppliers, given a level of industry promotional effort. In mature, stable markets total industry sales are usually taken as equivalent to market potential. In less mature, unstable markets the level of market potential is invariably in excess of total industry sales because every prospective purchaser does not have sufficient exposure and opportunity to purchase the product.

It is necessary to distinguish between absolute and relative market potential. Absolute potential refers to the total market, whereas relative potential is limited to one geographic area within the total.

Determining absolute potential

In some cases absolute potential can be taken as total industry sales, as mentioned above. Even in immature markets, total industry sales will be a guide since they will give a lower limiting value. A judgement would be necessary to establish how far above that figure lies the full potential. Use may be made of some relevant variable where total industry sales are not available, or where such sales are thought to be well below full potential. For example, a car accessory manufacturer may have research data showing the proportion of car owners who buy its product class each year. The firm, therefore, needs only fix the numbers of car owners to derive a measure of its market potential. An office machinery manufacturer may have derived a relationship between sales of his products and the number of clerical workers, so that it would expect total industry sales at saturation to be £x per thousand clerical workers. Government employment statistics would help in this estimate of market potential. But it should be appreciated that in both these cases the surrogate variables are themselves not absolutes. Car ownership and the level of clerical employment are clearly dynamic.

With segmented markets the study of each segment's potential may give a better opinion of total potential. A toothpaste firm may segment its market into heavy, moderate and light users. It could build an estimate of total potential by estimating potential in each of these segments. For instance, it may have determined the average buying volume, and the numbers of people in each segment, to obtain an estimate of the potential in each segment, and thus for the market.

More complex analysis would involve the use of several variables that were thought to influence sales. Consumer goods companies could investigate population, income levels, mean temperatures or whatever else was thought to have a bearing. Where a product was in joint demand it is only sensible to consult the sales of the related product.

In some markets an alternative approach to estimating market potential would rely upon various kinds of census information. There are industries which have regular surveys to determine the stock of equipment or machinery in use, and with repeated surveys it may be possible to estimate the flows in and out of that stock. If sufficient detail is available it may also be possible to study such stock movements within several segments. Growth curves may be fitted to the trends in the total stock and in the movements to and from that stock, and these may then be used in forecasting. Examples of products where such census information is available include machine tools and mainframe computers. To illustrate the amount of detail that can be found, reference can be made to equipment used in hospitals. Table 8.1 shows part of a national market research study on equipment in special care baby units in hospitals. The data, from Worldwide Medical Markets, report items of equipment in the eight hospital districts within the East Anglian Regional Health Authority's area.

With such data for all health authorities it would be possible to estimate market share nationally and regionally. By making international comparisons, and perhaps taking some expert opinion, it may further be possible to estimate the stock of equipment several years ahead. Additionally, studies of this kind can be useful for associated markets which may not have such detailed information available. It could be posited for example that sales are related to the stock of a particular piece of equipment. This might apply to consumable items.

Measuring relative potential

Perhaps the most frequent reason for estimating relative potential is to assess its relative spread within, or between, national markets. The most readily seen application is in the planning and control of salesforce activities.

Relative potential can easily be gauged if there is a suitable regional split of total industry sales. If this is done on a proportionate basis then it does not matter whether industry sales are the same as market potential – it can usually be assumed that the regional breakdown will be the same for the two. Where industry sales are not available on a regional basis then recourse may be made to some of the indexes constructed in the measurement of absolute potential. Regional statistics for employment, population, retail sales, new car registrations, income levels, and so on are readily found from government statistics.

Forecasting market potential

If current market potential has been measured, then its projection into the future could employ the same kinds of procedures that we considered in the earlier part of this chapter.

Table 8.1   *Equipment in special baby care units*

	District 1	2	3	4	5	6	7	8	Total
Total special care units	2	1	1	—	1	1	1	—	7
Number in sample	1	1	1	—	1	1	1	—	6
Total cots	48	12	16	—	22	5	16		119
Number in sample	24	12	16	—	22	5	16	—	95
Equipment installed:									
Incubators	18	10	7	—	11	6	10	—	62
Cardiac monitors	10	5	1	—	9	2	—	—	27
ECG machines	—	1	—	—	1		—	—	2
Ventilators	7	3	1	—	7	5	2	—	25
Humidifiers									0
Oxygen analysers	12	5	3	—	12	5	5	—	42
Infusion pumps	15	2	1	—	10	10	—	—	38
Suction equipment	18	12	7	—	12	14	12	—	75

Source: United Kingdom Special Baby Care Unit Study by Worldwide Medical Markets.

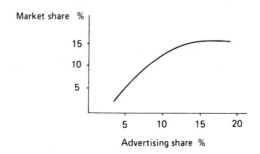

Figure 8.4   *Market share and advertising share*

Forecasting market share

A possible complication with derived forecasts is the nature of the market share figure applied to the forecast potential. It may be that a target share is used, in which case it is essential that this be made explicit. On the other hand, some attempt may be made to deduce an expected share, assuming some planned level of marketing effort. This deduction may find a relationship between market share and advertising share. Analysis of past data may reveal a situation like that depicted in Figure 8.4. It is unlikely that the relationship would be as regular as that shown in the figure, but correlation analysis would indicate the confidence that could be placed on any summary relationship that had been plotted. If the firm was tolerably happy that some significant relationship existed, then it could determine what advertising share it was willing to pay for, and derive the implied market share. Instead of advertising share it might have tried share of total industry salesforce or proportion of retailers stocking – or some combination of these in a multiple model.

Direct vs indirect forecasting

Now we return to the meaning and the place of forecasting in the planning process. It will be remembered that direct forecasts concentrate upon projecting the firm's sales without consideration of market potential. Derived, or indirect, forecasts first project market potential and subsequently forecast a market share. Each of these differs in the degree to which it is conditional. Direct forecasts tend to be partially conditional, in so far as they are made on the assumption that the level of past marketing activity continues during the forecast period. Forecasts of market potential tend to be more unconditional; it is only a tendency, because they imply assumptions about a steady technology and no radical change in other external variables. Derived forecasts can be more or less conditional: it depends on the market share forecast. If a higher market share were projected, and this was on the basis of higher marketing effort, then the derived forecast would obviously be conditional. If the market share were projected without extra marketing effort, then the derived forecast would be only as conditional as the market potential.

This underlines the need to recognise and to state the extent to which the forecast is conditional. If the forecast turned out to be sadly wrong it might be attributed to imprecise definition of the forecast variables, to the techniques employed – or to the failure to express the assumptions and conditions.

Should the firm use direct or derived forecasts? The short answer is both, because it will then be forced to appreciate the difference. At the beginning of this chapter it was noted that the planning process is never as rigidly sequential as some flowcharts lead one to believe. It must involve a plethora of false starts, revised assumptions and changed constraints, which require numerous full and partial iterations. No single person, and certainly no single technique, has a monopoly on the views of the future. Each has something to contribute to the evolving opinion that emerges from the planning process.

Direct forecasts are useful because they can be simply made from internal data. The use of the company's historical sales does also say much about its relationship to its competitors in the marketplace. Derived forecasts are less introspective. They use potentials as benchmarks and question the firm's objectives and strategy. But they may contain a larger element of judgement than direct forecasts. Interesting comparisons may result from the use of both approaches. Informed discussion of any discrepancy between the two can only help shape better opinions about the future.

Summary

Forecasts are opinions. Formal analysis may support the better opinions, and in so doing may breed a better forecasting procedure. Past failures from informal approaches are difficult to learn from since the assumptions and methodology are not specified.

It is useful to distinguish between conditional and unconditional forecasts, because that delineates the extent to which the forecast is dependent on some set of assumptions, e.g. about marketing activity.

There are many techniques that can be employed in forecasting. Most firms use several, since none is likely to be perfect. A spin-off from some methods could be better understanding of the variables affecting company sales.

Derived forecasts require the prior specification of market potential and the application of a forecast market share; direct forecasts work immediately on company sales.

Questions for review and discussion

1. What would you do if the forecasts from the salesforce were in opposition to the forecasts from a regression study?

2. Assume you had the results of a general survey of consumer confidence over a number of years. This showed the proportions feeling more, less or the same confidence in their overall economic position as three months ago. How could you use these data with the following product categories: packaged groceries, domestic applicances, machine tools? To what would you relate them and would you anticipate a direct or lagged relationship?

3. Search out time series for at least ten years for gross domestic product (and perhaps several other important macroeconomic variables, such as personal disposable income and capital spending). Relate these to one or more of the following: new car registrations, electricity generated, paint consumed in the domestic market. The analysis can be crude or more sophisticated depending upon whether the regression line is fitted by hand or mathematically. Apart from the frustration of obtaining a long, consistent time series, what does the exercise show about the value of such studies in forecasting? E.g. are these coincidental or causal relationships?

4. Now obtain a forecast about the macroeconomic variables you worked with in question 3, e.g. from the publications of the NIESR, OECD or elsewhere. What is the implied forecast for the dependent variable (i.e. car registrations, etc.)? Or was the correlation in question 3 too weak to use in forecasting?

5. A car accessory manufacturer has survey data showing the proportion of car owners with his kind of accessory fitted, for all brands. These statistics for this year, five years ago and ten years ago were respectively 7, 10 and 12 per cent. An estimate for the car population in those same years is 6, 9 and 11 million. He therefore deduces the stock of car accessories. On average be believes the product to have a five-year life, so that today's stock must have been purchased in the last five years.

    Estimate the average annual flow in and out of this stock. Adjust that average to take account of the varying proportions with the accessory fitted. (You will need to estimate that proportion and the car population for each year.)

    Now assume that in another country the market for this product was thought to have reached maturity with a fairly constant proportion of accessories per car of 15 per cent. You believe this might be the case in this country in five years from now, and that the car population could then be 15 million. Estimate the implications for market potential, and the stock of accessories in each of the next five years.

    What other kinds of study might help in checking the validity of the assumption made and the consequent projections?

References

1. Milne, T. 1975. *Business Forecasting: A Managerial Approach*. London: Longman, p. 1.
2. Makridakis, S. and Wheelwright, S.C. 1977. 'Forecasting: issues and challenges for marketing management', *Journal of Marketing*, vol. 41, October.
3. Saunders, J.A., Sharp, J.A. and Witt, S.F. 1987. *Practical Business Forecasting*. Aldershot: Gower. Provides a modern treatment of forecasting techniques.
4. Wotruba, T.R. and Thurlow, M.L. 1976. 'Salesforce participation in quota setting and sales forecasting', *Journal of Marketing*, vol. 40, April.
5. Similar surveys for all EU countries are published regularly by the European Union.
6. Good examples of the use of multiple regression in forecasting can be found in Wheelwright, S. and Makridakis, S. 1973. *Forecasting Methods for Management*. New York: John Wiley, pp. 115–21; and Luck, D.J. and Ferrell, O.C. 1979. *Marketing Strategy and Plans*. Englewood Cliffs, NJ: Prentice Hall Inc., pp. 118–23.
7. See the NIESR review.
8. Green, P.E. and Tull, D.S. 1975. *Research for Marketing Decisions*, 2nd edn. Englewood Cliffs, NJ: Prentice Hall Inc., p. 661.

Chapter 9

Developing marketing strategy

Company attitudes to strategy development have been changing. Aaker [1] traces four stages of evolution. From the 1900s the emphasis was on budgeting and control with an internal orientation which stressed managing complexity. In the 1960s long-range planning began to be influential, with an accent on anticipating growth. From then strategic planning emerged, and this gave weight to the need to change company strategic thrust and capability. In the 1980s strategic market management became a guiding ethos, reflecting the requirement to cope with strategic surprises and fast-developing opportunities and threats.

The approach to business strategy underlying all these phases is rationalist, and it emphasises planning and analysis. An alternative approach contrasts deliberate, planned strategies to emergent strategies. Critics of the rationalist approach, such as Mintzberg, offer a view which stresses the incremental, reactive and adaptive nature of strategies which, they argue, are emergent rather than directed. Despite the criticism, Kay [2] explains the continuing attention to the rationalist school as follows,

> Strategy is necessarily incremental and adaptive, but that does not in any way imply that its evolution cannot be, or should not be, analysed, managed, and controlled. (p. 357)

And that,

> To observe that organisations are complex, that change is inevitably incremental, and that strategy is necessarily adaptive, however true, helps very little in deciding what to do. Managers wish to be told of a process which they can at least partially control and, whatever its weaknesses, that is what rationalist strategy appears to offer. (p. 357)

This chapter takes a rational, analytical stance and considers current views on the planning frameworks which might assist understanding of the development of marketing strategy.

Strategy formulation

The earlier discussion of consumer behaviour was cast in terms of choices and problem-solving. The strategy formulation process can be cast in similar terms. Company executives need to establish goals, identify the issues, generate and evaluate the alternatives and then make and implement choices. Figure 9.1 shows the marketing management implications of this process, with slightly different words and a fuller statement of the issues.

A complication concerns the corporate 'ends', or where the organisation wants to be. There is no consensus about the terminology, and so the literature uses 'missions', 'goals' and 'objectives'. 'Missions' are distinguished from the other two in that they are very long term, very broad and are not time-constrained. Some writers draw distinctions between goals and objectives, but no distinction is drawn here. In Figure 9.1 goals could be introduced in at least two places: after the mission and before the development of marketing plans. The difference will be in how specific they are. In the first case they will be less specific with sales and profitability targets for the organisation as a whole. In the second case they could incorporate targets in particular 'businesses' or product/markets with an outline specification of product strategies required to achieve the targets, and identification of target customer segments. Lower-order goals would also feature in the marketing plans.

This highlights an important point in strategy formulation. Ends and means are linked in a chain; some means can themselves become ends for links lower in the chain. This is why the term 'goal hierarchy' is often used to indicate that there

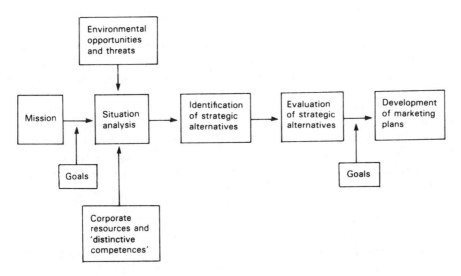

Figure 9.1   *Strategic marketing planning*

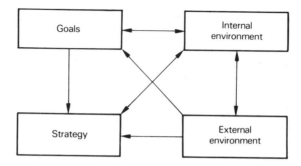

Figure 9.2   *Goals, strategy and environments*

will be a web of goals which becomes more detailed and shorter term the further down the organisational hierarchy.

Elements of strategy

Organisations are purposive. They strive to achieve their ends through the deployment of resources to the best means at their disposal. Having established their goals they determine appropriate strategies. These goals and strategies are heavily conditioned by the nature of the environment in which the organisation is placed. Analysis of external and internal environments is pertinent because they both influence and constrain what should be done and what can be done. Thus goals, strategies and the internal and external environments are all connected (Figure 9.2).

Strategic issues arise from the external environment because it is probably dynamic and so could create a stream (or a trickle) of new opportunities. This might lead to potential new products or processes, or to changes in the types of market segment served. Just as likely, the turmoil in the environment could be threatening. The unexpected arrival of a new competitor, a technological development or turbulence in the economy can all have serious impact on the selection of goals and strategies.

The internal environment relates to the relative competence of the organisation and to the nature and scale of the resources it has available. This leads to considerations of the strengths and weaknesses which are apparent. What can be done well? What cannot be done at present, and will that be the case in the future? What strength can be built on and what weakness needs to be overcome? Once more a series of issues emerges which needs to be engaged by the strategic planner.

Taken together these appraisals of the internal and external environments provide many of the points that need be addressed in the strategic planning process. One of the reasons underlying their importance is that they can illuminate a crucial phase in the decision process: that of problem recognition. Given a set of goals, then, a rational approach to decisions proceeds as in Figure 9.3.

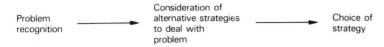

Figure 9.3 *Decision sequence*

Necessarily, if a problem is unrecognised or is given disproportionate attention then what follows will be misguided. The full and proper identification of the problems faced by the organisation thus takes on considerable strategic significance, and that identification will be a reflection of the quality of the environmental analyses.

The search for viable, apposite strategies cannot be boundless. An infinite search has no end. Boundaries are set, explicitly or implicitly, defining the domain within which the business operates. This definition of the scope of the enterprise is sometimes referred to as the organisation's mission. It may be cast in terms of technologies and markets and describe the organisation's long-term essential purposes, and thus its basic character and philosophy. Analyses of the environment would be partial, in keeping with the mission, so constraining the range of problems that might be recognised and so limiting the range of strategic options to be evaluated. That must be the case because the alternative would be no decisions and no actions. The judgement about what to look at in the environment has profound consequences. Too narrow a view could miss real opportunities and overlook developing threats. Too wide a view could result in unrealistic analyses and reports, easily dismissed as being 'inoperable'.

A further influential factor in strategic marketing planning is the quest for enduring competitive advantage. Ultimately the organisation must have strategies that result in it being at least as good as the competition, as perceived by customers. This may even be written into the mission statement. Acceptance of this view would influence much that is undertaken in the planning process and it would provide a major criterion in any evaluation. How that competitive advantage is to be achieved, through what actions, in which markets and against which competitors, permeates all marketing planning, at tactical as well as strategic levels.

Analysing the external environment

Systematic appraisal of the external environment will reveal problems and possibilities that will shape the strategy alternatives. Environmental scanning could point to changes in the age structure of the population, or to changes in society's attitudes to, say, health care or transportation or in the way particular businesses should be regulated. Any of these, and a host of other broad trends in the business environment, could have an impact on the firm's prospects. Monitoring the competitive environment might also uncover strategic issues. New competition may be emerging from unexpected quarters; what was an ailing rival may be revived; consumers may come to perceive a product from another industry as a direct substitute; the sum of marketing efforts in the industry may have changed palpably in quality or quantity. The industry may be getting old and its output judged by consumers as obsolescent. On the technological front, the company may be in the rear or the van, or moving from the one to the other. A static technology could be rendered obsolescent by some breakthrough. Additionally, the technology could be changing the entry and exit barriers to the industry: a rush of new firms may be predicted, or the scale of investment be so high as to chain the company to a troubled industry. Regarding markets, there could be step changes in growth rates, emerging opportunities in new segments or notable variation in the ways that consumers evaluate firms' outputs.

Tracking such developments establishes and projects the likely connection between these factors and the company's businesses. The prognosis might suggest a range of strategic imperatives. Careful analysis of the mix of opportunities and threats signals key issues in the search and development of strategic options.

Industry analyses

Studies of the present and predicted industry structure may focus upon the nature of the competitive forces apparent in the industry, upon the proper identification of rivalry in the industry and upon the evolutionary stage being reached.

Competitive forces

Porter argues that the state of competition is not just a function of the rivalry between existing members of an industry. Profits and other goals are also affected by four additional factors [3]:

1. Threat of new entrants.
2. Threat of substitute products.
3. Bargaining power of suppliers.
4. Bargaining power of buyers.

This leads to the concept of extended rivalry, in that all of the above groups will to some extent be competing with an industry's firms, and so the intensity and form of competition are derived from the sum of the several forces.

New entrants not only bring added productive capacity, but also a mixture of other capabilities. Their products may have novel and attractive features. IBM's late entry into the personal computer market had enormous impact because of their products' quality. Entry barriers were of no significance in that instance, but sometimes technical, production and marketing barriers can deter new entrants. The stress of the barriers can also change through time. New process technologies can heighten or lower a production barrier and new institutional arrangements could change a marketing barrier – such as a consortium of small hotels banding together to market nationally or internationally. The barriers in an industry should be well known, and the threat of new entrants to a degree predictable, though not always so. This threat has two strategic implications. First, whether or not the firm could or should try to affect the entry barriers by deliberately lowering prices, spending high levels on promotion or whatever else increases the stakes. Second, retaliatory strategies may be called for once an entrant arrives.

Substitutes are worrisome because of their unpredictability. They are unpredictable because they can emerge from totally unrelated industries, from unrelated technologies, and from overseas. Another problem is that it is the consumer, not the manufacturer, who judges what is a substitute. The benefit to be derived, or the function to be performed, is defined by the buyer, and this can mean apparently diverse products being perceived as competitors. Fortified wines compete with spirits; fountain pens with watches as presents and florists with confectioners. Research may help in identifying such relationships, and market intelligence may proffer news of burgeoning substitutes.

Both suppliers and buyers can attain sufficient power to adversely affect the profitability of an industry. This may be a function of their size, concentration or their expertise or prestige. The import of this for strategy is that the firm may attempt to reduce their power or influence by, for example, constraining the amount of business done with a major customer so that it does not dominate, or by searching for real or potential alternative suppliers.

Surveillance of direct competitors unfolds many issues that may be taken into the firm's strategic planning. Assessments of competitive positions on all aspects of the marketing mix disclose strategies that must be counteracted, or vulnerabilities that present openings. Undertaking assessments of this kind cannot rely upon vague feelings about assumed positions. Any knowledge gleaned will be partial enough even with a relatively formal and systematic procedure. Industries vary enormously in the intensity of the rivalry, and in how proprietary they believe information about their companies to be. Trade associations and informal meetings sometimes share information on a widespread scale, and just as likely the competition is so severe that nothing at all is shared. Informed judgements on all the main rivals for all their main strategies must be a key ingredient in the situation analysis.

Strategic groups

Fuller understanding of the competitive process may be derived from focusing not just on an industry or its individual firms, but from considering the extent to which there are distinctive groupings of rivals within the industry. Not all firms in an industry compete directly with all other firms. Each may have a primary group of direct rivals pursuing similar strategies in the same market segments. There may be also a number of other groupings in the industry, perhaps with firms operating at a different scale, targeting different segments and adopting different strategies. While direct rivals might condition much of the competitive activity of the firm, the other groupings could represent strategic threats or opportunities, since they may be moving to become a direct rival or because their markets are seen to be attractive targets.

Studies of these groupings within an industry have used the concept of the strategic group, which is a group of firms following the same or similar strategies. Tang and Thomas say,

> Theoretically, in contrast to the traditional industrial organization paradigm, which postulates that structure determines conduct, which in turn determines performance, the [concept of the strategic group] argues that the conduct (strategy) of the firm directly determines both the structure (group structure) and the performance of the industry. [4]

Managers can usually identify readily the strategic groups in their industry. A recent empirical study found that 'they are part of the way strategists organize and make sense of their competitive environment' [5].

Classifying and distinguishing between strategic groups has made use of the notion of mobility barriers. This is because they afford protection to firms within the barriers and because they deter movement between groups. McGee suggests these barriers may arise from market-related strategies, such as product and market segment decisions or geographic coverage; they may arise from industry supply characteristics such as scale economies, and from the nature of the ownership and management of the firm [6]. Alternatively, strategic groups have been identified in terms of their similarities in strategic actions, and particularly those relating to business scope and resource commitments [7]. Cool and Schendel show an application to the US pharmaceutical industry [8] and Johnson and Scholes one to the British brewing industry [9].

Industry evolution

Important influences on strategy development for the firm derive from the structure and the prospects for the industry in which it is participating, or that which it might consider entering. Industry structure and prospects evolve through time, presenting different sets of competitive pressures and consumer demand. Analysis of the forces driving industry change will reveal issues which must be incorporated into any assessment of strategy alternatives [10].

Through time the size, relative profitability and outlook for the industry change. Buyer segments evolve from a relatively small, select group of innovators as the product reaches the mass market; diffusion of the technology occurs as more firms learn its basics; mobility barriers become apparent, although the components may change in time, and new competitors may enter, and others leave the industry. Put together these factors describe a changing industry scene, with various phases offering quite different opportunities which require different strategic responses. Characteristics of these phases and possible developments in strategic emphasis are shown in Table 9.1.

Table 9.1 *Industry lifecycles: Some characteristics and strategic implications*

Embryonic
Slow then more rapid growth; technology evolving; unstable market; few, if any, competitors; innovators as customers – more sensitive to quality, availability and image than to price.
Strategic emphasis:
Testing and gaining market acceptance; conjectures about future industry structure; building future barriers based on scale, technology and image; establishing high quality distribution network.

Growth
Rapid growth and market expansion; clear trends in technology; new entrants and some 'me-too' products; increasing barriers; competitive turbulence may lead to shake-out in late growth.
Strategic emphasis:
Emergence of competitive groupings – some niche strategists; leaders try to consolidate market share; followers keen to build; promotion spend increases to reach larger market; some price-sensitivity; quality improvements and continuing product development.

Maturity
More stability in purchase patterns and market shares; mature technology; mature competitive groupings; well-established barriers; mass market and mass distribution.
Strategic emphasis:
High promotion spend with emphasis on sales promotion and advertising; increased price-sensitivity; product development stresses style changes and segmentation may focus on usage patterns; cost-reduction strategies.

Ageing/declining
Market contracts; some firms exit; competitive group disintegration; major threats, but some very different opportunities for some firms.
Strategic emphasis:
Decision on whether to survive or depart; voluntary or involuntary survivor; product-lines pruned; reduction of promotion; distribution networks thinned.

Empirical evidence on industry lifecycles indicates that each stage sets a different competitive circumstance because [11]:

1. New entries to the industry are at first high and then much lower.

2. Gross margins and profitability fall in later stages.

3. As markets evolve the extent of competitive differentiation declines.

4. Price rivalry dominates in maturity.

5. Marketing expenditures increase in late maturity to fund higher levels of promotional activity.

All these points are highly generalised; they may or may not apply in specific cases. That causes difficulties in the utilisation of the lifecycle concept because the current evolutionary stage may not be properly specified, let alone the great uncertainties in forecasting future stages. Yet the potential strategic potency of the prospects for the industry is so overwhelming that many firms use lifecycle as a dominant criterion in their evaluation of strategic options. This rests on the premiss that it is not perfect but it is powerful.

Technology

Some of the greatest upsets to business plans are caused by the advance of technology. Firms need to anticipate and to respond to technical change. Technological forecasting structures the anticipation and Taylor and Hussey advocate the writing of scenarios (hypothetical sequences of events) in order to generate opinions about the future technology [12]. They outline the common techniques used in setting the scenarios as:

1. Trend analysis – involves regularly scanning and analysing a number of publications inside and outside the enterprise to plot long-term trends.
2. Computer simulation – entails building a computer model of an enterprise or industry and making projections on different assumptions. The Department of Energy use computer models to forecast the total market for energy, the growth rate, the energy mix and the breakdown by type of usage.
3. A Delphi study – a systematic poll of experts, each of whom is asked independently to forecast future events, such as a technical breakthrough.
4. Cross-impact analysis – explores the possible impact of one future event upon another to determine if they will advance or delay each other.

Given the threat of a competing technology the firm will need to consider its response. Cooper and Schendel [13] propose that if the firm does not choose to participate in that technology it might:

1. Do nothing.
2. Seek to retard the technology by fighting it through public relations and legal action.
3. Increase flexibility so as to be able to respond to subsequent developments in the new technology.
4. Avoid the threat by decreasing dependence on the most threatened submarkets.
5. Expand work on the improvement of the existing technology.
6. Attempt to maintain sales through actions not related to technology, such as promotion or price-cutting.

They studied seven industries, and of twenty-two firms all except five made some effort to participate in a new, threatening technology. In all the industries the old technology continued to be improved after the introduction of a new technology, which shows that a combination of the different responses is normal.

Consumers

Trends in the size and composition of markets served, and those of potential markets, together with analysis of consumer requirements and consumer evaluations of products, can raise weighty matters that demand strategic responses. To structure this market opportunity analysis, three levels may be invoked. The first is generic product analysis, which would be broad product categories such as food or machine tools or financial services. Specific product analysis is the subdivision into more narrowly defined products like frozen vegetables, lathes or loans for house purchase. In some markets several layers of subdivision may be required to define adequately a specific product. For example, in lathes one of the subdivisions might be automatic turning machines, which could be further divided into single- or multiple-spindle and thence into bar or chucking types. Specific brand analysis is the third level which investigates the prospects of individual brands.

The virtue of generic-level analysis is that it 'forces managers to take a broad look at markets instead of concentrating on only the most likely potential customers' [14]. It proceeds by studying broad historical trends in sales and types of customer. This might mean, for example, tracing per capita food consumption, relating that to trends in income level, breaking it down into several demographic and geographic classes and then making forecasts about possible future food consumption patterns. This may reveal that the firm is in a low-growth sector and encourage it to consider entry into higher growth areas. Or it could throw up an emerging trend associated with the demographic distribution, such as older or younger people eating more or less of certain foods. At this level of analysis the enquiry might also be into very general, but very basic, values held by consumers. Are they becoming more 'convenience-minded' ? Are there changes in attitudes to desired diets? Is everybody now becoming more energy-conscious? Each of these could have impact for the company's present products and require strategies to respond. Changes in values and lifestyles might also encourage the firm to review the ways it presents itself. Should it persist with its outmoded portrayal of women in its advertisements? Does it wish to be seen as a leader among socially responsible companies?

Specific product analysis attempts to identify relevant market segments, which begs the question of the determination of the segmentation variable. If a simple demographic analysis revealed little difference between consumers, then what alternative should be investigated? Should degree of product usage be tried or lifestyles studied to uncover groups with potentially different responses to marketing efforts? Should there be consideration of benefits sought, or is it more likely that, for this product, discrimination between groups will be clearer from an analysis of usage situations? Alternatively, it may be that relative responsiveness to aspects of the marketing mix is more meaningful – dividing consumers according to their price responsiveness, or their reaction to promotions, might effectively spot distinctive groups. Such studies could point to strategic issues: a declining segment, one that is neglected or not properly served or one in which the firm has small penetration, and this leads to a decision to engage the issue and formulate appropriate strategies.

Along with segmentation analysis some knowledge of the evaluative criteria used by customers in this product category when making their purchases could be instructive. What product attributes do they rate, and how do they rate them? How important are consumption situations – does the rating vary by situation – and are other people's views taken into the valuation by the consumer? Speculations about how these criteria will change open avenues for fresh thought. As an example, many are now concerned about fuel consumption in cars, and it has become a salient evaluative criterion. In the future, how interested will new car buyers be in the aerodynamic design of cars? Will drag coefficient be a dominant choice criterion? If so, then it has implications for strategy development by car makers.

At the level of the specific brand, competitive analysis plots the extent and nature of the rivalry. Part of this contains judgements on the main basis of the competition – is it quality, service, availability, image or price? A listing of all rivals on these points might establish areas of concern. Further analysis could concentrate upon consumer perceptions of the brand in a brand mapping exercise (this was referred to as perceptual mapping in Chapter 2 and will be introduced again in product planning).

Analysing the internal environment

Potentially attractive opportunities might emerge from the analyses of the external environment, but the extent to which they can be acted upon is highly dependent upon the availability of resources and the nature of the organisation's competences. The notion of strategic fit is relevant: does the company have the competence to match the opportunity? If not, can it realistically gain sufficient competence and will it be able to compete effectively?

The dangers of straying into unrelated areas in which the firm has little established competence are illustrated by Goldsmith and Clutterbuck [15]. They quote a manager from Clarks the shoemakers who says that every time they have diversified it has been a disaster. They also relate the sorry consequences of a car maker buying a brickmaking machinery firm. Davidson also gives interesting examples of the fit between companies and markets [16]. He argues that Procter & Gamble have been most successful in markets like detergents, shampoos and toothpaste, where product quality can be objectively assessed. When they have attempted to enter markets where this is much more difficult to demonstrate, such as in snack foods and soft drinks, they have been far less successful.

Reviews of resources and competences are therefore necessary in any assessment once a potential opportunity has been spotted. Such reviews also have a role in defining the bases on which the company will attempt to build its long-term competitive advantage. An audit of capabilities can have both negative and positive impact on strategy search. It can be negative in that it could constrain acceptance of a market opportunity; perhaps the technical or marketing competence is incompatible with the opportunity or maybe the opportunity is seen as a diversion from the core business. It can be positive if it suggests lines for strategy search, derived from the need to capitalise on a business strength.

Resource reviews

Two phrases are commonly encountered in the study of business strengths and weaknesses: the marketing audit and the resource review. The former is the examination of the company's marketing environment, objectives, strategies and activities, while the latter takes a wider view and examines technical, production and financial factors in addition to those of marketing. Some of the areas that would enter a resource review are as follows:

Technical and operations	*Marketing*
Production capacity	Image and reputation
Production competence	Market knowledge
Research capability	Research capability
Design competence	Salesforce effectiveness
Materials utilisation	Sales promotion abilities
By-product utilisation	Distribution facilities
	Dealer relationships

Production capacity may be relevant in guiding strategy search in that if it were presently under-utilised then consideration may be given to alternative products that could be manufactured on the same plant. Obviously the degree of flexibility in the plant will limit the possibilities. Some plant is very inflexible, particularly in process industries; some plant in engineering industries is much more flexible, e.g. machine tools may be general rather than special-purpose. The same kinds of points can be made of labour skills, with the addition of the possibility of retraining.

The depth and breadth of the organisation's technical know-how could also limit the search. A very narrow technological base would be a considerable, though not necessarily insuperable, restriction. Licensing agreements, especially with overseas manufacturers, are common expedients for circumventing this limitation. Similarly, mergers and takeovers may be stimulated to get around this problem.

In some circumstances the firm may be operating on a scale such that it does not enjoy maximum discounts in its purchase of raw materials. It may, therefore, determine to find other viable products that could be produced using the same materials as those already being manufactured. For example, a manufacturer of a type of mechanical handling equipment may need to buy in fractional horse-power electric motors, but may not be able to place sufficiently large orders with suppliers to qualify for a discount. One of the elements in future strategy development might then be to find products that would use the same components, which would allow larger orders to be placed with suppliers and more substantial discounts to be negotiated. This point could be extended to include part of the case for backward vertical integration, with the manufacturer taking over his supplier. Another production factor that could guide strategy selection is the possibility of using scrap or waste materials from the manufacturing process.

Synergy

In the examples noted above there was the implication that by taking cognisance of resources there might be greater revenues or lower costs. This would be due to the possibility of synergy, which means that the whole is greater than the sum of its parts. Buzzell and Gale [17] offer four basic mechanisms to explain synergistic effects:

1. Shared resources to achieve scale economies.
2. Spill-over benefits in marketing and R&D.
3. 'Similar' businesses: knowledge and skills shared across businesses, especially high technology industries and situations where marketing skills are key.
4. Shared image: the gain from being identified with a highly regarded corporate whole.

The experience effect

The behaviour of costs is another relevant consideration in strategic analysis. In this context a concept that has attracted controversy is that of the experience curve. This plots unit costs against cumulative volume and exhibits the reduction in costs with progressive increases in volume. There may be, for example, 20 or 30 per cent reductions in unit costs every time cumulative volume doubles. Low unit cost is associated with high volume, and high volume implies the need to achieve high market share.

Sources of this effect may derive from learning, contributing to production efficiency, from scale economies and from technological improvements, which could come from the use of new production processes justified as output increases. Weitz and Wensley [18] believe this can be over-emphasised. Shared costs can be a problem. It may be impossible to allocate properly the costs of shared facilities or the advantage of common raw materials. Additionally, market share may not be indicative of cost advantage. Weitz and Wensley point to the hand-held calculator market where Bowmar was furthest down the experience curve and had the highest market share, but where Texas Instruments had the overall cost advantage due to their vast experience in semiconductor component manufacture, which accounts for 80 per cent of the cost of manufacturing calculators. That leads to an important issue in the application of this concept: Which costs should be studied and at what level of aggregation? In the above example what difference would it have made if it had been restricted to value-added? And should the analysis be on the basis of individual company cost curves or on industry aggregates?

Further criticism suggests that experience curves can exaggerate the effects of relative scale and experience [19]. This can result in undue attention being attached to the magnitude of the impact of market share, although market share considerations remain important. It must also be borne in mind that the striving for a low cost position is but one approach to the establishment of competitive advantage. Quality and differentiation may be better bases for competitive strategies for many companies.

Strategic thrust

Marketing strategy development is necessarily iterative, and in the iterations one crucial set of considerations can be summarised in what might be termed strategic thrust. This draws together five important areas in which the organisation will need to make decisions:

1. The bases on which the organisation intends to establish its competitive advantage.
2. The scope, or boundaries, of the area in which it intends to compete – its competitive arena.
3. The corporate positioning it intends to achieve.
4. The market segments it will serve.
5. The positioning it aims for in each competitive arena it enters.

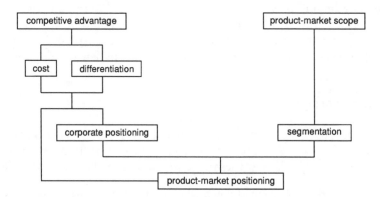

Figure 9.4 *Strategic thrust*

Taken together these decisions describe, and circumscribe, key aspects of strategic intent, laying down parameters within which strategies are elaborated (see Figure 9.4).

Competitive advantage

Broadly, the firm can seek to establish its distinction in the market by emphasising its lower cost, or by seeking other bases on which to differentiate itself. This decision conditions the nature of what the firm will offer in the market, and so it is fundamental in determining its relative attractiveness.

By making this choice on how it will develop its competitive advantage the firm deliberately constrains its strategic options. The choice concentrates the firm's resources, its efforts and its strategic thinking in particular ways. Building and sustaining the advantage, if it is to be followed rigorously, mean that some competencies will be developed and that some assets will be enhanced, at the expense of others. Strategic thinking will be channelled to provide strategies predicated on a given direction in the search for advantage, although this may be challenged sometimes due to some unexpected event or a new competence becoming available.

This channelling of strategic thinking gives a strong link with other decisions. The choice of competitive advantage shapes potential positioning strategies; it determines that some positions may be possible and that others may not. For example, a corporate positioning based on leading in the technology will effectively specify aspects of competence that must be available, if it is to be credible. The choice of competitive advantage is also linked with decisions on the competitive arena the firm chooses. There must be interaction between them because what could be done by the firm, based on its capabilities, must be appropriate to what should be done to take advantage of opportunities in a product-market. This is part of the process by which the organisation seeks strategies to match what it can offer to what is likely to be attractive in its target markets.

Cost-based sources of competitive advantage might relate to production or marketing efficiency, improved manufacturing systems, capacity utilisation, strengthening buying power or reducing materials and overhead costs. Differentiation-based sources of competitive advantage could relate to product attributes or performance, services provided, the quality of materials and processing, product availability or to special skills, experience and knowledge.

Competitive arena

Choice of where to compete can be as important as how to compete, and defining the arena could be in terms of products and markets. This has been called product-market scope, although Wensley uses the term product-market space when he says:

> A product-market is a group of potential customers with similar needs and sellers who employ similar methods (technologies and marketing programmes) to satisfy

Table 9.2 *Alternative growth paths*

	Existing products	New products
Existing markets	market penetration	product development
New markets	market development	diversification

Source: After I. Ansoff, *Corporate Strategy*, rev. edn, Harmondsworth: Penguin Books, 1989, p. 109.

those needs. A product-market space is a set of product-markets in a specific industry or business domain. Thus, the product-market space is the commercial arena in which sellers compete against each other for customers [20].

Ansoff structured the alternatives as being either existing or new, in the case of both products and markets, and they were presented as alternative growth paths for the firm (Table 9.2). More detailed discussion of this is left until the chapter on product planning.

Latterly Ansoff developed his ideas [21] by considering three dimensions: market need, product/service technologies and market geography. In each case they might vary from present to new. This is represented in Figure 9.5, with the origin indicating the present position. The firm could therefore stay as it is on each dimension, attempt to meet new needs with the same or new technologies, meet the same need with new technologies and vary the geographical area it serves. Many organisations need to develop their operations along all three dimensions. An example is in the supply of banknotes, dominated by government-owned facilities, but with seven private companies also competing worldwide. Market need is changing with the increasingly automated dispensing of notes; printing technology evolves continuously and new market areas are opening, such as new opportunities in Eastern Europe. Another example is given in the illustration overleaf, dealing with a producer of ink-jets.

Corporate positioning

Corporate positioning concerns how the organisation is, and wishes to be,

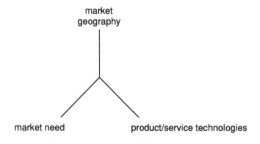

Figure 9.5 *Ansoff's three dimensions*

Domino Printing Science

Technologically advanced companies can be consumer-oriented. Domino Printing Science is an example. It manufactures a non-contact printing process which, when computer-controlled, can print variable data, such as a different number on every item, using a continuous ink jet. A major application is in putting sell-by dates on products, which following EC Directives are now compulsory on all food items. With subsidiaries in four European countries and the United States, Domino's profitable operation is built on reliability and assured quality. But most of all it is built on customer service: ensuring that it knows customer needs and delivering on time. Recently, it won an order for 500 printers from the Post Office, which was the largest single order ever placed for jet printers in the United Kingdom.

Until recently product-market scope was limited to sophisticated solutions to the printing problems of food manufacturers for dating packages and those of newspaper publishers in numbering individual papers. But it has acquired another company which uses much more primitive technology in order to serve a market in which it has not been operating. This concerns locating stock in warehouses.

Source: Based on J. Ferry, 'Domino jets ahead', *Management Today*, June 1992.

---

regarded by consumers relative to the competition. To be effective this positioning is built on, and should be consistent with, the choice made about the basis of competitive advantage. But some organisations, for good reason, do not articulate a corporate positioning strategy, preferring to concentrate upon a series of product positioning strategies. Further discussion is contained in the chapter on Segmentation and Positioning.

Segmentation

Target markets will be identified from the choices made about product-market scope and from the analysis of potential market segments. It is in these target markets that product-market positions are established.

Product-market positioning

Product-market positioning relates back to the bases of competitive advantage, from which it stems. But the relationship between product-market positioning and the bases of competitive advantage can be complicated. It may be direct, or it can be mediated by corporate positioning. In some cases a corporate umbrella is established, with all brands positioned consistently with the corporate identity, such as Kellogg. But, as shown in the discussion in Chapter 6, some products are not positioned within the context of a singular corporate positioning. This may be due to the way the organisation has developed over time, possibly through the acquisition of major brands which do not all fit neatly into the same positioning strategy. An example would be what is now Rover Cars in the days when it was BMC and then British Leyland. It may also be due to a policy of dealing in quite separate industries, say, consumer electronics and defence electronics, where the virtues promoted by a single corporate positioning may not be relevant.

Missions and goals

In the strategy formulation process missions and goals provide direction in the search for viable strategies, as well as subsequently offering targets for control purposes. They also provide the motivation or the drive in that they give expression to the organisation's purposes. Well-formulated strategies, therefore, depend on well-conceived and appropriate missions and goals.

At the highest level the organisation's purpose is defined in its mission. This gives very broad guidelines about what the organisation wants to become in the future. Harvey [22] puts it like this:

> The mission includes the basic thrust of the company, including its basic products, businesses and markets. The identification of the mission is an awareness of a sense of purpose, the competitive environment, and the degree to which the firm's mission fits its capabilities and the opportunities which the environment offers. The mission provides a starting point as to how the firm will deal with such issues as technological innovation, product quality, customer service, employee satisfaction, and socially responsible conduct.

An improperly defined mission can have dramatic consequences. Levitt's classic article, 'Marketing myopia' [23], posed questions about the company's mission and how it defined its business. His famous examples explained the decline of the cinema film industry as a function of companies defining their business as making films, and not more broadly as the provision of entertainment. Similarly, the railways were said to be in the business not of running trains over rails, but of providing transportation. Willsmer [24] sees virtue in so 'extending the business horizon', but notes a problem in determining how far that horizon should be pushed:

> The problem with extending the business horizon is how far do you go? If a newspaper is part of the 'communication' business, its potential competition is enormous. 'Communication' can encompass a whole range of audio, visual, audio-visual, transitory, permanent and semi-permanent media, sandwich boards and megaphones. The danger with such descriptive definitions is that they are too global, too nearly all-embracing.

Ultimately, the definition of the business becomes 'business', and that would seem to help nobody. But lifting the horizon can give a fresh perspective, although it has to be brought down to a meaningful level, one that has tangible application. That application should be market-oriented, and not confined to particular products.

From their empirical work on organisations' mission statements Hooley *et al.* recommend that mission statements should contain [25]:

1. The vision or strategic intent, setting out clearly the ultimate goals of the organisation.

Missions at Mars

Mars has gained a substantial reputation for growth and profitability. The company expresses its basic purposes in the five principles noted below.

Quality
The consumer is our boss, quality is our work and value for money is our goal.

Mars treats every single purchase as the most important, since it is the cumulative impact of countless purchases which sustains the company's success. Mars consequently strives to create products with unique benefits to meet specific consumer wants, combining best quality with the best value to offer the best buy.

Responsibility
As individuals we demand total responsibility from ourselves; as associates we support the responsibilities of others.

Individual Mars units and associates are asked to take direct and total responsibility for results. They are also mutually dependent. This demands open communication of business and individual objectives, and an egalitarian approach to avoid divisive privileges and to develop individual potential to the full.

Mutuality
A mutual benefit is a shared benefit and a shared benefit will endure.

Mars believes that every party contributing to its business should benefit from that involvement, recognising that the company's success depends upon the strength of the relationships it builds and the mutual benefits that result.

Efficiency
We use resources to the full, waste nothing and do only what we can do best.

Mars believes in organising all its assets for maximum productivity and minimum waste in order to manufacture at the lowest possible cost. It concentrates its activities on its areas of expertise.

Freedom
We need freedom to shape our future, we need profit to remain free.

Mars values freedom in its business activities, believing this to be in the best interests of the company and its millions of consumers. The creation of profit and its reimbursement in the business are both essential to freedom and an important part of it.

Source: Reproduced with the permission of Mars Confectionery.

2. How that vision will be achieved, in terms of the businesses the organisation will be in, customer needs served, products and services offered and technologies used to create them.

3. The competitive positioning that will be achieved, financial objectives to be pursued, the corporate philosophy that will be adopted and the corporate image that will be created and sustained.

Writers who have studied successful companies give great emphasis to mission statements as an articulation of organisational philosophy because, they suggest, the companies themselves stress their importance as a unifying, identifying set of principles guiding their corporate way of life. Mission statements can unify because, according to McBurnie and Clutterbuck [26], companies 'recognise that to capture and hold markets they need a vision of the future that will be understood and endorsed by all decision-makers in their organisations.' That a clear mission can identify a company is demonstrable from a listing of company names which immediately evokes clear images and associations: Marks & Spencer, IBM, Sainsbury, Clarks Shoes, Jaguar.

Goals have four components [27]. First, the goal or attribute sought, such as growth, efficiency, utilisation of resources or contributions to stakeholders (owners, customers, employees). Second, an index for measuring progress towards the goal or attribute, such as sales figures, profits, return on investment, dividends and so on. Third, a target or hurdle to be achieved on each index, and finally, a statement of the time period within which the target is to be achieved. Because these goals are likely to be to some extent interdependent, they necessarily need to be internally consistent, compatible and lead to an assignment of priorities. The clear statement of goals might uncover inconsistencies that should be resolved. For instance, is high growth consistent with high risk ventures? Is withdrawal from a market consistent with the required capital investment programme?

There is also the need for a tight link between goals and strategies because [28]:

1. Any particular goal is feasible only when a strategy can be devised that will attain it; if there is no way of realistically reaching a goal it would seem pointless to have set that goal in the first place.

2. The marketing planner knows what sort of strategy to seek only after being acquainted with the goal.

Missions and goals set basic parameters within which strategies are to be formulated, and give impetus and guidance to the process. They integrate, co-ordinate and motivate. Clearly a major task.

Strategy alternatives

Various approaches have been taken to categorise the types of marketing strategies that are, or should be, followed by organisations.

Porter's generic strategies

Porter discriminates three broad 'generic' strategies: cost leadership, differentiation and focus [29]. Cost leadership implies high market share with the requisite skills and resources to deliver low unit cost and tight cost control. A differentiation strategy seeks products that are unique and that are promoted on non-price attributes such as image, design, distribution or customer service. Focus relates to serving the needs of a narrow market segment, and may reflect cost or differentiation positions, but tailored to a relatively small target market.

Strategies and product-market scope

Consideration of product-market scope adds another dimension. Differentiation strategies may be concerned with defending a mature market, or with active attempts to enter new markets. Similarly, low-cost strategies may be pursued in mature, existing markets or with entries to new markets.

In any strategic review the product-markets to be investigated need not be confined to those in which the organisation is currently participating. Analysis would list and evaluate the main structural variables in each product-market to be considered, such as mobility barriers. The key uncertainties would be uncovered, perhaps related to stage in market evolution or to the rate of technical change. In tandem with this, the bases on which the firm could contend effectively in each product-market would be elicited. An overall rating of the relative attractiveness of each product-market would concentrate on a shortlist within which possible strategies could be developed.

Attractive current product-markets
Those product-markets in which the organisation is currently engaged, and which remain attractive, may be tackled with a range of strategies, sometimes in combination. A typical categorisation includes:

> Market penetration
> Market development
> Product development
> Maintain or hold
> Harvest
> Horizontal integration

Market penetration seeks to build market share through increased marketing activity, implying higher levels of promotion and/or lower prices. A structural limitation on this is the nature of the strategic groups in the industry. If the firm belongs to the leading group which contains, say, two or three others with comparable market shares then any competitive move is likely to be emulated and perhaps negated. In any event, there could be the prospect of diminishing returns to the effort.

Market development requires some slight change to product-market scope. The search here would be for new kinds of segment in which to offer the established product. This may mean exploring new regions or countries, new uses, applications or benefits.

Product development involves new products aimed at established markets. This may be conventional in an industry due to continuing technical change or chronic fashion changes. It may also be what the firm is particularly adept at doing, building on strengths in technical and marketing research and development.

Maintenance implies an essentially defensive posture, but not necessarily continuity in strategies. The firm would be satisfied with current performance and would adjust strategies in line with changes in the industry. This may require the reinforcement of mobility barriers or attention to the cost base.

Harvesting refers to short-term cash flow and is associated with later stages in the industry lifecycle and where the firm believes it has a defensible position. Horizontal integration may be followed if the firm believes there to be scope for synergy following the merger with a direct competitor. Economies may be possible in advertising or the salesforce, or from the rationalisation of purchasing, production or distribution.

Unattractive current product-markets

There may be situations in which the company finds that its current businesses are in fairly unattractive product-markets. The strategic response depends on the reasons for the poor performance. Turnaround may be possible; if not, then withdrawal from that product-market may result.

Attractive unrelated product-markets

Diversification into new product-markets could be a more or less radical move. Less radical moves include vertical integration, back to taking over suppliers or forward to the acquisition of distributors. Radical diversification covers moves into entirely new markets with technologies or products new to the firm. The high risk of such radical initiatives is not always rewarded [30].

Empirical typologies

Strategy types have been studied by Hooley, Lynch and Jobber [31] in an empirical analysis of firms in the United Kingdom. They discerned five broad types among the 616 firms studied:

1. *Aggressors*: operating in new, growing, dynamic markets and aiming at high sales growth across many segments with higher than average quality (113 firms).

2. *Premium position segmenters*: mature, stable market and aiming at steady sales growth from winning share and expanding the market in selected segments and with higher quality and higher price (172 firms).

3. *Stuck-in-the-middlers*: mature, stable market and aiming at some growth in selected segments but with average quality and average price (167 firms).

4. *High value segmenters*: new, growing markets and aiming at steady growth in selected segments with higher quality but average price (78 firms).

5. *Defenders*: mature markets and defensive aims, treating individual customers with average or higher quality but average price (86 firms).

Performance on financial and marketing-based criteria was best for aggressors and worst for defenders.

Strategic choice

Formulating strategies is the organisation's attempt to provide for the transition from the past into the future. Perceptions of the past, expectations about the future and the attitudes and values now held by those significant in the organisation, all influence how the transition is to be accomplished. All influence the kinds of strategies that will be chosen and the way in which the choice is made. For example, a company with a reasonable earnings record, a protected position in a static industry and a complacent management may preclude serious strategic planning. No strategic alternatives may be envisaged and so no choice is required. Change any of the elements in that company description and strategic choices are needed.

Assessments of current and past strategies are important for two reasons: they shape understanding of the efficacy of various actions and they place limitations on what can be done in the future. In marketing, the company will have a bundle of knowledge and skills, a present product line, established relationships with the trade and a set of consumer perceptions. It will know more or less about price sensitivity, customer quality consciousness, promotion elasticities and the norms in marketing to the trade. All that becomes part of the knowledge and assumptions held by company executives, albeit transmuted within the company culture, and has resulted in the current strategies being pursued. Radical departures from the broad strategic thrust would need considerable justification. That may well be provided if present performance is unsatisfactory or if there are major opportunities or threats.

Consequences of strategies on performance

It may be that company executives believe they have good understanding of the possible consequences of following various strategies. Analyses of past experience may have traced the connection between such variables as market share, product quality, stage in market evolution and profit as applied to the company's products-markets. However, even the most sophisticated organisations have sought to learn from more generalised empirical studies. The best known of these is PIMS (profit impact of market strategy), which began in the 1960s and now contains data on 3,000 business units. Buzzell and Gale summarise the six most important linkages between strategy and performance that have been established through the PIMS project as follows [32]:

1. In the long run the most important single factor affecting a business unit's performance is the quality of its products and services relative to competitors. In the short run, superior quality yields increased profits from premium prices. In the longer term it can lead to market expansion and increased market share, with consequent scale economies.

2. Market share and profitability are strongly related, because high share businesses derive higher profit margins from scale effects. Not that it should be inferred that high market share necessarily leads to high levels of profitability. The generality of this association has also been questioned. In a study of the US brewing industry, no strong correlation was found. Even where association is established, the direction of causality is sometimes questionable. Does high profitability afford the building of high market share, rather than vice versa?

3. High investment intensity acts as a drag on profitability. Crucial here is the ratio of investment to sales. New investment must seek to maintain or reduce this ratio if profitability is not to fall.

4. Cash flow is influenced by the same factors as profitability and not just by market growth rate and relative market share.

5. Vertical integration has a variable impact on profitability. Its effect is situation-specific.

6. Most of the factors that boost profitability also contribute to long-term value.

Portfolio planning

Most firms today do not operate in a single market with a single product; instead, they offer many products in multiple markets. In strategic analysis this multi-plicity brings with it some complexity, chiefly because it broadens the range of current and potential options, and because of the intricate connections that exist between the options. Strategic alternatives such as funding more production or promotion for an existing product, or investing in new product development, should not be evaluated without investigation of the impact on the rest of the firm's operations. Concern about this issue has led to the conception of the product portfolio, where options are evaluated within the context of all the

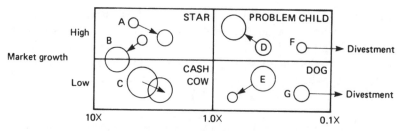

Market share dominance (relative to largest competitor)

A to G are products; arrows indicate planned directions of movement. The diameters of the circles are proportional to sales volume.

Source: G.S. Day, 'Diagonising the product portfolio', *Journal of Marketing*, vol. 41, no. 2, 1977.

Figure 9.6   *Share/growth model*

products or businesses in the enterprise, and with the implication that there is a search for an optimal portfolio, analogous to an investment portfolio.

Various portfolio models have been advocated [33]. The present discussion will illustrate the approach by reference to just two: the share/growth model and market attractiveness/business position models. The essential steps in these models are:

1. Definition of activities of each business unit.

2. Plotting each business unit on a two-dimensional grid.

3. Classifying the strategic goals for each business unit and allocating resources accordingly.

The *share/growth model* was conceived by the Boston Consulting Group. The market share dimension is employed in the belief that it represents the dominant measure of the company's position and is a summary of its relative strengths. This is also related to the previous points made about the relationship between market share and profitability and the experience effect. The market growth dimension is employed because it is held that the relative attractiveness of opportunities is a function of present and prospective growth rates, and is related to product lifecycles. An example is displayed in Figure 9.6.

Four quadrants are defined with different combinations of shares and growth rates. Low growth/low share products are given the label 'dogs' since their prospects and performance are dubious. The implication is that something would have to happen to them – improved performance or possible withdrawal. High growth/low share indicates a 'problem child' with good potential prospects, but perhaps currently under-performing. Such products may need considerable funding because of their growth, and this could be a drain on the total portfolio. High growth/high share will attract management attention because products here

Prospects for market sector profitability

	Unattractive	Average	Attractive
Weak	Disinvest	Phased withdrawal Proceed with care	Double or quit
Average	Phased withdrawal	Proceed with care	Try harder
Strong	Cash generator	Growth Leader	Leader

Company competitive position

Source: D. Hussey, 'Portfolio analysis: practical experience with the directional policy matrix', in B. Taylor and D. Hussey, *The Realities of Planning*, Oxford: Pergamon, 1982.

Figure 9.7 *Directional policy matrix*

are the 'star' performers. But the high earnings of the stars will require high fundings. This may be provided by the 'cash cow', with its low growth/high share.

Given the complexity of strategic planning it would be surprising if such a simple model did not attract substantial criticisms. The very reduction of all the issues to two dimensions is at best optimistic. Factors other than market share and growth should enter the analysis. Not all environmental, technological and competitive circumstances can be subsumed within these dimensions. Insufficient insight will be gleaned in judging two opportunities classified in the same box [34]. The model stresses cash flow and cash balances, but return on investment is usually taken as the critical criterion in evaluating portfolios. There is also the implication that high market growth is to be preferred, and no attempt to allow for differential risks in alternative ventures. Further comment on the relative usefulness of the share/growth matrix can be found in Morrison and Wensley [35].

Market attractiveness/business strength approaches attempt to overcome some of these problems by using composite dimensions. The directional policy matrix is one of these approaches, and uses as its two dimensions the prospects for sector profitability and company competitive position. It is illustrated in Figure 9.7, and a discussion of its application can be found in McDonald [36]. The following listing gives possible constituents of the composites:

Market sector prospects	*Company competitive position*
Market growth	Market position
Market quality	Market share

Sector profitability record	Marketing channel considerations
Margins	Production capability
Pricing practices	Production economics
Ultimate market size	Production capacity
Threat of substitutes	
Environmental factors	

A much fuller checklist can be found in McDonald [37]. The composition of the two dimensions is tailored to a specific company's circumstances, and Hussey gives examples of the way they were adjusted for Rolls-Royce Motors and for Guinness. To quantify the dimensions, judgemental scores are required for each factor, and relative weights attached to each of these scores. The weights reflect the significance of that factor to the company's strategic goals at that time, and so might not only vary between factors but could also vary for the same factor over time. Scores are aggregated for all the factors to arrive at an overall score for each dimension, and the overall scores position the business/product on the matrix.

The checklists that are an integral part of this approach can provide useful reviews, but their incorporation is dependent upon a deal of subjectivity. This can be seen in the initial selection of factors to be considered and in the relative weights attached to these factors. Interestingly, Hussey assesses the usefulness of this model as only partly being related to its contribution to strategy formulation [38]. He sees there also being:

> tremendous value in using the technique firstly to help managers to think as a group about their markets, the competition and the relative strategic value of their portfolio to the company. Secondly, the portfolio approach provides a useful way of communicating strategic guidelines to different business units.

A problem common to any portfolio model is the definition of the businesses or markets which are to be plotted on any matrix. Does Rolls-Royce supply the car market in its most general sense, or some more narrowly defined luxury car market, or does it have no substitutes? Is Guinness in the market for beer or stout? Should there be a geographical limitation to this definition? Wind urges great care and detailed analyses in market definition, and suggests analysis by customer segment, usage occasion, distribution outlet and different geographic units.

A further problem with all portfolio models is their reliability – are they consistent? To test this Wind *et al.* used the fifteen businesses of a large company and applied the different models [39]. Their analysis is not encouraging because they found enormous scope for quite divergent classification of the same business if different models were employed. This resulted from variations in definitions, and rules for dividing dimensions into 'high' and 'low'.

These kinds of problem and reservation have led Wensley to be very sceptical about portfolio models [40]. He argues that the central issue in strategy formulation is the identification and nurturing of sustainable competitive advantage, that classificatory systems may deflect management from this axiom and be harmful if 'used to justify some form of cash budgeting, since it is essential that any major project is assessed independent of its box classification'. Hammermesh and White are also concerned that too much attention is given to portfolio planning [41]. They show that organisational structure exerts considerable influence on performance and that executives can change this structure more easily than they can influence the competitive or environmental contexts.

Portfolio planning is clearly controversial. For some companies it is also a little perplexing because just as they are catching up with this trend in analysis, others are questioning its basic rationale. Proponents stress the analytical processes that portfolio models encourage; opponents stress the potentially damaging consequences if the output of the models is followed unreasonably while the input is so partial, or just wrong. Burke realises the limitations of market attractiveness and business strengths as the key dimensions, but still grants that the models can serve as frameworks to suggest possible strategies – although other factors should enter the final choice [42]. Haspelagh [43] also supports their use because:

> the approach can give companies a permanent added capacity for strategic control because it provides a framework within which the management process can be adapted to the evolving needs of the business. It also helps companies out of the dilemma between stifling centralization and dangerous decentralization.

The judicious use of portfolio models would not lose sight of the simplifying assumptions. They should be used to suit particular kinds of strategic goal and, as with all management techniques, their utility is as an aid to, not a substitute for, informed judgement in strategic decisions. The injudicious use of portfolio models breeds dogma that can obscure the much more fundamental situation analysis. Choice among strategic alternatives is instrumental in solving problems in the firm's situation. If the mode of analysis supplies constructs which distort the perception of that situation, then the problem is aggravated rather than solved [44].

Summary

Unravelling the constraints and possibilities acting upon the development of marketing strategy requires understanding of the interactions between the strategic trinity of environment, goals and strategy. Analyses of the external environment, including trends in industry structure, the technology and consumption will be influential in presenting opportunities and threats that need be addressed by company actions. The latitude the firm has in responding will be defined by its analysis of its internal environment, which might also add fresh ideas in the search for viable strategies. Audits and reviews of resources and competences could reveal primary sources of competitive advantage, strengths to be capitalised and weaknesses to be overcome. Broad direction and impetus are provided by the organisation's mission and goals, in the environmental analyses as well as in the specification of strategy.

Distillation of the strategic issues to be addressed may be aided by the construction of future scenarios, which could allow identification of rigidities in the strategic options being investigated. Consideration of product-market scope may encourage a wider view of the strategic alternatives, to embrace industries in which the firm is not presently participating.

Formulating strategies constitutes the firm's attempt to handle the transition from the past to the future. How that transition is to be accomplished is influenced by perceptions of the past, expectations of the future, and the attitudes and values of those significant in the organisation. Knowledge of the possible consequences of following various strategies will refine the strategic choice and planning frameworks, such as portfolio models, may add structure to the process.

Questions for review and discussion

1. Study of industry structure stresses a wide view of competitive forces. Contrast the nature of these forces in the inclusive tour industry (package holidays) and in retail banking.

2. How has technological development affected these competitive forces in those industries? Focus on transportation, information and communications technologies, drawing a matrix of the five forces and the three technologies.

3. Market opportunity analysis may be undertaken at the generic, specific product and specific brand levels. Trace some possible ways these different levels of analysis can influence the strategic alternatives to be evaluated and the strategic choices to be made. Give particular attention to consideration of current and potential product-market scope and to portfolio planning methods.

4. The experience curve, the primacy of market share as a goal, notions of lifecycles and product portfolios have all emerged as major topics in strategic planning. All have been variously discredited, resurrected and then questioned again. Does this indicate that marketing managers should ignore current developments in concepts and techniques, and only utilise those that have been well tried and acknowledged as classic?

5. If quality is king then why are many companies selling lower quality products?

6. Use the share/growth matrix to plot the positions of major car firms. Does it help understanding of that industry? Would it be as enlightening in the company as in the classroom?

References

1. Aaker, D.A. 1992. *Strategic Market Management*, 3rd. edn. New York: John Wiley, p. 11.
2. Kay, J. 1993. *Foundations of Corporate Success*. Oxford: Oxford University Press.
3. Porter, M.E. 1980. *Competitive Strategy*. New York: Free Press, p. 4.
4. Tang, M.-J. and Thomas, H. 1992. 'The concept of strategic groups: theoretical construct or analytical convenience', *Managerial and Decision Economics*, vol. 13, pp. 323–9. See also, Daems, H. and Thomas, H. 1994. *Strategic Groups, Strategic Moves and Performance*. Oxford: Pergamon.
5. Reger, R.K. and Huff, A.S. 1993. 'Strategic groups: a cognitive perspective', *Strategic Management Journal*, vol. 14, pp. 103–24.
6. McGee, J. 1985. 'Strategic groups: a bridge between industry structure and strategic management?' in Thomas, H. and Gardner, D. *Strategic Marketing and Management*. Chichester: John Wiley, p. 74.
7. Cool, K. and Schendel, D. 1988. 'Performance differences among strategic group members', *Strategic Management Journal*, vol. 9, pp. 207–23.
8. Cool, K.O. and Schendel, D. 1987. 'Strategic group formation and performance: the case of the US pharmaceutical industry 1963–1982', *Management Science*, pp. 1102–24; see also Cool, K. and Dierickx, I. 1993. 'Rivalry, strategic groups and firm profitability', *Strategic Management Journal*, vol. 14, pp. 47–59.
9. Johnson, G. and Scholes, K. 1988. *Exploring Corporate Strategy*, 2nd edn. Hemel Hempstead: Prentice Hall International, p. 74.
10. See Walker, O.C., Boyd, H.W. and Larréché, J.-C. 1992. *Marketing Strategy*. Homewood, Ill.: Irwin, ch. 5.
11. Buzzell, R.D. and Gale, B.T. 1987. *The PIMS Principles*. New York: Free Press, ch. 10.
12. Taylor, B. and Hussey, D. 1982. *The Realities of Planning*. Oxford: Pergamon, p. 222.
13. Cooper, A.C. and Schendel, D. 1984. 'Strategic response to technological threats', in Weitz, B.A. and Wensley, R. *Strategic Marketing*. Boston, Mass.: Kent, p. 466.
14. Cravens, D.W., Hills, G.E. and Woodruff, R.B. 1980. *Marketing Decision Making*. Homewood, Ill.: Irwin, p. 108. See also Cravens, D.W. 1994. *Strategic Marketing*, Homewood, Ill.: Irwin, ch. 5.
15. Goldsmith, W. and Clutterbuck, D. 1985. *The Winning Streak*. Harmondsworth: Penguin Books, p. 100.
16. Davidson, H. 1987. *Offensive Marketing*, 2nd edn. Harmondsworth: Penguin Books, p. 56.
17. Buzzell and Gale, op. cit., p. 230. See also Ansoff, I. 1987. *Corporate Strategy*. Harmondsworth: Penguin Books, ch. 6.
18. Weitz, B.A. and Wensley, R. 1984. *Strategic Marketing*. Boston, Mass.: Kent, p. 133. See also Hall, G. and Howell, S. 1985. 'The experience effect from the economist's perspective', *Strategic Management Journal*, vol. 6, no. 3; and Day, G.S. 1986. *Analysis for Strategic Marketing Decisions*. St Paul, Minn.: West, ch. 2.
19. Buzzell and Gale, op. cit., p. 78.
20. Wensley, R. 1987. 'Marketing strategy', in Baker, M.J. *The Marketing Book*, London: Heinmann, p. 32.
21. Ansoff, H.I. 1989. *Corporate Strategy*, rev. edn. Harmondsworth: Penguin Books.
22. Harvey, D. 1982. *Business Policy and Strategic Management*. Columbus, Ohio: Merrill, p. 16.
23. Levitt, T. 1960. 'Marketing myopia', *Harvard Business Review*, July/August. Reprinted Sept./Oct. 1975.

24. Willsmer, R.L. 1979. 'Market spectrum analysis for determining market position', *Quarterly Review of Marketing*, vol. 5, no. 1.
25. Hooley, G.J., Cox, A.J. and Adams, A. 1992. 'Our five year mission – to boldly go where no man has been before . . .', *Journal of Marketing Management*, vol. 8, pp. 35–48.
26. McBurnie, T. and Clutterbuck, D. 1988. *The Marketing Edge*. London: Penguin Books, p.107.
27. Hofer, C.W. and Schendel, D. 1978. *Strategy Formulation: Analytical Concepts*. St Paul, Minn.: West, p. 21.
28. Luck, C.J. and Ferrell, O.C. 1979. *Marketing Strategy and Plans*. Engelwood Cliffs, NJ: Prentice Hall, p. 5.
29. Porter, M.E. 1980. *Competitive Strategy*. New York: Free Press, ch. 2.
30. Porter, M.E. 1987. 'From competitive advantage to corporate strategy', *Harvard Business Review*, May/June.
31. Hooley, G.J., Lynch, J.E. and Jobber, D. 1991. 'Generic marketing strategies', *International Journal of Research in Marketing*, Special edition on strategic marketing.
32. Buzzell and Gale, op. cit., ch. 1.
33. Wind, Y. and Mahajan, V. 1981. 'Designing product and business portfolios', *Harvard Business Review*, Jan./Feb.
34. Abell, D.F. and Hammond, J.S. 1979. *Strategic Marketing Planning*. Engelwood Cliffs, NJ: Prentice Hall, ch. 5.
35. Morrison, A. and Wensley, R. 1991. 'Boxing up or boxed in? A short history of the Boston Consulting Group share/growth matrix', *Journal of Marketing Management*, vol. 7, no. 2, April.
36. McDonald, M. 1992. *Strategic Marketing Planning*. London: Kogan Page, p. 130.
37. McDonald, M. 1984. *Marketing Plans*. London: Heinemann, p. 94.
38. Hussey, D. 1982. 'Portfolio analysis: practical experience with the directional policy matrix', in Taylor, B. and Hussey, D. (eds), *The Realities of Planning*. Oxford: Pergamon.
39. Wind, Y., Mahajan, V. and Swire, D. 1983. 'An empirical comparison of standardized portfolio models', *Journal of Marketing*, vol. 47, Spring.
40. Wensley, R. 1981. 'Strategic marketing: betas, boxes and basics', *Journal of Marketing*, Summer; reprinted in Weitz, B.A. and Wensley, R. 1984. *Strategic Marketing*. Boston, Mass.: Kent.
41. Hammermesh, R.G. and White, R.E. 1984. 'Manage beyond portfolio analysis', *Harvard Business Review*, Jan./Feb.
42. Burke, M.C. 1984. 'Strategic choice and marketing managers', *Journal of Marketing Research*, vol. 21, no. 4.
43. Haspelagh, P. 1982. 'Portfolio planning: uses and limits', *Harvard Business Review*, Jan./Feb.
44. More detailed consideration of portfolio models can be found in Wilson, R.M.S., Gilligan, C. and Pearson, D.J. 1992. *Strategic Marketing Management*, Oxford: Butterworth-Heinemann, ch. 9; and in Kerin, R.A., Mahajan, V. and Varadarajan, P.R. 1990. *Strategic Market Planning*. Boston: Allyn and Bacon, chs 2 and 3; and in Hooley, G. and Saunders, J. 1993. *Competitive Positioning*. Hemel Hempstead: Prentice Hall, ch. 3.

Chapter 10
Competitive strategies

Marketing strategy would be sharpened by fuller consideration of the competitive domain. Success or failure in this domain rests on customer reaction to competitive offers, but first requires decisions to enter that competition in a given set of circumstances. These decisions and circumstances are the concern of this chapter.

Each firm will be seeking to build and sustain some competitive edge. As in any competition the astute participants choose what, how and when to contest, in relation to what they can do well. And, what firms can do well is to make better products and services, or produce at a lower cost. One of the issues in this chapter is the choice of the bases of the competitive edge.

A principal factor conditioning the firm's circumstances will be the structure of the industry in which it operates. The analysis of industry structure introduced in the last chapter is extended here to cover industry monitoring. This might allow definition of the apparent strategic or competitive groups and pick up important changes in the strategies of rivals, buyers or suppliers. Analysing strategic groups is a convenient way of introducing the range of options open to the firm in deciding on the types of competitive strategy it could adopt. Distinctions are drawn between its rivalry within its own group, its defence against attack from outside this group, and the attacks it might launch against firms in other groups. In all these options the stage of industry lifecycle, and the disposition of the strategic groups in the industry, affect what can be done and when. Industry ageing also prompts consideration of withdrawal from that arena, and the possible extension of the firm's product-market scope by entering other industries.

Competitive advantage

Striving for, securing and maintaining competitive advantage are the objects of competitive strategies. How this superiority is to be built depends on the nature of the advantage to be taken, and on how that is translated into a strong competitive position.

Day and Wensley [1] distinguish between the sources of advantage and their consequences for relative competitive position. Competitive advantage thus stems from two elements: the firm's distinctive competences (sources) and its positional superiority. For example, its particular competence might be in high precision manufacturing and it positions itself to serve a quality-sensitive market segment. If the source of the advantage was sufficiently distinct, and if it was effectively aligned to that market segment's needs, then superior performance in terms of share or profit could result.

Positional advantage

Two broad types of positional advantage are possible: those based on low cost and those on differentiation. Overall cost leadership may depend on the search for scale economies and on efficiency in purchasing, manufacturing, marketing and administrative systems. Davidson [2] gives a number of examples including that of Kwik Save who are said to have the lowest branded grocery prices in the United Kingdom. They have a narrow range of less than 1,500 products, against 7,000 or more in a large Sainsbury, and there is no individual price marking. In the personal computer market the past success of Amstrad could be attributed to its price leadership, underpinned by a low-cost position.

Differentiated positions may be based on any factor which is perceived by customers as providing valued benefits. This might embrace superior product features, better service, higher quality or more intangible benefits related to product branding and image. Much of companies' promotional activity is directed at nurturing customer perceptions of these differentials. To be effective this must be on dimensions rated as important by customers and ones on which the company can establish superiority, or at least something above par. An example is the Italian textile company Benetton. During the 1970s and 1980s their annual sales growth was above 20 per cent. Benetton's success has rested on keeping abreast of fashion, and especially in anticipating colour trends.

Low cost and differentiated positions are not mutually exclusive; they can be reinforcing. Differentiation can help protect a low-cost firm in a dynamic industry structure where, for example, suppliers or customers are gaining power. Similarly, low cost can aid a differentiated firm in a dynamic market whose brands are threatened by new product launches, or the onslaught of new substitutes. But it would be difficult, and impossible in many markets, for the company to be superior on cost and differentiation simultaneously. Competitive posture would tend to be more influenced by the one than the other.

Positional advantage may be sought marketwide or by focusing on particular segments. An example is the market for whisky. The major brands of blended whisky compete marketwide with mass distribution in every conceivable type of outlet. Minor brands and malt brands seek advantage by targeting smaller segments. Other examples are the markets for trade and consumer magazines. Some women's magazines attempt to build national circulations across the market, others focus on reader segments within narrower ranges of ages or interests. In trade magazines some are very broadscale dealing with 'engineering' or 'business' and others appeal to sharply segmented markets.

There is some evidence about the relative efficacy of differentiation and cost-based advantages. A recent empirical study found that 'differences broadly related to differentiation play a significant role in generating sustained intraindustry profit differentials, and differences related to cost, a somewhat less significant one' [3]. This study also found that differentiation-related advantages were absorbed in fatter margins and (in some cases) larger market shares, while cost-related advantages were taken primarily in increased market share.

Industry monitoring

Knowledge about the structure and strategies adopted in the industry is vital in the initial decision about the direction in which to build competitive advantage. It is of continuing significance as the market, the technology and the competitors change. These changes may be chronic short-term tactical adjustments within a strategic group, such as waves of promotion. Changes may signal strategic moves with new brand introductions within this group, or they may signal threats to the mobility barriers protecting the group, from other strategic groups within the industry or from outsiders.

To take window system manufacturing as an example it could be assumed there are two main strategic groups. Figure 10.1 shows that one group of firms stresses high quality and produces a wide range of systems in both aluminium and plastic, while the other group has restricted product lines and competes on value for money. There is strong rivalry within these groups, although they tend to compete between themselves along the same strategy dimensions. For each firm it will be important to map the tactical and strategic manoeuvres of its direct

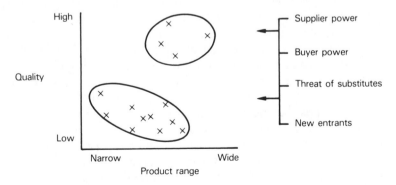

Figure 10.1 *Strategic groups and threats*

rivals, and it will be equally important to understand the wider industry context which impacts on strategy.

Are firms in one strategic group content to keep within the confines of that group? The quality group could be attracted to the value-for-money group in order to build volume, which may be necessary to reap scale economies in assembly, distribution or order processing, or to develop a power base against suppliers. On the other hand, the value-for-money group may see the possibility of higher profitability through increasing quality. For both groups the feasibility of these moves will be partly dependent on their ownership and management. Many of these firms will be subsidiaries of large enterprises. What role do they have in their parents' portfolios? Are they seen as core or peripheral? Are major investment programmes being undertaken in other parts of these enterprises, and what rate of return is demanded? In the case of any one competitor, the more it was able to glean of these issues the better able it would be to understand and predict rival strategies, and to assess the longer-term viability of its own positional strategies.

Are suppliers content? In some instances there could already be a web of ownership links from previous forward integration of suppliers into the industry. Aluminium and plastic extruders are well represented in window system manufacture, but what of paint and other treatment processes? Could chemical companies become interested in this industry, and, if so, would their strategic moves be in acquisition, and which strategic group would allow the easiest incursion? Intelligence on the power bases of suppliers should not, therefore, be restricted to medium-term predictions on their capacity utilisation, which would indicate how badly they needed the order. Broader understanding of the potential strategic thrust of suppliers is required since they could undermine positional strategies in the industry. This might be by changing the industry cost structure, by introducing new rivals into strategic groups or from the revitalisation of a relatively docile rival after acquisition.

In window systems some of the points made about suppliers can also be made about some buyers, and particularly the own-label companies. How are they expected to develop their business? Could they integrate backwards, and would they be allowed to? Will they take a large slice of total sales in the future? What does their power rest on – purchase volume, brand image, widespread outlets and intense sales coverage – and will these change? Again, knowledge and predictions about these factors are essential since they affect positional advantage. They could affect scale, experience and so costs. They could also affect differentiation. If a manufacturer was positioned to provide high level service to many hundreds of small distributors, and if the own-label firms took market share from these, then the positional advantage is devalued.

Threats from possible new entrants need also be monitored. An added complication is that they may arise from unexpected quarters. They could be from the same industry in other countries. Could a Japanese company launch into the British window system industry? Alternatively, new entrants could represent a diversification by a company in a quite different industry. Could a general building supplies distributor, a kitchen specialist or a DIY company move in? If there were such activity then how durable are the mobility barriers, and how easily could they be enhanced to frustrate entrance?

Substitutes could shake industry structure and strategies more or less profoundly. Suppose that in window systems a chemical company, unconnected with the industry, developed an entirely new material which could be employed in window assembly. It has the strength and durability of the highest quality materials now used, has the further advantage of being able to fix any colour indefinitely and can be moulded economically into any shape, allowing for windows which are not rectangular. How will the chemical company proceed, which strategic group is most at risk and what will be the industry reaction? The value-for-money group may be the least vulnerable. The quality group may be at risk depending on how the chemical company develops its product. It may believe that access to marketing channels is paramount and that it would take too long to break into the market itself. It may then be satisfied to be a supplier to the manufacturers. However, the existing suppliers to the industry would feel threatened and, through their ownership ties with some of the manufacturers, may attempt to impede the progress of the new material. But some manufacturers not tied to suppliers may seek to steal advantage by adopting the new material, or the chemical company may find an attractive acquisition amongst the manufacturers. A period of considerable instability might follow as competitors jockey for new positional advantage in the face of the changed circumstances.

Assessing competitors

Informed assessments of competitors depend on the knowledge available about their goals, strategies and capabilities. These factors bound their ability and willingness to initiate, and to respond to, competitive moves. Their significance is noted by Hooley and Saunders:

> The assessment of a company's capabilities involves looking at its strengths and weaknesses to determine what it can do. It is the final diagnostic step in competitor analysis. Whereas a competitor's goals, assumptions and current strategy would influence the likelihood, time, nature and intensity of a competitor's reactions, its capabilities will determine its ability to initiate and sustain moves in response to environmental or competitive changes. [4]

Dealing with these kinds of issue presupposes a timely flow of relevant information and intelligent interpretation, against a background of good understanding of structures and strategies. Constant monitoring of external sources such as the following could provide part of this flow:

Commercial databases
Trade publications
Published market research reports
Stockbrokers' industry and company analyses
Trade exhibitions
Competitors' promotional literature and advertisements

Annual reports and accounts of competitors, suppliers and buyers
Patent registrations
Government sources such as Office of Fair Trading, Monopolies
    Commission and industry research establishments

Just as valuable as these sources will be the wealth of contacts made routinely by company employees. An explicit part of the role of the salesforce would be to give forewarning of competitive strategies, and this may form an aspect of their normal reporting. Many others will have interesting contacts with established and prospective suppliers and distributors which may yield more news. The problem is that much of this information will be neglected because its significance is not appreciated, because it is inadequately stored, or because it does not reach the right people. Attempts to make this monitoring more systematic these days turn to computers and/or microfilming. Fuld gives warnings about mainframe systems in this context and recommends a mix of micro-based systems and hard copy with good indexes [5].

Just how seriously this monitoring is taken by companies is questioned by

---

Ice cream wars

For decades the ice cream industry in Britain was dominated by Wall's (Unilever) and Lyons' Maid (Allied-Lyons), although there was also a significant amount of retailer own branding. A major feature of these two companies' operations was very intensive distribution through tens of thousands of outlets. One way they protected their position was to supply freezers to their retailers without charge, but with the condition that these could only be used for their products. This practice was challenged by the Office of Fair Trading in 1982 and was found to be anti-competitive. Wall's then agreed that others could use their freezers if they could not supply the outlet. The Monopolies and Mergers Commission looked again at the supply of ice cream in 1994 and that time did not find the practice to be anti-competitive.

In 1988 Mars entered the industry with a significant technological development and the very successful launch of Mars Ice Cream. Another new entrant was Haagen-Dazs (Grand Met), brought over from the United States into the premium sector. Wall's responded in 1989 with new products, Gino Ginelli and Cadbury's Dream Ice Cream, and a 50 per cent increase in advertising. There was no large-scale response from Lyons' Maid which was running into difficulty, and becoming unprofitable. By 1991 it was sold to Clarke Foods. This firm in turn went into bankruptcy and was acquired in 1992 by Nestlé.

During 1993 Wall's dropped Cadbury's Dream because it was considered not to offer sharp enough branding. It was replaced by Cadbury's Dairy Milk Ice Cream. Wall's also moved into the premium sector to compete with Haagen-Dazs with the Ranieri brand. Later Nestlé launched new ice cream versions of its confectionery lines and repositioned Lyons' Maid as an economy brand in the take-home sector. From 1988 Mars continued to introduce new brands of ice cream products based on its confectionery brands.

Many of these developments in Britain were mirrored in other European countries, often with the same companies involved.

McBurnie and Clutterbuck. After their study of a wide range of firms in different industries they concluded [6]:

> If there has been reluctance in some companies to pay full regard to customers' needs, there has been just as little attention paid to competitors and their activities. An examination of most companies' business plans (or more specifically, their marketing plans) would reveal very little knowledge or analysis of competitors' current activity or how competitors are likely to respond to the company's strategy . . .

They ascribe this reluctance to cultural factors in the United Kingdom with executives shying away from the conflict inherent in handling competitors and:

> Playing the game still too often seems to be considered as important if not more important than winning. Business and especially the customer/competitor environment is all about winning and it is one in which many executives feel uncomfortable. The US culture is quite the opposite. Winners are acclaimed and losers are forgotten. In Japan, the penalty for losing face does not allow besting by a competitor to be accepted as anything other than temporary.

It may, alternatively, be a lack of appreciation of the logic of the analytical frameworks now available in strategic marketing planning, and the stress put on monitoring developments in competitive structures and strategies.

Competitive strategy decisions

Competitive strategies result from interpretations of the competitive circumstance and resolutions to respond appropriately. That prompts questions about the definition of the competitive circumstance and evaluation of feasible competitive responses.

Analysis of the competitive circumstance can be broad or narrow, more or less structured, and can tend to the pragmatic or the theoretical. The approach taken here owes much to the developments in recent years in industry and strategic analysis, and is influenced by the writers whose work was cited in the references to the previous chapter. Military analogies are sometimes used in describing competitive strategies and these are implicit in the following discussion. For explicit treatments of military analogies see Saunders [7] and Barrie [8].

The arena in which the firm competes is influenced by the competitive and industry structure. In that arena important contests for the firm will be:

1. Rivalry with direct competitors.

2. Defence against those anxious to move in to compete with these firms.

3. Attacks by the firm against other possible strategic groups in its industry.

But the arena is not static. The economics of the industry change as industry structure changes. Some of these changes result from the ageing of the industry as its market evolves through the lifecycle. Some changes result from the strategies of firms in the industry, such as an attempt by one firm to develop a new strategic position through radical differentiation. Firms' strategies could also lead to the erection of mobility barriers new to the industry, such as strong branding backed with heavy promotion being introduced into a market in which price or product features were previously the main competitive bases. Other changes may be due to suppliers or buyers becoming increasingly powerful. All these changes may affect the sources of competitive advantage by changing cost structures or by vitiating a particular differentiated position. Yet more change might derive from developments in the economy or the technology, again possibly affecting costs or differentiation and thus the basics of competition.

Additionally, through time, just who is contesting what in that dynamic arena needs redefinition. The strategic groups may not be static, especially if there are changes to the nature of mobility barriers, and group members will continue to skirmish between themselves while also contending with new entrants. Added to this, the rules may be changing, indeed powerful firms may have tried to change the rules themselves. For example, there may have been a tradition, even a dogma, that contests only employed certain kinds of promotional activity, or that the benefits afforded customers excluded some services, or that only established marketing channels were used. Car manufacturers hardly used television advertising before 1970, few hotels had en suite facilities and there were shopkeepers called ironmongers.

Results from the contests in the industry may not be proving satisfactory for the firm and it may look to other industry arenas, changing its product-market scope. These other industries could be in varying lifecycle stages. If the firm was the pioneer there would be no established strategic groups to fend off, and even if it entered in rapid growth it might be able to find a niche in the market. Later entry would prove much more difficult because firms already there would have established competitive advantages which could be used in immediate retaliation. Alternatively, if results in the present industry are unsatisfactory, and assessments indicate that it is moving into decline then the firm may decide to abandon that arena.

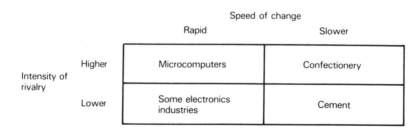

Figure 10.2   *Intensity of rivalry and speed of change*

From this background it can be seen that the firm may be engaged simultaneously in several contests in one or more arenas. Through time, its rivals may change, the rules may change, and the bases of its advantage may change. But the intensity of the rivalry and the speed and degree of change are likely to be highly variable. Industries with rapid change and intense rivalry are the most difficult to deal with, and are littered with casualties (Figure 10.2). Whatever the combination of degree of change and rivalry, there are commonalities in the need for continuing surveillance, for predictions about possible future industry structures and strategies and in the imperative for an unwavering preoccupation with the bases of competitive advantage.

Influences on competitive strategies

Two key elements in any description of the competitive circumstance are industry structure and lifecycle. Within industry structure a central influence on competitive strategies is the composition of the strategic groups and the depiction of dominant and subordinate groups. Stage in the industry lifecycle is relevant because it provides important determinants of the conditions in which firms compete. In addition, there will be the abiding possibility of threats from suppliers, buyers, substitutes and new entrants (Figure 10.3).

Industry lifecycle

A pervading influence will be the stage in the industry lifecycle with its fundamental characteristic of variability in the market growth rate. This affects the competitive orientation of the firm because in the early development phase the emphasis will be on testing and predicting market acceptance, on establishing and extending distribution networks and on developing manufacturing and logistics.

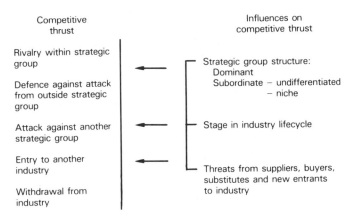

Figure 10.3 *Influences on competitive thrust*

Because there are few competitors there are no strategic groups yet established, but the rate of change in some new industries may be very fast and so there may be early conjectures on the possible future shape of industry structure, and planning about the future bases of competitive advantage and the nature of future mobility barriers.

During the rapid growth stage there could be a rash of new entrants, along with the beginning of strategic group formation as mobility barriers emerge and firms take up competitive postures based on decisions on their sources of advantage. Increasingly, the firm will be threatened by rivalry within its strategic group, threatened by other strategic groups and, depending on the attractiveness of the industry, by additional new entrants. As the industry matures so does the structure of strategic groups.

Apart from the growth, size and structure of the industry the lifecycle can exert other influences on competitive strategies. Market structure may change as new kinds of customer enter and this gives the possibility of segmented strategies, with the consequent decision by the firm about whether it will serve one or several segments. Its projections about future strategic group structures may affect this decision. Does it plan to remain in its present group and, if so, how will others in that group react to a segmented market? Simultaneously the segmentation decision will be constrained by the firm's present competitive position, and projections about the roots of its competitive advantage. It may have taken up a cost or differentiated position and both could be altered radically by the emergence of new customer types. Forecasts about the firm and industry economics may indicate erosion of the present bases of competitive advantage. For example, a heavily segmented market would reduce the possibility of some scale economies, or mute the effects of a singular differentiated position because it now appeals to only a minor segment.

Industry lifecycle will have further influence on the form of competition in that over time the effectiveness of competitive weapons may be sharpened or blunted. Very generally it is thought that price and sales promotional activities have more stress in later stages, that product modifications may impact more in growth, and that differentiation declines in significance late in the lifecycle. Testing and adjusting the marketing mix thus become a continuing activity throughout the lifecycle with the aim of trying to ensure that the sharpest set of weapons is to hand.

Dominant and subordinate strategic groups

There will be a tendency for there to be a dominant group and one or more subordinate groups in an industry, with the dominant group containing the high market share firms. In some industries, like grocery retailing, brewing and confectionery, the dominant group may have an overwhelming share and in others, like clothing, furniture or the distribution of many industrial products, there may be much less concentration. Which group the firm belongs to, its relative dominance, the strategies adopted in that group and the relationship to other groups, all condition appropriate strategic responses. This applies to rivalry within the group as well as to attack and defence of group boundaries.

Within and between group rivalry

Different industries may be characterised as having more or less rivalry within strategic groups, and more or less rivalry between strategic groups. Over time, for the same industry, there may be changes in the pattern of this rivalry: at one time there may be greater within group rivalry, and later there may be greater between group rivalry.

A study of the US pharmaceutical industry over a 20-year period found a shift: within group rivalry was important throughout, but in addition between group rivalry increased significantly later in this period [9]. The industry therefore experienced a much higher level of rivalry overall. This was explained by changing conditions of rivalry, caused by decreasing asymmetry in R&D resources, increases in generics, and new government regulations on testing and marketing. The effect was a substantial reduction in industry profitability.

This potential variability in the brunt and the direction of rivalry adds further complication for the competitive strategist. It reinforces the need to understand the factors which condition the structure of competition, and the need for continuous competitive monitoring. It also underscores the dynamic nature of competition and points to the requirement for the competitive strategy of the organisation to evolve as competitive conditions change. An effective strategy at one time, in one set of circumstances and against one set of rivals, may be far less effective later as the industry moves on.

Rivalry within the strategic group

Dominant groups

Rivals within a leading or dominant group have some common characteristics. Because they are high share firms they necessarily have, or have had, weighty competitive advantages. They probably have wider product ranges, appeal to many market segments and have competed successfully in the past. They have assessed properly the methods for obtaining superiority and adequately matched these to their own strengths.

Bases of the rivalry depend partly on lifecycle stage. In growth there may be emphasis on differentiation, tailoring the product range to cover major market segments and on securing a strong presence in the channels of distribution. In maturity, aggressive pricing and high level promotional spending become principal weapons. Each rival monitors the activities of the others, predicting and preparing to respond. They might engage in spoiling tactics and attempt to destabilise established patterns through, for example, developing product, packaging or service variants. In the consumer market such rivalry is epitomised in detergents, soft drinks, snack products and national newspapers. The insurance and car rental industries also exhibit this type of rivalry, as do telecommunication or aeroplane manufacturers on a worldwide scale.

Subordinate groups

There could be two classes of subordinate competitor: those with a clearly differentiated position and those without any strong competitive advantage. The differentiated firm will have identified a market segment and moulded its capabilities to provide a focused, high order set of benefits to this customer group. Such niche strategies attempt to establish a unique strategic group – of one. In some industries many companies might attempt to follow this strategy. The extent to which they can distance themselves relies on the dimensions chosen for the differentiation, and whether or not viable market segments can be uncovered and nurtured. If firms pursue the same dimensions, then distancing becomes frustrated. Much can depend on the technology. In electronics or pharmaceuticals small, protected niches are tenable, at least until the technology moves on. In the holiday market many of the smaller inclusive tour operators have identified novel market segments to serve.

The undifferentiated competitor could be one among many small-share firms. Rivalry here first requires the proper identification of contenders since not all need be competing with all others. There may be regional concentrations of rivalry, and a small firm may well have a large share in a small region. There may be several firms which take on the trappings of the dominant group, with wider product ranges and widespread distribution. These may be failed members of the dominant group, perhaps with less rigorous quality standards. Key factors

---

Competing for moments of refreshment

Coca-Cola says that its business is in the sale of a moment of refreshment, and that that sale is facilitated by ensuring that its products are universally acceptable, available and affordable.

The carbonated drinks market in Britain is worth about £1,300 million p.a. and has been growing steadily. In all there are almost 100 manufacturers, but two are dominant. Coca-Cola & Schweppes Beverages (CCSB), a joint venture formed in 1987 by Cadbury Schweppes and Coca-Cola, has a 43 per cent share with brands such as Coca-Cola, Sprite, Fanta and Lilt. Britvic, a joint venture between Bass, Allied-Lyons, Whitbread and Pepsico, has a 22 per cent share with brands such as Pepsi-Cola, Tango, R Whites and Corona. Twelve others have shares between 1 per cent and 6 per cent, and the remainder make for local markets.

Thirty to forty new products have been introduced annually, and up to 70 per cent of those have been unsuccessful. Entry to the market is easiest for manufacturers in adjacent markets, such as other soft drinks or alcoholic drinks. Thus Reckitt & Colman introduced carbonated drinks under its Robinsons brand; Bulmers franchised the Orangina brand; Taunton Cider has launched Piermont, and Grand Metropolitan Aqua Libra. The advertising/sales ratio in the industry is about 4 per cent, compared with 8 per cent for bottled water and 1.3 per cent for lager.

Gaining distribution is vital. About 80 per cent of carbonated drinks are sold by 'take-home' outlets and 20 per cent by leisure outlets such as pubs. CCSB and Britvic have a very high proportion of the trade in leisure outlets, including a number of exclusive supply arrangements.

Source: *Carbonated Drinks*. Monopolies and Mergers Commission, 1991.

determining the direction and intensity of the rivalry will be the aspirations of the owners and managers, and the level of commitment to the industry. Aspiring firms with commitment will be anxious to demonstrate this through ambitious, aggressive plans. However, these plans may rely entirely on extra effort being expended in head-on confrontations, since from the customer's viewpoint there would be little to choose between the rivals. Some other firms may be content with their position and concentrate on defence.

Defence against attack

Dominant defenders

Defence usually implies raising the mobility barriers, which may mean significantly increased marketing expenditures. Product lines may be filled out and new services added in order to establish a level of customer expectation which others would find difficult to satisfy without massive spending. Geographic coverage, and coverage of market segments, may be extended into less attractive areas to preclude easy access to the industry. Special inducements may be offered to distributors, perhaps with exclusive distribution rights, to secure the continued loyalty of the best. There may be forward integration to keep the attacker out. There may be attention to buyer behaviour with a search for methods of reinforcing their loyalty. Dedicated customer support facilities may be installed at customer locations, such as microfilming, computing and communications equipment, which would increase the cost of competitive moves. To forestall attack there may also be a policy of continuous product modification and enhancement, requiring sophisticated technical and marketing research.

Deliberate attacks may also have been made by the dominant defenders on a subordinate strategic group, as a by-product of raising the mobility barriers and as an indicator of how seriously they would retaliate. Often this defence would be by a single firm. Sometimes it could be by more or less concerted action, possibly through a trade association if the attacker was from outside the industry, and especially if it was from outside the country.

Not all attacks will be from companies aspiring to belong to the dominant group. Competitive threats can arise from technological change and change in customer needs. In computing the industry has been dominated by a few hardware manufacturers, but the burgeoning market requirement for open architecture and system integration (of rival mainframes through software) has brought leading software houses into powerful positions. The competitive rules have been changing and the dominant firms have had to invoke defensive strategies. In some cases joint venture companies have been established between manufacturers and software specialists, when manufacturers have realised they cannot hold out against the trend. The dominant group survives by adjusting to changes in the technology and the market, perhaps after having attempted to shape these.

The level and type of reaction might hinge on lifecycle stage. Full-blooded defence may be occasioned in late growth and early maturity when profit prospects are at their highest. In earlier stages the strategic group, and the mobility barriers, would not be fully formed. Barriers would none the less be in a formative stage and ambitious firms would already be anticipating future industry structure and would be keen to keep open future options in competitive position. In later stages attacks would test seriously the firm's resolve to remain in the industry, and to commit resources to shoring up the barriers.

Subordinate defenders

Undifferentiated small-share companies are vulnerable: they may offer little resistance to attack. It might be possible for them to imitate some of the dominant defenders' defensive ploys, if they had the funds and the competence. If they are independently owned, this may not be forthcoming, and if they are subsidiaries of large enterprises, their place in the parent portfolio may not justify expensive defence. They might attempt to find a more defensible position by pulling back into one region.

Niche strategists would probably be stout defenders and their first line of defence would be to emphasise the basics of their competitive superiority. Assuming the firm had not become complacent, then it would have been giving continued attention to the enhancement of its special expertise and reputation. Under attack it might raise PR and promotional activity and monitor extensively attitudes in its distribution channels to pick up any wavering. New product and service innovations may be brought forward. If the niche strategy is supported by a local or regional dominance, it can lead to a very strong position, in which case the attitude of the owners becomes the vital variable in conditioning the strength of the defence. Some service industries, such as hotels, accounting and legal services, show some of these characteristics.

Attacking strategies

Dominant attackers

Dominant firms in the industry would have considerable power in attacking undifferentiated small firms. The lines of attack would be along the bases of competitive advantage and against the mobility barriers. However, both may limit the attack. The dominant firm's advantage may be built on delivering a high quality; the small firm may satisfy less demanding customers. The dominant firm may reap scale economies from mass production; the small firm may have devised ways of handling batches relatively economically.

Retailing offers many examples of dominant firms successfully attacking small firms. The well-known developments in groceries, clothing, DIY and consumer electrical products are being extended into fields such as jewellery retailing.

Attacks on niche firms would need careful planning due to their established competitive edge. They might be vulnerable if the attack was based on some innovation in the technology. They may also be vulnerable if there was a fundamental change in the product/service bundle offered to customers, which was difficult to emulate and which customers thought valuable. This might mean 'unbundling' by breaking down a comprehensive product/service into components, with potential economies or superior performance from this concentration. Opposing that, there might be 'bundling' with a consolidation of products and services in order to provide single-point solutions to customer problems.

Motives for attacks by dominant firms may relate to industry structure and to lifecycle stage. The firm may feel there is the need for higher volume to obtain more scale economies and that this is easiest to build outside its strategic group. In late growth some industries experience substantial restructuring with a shake-out of marginal firms and a spate of mergers and acquisitions, helping to shape the structure of strategic groups in maturity. In this turbulence, dominant firms may attack smaller firms in the scramble to maintain membership of the dominant group by building market share.

Subordinate attackers

Small firms would usually find it impossible to launch credible direct attacks on a dominant strategic group. Certainly that applies if it were to be on a wide front. An exception would be the small competitor which was a subsidiary of a multinational and which was being used as the vehicle for expansion in the industry. More credible assaults would be on a small front and would best be pursued by niche firms, or by those which have accurately redefined customer needs and supply extra product features or services. Head-on competition between a minor and a major normally has but one result.

Astute subordinates can sometimes catch a major firm off guard. Gradual, hardly noticeable incursions during industry growth may be overlooked, especially if there are numerous small firms. The establishment of a dominant regional position can also be the bastion for national contention, as in snack products or newspapers. Some time ago the banking industry showed this feature and today it is apparent in some professional services.

Entry strategies

Timing the entry into an industry is complicated because some potentially unsatisfactory consequences may be largely out of the control of the firm. If entry is too early, there may be many unproductive years spent cultivating an unresponsive market, or there may have been assumptions that a substantial market could be developed which subsequent experience proved invalid. If entry is too late, then it may be very costly to make any impression against established firms. Such risks demand cool assessments of potential trends in industry lifecycle and structure and rigorous attention to the sources of competitive advantage [10].

Broadly, the firm may choose to be:

1. A pioneer – being an initiator of the industry.

2. A fast follower – entering in the development phase of the industry.

3. A late entrant – entering in rapid or late growth, or even in maturity.

Pioneers

Frequently, though not always, firms who eventually belong to the dominant strategic group in a mature industry originally entered as pioneers. Successful pioneering can lead to enviable long-term positions, deriving from two sources. First, pioneers can take positional advantage because of the open field. They may be able to manipulate some of the dimensions along which advantage will be gained, such as in influencing the criteria that customers use in their evaluations of rival offers. Second, pioneers can make an early start on erecting mobility barriers, thus contributing to the shaping of future industry structure.

Quality leadership may be a prime positional advantage accruing to the pioneer because, as Buzzell and Gale put it [11]:

> The products or services developed by a pioneering entrant frequently set the standard for later entrants and thereby achieve a leading quality position among customers – at least, until a new and better concept is developed.

This quality leadership can be generalised so that the firm becomes acknowledged as the first and the best, and this has other spin-offs as suppliers and distributors may clamour to become associated with this reputation. The pioneer then has first choice among these and would choose those that were superior. This would enhance further the quality image as the product is seen only in the best outlets and can boast the best materials and components.

Day [12] points to other advantages. The pioneer may elect to serve the largest market segments, leaving less desirable ones for later entrants. Customer loyalty to the first supplier in the market may be based on high switching costs, such as in the supply of electronic components where a customer's product may be designed around that of a supplier. The pioneer also gains early manufacturing experience which may contribute early cost reduction. Finally, the pioneer may be able to build a sustainable lead in the technology, which would be all the more powerful if it attracted patent protection. Davidson shows the advantages accruing to pioneers in British grocery markets. In his study of twenty-one markets the pioneer was only displaced by a competitor in seven cases [13].

Longer-term advantage might flow from the pioneer's ability to make early moves on the construction of mobility barriers. Some of these derive from the positional advantages noted above, and they imply that a potential competitor would need to make a substantial, high-risk investment in order to emulate the strategies. The more substantial the investment required, and the higher the risk, then the more effective the barrier.

Fast followers

Entry after the pioneer, but while the industry is still in a formative stage, has the advantage of the demonstration that a market exists, and an exemplar of the kind of product that appeals and the kinds of marketing strategy that have been tried. Rapid learning could mould effective differentiation and this may be allied to improved product design. There may also be the possibility of distinctive distribution strategies. The pioneer may have entered on a very small scale with extremely limited distribution outlets. The fast follower might have the confidence to plan for a much larger market becoming available and develop a substantial distribution network from the outset. This is complicated if the product of the new industry uses some of the same distribution channels as those of an established industry. In that case the feasibility of a distinctive distribution strategy relates to whether the pioneer or the fast follower belongs to the established industry.

Following with little distinctive advantage may mean that the firm will be relegated to a subordinate strategic group. If several firms enter at the same time after a pioneer then market share would go to those with superior products and strategies. The me-too firm would be destined to be an undifferentiated subordinate, with the associated vulnerability.

Late entry

Despite the inherent difficulties in coming late to an industry it may sometimes be considered. Entry in maturity would pose problems but may be warranted if projections indicated a long lifecycle. Such an entry would have to be undertaken seriously: firms in the industry would have a history of cost reductions and solid competitive advantage. An acquisition of a firm in the industry may be a route in, and the risks would be reduced if the entrant could offer a very positive product improvement, possibly extending the market opportunities, leading to an extension of the industry lifecycle.

Exit strategies

In declining industries, firms have to decide whether to withdraw sooner or later. Some firms may be able to ride the decline down and remain profitable as demand settles to some fraction of its peak in maturity. It would probably only be dominant and niche firms that survived into this lifecycle phase.

Strategic group structure may begin to disintegrate, although one or more reformed strategic groups may emerge in this new competitive circumstance, depending on how long the industry is likely to exist once it has entered decline. One of the ways of distinguishing these groups may be their motives for staying on, and whether they are voluntary or involuntary survivors. There may be some involuntary survivors: those tied in by the high cost of exit. This may be due to inflexible manufacturing systems, to contractual obligations or to the potential damage to the firm's reputation among customers or suppliers in other industries in which it is engaged. On the other hand, there may be some who promote actively their position as a survivor, declaring their commitment in the anticipation of attracting the remaining customers, and capitalising on the realignment in distribution channels as the industry shrinks. Dominant influences on these possibilities would be the rate of the decline of the industry and the reasons underlying the demise.

Slow withdrawal may be accompanied by a harvesting strategy which would centre on cost reduction, a minimum or maintenance level of promotion and little or no new investment.

Co-operative strategies

Co-operating can be as rewarding as competing. In extreme this could lead to collusion and cartels, and so to attention from regulatory bodies. But there are many other forms of co-operative activity.

At an industry level trade associations may act on behalf of companies in the industry. This may be to lobby government to shape favourable legislation, for example on the detailed definition of foodstuffs falling within the ambit of a piece of legislation. It may be to make representations about taxation, or about what the industry may see as unfair dumping by foreign suppliers, for example to maintain the 20 per cent tariff on Japanese photocopiers entering EU countries. It may be to establish and maintain standards on product or service performance, in order to achieve higher credibility among customers, or to build entry barriers. Examples are in house building and in travel and tourism.

Manufacturers in the same industry may also forge alliances with competitors to share knowledge and expertise. In computers IBM have linked with Apple, after a history of fierce rivalry. And in electronics more generally there have been widespread linkages. In Europe Philips has strategic alliances with five other electronics firms; Siemens is linked with IBM and Toshiba; SGS Thomson with Canon and GEC; Olivetti with Digital and two others. A prime motivation has been to share the huge costs of research, but in some cases there has also been rationalisation of production [14]. Co-operative agreements have been described as aiming to [15]:

> Develop market share.
> Gain access to new markets.
> Acquire new technologies.
> Diversify production.
> Obtain economies of scale.
> Reduce costs, time, risks.
> Rationalise the portfolio.
> Make the firm's technology profitable.

A different view of co-operative activity is seen in the case of Benetton [16].

They co-operate extensively with their suppliers and their distributors. Most of their manufacturing is taken care of by 400 subcontractors working exclusively for them. All materials requirements planning and production planning for this entire network are undertaken by Benetton. Most of their shops are owner-managed – again adhering to strict rules. Benetton see themselves as at the hub of a large, integrated network of suppliers and buyers.

Summary

The objectives of competitive strategies are to build and sustain competitive advantage. This may be based on two broad types of positional advantage – low cost and differentiation – which provide the general thrust in the establishment of a competitive edge. Industry monitoring attempts to reveal the structure and strategies apparent in the industry, and these define key elements of the competitive context.

A wide range of options is open to the firm in deciding the types of competitive strategy it will employ. The arena in which the firm competes is shaped by its strategic group membership in an industry structure. It will be competing with its direct rivals and at the same time may be defending against attacks from outside its group, and deploying attacks against other groups. Strategic group structure, with the possibility of there being dominant and subordinate groups, and stage in industry lifecycle influence the appropriateness of strategies. Threats from outside the industry can also influence competitive behaviour.

If the results from the contests in the current industry are disappointing the firm may contemplate broadening its product-market scope by finding a more attractive industry. Options in entry strategies cover pioneering or fast following. In later lifecycle stages consideration may have to be given to exit strategies.

Questions for review and discussion

1. Is it lack of competitive advantage which relegates many companies to holding small shares of the market?

2. The package holiday tour industry contains a wide range of companies. There are a few with high market shares, some generalists with lesser market shares, and various collections of firms specialising in particular countries, in particular age groups or activities, or in type of accommodation (e.g. villas or caravans).
    (a) Illustrate the kinds of competitive strategy adopted by these firms.
    (b) What is the apparent competitive advantage of these different types of firm and what is the nature of the mobility barriers?

(c) Consider the differences in how these various companies might deal with threats from suppliers, buyers, substitutes or new entrants.
(d) What stage in industry lifecycle would you say applied? Are there parts of this industry in different stages? How does stage in lifecycle affect competitive strategies in this industry?
(e) Assume a totally new concept in holidays was developed – perhaps related to some new activities, or related to some easy and very flexible kind of bundling or unbundling of the package/destinations, or to do with new types of accommodation or service. What factors should be borne in mind in the decision to enter this new market, whether to enter early or later, and would this vary for the different types of firm?

3. Now repeat questions (a) to (e) above for an industry of which you have knowledge. If you have no specific industry knowledge then apply the ideas to the car industry, newspapers, estate agencies, retailing or computer manufacturers. How much difference does the industry context make?

References

1. Day, G.S. and Wensley, R. 1988. 'Assessing advantage: a framework for diagnosing competitive superiority', *Journal of Marketing*, vol. 52, April.
2. Davidson, H. 1987. *Offensive Marketing*, 2nd edn. Harmondsworth: Penguin Books.
3. Caves, R.E. and Ghemawat, P. 1992. 'Identifying mobility barriers', *Strategic Management Journal*, vol. 13, pp. 1–12.
4. Hooley, G.J. and Saunders, J. 1993. *Competitive Positioning*. Hemel Hempstead: Prentice Hall, p. 125.
5. Fuld, L.M. 1988. *Monitoring the Competition*. New York: John Wiley, ch. 5.
6. McBurnie, T. and Clutterbuck, D. 1988. *The Marketing Edge*. Harmondsworth: Penguin Books, p. 140.
7. Saunders, J. 1987. 'Marketing and competitive success', in Baker, M.J. (ed.), *The Marketing Book*. London: Heinemann, ch. 2.
8. Barrie, B.J. 1988. 'Marketing: in search of a competitive role model', *Journal of Marketing Management*, vol. 4, no. 1.
9. Cool, K. and Dierickx, I. 1993. 'Rivalry, strategic groups and firm profitability', *Strategic Management Journal*, vol. 14, pp. 47–59.
10. See Kerakaya, F. and Stahl, M. 1991. *Entry Barriers and Market Entry Decisions*. New York: Quorum Books, ch. 2.
11. Buzzell, R.D. and Gale, B.T. 1987. *The PIMS Principles*. New York: Free Press, p. 183.
12. Day, G.S. 1986. *Analysis for Strategic Market Decisions*. St Paul, Minn.: West, p. 183.
13. Davidson, H. op. cit., p. 238.
14. Nakamoto, M. 1992. 'Plugging into each other's strengths', *Financial Times*, 27 March.
15. Urban, S. and Vendemini, S. 1992. *European Strategic Alliances*. Oxford: Basil Blackwell, p. 142.
16. Jarillo, J.C. and Stevenson, H.H. 1991. 'Co-operative strategies – the payoffs and the pitfalls', *Long Range Planning*, vol. 24, no. 1.

Chapter 11

Marketing planning and implementation

Strategic marketing planning leads to operational marketing planning. The difference between the two is in terms of the planning horizon and the organisational level involved. Strategic marketing plans may be for a five-year period, updated annually and involve the senior marketing executive in the organisation. Operational marketing plans may be for a one-year period and involve executives responsible for each major activity within the overall marketing function. Operational plans demonstrate the detailed ways of achieving strategic plans.

Five purposes explaining the function of the operational marketing plan have been identified by Luck and Ferrell [1]. They are:

1. To explain the marketing situation now and that expected in the plan period.
2. To specify the results expected so that the organisation can anticipate what its situation will be at the end of the period.
3. To identify the resources needed to carry out the planned actions.
4. To describe the actions that are to take place so that responsibility for implementation can be assigned.
5. To permit monitoring of the ensuing actions and results.

This chapter examines ways of fulfilling these purposes by considering key issues in developing and implementing marketing plans.

Planning marketing operations

The strategic trinity of environment–goals–strategy was introduced in Chapter 9 and can be used here to show the hierarchy of relationships between goals, strategies and plans. This turns on the strategies at one organisational level becoming the goals for the next level, as shown below:

Organisational level

Corporate	environment–goals–strategy
Marketing division	environment–goals–strategy
Marketing operations	environment–goals–plans

Environmental factors impinge at all levels. Forecasts about the national economy, for example, would impact right down the organisation, as would some step change in the competitive circumstances. Similarly, internal factors such as audits and reviews of the sources of competitive advantage would be influential in planning at all levels. There will be other environmental issues which intrude only at some levels, or their intrusion has a different stress. Examples might be in changes to mobility barriers and to cost structures. Mobility barriers in the industry may be crumbling and this would be taken as a paramount strategic issue, although its import in the next year may be minimal and operational planning little affected. Internally, cost structures may be changing, resulting from increased volume and experience, but strategic decisions may have been taken that preclude this having effect at the operational level.

It was implied above that marketing strategy supplies operational marketing goals. That relationship needs elucidation. Suppose a company had decided that the four main planks of its marketing strategy were:

1. Maintain market share within its strategic group (assume it is in the dominant group).

2. Defend against expected attack from own-label suppliers.

3. Attack several small regional companies and so increase market share in those regions.

4. Initiate product development to bring an improved range on-stream in order to counter competitive product launches that are expected.

Thorough reviews of positional advantage had been undertaken in developing the strategy and no fundamental departure from current positioning is envisaged. A radical change in the competitive circumstance would have thrown that into question, but even in the attack from own-label suppliers it has been decided to reinforce the present positioning.

If numbers and times were to be introduced into the four strategy statements they could be read as goals for an annual marketing plan. These goals would specify what would need to be achieved in the coming year in order for the longer-run strategy to be accomplished. So the marketing goals for next year could be:

1. Maintain 30 per cent share in strategic group, with projected 5 per cent real growth in total sales of that group; product line unchanged.

2. Prevent own-label companies increasing their share of industry sales from present 15 per cent by strengthening consumer attitudes and building on trade channel loyalty.

3. Increase market share in regions A and B from 20 to 30 per cent by targeting customers of competitors X and Y.

4. Improved product range ready to go into test marketing early in following year with initial marketing research complete.

Multiplying through by the relevant volumes would give the revenue goals, and applying established cost ratios would give a profit goal and so a profitability goal. However, that is too orderly and sequential. There would have been many iterations of this process. The cost and profit implications of each line of strategy would have been teased out, perhaps found wanting and adjustments made to the goals or the strategy. For example the greater penetration of regions A and B may originally have been set at 35 per cent. It may have been judged that, apart from other activities, that would need five more salespeople in each region, and with the lead-time in recruitment and training they would not be available until the second half year. Three extra could be available in each region from the second quarter by internal transfers, and the full five available from the second half. That more realistic level of salesforce activity is judged as being able to contribute towards a market share of 30 per cent in those regions. The revenue and cost implications are recast and found to be acceptable within the overall revenue and cost goals for the planned period, and so marketing goal 3 is established as an achievable target. The same testing and retesting would proceed for all the goals with the aim of twinning relevance and practicality. Fine-sounding strategy founders if it imposes impractical annual marketing goals.

Line marketing managers are involved heavily in explicating the annual marketing goals. In the example above, it would have been a sales manager's judgements that were most influential in getting the regional share goals down from 35 to 30 per cent. This would need to be within the context of checks and balances because some managers might otherwise seek to influence the formation of a goal related to their activity in a way prejudicial to other goals. The sales manager might have acceded to the 35 per cent regional goal if sales promotional spend in those regions was trebled, but that might reduce the spend available to fight the own-labels. Or a manager might seek to influence the establishment of goals which could be attained easily. So that in the regional case the goal is set at 25 per cent with the same level of extra sales personnel as was shown that would be needed for 30 per cent.

This involvement of line managers also points to another characteristic which may be evident in the planning process: the interaction of top-down and bottom-up planning. With bottom-up planning the broad functional or corporate plan is the result of an amalgamation of lower level plans with little central direction. In top-down planning a lower level plan is a direct output of a higher level plan. Often, marketing planning is a product of both perspectives, although company practice may tend more to one than the other. The implication is that plans may be traced while goals are still being formed, because of the top-down/bottom-up interaction and because of the many iterations of the process. In the examples above it was clear that the activity and resource implications of any one goal were being examined, by the manager responsible for implementation, before the goal was finally set.

Astute line managers may anticipate implementation problems, uncover inconsistencies and potential bottlenecks at the same time as they trace the activity implications of the tentative goals. Part of this might involve opening discussions with managers of related activities that can affect how easily the plan is accomplished. It may also entail early negotiation with subordinate managers to identify possible difficulties in meeting targets. During the planning process managers are therefore active in the following:

1. Influencing the goals to be set for their activity.

2. Tracing outline plans to achieve the goals.

3. Anticipating implementation problems.

4. Negotiating with managers of related activities and with subordinate managers.

Such a listing is indicative of some of the skills needed by successful marketing managers. Strong analytical abilities are necessary but insufficient. High-level communication skills, negotiating skills and adept personal influence strategies are all required for effective participation in the planning process. This fits in with the recent research evidence on marketing strategy formation in organisations, which emphasises a process, rather than content, view of marketing decision-making. Hutt et al. [2] used communication network analysis in tracing emergent patterns in the evolution of marketing decisions in an electronics company and comment that:

> Strategic processes are seen not as a linear progression from strategy formulation to strategy implementation, but as multilevel processes where the outcomes of decisions are shaped by the interests and commitments of individuals and groups, the forces of organizational momentum, important changes in the environment, and the manipulation of the structural context surrounding decisions.

The integrated marketing plan

Once the annual marketing goals are set then more detailed planning of the marketing mix can proceed. In fact, as indicated, some of the details may have been anticipated and possible directions for particular activities already shaped. In some areas it may also be that a large part of the plan is a continuation of last year's activities, so that planning does not commence with a blank sheet of paper or a blank computer disk.

Each goal is likely to require several different activities for its attainment, as in the maintenance of market share goal in the example, which would need the deployment of all marketing activities. There is thus the necessity for an integration of effort in order to:

1. Take advantage of possible synergy.
2. Ensure consistency.
3. Anticipate mutual dependency.
4. Co-ordinate timing.

Possible effects of synergy might emerge as one activity, like advertising, prepares the ground or reinforces the effect of another, like the salesforce. Integrated planning of the mix is also a prerequisite of assured consistency, so that the efforts in one activity to develop product positioning are not frustrated by other activities. A premium price would be consistent with a high quality image and the use of exclusive distributors, but the plan would be totally undermined if the product employed inferior materials. Disparate efforts also need to be integrated if they are mutually dependent. Some sales promotional activities rely entirely on the salesforce for their effect; a new product launch relies on adequate marketing research and a price plan needs the full co-operation of field sales. Finally, integration is essential in co-ordinating the timing of marketing efforts. A promotional plan may stipulate a start date of early March. Advertising to the trade may run in February, the salesforce ready to sell in during that time and a coupon drop to consumers arranged for the first week of March. The effect of all that would be reduced if a planned major national television campaign, supporting the promotion, could not be booked to run in the weeks and in the slots needed to deliver the message to the target segment.

Plans need be detailed for each marketing goal, and the overall set of plans for any one activity would comprise the summation of its plans for each of those goals. Resource allocation would follow, indicating the disposition against each of the goals (Table 11.1).

The overall marketing plan would need to be refined into plans for each marketing activity, such as those listed in the table. These would show in detail how that activity was to contribute to the marketing goals, when particular tasks were required to be effected and by whom. For instance, the bulk of the advertising plan would cover the tasks needed to maintain the 30 per cent market share. This might involve targets for consumer awareness levels of the main company brands and for the reinforcement of consumer perceptions of particular brand claims. Preliminary discussions would probably already have been held with advertising agents to outline the creative strategy. Judgements would show the number of advertising impressions needed to deliver those targets, and product usage and media data supply information to derive a media schedule to reach the target customer groups. Timing might reflect practice in recent years, as influenced by seasonal considerations and

Table 11.1 *Marketing goals and plans*

Goal	Sales calls 000s	Advertising £000	Consumer promotions £000	Trade promotions £000	Marketing research £000
1. Maintain 30% market share	100	3,000	1,000	200	100
2. Defend against own-labels	10	1,000	200	0	10
3. Regional attacks	5	100	100	50	5
4. Improve product range	0	0	0	0	100
Total	115	4,100	1,300	250	215

competitive activity, and the need to co-ordinate advertising with other sales promotional plans.

Increasingly, other dimensions are being added to the way the overall marketing plan is specified. It may not be sufficient just to have plans for each of the main marketing activities. There may be cross-cuts to derive plans by products, market segments or marketing channels. If the company has product or brand managers then product plans would feature significantly. These would show how each product or each product group was going to assist in the achievement of the marketing goals, along with its share of the resources devoted to each of the marketing activities. If the company had trade marketing managers there would probably be a trade marketing plan, this time detailing activity by the channels for which they are responsible. Breaking plans down along these dimensions can be very revealing, and at the same time possibly confusing. A great deal depends on the clarity of the definition of these managers' roles and their relative status within the organisation. A product plan is looking at promotional activity across all channels for a group of products, and a trade marketing plan is looking at promotional activity for all product groups just in trade channels. For part of the time they are both looking at the same activity, and there is additionally an activity manager (such as a sales manager) responsible for planning that activity across all products and all channels. In these circumstances the potential for confusion is high, with the corollary that great attention needs to be given to co-ordination and role clarity for the planning to be effective.

Important constraints on the way the overall marketing plan is to be broken down are the organisational structure and the information system. Plans are meant to crystallise who does what and when, and with what resources, and to determine who is responsible for making sure it happens. It would be logical for this to mirror the organisational structure. In the same way, the information system should be tied to the organisational structure, since the information system feeds decision-making, and decisions are implemented through the organisational structure. A straightforward, functionally-based marketing organisation might just have functional (activity) plans. More complex organisational forms might superimpose other types of plan, such as by product or channel. A limitation on the efficacy of a complex of plans would be the kinds of information available. A trade marketing plan would lack credibility, as well as being difficult or impossible to implement, if basic data on marketing channels were not routinely available. This would include cost as well as market data. Some companies have ready access to such market data, perhaps bought in from a market research firm, but may not have cost data analysed by marketing channels. Their plans might then stress volume goals because profitability cannot be derived. In other cases, potentially useful ways of specifying the overall plan, such as by market segment, may be infeasible because little relevant information is available regularly.

Sales response functions

Plans are built on judgements and marketing plans require judgements about the potential effect of various levels of effort in the activities being planned. Some examples were seen in the past few pages. Ultimately it is the sales response to various levels of effort which most interests marketing managers. Sometimes, because of the tenuous relationship between a particular marketing effort and sales response, an intervening variable is employed, which it is assumed links the two. The judgement then centres on the response of that variable to changes in the marketing effort. In advertising, the intervening variable could be brand awareness or attitudes, and the judgement is about how much advertising is needed to change awareness or attitudes. Very often, though, no such intervening relationships are considered: despite the difficulties, or because of them, managers judge how much effort will result in how many sales. Explicitly, or implicitly, they employ a sales response function.

The choice of marketing instrument, or mix of instruments, which is to be applied in order to reach the goal is contingent upon the potentiality of the instrument and, more pertinently, how much the firm knows about that potential. Variations in the balance of the mix, and in the levels of effort on each mix component, will have different impact on sales and profits, and so some knowledge of the sales response to the mix elements is a necessary foundation for marketing planning.

Sales response functions describe the relationship between sales and one or more marketing variables. A demand curve is one particular form, which describes the relationship between amount demanded (sales) and alternative price levels. Other examples might relate sales to various sizes of salesforce or advertising appropriation, or to combinations of several marketing variables. The usefulness of such studies will plainly depend on the validity of the assumed relationship, which in turn depends on how it is conceived and specified.

Estimating and employing sales response functions are a blend of analysis and intuition. Analysis alone would be sterile, and frequently erroneous, since the methodology requires objective data which sometimes do not exist (although in

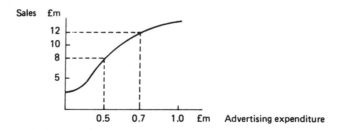

Figure 11.1   *Single variable sales response function*

some cases, e.g. direct response marketing, very reasonable data may be available). Intuition alone can be equally misleading because the basic parameters are unspecified and this may lead to unproductive debate or the acceptance of dogma. The logical, problem-solving approach is to leaven analysis with intuition in a structured manner.

A general supposition is that a single variable sales response function takes a form similar to that shown in Figure 11.1. With no advertising some sales may be made; with a little advertising some increase would be anticipated, and successive increments to advertising could have a more than proportional effect, until the sales response once more begins to weaken. In the figure an increase in advertising from £0.5 million to £0.7 million (+40%) leads to a sales increase of 12/8, or +50%. The response coefficient over these ranges is therefore 1.25 (50/40). At lower and higher levels of advertising the coefficient tends to be inelastic.

Decisions often relate to changes in not one, but several, marketing variables, and so some estimate is required of the multiple sales response function. Kotler's approach provides the classic framework for this estimation.

With more than one independent variable (in this case element of the mix) there are two main problems: first, the possible sales levels with each variable acting independently; and, second, the possibility that the variables may interact and the resulting synergy produce a more marked effect. The latter point is illustrated in the situation where the advertising response coefficient might be 0.2 (e.g. a 10 per cent increase in advertising leads to a 2 per cent sales increase) and the coefficient for the response to saleforce effort was 0.5. But, taken together, the sales increase might reflect a combined coefficient of 1.0, the extra 0.3 perhaps being caused by the fact that the sales force received a better reception because of the increased advertising.

An example, taken from Kotler, of a sales response function with two marketing mix variables is shown in Figure 11.2. There advertising spending of A_1 and selling expenditure of D_1 combine to produce sales of Q_1. The higher expenditure of A_3 and D_3 produce Q_3. The extent to which any systematic relationship existed between these variables could be estimated by multiple regression analysis.

An interesting interaction between mix elements is that of advertising and price. It may be supposed that higher advertising reduces price elasticity, by creating stronger differentiation, but Lilien and Kotler [3] are unconvinced:

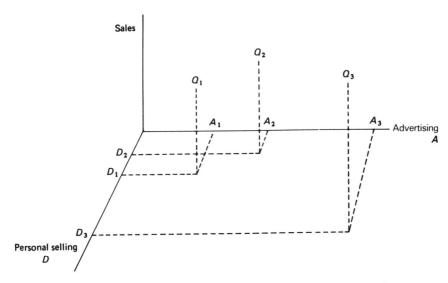

Source: P. Kotler, *Marketing Management Analysis Planning and Control*,
8th edn, Englewood Cliffs, NJ: Prentice Hall, Inc. 1994, p. 118.

Figure 11.2 *Multiple sales response function*

many practitioners believe that advertising reduces price elasticity and also that advertising is more effective at higher prices. However, empirical evidence does not support this view. It seems that the specific structure of the market studied, as well as the nature of the advertising (medium, message) may affect the sign and the magnitude of the interaction.

Response elasticities may not only vary due to interactions between mix elements, they may also vary over time and possibly between market segments. In reviewing research in this area Parsons found some evidence of advertising elasticities falling through the product lifecycle, and for price elasticity to reach a minimum in maturity [4].

In both the single and multiple variable examples the abiding problem is the sales revenue estimation. A starting point would be the analysis of historical data. Indeed, both of the examples could have been based on that. This might be enriched by experimental data, for instance from test markets, and by the use of direct analogies – such as company experience with similar products. However, it is likely that insufficient data are available and so expert judgement must be employed, which on the face of it may appear to make the whole exercise highly impressionistic and subjective. As Luck and Ferrell [5] say:

> But marketing management, you might well protest, rarely has accurate data on each variable's effects on sales volume; and even when it does, those data tend to be limited to a handful of observations or a narrow range of intensity – or to relate

to other products or market situations than one particular one being faced. Granting this, it is desirable to employ a market-response formula, even if all the ratios used are intuitive and the basic market size in substantial doubt. Any decision maker who determines the amount of marketing expenditures of effort for any product, function or firm can do so rationally only with implicit assumptions of such relationships. The use of a formula and actual calculations forces the decision-maker to explicate her or his calculations and thus realise how the decision is being reached and with what assumed values.

That the output from such analysis will be somewhat less than perfect is partly because many variables will not have been taken into account. Concentration on sales response functions implies the assumption that variations in our sales are mainly a function of our efforts. This may not be the case, as demonstrated by Fitzroy's general model of market response which takes the form [6]:

$$S_t = f_t(X_t, C_t, E_t, S_{t-1}) + e_t$$

where:

S_t = sales of the product in period t
X_t = marketing mix variables in time t
C_t = competitors' strategies in time t
E_t = environmental variables in time t (e.g. population)
$S_t - 1$ = sales in period $t - 1$ representing the effect of past marketing, competitive and environment factors
e_t = error term

This shows that there are substantial variables outside the control of the marketing manager, and particularly the competitors' strategies and the environmental variables. In some circumstances these may account for much more of the variation in a company's sales than any of the changes it makes to its own efforts, and may considerably frustrate the search for the definition of sales response functions. Recognition of the extent of what is uncontrollable, yet germane to goal accomplishment, is an important aspect of goal setting. On one level it defines the manager's latitude in achieving the goal and on another level it directs analysis and research into factors affecting market performance.

Empirical studies of marketing planning practice

Surveys and empirical studies on British marketing practice have been reported by Doyle [7], Greenley [8], Hooley *et al.* [9] and by Leppard and McDonald [10]. Generally, they find that between a half and three-quarters of firms surveyed undertake some form of marketing planning – meaning a quarter to a half do no marketing planning. Greenley assessed that only in a tenth to a fifth of the cases was the planning comprehensive, and in Doyle's and Hooley's samples only a half undertook annual planning within the context of longer-run strategic plans.

Interpretations of such figures obviously start with a value judgement, and in this case it is no surprise that marketing academics take the view that higher is better. Support for such a judgement comes from another survey of over a thousand companies by Lynch *et al.* [11]. They found that two-thirds had at least annual marketing plans, which is within the range of the other surveys. This survey also compared 'better performers', defined on a range of financial and market-based measures, with other companies and found a significant difference in that the successful companies were much more inclined to undertake formal, longer-term marketing planning.

Several factors seem to be important in determining a company's attitude to marketing planning. Doyle and Leppard and McDonald point to the role of the chief executive and the company culture. The chief executive must understand, and actively support and promote, a marketing planning system for it to stand much chance of success. This might express itself in the extent to which short-run financial goals are emphasised, as against longer-run market position. The latter presupposes systematic strategic marketing planning. Similarly, the company culture, its management style and values, needs to be sympathetic to planning. In addition Leppard and McDonald place importance on the stage of development of the organisation. They trace five phases in this development with marketing planning taking a different role in each. In the first phase of evolution there is little evidence of planning. In the second phase marketing planning is directed by the senior executive. This gives way to a phase of delegation, with an emphasis upon bottom-up planning. In the fourth phase a more co-ordinated approach is taken and:

> In many ways, the marketing planning processes which are the stuff of textbooks and the like appear to be most suited for a company at this stage of its development. However . . . it is possible for the planning process to degenerate from essentially a problem-solving process into a meaningless, bureaucratic ritual. [12]

The fifth phase might be one which overcomes any bureaucratic tendencies and combines effectively creativity with expediency.

Implementing marketing plans

Planning is futile if nothing actually happens. For their accomplishment, plans require that numerous people undertake a wide range of actions in a controlled and co-ordinated manner. This section considers the process and the problems of this implementation.

The implementation process

Budgets for costs, efforts and outputs provide targets for the programme of implementation and are directly derived from the plans. The process determining the extent to which these targets are achieved in the execution of the plans has been explained by Greenley [13] within a framework of five components:

Delegation
Participation
Motivation
Leadership
Integration

All five have significance in planning as well as in implementation because the way each element is treated in the process of planning conditions the effects of each during implementation. The very process of planning sets up expectations about implementation: about the activities required and, crucially, about the management style. Participative management styles are frequently advocated as a means of securing commitment in the execution of plans. Problems can occur if there is a mismatch between the planning and implementation styles; if there is, for instance, little delegation and participation in planning followed by the inevitable delegation in implementation.

Where aspects of planning have been delegated to particular managers, other than 'planning' managers, it is consistent that the associated implementation should be delegated in the same way. An activity manager therefore assists in drawing up the plans for his activity and then becomes responsible for their successful implementation. Greenley sees potential difficulty, though, in the demarcation of authority if the firm has product managers, marketing planners and marketing services managers working in tandem with activity managers. This emphasises the point made earlier about role clarity, with the possibility that where role perceptions overlap there may be conflict and duplication, or the chance that 'difficult' tasks will not be undertaken because they can be avoided in the confusion. Such difficulties may be lessened in small organisations, which often seem to thrive on less mechanistic organisational structures.

The organisation's approach to control will also influence the process of implementation. Control systems monitor implementation and report deviations from planned targets so that corrective action is taken. This control can be more or less detailed, and more or less concerned with the overall marketing plan and with its component parts. It can also be more or less sophisticated: dealing with some uncomplicated costs or involving the rigorous analysis of market share variances in specified market segments. The information system supporting the control system might also be crude or advanced. Because of these variables the effectiveness of control will itself be variable, and implementation may not run to target because early warnings of deviation are not picked up.

Specification of the control system can shape behaviour in implementation. Managers will be keen to ensure their activities achieve what is being measured, and pay less regard to what is not being measured. The measures may attract more attention than the activities, and their calibration might be of costs, efforts and outputs which are the easiest to gauge. Efforts and outcomes which are difficult to measure are overlooked; the measures may be seen as 'soft' or fuzzy and thus incredible. As an example, the accounting system might routinely report price and cost variances, and because of this visibility managers might do all they can to keep these measures within budget. Prices and costs are clearly relevant, but for marketing purposes equal importance might be attached to market size and share. Price and cost variances would be calculated but market size and share variances probably not. Controls therefore emphasise price and cost, and managers could divert some of their attention from market size and securing market share in order to meet the targets that are being monitored. The control system becomes a strong influence on plan execution, often in a very positive way directly related to the achievement of marketing goals, but with the potential to stress goals and actions which are the more easily measured.

Implementation problems

Bonoma [14] has identified several sets of implementation problems from his studies of a range of organisations. These concern actions, systems and policies. Actions refer to the marketing mix and he sees two main causes of problems: assumptions and contradictions. Management by assumption is where senior executives sweep away the practicalities of implementation. Thoughtless assumptions are made that more can be done with the same resources; the salesforce can take on an additional product line or the physical distribution system can handle a 20 per cent increase without extra resourcing. Contradictions creep in when mutually inconsistent plans are made, as in the company which targets a quality sensitive segment with a good product and weak after-sales care, or the introduction of a technically advanced new product to a market with sophisticated buyers when the salesforce was poorly trained. Muddling through becomes the mode of execution.

Marketing systems comprise the formal and semi-formal organisational and control devices. A ritual may be made of these and the sheer weight of bureaucracy frustrate actions. Alternatively, the systems may be politicised: trivial deviations from plan fanned out of proportion to divert attention from other variances, or to 'prove' inefficiencies that can only be rectified by organisational changes. Effective execution of the plans can become inhibited rather than facilitated by the systems.

Marketing policies give the broad purpose and direction; they supply the vision and theme. Clarity in all these assists the proper implementation of plans. Shared understanding in the company of prescribed patterns of behaviour – what kind of organisation it is and how it conducts its business – can ease the accomplishment of tasks. Valid assumptions can be made about related parts of the organisation and how they will behave in putting the plan into action. Many details may not need to be explicated because they are well covered by company policy – the way things are done. On the other hand, confusion and conflict in marketing policies would require much more detailed, elaborate plans if problems are to be avoided in implementation.

The impact of some of these problems is reduced by skilful managers. Bonoma suggests four groups of skills which facilitate implementation:

Interacting skills
Organising skills
Allocating skills
Monitoring skills

Managers work with and through other people, and the formal organisation provides the framework for these interactions. Relationships can be stilted and sometimes dysfunctional if confined to formal structures since the formal organisation cannot predict and prescribe every eventuality. Managers therefore work through both the formal organisation and through the informal or emergent organisation. Effective interacting skills in these contexts are based on knowledge of self and others, against the backcloth of perceptions of relative power, prestige and expertise. In the process of implementing plans managers often need to make compromises, trade-offs and exchanges with other managers. Such negotiations are influenced by the quality of the knowledge and the accuracy of the perceptions that the manager holds about self and others.

Working through the informal or emergent organisation requires a related set of organising skills: networking. Bonoma describes this as recreating the organisation to solve each problem. The manager expedites by informally cutting across the organisation, by seeking out bottlenecks, finding just who can help and by striking bargains. In this sense, organising skills require the cultivation of wide formal and informal connections across the organisation.

Allocating skills are more analytical and depend on what is known about how much and what types of effort are needed to accomplish a given task. How many orders will be generated by how many sales calls? How many mailings are needed to achieve how many customer enquiries?

The formal monitoring system may be to some extent inadequate: too little, too late or too much of the wrong measure. In these circumstances the manager will need to develop supplementary monitoring. Bonoma argues that this should be elegantly simple and based on deep background knowledge. He concurs with the writers on success and excellence in business who advocate MBWA – managing by walking about [15].

Summary

Strategic marketing planning leads to the shorter-term operational marketing planning, which may be for a one-year period. Goals for the annual marketing plan are supplied by the longer-run marketing strategy. The process of specifying these goals goes through many iterations, involving line managers testing their feasibility and practicality. Outline plans may be traced, and possible implementation problems anticipated, while goals are still being formed.

Detailing the plans stresses the need for integrated efforts, to take advantage of synergy, to assure consistency, to highlight mutual dependency and to co-ordinate timing. Plans may be cast in terms of each main marketing activity, such as the salesforce or advertising. Increasingly, companies are adding other ways of structuring these plans, such as by product or marketing channel. The effectiveness of these kinds of plan depends on the clarity of the definitions of the roles of responsible managers and on a deal of co-ordination. The organisational structure and the information system also affect how well such plans are accomplished.

Marketing planning is judgemental, and central to this are judgements about the sales response to various marketing efforts. Managers use sales response functions either explicitly or implicitly. If it is implicit the necessary assumptions are hidden and learning may not ensue.

Empirical studies show that a half to three-quarters of companies undertake some marketing planning, with a much lesser proportion making comprehensive plans. Attitudes held by chief executives and the company culture influence the extent and type of marketing planning. Companies may go through different evolutionary phases which also affect planning modes.

The organisation's approach to delegation and control is crucial to how implementation proceeds. Managers seek to achieve what is being measured and what is being measured may accentuate activities that are most easily gauged. Implementation problems may arise if gross, unrealistic assumptions have been made in planning, if plans build in contradictions, if system controls become bureaucratic and if overall policies are confused or conflicting. Skilful managers reduce the impact of such problems by working through the informal, emergent organisation, developing sensitive monitoring procedures for their activity and by learning what impacts on the key factors that affect the outcomes.

Questions for review and discussion

1. Show how environmental factors can have a different impact on planning marketing at different organisational levels. Illustrate by reference to the following:
    (a) Sterling exchange rates (for a firm exporting).
    (b) Substantial, and supposedly long-run, increases in raw material prices.
    (c) Much increased supply of television advertising opportunities (from cables and satellites).
    (d) A policy announcement by a large retailer that in future no sales calls will be allowed at outlets.

2. Marketing plans need to be integrated. More complex ways of specifying these plans, by product, channel or segment, are being developed. In what ways might this complexity frustrate the preparation of integrated marketing plans?

3. Would you agree that discussions of sales response functions are merely sophisticated ways of disguising guesswork?

4. Control systems can channel managerial behaviour. More senior managers would be alert to this and ensure that distortions in the allocation of effort were minimised. It therefore follows that plans will be accomplished whatever the formal controls. Discuss.

5. All management planning must be by assumption because it is about the future. Would you say that Bonoma is wrong in highlighting management by assumption as a potential problem in implementation? Illustrate by reference to the following:
    (a) Sales response functions.
    (b) Issues in distribution logistics.
    (c) The co-ordination of several disparate activities in the launch of a new product (e.g. timing promotions, the flow of promotional materials to sales outlets, stock levels at various points in the channels).

6. Getting things done sometimes requires cutting across the formal organisation and ignoring formal procedures. On the other hand, plans are formal and lay down prescribed behaviour. In consequence there must always be a tension between planning and implementation, with more detailed planning leading to greater tension. In these circumstances, is the construction of detailed marketing plans just a charade?

References

1. Luck, D.J. and Ferrell, O.C. 1985. *Marketing Strategy and Plans*, 2nd edn. Englewood Cliffs, NJ: Prentice Hall Inc., p. 468.
2. Hutt, M.D., Reingen, P.H. and Ronchetto, J.R. 1988. 'Tracing emergent processes in marketing strategy formation', *Journal of Marketing*, vol. 42, January.
3. Lilien, G.L. and Kotler, P. 1983. *Marketing Decision Making*. New York: Harper & Row, p. 662.
4. Parsons, L.J. 1981. 'Models of market mechanisms', in Schulz, R.L. and Zoltners, A.A. (eds), *Marketing Decision Models* New York: North-Holland, p. 90.
5. Luck and Ferrell, op. cit., p. 478.
6. Fitzroy, P.T. 1976. *Analytical Models for Marketing Management*. Maidenhead: McGraw-Hill, p. 310.
7. Doyle, P. 1988. 'Marketing and the British chief executive', *Journal of Marketing Management*, vol. 3, no. 2.

8. Greenley, G.E. 1985. 'Marketing plan utilisation', *Quarterly Review of Marketing*, vol. 10, no. 4.

9. Hooley, G.J., West, C.J. and Lynch, J.E. 1984. *Marketing in the UK: A Survey of Current Practice and Performance*. Cookham: Institute of Marketing.

10. Leppard, J. and McDonald, M. 1987. 'A reappraisal of the role of marketing planning', *Quarterly Review of Marketing*, vol. 13, no. 1.

11. Lynch, J.E., Hooley, G.J. and Shephard, J. 1988. 'The effectiveness of British marketing: a resumé of preliminary findings', *Proceedings of the 21st Annual Conference of the Marketing Education Group, Huddersfield*.

12. Leppard and McDonald, op. cit.

13. Greenley, G.E. 1986. *The Strategic and Operational Planning of Marketing*. Maidenhead: McGraw-Hill, ch. 12.

14. Bonoma, T.V. 1985. *The Marketing Edge*. New York: Free Press.

15. See also Piercey, N. 1992. *Market-led Strategic Change*. Oxford: Butterworth-Heinemann, ch. 9.

Chapter 12
Product planning

The essential vehicle for the provision of customer satisfaction is the product or service that the company offers in the marketplace. The array of decisions associated with that offer becomes the base ingredient in the development of the total marketing plan. All other marketing mix decisions need to be integrated with those of product planning, since they are about how to promote, price and distribute the product.

Discussion of product planning should not be limited to the physical composition of the products. The firm manufactures a physical object, but consumers make purchase choices between physical objects which they evaluate as offering different propensities to convey valued benefits. The physical object is consumed not for itself, but for what it can do to meet one of the consumer's needs. It follows that the consumer's perception of the product should be the cornerstone of all company thought about its product range. That product perception will not only be influenced by the physical properties (taste, texture, colour, smell, etc.), but also be affected by the individual's perception of any associated services. The package, the brand name and the generalised image might also be important, as could a whole range of social and cultural associations that had come to be attached to the product.

Once it is acknowledged that a simple physical definition of product meaning is insufficient, then much more complex, and potentially variable, psychological definitions are needed. Ultimately, each customer could have a unique perception. Generalisations are required, and it could be argued that the firm's competence in arriving at adequate generalisations of these product perceptions is among its most important activities.

Influences on product decisions

Product strategies are a fundamental set of choices that an organisation makes within its understanding of the external environment and given its resources and

236

competences. Key choices in this set are product-market mix, product positioning and branding. Crucial aspects of the external environment concern consumers, competitors and product lifecycle, because all three can affect all product decisions. Important resources and competences influencing the choices are in manufacturing, finance, marketing and R&D. Product decisions result from the simultaneous interpretation of the external and internal environments, features of which are shown in Figure 12.1.

Almost all the elements in the figure may have some bearing on all the other elements. For instance, how well consumer needs are understood depends on the organisation's marketing knowledge, skills and research abilities. How well those needs are translated into product offerings depends partly on R&D and manufacturing/operations competence. This also depends on marketing channels and on the appropriateness of the decisions on positioning and how that is communicated in the market. Consumer perceptions of the product offering are influenced by what they know of competitive offers. And just how many and which consumers are in the market adds another variable: through the product lifecycle the numbers and kinds of consumer are likely to change.

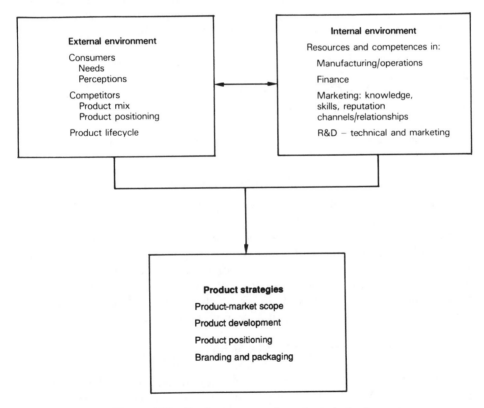

Figure 12.1 *Environment and product strategies*

Two other factors overlay the interaction between environment and strategy, and these are the overall marketing goals and product history. The requirement to contribute to the attainment of marketing goals supplies the drive in the search for appropriate product plans and gives benchmarks for their acceptability in sales and profit terms. The relative effectiveness of past product strategies informs current decision-making by constraining the options to be considered. A previously successful strategy, with no radical environmental change, may be continued. Alternatively, a past experiment may have had unfortunate results and so similar ventures may be ruled out.

Six of the elements in the figure will be investigated in more detail in this chapter. They are product lifecycle, product-market scope, product development, product positioning, branding and packaging.

Product-market evolution

Ideas about how product-markets evolve will be influential in product strategy. Central to this will be views on prospective sales levels in product-markets in which the organisation is participating, and in those which it might consider entering. Such views are often related to the notion of the product lifecycle (PLC), but it is useful to set them within the wider context of evolutionary processes.

Lambkin and Day [1] consider that three groups of forces facilitate or inhibit product-market evolution. These are:

1. The demand system – the market environment and the pattern of diffusion.

2. The supply system – the competitive environment and supplier behaviour.

3. The resource environment – exogenous and industry factors.

Diffusion of innovation theory has been used widely as an explanation of the rate of adoption of a product by buyers over time (see Chapter 4). In this theory attention is focused on the role of interpersonal communication in encouraging or discouraging the adoption of new products, and on attempts to understand the characteristics of buyers which might be related to their adoption propensity. The rate of adoption by buyers will be a major factor shaping the way a market evolves.

Suppliers influence the speed with which a market evolves. The numbers and size of suppliers entering a market, and the scale of their resource commitments, will determine the productive capacity available, which in turn will be one determinant of costs. And these factors will condition the intensity and the form of competitive activity, with very intensive competition being likely to encourage sales growth. The volume of informative and persuasive marketing communications put out in the market will also be partly a function of the numbers of suppliers and their resources. High volumes of marketing communication would assist suppliers in their attempts to 'grow the market'.

Strategies chosen by the competitors on how to proceed in developing the market will be another main force driving the evolutionary trends. Some competitors may prepare for rapid market penetration and use strategies to encourage this. Pricing and promotion decisions will have especial significance; low prices with heavy promotion would usually be expected to stimulate higher demand levels. Strategies may also be implemented because of the concern that present competitors have about potential new competitive entrants to the market and this may lead to the active construction of entry barriers.

The resource environment, trends in product and process technology, in input costs, and in the economy, all have bearing on the rate of market development, and mediate the behaviour of the demand and supply systems.

Product lifecycle

The basic idea of the PLC – that through time the sales of a product increase, level out and then decline – has been widely disseminated but, 'few management concepts have been so widely accepted or thoroughly criticized . . .' [2]. It is widely accepted because it is easily understood, it is intuitively appealing and because examples have been published from many industries where some lifecycle pattern has been evident [3]. It is criticised because of its normative approach in offering prescriptions about appropriate strategies at each phase in the product's life, which may not have any empirical justification. Its lack of predictive ability, in terms of the sales trend and competitive and customer behaviour, is another weakness. Hunt [4] finds the notion tautological because:

> if the level of sales determines the shape of the lifecycle, then the stage in the lifecycle cannot be used to explain the level of sales. Unless and until the product lifecycle can be refined to a point where the stages can be identified independent of the sales variable the lifecycle concept will remain impotent and void of explanatory power.

Studies of lifecycle phenomena deal with evolutionary trends and normally offer descriptions of birth, growth, maturity and decline. A body of knowledge has developed about these stages and it is a reference point for any lifecycle analysis. That can lead to confusion if there is the expectation that the classic lifecycle stages should be observed irrespective of how the basic parameters are defined. The reference point stands, but may or may not hold in particular applications.

Careful definition is needed of exactly what sales are being aggregated in any study of trends through time. That is all the more so if the resultant curve is to be compared with a generalised model, and if strategic inferences are to be drawn. Distinctions need to be made between product class, product form and brand lifecycles. Product class is a highly aggregated, generic category such as cars. Product form is a subcategory, such as family saloons, within which there may be a variety of brands. Often, product class can be equated with industry, though this need not always be so. Much depends on what the study is attempting to illuminate. For example, to what level should furniture manufacturing be studied? Should there be distinctions between domestic and institutional markets? Should there then be a distinction between major usages, and a further one between various quality levels? Where should one strike the product class, and would that also define an industry?

If the object of the study were to offer insights for broad strategy development, taking a very long-term view, then a very high level of aggregation would be of use, perhaps defining the industry as all types of furniture. Product-market scope in that instance takes a broadscale view of firms' competence in meeting market needs. Output of the analysis might be opinions about long-term demand levels, overall industry structure and long-run trends in competitive strategies. This would contribute to an appreciation of how attractive it might be to participate, or to continue participation, in that industry. Alternatives might be in radically different technologies which might require basic changes in firms' competences, but which could none the less be worth developing or acquiring.

If there were a more limited object to the study, then a different specification would be warranted. Say the planning horizon was three to five years, and that the perspective was not that of long-term corporate strategy but of medium-term product management. Trends in the broadscale furniture industry would not be as immediately relevant. Now the 'industry' might be defined as the manufacture of high quality domestic furniture for use in living rooms, dining rooms and bedrooms. Specific competitors could be identified, including imports, and 'industry' sales defined as the aggregate of their sales. The plot of these figures could be read as an industry lifecycle or a product class lifecycle, and this analysis would probably be taken down to the study of product forms and the main brands in each form. One output from the investigations could be a recommendation on product development, such as the need to extend the product line in one of the forms. Another output could be the demonstration of the need to sharpen product positioning, perhaps because of style changes by a major competitor; or it could suggest the possibility of combating a quality retailer's dominance by changing brand policy to include manufacturing for own-labels.

Lifecycle stages

Differences in three groups of factors explain much of the variation in the four stages usually distinguished in lifecycle analysis. These factors are: total market size, the kinds of customer in the market, and the number and types of competitors. Over time all three are likely to vary and so constitute different market and competitive circumstances, which may prompt different marketing strategies.

In the introductory phase, sales levels are a small fraction of what they may later become and so total market size is small. The innovators are, by definition the first to buy a new product. Study of their needs, characteristics and media use habits would be useful in attempting to design targeted strategies in the hope of speeding market acceptance. The market will be less price-sensitive than it later becomes, and with restricted production volumes and high unit costs, prices will be high. Only one firm is in the market initially and it is not competitive. The product is not widely available and often there is relatively little presence in marketing channels. It is a speculative and unprofitable period. But the pioneering company may be building substantial competitive advantage, and in particular may be establishing an enduring quality leadership and gaining valuable operations and marketing experience.

Competitors, probably with some product variants, enter in the growth phase, attracted by the possible geometric increase in sales volume. This ushers in major attempts to establish brand identities, to secure the best distributors and to attain a strong market presence. Recognition may be given to smaller segments of the market, with tailored marketing plans. Some competitors may begin to map out niche strategies in the hope of establishing clear superiority in attending to just one or two segments. Price competition emerges, although unit costs will be falling to make this the most profitable phase.

By maturity the product has reached the mass market. The sales curve begins to flatten and even to weaken. Price competition may be fierce in the early part of this phase, and non-price competition may dominate the remainder. Profits may begin to dwindle. In some industries there could be a shake-out in early maturity and several of the weaker competitors are forced to leave.

Finally, the product enters decline. The fall in sales becomes increasingly apparent and projections only indicate further decrease. Many firms decide to leave, and it is only a matter of time before they are all forced to face the possibility.

This generalised model is often shown in the form of a normal curve and sometimes as S-shaped (Figure 12.2). The time dimension is not specified because it could be a few months for some fad to many decades for some basic machinery. A number of studies have questioned the shape of this curve and just how universal it is [5]. Some argue that the lack of evidence of anything like a normal curve at the brand level means that we should forget the lifecycle altogether. A

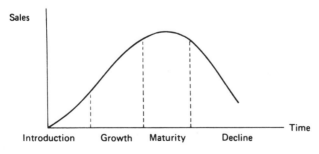

Figure 12.2 *The classic product lifecycle*

modern view would not be that extravagant. Provided that it is clear which life-cycle level is being discussed, and that there are clear definitions, then the concept has considerable utility, although it must be granted that the general model would not be expected to operate at the level of the individual brand. Investigations incorporating lifecycle analysis therefore approach the study by first testing the extent to which it applies in the particular circumstances.

Distinctions between product class, form and brand cycles allow the possibility that contrary trends may be apparent at these three levels. This can be illustrated by noting the varied fortunes of the three lifecycles in Figure 12.3.

Suppose that Figure 12.3 covers a five-year time-scale. The class cycle shows some growth, and with other evidence it is believed to be in late growth. At the form level, the decline seems to indicate a later stage, and so any predictions of these two cycles would give entirely different futures. At the brand level there is more confusion, with the two shown experiencing different fortunes. Appreciation of the sales trends at each of the levels is therefore crucial. Two further examples will help.

Example 1

Continuous monitoring reveals the beginning of weakness for a brand which is consistent with the class cycle but contrary to the form cycle. Research may suggest that consumers perceive the brand is part of the product category, but think of it as belonging to an old-fashioned form and not the form management assumed.

In this case management would wish to explore further the relationship between the form and class cycles. Does the decline at the class level presage a decline at the form level, or is that particular form sufficiently differentiated to sustain an alternative trend? Investigations would also be required into why the brand is associated with an old-fashioned form. Perhaps it was one of the first in the field and its style has not kept pace with competitors. Perhaps its appeal was to one age group, now grown older, and successive generations have identified with newer brands.

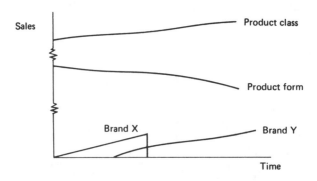

Figure 12.3 *Product, form and branded lifecycles*

Example 2
Gradual, long-term decline at the class and form levels is opposed to a slow increase at the brand level.

The strategic problem here is the seemingly good performance of the brand, since it is increasing its market share. Some competitors may have withdrawn. Should the decision be taken to pre-empt later problems by phasing out a currently healthy brand? The major variable will be time. The decline may settle on a plateau. An instance of this is the British washing machine industry in the 1960s when seven manufacturers withdrew as the total market contracted, but four remained.

Pursuing the distinction between the several levels of cycles, another example will serve to show that is not as obvious as it may at first appear. In the machine tool industry it would be insufficient to say that the class was machine tools and that the forms were drilling machines, boring machines, and so on. Numerous subforms would have to be identified to ensure that like was being compared with like. A surface grinder is quite different to an external cylindrical grinder, and their lifecycles and prospects are quite different. Careful definition is essential.

Technological development may be one of the critical influences on the lifecycle. In the case of nylon, developments in technology have meant that successively larger markets have been opened, from stockings to shirts, carpets and all kinds of industrial applications. Improvements to an existing class can rejuvenate it. Electric typewriters, automatic washing machines and jumbo jets are all examples of new forms in established product classes. But the implications of a new form can be very varied, and sometimes can have disastrous effects, as in the cash register industry. Gross Cash Registers had a 50 per cent market share in the United Kingdom in the 1960s. They produced a mechanical cash register and were apparently taken by surprise by the rapidity of acceptance of electronic registers. Their market share plummeted in the late 1970s and a desperate attempt to catch up with the new technology almost sent them bankrupt. They were an easy takeover situation for Chubb, and the new company is now trying to re-establish itself with electronic machines, but faces twenty-two foreign competitors in its domestic market. Thus, while technical change has beneficial effects on some lifecycles, it can lead to premature obsolescence for others.

Some of the important strategic implications of the product lifecycle have been summarised by Doyle and they appear in Table 12.1. The table also depicts some of the main characteristics associated with each phase. More detailed strategic implications of the lifecycle can be noted from the research of Corkindale and Kennedy. Their empirical study revealed important changes in advertising objectives set for a number of brands in different stages of the lifecycle (Table 12.2). They categorise seven groups of objectives; most are readily understandable. 'Information' concerns factual statements about the brand; 'messages' are more subjective and include claims of higher quality and value for money.

Table 12.1 *Implications and characteristics of product lifecycles*

	Introduction	Growth	Maturity	Decline
Characteristics				
Sales	Low		Slow growth	Decline
Profits	Negligible	Peak levels	Declining	Low or zero
Cash flow	Negative	Moderate	High	Low
Customers	Innovative	Mass market	Mass market	Laggards
Responses				
Strategic focus	Expand market	Market penetration	Defend share	Productivity
Marketing expenditure	High	High (declining %)	Falling	Low
Marketing emphasis	Product awareness	Brand preference	Brand loyalty	Selective
Distribution	Patchy	Intensive	Intensive	Selective
Price	High	Lower	Lowest	Rising
Product	Basic	Improved	Differentiated	Rationalised

Source: P. Doyle, 'The realities of the product life cycle', *Quarterly Review of Marketing*, Summer 1976; reprinted in M.J. Thomas and N.E. Waite, *The Marketing Digest*. London: Heinemann, 1988.

Branding is important throughout the cycle, but will be different as the brand matures. Apart from this, the distributions in the table appear to be reasonably consistent with what traditional lifecycle theory would predict. Information, awareness and trial are important during introduction. Increased competition in growth leads to more messages, claiming distinction of one kind or another, and to information on usage and maintenance of favourable attitudes. Maturity is often the most competitive phase, and so the trends apparent in growth are magnified. During decline the wide spread of objectives reflects the contrary strategies that the remaining competitors adopt – some will be preparing to leave the market, while others will wish to ride the cycle down.

It is tempting in product lifecycle studies to conclude that stage in lifecycle

Table 12.2 *Advertising objectives through the lifecycle*

Objective	Number of objectives per brand			
	Introduction	Growth	Maturity	Decline
Branding and image-building	1.0	0.54	0.77	0.5
Information	0.71	0.36	0.44	0.5
Messages	0.42	0.73	0.66	0.66
Attitudes	0.28	0.36	0.66	0.33
Awareness	0.57	0.27	0.0	0.33
Trial	0.28	0.09	0.0	0.33
Loyalty	0.0	0.09	0.44	0.16
Number of brands in sample	7	11	9	6

Note: Lifecycle here is for 'markets'.
Source: D.R. Corkindale and S.H. Kennedy, *Measuring the Effect of Advertising*. Farnborough: Saxon House, 1975, p. 195. Copyright © Saxon House, 1975.

is the dominant influence on the product's viability. In warning against drawing such a conclusion Wind [6] states that:

> it is implicit in such an assumption that, at any one stage in the product lifecycle, the firm has only a single 'reasonable' marketing strategy it can follow. This implicit assumption is not only misleading but also dangerous, since it can constrain management's creativity in generating new marketing strategies.

The example of the battery market overleaf demonstrates that stage in product lifecycle can be less immediately important than many other factors. Thus, while the notion of a lifecycle can have significance it should not obscure other, perhaps more complex, issues of relevance in product planning.

Product differentiation

Through product differentiation the firm attempts to mark its product as being superior to competitive offerings, or as being unique. The possibilities for product differentiation can be seen from Levitt's [7] analysis of the four levels on which products can be considered. These are:

1. *The core product*: the essential elements of the product or service without which the firm could not compete in a given product-market.

2. *The expected product*: what customers have come to expect as normal additions to the core.

3. *The augmented product*: the features and services that go beyond the normal customer expectation.

4. *The potential product*: all the potential features or benefits which could be offered and which customers would see as beneficial.

Christopher *et al.* [8] illustrate these differences in respect of cameras,

> the expected offer may include a series of lens choices, attractive packaging, easy-to-read instructions, a network of service agents, and so on. The augmented offer could include a wide range of differentiating factors such as longer warranties, etc. The potential offer involves creative options or innovations which will add value for the customer. This might involve new applications being worked on, new materials being used in the camera constitution, or new ideas for varying the camera's features for different user requirements.

Strategies for augmenting the product are discussed by Hooley and Saunders [9]. They suggest that augmentation may be through attention to one or more of the

Battery lifecycles

It is important to realise that product lifecycles are but one input to a situation analysis. This can be illustrated with reference to the market for batteries where to an extent the traditional lifecycle concept can be applied. Zinc carbon batteries have been dominating the market since before the 1920s with growth in the 1950s and 1960s as more types of small appliances and toys needed portable electric power. Growth rates slackened in the 1970s, indicating that maturity had been reached, and by the early 1980s sales had reached a plateau. However, a fuller analysis would need to take account of substantial developments in technology, changes in competition and in consumer behaviour.

Ever Ready has held about three-quarters of the zinc carbon market. But its commanding position in the overall battery market has been eroded by the rapid growth of the long-life alkaline products, in which Duracell has more than an 80 per cent share. Ever Ready had maintained its position because it was well down the experience curve and had low unit costs. It also had an intensive distribution strategy with two-thirds of sales being made by 280 vans which call regularly at retail outlets. By the late 1970s and early 1980s grocery stores had taken a quarter of all sales, but the chain grocers would not deal with direct shop deliveries; most preferred deliveries to their central warehouses. Along with this shift there was a change in buyer behaviour: more women were buying batteries.

Against this background the competition stiffened and advertising budgets multiplied. Ever Ready responded by launching an alkaline battery in 1979 under the brand name Super Plus, which was sold alongside its three zinc carbon products called SP, HP and PP Confusion that consumers might have had about alkaline and zinc carbon was thus compounded by seemingly meaningless brand names. Attempts to retrieve the position led Ever Ready to another launch in 1984 and the introduction of Gold, Silver and Blue seals; Gold is the alkaline and the other two are zinc carbon.

This market therefore shows lifecycle studies to be of some use, but the fortunes of Ever Ready have been much more influenced by environmental factors and by its own strategic choices.

It is also instructive in this case to examine again the meaning and the definition of a product. From a marketing viewpoint the only valid definition is that which the consumer makes, and that is a function of the benefits derived. Thus consumers do not buy batteries, they buy the benefits of portable power, and that should influence the way that products are explained to consumers. Infinitely more complex products are bought by consumers, often with no mention of the technicalities.

product features or performance, the perceived quality of the product, its packaging, style, image and the services that could be provided, such as advice, installation, parts availability, delivery and repair.

This perspective on product differentiation can show another consequence: the position is dynamic. Competitors and customers change. Many points of differentiation can be copied and so their worth as a competitive distinction deteriorates over time. Customer expectations also develop as they come to accept the augmented product as normal – it becomes the expected product. Companies cannot therefore be complacent and the search for differentiation can never be said to have been completed.

Product-market scope

Discussion in previous chapters showed the importance of defining the scope of the competitive arena. Definition of the area in which the business is to compete has equal significance at the level of product strategy, and the term product-market scope is used in this context.

Product plans rest on decisions about the product-markets in which the firm should participate. There are a number of ways of characterising the range of possibilities, and Table 12.3 shows one approach with several categories of products and markets, graduated according to how new they are to the organisation.

Market development suggests meeting rivals head-on in existing markets with existing products. Any growth would come from increased market share, or from secular growth in the market. The PLC stage would be relevant because this approach is likely to be more easily accomplished in the growth phase. For it to work in maturity it presupposes an increase in funding, and the deployment of much extra effort, perhaps in price-cutting, sales promotion or advertising. There is a limit to how far this can be taken since the incremental returns to this effort will diminish. Estimates of response coefficients would be helpful in determining just how valuable any increased effort might be. However, this might be a particularly difficult decision because argument might revolve around the quality, and not the quantity, of the effort. While the estimated response to, say, advertising might indicate relative inelasticity, that would be on the basis of an assumed similarity between past and present advertising. Some members of management might sidestep this by taking the view that a radically new advertising approach could overthrow the previous relationships between advertising and sales. In that case the use of past response coefficients would be irrelevant, and there would be the implied assumption that the new advertising would achieve much more responsiveness. Some small-scale research might lend this argument a little credence; but a large area of judgement would remain.

Product development implies some more or less significant modification: enhancing performance, adding features, providing new services, making changes in design or packaging. But essentially the same product is offered in the same

Table 12.3 *Product-market scope*

Markets	Products			
	Existing	Modified	New: same technology	New: new technology
Existing	market development	product development	new product	radical new development
New	market development	product-market development	new product/ new market	diversification

markets. An example is Pampers disposable napkins, quoted in an earlier chapter, which underwent a series of developments in the 1980s from improvements to their absorbency, the introduction of boy and girl formats and the addition of variants for babies of different ages.

New product development may involve working with the same technology or with a new technology. Examples of the former case are Black & Decker, and their frequent introductions of new types of portable electrical tools, and many food and drink manufacturers. Examples of the latter case are the adoption of ATM's by banks, or electronics being employed by a toy manufacturer in a new product range.

Market development covers the search for new uses, or for new market segments, for the existing product. Firms already established in one consumer segment may seek another. A notable example is Johnson's Baby Powder being promoted to adults. Another example is from the range of Heinz tinned baby food: strained apples for babies can be apple sauce for adults when the tin has a different label. Changing the geographic area served may also provide possibilities for market development.

Sometimes the search for new markets may require some adjustment to the product. Firms selling in the industrial market may find new opportunities in the consumer field. Industrial adhesives have been repackaged into small tubes for sale in the consumer market, as have various industrial cleaning agents. Fast food restaurants may modify their product offering in order to attract business at breakfast.

Developing new products to enter new markets poses problems. The firm moves deliberately from what it knows, in terms of its products and markets, to the more or less unknown. With all of the options discussed above there was always the security of familiarity with at least one of these dimensions. Diversification is the most radical departure from existing strategies. New products, in new technologies, and aimed at new kinds of markets are high risk strategies. They may be prompted by a lack of growth possibilities elsewhere, and the prospect of high returns.

Pursuit of any of the strategies mentioned in this section reflects the organisation's choices based on its understanding of its competence and its environment. It tests the rigour of its planning and its attitude to innovation.

Product development

More operational issues emerge from concentrating the discussion on the product dimension of product-market scope. Johne and Snelson [10] show that the options for both new and existing product lines centre around increasing or decreasing the following six marketing mix variables:

1. Changing the performance capabilities of the product.
2. Changing the application advice for the product.
3. Changing the after-sales service for the product.
4. Changing the promoted image of the product.
5. Changing the availability of the product.
6. Changing the price of the product.

The objective in any change would be to enhance differential advantage. How far that is accomplished will depend on how realistic a view was taken about customer reactions to the move. In turn that depends on the accuracy of current knowledge about customer perception of these elements, and on assumptions about competitive moves. This points to the need for continuing tracking of customer perceptions and continuing surveillance of prime competitors.

Traditionally, decisions about the first three elements noted above have been the responsibility of technical specialists and the remaining three the responsibility of marketing personnel. In their empirical study Johne and Snelson found that [11]:

> What characterises the approach to product planning in active product developer firms is that it is market-led (as opposed to being functionally-led by the marketing or technical department). It is based on careful prior analysis of market opportunities perceived by a mix of key functional specialists and co-ordinated by a committed chief officer. This task is contributed to substantially by marketing specialists but is not delegated to them totally . . . . The situation in less active product developer firms is usually quite different . . . . Product development in such firms is typically either predominantly technically-led or marketing-led . . . top management has difficulties in achieving an explicit balance between old product developments and new product developments.

Most companies have a portfolio of products and face an external environment which is likely to be dynamic. Ideas from the product lifecycle concept suggest one source of this dynamism. Ideas from the study of competitive strategies suggest another source. A portfolio which was entirely new or entirely old may not represent the best adjustment to the environment. A balanced portfolio of new and old product development is usually advocated. This theme of balance is also taken up in product innovation strategies.

Product innovation strategies

Cooper has conducted an interesting empirical study of the product innovation strategies of industrial product companies [12]. He found that in the 122 firms studied their new product strategies could be distinguished on two dimensions:

the degree of technological sophistication and orientation, and the degree of market orientation. Five clusters were evident:

1. Technology driven (25 per cent of firms) – non-market-oriented; high degree of technical sophistication; high risk, state-of-the-art, innovative; not among the top performers on success rate for new product introductions.

2. Balanced strategy (15.6 per cent of firms) – most successful firms; high success rate in new product introductions; both market-oriented and technically sophisticated; new products fitted existing products and markets; sought out high growth markets.

3. Technically deficient (15.6 per cent of firms) – lack technical sophistication; brought out 'me-too' copies of competitive products; simple mature technology; low-risk, defensive attitudes; dismal performance.

4. Low budget, conservative (23.8 per cent of firms) – low R&D spending; 'me-too' products; but capitalised on strengths; close fit with existing products and markets; good results.

5. High budget, diverse (18.9 per cent of firms) – small firms but not as small as type 3; high R&D; attacked radically new markets with high growth rates; high-risk strategy.

Overall the new product strategies were successful with a 67 per cent success rate. It is interesting that the most and the least successful were market-oriented– the former were also technically sophisticated whereas the latter were technically deficient. Thus in industrial product markets, market orientation is necessary but not sufficient whereas although technical sophistication is not always necessary, it is also not sufficient.

Product positioning

Analyses of customer perceptions and preferences concerning the firm's products, and those of its competitors, provide important ingredients in assessments of product strategy. They can furnish a snapshot of customers' views of current market structure and may be able to uncover gaps in the provision. Over time they may reveal something of market evolution, with different customer groups being attracted as adoption of the product spreads. This could deal with conventional customers and well-rehearsed customer choice criteria. But such studies might uncover dynamic market features by identifying changes in customer choice criteria and by spotlighting unconventional or emergent rivals. Early warning on such structural change in the market could indicate the possible erosion of established competitive advantage and might prompt thought on possible defensive strategies. This could entail attempts at shoring up customer belief in the traditional choice criteria, some more focused strategy on segments likely to stay loyal, or a general attack on the new competitors. More positive response may open the possibility of creating new kinds of advantage in the changed market, with implications for product development.

Consideration of positioning strategy can permeate all levels of tactical and strategic planning. On one level it can lead to small, short-term changes in advertising copy, perhaps as a rejoinder to a rival. On another level it might reach deep into the basics of the business by triggering an appraisal of the fundamentals of competitive superiority, perhaps because cost leadership has been lost or because a differentiated position is threatened by technical change.

Fuller discussion on positioning strategy, on procedures for the determination of product position, and on problems in positioning, can be found in the chapter on Segmentation and Positioning.

There are numerous approaches to product positioning. Aaker [13] discusses eleven types and Wind emphasises the following six [14]:

1. Positioning *by product features*: this would emphasise performance on particular attributes such as convenience in use, speed of application or ruggedness of construction. An example is the Citroen BX19 which claims to need only two and a half hours servicing a year.

2. Positioning *by benefits or problems solved*: many services offer solutions to specific consumer problems but products too are positioned in this way. Examples are Anadin – the 'fast relief for headaches'; complete reliability from parcel delivery companies; Oil of Ulay for younger-looking skin.

3. Positioning *by usage or use occasion*: this would relate the product to specific occasions or usage situations. Examples are products and services associated with particular festivities or seasons of the year. Many hotels, restaurants and specialist retailers use this strategy. Some products announce they are the one 'for the big job' or for the light snack.

4. Positioning *by user category*: some brands define their positioning in respect of consumers, by emphasising the kinds of people who use the product. Examples are Empathy shampoo for the over-forties, Flora – the 'margarine for men', some financial products aimed at the over-fifty-fives and a number of holiday tour packages.

5. Positioning *against another product*: this can be head-on comparative advertising with explicit 'knocking copy' or more general comparisons against 'another leading brand'. Cars, lawnmowers and washing powders are notable examples. This can make specific brand comparisons or take a more defensive line such as 'if it doesn't say Kellogg's on the pack it isn't Kellogg's in the pack'.

6. *Product class dissociation*: this positioning can be used to appear to be different from the crowd – Alliance Building Society, 'not all building societies are the same'. It can also be used if the product class as a whole is meeting problems. The attempt would be made to encourage consumers to reclassify the brand, perhaps as part of another product class, by surrounding it with a new set of associations.

In selecting a positioning plan several possibilities may be combined. The choice will be influenced by the competitive situation, the positions taken by others, customer perceptions and the historical position of the product class and its brands. The practicality of a desired positioning will be limited by the resources available and by the ability to translate the position into an effective communication to consumers. Positioning takes on particular importance in developing new products, in revitalising established products, when competing products change their positions or new competing brands are launched, and when new product classes emerge that might be threatening.

Branding

Products can be sold as unbranded commodities. Raw materials are still treated in this way, but increasingly branding is becoming dominant, even in the supply of industrial components and in hitherto unbranded areas such as vegetables.

What is the power of brands? Would you buy unpackaged, unbranded breakfast cereal from an itinerant street-trader? Would you buy perfume as a present for a female relative if it came in an unlabelled brown bottle? Would you buy an anonymous microcomputer from an anonymous source? Branding saves us much time as consumers. A simple word or two comes to represent a wealth of associations, for us and for others, and can offer detailed expectations. So that we do not need to ponder on the possibly murky channels used by the trader in obtaining supplies of breakfast cereal. We know the female relative will like the perfume – she may have even previously specified the brand. We know the range of compatible software for the microcomputer. Consumers learn to place some reliance on brand names when evaluating competing products. In services, too, branding can serve the consumer by offering consistent, identifiable services which might reduce confusion and save on search time [15].

From the organisation's point of view branding relates to fundamental strategic issues. Normally, brand strategy is an integral aspect of positioning strategy. Differentiation is possible without branding, but it would be a laborious task to reiterate a litany of points of difference in every communication, internally as well as with customers. It is also very doubtful that customers would bother to learn all the company's claims without some shorthand device. If the firm did not supply some cue then customers would probably construct their own, with massive variation and a good deal of distortion. Brand names are an economical communication device and allow the organisation to attempt to influence consumer perceptions, and so to establish a differentiated position with more clarity.

The potential influence of brand names is enormous. Porter [16] sees product differentiation in convenience goods as the major factor in sustaining the manufacturer's power against retailers, and branding has come to represent this differentiation. Table 12.4 indicates the difference that brand names make to consumers. Scrutiny of the responses of the exclusive users of brand B reveals a huge shift across the rows. Many prefer brand A in the blind test, which is quite contrary to the branded test. This anomaly is supported in the third column where these respondents tested brand B marked as brand A, and many said they preferred the other brand (i.e. brand A, thinking it to be brand B).

Marks & Spencer is the top brand in Britain according to a survey in 1988. It scored highest on awareness and on how highly regarded it was by members of the public. An interesting comparison is between Britain and Europe. Top brands across Europe are dominated by car manufacturers (Table 12.5). In all these cases it is the corporate identity that dominates.

There are several options in brand strategy. A company can sell under its own brand or under that of another company. In the latter case it is often a retailer's own label. In using the company's brand a choice will be needed between using a 'family' brand name for all that firms' brands, as opposed to giving each product an individual brand name.

Some companies attempt to obtain the benefits of both strategies by family branding and at the same time having several 'sub-brands'. Ford puts its name on all its cars, which also have individual brand names. The Lever subsidiary Birds Eye Wall's created sub-brands in frozen foods with Menu Masters and Captain Birds Eye. An alternative trend is seen in Reckitt and Colman's food and wine division, where strong brands in several product fields (Colman's mustard, Gales honey, Jif

Table 12.4 *Consumer response to brand names*

	Blind test brand A vs brand B %	Brand test brand A vs brand B %	Brand test brand A (branded as A) vs brand B (branded as A) %
Total sample	+12	+ 6	− 2
Exclusive users of A	+ 6	+42	+28
Exclusive users of B	+22	−29	−22
Users of A and B	+18	+ 2	−12
Users of neither	+ 8	+ 2	− 4

Note: Data are for net preferences for brand A, which is the percentage difference in these paired comparisons.
Source: J.C. Penny, I.M. Hunt and W.A. Twyman, 'Product testing methodology', in P. Law, C. Weinberg *et al.*, *Product Management*. New York: Harper & Row 1974.

Table 12.5 *Survey of brand names*

Top brands in Britain	Top brands in Europe
1. Marks & Spencer	1. Mercedes
2. Cadbury	2. Philips
3. Kellogg	3. Volkswagen
4. Heinz	4. Rolls-Royce
5. Rolls-Royce	5. Porsche
6. Boots	6. Coca-Cola
7. Nescafé	7. Ferrari
8. BBC	8. BMW
9. Rowntree	9. Michelin
10. Sainsbury	10. Volvo

Source: Landor Associates, 1990.

lemon, Robinson's barley water, Moussec, Veuve du Vernay, Bull's Blood) were brought under the umbrella of the corporate brand of Colman's of Norwich.

Manufacturer's brand or distributor's brand?

Most retail chains now carry a large proportion of their merchandise under their own label. Manufacturers therefore need to determine their response to this development. They can refuse to make for retailers' own labels (as a few do); they can give over all their output to this type of brand policy (again as a few do); or they can adopt a mixture, as most seem to do.

By using retailers' brand names the manufacturer stands to gain additional volume, or at least fill the gap that may otherwise have emerged following the retailer's use of a competitor's output for own branding. This volume can lay down a base load which, within annual periods, may be relatively stable, and so ease production planning. It also requires minimal promotional expenditure, and sometimes may be the only way to deal with some outlets, e.g. Marks & Spencer. However, this strategy does have its drawbacks because it shifts the balance of power very firmly to the retailer, and in consequence the manufacturer's margins are likely to be squeezed. Retailers will also be anxious to ensure that delivery and stocking arrangements work to their advantage.

From the retailer's viewpoint the attraction of own brands is to build store loyalty, yet attitudes display marked diversity. Marks & Spencer trade almost exclusively under their own brand and Tesco have about 30 per cent of their grocery sales from their two own brands. In furniture it is interesting to note that the Great Universal Stores (GUS) retail subsidiaries have different strategies. Ornstein [17] reports that Cavendish Woodhouse aim at C2–D consumers for credit sales with a high proportion of own brands. On the other hand, Times Furnishing aims at B–C1 groups for cash sales with national brands. Another GUS subsidiary, National Discount Stores, carries national brands in order to achieve clear price comparisons.

Ornstein summarises the conditions necessary for successful own brands as follows:

1. The stores must have a high reputation.

2. Where the brand is a copy of a manufacturer's brand, then there should be a marked price differential.

3. Merchandise innovations can be made only if the stores have a very high reputation.

4. Own brands are viable only in large markets, permitting mass production for the same outlet nearly comparable to the mass production of manufacturer's lines sold through many outlets.

The phenomenal rise of the large grocery retailers over the past thirty years, in particular Sainsbury and Tesco, has had other implications for branding. In many grocery markets these retailers' brands are as prestigious as, or are more prestigious than, the manufacturers' brands. This gives the retailer enormous power, and one reflection of that is that they are willing to compete directly with the strongest brands, even sometimes mimicking their distinctive packaging.

Multi-product brands or multi-brand products?

Should the firm have one brand name for all its products, or should it have several brands in the same product category? Multi-product brands conform to the first case and imply that the company stamps the same name on quite different products (e.g. Heinz, Cadbury and Kellogg). Multi-brand products on the other hand occur where the same manufacturer has several different brands of the same product (e.g. soap companies).

Multi-product brands, sometimes called 'family brands', have distinct promotional advantages. Heavy advertising spending on major items in the product line could have a carry-over effect on all the range. With favourable past customer experience, substantial reputations can be built for the whole product range, easing new product introductions since both retailer and consumer are already impressed by the company. This can, of course, work in reverse; minor brands which do not fulfil customer expectations can damage the prospects of major brands. Stereotyping can therefore be both beneficial and potentially harmful. Additionally, an established company with a solid reputation for middle-of-the-road design could find it extremely difficult to introduce a new trendsetting line.

In some market circumstances a number of brands in the same product field may be justified. Several market segments may be better served with separately defined brands from the same manufacturer. Each of the brands would be designed to cater for the particular requirements of each of the segments.

Brand extensions

Using an established brand name in order to move into another related or unrelated product class has been a source of growth for many organisations. Unrelated brand extensions are sometimes referred to as brand stretching.

The attraction of brand extensions is the reduction in the cost of gaining a place in the market. Consumer awareness can be more easily built, there may be favourable associations to carry over and distributors may be more inclined to stock. The investment in the original brand may then gain a more substantial payoff, and in some cases the brand extension could even take over as the firm's leading product, thus giving assurance to future payoffs.

When the extension is complementary to the original product consumers may perceive a natural carry-over of competence, but not all successful extensions are complementary to the original. Aaker suggests that effective extension strategies have the following characteristics [18]:

1. The original brand has strong, positive associations which set up consumer expectations, reduce the communication task and help to establish differentiation.

2. There is high perceived quality of the original brand.

3. The original brand is well known and easily recognised.

Given these points the introduction of the extension is eased because the risk to the consumer in a trial purchase is reduced, since the new product is seen to come from a reputable source. There could be further benefit if the extension enhances the original by supporting it, adding to and deepening its image, and carrying it to new market segments.

Alternatively, an extension would be problematic if:

1. The original brand name does not add value in the specific context of the market in which the extension is placed – the original might not be well known to the particular segment or it is might be seen to be irrelevant to their needs.

2. There are incredible associations – disbelief that competence in one product class can be carried to another.

3. The image and associations of the extension do not fit comfortably with the original.

4. The new brand is not of the same quality as the original.

Arnold warns that [19]:

> The biggest single danger with a brand extension programme is that of diluting the original personality of the brand. If this is allowed to happen, consumers will become confused and the bond between them and the original brand will be lost. Consistency is the prime criterion – as long as the extension offers the market similar satisfactions to the original brand, the extension can be considered. If it does not, then even if the new brand does well (unlikely) it may only be at the expense of the original core brand.

Examples of brand extension strategies can be seen in the illustration overleaf. It is interesting to consider those in the light of the discussion above.

In analysing brand extension strategies Doyle [20] suggests that two factors are important: the differential advantage of the brand and the target segments. In both of these the brand extension and the original brand may be similar or they may be different. This gives four possibilities:

Similarities and differences between a brand extension and the original brand	*Doyle's recommendations*
1. Similar differential advantage; similar target segment.	Consistency in positioning strategies allows the sharing of the same company or range name, e.g. IBM, Timotei.
2. Similar differential advantage; different target segments	Similar benefits offered; same name can be used but distinguish type or grade e.g. Mercedes 200 or 500.
3. Different differential advantage; similar target segments.	Use separate brand names, perhaps with company name, e.g Kellogg.
4. Different differential advantage; different target segments.	Use unique brand names with unique positioning.

Packaging

Self-service shopping has an obvious and enormous implication: nobody is there at the point of sale to talk to the customer. The friendly shopkeeper no longer directs the customer's attention to a new line with the assurance that his wife has tried it. Add to that the sheer scale of the modern superstore with its thousands of brands on offer, and the manufacturer's problem in attempting to gain some attention can be appreciated. Packaging has taken on a sales promotional role to alleviate this problem. Visibility clearly counts, and so packaging research, using fairly straightforward techniques, aims at improving the pack's impact.

Packaging can also convey information – literally, graphically or by using transparent materials. This information may give instructions or legally required information about the contents, or be tied in with other sales promotional activities. Additionally, the pack could have some emotive effects. It could be suggestive of the quality of the product, as in cosmetics, or it could reinforce favourable

---

Brand extension strategies

Kenwood has been making food mixers since the 1950s and its Kenwood Chef has held a leading position in many countries. In 1993 it diversified by launching two ranges of new products with the Kenwood branding – hairdryers and shavers. Its marketing director is reported as saying that cookware is the next likely brand extension, and that lawnmowers and luggage may be possibilities.

Gillette began its business with razor blades and carried the brand name to related shaving products. But it did not extend the name to deodorants, preferring the Right Guard branding, nor to electric shavers, and other small electrical appliances, where it retained the Braun name, or to writing implements where it has the Papermate products.

Wilkinson Sword originally made swords and then it went into razors. Subsequent brand extensions were into gardening equipment such as shears and secateurs.

Bic made ball point pens. And then it made disposable plastic razors and disposable lighters under the same brand name. Later it experimented with perfumes.

---

impressions delivered by advertising. A summary of factors to consider in packaging decisions is given in Table 12.6 which is taken from Davidson.

It was noted in the discussion of branding that the organisation seeks economical ways of communicating effectively with customers. Modern packaging is viewed as a vital part of that communications mix. It has strategic significance in so far as it reflects and reinforces brand and corporate identities and it has operational significance in that it provides point-of-purchase stimulation, in addition to its functional role.

Table 12.6　*Checklist for packaging development*

The pack may offer:	Check points
1. Protection against . . .	moisture, air, heat, cold, separation of products, leakage, staleness, breakage, crushing, dirt, corroding, scuffing
2. Consumer convenience . . .	ease of opening, disposal, storage, dispensing and handling, safety in use, reusable, reclosable, clear instructions for use, light to handle, stands easily
3. Trade appeal . . .	ease of stocking, shelving, displaying, identification of both individual products and outer cases, economic utilisation of space and good protection
4. Consumer sales appeal . . .	good size impression, attractive shape and design, easily identifiable, distinctiveness from competitors, tie in with product purpose

Source: J.H. Davidson, *Offensive Marketing*, 2nd edn. Harmondsworth: Penguin Books, 1987, p. 205.

Summary

Product plans must necessarily depend on the view taken about possible future sales levels. A central consideration in this view will be the product lifecycle, although it is relevant to distinguish between the product class, the product form and the brand level. Technological development could be a crucial influence on lifecycles inasmuch as it can innovate new products, rejuvenate established products and make others obsolete. Just as basic to product planning is the choice that the firm makes with regard to its growth path. Does it stay with existing products aimed at existing markets, or will it seek further development by changing its product-market mix? The choice of growth path interacts strongly with the strategy chosen for product positioning, and a highly differentiated positioning strategy is supported by decisions on both branding and packaging.

Questions for review and discussion

1. What extra insights can be derived from an analysis of lifecycles at the form and brand level, in addition to the product class level?

2. List some major technological developments. What product lifecycles have they affected, and how?

3. Using Ansoff's growth matrix, derive further examples of companies employing each path.

4. Examine product positioning in a particular market. How do the firms attempt to distinguish themselves, and on what basis? Is product positioning simply tied to advertising strategy?

5. Review the six positioning strategies suggested by Wind. Find new examples for each type, and illustrate with advertisements.

References

1. Lambkin, M. and Day, G.S. 1989. 'Evolutionary processes in competitive markets: beyond the product life cycle', *Journal of Marketing*, vol. 53, July, pp. 4–20.
2. Ibid.
3. Urban, G.L. and Star, S.H. 1991. *Advanced Marketing Strategy*. Englewood Cliffs, NJ: Prentice Hall, shows many examples in ch. 6.

4. Hunt, S. 1991. *Modern Marketing Theory*. Cincinnati, Ohio: South-Western, p. 95.

5. Day, G. 1986. *Analysis for Strategic Market Decisions*. St Paul, Minn.: West; Midgley, D. 1977. *Innovation and New Product Marketing*. London: Croom Helm; Cox, W. 1967. 'Product lifecycles as marketing models', *Journal of Business*, vol. 40, October.

6. Wind, Y. 1982. *Product Policy*. Reading, Mass.: Addison-Wesley, p. 59.

7. Levitt, T. 1986. *The Marketing Imagination*. New York: Free Press.

8. Christopher, M., Payne, A. and Ballantyne, D. 1991. *Relationship Marketing*. Oxford: Butterworth-Heinemann, p. 58.

9. Hooley, G. and Saunders, J. 1993. *Competitive Positioning*. Hemel Hempstead: Prentice Hall, p. 210.

10. Johne, F. and Snelson, P. 1988. 'The role of marketing specialists in product development', *Proceedings of the 21st Annual Conference of the Marketing Education Group, Huddersfield*, vol. 3, pp. 176–91.

11. Ibid.

12. Cooper, R. 1984. 'The performance impact of product innovation strategies', *European Journal of Marketing*, vol. 18, no. 5.

13. Aaker, D. 1991. *Managing Brand Equity*. New York: Free Press, ch. 5.

14. Wind, op. cit., p. 79.

15. Murphy, J. 1987. *Branding: A Key Marketing Tool*. Basingstoke: Macmillan, p. 129.

16. Porter, M. 1967. *Interbrand Choice, Strategy and Bilateral Market Power*. Cambridge, Mass.: Harvard University Press, p. 89.

17. Ornstein, E. 1976. *The Retailers*. London: Associated Business Programmes, p. 69.

18. Aaker, D. 1991. *Managing Brand Equity*. New York: Free Press, ch. 9.

19. Arnold, D. 1992. *The Handbook of Brand Management*. London: Century Business, p. 143.

20. Doyle, P. 1994. *Marketing Management and Strategy*. Hemel Hempstead: Prentice Hall International, p. 177.

Chapter 13

Planning new and mature products

The product plan will determine the overall product range to be offered by the firm. The desired product mix delineates the need, if any, for new products, indicates the requirement to reposition established products and isolates the products which might be candidates for withdrawal. This chapter considers the influences on these decisions and introduces techniques that could be employed.

New product planning

There is wide belief in the notion that the mortality rate for new products is extremely high. Insight into the reasons for new product failure is offered by Davidson's analysis of fifty successes and fifty failures in the British market since 1960. He sees significant price or performance advantage as crucial (Table 13.1). As can be seen, 80 per cent of the failures had nothing to distinguish them from the brands already on the market, and 74 per cent of the successes were exactly

Table 13.1 *Price and performance advantage in new product launches*

	50 new product successes %	50 new product failures %
Significantly better performance, higher price	44	8
Marginally better performance, higher price	6	12
Better performance, same price	24	0
Same performance, lower price	8	0
Same performance, same price	16	30
Same performance, higher price	2	30
Worse performance, same or higher price	0	20
	100	100

Note: Performance was, as far as possible, evaluated by blind product tests among target consumer groups.
Source: J.H. Davidson, *Offensive Marketing*, 2nd edn. Harmondsworth: Penguin Books, 1987, p. 336.

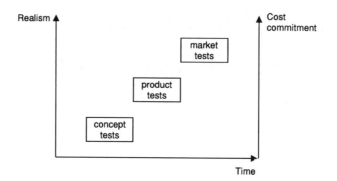

Figure 13.1   *Tests in new product development*

opposite. The 20 per cent of failures with good product performance are interesting. Davidson explains their demise by their high prices, their promotional failings or the small size of the segment to which they appealed.

Broadly, three kinds of test are used during new product development in order to generate the kinds of information required by marketing managers. Concept tests and product tests are discussed in this chapter and market tests in the next chapter. Figure 13.1 depicts the sequencing of these tests. It shows that the realism, and possibly the amount of reliance that can be placed on test results, increase with the move from concept to product to market tests. At the same time cost commitment increases. This relates to the costs sunk in the new product project, and to the capital committed. Each of the three categories of testing also have costs of entirely different orders: concept tests are relatively inexpensive, product tests can be more expensive and market testing moderately or very expensive.

A crucial factor in new product introductions is the reaction of distributors. If they are not convinced of the virtues of a new brand then they will not stock it, or will give only minimal support. Kraushar and Eassie, new product consultants, have undertaken regular surveys of the attitudes of buyers in multiple grocers to new products. Between 1970 and 1982 they monitored some interesting changes in the reasons given by grocers for not taking new products: product quality, advertising support and introductory bonuses had improved and were much less frequently the reasons for refusal in 1982. The lack of a perceived product advantage reinforces the conclusions in Davidson's work referred to above, and the lack of shelf space is a reflection of the great number of new products introduced over the years.

The theme of differential advantage is echoed in the research by Cooper who emphasises three composite factors as dominating new product success [1]. These are:

1.   Product – having a product with a differential advantage in the eyes of the consumer.

2. Market – obtaining a sound knowledge of the marketplace and customer together with proficiently carrying out the market research and launch studies.

3. Technical production – having synergy between project and firm in terms of production and technical resources, and well-executed technical and production activities.

Balance both in strategies and in resources is therefore a requisite. Take any one of the three elements out and the resultant imbalance contributes to a fall. Cooper's empirical studies on 200 new products demonstrate a systematic relationship from those low on all three factors (7 per cent successes) to those high on all three (90 per cent successes).

This background is suggestive of the risk the firm may encounter once it decides to introduce new products. Before examining approaches to contain this risk we need to consider further the pressures that might impel organisations into this potentially dangerous strategy. This can be done by referring once more to the environment–goals–strategy triad. Substantial changes in environments or goals will prompt strategic responses, which could include product development. Table 13.2 shows some changes in environments and goals that might trigger consideration of new product development.

Change in any of the factors in Table 13.2 could cause a firm to review its product strategies. Reviews of past performance might spur thoughts of new products and could be seen as a symptom or consequence of the other changes. Previous goals may not have been met, and sales and profit projections may reveal a gap between desired levels and those that might be achieved without change in strategies. There may also be change in corporate expectations, perhaps because of change in ownership or top management. The firm's resources and

Table 13.2 *Changes in environments and goals*

Changes in external environment	Changes in internal environment	Changes in goals
Societal values/ expectations	Ownership	Reviews of past performance
	Management	in meeting goals
Consumers	Resources and competences	
Income effects	Cost effects	
Fashion/taste	Manufacturing ability	New goals
Demographic effects	Marketing ability	
	R&D ability	
Competitors		
Attacks with new products		
Repositioning		
Technology		
Product obsolescence		
New opportunities		

competences will not be constant: cost structures may be changing, making some products more expensive and alternatively releasing opportunities which were previously thought too costly. Manufacturing ability may be enhanced through experience, allowing the production of higher quality products, or marketing competence increased to allow effective attacks on product-markets which had hitherto been ruled out. New products could additionally be on the agenda because new R&D competence has been acquired.

External factors will have at least as much impact, and for many firms may be the most powerful. Broad changes in society could result in new patterns of values and behaviour which could mean that consumers seek new benefits from products and services, or reduce their demand for old products. This might also be expressed in changes in fashions and tastes. Competitors will not be idle and may make fast response to these changes. New rivals may emerge from within the industry or there may be new entrants. Established firms may redefine their search for competitive advantage and reposition with threatening new products. Further turmoil may be caused by the technology: some products may be rendered obsolete and entirely new classes of products emerge.

Faced with these kinds of pressure the firm may choose to respond by developing new products. Some will be attracted by the pay-off often achieved by pioneers; others may attempt to stake out a distinctive niche in a growing market, whilst many may only be trying to catch up with the leaders.

Generating new product concepts

Strategic factors, as well as the firm's competence in new product development, will influence how rigorous the search will be for a new product concept. The issues prompting the product review will have a significant bearing. If they concern chronic change affecting the fortunes of a key product then considerable attention may be given to the search for new opportunities, with the employment of a very wide range of sources and techniques, and possibly resulting in quite radical new products. If the issues are less stressful, then more moderate search may be undertaken, perhaps confined to existing product-market scope and resulting in a modified product rather than a radically new product. The initial stimulus for generating product concepts arrives with much variation in urgency, significance, parameters for the search and levels of work already done. It is set against equal variation in the multitude of sources and techniques that might be employed. The process does not have a singular rationale for its inception and there is not automatic choice of source or technique. This argues for a systematic procedure fitted to the scale and nature of the problem originally posed.

Approaches to concept generation have been classified by Crawford as being based on either consumer problems or reappraisals of products already on the market [2]. In the first case the object is to discover unmet needs or problems the consumer might have, and so to attempt to solve them through the development

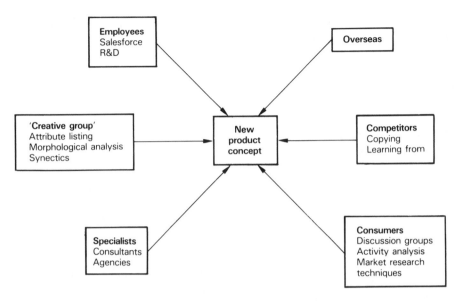

Figure 13.2 *Generating concepts: sources and techniques*

of a new product. In the second case the approach is to consider the needs and problems that are currently being served by products, and then to address them in new ways. On the other hand, Sowery classifies techniques into two groups: creative and analytical [3]. Figure 13.2 is an amalgam of some of the principal sources and techniques.

Copying from competitors has been a widely used source. The earlier analysis of new product launches with little to distinguish them from those already available is indicative of the scale and of the inherent problems. It is used because there is the demonstration that a market exists. It is abused if it results in a me-too product, destined to be a market follower. Learning from competitors is different, and could lead to improved products, better design and to enhanced promotion and distribution strategies.

Bringing in product ideas from abroad has been lucrative in some markets: lager, pharmaceuticals, confectionery, cars, office machinery and some engineering products have flourished after the transplant. Sowery lists a number of successful products which came from overseas including Cadbury's Smash, Crawford's Tuc, Lever's Shield and St Ivel Gold. But Davidson believes it has not always worked well in grocery markets. In his analysis of success rates 18 per cent of the successes were of American origin, as were 30 per cent of the failures. Despite the common language the differences in the market environments have been 'sufficiently serious to trip up a long line of American transplants to the UK – Betty Crocker (General Mills), Campbells, Gerber, Cheseborough-Ponds and Bristol-Myers being among the prize examples' [4].

Salesforce personnel have a unique position at the boundary of the organisation. Their routine contact with the trade, customers and competitors allows them to act as a channel for ideas from the market and possibly to conceive of new solutions to customer problems. Ideas may also stem from internal R&D. In science-based industries this may be by far the best source of innovation for some firms. In consumer product industries the emphasis in R&D may be the development of products after a concept has been generated.

In Figure 13.2 'creative group' indicates any group specifically charged with generating concepts, in the firm or an agency. Numerous techniques have been employed. Lateral thinking has been advocated by de Bono [5], and Hisrich and Peters review many other possibilities, a few of which are noted below [6].

1. *Attribute listing* – a list of attributes relating to the problem is considered from a variety of viewpoints; each attribute may be modified in turn and the consequences investigated.

2. *Morphological analysis* examines the relationships between all the possible variables in solving a problem. It requires the construction of relevant dimensions and the generation of solutions in every combination of the dimensions. Cafarelli illustrates this by taking five consumer benefits as one dimension and five product attributes as a second dimension [7]:

Product attributes	Consumer benefits
Shape	Nutrition
Colour	Flavour
Size	Eat wet or dry
Smell	Easy to eat or digest
Texture	Non-fattening

For each of the twenty-five combinations of these dimensions a new product concept is conceived. As an example, if this were related to cereals then the shape/nutrition cell might lead to a totally different idea to the smell/nutrition combination or the colour/easy-to-eat cell.

3. *Synectics* is a group process which uses analogy to unlock new ideas. How does nature solve that problem? How does another industry or culture view that problem? Cafarelli gives the example of cleaning teeth. The analogy was with cleaning an office block and the creative group had to imagine they were the cleaners moving in at the end of the day. They envisaged the kinds of problem they would meet and how they would tackle them.

Customers might be a fruitful source of ideas. In industrial markets they may be able to articulate fully a problem they have and lay down lines along which solutions can be found. They may search actively for potential suppliers. In consumer markets it is usually necessary for the firm to initiate the contact with customers and to structure the procedure for obtaining their ideas. This could be simple observation of user activities: how they prepare, cook and eat their meals; how they use their time or how they approach particular problems. It could involve bringing together a group for semi-structured discussion or more imaginative role-playing and other qualitative research. It might also use perceptual mapping.

Obtaining product ideas is but the first step; the remainder of the development process is aimed at whittling down the number to retain those most nearly matching the objective set when the process was initiated, and to refining the concept so that it meets market acceptance.

Screening

Only some ideas will justify the expense of development work, so some mechanism is required to sift out the few that deserve further attention. There are two essential features in this screening process:

1. The establishment of a set of evaluative criteria, i.e. a list of the important factors that should be considered when making a choice.

2. Judgements about the extent to which each product idea meets each of these important factors.

O'Meara produced one of the most widely known screening techniques, involving seventeen criteria [8]. The steps in this procedure are as follows:

1. Each criterion is given a weight to distinguish its relative significance, assuming that they are not all equally important.

2. Judgements are made of the product performance in respect of each criterion. Three possible levels of performance could be considered: 'good', 'average' and 'poor'.

3. These judgements could be restricted to a statement that the performance will be at one of these levels. However, we may not be able to be that certain. In this case we would assign a probability distribution across the different levels of possible performance; e.g. we might judge that there is a 30 per cent chance of the product being 'good' in respect of one criterion, a 50 per cent chance of it being 'average' and a 20 per cent chance of it being 'poor'.

4. Each performance level is then given a weight, e.g. 3 for 'good', 2 for 'average' and 1 for 'poor'.

5. The expected probabilities derived at step 3 are then multiplied by the performance level weights determined at step 4. This gives the 'expected value'. So the expected probability might be 0.3 and the performance weight 3, to give an expected value of 0.9 (see the third criterion in Table 13.3).

Table 13.3 *A new product idea screening device*

Criterion	Criterion weight	Performance level						Total EV	Criterion score
		Good Weight 3		Average Weight 2		Poor Weight 1			
		EP	EV	EP	EV	EP	EV		
Relation to present channels	0.2	0.5	1.5	0.5	1.0	0	0	2.5	0.50
Relation to present products	0.3	0.0	0.0	0.7	1.4	0.3	0.3	1.7	0.51
Breadth of market	0.1	0.3	0.9	0.5	1.0	0.2	0.2	2.1	0.21
Resistance to cyclical fluctuations	0.4	0.2	0.6	0.8	1.6	0	0	2.2	0.88
	1.0								2.10

Notes:
This example uses just four of the seventeen criteria suggested by O'Meara.
EP = expected probability that the product would achieve that performance on that criterion; first case 0.5 good and 0.5 average.
EV = expected value = EP × performance weight (not criterion weight); e.g. on the first criterion there is a 0.5 *EP* that the product will be 'good' and 'good' has a weight of 3; therefore *EV* = 1.5.
The criterion score is given by total *EV* times the criterion weight, e.g. in the first case (2.5 × 0.2) = 0.5.
Source: Adapted from J.T. O'Meara, 'Selecting profitable products', *Harvard Business Review*, Jan./Feb., 1961.

6. The 'expected value' at each performance level is then summed to obtain the 'total expected value' for each criterion. In Table 13.3 for the third criterion this is 2.1 (0.9 + 1.0 + 0.2).

7. The 'total expected values' are then multiplied by the criterion weight to take account of the fact that performance against different criteria will have differing impact. For example, in the table the fourth criterion is thought to be far more significant than the third (for that particular company at the particular time).

8. An overall score for the product idea is computed by summing the scores at step 7.

9. Some decision rule is now needed – some benchmark, which should be exceeded for the product to proceed. This is usually derived from past experience. In the example in the table, if the benchmark were 2.0 the product would pass the screening.

Such a procedure can help to sharpen a company's critical evaluation of a new product idea, although reservations have been expressed about its validity. The units of measurement for each criterion may be quite different, and some of the criteria may well be subsumed within others so that the overall score may contain unspecified interaction effects [9]. To meet such objections it is necessary first to list out the relevant criteria and then to rank – not weight – each of them. Every member of the new product screening team then rates the possible performance on each criterion, and an average is determined. The average for the first criterion is then set against some prearranged benchmark. Those ideas that pass on the first criterion are then evaluated on the second, and so on.

Whichever procedure is employed the cardinal step is the prior choice of relevant evaluative criteria. There is no universal set of such criteria; they must be specific to each company's experience and expectations. The clear specification of these criteria is a valuable exercise in its own right, because all of them should be related to the firm's ultimate goals. If sales or profit criteria could be used, then more detailed criteria would be redundant. But since this is at the product concept stage – and there is no physical product – then sales and profit guesses are likely to be wild. By discovering more detailed implications of a potential product, such as effects on channels of distribution or other elements in the product range, it is hoped to obtain an approximation of the effects on sales and profits. The burden of this study therefore sets some very challenging questions about the variables that produce given sales and profit levels. A corollary is that companies that have a better understanding of such variables should be able to make better screening decisions.

Some firms have to make literally hundreds of screening decisions every year; others, very few. The consequences of these decisions are also very varied. In some instances they affect the survival of the organisation, and in others they might have only marginal impact. In some cases, of necessity, they become routine; in others each screening decision is unique. Whatever the particular circumstances, a planned and systematic approach to screening new product ideas seems wise. Above all, an agreed set of evaluative criteria is required, otherwise different people will arrive at contrary judgements because they evaluate the idea against different criteria. The resulting impasse will be at least embarrassing. Good ideas could wilt because of inattention and bad ideas survive because of 'political' pressure.

Concept testing

One of the main worries about new products is the likely level and type of consumer response. Advocates of consumer orientation rightly argue that some evaluation of this should be incorporated at all stages of development. If valid assessments could be made, then sales forecasts would be improved and the direction of product development more properly aligned to market requirements. Concept testing is designed to gauge something of consumer reaction at an early stage.

Group discussions are a widely used means of concept testing. Groups of about eight consumers are convened to discuss the product, or the concept. Sometimes a set of written statements forms the stimulus for such discussions. Confusion and lack of comprehension of the product idea are very possible with this kind of stimulus alone; and so for convenience goods, resort may be made to dummy packages and mock-up advertisements to convey a more meaningful impression of the product. The product itself would not be available for testing because concept testing comes before a decision even to develop a prototype.

Research conducted in such a fashion is bound to be speculative. None the less it can have some limited value. The discipline of having to explain the product idea to a group of consumers is always helpful, and the associations that the concept has for these people may be instructive. Advance warning may be derived that the concept would meet resistance because it was linked in unforeseen ways with other concepts that consumers held. They may label it as not really being very new since they expected its performance to be similar to another existing product, and this despite important innovations in product design. They may totally discount what the company conceived as being the major feature and, instead, focus on a minor element. For example, a new foodstuff may be seen by the manufacturer as having the important advantage of reduced preparation time. Consumers in discussion groups may centre on its novel storage requirements. That introduces another problem: what is most talked about in a discussion group may not be what is most valued by the eventual consumers. Clearly, nothing is going to be proved in such exercises, although they could provide a host of hypotheses.

It is tempting to link this procedure with purchase intention: to ask group participants if they would buy the product being described. Rating scales with five points from 'definitely would buy' to 'definitely would not buy' could be administered. Tauber has conducted a study to assess the validity of purchase intentions questions [10]. He found that those expressing positive intentions were subsequently much more aware of a product that was launched nationally, but the five-point scale did not adequately discriminate between those who 'would probably buy' and those who 'might or might not' among those who in fact did buy the product once. And the purchase intention scale could not differentiate on repeat purchases. It would be dangerous to put too much reliance on purchase intentions in such artificial circumstances, but companies which undertake frequent concept tests might develop benchmarks to be used for screening out the weakest ideas. In this way concept testing becomes a screening and development technique rather than a sales prediction technique.

Problematical as it is, concept testing represents the product's first encounter with the market. Apart from gaining broad impressions of the idea's acceptability, more detailed benefits may be apparent. Participants in the discussions may spark off a hitherto neglected aspect: a new use not previously considered, a competitive position not recognised, a minor attribute that with development may be important, or a design change that could make it more flexible or open up joint consumption possibilities with other products. Concept testing can also be instructive in the initial development of communication strategies. It can establish some of the difficulties in describing the product to consumers, such as whether or not product attributes should feature in the communication, whether better understanding would follow from using reference groups, or stressing consumption situations, or whether the concept would be better assimilated if it was associated with other firmly established concepts or products.

Table 13.4 *Ranking of hand trowels*

	Short handle	Medium handle	Long handle
Narrow blade	8	5	9
Medium blade	2	1	4
Broad blade	7	3	6

1 = Highest rank.

Table 13.5 *Utility scores for calculators*

Memory type	Score	Function type	Score	Shape	Score
None	6	Arithmetic only	10	I	35
Constant operand	33	With automatic %	29	II	30
All-functions single	40	With square root	44	III	36
All-functions dual	49	With reciprocal	48	IV	30

Trade-off analysis

The product concept may have been developed sufficiently to specify the product attributes in some detail. The problem then becomes one of determining which combination of attributes the consumer prefers. A quantitative approach to this problem could employ trade-off analysis. The basis of this approach is consumer rankings of various combinations of attributes. For example, with hand trowels used in gardening the two attributes might be length of handle and breadth of blade, and the rank order of combinations given by consumers is shown in Table 13.4 (1 = highest rank).

The medium blade gets the top ranking, except when it has a long handle, and in that case a broad blade is preferred with a medium handle. The aim of the exercise is to determine how much of one attribute will be sacrificed to obtain a given level on another. Advanced statistical techniques can derive 'utility values' from such rankings, and Lunn and Morgan illustrate this in a study of calculators [11]. They considered nine attributes, each at several levels. Some of the 'utility scores' are shown in Table 13.5.

Type of memory and function affect the utility much more than the shape, although with more sophisticated memories and added functions the incremental worth declines. If the sample size had been sufficiently large it might also have been possible to discriminate between different segments, in order to investigate if different groups trade off different attributes.

Product testing

Once prototypes are available then deeper evaluations are possible. Selecting an appropriate sample of consumers is contentious. Current practice employs a judgement sample in the target segment. Midgley [12] argues against this by

---

Concept and product testing for the Ford Fiesta

Ford's move into the small car segment in 1976 was a major step, and it was preceded by very large-scale marketing research. This research was in three phases:

1. Mid-1972 to mid-1973 – selecting the right concept.
2. Mid- to end-1973 – determining the specific product proposal: its precise dimensions, styling, interior space.
3. 1974 to mid-1976 – detailing aspects with shorter lead-time, e.g. seat design, door panel design, detailing exterior styling.

Phase 1 research methods included a survey among owners of existing small cars aimed at uncovering the strengths and weaknesses of different concepts in terms of performance, handling, roominess, styling and economy. Surveys were also undertaken in specific segments, such as where a small car was a second car and among first time buyers. Two waves of 'product clinic' were also conducted in each of the five main European markets. Models had been built of alternative exteriors and interiors. Although these were of clay they were entirely realistic, even at close range. Samples of new car buyers were invited to these 'clinics' and co-operated in group discussions, individual unstructured interviews and self-completed questionnaires. Results from this were:

1. The essence of the interior design was settled.
2. A clear direction for styling was provided.
3. It demonstrated that an Escort-derived, rear wheel drive, small car would be a risk.
4. A range of possible sales volumes was derived.

Phase 2 research employed fibreglass models of four alternatives devised from the initial research. 'Beauty contest' clinics were used to evaluate these. There was one consistent winner among the four: this was approved, and tooling for large-scale production began.

Phase 3 lasted two-and-a-half years and filled in all the final 'detailing'. More clinic studies led to progressive refinement and allowed checks against new products from competitors. In this phase there was also research into the brand name and the launch advertising strategy.

Source: R.P Smith and C.A. Malloy, 'Fiesta: the marketing research contribution to the development of Ford's small car for Europe', *ESOMAR Congress 1976, Research that Works for Today's Marketing Problems*. Amsterdam: ESOMAR, 1976, pp. 195–212.

---

pointing out that new product success is dependent on the purchase intentions of the innovators, and that these may not be represented sufficiently in such a sampling plan. He advocates Ostlund's methodology [13] for discerning innovators along dimensions of perceived risk and so on, which was discussed in Chapter 4. A questionnaire on 'innovativeness' would therefore be administered in order to choose the sample. A self-report scale to measure innovativeness could also be considered and this might elicit scaled responses to a series of statements such as 'Compared to my friends I own few new fashion items' [14]. Since innovators may be different from the rest of the population in their product perceptions, it would probably also be useful to include a study of non-innovators. Apart from anything else this could provide valuable clues about how advertising strategy should change as the market evolves.

The next issue in product testing is the choice between single or comparative tests. A common technique is to place a pair of products in plain packages for evaluation by a sample of consumers – the 'blind paired comparison'. It is possible that this exaggerates differences. Because they are given two products, the respondents impute that there must be differences, and so look for them. One answer to this problem is offered by Penny et al. [15]:

> If some kind of market acceptability rating is required then the best strategy appears to be to make the test conditions as much like real life usage as possible, which may mean monadic [single] testing, and to rely on past experience or other research to indicate the meaning of the rating obtained.

Questions posed to respondents in product testing usually concern overall disposition towards the product and evaluations of particular attributes. Intentions-to-buy may also be investigated. All of these could employ scaling devices to elicit respondents' feelings about the sample. Alphanumeric and pictorial descriptions are used to describe each of the scale positions.

Product testing can appear deceptively simple. A group of consumers merely says whether or not the product is liked. Such simplicity disguises many pitfalls. For instance, do consumers make their evaluations in a laboratory setting (or in halls in various parts of the country) or do they make evaluations after using the product at home? Realism and cost need to be balanced, but a cheap test giving the wrong result is worse than no test at all. Boyd suggests multi-stage testing with central testing on a larger number of product options, and in-home testing on a subsequently reduced number of options [16]. It would be expected that the kind of evaluation and the circumstances in which it was made would affect the consumer's reaction. Watkins [17] found this to be so in his survey of company practice and says:

> a large company reported . . . high scores in terms of intention to purchase are obtained using monadic, in-hall tests with an interviewer-completed questionnaire after the respondent has tried the product first and been shown the packaging. Low scores are obtained with comparative in-home tests with self-completion questionnaires.

Determining who is to do the testing can cause difficulties. Family products are obviously problematic; the person who buys may actually hate the product. Pet foods can also be difficult to evaluate. Tull and Hawkins recount the case of a new dog food that was launched after extensive packaging and advertising research and which obtained good initial market penetration. Several months later sales declined heavily and it was only then that it became clear that the product had not been tested on dogs: few would eat it given any choice [18].

The way that test information is presented can also deceive. Haller [19]

Table 13.6   *Different interpretation of consumer preferences*

	Consumer preferences			
	A	B	A	B
Number preferring each	210	90	210	90
Base for %	210	90	300	300
Reasons for preference:				
Makes more suds	33%	30%	23%	9%
Cleans better/more easily	23%	21%	16%	6%
Easier to use	18%	16%	12%	5%

argues that 'reasons for preference' are central to understanding a product's reception, but that slight changes in the way data are displayed can obscure the interpretation. If 300 consumers had expressed a preference for two products, with reasons, the data could be shown as proportions of the 300, or as proportions of those preferring product A and those preferring B (Table 13.6).

Expressing the reasons as a proportion of those preferring each product reveals little discrimination between A and B, and it might be concluded that the reasons given are not related to determinant attributes. Whereas changing the base for the proportions to all those expressing a preference (either for A or B) uncovers 'sudsiness' as a powerful discriminator. A trivial change results in a radically different interpretation. The point is that researchers can be trapped by their own mode of analysis; they develop routines for analysis, some things are taken for granted and others appear 'obvious'.

Despite the problems, product testing is another step closer to the market and should furnish more opinions on the degree of success to be expected. Just as purchase intentions may have been elicited at the concept stage, they could again be tested. Interpretation of these intentions is easier if the company has long experience and has been able to establish benchmarks. For example, Black & Decker developed the Paintmate system with Berger and conducted six product tests with two thousand respondents. Those saying they 'would buy' amounted to 50 per cent, and this compared with 25 or 30 per cent for previous successful new products launched by Black & Decker [20].

Test marketing may be the final extension of the search for knowledge about buyer reactions, and this will be considered in the next chapter.

Changing positioning strategy

Developments in industry structure, competitive strategies and product lifecycle may occasion a rigorous assessment of the product's performance and could lead to changes in positioning strategy. Structural changes in the industry could erode the product's established competitive edge, such as in cost increases or new entrants to the industry. Direct rivals may become more competent or aggressive, sharpening the sources of their competitive advantage and perhaps bringing out successful product variants. The product lifecycle may mature, capping total market size and meaning that further growth can only derive from larger market share.

Approaches to repositioning relate to the fundamentals of competitive striving and so are based on the following broad directions:

1. *Cost effects*. Experience effects may allow the firm to compete for the first time as a low cost operator, possibly by cutting prices.

2. *Segment focus*. Market extension may be afforded by directing effort to serve segments new to the firm; this might mean widening the number of segments served or attempts to establish a specialist niche.

3. *Differentiation*. Changes may be made to the bases of differentiation with style, functional or quality changes.

Any of these could be considered at any stage in the product lifecycle. Just how appropriate they are will depend on analysis of the relationships between product class, form and brand cycles.

Detailed analysis of the relationships between the three levels of lifecycles will assist this investigation. To generalise, say, each of the products form and brand cycles may be on a trend that is up, static or down. Table 13.7 details the nine combinations when the product cycle is static. Each of these combinations poses different implications. The six cases where the brand cycle is down or static are most interesting in the present analysis. Supplementary pieces of information which will further the investigation are historical brand shares within the form and knowledge of entry dates of competitors. Add in opinions about the brand's standing with respect to each of the main competitive elements of the marketing mix, and there are the ingredients of a product review. Naturally, a key set of data will be the trend in profit. Some illustrations, all of which assume good competitive standing on price, promotion and distribution, are given below:

1. Form up/brand down or static – a candidate for revitalisation.
2. Form static/brand down or static – a more marginal candidate for revitalisation.
3. Form down/brand static – possibly continue brand without revitalisation, but continuous reviews.
4. Form down/brand down – probably withdraw.

Table 13.7 *Static product cycle with variable form and brand cycles*

Product cycle	S	S	S	S	S	S	S	S	S
Form cycle	U	U	U	S	S	S	D	D	D
Brand cycle	U	D	S	U	D	S	U	D	S

U = up   S = static   D = down

Searching for a new market segment for the same product is widely encountered. Products associated with one kind of use occasion can seek other use occasions. Breakfast cereal producers have tried to encourage consumption at other times of the day. Ice cream consumption has been promoted during the winter. Stones Ginger Wine is now trying to stimulate sales at times other than Christmas. Heinz are stressing the nutritional content of baked beans to attract new types of consumer. Clairol launched their Glints brand to reach younger women who had not been in the market for hair colouring. The virtue in all these strategies is that the production expertise already exists, and the firm will be some way down the experience curve. The difficulty is locating segments that are large enough to warrant the cost of reaching them. If a major promotional campaign is needed it would be self-defeating if media could not be targeted at the newly identified segment. Equally well, it would not be sensible to embark on such repositioning if an entirely new distribution system was required, or some other suitable arrangements made. Some firms find their new segments in overseas markets.

The requirement for a style change can be stimulated by a competitor. Cuprinol was for years the main outdoor wood preservative. Its brand name had almost become synonymous with the product class. The launch of Dulux Weathershield changed consumer perceptions: it was no longer a commodity market, but a branded market. Cuprinol reacted with a campaign designed to sharpen its traditional image and to differentiate it from 'technological' newcomers. Style changes are widespread amongst retailers, such as in the moves by Burton and Hepworth to reposition to attract new market segments.

Functional changes may render the product open to new uses and tap new markets. Product variants incorporating functional differences may appeal to smaller segments not adequately served by existing products. Farmer's Table provides an illustration. This company was well established in the poultry industry, selling whole frozen chickens. Massive overproduction in the industry in the mid-1970s led to a reappraisal of product policy. Farmer's Table reduced its dependence on whole chickens by devising economy portions. Subsequently it generated 700 concepts for product variants and finally launched a range of chicken burgers, chicken fingers, chicken rissoles and chicken sausages.

On occasion, packaging may be the basis for the functional change. The mode of application of some products is dictated by the kind of pack used. Household polishes and window cleaners can be solid, liquid or somewhere between, and come in tins, bottles or plastic containers, and with or without an aerosol applicator. Various combinations of these elements will have a differential appeal to several segments. If all competitors move in one direction, say to aerosols, that might leave an opportunity to reposition to cater for those with more traditional attitudes.

Devising a product variant to attract a new segment can be applied in services. In hotel marketing the 'club concept' partitions a floor to resemble a club, with its own bar and lounge. The target segment is 'executives' who might otherwise stay at another hotel. Various weekend packages in hotels are also examples of functional changes aimed at spreading the segment base.

Changes in quality might also provide the desired product modification. This could involve the use of superior or inferior materials and more or less rigorous manufacturing. Higher quality may be called for if consumers become more quality-conscious and this is not exploited by competitors. Lower-quality decisions may stem from recognition of increased consumer price sensitivity. Besides this, quality changes could be triggered by technological development. The availability of new materials or new production processes always presents problems about the quality of existing products.

Style changes may be reasonably straightforward, although consumer reaction may be highly volatile. Buyer perception is sometimes greatly influenced by trivial points of appearance. A brand may be labelled 'old-fashioned' because its style has not kept pace with fashion trends, and this is not just restricted to fashion products – everyday grocery items may be equally open to these perceptual factors. Slight changes to packaging may bring it back into line, and this might be as perverse as resuscitating forty-year-old designs if nostalgia happens to be the current design fad. More substantial style changes are necessary in consumer durables. The classic instance is in the car industry, where an uncomfortable balance needs to be struck between appearing patently out of date and launching into extraordinarily high retooling expenses. Another case provides an example which had considerable success with style change. Boots No. 7 cosmetics had for a long time appealed to older ladies. Some product formulae were outdated and the packaging was similarly outmoded. A revamp of both of these established No. 7 as a major brand for the first time.

Withdrawing products

'In spite of the widespread reluctance to recognise it, the viability of a company's product mix can be just as much a function of pairing it as proliferating it' [21]. In some cases, attempts at product modification would be unwarranted. A secular downtrend on all three lifecycle levels is ominous for the product's continuation. In fact, a downtrend at the form level, whatever the other two, is unhealthy for the long-term survival of the brand. There could come the time when consistent losses are incurred.

Multi-product firms encounter very complex decisions in this context. Shared manufacturing plant may be a problem. A production system might entail several processes, some of which are common to both sick and healthy products. Withdrawal of the doubtful product could shift a higher overhead on to the healthy one, and this in turn could jeopardise the latter's future. Similarly, joint products and by-products have complicated economies which need to be disentangled before the decision can be made. An alert accounting system is obviously essential.

Distributor, consumer and supplier response must also be anticipated. Distributors and consumers may see the product as necessary to ensure the

Table 13.8 *Phase-out strategies*

	Drugs %	Minor appliances %	Food %	Clothing %
Drop immediately	44	62	53	78
'Milk' or slow phase-out	33	29	34	15
Both drop and 'milk'	21	9	13	7

Source: T. Rothe, 'The product elimination decision', in P. Law *et al.*, *Product Management*. New York: Harper & Row, 1974.

company's credibility as a manufacturer of a complete range; or they may be favourably impressed by its replacement. Suppliers should also be considered, because they may be less willing to continue preferential terms for reduced volumes.

There are several strategy alternatives dependent upon its perception of the problem that the firm must study. An appropriate way out could be to continue manufacturing, and to leave the marketing to another company. Alternatively, it could withdraw from production and concentrate on marketing the product, subcontracting the manufacturing. It depends very much on the company's strengths and weaknesses, how compatible the existing brand is and how development of new products affects both manufacturing and marketing. With regard to the timing of withdrawal, Rothe reports that most commonly firms decide to drop immediately (Table 13.8).

Hart [22] has studied the product elimination decision in a sample of companies and emphasises the need for adequate monitoring and control procedures because:

> much top-level management activity is being absorbed by deliberations on the fate of products that might have been eliminated before reaching the crisis stage. If top management can delegate control activity more effectively, they would be able to concentrate on planning changes to the whole range (new products, replacements, modifications and deletions), effectively resolving problems before they became urgent.

Summary

The product plan lays the foundation within which decisions about new products, and about the continuance of mature products, can be taken. New product introductions constitute a high risk strategy, depending on the amount of experience the firm has with the product category and its knowledge of the market segment. Despite high failure rates, many companies feel obliged to undertake product innovation because of their dynamic technological and competitive environments. A planned approach to new product development attempts to reduce the risk of failure by careful assessments of the product concept, and a systematic procedure in screening new product ideas. Proper interpretation of buyer requirements may involve trade-off analysis to identify appropriate combinations of product attributes. Subsequent product tests may further refine the proposed market offering.

Mature products may require revitalisation through product modification or market repositioning. This could cover the search for new segments, style changes, functional changes or quality changes. Repositioning clearly depends on the original product positioning strategy, competitive positions and developments in the market since the original launch. Eventually, withdrawal from the market may be the only course left open. This decision is difficult because of the ramifications on other products in the range, and because of reactions of suppliers, distributors and customers.

Questions for review and discussion

1. 'New products are a necessary evil.' From whose viewpoint are they necessary and from whose viewpoint are they evil?

2. 'It is easier to copy than to be creative, but in new product planning copying reduces the risks and so it is the preferred strategy.' Is that so?

3. What advantages are there in making new product screening procedures systematic? Are there any circumstances where this would be less pertinent?

4. Examine the problems that might occur in concept testing the following: (1) dehydrated marmalade or other fruit preserve; (2) a revolutionary ultrasonic cleaning device for domestic use in place of conventional washing machines; (3) a robotic mechanical handling system for factories.

5. Compare the advantages and disadvantages of blind/open, single/paired and in-use/laboratory methodologies in product testing.

6. Clairol repositioned their Glints brand of hair colouring to reach younger women who had not been in the market previously. What would be the main problems in such a strategy?

References

1. Cooper, R.G. 1980. 'Project NewProd: factors in new product success', *European Journal of Marketing*, vol. 14, nos 5/6. Reprinted in Greenley, G.E. and Shipley, D. 1988. *Readings in Marketing Management*. Maidenhead: McGraw-Hill, p. 97.

2. Crawford, C.M. 1987. *New Products Management*, 2nd edn. Homewood, Ill.: Irwin, ch. 5.

3. Sowery, T. 1987. *The Generation of Ideas for New Products*. London: Kogan Page.

4. Davidson, J.H. 1975. *Offensive Marketing*. Harmondsworth: Penguin Books, p. 256.

5. de Bono, E. 1978. *Opportunities: A Handbook of Business Opportunity Search*. London: Associated Business Programmes.

6. Hisrich, R.D. and Peters, M.P. 1984. *Marketing Decisions for New and Mature Products*. Columbus, Ohio: Merrill, ch. 8.

7. Cafarelli, E.J. 1980. *Developing New Products and Repositioning Mature Brands*. New York: John Wiley, p. 67.

8. O'Meara, J.T. 1961. 'Selecting profitable products', *Harvard Business Review*, Jan./Feb., pp. 83–9.

9. Midgley, D.E. 1977. *Innovation and New Product Marketing*. London: Croom Helm, p. 220.

10. Tauber, E.M. 1981. 'Utilization of concept testing for new-product forecasting: traditional versus multiattribute approaches', in Wind, Y., Mahajan, V. and Cardozo, R.N. *New-product Forecasting*. Lexington, Mass.: Lexington.

11. Lunn, J. and Morgan, R. 1982. 'Some applications of the trade-off approach', in Bradley, U. (ed.), *Applied Marketing and Social Research*. Wokingham: Van Nostrand Reinhold, ch. 7.

12. Midgley, op. cit., p. 231.

13. Ostlund, L.E. 1974. 'Perceived innovation attributes as predictors of innovativeness', *Journal of Consumer Research*, vol. 1, September.

14. Goldsmith, R. and Flynn, L.R. 1992. 'Identifying innovators in consumer product markets', *European Journal of Marketing*, vol. 26, no. 12, pp. 42–55.

15. Penny, J.C., Hunt, I.M. and Twyman, W.A. 1974. 'Product testing methodology' in Law, P., Weinberg, C. *et al.* (eds), *Product Management*. London: Harper & Row.

16. Boyd, K.T. 1982. 'Product testing', in Bradley, U. (ed.), *Applied Marketing and Social Research*. Wokingham: Van Nostrand Reinhold, ch. 6.

17. Watkins, T. 1984. 'The practice of product testing in the new product development process: the role of model-bases approaches', *European Journal of Marketing*, vol. 18, nos 6/7.

18. Tull, D.S. and Hawkins, D.I. 1980. *Marketing Research*, 2nd edn. New York: Macmillan, p. 616.

19. Haller, T. 1983. *Danger: Marketing Researcher at Work*. Westport, Conn.: Quorum, p. 28.

20. Rines, M. 1981. 'Decorating gets brand new look', *Marketing*, 29 April, pp. 16–17.

21. Hart, S. 1988. 'The managerial setting of the product deletion decision', *Proceedings of the 21st Annual Conference of the Marketing Education Group, Huddersfield*, vol. 2.

22. Ibid.

Chapter 14

Market testing

Central to new product development is the search for information. Numerous choices are made during the development process and, to improve the quality of the decisions, three streams of information are generated concerning the following:

1. Product design and performance characteristics.

2. Manufacturing requirements and costs.

3. Marketing activity and sales prospects.

Throughout all development phases a main aim is to obtain fuller knowledge and more accurate understanding of each of these. New data will be assimilated on all three and revised projections made at frequent intervals. Revenue projections will weigh heavily and that explains the preoccupation with attempts to provide better and earlier sales forecasts. Ideas about the most appropriate marketing plans will also be evolving during development, with refined assumptions about the effects of alternative plans. Important parts of the information search therefore relate to sales forecasts and to plan effectiveness, and this search process may make use of what can broadly be referred to as market testing.

One of the purposes in market testing is to reduce the risk in new product launches. But no amount of testing will guarantee success. Even large companies make mistakes in new product launches. In 1990, Heinz launched a range of frozen ready meals called Memories of China, but the brand never reached expectations and was withdrawn within a year. Heinz also aborted the pasta sauce they launched under the brand name Spagheroni, because it was never able to contend effectively against the market leaders, which are Unilever's Ragu brand or Mars's Dolmio.

Testing the market can take many forms, ranging from informal discussions with potential buyers, through more formal experiments with or without sales being made, up to regional or national launch with full-scale marketing activity. This chapter deals with several topics in market testing. Limited experiments, which may be conducted before or instead or test marketing, are discussed first.

Test marketing is then introduced, followed by some consideration of the applicability of market testing in industrial and service markets. Finally, there is further discussion of some techniques that could be employed in testing or in the analysis of the launch of the product.

Which test?

Judgements are needed about whether to test, when to test and how to test. Influences on these judgements include the following:

1. Levels of confidence in the product concept.

2. Indications already received about possible market reaction.

3. Whether the product is durable.

4. Competitive circumstances.

5. The significance of the new product in the overall portfolio.

6. The acceptability of the testing procedures.

7. Costs of the tests.

There may be grounds for feeling fairly confident about projections that had been made about the product's prospects. The company may have extensive, sophisticated knowledge and experience of operating in the market segment. If that was backed by preliminary market research, and if there were strong favourable indications from concept and product testing, then subsequent testing may be forgone. But even with this set of circumstances there could be an argument for some types of testing, especially connected with the marketing plan. For example, there could be great uncertainty surrounding the extent to which various advertising approaches correctly underscore the positioning strategy, or conflicting views about alternative sales promotion plans.

In some durable product-markets many kinds of experimentation may not be at all feasible because of the cost and lead-time in manufacturing. Full-scale tooling cannot proceed simultaneously for several possible new washing machines or cars, in order to mount a test market. Apart from anything else, the company's reputation could be damaged if it became known that it was putting experimental products on the market. Such firms are forced to rely on earlier testing.

Guesses about competitive reaction can also affect test decisions. It may be known that several companies are rushing to bring out similar new products. Market experiments would delay national launch and give competitors the chance to evaluate rival products and plans. It would be expected that competitors would monitor any experiments, commissioning special market research on their rival's new product. Disruptive, spoiling tactics may also be used, with competitors buying up product, putting in extra promotional activity in the test area, dropping prices or attempting to influence the trade against the newcomer. Aggressive competitive reaction could preclude or curtail test marketing and make more limited experiments attractive [1].

The new product might be of variable significance in the portfolio. If a major investment were at stake, there would be greater reason to employ a wide range of tests. If the product were an extension of a range, and much smaller investment were being risked, then less testing would be likely.

Testing also imposes costs. With test marketing, unit production costs would be high and, if calculated, the same could be said of unit promotion costs. Management costs might also be of a high order because of the attention given to high-profile endeavours such as new product introductions. It would be pointless to mount a test without considerable measurement being taken, which adds to the costs. And, considering research, some firms have been stultified by 'grey' results showing that their efforts would be neither hugely successful nor abysmally unsuccessful, providing misgivings about testing at all.

For these reasons, attempts to improve testing procedures and to allow much earlier predictions are always in hand. Reducing the risk in new product launches, within acceptable time and cost limits, is the goal.

Limited testing

Increasing attention is being paid to attempts to make better and earlier forecasts, and this has led to refinements in research procedures and modes of analysis. In deriving forecasts of new product sales, the focus is usually on the following three types of question:

1. How many of the buyers in the market will make at least one purchase?

2. Of those, how many will repurchase?

3. When they repurchase what will be their average purchase volume?

The first of these factors is referred to as the penetration rate, the second the repeat rate and the third the buying rate index. The three were incorporated into a model by Parfitt and Collins [2] so that:

Brand share = Penetration rate × Repeat rate × Buying rate prediction

For example, assume that of all buyers in the breakfast cereal market the ultimate penetration rate for a new brand is 50 per cent, and say repeat buys as a proportion of total purchases in a period settle at 20 per cent. That means that a half try it at least once, and a fifth of those that try go on to buy more. A first estimate for brand share would then be 10 per cent (20% × 50%), simply because a fifth of those that buy at all keep on buying. Now if repeat buys are at a rate different from the average of all buys, then that estimate needs revision. If the buying rate index is a tenth higher than the average, then the market share estimate increases to 11 per cent (10% × 1.1). With a prior estimate of the total market size this share estimate could be used to derive a revenue forecast. Further discussion of this model and potential applications appears at the end of this chapter.

A variation is to estimate sales from awareness, trial and repeat. Thus it may be estimated that there are 2 million buyers in the market, and 1 million become aware of the new product. Half a million try it once and 0.2 million become repeat buyers. If repeat buyers are estimated to buy an average of four units a year then the sales volume forecast is 0.8 million units a year (0.2 m × 4).

Either of the above approaches could become the basis for developing a new product forecast. Because of the considerable interest in making reliable estimates of the key variables as early as is possible a number of commercial services has become available. Saunders [3] reports some of these.

One service recruits 100 or 200 buyers in the relevant product field who agree that an interviewer can do their shopping for that class of product for them for a few months. They are shown the test item, its advertising and that of competitors. The buyers choose from a catalogue, with regularly updated prices, which includes a test item that, if chosen, is delivered from a special stock; other choices come from local shops. Interviews obtain reactions to the product and its advertising.

Another service uses simulated shopping. Up to 100 respondents are recruited at a central location, interviewed to establish brand awareness and preferences, and are then shown videos of the test product and competitors. They are given a cash voucher which they can exchange for products chosen from a simulated shop shelf, and a free sample of the test item is given to those who did not choose it. Later, interviewers visit their homes, check awareness and preferences, and prompted by a photographic display offer respondents the opportunity to make purchases with their own money.

Much longer-term consumer panels are employed in one other approach. Five hundred housewives in two cities are visited weekly by a mobile self-service shop. They believe they are in a shopping club. The vans carry 1,500 product lines, including a unique own label, with perhaps a dozen test items. Purchases are made from this stock. Different prices can be tested in the two panels. An example of the use of this service is provided in the case of Sunlight Lemon Liquid.

Some other procedures use a small number of real shops that agree to participate in a test. Panels of consumers are recruited at these locations and they record their purchases in a weekly diary. Electronic data capture has allowed sophisticated extensions to this basic idea. A panel of regular shoppers at a store is recruited and given plastic cards which are scanned at the checkout each time they visit. Demographic and attitudinal data are obtained from those co-operating. Test products can be introduced to the store and sales to panel members monitored. Special analyses of penetration, repeat and buying volume rates within demographic or attitudinal grouping are therefore possible. There

---

Sunlight Lemon Liquid mini-test market

Lever Brothers had a 9 per cent market share standard for the introduction of this brand into the washing-up liquid market. The formulation of this product was efficient and therefore expensive, and so a main concern was how much higher its price could be over that of Fairy Liquid. A high and a low price were experimented with and the mini-test results were:

	High price	*Low price*
Cumulative penetration (of product field buyers)	42%	50%
Repeat buying rate	13%	18%
Buying rate index	1.0	1.0
Predicted brand share	5.5%	9.0%

At the time the test was undertaken the 3.5 per cent brand share difference represented £1.5 million retail value in the market nationally. The company planned a regional test market, but a competitor appeared with a similar product and so the decision was taken to launch nationally at the lower price without further research. Twenty-four weeks after this launch Sunlight Lemon had a 14 per cent market share which gradually fell back to 9 per cent 56 weeks after the launch.

Source: B.C. Pymont, D. Reay and P.G.M. Standen, 'Towards the elimination of risk from investment in new products', *ESOMAR Congress 1976: Research that Works for Today's Marketing Problems*. Amsterdam: ESOMAR, 1976, p. 169.

---

could also be some degree of control over the promotion of test items, possibly using direct mail to panel members or special editions of free newspapers. In the United States cable television is used to screen test advertisements to such shopping panels and their viewing recorded electronically. This provides integrated product and media data [4].

Saunders suggests that there are two reasons for the shift from full-scale test marketing to earlier, more limited testing. First, competitive pressures give the need for faster response and more secure product development processes. Second, new types of testing service have been introduced and their accuracy improved. He quotes one service which, in a study of 74 products tested, found that 63 per cent of those classified as likely to be definitely or probably successful were in fact so in test markets. This compares with a Nielsen study which showed that the average success rate of test market products was a little over a third.

Test marketing

Although there has been considerable development of new pre-test marketing procedures the full scale test is still widely employed. This is because test

Table 14.1 *Purposes in test marketing*

Pilot launch	Marketing mix testing	Sales testing
Logistics check: investigation of production, product packaging and distribution problems	Marketing mix check: investigation of mix components and interrelationships	Sales check: generating data on penetration and repeat

Source: Adapted from J. Davis, *Experimental Marketing*. London: Nelson, 1970.

marketing can do things other tests cannot. The very act of placing the new product on sale in a reasonably large area provides a much more natural test than the services noted above. For example, the preoccupation in limited testing is the reactions of consumers. This misses a vital set of reactions which will be just as powerful in determining the product's prospects: those of the trade. There might also be significant problems in the logistics of bringing out a new product which need to be evaluated in a natural setting. Additionally, the impact of the full marketing mix can only be realistically evaluated in a fairly large test operation. Fuller information on the key variables to be used in estimating sales levels may also be collected. All this argues for test marketing despite its cost, the time it takes and the exposure of company plans.

Davis has put forward a threefold classification of the purposes in test marketing (Table 14.1). The pilot launch checks the logistics, marketing mix testing investigates the returns to alternative marketing efforts, and sales testing yields insight into possible national sales levels. All three could be of equivalent moment, but frequently there would be more uncertainty about one of these areas and so most attention would be paid to that.

Sales testing

This check has objectives similar to those in limited testing. The aim is to generate data which can be used to make estimates of sales once the product is nationally launched. As in limited testing the key variables are penetration, repeat and buying volume rates. These data are normally obtained from a consumer panel, often based on diary records. Retail audits may give market share estimates, which could also be assessed, but it is often found that the study of repeat purchase rates is vital. Increasingly though, the retail outlet could become the data source even for repeat rates, given the introduction of shopping panels whose purchasing behaviour is monitored electronically at the point of purchase.

Pilot launching

Pilot launching is a readily understandable objective. Any pilot operation aims to determine whether or not the system works as well as intended, and at discovering design errors and weak components. For example, the pilot launch may uncover production problems. Until now only prototypes have been made, probably on experimental plant. The pilot requires higher volumes, and this will test the system. Occasionally, severe problems will be revealed, as in the case of the plastics company that developed a revolutionary honeycombed product with tremendous impact resistance. Their prototypes received much praise and many diverse applications were discovered in transportation and packaging. They made the prototypes by pouring the substance into small tanks containing metal rods, and allowing it to set. For large-scale production however, they grossed up the size of the tanks only to find they could not extract the rods without breaking the honeycomb. Another example is the food company that was encouraged at the product testing stage because respondents found the distinctively shaped glass container impressive. Unfortunately, the preparations for the pilot launch revealed that the glass manufacturer could not produce to the desired specification in the requisite numbers.

Another illustration of a pilot test revealing production difficulties is provided by Cadbury's Wispa chocolate bar. This was put on test in the Tyne Tees television region in late 1981, but was withdrawn in a matter of weeks because the production plant could not cope with unexpectedly heavy demand. A decision was taken to invest £12 million in new plant and the product was launched nationally in 1984 [5].

Consumer reaction to the product can also be more realistically assessed. Product testing, even in natural settings, is artificial. The pilot launch gives the opportunity to derive consumer ratings and to study how they use it. This may reveal that they do not use it in the predicted manner, or on the predicted occasions. Instructions for use on the package may be shown to be inadequate; some consumers may be using the product inappropriately. Household cleaning products may be applied to some materials with deleterious effects, and foodstuff wrongly prepared or incorrectly stored. Of course, not all this feedback need be negative. Unforeseen uses in non-target segments could appear and product improvement result.

Pilot testing will also allow the distribution system to be tested. Storage and handling characteristics of the products may be of interest. Silly problems may be encountered such as an insufficiently strong glue being used on the outer cases. Deeper problems may be uncovered in, say, a new palletised handling system.

Retailers' attitudes and behaviour decide the ultimate fate of many new brands. The test market is a forum for receiving information on these. Their willingness to stock is the acid test for a brand's launch. Obtaining 'listings' in the key multiple accounts is crucial. Some firms set launch objectives in terms of gaining distribution in 30–40 per cent of relevant shops. Nielsen [6] suggests that successful brands need to be stocked by shops that account for at least 40 per cent of total grocery turnover, and that that level of distribution needs to be attained within four months of launch. It will therefore be necessary to monitor retailer acceptance and investigate reasons for unsuccessful attempts to gain distribution.

Marketing mix testing

This is an experimental approach to evaluating the marketing mix. Marketing executives will have made judgements about many of the issues in devising the total mix. Some of these judgements will have been on the basis of research information generated prior to test marketing, and some on seemingly analogous situations encountered previously. Inevitably, these judgements could be improved; few would care to claim that they had optimum strategies. Frequently the company just does not know which of two advertising approaches to use, which of two media schedules or which of several promotional devices to employ. Obviously a great deal of judgement would have gone into whittling down the options to these few. Practicalities necessitate such reduction since a ridiculously high number of experiments would be required to test every feasible combination of mix elements.

Pure experimental design seems absent from many test operations. Proper controls are often not incorporated into the design. Sometimes 'experiments' are monadic (single-area), and when comparative may just be two areas without a control. These inadequacies are disquieting although, to an extent, understandable. Take the company that was unsure of its television advertising message. A natural setting test of two alternatives, with a control, would involve the use of three television regions, and in the United Kingdom this might cover perhaps a fifth of the national population. Some television areas can be split to reduce the scale of this problem. Experienced companies may also replace control areas by using predetermined benchmarks of consumer attitudes and behaviour. The point is that the marketplace is not an experimental laboratory. The marketing experimenter does not control the experimental environment and has influence over only a few of the experimental variables. Because of this it would be quite wrong to read test market results as conclusive evidence. How far short of this they fall depends on how carefully the experiment was designed and, importantly, the exact measuring instruments employed to gauge which more or less relevant variable (or surrogate).

Furthermore, sample size used in the research is a problem – the scale of which seems to evade some managers. Corkindale and Kennedy [7] nicely illustrate this at the national level. To be 95 per cent sure of detecting a 0.9 market share point change one would need a sample of 6,000 product class users. If product class users were only 10 per cent of the sample, then that sample would need to be ten times larger. For many product classes the users could well be less than 10 per cent of the population, making the multiple much higher. Few people, other than government, would ever conceive of using a sample size of 60,000; few even go to 6,000.

Planning the test market

Above all, test areas should be representative; it is widely judged that they should be as nearly as possible a microcosm of the total population. Dhalla [8] contends that one can become obsessive about this, and that all that is needed is a relatively representative area. Typically, demographic and socio-economic profiles of possible test areas are compared to national profiles. Product class history and consumption trends are also compared. Some manufacturers choose their test areas on different criteria. Confectionery companies often use central Scotland as a test area because it has the highest per capita consumption of confectionery in the United Kingdom. Presumably they feel that if a new brand is successful there it will be so elsewhere.

Advertising plans for a test market should resemble the advertising plans for a national launch. The first aspect of this is the level of advertising expenditure. A simple method would be to scale down the spending on a population basis. A more complicated approach would be to scale down according to the total exposures expected from advertising in different media. That is to have an idea of the number of times the campaign would be exposed to individuals at the national level – say 10 or 20 million exposures. Then the estimate would be made of the segment size in the test area, and the expected proportion of the national market that that segment represents. Applying the national exposure levels to the individuals in the tested area would yield the desired total exposures there. Media would then be checked to ascertain the cost of delivering those exposures in the test area, and this would provide the scale of the advertising expenditure.

A second problem with advertising is the choice of media. Town tests cannot employ television in the United Kingdom. National press is also difficult to scale down, although some national magazines do offer regional splits. The largest women's magazines do have a reasonably controlled distribution which might allow area testing. The local and regional press are also anxious to demonstrate their usefulness in test marketing, and offer special deals to encourage this. Broadbent [9] feels that local newspapers can stand in for the national press, but that would depend on the nature of the product, the advertising message and the purpose of the test.

As with advertising, the attempt should be to ensure salesforce activity is typical. This may be problematical because the sales representatives are bound to be aware that management attention is focused on the new brand. If they carry several lines, then a disproportionate amount of their time could be devoted to the test item. Similarly, the test brand may receive an inordinate amount of management time. Sometimes a special sales taskforce is hired to develop retailer co-operation. Again this needs to mirror national plans.

Data requirements in test marketing

Any experiment requires measurements, otherwise there is no yardstick for determining its success or failure. Test marketing can stimulate a voracious appetite for data. Table 14.2 gives some impression of the span of the data that might be useful in monitoring an experiment.

Table 14.2   *Data requirements in test marketing*

Data	Source
Channels:	
retail sales	Retail audits
% outlets handling	Retail audits
Stock levels	Retail audits
Displays and shelf position	Retail audits and salesforce
Prices	Retail audits and salesforce
Retailer attitudes	Surveys and salesforce
Customers:	
Customer profiles	Consumer panels
Trial and repurchase rates	Consumer panels
Usage and attitudes	Panels and surveys
Advertising recall	Surveys
Response to other marketing activity	Panels and surveys

Retailers and test marketing

Retailers are important to test marketing in two ways. First, their co-operation is needed in order to obtain distribution in the test area. Second, they do a lot of testing for themselves. Ornstien records major retailers' use of tests as follows [10]:

Tesco:	20 stores used for a minimum of 13 weeks (out of 450 stores)
Sainsbury:	10–12 stores employed (out of 200)
Safeway:	Up to 6 branches used (out of 67)
British Home Stores:	6 stores for a month (out of 100)

In choosing test stores most seem to go for typicality, although some deliberately select less successful branches as an 'acid test'. All agree that testing is used when there is some doubt, but there is some divergence in opinion about the amount of doubt aroused by new product decisions. Many retailers appear to feel that they can make adequate judgements about the prospects for new lines without testing. Manufacturers would undoubtedly like to share that optimism, but few can. A major difference is caused by the relative impact of bad new product decisions on a manufacturer and a retailer. The manufacturer may be irreparably harmed by such a decision; the retailer would find it had little long-term significance since it was just one out of thousands of lines carried.

Projecting test results to national equivalents

One area fraught with difficulty in any assessment of test market results is the

Table 14.3   *Controlled brand share estimation*

| Brand | Market share (%) | | | | | |
| | Control area | | | Test area | | |
	Pre-launch %	Post-launch %	Change %	Pre-launch %	Post-launch %	Change %
C	20	18	−2	20	14	− 6
D	40	44	+4	40	30	−10
E	40	38	−2	40	36	− 4
X	−	−	−	−	20	+20

Source: F. Buttle, 'Test marketing: go national or go broke', *Management Decision*, vol. 14, no. 1, 1976.

possibility of 'grossing-up' the test results to national equivalents. At its simplest level is it to be supposed that a 10 per cent market share in the test is equivalent to a 10 per cent share nationally? Common approaches to this are to gross up on a population or a 'buying power' basis. Buttle shows that these methods can lead to national estimates of a wide range – and these from the same test data. He suggests an alternative, termed 'controlled brand share estimation'.

Table 14.3 gives brand share data for a control and a test area. Brand X is the test brand. Buttle's procedure is to adjust the changes in the test area for the changes in the control; otherwise 'normal' market dynamics would be confused with changes due to the introduction of the new brand. In this case brand C's change of −6 in the test area would be corrected to −4/20 to allow for the −2 change in the control, and the 20 per cent brand share it originally had. Brand D would be corrected to −14/40 and brand E to −2/40. This is equivalent to saying that only 24/40 of the market share obtained by brand X was due to the marketing of that brand (i.e. 4/20 + 14/40 + 2/40). The other 16/40 are attributable to market dynamics. Market share for brand X would therefore be adjusted down to 12 per cent (i.e. 20 × 24/40). This technique also allows better recognition of the brand suffering from the introduction of a new brand. In this instance it is brand D, which actually increased its share in the control.

Market testing industrial products

There are three important characteristics that distinguish industrial markets in the context of market testing. First, it is probable that industrial marketers will have much closer relationships with customers than is normal in consumer markets. Key customers may be extensively involved throughout the new product development process. Second, those customers may be much more active, volunteering to undertake product testing because they may see a more immediate pay-off than customers in the consumer market. Third, most industrial products are durable, so that repurchase cycles are lengthy and not likely to emerge during a test. For these reasons the classic consumer market testing techniques are less appropriate.

Industrial customers may be able to understand a great deal more about a product just from descriptions than those in consumer markets, and their evaluations of new products may be dominated by assessments of performance characteristics. More emphasis might, therefore, be placed on intentions-to-buy questions. These may be administered in some type of group discussion, although these may be events with other names, such as a 'customer technology update' or a 'new trends seminar'. Alternatively, salesforce involvement may allow them to 'sell' the product to customers although the only form they write is an intentions questionnaire.

Placing products for trial by major users may take on major proportions. In some markets an externally imposed benchmark on technical performance must be achieved, and sometimes these benchmarks are determined by the key users. Their trial of the product becomes the critical event in new product development, and success in these trials can make massive difference in subsequent penetration.

There are some industrial markets, though, which have some of the characteristics of consumer markets and in which some derivation of consumer market testing is feasible. Industrial consumables sometimes have extended distribution networks with several layers of agents and distributors. Test marketing is possible. Its viability is dependent on how easy it is to control distribution, confining it to particular geographic areas or to specified market segments. Taking a multinational view, the test could be in a small country, but that would raise issues of typicality. Questions about the availability of research data would also be raised, and something equivalent to consumer panels or retail audits may be needed in order to obtain penetration and repeat rates, assuming distribution is not direct to the user. In these markets too, electronic data capture is having an impact, especially if the manufacturer has established appropriate communication links with distributors.

Market testing of services

For some services, many of the techniques in market testing can be directly applied. Some service companies have major advantages in test marketing. If a nationwide firm has a comprehensive network of distributed service points then it has considerable opportunities for testing. It can experiment with much greater control than is the case in most markets and derive many of the key data itself. Professional services, rental companies, many financial service operations and various franchise networks can potentially make great use of market testing.

In other kinds of service organisation there may be less scope, but market testing in some form is still possible. Within a hotel a battery of services is offered. New services can often be added on an experimental basis with relatively little cost. Similarly, tour operators can sometimes test new destinations on a very limited basis.

Public sector services can also be tested using some of the techniques in market testing. Depending on the service, it could be analogous to the network of distributed service points or to the single service point offering multiple services. In either case some form of test marketing or other experiment is feasible. A difference would be in the variables to be forecast. Market share would probably not be relevant, though that may not be universally so. Notions of penetration and repeat usage would also have to be revised, but the essential idea of measuring, trial and repeat might be appropriate for some services. In other cases there may be no repeat usage and the problem becomes one of defining the size of the relevant population and establishing an acceptable benchmark against which penetration estimates can be compared. Control of the experimental variables presents an equally rich variety. Some public services are provided in a tightly defined and completely closed system; others are provided in a diffused, ill-defined system. Furthermore, the types of marketing effort in a test may not reflect those needed in a full-scale launch, possibly because research and experimentation may not have the same claim on resources as in the private sector.

Analysing penetration and repeat

Estimates of penetration and repeat rates are of significance in market testing and in the analysis of the launch of the product. These estimates can be of utility both in forecasting and in diagnosis. The discussion in this section relates to the Parfitt and Collins model which was introduced earlier in this chapter. More complex models are discussed in Wind [11], Wind et al. [12], Lilien and Kotler [13] and Urban and Hauser [14].

Penetration and repeat rates

These are the most widely used bases for such analysis. Penetration is the proportion of the market (either individuals or households) that buys at least once, and cumulative penetration curves plot the build-up in this statistic from launch into the test. These data come from consumer panels and, for this purpose, are usually weekly. Repeat purchase rates may be measured as the proportion of total purchases in a period not made by first-time buyers.

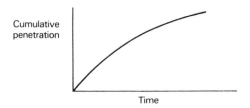

Figure 14.1 *Cumulative penetration curve*

Ehrenberg [15] has found that in some market circumstances the major determinant of market share differences is penetration level. This will be the case where purchase frequency is relatively constant between all brands. Where this does not apply, penetration levels will still be of significance, and so some estimate of the eventual stable penetration rate is useful.

Forecasting penetration ratio

The aim is to forecast the position and shape of the cumulative penetration curve (Figure 14.1). Various growth models have been tried in projecting this curve. A simple model assumes an ultimate penetration level below 100 per cent and a constant proportional increment up to that point. This requires an estimate of the ultimate penetration and the incremental constant. With a few periods' data a 'line of best fit' might be used for this estimation. Parfitt and Collins have done this with the launch of Signal toothpaste. Consumer panel data provided weekly estimates of penetration and after sixteen weeks they predicted an ultimate penetration level of 37 per cent of households using toothpaste, which later proved to be quite reliable. Rawling and Sparks have fitted modified exponential curves to assist in this forecasting with some success [16].

Forecasting repeat rates

Success in forecasting repeat rates depends upon how stable the ultimate repeat rate becomes. In low-risk grocery markets the current consensus is that, after introduction, a new brand eventually settles to a fairly stable repeat rate. If that is the case, then analysis of data for the first few weeks into test can give a reasonable basis for extrapolating to the stable state. Simple estimations may sometimes be sufficient.

Total brand sales are composed of purchases by new buyers, purchases by first repeaters, by second repeaters, and so on. Just as a growth curve may be fitted to new buyer data to analyse penetration, so similar curves may be found to be appropriate in approximating the temporal growth in subsequent trial classes. A trial class would be, for example, those buying for the second time, or

Table 14.4 *Empirical test of the Parfitt–Collins brand share predictor*

	A	B	C	D	Brand E	F	G	H	I
Predicted share (%)	7	12	7	1	14	6	3	8	4
Actual share (%)	6	13	8	2	10	15	3	8	9

Source: T.C. Rawlings and D.N. Sparks, 'The use of repeat buying measures in evaluating new product launches', *Proceedings of the 18th Annual Conference of the Market Research Society*, 1975.

those buying for the third time. Say, first-time buyers were estimated at 20 per cent of the segment, that 50 per cent of these go on to make a second purchase, and 80 per cent of this 50 per cent make a third buy. Further assume that those that make three buys thereafter remain fairly loyal. Thus 8 per cent of the segment will be regular buyers in the steady state: $0.2 \times 0.5 \times 0.8 = 0.08$.

Combining penetration and repeat rates

In the Signal case referred to above Parfitt and Collins made forecasts of ultimate brand share by combining penetration and repeat rates. As shown above, estimates of repeat rates can give the proportion of a segment becoming regular buyers. Estimates of penetration give the proportion of a segment that try the new brand at all. If repeat rates are expressed as a proportion of total product class purchases by those who have ever tried the brand, an estimate can be made of brand share by applying this statistic to the penetration level. For Signal, repeat purchases settled down to 40 per cent of total toothpaste purchasing by those who tried Signal at least once. The proportion who tried it at least once (i.e. penetration) was 37 per cent. Forecast brand share is 40 per cent of 37 per cent, which is 14.8 per cent. Other tests of the Parfitt and Collins approach are included in Table 14.4.

Possible variations in usage rates have so far been ignored. Repeat buyers may buy more heavily in a given time period than all buyers. A buying rate index would have to be calculated, relating the volume bought by repeaters to the total volume in the product field. Heavy buyers may have an index of 1.3 and light buyers 0.7. The relevant index would be applied to the brand share estimate made above. For example, if the Signal repeat buyer's index was 1.3, then brand share would be 19.2 per cent and not 14.8 per cent.

Further analyses using penetration and repeat data

Simple comparisons between penetration and repeat rates may yield useful insights into the product's market performance and be suggestive of problems in marketing activity. For example, any of the following combinations may be apparent:

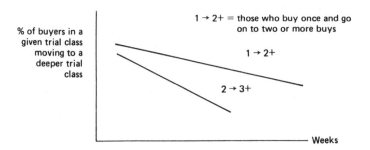

Figure 14.2 *Conversion rates between trial classes*

Penetration rate	Repeat rate
High	High
High	Low
Low	High
Low	Low

In the first case it could be supposed that the promotion was successful in encouraging trial, and that those that tried liked the product. Both the product and the marketing activity therefore seem successful, and presumably national launch will follow. But in the second case the effective promotion is followed by disappointing repeat purchase levels. The product does not live up to the promises in the promotion. Further investigation of the product and its usage would be warranted. In the third case the problem is with the promotion. Not enough are tempted to try, but once they try they keep on buying. It might be the lack of advertising or the media plans that are at fault, or it could be that the message is inappropriate. In the final case there is failure on both counts. The product would be dropped, or certainly not pursued in its present form.

Other investigations using penetration and repeat rates include depth of trial,

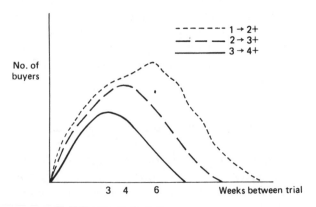

Figure 14.3 *Periods between trial for three trial classes*

conversion rates between trial classes and periods between trial. These are considered below.

Depth of trial refers to the number of repeat purchases made by the individual. Each successive try reaches a greater depth of trial. Some reasonable depth is required for brand loyalty to be assumed. With weekly panel data, total brand purchases can be broken down into those buying for the first time, those for the second, and so on. A cumulative plot for each category may help identify problems. It may also assist in the evaluation of an on-pack coupon offer, which was designed specifically to encourage first-time triers to make a second buy.

Conversion rates are an extension of the depth of trial analysis. These are studies of the rate at which consumers convert from one depth of trial to another. The proportion of first-time buyers moving to two or more purchases may be compared with the proportion of second-time buyers moving to three or more buys (Figure 14.2). In this case the position is fairly straightforward, with the proportions descending in time. More varied situations might show the $1 \rightarrow 2 +$ curve falling sharply and the $2 \rightarrow 3 +$ curve at first rising dramatically and then falling. Such analyses are useful in assessing the marketing effort. In the situation just described a successful advertising campaign might have generated high penetration but significantly lower repeats, although those who bought a second time became more likely to buy a third time.

Periods between trial – that is, the length of time between first and subsequent purchases may also be interesting. Figure 14.3 depicts a comparison of periods between trial for three trial classes. Average repurchase frequencies are clearly relevant to the assessment of a brand's prospects. This study extends the analysis into different trial classes. As can be seen, the average repurchase frequency is becoming shorter as buyers move to deeper trials. The company would be worried if the reverse were the case.

Epidemics and contagions

The essentially social nature of the new product adoption process has led some researchers to investigate its contagious nature. Bass [17] has derived a growth model for application in consumer durable markets, i.e. with an absence of repeat buys in the launch phase. He distinguishes between innovators and imitators. Innovators are assumed to have a constant probability of adoption, while imitators are substantially influenced by the number of existing adopters. In other words, the spread of the new product is likened to an epidemic.

Goddard has investigated the contagious nature of brand choice [18]. He extends Ehrenberg's view of the overriding significance of penetration to include a measure of 'patronage', that is, the proportion a brand takes of its buyers' total purchases in a product class. He equates penetration to 'fame' and patronage to 'appeal' and finds that appeal is dependent on fame. Perceived popularity breeds appeal; success brings success since people prefer what is popular.

Summary

Competitive and cost pressures have caused some companies to consider alternatives to test marketing in the search for reliable indicators of the likelihood of new product success. Developments in research procedures and technology have allowed the introduction of a range of commercial services for this purpose. But the important contribution of test marketing remains, not least because it can serve quite other purposes such as in pilot launching and in marketing mix experimentation. Market testing has some application both in industrial markets and in services, and some of the techniques can be adapted for the testing of public services.

Studies of penetration and repeat rates can be instructive for forecasting and diagnostic reasons. Taken together they might yield brand share estimates. More detailed analyses of repeat rates can uncover problems in promotional plans and in product acceptability.

Questions for review and discussion

1. What are the advantages and disadvantages of shopping panels with electronic data capture in the following cases?:
    (a) A limited test based upon two superstores where the object is to estimate potential market share.
    (b) As above but where the object is to test price sensitivity.
    (c) As above but where the object is to test advertising plans.

2. Assume that cable or satellite television allowed the selection of audiences to match shopping panels as in the first question. Would that make test marketing redundant for fast-moving consumer goods?

3. 'National equivalents' are a major problem in estimating brand shares from tests and in calibrating marketing efforts during tests. Why is this so?

4. How might a large car rental firm use market testing?

5. Do you expect that market testing techniques will be increasingly applied in public sector services? Contrast possible applications in the Post Office and in the National Health Service.

6. Why does penetration rate × repeat rate give a market share estimate?

7. Which is better, a high penetration with low repeat or vice versa?

8. Suppose that a company planned to avoid test marketing an important new product because of competitive pressures. Product tests had been reasonably encouraging but a limited market test showed moderate penetration and mediocre repeats, which indicated a brand share below expectation. What factors might influence the next steps?

References

1. Assmus, G. 1984. 'New product forecasting', *Journal of Forecasting*, vol. 3, no. 2.
2. Parfitt, J.H. and Collins, B.J.K. 1968. 'Use of panels in brand-share prediction', *Journal of Marketing Research*, vol. 5, May. Reprinted in Wind, Y., Mahajan, V. and Cardozo, R.N. 1981. *New Product Forecasting*. Lexington, Mass.: Lexington.
3. Saunders, J. 1985. 'New product forecasting in the UK', *Quarterly Review of Marketing*, July.
   Saunders, J.A., Sharp, J.A. and Witt, S.F. 1987. *Practical Business Forecasting*. Aldershot: Gower, ch. 8.
4. Crawford, C.M. 1987. *New Products Management*, 2nd edn. Homewood, Ill.: Irwin, p. 306.
5. Huxley, J. 1984. 'Bar Wars', *Sunday Times*, 6 January, p. 57.
6. 'Realities of new product marketing', *Nielsen Researcher*, Jan./Feb. 1970.
7. Corkindale, D.R. and Kennedy, S.H. 1975. *Measuring the Effect of Advertising*. Farnborough: Saxon House, p. 104.
8. Dhalla, N.K. 1977. 'How to set advertising budgets', *Journal of Advertising Research*, vol. 17, no. 5.
9. Broadbent, S. 1975. 'Markers in miniature', *Marketing*, November.
10. Ornstien, E. 1976. *The Retailers*. London: Associated Business Programmes.
11. Wind, Y. 1982. *Product Policy*. Reading, Mass.: Addison-Wesley, ch. 15.
12. Wind, Y., Mahajan, V. and Cardozo, R.N. 1981. *New-product Forecasting*. Lexington, Mass.: Lexington.
13. Lilien, G.I. and Kotler, P. 1983. *Marketing Decision Making*. New York: Harper & Row, ch. 19.
14. Urban, G. and Hauser, J.R. 1980. *Design and Marketing of New Products*. Englewood Cliffs, NJ: Prentice Hall Inc., ch. 15.
15. Ehrenberg, A.S.C. 1972. *Repeat Buying*. Amsterdam: North-Holland.
16. Rawling, T.C. and Sparks, D.N. 1975. 'The use of repeat buying measures in evaluating new product launches', *Proceedings of the 18th Annual Conference of the Market Research Society*.
17. Bass, F.M. 1969. 'A new product growth model for consumer durables', *Management Science*, vol. 15, no. 5. Reprinted in Wind, Mahajan and Cardozo, op. cit.
18. Goddard, J. 1977. 'Some general properties of brand leadership', *Proceedings of the 10th Annual Conference of the Marketing Education Group*, London.

Chapter 15
Promotion planning

Organisations promote their products through a variety of means, such as advertising, selling, point-of-sale displays, competitions, exhibitions and numerous other activities. These means have the common end of attempting to fulfil the firm's goals, although the exact relationship between them and the goals is often unclear. Lack of adequate definition of the goals is one of the principal complexities. A vague statement that the aim of advertising is to increase sales does not aid understanding of the process, furnish guidelines for the development of specific advertising plans or place its role relative to the other promotional tools. To specify goals requires some prior insight into the nature of marketing communication, and the limitations to its effectiveness.

Communication theory

Communication implies that someone wishes to share a meaning with another person and that a message passes between them. The source needs to encode that message in such a way that the receiver has no problem in decoding, and needs to use an appropriate signal strength and duration. Schramm's model depicts the process (Figure 15.1).

A military analogy can help to clarify this model. Military radio commun-

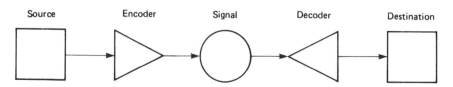

Source: W. Schramm, 'How communication works' in W. Schramm (ed.), *The Process and Effects of Mass Communication,* Urbana , Ill., University of Illinois Press, 1961.

Figure 15.1   *Schramm's model of communication*

ications present an effective system for a number of reasons. First, the source often has prescribed reasons for wanting to communicate, e.g. to summon supplies. Second, there will be prescribed ways in which the message should be encoded: both the source and the receiver will employ common coding manuals. Third, the source knows with some certainty that the receiver is waiting for the message and that on receipt it will be given more or less undivided attention. Fourth, the message will be easily understood and the consequent action will probably be what the source required. From this it can be seen that the system's behaviour is predictable because it is a closed network and because the components are controllable.

If the analogy is dropped, it is possible to discover where inefficiencies creep in, inefficiencies that cause great trouble in promotional management: they arise in each of the system components.

Source problems

Source problems might be a comment upon management. If managers do not know what they are trying to accomplish, or do not understand how they might achieve their goals, then the system will be haphazard. But there are other source problems.

In the analogy above, the receiver's attitude to the source was largely irrelevant. The receiver will act in the prescribed manner irrespective of the opinion he holds about the source. However, in the marketplace the generalised opinion that the receiver has of the source is crucial to the reception and interpretation of the message. The potential effects of source credibility have already been investigated in Chapter 5. An extension is derived by Lowe-Watson when he suggests that the relationship between the buyer, the 'personality' of the brand and the 'personality' of the seller affects persuasive communication. He uses Emery's theory (see Figure 15.2) to expose the need for balance and congruity between these three elements [1]. In the A–B relationship, if A has an unfavourable image of B, then the advertisement will be discounted; the audience needs to feel that the advertiser is competent.

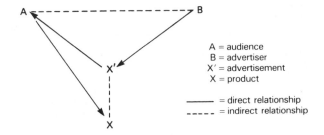

A = audience
B = advertiser
X' = advertisement
X = product

———— = direct relationship
- - - - - = indirect relationship

Source: D. Lowe-Watson, 'Advertising and the buyer/seller relationship', in R. Lawrence and M. Thomas (eds), *Readings in Marketing Management,* Harmondsworth: Penguin Books, 1972.

Figure 15.2 *Emery's model of persuasion*

In the B–A relationship a critical point concerns the posture that the advertiser adopts in respect of his audience. Is he authoritarian, and if so will the audience accept that stance as legitimate? Or is he conspiratorial, and if so will the audience enter the conspiracy? These ideas relate to 'transactional analysis', which stresses the need for harmony between the perceived roles of both receiver and source. Use is made of three possible postures: to behave like a parent, like an adult and like a child. In the examples above the authoritarian posture is consistent with a parent–child relationship and the conspiratorial with a child–child relationship.

This analysis views communication as a transaction between participants, and for effective communication both the source and receiver need common assumptions about their respective roles. Some good advertising can be interpreted in this fashion. There are many examples where the audience is cast as children to be talked down to and to be shown the proper way to do things, e.g. some pharmaceutical and technical products. Some advertisements are quite childish, appealing to childish motives and perhaps using cartoons. Entreaties to 'spoil yourself' sometimes strike the right chord. But to be effective, the role assigned to audience members has to be mutually acceptable. That is, they have to see it as legitimate that they are being addressed as children or as adults. If a childish role is assigned and rejected, then the communication can be counterproductive. A further problem with such approaches is that it can be difficult to carry them across several types of medium because some media are perceived as being serious or expert and others as lighthearted.

The indirect relationship between the advertisement and the product will also condition the effectiveness of the persuasion. The audience needs to believe that the advertisement is truthful and relevant in respect of the product. Some

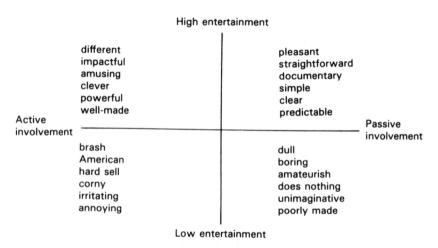

Source: W. Gordon, 'The big name TV switch-off', Campaign, 18 March 1983.

Figure 15.3 *Presenter effects*

exaggeration seems expected, but over-ripe claims could be counterproductive in the initial persuasion as well as in any possible post-purchase dissonance.

Many advertisers use a presenter for their message, such as famous actors or sports personalities. In Emery's model the presenter would come between the audience and the advertiser. Once more there is a need for consistency. To be effective the presenter would have to be seen to be competent to talk about the product and to fit the role in the 'transaction'; that is, he would have to be perceived as adult, child or parent. Some choices of presenter seem unfortunate, others quite congruous.

Endorsements and testimonials can improve or hinder communication. A study of consumer perceptions of this type of advertising undertaken by a research company showed two dimensions to be important [2]. Entertainment value and degree of audience involvement differentiated consumer reactions. Figure 15.3 uses the words consumers employed in describing their response to advertisements in each of the four quadrants. Commercials in the top left quadrant, such as the PG chimps or anything by John Cleese, elicited strong positive feelings towards the brand. Those in the bottom left, such as some margarine and soap powder advertisements, using famous personalities or members of the public, may generate hostile reactions but still be remembered. Such commercials are perceived as having little credibility but may work to the extent of being recalled. In the consumers' view they are designed to be believed and fail on that count. Advertisements in the two quadrants on the right do not elicit strong reactions. They are 'simple and clear' or 'dull and unimaginative'. But to be effective does not necessarily require strong, conscious reactions. Low key communications, with repetition, may be sufficient in registering a few flakes of information or in breeding familiarity.

Encoding problems

Advertisers would welcome a code book that they knew was being used by their audience. Copywriters could then consult this and be sure that they encoded particular meanings in a readily and predictably understood fashion. It might be supposed that dictionaries could fulfil this role, but the problem is that even trivial words have a plethora of formal meaning, and everyday usage might radically depart from these definitions. On the face of it, advertisers have little assurance that they are using a code that will be consistently interpreted in the desired manner by all members of their audience. For straight, factual information the problem is reduced though still apparent because they might use unfamiliar language. For more imaginary copy there is substantial potential for misunderstanding and confusion. Copy testing may go some way to reducing this potential.

Message problems

What is the right signal strength and duration? How many repetitions are required for the message to be understood? Should the signal be sent more or less

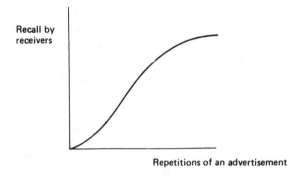

Recall by receivers

Repetitions of an advertisement

Figure 15.4   *Effects of repetition*

continuously or in intermittent bursts? These are just some of the vexing problems. Considerable research has been undertaken into repetition and forgetting, and some generalised ideas about this are shown in the Figures 15.4 and 15.5. In Figure 15.4 repetition is thought to have the effect of building recall levels. In Figure 15.5 forgetting depresses recall levels, but extra repetitions push it up. Naturally, these are only generalised models.

Audience feelings about media

Media are not passive conveyors of messages. It was seen earlier that how the audience perceives the source can affect message reception. Similarly, audience perceptions of media can affect how they react to the message. Some media might be considered expert or prestigious and other media trivial or amusing. They provide different environments for advertising messages which can influence the communication effects. Attempts are made to investigate the nature of these effects and to build in allowances for these differences in media planning. This is referred to under 'media weights' in Chapter 17.

Recall

Time

Figure 15.5   *Effects of forgetting*

Table 15.1 *Opinions about media advertising*

%	Newspapers	Radio	Television	Magazines
Like a lot	4	3	7	5
Quite like	23	16	44	29
Neutral	54	23	27	32
Rather dislike	9	10	15	6
Dislike a lot	2	3	4	2
Don't know	1	3	1	2
Never see/hear	8	43	1	24

Source: Viewpoint Magazine. February 1985.

The general opinion held about advertising in different media may also influence the communication. In the military analogy, any thought that the receiver had about the medium was redundant. In marketing communication any strong feelings can disrupt or distort the message. If advertising was judged to be unduly intrusive or irritating, then for at least some section of the audience its effect could be counterproductive. Advertisers, agencies and media owners are all interested in this topic and regular monitoring of public opinion takes place. The Advertising Association reports these surveys. Television companies have a Television Omnibus Monitor, and Table 15.1 gives opinions of 1,200 adults on four media classes [3].

Decoding problems

These problems have been partially subsumed within the discussion of encoding problems. A further set of complications is connected with the receiver's perception of the message. The selective nature of perception and retention seriously impairs the working of the communication system from the advertiser's viewpoint. Receivers may distort the message to make it fit their preconceptions; they may magnify small parts of the message to derive a different impression from that intended; they may ignore what the advertiser thought was the main platform of the message; or they may simply not like it because the people featured in the message were not 'acceptable'.

Receiver problems

Perhaps the most profound problem of all is the simplest one: the receiver may have switched off. Nobody is compelled to watch television commercials, read newspaper advertisements or listen to a sales representative. The desire to know how many people actually receive advertising messages has led to the growth of one of the most important branches of marketing research. A traditional approximation has always been the circulation statements of publishers. The

Psychographic segmentation and communication

In today's markets mass communication is often targeted at specific segments. Advertisers try to learn as much as they can about these segments. On the premiss that improved communication will follow from knowing the receiver's 'field of experience' many attempts are made to uncover the lifestyle and attitudes of audience members. The resultant 'portraits' may help encode messages more clearly keyed to particular groupings of the population. An example is from the McCann-Erickson advertising agency's study of men. From 1,000 interviews eight clusters were identified and these are given below.

A male typology
1. *Passive endurers*
   Traditional view of masculinity; tend to be intolerant and pessimistic; uninvolved; find difficulty in expressing feelings; older and lower social class than average in sample.
2. *Sleepwalkers*
   Remote, uninvolved; traditional view of masculinity; contented underachievers; independent and unsentimental.
3. *Token triers*
   Try hard but fail; strive to improve; respond to new things; find difficulty in coping with life; biased toward under-35s.
4. *Self-exploiters*
   Self-starters; individualists; success comes from hard work and imagination not from luck; confident and manipulative.
5. *Self-admirers*
   Narcissistic and striving; intolerant and innovative; gregarious and see themselves as well-liked.
6. *Chameleons*
   Contemporary view of masculinity; other-directed; trend follower rather than innovator.
7. *Avant guardians*
   Optimistic and contemporary view of masculinity; expressive and concerned; tend to be younger and higher social class.
8. *Pontificators*
   Opinionated but with contemporary view of masculinity; respond to integrity and discipline.

Source: C. Bowring, *The Manstudy Report*, London: McCann-Erickson, 1984.

inadequacies of some of these has led to independent audits, e.g. the Audit Bureau of Circulation (ABC). But circulation statements tell only how many copies are sold, not how many people read them. Thus 'readership' studies are put out by publishers indicating how many 'readers per copy' they have. In the industrial market, and in local media, this is often the best available. For national press media a much better source with comparable data for all publications covered is the National Readership Survey. This will be considered in Chapter 17.

If the advertiser has a very particular audience in mind – some relatively small segment – then he has added problems since no single medium may give him adequate coverage of his segment. In fact, he may have to use several media knowing that just a few per cent of the audience for each is relevant to his campaign. His costs for reaching each one of these select few can be extremely high.

On top of this, most of the media employed for promotion are one-way. They have no in-built feedback mechanism. In the military analogy, if the receiver did not fully comprehend the message he could instantly ask for a repetition. If what the source asked for could not be done, then alternatives could be discussed. Advertising is one-way communication. Effective communication – the sharing of meaning – frequently has to be two-way. Research may very crudely attempt to perform the feedback function, but at best it is partial and late.

Finally, it should be remembered that marketing communication operates in an open system. All kinds of 'noise' and interference impinge. Competing messages are carried by the same media, and receivers usually only have a casual interest in the system.

The so-called power of advertising is, therefore, highly questionable. It is a relatively inefficient means of communication, but it continues to be used because other means are less effective or far more expensive.

The promotion mix

There are four categories of promotional means:

1. Advertising – paid, non-personal communication in a mass medium.
2. Personal selling – personal communication which is usually face-to-face, though sometimes by telephone.
3. Publicity – non-personal communication in a mass medium, which is not paid for by the source, e.g. favourable editorial comment or news stories.
4. Sales promotion – persuasive activities not included above, which may involve in-store displays, demonstrations, exhibitions, competitions, direct mail pieces, coupons, samples.

Table 15.2 *Influences on the promotion mix*

Company factors	Consumer factors	Product factors	Promotion instrument factors
Strategic issues	Desired consumer response	Product type	Relative capabilities
Distribution and service plans	Target market size and location	Lifecycle	Relative costs and effectiveness

The specific combination of these four types of means used by an organisation is its promotion mix, which is a subset of the overall marketing mix. Factors that could influence the mix adopted are set out in Table 15.2 and considered in more detail.

Company factors

Strategic issues

Tasks to be accomplished by the promotion mix are determined by the marketing goals and strategy, and so the kind of strategy being pursued is highly influential. Different strategies will present a variety of problems which may necessitate quite different promotion mixes.

If the central thrust of competitive strategy is rivalry with the main established competitors, then the promotion mixes of those rivals will be significant. If heavy advertising and special sales promotions are the norm among the group of competitors then this may need to be mirrored in company plans. Competing for visibility in the marketplace might require at least parity in the scale of promotional spending, and it may be judged that the best way to achieve a strong presence is to employ the same kind of promotion mix as the chief rivals. Attacking, defensive and market entry strategies all have different implications for promotion. In particular, the type of salesforce and advertising effort may vary. With each of those strategies, salesforce effort may be crucial in influencing the attitudes in trade channels. Advertising would have a special role. It may support awareness and trial objectives in market entry strategies and may be employed to emphasise differentiation in attack and defence.

Positioning strategy would also affect the promotion mix. Some kinds of positioning may be best explained to consumers through advertising, especially if there is reliance upon the development of strong sets of associations and images. The use of the rest of the promotion mix would need to be consistent with, and supportive of, the planned positioning.

Distribution plans

Promotional and distribution plans are mutually supportive. Plans made for distribution can condition the plans made in promotion. This can be seen where the firm adopts a 'push' or 'pull' strategy in respect of its distribution channels.

With a 'push' strategy the aim is to concentrate efforts upon the trade or middlemen. The rationale for this strategy is that product availability is crucial and that with sufficient incentive the middlemen will co-operate in developing end-user preference for the brand. This might be in allocating shelf space, point-of-sale promotions, competitive pricing and, if appropriate, in providing customer advice and after-sales services. In this case the promotion mix of the producer would emphasise dealer relations, with priority being given to salesforce and promotions to the trade. These could encompass advertising in trade magazines, and various dealer incentives such as special discounts, competitions and rewards keyed to displays and customer demonstrations.

A 'pull' strategy focuses upon the end customer. The aim is to stimulate strong brand preference so that customers demand that the product is made available. Middlemen need to perceive this demand and so some effort is made to demonstrate this by planning high-level national advertising. This has the dual effect of creating customer awareness and interest and at the same time convincing the trade that there will be heavy demand for the brand simply because it is being widely advertised. With this strategy the promotion mix stresses consumer advertising and consumer promotions.

Some firms may give great attention to one or other of these strategies, but other firms may adopt a mixed approach. Even so there would probably be rather more emphasis upon one than the other. It is also possible that the strategy will change through the product lifecycle: sales appeals and resale activities could evolve as the product matures. In earlier phases the emphasis will be on building customer awareness and encouraging trial. Manufacturers might persuade middlemen to offer product demonstrations and pass promotional material through the channel. In later stages middlemen might have less reason to push one brand any more than another, and so some manufacturers may tend to a pull strategy [4].

Service

Some markets are highly responsive to personal service. The product may be fairly homogeneous and the brunt of competition is in the service offered. Merchants and distributors of some standard engineering products rely entirely on their salesforces for product promotion. Advertising may be irrelevant because all potential customers know the competing distributors, and perhaps have used them all before. There may be some limited scope for sales promotion, and thus the use of calendars, diaries, and so on.

Consumer factors

Desired consumer response

Potentially, promotion can contribute to the desired consumer response by influencing a range of attitudes and behaviours. It can develop consumer awareness of the product and its claims. It may encourage the formation of favourable attitudes, stimulate consumer trials of the product and attempt to maintain brand loyalty. Each element of the promotion mix contributes differently in this context and this is considered later.

Additionally, the kind of consumer response sought may tend to one of 'thinking' or 'feeling', being relatively rational or emotional. There might also be differences in the level of involvement by the consumer in the product field. High involvement is characterised by high financial and social risk, often with considerable ego involvement, and because of this the consumer finds the product category interesting or important. Response to promotion may be thoughtful; there may be active search and evaluation of competitive products. Alternatively, there are less involving product fields in which there may be no massive differences in the physical properties of competing brands. In this case promotion may have the task of establishing differentiation through a 'feeling' response, by emphasising images and associations. Different promotion mixes would be derived depending on whether a thinking or feeling response was sought and on the extent of consumer involvement. The 'thinking' mix might employ print media, encourage visits to distributors, a large volume of promotional literature and with active salesforce support. The 'feeling' mix might use television and a collection of spurs for product trial such as coupons, samples and point-of-sale inducements.

Market size and location

Large, widely dispersed markets have different promotional requirements from smaller, geographically concentrated markets. A nationally distributed grocery product usually features mass advertising and sales promotion as the key elements of the mix, with personal selling taking a distinctive role in supporting these and in developing trade relations. A localised dairy producer or bakery can consider a promotional mix emphasising personal selling with the sales representatives delivering the product. In industrial markets the relatively small number of potential customers also allows a mix stressing personal selling.

Product factors

Product complexity

For complex products, where detailed technical evaluation by the buyers provides important evaluative criteria, the promotional mix needs to be designed to supply the desired information. This invariably means personal selling backed up with sales promotional aids, such as catalogues, technical data sheets and demonstrations. This is the usual case in industrial markets. For complex products where the buyer does not use technical evaluative criteria (e.g. in some consumer durables) there is less need for such a mix. In fields where the product is readily understandable, promotion may stress advertising rather than personal selling.

Table 15.3   *Promotion from introduction to decline*

| Introduction | Promotion mix | | Decline |
	Growth	Maturity	
Publicity	Mass media	Mass media	Gradual
Personal selling	Personal selling	Dealer promotions	phase-out of
Mass media	Sales promotion	Sales promotion	all promotion
	Publicity	Publicity	

Source: Adapted from C.R. Wasson, *Dynamic Competitive Strategy and Product Life Cycles*. St Charles, Ill.: Challenge Books, 1974, p. 284.

Product lifecycle
During the introductory phase of the lifecycle publicity will be highly prized, and may be far easier to obtain than in later phases of the lifecycle. Selective advertising to innovators and retailers and pioneering work by the salesforce may be the promotion mix employed. In subsequent lifecycle stages the mix is likely to change. Some possibilities are shown in Table 15.3.

Promotion instrument factors

Relative capabilities of promotional methods
Each promotional element has a different communication capacity. Sales representatives can talk to only a relatively small number of people, although their potency for persuasion is high. Advertising may expose a simple message to millions, with a more limited potency. Publicity may be more credible than advertising, and thus more effective communication, but the opportunities are restricted since the decisions to use publicity material are with editorial staff in the media. Sales promotion has highly variable communication effects. In-store activity may be the final link in prompting a purchase. Samples and coupons may generate the important first trial. Demonstrations and exhibitions may increase comprehension. Sponsorship may stimulate awareness. These various capacities may be related to stages in the persuasion process, as shown in Figure 15.6. It follows that reliance on just one of these methods is exceptional: most organisations use a combination.

Relative costs and effectiveness
Choice of the mix should, theoretically, be reduced to an assessment of the

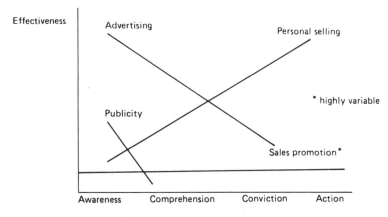

Figure 15.6 *Effectiveness of the four promotional means*

relative cost and effectiveness of the various elements. Costs can usually be reliably estimated: measures of effectiveness can be inordinately difficult.

If something of the sales response to each promotional element were known, then an optimal mix could be derived. The classic economic cost and revenue curves could be plotted, and with a mix of, say, advertising and personal selling, the optimum may be determined by holding one steady, varying the other and calculating the marginal effects on profit, then adding to the one with the greatest effect until there is no further increase in profit. Clearly, one first needs the response functions, and these are likely to be difficult to obtain. Management judgement, and perhaps experiments, could be used, and this procedure would then give some impression of the results of alternative mixes. But carry-over effects of advertising will not be felt in any single budget period – it is cumulative. This is ignored in the procedure above. Some guesses would also have to be made about the interaction of the elements. More advertising may generate more enquiries, needing more sales representatives. That is, advertising may increase the marginal profitability of sales personnel [5]. Despite these weaknesses, the marginal approach is probably a useful starting point in discussions about the balance of the elements in the promotion mix.

In practice, the problem is not as open-ended as theory supposes. In the short run, and perhaps for a few years, the size of the salesforce may be relatively fixed. Certainly, effective increases to size cannot be accomplished for at least a year. Decreases may be more difficult, given legislation about employment protection. The major decision, then, assuming a fixed salesforce in the short term, is the balance between above and below-the-line expenditure (advertising and sales promotion respectively). Kennedy and Corkindale [6] have commented on this:

> This decision is subject to the historical behaviour of the industry as well as the task to be accomplished. It is generally agreed that below-the-line expenditure will elicit a rapid growth in the sales curve in the short term, but that it will do little to build long-term brand loyalty, or to lift the curve to a higher level in the longer term. Hence this type of activity should only be used to meet immediate objectives. The historical point is of importance, however, for in those markets where the large segments have become promotion-dominated it is very difficult, if not impossible, for all brands to follow suit.

Goals

Clear specification of the objectives of each promotion element is a necessity in choosing the mix. If the role of each is defined, then cost estimates can be attached to the attainment of the goals. This again is, unfortunately, difficult to determine precisely. Because of the problems in measuring the sales effects of each promotional element, companies are increasingly trying to measure intermediate responses. They are moving away from a 'black box' approach, which considers just inputs (say advertising) and outputs (sales) and ignores the intervening processing, and are now beginning to explore the nature of the intervening responses. If discrete processes occur between input and output, then it may be possible to set communication goals for promotion in terms of movements in these intervening variables. So, rather than fix the objective as sales, the goals may be how well the audience remembers the brand's claims, or some change in customer evaluations of an attribute.

These attempts to measure communication effects rest on how well the intervening processes are understood. They may lead to the use of the wrong variables, or ones that cannot be effectively quantified. The nature of the variables currently thought relevant, and views on how they might be related, are explored in the next chapter. Before proceeding it is worth remembering that nothing is settled. There is no lasting agreement as to the 'right' variables, but because it is so central to marketing theory and practice it is one that requires an appreciation of the main issues and presently conceived arguments.

Summary

Schramm's model was used to introduce communication theory and the effectiveness of military communications was examined to establish a benchmark for marketing communications. Inefficiencies in the latter can be discerned in each of the components of the communication system.

A potential source problem is caused by the receiver's perception of that source. The reception and interpretation of the message can be affected by the receiver's opinion of the source. Coding problems are due to the differing frames of reference of the source and receiver. They may not share common understanding of some words and images. Message problems include those of determining the right strength and duration of the signal, and receiver problems are associated with the probability that they may not be there attending to the message.

Important influences on the promotion mix adopted include strategic issues, plans in other marketing mix decision areas, consumer and product factors and the relative capabilities, costs and effectiveness of the various promotion tools. The possible use of marginal analysis in the choice of promotion mix was considered, and finally the need for clear promotional goals was underlined.

Questions for review and discussion

1. Use transactional analysis to investigate some current advertising campaigns. What role is the advertiser allotting to himself and his audience? Will the audience accept that role?

2. Think of some presenters employed in television commercials. What role do they take, and is it congruous with the product and the advertiser? Are there any circumstances when an incongruous presenter can be effective?

3. Define the following words: dig, digit, double, down, drain, dress. Now check the dictionary definitions. Is there any problem in using these words in copywriting? Would the context overcome possible ambiguities?

4. Why is it usually thought that personal selling can be more potent than advertising? Are there any exceptions?

5. What are the difficulties in using the marginal approach to choosing the promotional mix?

6. What promotional mix would you suggest in the following instances: (1) a new brand of baby food; (2) a new expensive restaurant; (3) a new kind of automatic sprinkler system for fire control; (4) an established distributor of building contractor's plant?

References

1. Lowe-Watson, D. 1972. 'Advertising and the buyer/seller relationship', in Lawrence, R. and Thomas, M., *Readings in Marketing Management*. Harmondsworth: Penguin Books.
2. Gordon, W. 1983. 'The big name TV switch-off', *Campaign*, 18 March.
3. Bennett, B. 1985. 'Growing public regard for TV ads', *Viewpoint*, February.
4. Engel, J.F, Warshaw, M.R. and Kinnear, T.C. 1983. *Promotional Strategy*, 5th edn. Homewood, Ill.: Irwin, p. 466.
5. See, for example, Boyd, H.W and Massy, W.F. 1972. *Marketing Management*. New York: Harcourt Brace Jovanovich, p. 200.
6. Kennedy, S.H. and Corkindale, D.R. 1976. *Managing the Advertising Process*. Farnborough: Saxon House, p. 235.

Chapter 16
Advertising objectives and assessment

Advertising spans the boundary between an organisation and its environment, and consequently it can have many purposes. It is an important voice for the organisation and so carries many of its messages to quite varied audiences. Sometimes these are straightforward, objective announcements concerning topics such as financial results or employment opportunities. But the bulk of the national advertising spend has informative and persuasive purposes in furtherance of marketing objectives.

This chapter investigates the problems in specifying advertising's role in the marketing mix. Some of these problems are due to the difficulties in defining advertising's capacity to persuade. Views are still evolving, and several approaches are discussed. Despite the continuing debate about this capacity, advertising executives operate in real time and decisions are needed. Advertising objectives are set and campaign effectiveness evaluated, and so important parts of the chapter review these activities.

Strategy and advertising

Fundamental parameters for the advertising plan are set by the overall corporate and marketing strategies. These parameters include:

1. The basis on which competitive advantage will be built (cost or differentiation).
2. The thrust of competitive strategy (competitive rivalry, attack, defence, market entry).
3. Positioning strategy.
4. Segmentation strategy.

Much of advertising's role in the marketing mix is determined by the extent to which it can contribute to enhancing positioning in the target segment, with the object of countering competitors in order to sustain competitive superiority. Typically, there will be an annual advertising plan showing this contribution, although the role goes on year after year. The annual plan is a convenient division, and is probably needed for media buying, but large-scale advertising spending is seen as part of a long-run stream. Pedigree Petfoods spends more than £20 million annually on advertising and its media controller explains this commitment as [1]:

> a long-term investment to stimulate trial and to change purchasing behaviour . . . to establish long-term franchises by:

- Communicating and generating brand images.
- Communicating more tangible messages – lower prices, tastier recipes, new varieties.
- Gaining 'top of mind' awareness.

Advertising in any one period is therefore a section of the stream, and decisions in that period are influenced by the stream's strength and direction.

Understanding advertising

Use of advertising requires some understanding of how it functions. This requirement has yielded various attempts to model the process, and several are reported in the next section. Reservations can be expressed about all these models. Recently, attention has been turned to attempts to understand more about consumer responses to advertisements in terms of their involvement and feelings; these are discussed in the subsequent section. Some practitioners and researchers remain unconvinced by attempts to derive behavioural models, and so there is continuing interest in more quantitative approaches. This leads to some consideration of econometric models.

Sequential models

Earlier models

AIDA (attention, interest, desire, action) was formulated in the 1920s and suggests that the buyer passes through the successive stages in the order presented. Advertising would be expected to act on the first three stages and good advertising would contain elements to capture attention, stimulate interest and kindle desire. For some this simple conception remains the default model despite the shallow prescriptions it can offer.

DAGMAR (defining advertising goals for measured advertising results) was conceived by Colley [2] in 1961 and offers the following sequence through which the audience member moves:

Unawareness → Awareness → Comprehension → Conviction → Action

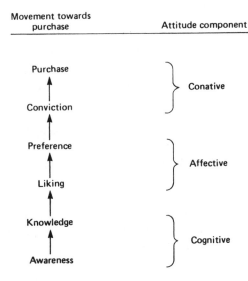

Figure 16.1 *Lavidge and Steiner's hierarchy of effects model*

Advertisers are recommended to set communication goals in terms of moving potential customers up through these various levels. A preliminary step would be to determine where relevant segment members are presently located in this progression. A goal would be established to increase the numbers at one or more of the stages, and a campaign devised and run with that declared aim. Its effects could then be measured by determining the degree of movement that had been accomplished.

A third approach, the hierarchy of effects model, was proposed by Lavidge and Steiner [3] and has been one of the most influential sequential models. It is shown in Figure 16.1.

All these models have been criticised because they describe the movement towards a purchase as necessarily following the established order sequence. Each was a valuable contribution in attempting to make advertising thought more systematic. But each is only an hypothesis and there are reasonable grounds for questioning their validity.

Palda [4] has presented a rigorous critique. He questions the logic of the models and criticises the lack of adequate measurement devices that would be necessary in making them operational. Awareness and knowledge do not always have to precede purchase by any appreciable amount of time. Similarly, the liking/conviction progression is challenged. It may or may not be necessary to like a product a lot before one buys it for the first time. Then again, how are the various stages to be measured? There are conceptual problems with each of them. Attempts are made, but the operational definitions required to actually collect data in the field often leave open whether or not the desired construct has actually been measured at all.

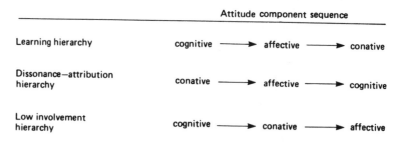

Figure 16.2 *Three-order hierarchy*

Palda's objections have triggered new work on both categories of criticisms. Data collection and analysis have improved, and the logical flaws are addressed by less dogmatic sequential arrangements.

Three-order hierarchy

Ray [5] and his colleagues freed the original hierarchy model from some of its rigidity. They proposed that communication responses could take three forms, as shown in Figure 16.2. The learning hierarchy is the traditional Lavidge and Steiner model. It is suggested that it applies only in some communication situations. Audience involvement with the product category and clear differences between alternatives are thought necessary. Typically this could be the case in the adoption of a new product, where mass media learning could be important. This then is a logical sequence of absorbing information, making evaluations and trials.

In the dissonance–attribution model, behaviour occurs first, followed by an affective change; finally, learning leads to a new cognition. It is exactly the reverse of the learning hierarchy. It posits an involved but uncertain consumer who may be confused by the lack of clear brand distinctions, or by his lack of confidence in making judgements, or by his inability to interpret which brand is related to a reference influence that he is attempting to follow. Non-media sources may be important in prompting his purchase decision. Once made, post-purchase dissonance leads to the justification of the choice through the development of affection. Advertising messages, and selective learning through experience with the product, support and secure the choice.

This model may be extended to include impulse purchasing in some instances. Children buying confectionery may follow this sequence. To them this product category may be an involving one. Impulse buying may be on the basis of no knowledge at all.

The third sequence has been evolved after the work of Krugman [6] and has been applied to television advertising. Krugman postulates that the audience is not involved with the medium and its messages; it is a passive medium. The audience's perceptual defences are down and the television message registers by changing the frame of reference – not by developing a strong affection for a brand. Repetition leads to a change in cognitive structure, which, for example, could be related to a change in the relative salience of attributes to be used in evaluating a given product category. Repetition also breeds familiarity. This is insufficient for the purchase act and some stimulus at the point of purchase may be required, e.g. a price incentive or distinctive merchandising. Some empirical support is offered by Bird and Ehrenberg [7] who establish a standard relationship between attitudes and usage, and who report that long-run past advertising is more important in explaining deviations from that standard relationship than is recent advertising. That is, carryover effects are substantial, and the gradual and consistent development of brand comprehension is critical. In this model, affection is a function of experience.

The resuscitation of the hierarchy of effects model by dropping its rigid, single-sequential arrangement was an important development in advertising theory. But problems remain in the operational definition of the constructs, and a new one has been added: the appropriate model needs first to be chosen. In general it is thought that the learning hierarchy applies to new products and to consumer durables; the dissonance–attribution model to involving product categories attended by pre-purchase confusion; and low involvement to much of the grocery market. What happens, though, when there is a radically new grocery product surrounded by a mass of preconceptions? There may be different audience segments whose communication response could be typified by different models. Should there be several campaigns each based upon a different model? Such confusions are, unhappily, more realistic than the assumption of homogeneity in DAGMAR.

Involvement and feelings

While debate continues about sequential models there has been further elaboration of the influences upon consumer responses to advertising. This has extended the earlier work on involvement and elevated the significance of the audience's associations and feelings about brands and advertising.

Involvement

Krugman's work referred to earlier in this chapter used the term low involvement. That was essentially in respect of consumer involvement with the advertising medium. Here involvement is with the product.

Involvement concerns the extent to which consumers care about the product field, and particularly the extent to which they care about individual brands. Factors influencing the level of involvement include the cost of the item, whether or not there is some social risk attached to its consumption and the extent to which there may be ego involvement. Therefore, high cost, socially conspicuous products with considerable implications for ego would be deemed as high involvement purchases. Cars, some consumer electronics, fashion and personal grooming products are examples. Some financial services, holiday and entertainment services may also be included. On the other hand, many products and services are the opposite on those factors. They may be perceived as mundane and uninteresting, even boring, or arouse no particular response at all.

Rothschild [8] has contrasted the implications for the way advertising may be used in high and low involvement as follows:

High involvement
Awareness → Attitude → Behaviour → Long-run behaviour

Low involvement
Awareness → Trial behaviour → Attitude → Long-run behaviour

He sees advertising operating in different ways in these situations and within different promotion mixes. For example, at the awareness stage with high involvement, advertising would play a significant role and may be primarily in print media using lengthy, informative copy with relatively few repetitions. In contrast, trial behaviour with low involvement might give emphasis to other promotional means and advertising might contain a coupon or other offer.

Associations and feelings

It has long been recognised that some advertising elicits a 'thinking' response from consumers, and some a 'feeling' response [9]. Some advertising works by emphasising words and some by emphasising pictures; some presents arguments and facts, and other advertising attempts to engage emotions and to create moods and images. The thinking/feeling dichotomy could be added to that of low/high involvement to derive four categories of consumer response to advertising:

	Examples
Thinking with low involvement	Groceries
Thinking with high involvement	Durables
Feeling with low involvement	Confectionery, drinks
Feeling with high involvement	Cosmetics

This can be accommodated to an extent by the hierarchical models considered earlier. In both low involvement cases the hierarchy steps might be do–feel–learn (conative–affective–cognitive). The thinking/high involvement hierarchy might be learn–feel–do and that with feeling/high involvement might be feel–learn–do. But the greater attention now given to audience feelings has wider implications because it asserts the consumer's perspective and the use that consumers make of advertising.

Taking this perspective leads to another complex set of issues. The consumer is not seen as a passive recipient of mass communications but as a sophisticated, even sceptical, user of advertising. He may not control the issue of the communication but does control what happens to it. It is a part of the context in which the consumer may come to attach symbolic, as well as functional, utilities to products. And the symbolism serves the consumer's purposes. It can evoke images and feelings and express to others something about the individual. Necessarily, it is the consumer's perception which operates. The advertiser may project images, but the associations and feelings can only be those of the audience and may or may not resemble the advertiser's intentions. Some products become highly symbolic without any advertising at all and others come to stand for things that manufacturers try to disown.

Research in this area studies the nature of the symbolism, and specifically the associations and feelings aroused by brands and by advertising. It has led to renewed interest in the relationship between the brand, its advertising and the consumer's feelings about both. It is suggested that where the consumer's response to the advertising is basically one of 'thinking' then it is immaterial whether or not the advertisement is liked. Where the response is essentially 'feeling' it is more important for the advertisement itself to be liked. Thus the preoccupation with highly creative, visually pleasing advertisements, often using a touch of humour.

Involvement and motives

The four involvement and thinking/feeling categories noted above have come to be known as the FCB grid, after the agency (Foote, Cone, Belding) which developed some of these ideas. Another advertising planning grid has been proposed by Rossiter and Percy [10]. They retain an involvement dimension which they define in terms of the risk perceived by the typical audience member in purchasing a brand. But they replace the thinking/feeling dimension by a purchase motivation dimension. On one side of this motivation dimension they put forward a 'think' class of purchase motives, which they term informational motives and which, they assert, can be satisfied by providing information about the product or brand. These motives are problem removal, problem avoidance, incomplete satisfaction, mixed approach–avoidance and normal depletion. On the other side of the motivation dimension they place 'feel' motives – in their terms, transformational motives – which 'promise to enhance the brand user by effecting a transformation in the brand user's sensory, mental or social state'. These motives relate to sensory gratification, intellectual stimulation (achievement, mastery) and social approval.

There are then two dimensions to this framework: involvement and purchase motivation. On each dimension there are two subdivisions: high or low involvement and informational or transformational motives. Taken together they form four categories:

	Involvement	Motives	Examples
1.	low	informational	aspirin, detergent
2.	low	transformational	confectionery, beer
3.	high	informational	insurance, microwave ovens
4.	high	transformational	holidays, fashions, cars

Econometric models

Some researchers remain unhappy about behavioural models of advertising. They see the models considered above as too simple, and attempts to make them more realistic are confounded by the variability of human behaviour. An alternative approach is to investigate advertising's direct effects on sales. Doyle and Corstjens [11] have demonstrated a model in a mature market which estimates advertising elasticity and advertising's marginal revenue product. Broadbent suggests that typical price elasticity of brands he has studied is −1.3 and typical advertising elasticity is +0.2 [12]. An example of such exercises is provided by Kellogg's Bran Flakes, reported by Elliot [13]. The model developed took Bran Flakes' market share as the dependent variable and attempted to explain variations in that share by changes in several independent variables. The independent variables are listed below, together with their estimated influence. In the case of the first variable the +0.2 per point means that Bran Flakes' market share increased 0.2 per cent for every 1.0 per cent increase in the combined share growth of other bran cereals.

The bran boom –	simulated combined share growth of other cereals	+0.2 per point
Competitive brands –	market share of other brands	−0.5 per point
	market share of Special K	−0.6 per point
Price elasticity		−0.6
Advertising elasticity –	Television 1980	+0.1
	Magazines 1981	+0.1
	Television 1982 'Tasty'	+0.3
	Television 1983/84 'Waiters'	+0.4

$R^2 = 0.91$

Advertising models: a practical consequence

While debate continues about whether it matters that advertising may work in different ways in different circumstances, advertising planners still have to make decisions. Some argue that thought about how advertising works is so inconclusive that the whole question should be ignored. But the problem cannot be escaped: some kind of model is necessarily used in all advertising. The only issue is whether that model is made explicit.

An intriguing example of the impact of the view taken about how advertising works is provided by Knirps umbrellas. The market had not been brand-conscious and so Knirps set about establishing itself as the brand leader by implementing an intensive advertising campaign. The theme was 'you can't knacker a Knirps' and £300,000 was quickly used up on television advertising. Brand awareness increased by 30 per cent, but there was little increase in sales. The advertising bill had to be met and unfortunately the company went into liquidation.

Subsequently a managerial buy-out led to the relaunch of the umbrella. This time there was no advertising, but great attention to point-of-sale activities. The view had changed and strong brand identity was seen as less important. It was now believed that umbrella purchasing was impulsive, and so product availability and merchandising were the key factors.

In this case the view adopted about the advertising model which was appropriate was as dramatic as contributing to company failure. It is difficult to get much more basic than that.

Source: Based upon an article in the *Sunday Times*, 24 October 1982.

The varying advertising elasticities are interesting, with the earlier campaigns having less effect than Broadbent's norm noted above, and the later campaigns exceeding that norm. Sales of this brand also seem to be much less price-elastic than normal.

Sometimes such models take into account the notion of 'adstock', to allow for the cumulative effects of advertising. Advertising's effects are partly a function of spending in the current period and may also be a function of the carry-over of past advertising. 'Adstock' adds in recent advertising, deleted or decayed, to current advertising. In the case of television advertising this week's adstock might be this week's advertising plus 0.6 of last week's, 0.4 of the week before and so on. The decay rate applied is obviously important and perhaps several would be tried to discover which gives the best fit.

Advances are being made in the application of econometric models in advertising. Twyman [14] believes they can be useful in measuring short-term effects, but that advertising's longer-run effects may be too variable and inconsistent to yield to this approach. Broadbent and Jacobs [15] see virtues in this approach but point out that it is an art as well as a science:

> Multivariate statistics applied in this area require assumptions, checks and comparisons with other information, and it is not a sausage machine. Both in the selection of the model and in the jump from association to the statement that A caused B, the analyst is often on very thin ice. Nevertheless, analysis can give convincing explanations in particular cases.

These models therefore need to pass a reality test: Do they make sense and can they be believed? And while they can shed considerable insight they cannot offer comprehensive explanations. Their empirical basis could also lead to the charge that they derive 'facts without theories' in contrast to the behavioural models which could be charged with producing 'theories without facts'.

This is a controversial area, but it should not be taken that the behavioural and econometric approaches are mutually exclusive. Dogged reliance on one, in ignorance of the other, is myopic. Econometric models do not say how advertising works, though they might detect something of the effects. Behavioural models postulate how advertising works, as yet inconclusively.

Setting advertising objectives

The goals established for advertising must be set squarely in the context of a view of how advertising works, otherwise unrealistic or inappropriate targets may be chosen, and strategic development given hopeless parameters.

The need for advertising objectives

Advertising decisions concern the following six elements [16]:

1. How much should be spent?
2. What should comprise the content and presentation of the advertisements?
3. Which media are most appropriate?
4. What should be the frequency of display of advertisements or campaigns?
5. Should any special geographical weighting of effort be used?
6. What are the best methods for evaluating the accomplishment of advertising?

It is difficult to see how any of these decisions can adequately be made without the prior clear specification of objectives.

Empirical evidence on advertising goal-setting

A study of British and European companies found that 70 per cent appeared to set objectives, although only 55 per cent were in written form and many of these were crude [17]. Most had as the main objective to increase sales, which is an overall marketing objective that is unreasonable to expect advertising alone to achieve. Britt has reported on 135 American campaigns [18] and concluded that most did not have objectives stated in a quantifiable, detectable way.

The most rigorous published empirical work is due to Corkindale and Kennedy. Table 16.1 shows what kinds of objective were set for thirty-three important products. They include some of the very largest British consumer goods companies, and are indicative of current best practice. As can be seen, the predominant goals are rightly those that advertising could have some direct impact on – image building, attitude development, informative and persuasive messages. Moreover, in most cases reported in Table 16.1 some type of assessment was attempted. However, Table 16.2 shows some inconsistencies. While the most frequently cited assessment method is some form of attitude/image study, the next most common is a sales measure. It is difficult to see how the advertising objectives in the top half of the table can be reliably assessed by sales measures.

More detailed analysis led the researchers to probe the widespread uses of attitude/image measures. The companies apparently use these to gauge something of the effects of nearly all their advertising goals, but [19]:

> it was realised that companies actually use attitude/image studies primarily for monitoring consumer reaction to the product. Using the surveys to assess the effectiveness of any particular campaign is almost an incidental check, and not a formal assessment. As such, these measures almost constitute an 'informal' evaluation. For those product situations where these surveys are used for formal

Table 16.1 *Advertising objectives and assessment*

Objectives	Frequency of mention	Number of occasions on which assessment was undertaken
Advertising objectives		
To create branding and image-building	23	19
To convey particular messages	21	18
To educate and convey information (distinguished from messages by the more factual and objective basis)	16	10
To affect attitudes	13	13
To create awareness	8	5
To affect loyalty intentions	6	4
To gain willingness to try	5	3
To act as a reminder	2	1
To motivate enquiries	1	1
Marketing objectives (set for advertising)		
Buyer behaviour*	13	8
Market share	9	8
Penetration/distribution	6	3
Influence on buyer behaviour†	5	5
Relating to 'own-label'‡	5	5
Total market development§	3	3
Sales	2	2

Notes: This information was derived from thirty-three products made by companies such as Beecham, Cadbury Schweppes, CPC, Heinz, Lyons, Spillers and Watney Mann.
* Buyer behaviour includes such as 'to improve frequency of purchase' and 'to gain new users'.
† Influence on buyer behaviour includes 'to win back previous product users' and 'to stop existing users turning to a competitive product'.
‡ Own-label includes 'to defend against "own-label" products'.
§ Total market development includes 'to expand whole market'.
Source: D.R. Corkindale and S.H. Kennedy, *Measuring the Effect of Advertising.* Farnborough: Saxon House, 1975, p. 154.

assessment, the assumption is that favourability of attitudes is the best available predictor of consumer purchase.

Prescriptions for setting advertising objectives

There can be no ready-made collection of advertising objectives. Prescriptions about goal-setting are therefore meant to establish a logical and objective process which might enhance diagnosis, evaluate feasible alternative means and allow critical appraisals of how far advertising goals and means might achieve higher-order objectives. Once more, then, it is an analytical process that is recommended.

Some of the more important elements in this process are depicted in Figure 16.3. This figure should not be interpreted as a sequential flowchart. The arrows

Table 16.2 *Relating objectives to assessment methods: Corkindale and Kennedy's 33-product sample*

Objectives	Method of assessment									
	Attitude/ image response	Sales	Advertising content monitor (e.g. recall)	Consumer reaction monitor (pre- and post-testing)	Buyer behaviour	Trade response	Audience achievement	Experimental response	Coupon response	No formal assessment
Advertising objectives										
To create brand/image building	17	3	3	1		1	1			8
To convey particular messages	13		5	2	1			1		4
To educate and convey information	7	2	2	2		1				7
To affect attitudes	11	1	1	1				1		1
To create awareness	4	1	2	1		1		1		3
To affect loyalty intentions	2	2		1				1		2
To gain preparedness to try	2	2	1	1				1		1
To act as a reminder	1									1
To motivate enquiries									1	
Marketing objectives										
Market share		8								2
Penetration/distribution		3				1				2
Total market development		3								
Sales		2			1					
Influence on buyer behaviour	2	4				1				
Buyer behaviour	1	8		2			1			4
Related to 'own-label'	3	5		1						
Total	63	44	14	12	2	5	2	5	1	35

Source: Corkindale and Kennedy, op. cit., p. 169.

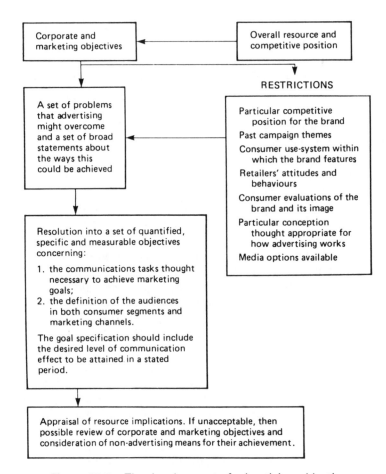

Figure 16.3 *The development of advertising objectives*

show directions of influences not temporal orderings of a 'right' way in which the factors should enter decision-making. Even then it is highly partial: it assumes that higher-order objectives are already determined, shows little of the influences on these; and does not demonstrate the essentially circuitous nature of the process, e.g. the effect of the restrictions on the establishment of marketing objectives. The diagram should have arrows pointing in all directions, links between every box and any amount of feedback and iteration. That would effectively disguise the burden of the argument.

Clear, detailed marketing goals do not necessarily begin the process, although they must feature importantly in it. From these, some initial role will have been assigned to advertising and to the rest of the promotion mix. This role will be tested and adjusted in the light of what are here termed 'restrictions'. Each of these could subsume a wealth of circumstances. The competitive circumstance might cover good or bad standing in respect of traditional competing brands, newly launched brands, own-label brands, or perceived competition from a separate product class. This could yield problems that need to be taken into account when formulating marketing objectives; it could also provide specific advertising tasks and set limits to the effects advertising might have. Advertising has to compete with other advertising; competitors may have pre-empted some claims/appeals and their previous advertising may require a competitive answer.

The consumer-use system may be developing: complementary and substitute product classes may be changing and consumer lifestyles may be taking new directions. These pose both opportunities and threats. Similarly, retailer reaction to and consumer evaluation of the product and its image may well be dynamic, though perhaps they will evolve relatively slowly.

Another concern will be the view that the company takes on how advertising performs its tasks. The earlier discussion pointed to the several conceptions currently held.

All of the above feed from the marketing information system, and from the analysis some detailed problem areas should emerge. These must necessarily be tractable from an advertising viewpoint, since it is meaningless to set goals for advertising which advertising cannot hope to achieve. Accompanying this should be some statement about how advertising might alleviate the problems. Now comes a major step. These ideas need to be translated into specific advertising objectives. Sometimes these may be readily deduced. For example, a new brand launch needs information and trial objectives. Benchmarks for the desired level of these may be more difficult to fix. A company with long experience in similar markets may feel it knows enough of consumer behaviour to set a level by rule-of-thumb, e.g. 40 per cent aware and 20 per cent penetration in a target segment within six months of launch. Research information may be available about previous launches. In another instance the problem may have been determined as a sudden decline in consumer evaluations on one attribute. The goal might then be to regain the former level on this dimension. In yet another case the problem may be the introduction of a new competitive brand with a notable packaging feature. The objective here may be to denounce the new feature as irrelevant – in which case the assessment of effectiveness must include a measure of consumer reactions to the new brand's packaging. Or the judgement may be to side-step the new feature and defend the current image. In that case another judgement would be required on the volume of advertising required to maintain the existing profile, and that volume may be more than previously needed.

Goals evolved from this process would not be accepted without question. It could well be that the cost of reaching them is too high. Other plans might be discussed and more modest advertising objectives established. Alternatively, if advertising were a fundamental part of the marketing mix, the total marketing task might be redefined. Additionally, other promotional tools may be considered as substitutes for advertising.

What should now be clear is that setting advertising goals is not an obvious process. It is an analytical procedure where great care should be taken in making the host of necessary assumptions as explicit as possible. Advertising problems never present themselves with tailor-made solutions. The advertising executive's skill is in formulating the problem and tailoring possible solutions. An example demonstrating the complex mix of factors contributing to the development of an advertising campaign is shown below in the case of Pirelli tyres.

Assessing and improving advertising effectiveness

Advertising without specific aims is pointless, and if specific aims are set then a logical corollary is to attempt to measure the degree to which they are achieved. That is the argument for post-exposure measurement. To rely only on assessments after the campaign has run means that improvements can only be incorporated into the next campaign, which may or may not have the same objectives. Prior to exposure few people would claim that they have devised the singular best campaign, and so there must inevitably be scope for improvement. Pre-testing attempts to define that scope.

Pirelli tyres: developing an advertising campaign

Situation
The passenger car tyre market has been fairly static in recent years. Total sales have been around 15 million annually, and Pirelli has about 10 per cent of the market. Low profile tyres have, however, been a growth sector associated with the increasing number of performance saloon cars, and Pirelli has about 20 per cent of this sector.

Segmentation
Pirelli commissioned awareness and image research prior to its 1984 campaign. The brand did not show up well on the main image dimensions of 'gives excellent mileage', 'safe', 'suitable for family car', 'good wet grip' and 'good handling'. It was considered expensive, and this confirmed qualitative studies which indicated the tyre was associated with Italian sports cars, and for a substantial part of the population it was regarded as 'not for me'. Deeper analysis revealed a segment which would demand and pay a premium price for a high quality product. This represented 11 per cent of the total and there was a further 41 per cent who claimed that they were susceptible to a quality/price argument. The segment was further defined as ABC1 male performance car drivers who were driving enthusiasts or non-enthusiasts particularly interested in safety. The enthusiasts thought Pirelli was 'for me'; the non-enthusiasts the opposite.

The target segment chosen was the enthusiasts and geographic analysis found them to be strongest in London and the South East.

Campaign objectives
1. To build on current brand awareness levels amongst ABC1 males primarily in London and the South East.

---

2.   To justify a premium price by presenting an image of superior road-holding ability.

Developing the advertisement
Research had identified the enthusiast's association with the emotional benefits of road-holding and the desire to be a confident, skilful driver. Further research assisted creative development by stressing the need to demonstrate 'driver involvement', and it also showed that the use of 'relevant' cars could help select the target audience. The final advertisement entitled 'Riders on the Storm' featured an Audi Coupé on a night journey in adverse weather conditions. The treatment was menacing and surreal.

Campaign results

Coverage and frequency
TVS region – ABC1 male ratings of 418; 84 per cent coverage with 5.0 o.t.s.
London – ABC1 male ratings of 418; 89 per cent coverage with 4.6 o.t.s.

Spontaneous awareness
Increased from 57 per cent before campaign to 71 per cent.

Prices
Market prices were cut 10 per cent in the first half of 1984; Pirelli prices were maintained.

Image tracking
Improvement on all key image dimensions.

Sales and profits/
Company sales maintained and profits up.

Source: *Viewpoint*, no. 33. 'Marketing case studies from TV advertisers'.

Research also has other roles during the development of the campaign. It may assist the understanding of what have here been called the restrictions. Investigations into image and competitive standing can supply the problems to be addressed by the goals set for advertising. Research may also help management over the hurdle from problem definition and goal specification, to strategy determination. It is one thing to say that the problem is a slip in user evaluations of one attribute: it is quite another to formulate a specific campaign to overcome that weakness. Say that the attribute was convenience of use, that all physical product properties were constant, and that the cause of the decline was thought to be new competitive messages. Past and current research may fix the problem to just one segment, and it may give its relative salience. Research may also help develop creative ideas to address the problem and screen alternative approaches.

Furthermore, an advertising objective of lifting attribute rating does rest on the assumption of a relationship between message registration and attribute rating. Research may give some broad impression of that relationship. It would

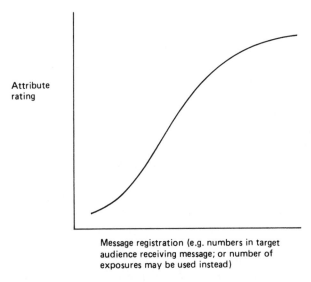

Figure 16.4 *Message registration and attribute rating*

fall far short of being able to plot the exact shape and position of the curve shown in Figure 16.4. But it would help. Because this is likely to be impressionistic – perhaps based on analysis of past campaigns and similar brands – it has the danger that dogma will creep in about the elasticity of the curve. Emphasising the assumptions and tenuous nature of the analysis might guard against this.

Research has further potential contributions during the development phase. The discussion has taken the creative execution of the campaign theme for granted. The visuals and copy may be better or worse than average and they may, or may not, fit the desired effect squarely. They may also have beneficial or harmful side-effects. Some 'copy testing' may indicate the closeness of the fit and, before that stage, group discussions may generate ideas relevant to the creative formulation.

Drawing these points together, the role of research in assessing and improving advertising efficiency may be summarised as follows:

1. To assist problem definition.

2. To guide strategy development:
   (a) creative;
   (b) type and level of effort.

3. To evaluate strategy achievements post-exposure.

Both advertisers and advertising agencies are involved in the research process. But both have differing interests and perspectives, and Flandin *et al.* have surveyed their approaches and attitudes. Very generally much of the research undertaken by agencies seems to concentrate upon the evaluation of creative ideas and copy during the development of the campaign, and great use is made of qualitative research. Clients are concerned with measuring the subsequent effectiveness of campaigns and 'are preoccupied with proving immediate sales increases during or following a particular campaign', and so there is always the need for 'a compromise between the short-term bottom-line focus of the client and the creative orientation and interest in longer-term brand building of the agency' [20].

Before considering the specific techniques employed it is necessary to recognise that these tools are used to test particular advertisements and campaigns. This presupposes that an advertisement has meaning in itself. This is justifiable because advertisements do carry information about the products, and/or the situation. However, Leymore, using structural linguistic analysis, contends that the full meaning of an advertisement cannot be deduced in isolation. She argues that the structure of advertising can be understood only in the context of the full system of all advertising for a product category. This is based on the notion that advertising can be reduced to certain underlying themes or dimensions, and that these are apparent only from the totality of all advertising in a product class. Appeals made by one brand interact with appeals made by all other brands to shape the perception the individual has of any single advertisement or campaign. Brand A might claim to be 'bright' and brand B to be 'white'. Assessments of the brightness claim and its effect on consumer responsiveness can be made only in so far as it is related (opposed?) to the whiteness claim. Interestingly, Leymore analyses soap powder advertising and reduces whiteness to 'good' and brightness to 'not good'. Most soap powder advertising in fact stresses whiteness – only a small minority of brands proclaim brightness [21].

This means that advertising research using the common methods described below is essentially aimed at assessing and improving the impact of individual advertisements. Deeper insights into the nature of the concept formations affected by advertising messages are coming to be investigated, and it is this area that may receive increasing attention in the future. This ties in with the developing information processing tradition in consumer behaviour. Not that structuralism is without its critics: one limitation is its preoccupation with verbal content; another is the assumption that individuals are sensitive to 'deep structure', e.g. basic cultural themes [22].

Research using structural linguistics in advertising has so far been extremely limited. That it may offer interesting speculations is demonstrated by Leymore's analyses of advertising for soap powders, cheese and ready meals. These studies attempt to trace the meanings of this advertising to major cultural themes such as life and death, nature and culture, war and peace, and happiness and misery. Hence the theory that advertising performs the function in modern society that myths performed in earlier societies.

We now look at some of the principal techniques used in the research tasks determined earlier, omitting research for problem definition since this could include marketing research in its widest sense.

Measuring cognitive effects

Recall tests

Tests to indicate the amount that a respondent can remember of an advertisement are frequently used to measure cognitive (awareness and comprehension) effects. These 'memory tests' usually involve a measure of 'recall' and show the percentage of a sample of respondents that could correctly recall having seen the advertisement, and sometimes they give scores for those remembering individual elements in the copy, e.g. headline, illustration, text. There are four main variables concerning the design of these tests. First, there is the nature of the material to be tested. As Hedges [23] says:

> One of the real difficulties . . . is finding adequate stimulus material. Much imaginative work has been done with animatics, narrative tapes, concept boards and the like.

There is a trade-off between cost and realism in the selection of material. With television, a finished film with the final actors and locations will be expensive, but is an animated cartoon a suitable surrogate? Second, there is the method of exposure. Print advertisements might be shown in a loose folder with other recent advertising, or in a dummy magazine or newspaper. Television advertisements could be shown on a small monitor to individuals, or on a large screen to

---

Undertaking the research

How and when the research is undertaken can affect how it is interpreted. The following case illustrates.

the example of a pre-test for a Fisher-Price (UK) ad called 'Baby'. The ad opens on an empty, sunfilled room with net curtains billowing in from the high windows and a polished wood floor. A dramatic chord heralds the magical appearance of a perfect little boy on a white blanket. An enthusiastic but gentle voice-over suggests the baby's thoughts: 'Where am I? How d'I get here?' Another chord and the baby is surrounded by Fisher-Price toys: 'What's this box? What If I push?, What if I pull? . . . etc.' The ad closes with the thought: 'Fisher-Price, for the most enquiring minds in the world.'

The agency loved the ad and it researched well among focus groups of women talking about babies, toys and toy manufacturers. However, when the ad was presented, without introduction, in a reel of general advertising (in fact, to test impact) many mothers said they had been terrified by the opening sequence. The billowing curtains and dramatic chord had suggested Alfred Hitchcock rather than creation. When the baby arrived the mothers expected a harrowing public warning film . . . the point is that anyone viewing the ad knowing it was for toys missed the decidedly sinister overtones at the start.

Source: J. Corstjens, *Strategic Advertising*. Oxford: Heinemann, 1990, p. 145.

groups. Third, there is the type and sample of respondents; and, fourth, the kinds of question asked and the amount of permissible prompting ('aided recall' is where the interviewer gives prompts, such as showing a card listing brands, or asking whether advertising in a specific product category can be remembered).

Superficially, recall tests are appealing. They generate columns of percentages that some users take to be an index of the relative performance of different advertisements. Advertising industry awards, especially those given by the media, sometimes use high recall scores as evidence of advertising excellence. Recall studies are very pervasive in advertising, yet they are severely criticised by many commentators. Assuming reasonable research discipline (which is debatable when only small samples are used), the main contentious issue is the interpretation of the recall score. There is no logical necessity for these scores to be positively correlated with purchase behaviour, as can be inferred from the earlier treatment of advertising models. But frequently in practice high positive correlation is assumed unquestioningly, and so recall scores would be used as the basis for choosing between alternative advertisements that were being tested before a campaign was run. If it was explicitly decided that a learning model was appropriate, then recall measures would have a little more validity. Just how much validity would be a function of the methodology. Small judgement samples are often employed, and so the results can be at best impressionistic. Such tests would, however, be relatively inexpensive and easy to employ.

Less dispute is usually aroused over the use of recall on individual elements of the copy. In this case it is not the total impact of the advertisement that is the question, but the proportion of the sample remembering the headline, and so on. The verbatim comment from subjects is also sometimes useful in such studies. Qualitative work of this kind can help both analysts and creative personnel.

The doubts and uncertainties surrounding this type of advertising research have led Ostlund and others to point to what they describe as inertia in copy testing [24]. In a survey of American advertisers and agencies they found extensive use of recall methods, especially day-after-recall (DAR) for television advertisements, yet found it uncommon for users to check on the reliability or the validity of the methods.

Laboratory tests

Physiological changes resulting from exposure to an advertisement are sometimes measured. Arousal is usually the focus of attention and is monitored by the psycho-galvanometer, which reacts to changes in the activity of the sweat glands, or a camera recording pupil dilation. Neither is widely used. They rely on the assumption that an emotional reaction is necessary and that positive and negative arousal can be distinguished.

Tachistoscopes attempt to measure impact. They are instruments that allow the test material to be illuminated for controlled periods of time varying from one-hundredth of a second. The subject looks into the tachistoscope, the material becomes visible for the controlled time, and the researcher asks what the subject saw. The procedure is repeated until the whole advertisement can be recalled. Successively longer time periods of exposure are allowed with each repetition to each subject. This is a useful device in advertising and packaging research, and can be used to investigate the impact of variations in copy elements, layout, colour, size, typography and shape. It is the only laboratory technique that has become standard, although its popularity does wax and wane.

Measuring comprehension
Individual interviews and group discussions are commonly used to assess comprehension. The purpose is clear: to gauge how well respondents understand the point of the message. Groups may be asked to comment on test advertisements with probes on the credibility of the situation and characters portrayed. Are the actors acceptable? Are they convincing in that role? Does the product fit that situation? Does the message emerge with clarity? Is it distorted or fuzzy? Does the presentation confuse or have unforeseen side-effects?

This research is on the basis of very small samples. Groups of six to eight respondents and three to eight groups in all are normal. To compound the difficulty, the recruitment of discussion participants is open to criticism. If the campaign is aimed at a specific segment, then individual members of that segment need to be located for the discussion group. Thirty-five- to fifty-year-old men who do all their own car maintenance (who may constitute the segment) are not easily found and persuaded to join a discussion. This is an awkward problem which advertising or research agencies may subcontract to specialist recruitment agencies that exist in many large towns. There has been considerable talk in market research circles about the need to control such recruitment because it can be questionable. Despite these problems, this qualitative work can be beneficial. An important use is in screening for unfavourable associations in the copy, or for unfortunate phrases and incredible situations – if these were not intended.

Measuring affective response

Quantitative and qualitative researchers have been active in developing techniques to explore affective responses to advertising, particularly for use in the development of campaigns. Quantitative research tends to focus upon attitudes, and qualitative research upon feelings. Apart from their potential usefulness in advertising research both could also have more basic use in developing positioning strategy.

Microsimulation of attitudes
Advances in computer technology are allowing greater utilisation of simulation in marketing. One application uses multi-attribute models of consumer attitudes to simulate response to product concepts and to advertising. SCRIBE uses a computer-aided interviewing technique to elicit feelings against attributes for brands in a product field, and to locate 'ideal' levels on up to forty attributes. Buying intentions data are also gathered. Assuming a relatively robust model is developed then it should relate reasonably to market shares, and it could then be

inferred that determinant attributes had been isolated. Various simulations could proceed [25].

A new advertising treatment could be researched. Respondents would be exposed to the advertisement and their feelings on relevant attributes gauged. This would be compared with the attribute ratings in the original model, differences noted and the implications for buying intentions and for possible market shares projected. Alternatively, in the case of a new product, a desired attitude profile may have been established by the company. The research would then attempt to measure differences in attitude profiles with alternative copy approaches.

Simple research with a small number of respondents and a handful of attributes could always be undertaken. The difference with microsimulation is that hundreds of respondents can be involved and forty attributes simultaneously tested – and a more convincing model can be established in the first place. The potential speed and flexibility of the new technology allow much greater experimentation. Of course, problems remain in the validity of the attitude model used and in the way that the advertising material is exposed. There is also an assumption that exposure to an advertisement should have some impact upon feelings about product attributes. In reviewing research in this area Leckenby and Wedding [26] are not at all conclusive. Some studies on the reliability of attitude change measures show reasonable results and others give wide discrepancies in test/retest scores using the same advertisement.

Exploring feelings

It could be argued that multi-attribute attitude models deal with a 'thinking' response and may be most appropriate where there are clear differences between brands. In some product fields there are less clear distinctions and there may be parity between brands on their physical properties. Companies seek differentiation through the development of the brand image and this may depend on a 'feeling' response from consumers.

Exploration of feelings has employed various qualitative approaches. Cooper contends that brands are used by consumers as a sort of language; as expressive gestures and as part of rituals [27]. Imagery and symbolism feature strongly in this view and, to get past the rationalisations we all make about some of our purchase behaviour, use is made of projective techniques (often with groups of respondents) such as sentence and picture completion, role playing and drawings to express feelings. This may assist the creative process by offering a richer understanding of how consumers perceive that both the product and its advertising relate to their lives. It may help to clarify the images, associations and moods perceived to be represented by the brand and its advertising. It may spur a new creative approach or, more fundamentally, unlock a new interpretation of positioning strategy.

Measuring intentions and behaviour

Intention to buy or 'buying predisposition' can be scaled, and once more presents a contentious area. Potter and Lovell [28] argue that such scores are not an index of the persuasive power of an advertisement, but could be used in a more limited role. If they are employed as an additional probe they might reveal symptoms worthy of further investigation. Questions could be asked after exposure to a test advertisement as to the extent of change in respondents' interest in buying. Probing those with negative reactions may spotlight a weakness in the creative presentation. Crimp reports the use of intentions data by Research Bureau Limited, where a long history of using such studies has shown some correlation with purchase [29].

More controversial techniques attempt to predict behaviour in various laboratory, hall or theatre tests. Respondents might be invited to choose from several brands prior to the screening of a commercial – which might be shown alone, with other commercials or within the context of a feature film or documentary. After the screening, respondents would be asked to make a further choice among the brands, and this might be a 'real' choice in that they might be allowed to take it away with them. While the commercials were being shown, the audience might have had a button by their seats which they could push when they saw something which pleased or displeased them. The result would be a measure of 'brand preference change' and detailed assessments on copy elements. Such services are still available in the United States, although they have had a mixed reaction in the United Kingdom.

Coupon responses could be helpful in pre- and post-testing where the aim was to generate enquiries or requests for literature, for instance where the advertisement included a coupon to be cut out and returned. In industrial advertising many journals have well-organised reader service enquiry systems and this procedure is extensively used.

Sales measures are appropriate in direct response advertising. Even in other circumstances they may give some insight into possible advertising effects. Caution is required, but Bloom *et al.* [30] argue from their study of Horlicks and Ribena for the inclusion of some sales measures; the earlier treatment of econometric models would support this.

Choosing the test instruments

This brief review has indicated a wide range of techniques that are used in assessing advertising effectiveness. There is no universal test battery that has been found to be *the* way to conduct advertising research – it all depends. The following quotation sets up the problem:

> the *sine qua non* of a pre-testing programme should be awareness of the fact that an effort of judgement is involved in choice of technique and specification of the parameters on which measurements are to be sought. [31]

Important factors that could enter the judgement are the following:

1.   The advertising model thought relevant.

2.   The advertising problem in relation to that model.

3.   The objectives of the campaign.

4.   The significance of the campaign relative to total marketing effort.

5.   The amount of uncertainty perceived by management.

6.   The amount of company experience with the brand in that segment.

7.   The research budget available.

8.   The time available.

9.   Whether research is aimed at assisting creative development, the choice between alternatives or checking post-exposure effectiveness.

Some instruments are widely used, others rarely. Currently, it appears that recall tests and group discussions are dominant. Both relate mainly to cognitive development. Attitude rating is probably the next most widely used among large advertisers, and increasing attention is being given to researching consumer feelings about brands and advertising.

Summary

Various conceptions of the advertising process were reviewed. Several behavioural models were considered, and their limitations discussed, before a brief report on econometric models of advertising effects.

Empirical evidence on advertising goal setting was presented, as were the types of method employed in measuring goal accomplishment. The complex process of establishing realistic advertising objectives was investigated and prescriptions offered.

The possible contribution of research in assisting problem definition, guiding advertising strategy development and assessing its effectiveness was studied prior to a review of some major research techniques.

Questions for review and discussion

1.   If it is possible to have good advertising without specific knowledge of models of the advertising process, then what purpose is served by understanding such models?

2. How might selection of a particular model of advertising as a basis for campaign planning affect the choice of research method used to test its effectiveness?

3. Refer back to the section in Chapter 2 on attitude-to-object and attitude-to-behaviour. Can attitude-to-object theories be fitted into each of the models in the three-order model of advertising?

4. Does the attitude-to-behaviour theory have to be treated as another model of the advertising process? Is it inconsistent with theories of advertising considered in this chapter, or merely tangential to them?

5. Suggest illustrations for each of the 'restrictions' in Figure 16.3 and show how they could affect the development of advertising objectives.

6. The validity of recall tests has been seriously questioned. Why are they still so widely used, and why are they criticised?

7. How might an advertising copywriter benefit from group discussions among potential consumers?

References

1. Haselhurst, L. 1988. 'How Pedigree Petfoods evaluate their advertising spend', *Admap*, June.
2. Colley, R.H. 1961 and 1973. *Defining Advertising Goals for Measured Advertising Results*. New York: Association of National Advertisers.
3. Lavidge, R.T. and Steiner, G.A. 1961. 'A model for predictive measurement of advertising effectiveness', *Journal of Marketing*, October.
4. Palda, K.S. 1966. 'The hypothesis of a hierarchy of effects: a partial evaluation', *Journal of Marketing Research*, vol. 3, no. 1.
5. Ray, M.L. 1973. 'Marketing communication and the hierarchy of effects', in Clarke, P. (ed.), *New Models for Mass Communication Research*. Beverly Hills: Sage. See also Ray, M.L. 1982. *Advertising and Communication Management*. Englewood Cliffs, NJ: Prentice Hall Inc.
6. Krugman, H.E. 1965. 'The impact of television advertising: learning without involvement', *Public Opinion Quarterly*, vol. 28, no. 3.
7. Bird, M. and Ehrenberg, A.S.C. 1966. 'Non-awareness and non-usage', *Journal of Advertising Research*, vol. 6, no. 4.
8. Rothschild, M.L. 1987. *Marketing Communications*. Lexington, Mass.: Heath, p. 74.
9. Aaker, D.A. and Myers, J.G. 1987. *Advertising Management*, 3rd edn. Englewood Cliffs, NJ: Prentice Hall Inc., ch. 10. See also Vaugh, R. 1980. 'How advertising works', *Journal of Advertising Research*, vol. 20, Oct./Nov. Reprinted in Govoni, N., Eng, R. and Galper, M. 1988. *Promotional Management*. Englewood Cliffs, NJ: Prentice Hall Inc.

10. Rossiter, J.R., Percy, L. and Donovan, R.J. 1991. 'A better advertising planning grid', *Journal of Advertising Research*, Oct./Nov., pp. 11–21. See also Rossiter, J.R. and Percy, L. 1987. *Advertising and Promotion Management*. New York: McGraw-Hill, ch. 7.

11. Doyle, P. and Corstjens, M. 1982. 'Budget determination for highly advertised brands', *International Journal of Advertising*, vol. 1, no. 1. See also Broadbent, S. 1989. *The Advertising Budget*. Henley-on-Thames: NTC Publications, p. 198; and Corstjens, M. 1990. *Strategic Advertising*. Oxford: Heinemann, pp. 177–85; and Mercer, A. 1991. *Implementable Marketing Research*. Hemel Hempstead: Prentice Hall International, ch. 2.

12. Broadbent, S. 1983. 'Practical economics and computing at the brand level', *International Journal of Advertising*, vol. 2, no. 1.

13. Elliot, J. 1985. 'Breaking the bran barrier – Kellogg's Bran Flakes', *Admap*, vol. 21, no. 2.

14. Twyman, W.A. 1980. 'Are long-term effects possible or measurable?', in Broadbent, S., *Market Researchers Look at Advertising*. Amsterdam: ESOMAR.

15. Broadbent, S. and Jacobs, B. 1984. *Spending Advertising Money*. London: Business Books, p. 369.

16. Corkindale, D.R. and Kennedy, S.H. 1975. *Measuring the Effect of Advertising*. Farnborough: Saxon House.

17. Majoro, S. 1970. 'Advertising by objectives', *Management Today*, January. Quoted in Corkindale and Kennedy, op. cit.

18. Britt, S.H. 1969. 'Are so-called successful advertising campaigns really successful?', *Journal of Advertising Research*, vol. 9, no. 2.

19. Corkindale and Kennedy, op. cit.

20. Flandin, M., Martin, E. and Simkin, L. 1992. 'Advertising effectiveness research: a survey of agencies, clients and conflicts', *International Journal of Advertising*, vol. 11, pp. 203–14.

21. Leymore, V.L. 1975. *Hidden Myth: Structure and Symbolism in Advertising*. London: Heinemann.

22. Baggaley, J. and Duck, S. 1976. *Dynamics of Television*. Farnborough: Saxon House, pp. 35–42.

23. Hedges, A. 1985. 'Testing to destruction', *Admap*, vol. 21, no. 2. See also Butterfield, L. 1987. 'Creative product development', in Cowley, D. *How to Plan Advertising*. London: Cassell, ch. 6.

24. Ostlund, L.E., Clancy, K.J. and Sapra, R. 1980. 'Inertia in copy research', *Journal of Advertising Research*, vol. 20, February. See also Clark, E. 1989. *The Want Makers*. London: Coronet, ch. 3.

25. Frost, A. (undated). *SCRIBE: A general approach to product and advertising optimisation*. London: Frost International.

26. Leckenby, J.D. and Wedding, N. 1982. *Advertising Management*. Columbus, Ohio: Grid, ch. 11.

27. Cooper, P. (undated). *The New Qualitative Technology and Other Papers*. London: Cooper Research and Marketing.

28. Potter, J. and Lovell, M. 1975. *Assessing the Effectiveness of Advertising*. London: Business Books, pp. 39, 110.

29. Crimp, M. 1985. *The Marketing Research Process*, 2nd edn. Hemel Hempstead: Prentice Hall International, p. 165.

30. Bloom, D., Jay, A. and Twyman, T. 1977. 'The validity of advertising pre-tests', *Journal of Advertising Research*, vol. 17, no. 2.

31. Lovell, M., Johns, S. and Rampley, B. 1972. 'Pre-testing press advertisements', in *Ten Years of Advertising Media Research*. London: Thomson Organisation, p. 183.

Chapter 17

Planning advertising and sales promotion

This chapter considers some additional areas of advertising planning. They all concern the media: audience research, the development of media plans, the allocation of funds to advertising and media scheduling problems. Some major aspects of the planning of sales promotion are also introduced.

There are five main media classes: press, television, outdoor, cinema and radio. Within each class there are specific media vehicles, such as a particular newspaper or television station. A fundamental difficulty is that each class and each vehicle has a different capability to expose an advertiser's message and each class has a different means of making that exposure. Comparisons are complicated, but the rational allocation of the advertising budget necessitates such comparisons. The relative size of audience is a common yardstick for measuring exposure capability, but more subjective evaluations are made about the technical differences in means of exposure. The latter are called media weights and will be dealt with shortly, but to begin with, the first topic is research into media audiences.

Audience research

A first approximation for the size of a newspaper's audience could be its circulation, as shown by the publisher's statement of the number of copies sold. Until the early 1960s that was the principal method of comparison. For many smaller publications, and particularly those in the industrial market, it remains so. A refinement is to obtain independently audited figures from the Audit Bureau of Circulation which can be found in *British Rate and Data*. However, circulation may or may not be a reliable guide to audience size. Some estimate of readership, or numbers viewing or listening, is a better approximation. Before describing well-known regular audience studies it should be borne in mind that readership figures are normally for the publication, not the advertisement. The size, position, creative endeavour and intrinsic interest in the product category are variables that could attract larger or smaller audiences to several advertisements in the same vehicle. Despite that, the total vehicle audience must be the first basis

Table 17.1 *Audience research*

	Press	Television	Radio
Frequency	Twice yearly	Daily	Quarterly
Report format	Hard copy and electronic	Electronic	Hard copy; electronic from bureaux
Sample	37,500 individuals survey	4,435 households panel	14,500 adults survey
Measures	Computer-assisted personal interview – readership in the past year	Meters record live and playback viewing; push-button hand-held set records numbers of individuals viewing	Self-completion diary completed over a week; records listening to any 5 minutes in each quarter hour
Coverage	230 national newspapers and magazines	Terrestrial and satellite stations	National and local; BBC and independent stations
Sponsor*	National Readership Surveys Ltd	BARB*	RAJAR**

* BARB: Broadcasters' Audience Research Board.
**RARJAR: Radio Joint Audience Research.
Source: Publications by the sponsors.

for comparison. Table 17.1 summarises details of some of the main audience research methods in the United Kingdom.

National Readership Survey (NRS)

Readership is some multiple of circulation because most publications have secondary or 'pass-along' readers. The NRS estimates the total readers by a sample survey. Respondents are asked whether they have 'looked at' any copies of the major newspapers and magazines. The reports yield a vast amount of data compared with circulation statements because they contain detailed classifications of types of reader. Generally, circulation statements are confined to numbers of copies sold, but controlled circulation publications are able to give breakdown by job titles or industry types.

The NRS can be used to determine total audiences for the major publications and the profile in age, sex, social class and other demographic terms. The profiles of different publications can be compared to deduce such things as that nearly 90 per cent of *The Times* readers are ABC1 whereas only about 25 per cent of

Daily Mirror readers are such. Regional comparisons are made, and even the number of men reading women's weeklies is estimated. Additionally, the NRS includes data on television viewing, cinema attendances and, periodically, ownership of various consumer durables (all cross-classified by press readership). An extract from the NRS is shown in the appendix to this chapter.

Business Readership Survey (BRS)

The *Financial Times*, *Daily Telegraph*, *Guardian* and *The Times* all have a large number of readers who are business executives, and many advertisers wish to reach such a segment. Detailed readership figures, similar to the NRS, are contained in the annual BRS reports. They cover national newspapers and major business and trade journals. As well as total readership the analyses classify the data by industry type, occupation, salary levels, education, and so on.

For both the NRS and the BRS perhaps the greatest benefit is that they present directly comparable data. The definitions used within each of these studies and the samples consulted are constant – there is also good comparability between the two surveys. This uniformity is absent from ad hoc studies carried out by individual publishers.

Television audience measurement

Unlike the NRS the television audience is measured continuously. This is accomplished through the operation of a panel of households which agrees to have a meter attached to their television. It records automatically whether the set is on or off, whether a live or recorded programme is being viewed and, if live, which station is being watched. Video playback of recorded programmes is added to the live audience number if it takes place within seven days. To determine the number viewing the panel members agree to use a hand-held push button device.

Audience reporting is on a minute-by-minute basis with 3-minute rolling averages. The essential statistic is the TVR – television rating. This is an estimate of the percentage of the audience viewing at any one time. If it is given without further qualification then it refers to the percentage of the total national audience. But frequently it is given as a TVR for a specified subgroup. This might be a 'housewife TVR' which is the proportion of all housewives, or it could be 'adults TVR'. In the weekly reports each commercial is given an estimated TVR and this is divided by the rate card cost to deduce the 'cost-per-thousand' estimated viewers. The periodic audience composition reports give detailed demographic analyses for time slots and for programmes.

Whole campaigns are sometimes evaluated in terms of total or accumulated ratings by summing the rating for each spot. Objectives may be set to achieve a given accumulated TVR, such as 500, and this might take twenty or thirty spots. The television contractor's rate card may also guarantee a TVR for a number of spots, and repeat the commercial until that level is attained.

Exposures, reach and frequency

From the description of the audience research methodology it is apparent that what is being measured is the opportunity to see (o.t.s.) an advertisement. It is implicitly assumed that:

o.t.s. the vehicle = o.t.s. the advertisement = actually seeing the advertisement

For television the weekly schedule makes it a little easier than this because the estimates are for each advertisement. But, for the NRS the data are for the vehicle as a whole. 'Page traffic' studies are sometimes undertaken to determine the average readership for each page within the publication, but these are ad hoc and do not necessarily give the o.t.s. for a particular advertisement. Recall tests attempt to check advertisement o.t.s., but again these are ad hoc and do not usually cover more than one vehicle.

The problem is not as severe when comparisons are being made within one media class. Whatever o.t.s. means, and however it is measured, if definitions and measurements are constant then reasonable comparisons can be made.

A high o.t.s. may be achieved by a large number of people being exposed once or a small number being exposed several times: 50 per cent of a segment being exposed once would give the same total o.t.s. as 10 per cent exposed five times. To specify a campaign goal just on o.t.s. is therefore insufficient, e.g. the accumulated TVRs noted above. The total number of individuals exposed and their frequency of exposure need also to be declared. These notions are set in the concepts of reach (or coverage) and frequency:

- Reach – the number or proportion of an audience group or segment exposed to an advertisement at least once.
- Frequency – the average number of exposures per individual reached.

Table 17.2 gives an application of these ideas to magazine advertising. Five possible schedules are presented to reach a target segment of C1 women. The six magazines are variously combined to give different schedule performances. The total cost of each schedule is between about £45,000 and £50,000, but variations in reach result in a spread of cost-per-thousand from around £18 up to £25. None of the schedules is the best on all criteria, and so the choice amongst them will depend upon the relative importance attached to reach and frequency – bearing in mind the cost-per-thousand. If the advertisement centred on an announcement of some product change, then coverage may be valued more than frequency and schedule 2 chosen. If it was believed that the nature of the advertisement required a minimum number of repetitions (say 3), then the relatively expensive schedule 4 would be chosen. This might be where lengthy body copy was used to explain a complicated product claim.

Table 17.2   *Magazine schedule evaluation*

Target: C1 women	Schedule				
Publication	1	2	3	4	5
Woman's Realm	1	1	1	0	0
Woman	1	2	0	0	0
Woman's Weekly	1	1	0	4	0
Woman's Own	1	0	3	0	2
My Weekly	1	1	0	3	4
People's Friend	1	1	0	3	4
Total insertions	6	6	4	10	10
Reach	50.0	50.6	44.6	37.1	45.8
Frequency	2.1	2.0	2.2	3.4	2.7
Total cost (£000s)	48.2	47.6	50.1	48.4	45.8
Cost-per-thousand (£)	18.8	18.3	21.9	25.4	19.5

Source: Based on tables in S. Broadbent and B. Jacobs, *Spending Advertising Money*, 4th edn. London: Business Books, 1984.

A similar approach can be taken to television schedule analysis. In this case the various schedules could be for different times of the day, or weekday against weekend. An additional consideration might be introduced related to 'impact'. It might be felt that to command attention the advertisement must have an average exposure of at least a given level. A common yardstick is 'four-plus', which is the proportion with an average frequency of at least four times.

Response functions

Theoretically, it is possible to optimise reach and frequency, as the graphs in Figure 17.1 demonstrate. Economists will be well used to the methodology used in this approach to optimising reach and frequency. Figure 17.1(a) shows that media costs rise with reach and that these will vary with frequency level. Figure 17.1(b) shows how awareness changes with reach. The assumption here is that awareness is the objective and so the aim is to find that reach (and later frequency) where increments to awareness equate increments to media cost. Thus in Figure 17.1(c) R_1 is the optimum reach for $F = 5$ since until then extra awareness is gained with less than proportional marginal cost. Similarly, reach above R_1 increases awareness but only at high marginal cost. To find the theoretical optimum for frequency the exercise is repeated for all other feasible frequency levels and the one with the greatest distance between the awareness and cost curves would be the best.

The great unknown in this sequence is the awareness reach relationship; it is another kind of response function. Broadbent [1] recommends six possible ways of learning something of the nature of this function.

1. Coupon return analysis – in some controlled circumstances.
2. Single interviews – it *may* be possible to make deductions from post-exposure surveys, seeking to relate individual awareness or recall to frequency of exposure.

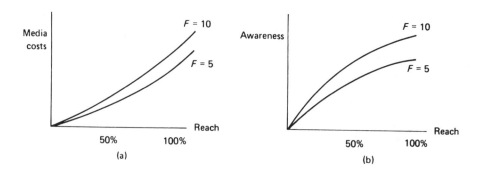

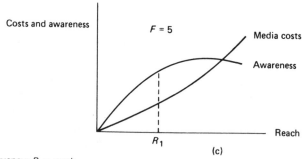

F = frequency; R = reach

Source: P. Kotler, *Marketing Decision Making*, New York: Holt, Rinehart & Winston, 1971, p. 452.

Figure 17.1   *Optimal reach and frequency. (a) Media costs varying with reach and two frequency levels. (b) Brand awareness varying with reach and frequency levels. (c) Optimum reach for frequency of 5*

3.   Before-and-after interviews – Broadbent quotes a Swedish study of the Esso Tiger campaign where a linear response function was found. Those heavily exposed increased their visits to Esso stations.

4.   Experiments – of these Broadbent says, 'Normal experimentation is . . . not an ideal method for measuring response . . . [but] used with care, the results of experiments are valuable.'

5.   Observation – e.g. in direct response advertising.

6.   Study of individual behaviour – the build-up of comprehensive media and product data for individuals.

Studies of response functions in advertising are potentially confusing because of the great difficulties in defining both the dependent and the independent variables. In the theoretical example above awareness was taken as the critical dependent variable to be related to the independent variable of reach. And even then awareness was itself a surrogate for sales. Quite other specifications have been employed. Reach may be interpreted as 'impressions', which would be an estimate of the number seeing an advertisement rather than just having the opportunity to see. The dependent variable could be related to a specific campaign objective, such as improved user evaluations of a product attribute. In reviewing this area Broadbent and Jacobs [2] comment:

> The difficulties in using response functions are dismaying . . . But the reasons for using a model at all still apply. In particular, the response function may be treated simply as a working tool. That is, no actual relationship between impressions and response is assumed – the response function is just part of the method of schedule analysis or construction which is expected to lead to better schedules. The criterion here for 'better' is not sought in the function itself but in inspection of the schedules resulting from the system.

They also point out that 'over the range in which the function is usually thought to lie, very different media decisions are unlikely', and that qualitative factors will be critical, especially when constructing schedules employing more than one media class.

Multi-media schedules

Evaluations within a media class could proceed as outlined. Evaluations across media classes require more judgements. On the face of it, similar terms are being used, and so it might be felt that straightforward comparisons can be made. This is not so. In the magazine example the basis was for a full page in each publication. What would be comparable to that in the case of television? A 30-second commercial? A 60-second commercial? No convincing case can be made for any particular comparability. Therefore the decision between media classes relies on a range of other judgements. These include what the competition is doing, the segment coverage, the creative suitability, the total cost and budget available and the past experience with various media.

Audience duplication

Only in special circumstances will the target segment match the audience profile for a particular vehicle. Maximum segment coverage often requires the use of several vehicles, and perhaps two or more media classes. However, audiences for these are unlikely to be discrete: there will be overlap. The degree of this overlap is a variable that needs to be estimated, otherwise calculations of total reach will be artificially inflated. Thus in bringing in vehicles to a schedule it is not sufficient to discriminate between total and segment readership: the net unduplicated segment readership should also be estimated. The cost-per-thousand of such readers rises progressively as more vehicles are brought in, because each additional vehicle will probably display increasing duplication with the vehicles already in the schedule. This problem may be so severe that it becomes necessary to consider using vehicles that have only a small proportion of their total audience in the desired segment, but which have mass audiences in total. Thus television could be employed in a segmented strategy even though only a small proportion of viewers are in the segment – it may have a lower cost than the total for twenty magazines' net unduplicated audiences.

These analyses can be complex and several researchers have developed models incorporating unduplicated reach [3]. A prerequisite is some estimate of the amount of duplication. Both the NRS and the BRS contain duplication tables so that, for example, the number of *Sunday Times* readers who also read the *Sun* is given, and that for every possible combination of the 100+ publications surveyed. The BRS does the same. The real problem of data inadequacy is in studies across several media classes. The number of viewers to a particular television slot who also read a particular magazine is not reliably available. Generalisations are often made. These may analyse the duplication between a publication and 'heavy' or 'light' ITV viewers, which takes it part of the way.

Media weights

Media planners have focused most attention on estimating reach and frequency, but they do appreciate that such quantities do not encompass all of the factors that need enter a scheduling decision. There are four other elements classified by Gensch [4] as being influential in media selection. The generic term for these considerations is 'media weights'.

Target population weights

Target population weights recognise that a publication's audience will contain members of differing worth to the advertiser. Thus ABC1 housewives with two children may be given a weight of 1.0 and those with more or fewer children weighted below 1.0. In another case, men aged 18 to 25 may be highly weighted and other age groups much less so. The assignment of these weights is subjective because nobody is likely to offer proof that a woman with (say) above-average education is only worth 65 per cent of a woman of average education.

More specific target population weights may be applied if something was known about the product usage by audience members of the various media. There are several approaches to this problem. Product U&A (usage and attitudes) surveys may have indicated the media habits of heavy and light product users. Alternatively, media surveys may indicate product usage by media vehicle. Integrated product/media surveys – such as TGI – are usually held to offer the best prospect in this area. A media vehicle's audience could be divided into heavy users, light users and non-users of the product. Depending on the campaign objectives these would be differentially weighted. Assuming the goal were to stimulate light users into greater product usage then they might be weighted 1.0 and the others 0.5 or 0.2, or simply 0.0. The arbitrary nature of these weights is clear, and changes to them can alter significantly the media schedule decision. This arbitrariness worries media planners, but is seen by media owners as a platform on which their sales representatives can build a case for the inclusion of their particular vehicle.

Media vehicle appropriateness weights

It has long been assumed that the vehicle affects the message; that the same advertisement in separate vehicles could have a differential impact. It is often thought that Sunday newspapers are 'relaxed', dailies 'urgent' and local press 'chatty'. It is also reasonable to assume that a food advertisement would be perceived differently if run on a television station showing a documentary on poverty in the Third World and one carrying a 'soap opera'. Traditionally, such considerations have entered media planning in an unspecified manner, but the advent of computer-based models has required that they be specified and quantified.

This analysis refers to source effects: media class source effects and vehicle source effects. Just as it is possible to consider source effects when the advertiser is the source, it is also possible to investigate the effects that the media and vehicle may have. The potential for a media class source effect is illustrated in Table 17.3. Nolan derives four consequences from these media class comparisons:

Table 17.3 *Press and television advertising: the different processes of influence*

Television					Press
More involuntary attention	Sound	←	Stimulus feasibility	→	Lengthy exposition	More voluntary attention
		←				
More unconscious effects	The medium	←	Control of perception	→	The reader	More conscious effects
	Less reliable	←	Attitudes to media	→	More reliable	
More gradual effects	Not decision-oriented	←	Circumstances of exposure	→	Decision-oriented	More discrete effects

Source: J. Nolan, 'Combined media campaigns', in *Ten Years of Advertising Media Research*. London: Thomson Organisation. 1972.

1. Television commercials are better able to command attention.

2. Press advertisements are better able to arouse personal involvement.

3. Press advertisements tend to exert a more conscious influence.

4. Television commercials have gradual effects; press advertisements are 'all-or-nothing'.

With respect to vehicle source effect Aaker and Myers [5] conclude that three factors are significant: expertise, prestige and mood created. A magazine related to a special interest may have developed a reputation for being authoritative in connection with that interest. Advertisements in such a magazine may gain by association. Similarly, prestige may be important; some publications are far more prestigious than others. An advertiser wishing to build a prestigious image might find the 'editorial environment' in a quality magazine more consonant than that in cheap magazines. With regard to mood creation, the notion is that the vehicle may induce a distinctive mood among its audience and that mood may affect the reception of the advertisement. The mood created is probably not simply a function of the vehicle. Time and place of exposure may be more important. People may select media to support a desired mood, e.g. many women read magazines in bed. The effect of the interaction between vehicle and circumstances of exposure could be the association of a vehicle with a specific mood. Studies of how people use media and the nature of the gratifications they derive are therefore relevant in establishing this association.

Attempts have been made to explore the relationship between these factors and alternative copy approaches. Aaker and Brown [6] experimented with two kinds of copy, which they termed 'image' and 'reason-why', and questioned a sample of women to determine which magazines could be considered prestigious and which expert in respect of cooking, foods and kitchenware. Four test magazines were chosen, two from each category. Folders were made up with the cover pages of these magazines and several advertisements included with a test specimen. Various measures were taken of the expected price, quality and reliability of the brands being investigated. It was found that image advertisements did best in prestigious magazines and reason-why advertisements in expert magazines. Experiments may therefore help to quantify vehicle source effects.

Advertising exposure weights

Advertising exposure weights try to establish the difference between vehicle o.t.s. and advertisement o.t.s. They concern the conditional probability of individuals being exposed to advertisements given that they are exposed to the vehicle. Reading frequency and page traffic studies of a publication may be relevant here. It may be known that the readership for a magazine is one million in a target segment, but that does not mean that all those will read any single issue. The NRS includes reading frequency tables, e.g. for a daily newspaper six times per week.

The overall readership figure can then be reduced to probable issue readership. Page traffic refers to numbers of total readers who read each page – only half may read, say, page 21. Assuming that it was found that issue readership is 80 per cent of total readership and only a half of those are likely to read a specified page, the advertisement o.t.s. can therefore be at most 40 per cent of total readership. Broadbent and Segnit give an indication of the impact of these problems on an actual schedule (Table 17.4). Without media weights the schedule in the table is estimated to have a reach of 90 per cent and a frequency of about 12. With the adjusted o.t.s. reach falls only slightly, but frequency is halved. In the first case nearly a half of these publications' audiences were thought to have an o.t.s. of above 10. The adjustment takes this down to 14 per cent. It is clear that the introduction of this type of media weight has considerably revised the assessment of potential campaign effects.

Some market research agencies and some media owners attempt regular monitoring of advertising exposure. The longest running is American Starch 'reading and noting' studies. These are to be distinguished from recall studies in that the interviewer asks the respondent to go through the current issue of a publication 'in the way they first saw it' and to point out editorial and advertising items they remember having seen. In some media owner studies it is 'seen with interest'. In the industrial market such research can be conducted by post because the journals have addresses for subscribers or for 'registered readers', i.e. controlled circulation. With long runs these studies develop analyses by product groups and show averages for 'run of book' or 'facing matter' (the first of these means anywhere in the bulk of the advertising pages and the second means facing an editorial item). They also show averages for the cover pages and for right-hand or left-hand pages. Of course, the usefulness of all this is a function of the research methodology. If recall studies are controversial, then these 'recognition' studies are generally even more so.

Table 17.4 *Weighting a schedule to obtain vehicle o.t.s.*

Publication	Insertions	Media weight	Publication	Insertions	Media weight
Woman's Weekly	7	55	*Radio Times*	6	38
Woman's Own	6	48	*Woman and Home*	2	59
Woman	6	52	*Family Circle*	2	61
Woman's Realm	6	52	*Good Housekeeping*	2	65
TV Times	6	53	*Reader's Digest*	2	32
TV World	6	45	*Housewife*	1	57

	0	1–10	11–20	Over 20	Average frequency
O.t.s. insertions without media weight	10%	44%	33%	14%	12.4
O.t.s. adjusted for page traffic with media weight	16%	70%	13%	1%	6.3

Source: S. Broadbent and S. Segnit, 'Beyond cost-per-thousand – an examination of media weights', in *Ten Years of Advertising Media Research*. London: Thomson Organisation, 1972.

Advertising perception weights

Advertising perception weights attempt to bridge the gap between o.t.s for the advertisement and the perception of the advertisement. Page size, colour, quality of reproduction and interest in the product field are thought to be important variables. Recall tests have been used to discern something of their impact. These may lead media planners to apply generalised rules of thumb. For example, a half page is worth 60 per cent (or 40 per cent) of a full page; similarly a 15-second television spot compared with a 30-second spot. Four-colour may attract a 50 per cent greater weight than black and white, and high quality reproduction may be thought 20 per cent better than average reproduction. Obviously it is preferable if such generalisations are based on some research evidence.

Determining the advertising budget

Marginal analysis

Marginal analysis for budget determination has considerable theoretical appeal. But if the objective function is sales, then the tortuous link that may exist between advertising and sales need hardly be reiterated. Regression analysis on historical data may uncover just how tortuous, or direct, that link may be. If a reasonable correlation did exist, the regression line might be used for budgeting. However, much of the discussion in this and previous chapters disputes the universality of a high advertising/sales correlation, i.e. variances in sales may be only very partially explained by changes in advertising volume. For this reason, the typical approaches to the budget decision are usually far more pragmatic [7].

Percentage of sales

This method is widely used. It applies some fixed ratio of advertising to some forecast sales level. Sometimes it is used on a pence-per-pack basis. Here the forecast sales volume is determined and some more or less arbitrary figure for advertising per pack applied. It is a simple approach, and that is probably its only virtue. Accountants may like it because the advertising budget is seen to be affordable, and if it is not, then it can be adjusted before the decision is taken. The difficulty is that the magic ratio may become encrusted in the firm's behaviour. Blind acceptance of a given figure, which may have been established a long time ago, is not the hallmark of dynamic management.

Competitive parity

Another common guide is to fix the budget to match or exceed the budgets of competitors. The rationale is that the brand must be seen to be competing. A

Table 17.5 *Market share and advertising share*

Brand ranking in its market	Market share %	Advertising share %
No. 1	30	35
No. 2	17	21
No. 3	11	13
Average for 75 leading brands	19	23

Source: Nielsen Researcher, 1983 no. 2.

Nielsen study of 75 leading brands demonstrated the importance of considering share of total advertising as well as market share. Table 17.5 shows that brands which were ranked first, second or third in their markets had advertising shares which were higher than their market shares.

Adams [8], Peckham [9] and Broadbent [10] have used advertising share and market share in MAP (marketing advertising patterns) analyses. Investigations into the relationship between these can be useful and an example is shown in Figure 17.2.

The horizontal axis in the diagram is the difference between advertising share this year and market share last year. Where advertising share (*AS*) this year is greater than market share (*MS*) last year then this indicates a proportionately heavy advertising budget (assuming the total market is not in decline). If *AS* this year were 20 per cent and *MS* last year were 15 per cent, and if the 5 per cent difference were associated with an increase in *MS* this year, then the brand is responding to the heavy *AS*. This would apply to all observations in the top right quadrant of the diagram, and the steeper the curve the stronger the response. Observations in the bottom right quadrant would indicate a poor response and lead to the supposition that the volume of advertising may be past saturation level. Observations in the top left quadrant would arouse some curiosity, because

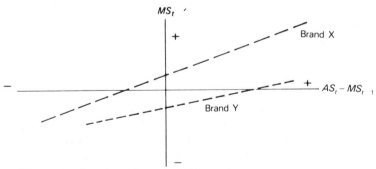

MS_t = market share change from year $t-1$ to year t
AS_t = advertising share in year t
MS_{t-1} = market share in year $t-1$

Figure 17.2 *MAP analysis*

a declining *AS* is associated with an increasing *MS*. This might be rationalised as being a reflection of a qualitative difference in the advertising's creative content, or evidence that something other than advertising was much more important – such as price or product quality. Observations in the bottom left would support the idea that this brand was responsive to changes in *AS*.

Historical data for brands can be plotted against these two axes and regression lines fitted. Reasonable fits with simple linear regression have been found in practice – but if a very dispersed distribution was found, that in itself would be interesting. In the case of brand X in Figure 17.2 the position and slope of the curve indicate *MS* responding to higher *AS*.

To use this analysis for budget determination two things are needed: an estimate of total industry advertising next year and a target market share for next year. The change in *MS* next year from *MS* this year will imply the difference between *AS* next year and *MS* this year. That is, the *MS* change would be entered on the diagram and the implied difference between *AS* next year and *MS* this year deduced. That would give the target *AS* next year, and for this to be translated into the actual budget the total advertising spend for all competitors would have to be estimated. This estimation may be informed by analysis or market intelligence. Analysis might be time-series statistical analysis; intelligence would use various trade and agency sources.

Using competitive parity as the basis for the advertising budget is not without problems. In some heavily advertised markets it can lead to escalation quite unconnected to sales response, and all major competitors exceed a spending level that any other method would advocate. This could be a deliberate policy to establish entry barriers.

What can be afforded

With this approach advertising is treated as essentially passive: it can do nothing dynamically to affect the company's position. Profit forecasts are made, and only at that point is it determined that a given sum is allowed as the advertising appropriation. For small firms this may be sensible, in so far as large advertising costs will not be incurred to send it bankrupt. Larger companies often see advertising in a more positive light. They believe the volume of advertising may materially change their position.

Advertising by objectives

The essence of this approach is the prior statement of the precise, quantified advertising goals. This is followed by estimates of what is felt is needed to achieve those aims, and then the costs associated with these are calculated. Goals may be set regionally and the total budget built up from regional costs.

Given a set of communication tasks, the problem is to estimate the costs that need to be incurred for their achievement. Of the numerous possible tasks, suppose some specified increase in awareness was featured in the goals of a campaign. When discussing optimal reach and frequency it was concluded earlier that the central difficulty was in estimating the response function. That is equally relevant here. The research procedures advocated in that earlier section may yield some insight into how much reach and frequency would be required to obtain a desired awareness level. In the absence of such knowledge a judgement would have to be made. Once the necessary reach and frequency had been determined, the media costs required to give those levels of exposure would be estimated. These costs would indicate the size of the advertising budget.

Budget by experiment

Whatever research is carried out to estimate the advertising exposures required to obtain a communication goal, there is inevitably an area of subjectivity. A scientific approach would advocate: if in doubt, do an experiment. Aaker and Myers [11] quote three such experiments carried out in the United States:

1. *Teflon.* Four cities received 10 minutes of commercials per week, five cities 5 minutes per week, and four cities no commercials. Sales in '10-minute cities' were 30 per cent above the others.

2. *Missouri Valley Petroleum.* Four groups of cities were tested for three years. The group with twice the advertising of the control group registered sales increases for each year of 17, 23 and 36 per cent. Those with three times the advertising spending registered increases of 16, 11 and 16 per cent.

3. *Budweiser beer.* This involved a two-year experiment with samples from 200 geographical areas. The conclusion was that the company was spending too much on advertising. A vice-president of the advertising agency involved said, 'To return to our stylized [S-shaped] response curve, we might say that spending for Budweiser advertising was too far up the curve and that we could slide back some.'

But Corkindale and Kennedy [12] warn that such experiments in the United Kingdom often have disappointing outcomes. They emphasise the need for sound experimental discipline if the results are to be meaningful. Given this discipline, Dhalla [13] argues that tests to determine media weight (here meaning volume of advertising) are feasible.

Timing patterns

There are numerous possible alternative time patterns that may be adopted in scheduling a campaign. Kotler [14] has presented twelve broad types of time pattern and these are shown in Figure 17.3. AGB, the research firm, has commented on these patterns [15]. It suggests that concentrated patterns are used in situations such as new brand launches to swamp competitive advertising during the launch

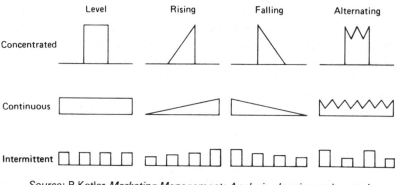

Source: P. Kotler, *Marketing Management: Analysis planning and control*,
6th edn, Englewood Cliffs, NJ: Prentice Hall, Inc., 1968, p. 636.

Figure 17.3   *Advertising timing patterns*

period and to 'force' distribution and sampling. Part-work publications (issued in instalments) fit this pattern, as do products with marked seasonal demand.

Continuous advertising can be very expensive. Brand leaders with considerable appropriations and in product categories with high advertising/sales ratios may choose this pattern. Some slight seasonality may cause rising or falling patterns, although AGB feels that heavy continuous advertising often takes an alternating pattern in order to achieve the following:

1.   Exploit seasonal cost efficiency variations (television rate card prices vary through the year).
2.   Support other promotional activity.
3.   Exploit 'gaps' in competitive activity.

Intermittent bursts are widely used, mainly because continuous advertising is too expensive – particularly on television. A 30-second spot each day will give 15 minutes of airtime each month, or less than 1 per cent of the total time allowed for commercials. That rate of advertising nationally would soon reach a cost of many millions of pounds, and yet it represents a minute amount of all television advertising. Thus many advertisers plan bursts to achieve more concentrated impact periodically.

Advertising agencies

Most advertisements are created in agencies, and most advertising space and time is bought by them. But an interesting development in recent years has been the growing attention given to all aspects of advertising planning within the client companies. Traditionally, many relied on their agencies for wide-ranging marketing advice, apart from creating and placing the advertisements. Many large advertisers now have their own advertising departments which undertake extensive research – market, advertising and media – or have brand managers with advertising responsibility. This has led a few to experiment with specialised media broking services and limited service creative agencies in place of full service agencies. A problem is the nature of agency remuneration. They work on a 10 or 15 per cent commission (depending on the media), which they are paid by the media owner. Some large advertisers feel that with, say, a £1 million account they do not receive £100,000 to £150,000 worth of services, particularly if they employ their own specialists. Agencies, on the other hand, are careful not to offer too many free additional services. The negotiations for special fees for extra agency services is therefore a contentious issue for large advertisers. Forty per cent of agency income now comes from fees rather than commission.

With well-publicised movements in accounts between advertising agencies, there has been an assumption that there is almost continual turnover. Michell [16] found that in the period 1975–80, about half of all accounts switched agencies, but that larger accounts were much less likely to do so. Fast-moving consumer goods accounts were more loyal, and larger agencies maintained accounts longer.

Sales promotion

Sales promotion covers a variety of techniques employed for a variety of purposes. Something of this variety is indicated in Table 17.6, which distinguishes between promotions aimed at the consumer and those aimed at the trade. The wide range of techniques available means that this is a very flexible set of tools. No accurate figures are available on the total spending on sales promotion, but it is often thought to be at least as much as the total spending on advertising, which is about £8 billion p.a.

Consumer promotions often have short-term objectives such as boosting sales in a short time-period. This could be to counteract rival activity nationally, in particular regions or at particular times. Special price offers are common means for achieving this. In new product launches promotions would be aimed at inducing distributors to stock the product and at inducing consumers to try it. Special price offers, coupons or free samples are used for this purpose.

Another aim could be to encourage heavier usage in segments already using the product. Multi-packs might be employed, such as 'buy three get one free', or some type of customer loyalty scheme might be devised. In services this could be the dry cleaner offering three items to be cleaned for the price of two. It could be a 'club' for frequent users of a hotel or airline, or a form of stamp or coupon to be collected which might give some privileges. One further goal may be an attempt to 'cross-sell' by introducing users of one product to other products in the company's range by physically banding packs together. An example is a

Table 17.6 *Sales promotion techniques*

Consumer Promotions	
Multi-packs:	Several units of the product sold together at a reduced price.
Banded packs:	Two related products banded together and sold at a reduced price.
Give-aways:	Free gifts, related or unrelated to the product, which may or may not require proof of some level of product purchase.
Self-liquidators:	Offers of merchandise, related or unrelated to the product, priced to cover the cost of the promotion.
Contests:	Competitions.
Reduced price:	Initiated by the manufacturer, the retailer, or by both.
Coupons:	Money-off offers distributed in-pack, on-pack, in-store, door-to-door and in advertisements.
Free samples:	Distributed in-store, door-to-door, at events and exhibitions.
Direct mail:	Brochures and announcements which may also include coupons or samples.
Exhibitions:	Ranging from those organised by an individual firm to participation in an international exhibition.

Trade Promotions	
Price discounts:	For volume or as inducements for special activities, such as introducing a new product.
Contests:	Competitions for the trade customer or its employees.
Gifts:	
Credit/invoicing:	Extended credit and delayed invoicing.
Special allowances:	For advertising, in-store displays, test marketing or introducing new products.
Direct mail:	Brochures and announcements.
Exhibitions:	For the trade, and inducements for trade participation in consumer exhibitions.
Training and advisory services:	Technical and sales.
Equipment and materials:	Providing free, or low-cost, equipment and materials useful in promoting to end-user.

setting lotion banded to a hair shampoo. An equivalent in services would be the fast food restaurant offering three or four products together at a reduced price.

Sales promotion can have informational as well as persuasive intent. Brochures and other promotional literature can contain a great deal more information than advertisements. They can be distributed in a reasonably controlled way door-to-door, by direct mail and can be available in distribution outlets. Exhibitions may be able to give even more information and may include product trials. They can be local, national or international. Companies can participate in exhibitions arranged by others or they might organise their own at a fixed location, such as the LEGO theme park near Windsor, or they might arrange a 'roadshow'. In industrial markets catalogues and technical literature are important sources of information for buyers. Distribution of these may be by the salesforce or by direct mail, and in some markets, such as in the building industry, specialist agencies may offer a collection, binding and distribution service for these catalogues. In the future the development of dedicated television channels, terrestrial or satellite, may come to have a role in the provision of this kind of promotional activity.

Trade promotions can have specific short-term sales objectives, but can in addition include activities which are part of longer-run goals. These might be to maintain a strong presence in distribution channels by tying dealers in with the provision of extra training or advisory services, or by supplying them with equipment and materials which may be used for promotional purposes. There might also be attempts to develop the quality of those channels. For example, contests could be arranged for the best product demonstrations or for the best after-sales care by a distributor. For some fast-moving consumer goods, companies' trade promotion spending has come to be dominated by special allowances to retailers, which are given as quantity discounts, 'facing' allowances for particular shelf-space and 'market development' allowances for local advertising.

Organisations are not free to design any form of promotion they have a mind to. Promotions must be legal, comply with codes of practice and be within government and EU competition policy. An example of a promotion which was deemed to transgress competition policy was that operated by British Coal. They had a 'Loyalty Rebate Scheme' under which coal merchants received a rebate of £1.50 per tonne if they did not deal in coal originating outside the European Coal and Steel Community. In 1991 the Office of Fair Trading found this to be an anti-competitive practice.

It is common for sales promotions to be planned in short bursts over the year as a component of the overall promotion mix. Decisions on the timing of these bursts would consider the full plan for all brands in the portfolio, and the need for the integration of sales promotion plans with advertising and salesforce plans. This would necessitate the detailed charting of the full promotion mix for all brands on a monthly basis. Promotions are planned in bursts partly because of the expense of continuous promotional spending. A succession of activities is planned in order to maintain interest and in an attempt to keep a freshness and a vitality in the marketing effort. And this is not just for consumers and the trade; it is also for the product management team and the salesforce.

Measuring the effectiveness of sales promotion can be as difficult as measuring the effectiveness of advertising. There are the same problem areas which include:

* Multiple cause–effect relationships.
* Time-lags between the promotion and its impact.
* The adequacy of the goals established for the promotion.
* The research techniques available.

But because some promotions have definite and short-term goals, the measures of effect may be easier. Coupon redemption rates can be calculated, and they may vary from 1 per cent for coupons in newspapers, 5 per cent or so for door-to-door distribution, to 10 per cent or more for coupons in or on the package [17]. The numbers participating in a self-liquidating offer, writing in for free gifts or those taking part in competitions can also be readily identified. Sales measures are generally thought more appropriate for gauging the effects of sales promotion than those of advertising. No manager would ignore sales figures when evaluating a reduced price offer, and in many markets electronic scanning at the point of sale means that such data are quickly available. In cases where direct mail is the principal marketing activity of the organisation, the evaluation is much more straightforward, with few of the complications referred to above.

Much sales promotion is tactical, short-term and a response to competitors' activities. As such it might prove beneficial over short promotional periods in resisting rivals, but its injudicious use could be damaging in the long run. Aaker warns [18]:

> Unlike brand-building activities, most sales promotions are easily copied. In fact, competitors must retaliate or suffer unacceptable losses. When a promotion/price-cutting cycle begins it is most difficult to stop because both the customer and the trade become used to it and begin planning their purchases around the promotional cycle. The inevitable result is a great increase in the role of price. There is pressure to reduce the quality, features, and services offered. At the extreme, the product class starts to resemble a commodity, since brand associations have less importance.

Large-scale national promotions require careful co-ordination. Many organisations could be involved, including several sales promotion agencies, list suppliers, mailing houses and suppliers of materials. There have been notorious mistakes, such as Hoover's 'free flight' fiasco and many less publicised errors. Promotions therefore have the potential to damage the organisation as much as they can assist.

Some organisations are reappraising the relative roles of sales promotion and advertising. Much publicity accompanied the move by Heinz to drop product-specific advertising and to develop its direct marketing activities on a large scale. A reason put forward for this switch is the ever-increasing share of grocery sales taken by own labels, now with a third of the market. Retailer brands have become strong, credible brands in their own right. Heinz believe the way to counter this retailer power is through targeted, direct promotional campaigns offering purchase incentives and a loyalty scheme, backed by an annual spend of perhaps £12 million on corporate advertising. Building direct relationships with customers may also allow the development of fuller market information as another way of competing with the retailers who have unique access to market trends from their EPoS systems.

Similar motives stimulated Nestlé to use its Buitoni brand of pasta as an experiment in direct marketing in the United Kingdom [19]. Its 200,000 name database is being increased by magazine and television advertising inviting people to ask for a free recipe booklet. Those interested can join the Casa Buitoni Club which the company says is one way of developing the feel of a one-to-one relationship with its customers.

Database marketing

The application of relational databases in marketing allows the accumulation of vast amounts of customer information and its utilisation in individual communications, by direct mail, telephone or by the salesforce. Fletcher says that the aim is not just to sell, but to build up a long-term relationship with existing and potential customers:

> This means that a company must know its customers, not just in general segmentation or customer profile terms, but in a much more detailed way by individual customer. Each record on the customer database will contain not only name and address of existing and potential customers, but also information on customer needs and characteristics, past purchases and past communications (and the individual's response, if any). [20]

Sources of information for the database include sales, enquiries, coupon responses, salesforce reports and bought-in lists. Car manufacturers make use of sales information and also invite buyers to complete questionnaires which include questions on their frequency of purchase, other cars owned by the household, usage and sometimes lifestyle. Some car firms then mail their own magazines and further questionnaires on topics such as customers' evaluations of the effectiveness of their distributors.

Database marketing at Thomas Cook

Thomas Cook has a 2 million name database. Originally the data were structured for accounting purposes – identifying who owed money, but not what products they had bought – and much of the information, since it was captured at the point of sale by hand, did not include important details like which branch had made the sale. Now the database is used to cross-sell products and to capture information on customers' future travel plans. And so if a customer from the ski programme says he will not travel again until August and then to Italy, the mail programme sends the information two months beforehand. Another related development has been the introduction of telephone booking.

As the Group Database Marketing Manager says, 'We are creating a dialogue programme with our customers. Not with the whole database at present – we are taking a couple of areas of the country and carrying out a full customer care programme to test how often they want to be mailed, when the best time is to mail, what they want to hear about.'

Source: Extracts from, 'Cooking with data', *Direct Response*, October 1990 p. 46.

Software developments now enable more sophisticated analysis, planning and implementation of marketing activities. Six broad categories of marketing software can be identified [21]:

1. Market analysis software – that has analytical functions and can import internal data and market research.

2. Campaign management software – for planning and evaluating promotion campaigns.

3. Direct mailing software – including 'cleaning' and de-duplicating names and monitoring responses to direct mailings.

4. Telemarketing software – tracking systems to guide and to record the results of telephone calls.

5. Account and salesforce management software – gives account status and history, including previous order volumes and values; records the results of each communication episode including sales orders and enquiries.

6. Customer service software – some similarities to telemarketing software; may be employed by organisations with many repeat customers, and these are often trade customers.

Banking with technology

Since 1989 Firstdirect has been offering a banking service over the telephone 24 hours a day, every day of the year. Research showed that customers wanted that kind of availability and that they also wanted service from another person and not from a machine. Firstdirect's customers therefore telephone to talk to a banking representative who can deal with simple enquiries or arrange personal loans and mortgages. Sophisticated computerised systems allow screens of customer banking history to be accessed immediately by the representative, allowing them to deal promptly with queries. Customer information is pulled down to the marketing database for analysis and this information can then be used in promotional campaigns. The company's Commercial Director illustrates this by saying

> From this we make predictions. For example, we would predict that a 30-year-old family man with a mortgage might make his next major purchase a new car, so we will target car loan information to customers in that category.

The marketing database automatically manages in-bound calls and out-going company marketing activities, prompting staff to send out information packs, to make follow-up calls and chase letters. Firstdirect has a third of a million accounts and is growing rapidly.

Source: Extract from J. Howells, 'The direct approach', Software Solutions Supplement, *Marketing Week*, 25 June 1993, pp. 27–8.

Summary

Some of the major audience research methods were described at the beginning of this chapter. This led to a discussion of reach and frequency as important notions in media planning, and to the problems in utilising these. The complications caused by audience duplication were then met and the need for estimates of net unduplicated reach determined. But quantitative analyses such as these are insufficient bases for media decisions. Media weights are applied to assess what are essentially qualitative elements in media planning.

Several methods of setting the advertising budget were reviewed, and the more analytical procedures commended. A second level of allocation problem in advertising planning, concerning timing patterns, was given some attention.

Sales promotion techniques were reviewed, as were issues in the planning of sales promotion activities.

Questions for review and discussion

1. What are the advantages of readership data over circulation data?

2. What are the following: BARB, NRS, BRS, o.t.s., TVR, reach, frequency, duplication, media weights?

3. Considering Figure 17.1:
    (a) Explain why media costs increase with reach and are at different levels for different frequencies (what data would be required?).
    (b) Would it ever be possible to obtain even broad impressions of the awareness/reach relationship?
    (c) Why is R_1 the optimum reach for a frequency of 5?

4. Distinguish between media class source effect and vehicle source effect. Outline research procedures that might gauge something of these effects.

5. Assume that you have been given a MAP analysis of advertising and market shares as justifications for a marked increase in advertising appropriation. What questions would you ask before accepting the validity of the case?

6. Find examples for each of the twelve timing patterns shown in Figure 17.3.

7. In what kinds of advertising problem would you stress reach more than frequency? When would frequency be more important, and what is the connection with: (a) positioning strategy, (b) the view taken about how advertising works, and (c) ideas thought relevant to consumer concept formation?

References

1. Broadbent, S. 1975. *Spending Advertising Money*, 3rd edn. London: Business Books, pp. 293–8.

2. Broadbent, S. and Jacobs, B. 1984. *Spending Advertising Money*, 4th edn. London: Business Books, p. 386.

3. Agostini, J.M. 1961. 'How to estimate unduplicated audiences', *Journal of Advertising Research*, vol. 1, March.
Claycamp, H.J. and McClelland, C.W. 1968. 'Estimating reach and frequency and the magic of *K*', *Journal of Advertising Research*, vol. 8, June. A valuable review of the literature can be found in Corkindale, D.R. and Kennedy, S.H. 1975. *Measuring the Effect of Advertising*. Farnborough: Saxon House, ch. 7.

4. Gensch, D.H. 1970. 'Media factors: a review article', *Journal of Marketing Research*, vol. 7, no. 2.

5. Aaker, D.A. and Myers, J.G. 1987. *Advertising Management*, 3rd edn. Englewood Cliffs, NJ: Prentice Hall Inc., pp. 474–80.

6. Aaker, D.A. and Brown, P.K. 1972. 'Evaluating vehicle source effects', *Journal of Advertising Research*, vol. 12, August.

7. For a review of sales and non-sales measures of advertising effects and approaches to determining budgets in industrial markets, see Lilien, G.L., Silk, A.J. and Choffray, J.M. 1976. 'Industrial advertising and budgeting practices', *Journal of Marketing*, vol. 40, no. 1.

8. Adams, J.R. 1973. 'A new look at the determination of advertising expenditure', *European Research*, vol. 1, no. 5.

9. Peckham, J.O. 1980. 'Marketing advertising patterns', in Broadbent, S. (ed.), *Market Researchers Look at Advertising*. London: Sigmatext, pp. 179–88.

10. Broadbent, S. 1989. *The Advertising Budget*. Henley-on-Thames: NTC Publications, p. 242.

11. Aaker and Myers, op. cit., p. 68.

12. Corkindale and Kennedy, op. cit., p. 100.

13. Dhalla, N.K. 1977. 'How to set advertising budgets', *Journal of Advertising Research*, vol. 17, no. 5.

14. Kotler, P. 1988. *Marketing Management: Analysis, Planning and Control*, 6th edn. Englewood Cliffs, NJ: Prentice Hall Inc., p. 636.

15. 'Do you plan to burst your advertising schedules?' *Audit Magazine*, Audits of Great Britain Ltd, April 1971.

16. Michell, P. 1983. 'The grim facts behind agency account moves', *Campaign*, 18 July.

17. *Marketing Pocket Book 1993*. Henley-on-Thames: The Advertising Association, p. 81.

18. Aaker, D.A. 1991. *Managing Brand Equity*. New York: Free Press, p. 11.

19. Rapp, S. and Collins, T. 1994. *Beyond Maximarketing: The New Power of Caring and Daring*. New York: McGraw-Hill, ch. 8.

20. See *Price Waterhouse Sales and Marketing Software Handbook*, 1993. London: Pitman.

21. Fletcher, K. 1990. *Marketing Management and Information Technology*. Hemel Hempstead: Prentice Hall International, p. 283.

Appendix: Readership data for daily morning newspapers

| | Total | | Social grade | | | | | | | | | | |
| | | | A | | B | | C1 | | C2 | | D | | E | |
	000	%	000	%	000	%	000	%	000	%	000	%	000	%
Unweighted sample	28,500		760		4,121		6,421		7,910		5,222		4,066	
Est. population 15+ (000s)	44,775		1,219		6,605		10,201		12,389		7,985		6,375	
Sun	11,340	25	57	5	644	10	2,032	20	3,939	32	2,975	37	1,693	27
Daily Mirror	9,062	20	49	4	513	8	1,648	16	3,310	27	2,353	29	1,189	19
Daily Mail	4,531	10	172	14	911	14	1,461	14	1,157	9	488	6	341	5
Daily Express	4,306	10	108	9	794	12	1,319	13	1,190	10	518	6	378	6
Star	3,920	9	20	2	137	2	612	6	1,434	12	1,160	15	557	9
Daily Telegraph	2,765	6	388	28	1,082	16	816	8	325	3	107	1	97	2
Daily Record	2,207	5	13	1	132	2	399	4	713	6	562	7	388	6
Guardian	1,465	3	106	9	634	10	400	4	183	1	102	1	40	1
The Times	1,213	3	190	16	500	8	318	3	113	1	59	1	33	1
Today	1,060	2	14	1	150	2	269	3	327	3	238	3	62	1
Independent	912	2	77	6	387	6	271	3	118	1	47	1	11	*
Financial Times	757	2	94	8	303	5	252	2	63	1	39	*	6	*
Sporting Life	340	1	3	*	26	*	69	1	103	1	88	1	51	1
Racing Post	130	*	–	–	4	*	33	*	45	*	33	*	15	*
B'ham Daily News	515	1	15	1	77	1	103	1	113	1	92	1	115	2
Glasgow Herald	365	1	29	2	106	2	104	1	73	1	36	*	17	*
Dundee Cour & Adtsr	310	1	7	1	52	1	61	1	86	1	59	1	46	1
Ab'deen Press & Jrnl	292	1	6	1	50	1	62	1	82	1	59	1	31	*
Yorkshire Post	285	1	16	1	63	1	93	1	63	1	30	*	21	*
Wales Western Mail	234	1	7	1	64	1	61	1	57	*	30	*	14	*
Scotsman	203	*	17	1	92	1	53	1	22	*	10	*	8	*
Daily Mirror/Record	11,187	25	62	5	636	10	2,037	20	3993	32	2,892	36	1,566	25
Any national morning	30,322	68	900	74	4,416	67	6,787	67	8,652	70	5,784	72	3,783	59

Readership analysed by social grade – all adults.
An asterisk signifies less than 1%
Source: *National Readership Survey 1987*, JICNARS.

Chapter 18

Salesforce planning

Personal selling is an important cost element for most companies, and for some it is the dominant part of the marketing budget. Because of this, concern about the relative effectiveness of salesforce activity in the overall marketing mix is usually very marked. Unique costs, associated with potentially unique contributions to total company efforts, elevate this to one of the major realms within which marketing managers make decisions.

Two chapters are now devoted to these decisions. Chapter 18 investigates influences on the role to be assigned to the salesforce, considers some important trends affecting that role and introduces the central decision problem of allocating efforts. Aspects of that problem include the determination of the size of the salesforce, the design of sales territories and the assignment of representatives to territories and customers. Chapter 19 concentrates on the abiding issue confronting the sales manager: salesforce motivation and control.

The role of the salesforce

Figure 18.1 depicts some of the main factors that will condition the role of the salesforce. The obvious and distinctive feature of salesforce activity is that it involves personal contact with customers. Need for such contact presents two kinds of variable: the need to persuade through personal visits, and the need to undertake other activities not directly associated with persuasion. Persuasive visits recognise the potency of sales representatives in communication with customers. Their ability to engage attention, to adjust a message to the audience's interests, to answer questions and overcome objections is unrivalled by other marketing communication media. Historically, face-to-face persuasion has been the prime marketing tool. But other things have changed, especially the size of markets and the size of companies. So personal persuasion is now seen to be potent but expensive.

Personal contact is required not just to develop attitudes and influence customer behaviour. The distance between producer and consumer means that

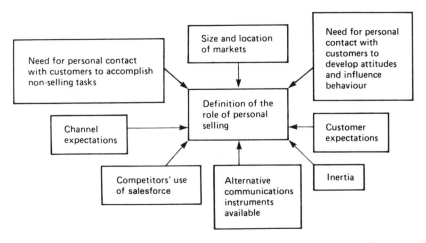

Figure 18.1 *Salesforce role determinants*

many non-selling tasks need to be undertaken by the salesforce. In the industrial market, the salesperson might be viewed as a consultant in a given technology and would advise customers on applications of that technology. This need not be brand-specific advice, and the impact on sales may be felt only in the long term. The salesforce may also serve important marketing research functions in defining DMU membership, gleaning customer attitudes, monitoring competition and providing sales forecasts. Additional duties may involve collecting bad debts, returning rejects and handling complaints on quality or delivery. In the consumer market, ancillary tasks could be associated with merchandising: erecting display material, stocking shelves and auditing retailer stock levels. All these activities require personal visits, although they need not necessarily be performed by the salesforce. Many firms define their salesforce job to include at least some of these non-selling tasks, because it may be less expensive and more convenient than employing a separate body to undertake them.

Market factors also condition the role of the salesforce. Small, geographically concentrated markets can be easily reached by personal contact. Large, widespread markets can be so reached only at great cost. Some companies have decided that this cost is necessary and so employ a huge salesforce, many hundreds strong. However, it should be noted that some firms with a large salesforce in the consumer market now feel that if they were beginning again they would employ only a small proportion of their current numbers. This is an important point which requires further comment.

In Figure 18.1 a significant element is inertia. The role and size of a salesforce at one time are greatly influenced by its past role and size, perhaps irrespective of current best views. Thus in the past an appropriate role may have been assigned to personal selling in the light of conditions then pertaining. Market size, structure and location are dynamic. The structure of retailing can also change radically, as can the kinds of mass media available. This means that, through time, the appropriate role of personal selling can change, but it is extremely difficult to dismember a large, established salesforce. The ramifications are dramatic and can affect every aspect of the company's operations, structure, internal and external power relations and all its employees. Such decisions can never be taken lightly, and the argument is that they may not be taken at all. But this inertia has a more subtle twist. The absence of a decision to cut the salesforce may lead to decisions actively to maintain it. Vacancies are filled and training programmes continue in the attempt to ensure efficient sales operations. The company continues with efficient salespeople and efficient sales procedures, but a relatively ineffective total marketing operation. It is suboptimising through inertia. If it were starting afresh it might conceive an optimum salesforce of forty people, calling on key accounts concentrated at the head offices of retailers. With inertia it maintains 400, calling on 80,000 retail outlets. In consequence it builds a marketing mix around its salesforce. The advertising budget becomes a secondary consideration, whereas ideally perhaps it should be more important.

Customer expectations can hardly be ignored. Once more inertia may be apparent through established custom and practice. In industrial markets, customers may go to the extent of partially evaluating suppliers in terms of the frequency and helpfulness of sales representatives' visits. Customer responsiveness to sales visits needs investigation. Often this is done through a critical appraisal of experience. It may be possible in some situations to experiment or to learn from analogous situations faced by other companies.

Channel expectations refer to the views held by middlemen about the role of supplier salesforces. Visit frequencies and activities may have been developed into a regular pattern. Channel members may have become accustomed to that pattern and ordered their own activities around a constant cycle of visits. Departures from routine may be seen to be disruptive and could result in antagonistic reactions.

Equally well the salesforce role will be influenced by the availability of alternative communications instruments. The employment of personal selling will always be a function of an evaluation of its relative effectiveness given a cost constraint. Measures of relative effectiveness are bounded by the established objectives. These may change. At one time the goal could be user awareness of a new product, at another time increased sales in a particular market segment. Each goal could lead to a different relative effectiveness for the various communication instruments. In addition, comparisons between instruments will also be affected by the nature of the instruments available. Over the past twenty years we have witnessed massive changes with the increased use of television and radio advertising and the widespread use of coupons and samples: over the next twenty years novel media can be expected to complicate further any evaluation of the relative role of the salesforce.

Finally, competitors need to be considered. Their use of personal selling must affect other companies since customers will make comparisons. Competitors may also set the norm for pay and conditions.

Variations in these factors as perceived by the management of a company will lead to quite different roles being assigned to personal selling. When considering advertising it was emphasised that it was heterogeneous. Salesforce activity is much more diversified. The only logical way to handle decisions given great diversity and disparity is through analysis, with as little recourse to dogma as possible. The task is to build a logical framework for the analysis of salesforce decisions. This will be done by concentrating on the allocation problem as the primary planning problem in sales management, and by some consideration of the control of sales plans. Recruitment and training of salespersons will not be studied, since these are specialist activities which properly require specialist treatment, such as in Lancaster and Jobber [1].

Throughout the discussion of salesforce activity it is worth bearing in mind the similarities with advertising problems. Judgements about reach and frequency are every bit as relevant to salesforce allocation. But measures of effectiveness are often taken as being less complicated in the case of personal selling because it is sometimes assumed that sales measures are more directly meaningful.

Salesforce trends

Salesforces operate in a dynamic environment, as indicated in the previous discussion. Trends in addition to those implied above are now considered.

Account management

Concentration in buying power has meant that large customers have taken on increasing significance. Their importance is reflected in the special treatment that they are receiving, and this is not just in terms of the discounts that they demand and obtain. One aspect of this treatment is the development of account management [2].

The essence of account management is the devotion of considerable and continuing time and effort to individual customer care. It is partly a direct selling function, but is likely also to involve high-level negotiation on long-term contracts. The range and scope of the negotiations will be wide and include a package of products, services and complex financial arrangements and contractual agreements. From the customer's viewpoint, once the relationship is established the account manager is his representative in the selling company, assuring the buyer's needs are attended to with urgency. The account manager would also be the first-line consultant on his products' applications, and anxious to see that more detailed consultancy is available if required by the buyer. From the selling company's viewpoint, the account manager will develop intimate knowledge of customer demands and buying practices. He will supply sales forecasts, detailed monitoring of customer attitudes, insights into developing needs for new products, triggers for possible new contracts, and a deep knowledge of customer DMUs.

Organising for account management has led many firms to establish separate salesforces, which may deal with national accounts. Others have a longer tradition of house accounts handled by senior sales management, although that does not always imply account management as described above. Some firms have tried separate account management structures but have reverted to a single salesforce structure. In this case, the rationale would be that account management requires some of the best representatives, and that to deprive the normal salesforce operation of these people reduces its effectiveness. To give first-level regional management added incentive they may be allocated account management responsibility in addition to their supervisory functions.

Effective account management has two kinds of financial implications. First, the need for efficient accounting procedures to establish and to maintain account profitability. Second, the need for account managers to be conversant with modern management accounting. As Kirkby [3] says:

> Unfortunately, all too often even senior people are financially naïve, or top management mistakenly believes that either its salesmen do not need financial skills in order to sell, or, worse, that for dubious security reasons they should be kept ignorant of internal cost, margins, costing systems and break-even quantities. Inevitably the salesman is handicapped in being able to negotiate the terms and conditions of the contract after agreement in principle has been reached.

Burnett [4] suggests that there are four groups of ways of developing a strong, lasting relationship with major customers. These are:

1. Developing trust
   - high frequency of contacts; social activities,
   - special events for the customer; keeping promises,
   - open communication; sharing mutual problems,
   - being flexible and empathetic.

2. Creating entry barriers:
   - low competitive pricing; superior products and applications,
   - electronic links; network of relationships,
   - joint innovation teams.

3. Reinforcing exit barriers:
   - making customer dependent on technical support,
   - loaning equipment; signing long-term contracts,
   - financial support, e.g. leasing; forming customer clubs,
   - incorporating unique component design,
   - giving training support.

4. Joint venture projects:
   - assigning staff to customer; creating joint project teams,
   - pooling research and development; joint marketing research,
   - shared customer database.

Table 18.1 *Account strategy options*

Customer attractiveness	Business position of supplier		
	Strong	Average	Weak
High	Defend/develop	Develop	Maintain selectively
Medium	Develop	Defend/ maintain	Maintain minimally
Low	Defend selectively	Maintain minimally	Withdraw

Source: Based on K. Burnett, *Strategic Customer Alliances*. London: Pitman, 1992, p. 53.

In planning activities regarding major accounts, Burnett argues that there are four generic strategies that could be considered; to target for development; to defend from competition; to maintain with minimal resource; and to withdraw. In assessing which of these is appropriate he recommends a variant of the portfolio planning models discussed in Chapter 9.

Two dimensions are employed: attractiveness of the customer and the business strength of the supplier, and each is a composite of factors. Customer attractiveness includes sales potential, possible profitability, length of term of supply and exclusivity. Business strength includes share of customer's business, contract basis, age of relationship, price and quality competitiveness. Scores and relative weightings are attached to these factors in order to determine whether customer attractiveness is low, medium or high, and whether business strength is weak, average or strong. Analysis would position accounts against both dimensions and a guide to possible strategy can be seen in Table 18.1.

Industrial selling: an interactive process

Account management in industrial marketing recognises the crucial importance of the need to manage the relationship between buying and selling organisation. The interaction model was introduced in Chapter 5 and it was seen that in industrial markets the relationships were likely to be long-term, complex, active interactions between companies.

The web of communication ties between organisations is a central facet in the development and maintenance of such relationships. This web can be viewed as a series of episodes of communication exchanges concerning goods, information, money or social relations. From the seller's viewpoint, considerable effort would be devoted to nurturing these ties. Some may become routine and there may be some mutual adaptation to systems and procedures between the firms to strengthen and improve the relationship. The effective account manager would be active in monitoring the ties, in encouraging routine adaptations and in smoothing any friction.

Another dimension to the role of the account manager would be as a major player contributing to the atmosphere in which the exchanges take place. The tone of the exchanges might vary between conflict and co-operation. Tension is bound to arise at times, particularly in transition caused by changes in the balance of power in the relationship, by technical change, or changes in industry structures. The stream of past communication ties may have been variously satisfactory and also contribute to future expectations. The account manager would need to be sensitive to how such factors would affect the atmosphere of future exchanges and would be active in creating and sustaining a favourable backcloth to communications.

Selling by a team

Account management may or may not be associated with team selling. Key accounts may require the skills of more than one person. In industrial marketing this may involve engineers and designers calling on customers in support of the sales representative. It may involve the manager of customer training programmes, or legal and accounting personnel. In consumer markets the team may comprise sales representatives, canvassers, merchandisers and delivery personnel.

As with any team the biggest problem is likely to be co-ordination. Clear roles and objectives for each team member are a necessity, otherwise there is the possibility of conflicting efforts and only partial customer coverage.

Selling to a team

The discussion of organisational buying behaviour stressed that the DMU is likely to be composed of several people. With large sales to large organisations the DMU will be at various authority levels, and represent different interests. Matching authority levels and specialist interests between the buying and selling organisations may be required and may even be insisted on by the buying organisation.

Selling to several customers at the same time

Personal persuasion, especially if coupled with product demonstration, is recognised as an efficient means of customer communication. The problem is its cost. One way around this problem, which is being employed by an increasing number of companies, is to sell to several customers at the same time. A usual vehicle for this is some form of 'seminar', 'product briefing' or 'customer update'. This entails bringing a number of customers and prospects together, making presentations, giving demonstrations and allowing examination of the product. Naturally, this needs to be undertaken with consummate professionalism.

This 'shotgun' approach can be compared with the 'rifle' approach of the personal interview. It cannot attune the sales message to the specific problems of the individual prospect. Nor is it likely to uncover and overcome specific objections. But some companies, particularly in electronics and computing, have found it expedient to adopt this approach because of the cost of intensive customer coverage with personal visits.

Communications technology

Communications technology, together with information technology, have aided the work of the salesforce and its management. Portable telephones, laptop computers and modems assist recording, reporting, analysis and communication. But technological developments have other implications.

At the simplest level the telephone can replace the personal visit. More and more companies are employing telesales to supplement or supplant sales representatives. In the consumer market this may be the brewery, ice cream, soft drinks or publishing company. In the industrial market it may be the coffee vending or electronics components firms or engineering distributor. This technology may soon be enhanced by visuals and by improved telephone conference facilities.

More sophisticated implications may be set in train by video and cable television developments. Initially, video presentations may assist the representative in personal visits. Verbal presentations with static visuals have their limitations, which video may overcome. Some companies are already posting video cassettes to prospects in place of salesperson visits, and this is not restricted to the industrial market since travel companies have also introduced this service. Teletext services are also developing and specialist catalogue presentations are emerging. Whether this will be considered to be a substitute for advertising or salesforce effort remains to be seen. Finally, special cable television networks could be envisaged, or maybe direct broadcasting by satellite, which had no intent to entertain. They could be purely for business, and perhaps 'narrow-casting' with high definition market segments. If direct audience feedback were to be incorporated, it would have far-reaching implications for the future role of the salesforce.

Merchandising

Earlier it was noted that one of the tasks that may be required of the salesforce was merchandising. Buttle [5] defines merchandising as:

> any form of behaviour-triggering stimulus or pattern of stimuli, other than personal selling, which takes place at retail or other point-of-sale.

These tasks need not be undertaken by the salesforce, as traditionally has been the case. There has been a trend to reduce the size of saleforces by the employment of separate merchandising forces. For some firms these are specific to their organisation, and may be restricted to part-time staff. For other firms, merchandising may be carried out by specialist merchandising companies.

Determining salesforce size

Most sales managers work with an established salesforce. The size issue may therefore appear redundant because short-term rigidities will not allow adjustment to the numbers employed. That argument is clearly myopic. If a company does not know by how much it is suboptimising, then it will always assume that it is optimising, and even in the long term will keep the same size salesforce. Then again, some experienced sales managers suggest that close investigation of the size issue with new salesforces is unwarranted. In these cases they would argue that a very small beginning, with just one or two sales personnel, is decided by the scale of funds available. That is a more valid argument, but applies to an insignificant proportion of total selling effort by all companies.

Marginal analysis

Theoretically, the best decisions could be derived from marginal analysis. As ever, the practical problem is with estimating marginal revenue. The sales response function is often impossible to tie down with any accuracy, although in some situations approximations may be possible. Where salesforce effort is the dominant element of the marketing mix, the complications in tracing sales response are reduced. A regression analysis may indicate the sensitivity of sales volume to numbers of sales persons, though lag effects may be difficult to handle. Wotruba quotes a study by Lambert from the X-ray film market where an attempt was made with some success to apply the marginal approach [6].

Workload method

Talley [7] proposed a practical procedure which had the virtue of being readily understandable and easy to employ. It is based upon estimates of total effort required and total effort available. Effort required is a judgement about reach and frequency. Effort available results from study of sales representatives' present call load and the determination of average hours available for selling. An example will clarify the approach.

Suppose that a decision had been made to reach all established customers during a year. Further suppose that a decision was made to reach them with differential frequency according to size of account. Thus the 100 large accounts would be visited twelve times per year, the 1,000 medium-sized accounts six times per year and the 5,000 small accounts three times per year. This gives the total required call load of 22,200.

Estimates will now be made of the number of calls that each salesperson could make during a year. Analysis of past performance may indicate an average of 40 calls per week or 1,920 calls for a 48-week year. Thus 22,200 calls would require 11.6, or 12, sales representatives.

This basic approach can be refined in a number of ways. The analysis of effort required could have been very detailed. The starting point could have been small geographical areas – in the grocery market district council areas or census enumeration districts. Analysis of account types in each small area would give a workload for each of these which would be useful for the later assignment of salespeople to territories. Another refinement could be the nomination of several classes of call, perhaps by duration. Large accounts may require not only more but also lengthier calls. Finally, the analysis of effort available could be far more detailed. Eight calls per day were assumed for the sake of the example; a fuller study [8] may have revealed a breakdown of the average representative's time into hours spent travelling, waiting, report-writing and in sales interviews. The whole analysis would then be in terms of 'selling hours' required and available, rather than the rather vague 'calls'.

This approach is as valid as the fundamental judgements that it requires about reach and frequency. The example was confined to established customers, irrespective of definition. There will obviously be a whole range of possibilities, from accounts placing large orders every month to those that have not placed an order for years. When does an account become 'established' or 'disestablished'? There will also be prospective accounts in various states of readiness to place an order. There might be little chance of orders in the short term from some, but calls would none the less be necessary to build up a relationship and to monitor the critical times when switching may be possible. The approach also rests on judgements about frequency. Some sales managers will feel their experience is sufficient to make this judgement; others have attempted to experiment.

Sales potential method

If it can be assumed that past variations in sales are largely a function of variations in the number of salespersons, then Semlow's approach may be useful [9]. The essence of the method is a study of the sales potential and actual sales volume in all territories in the past. Sales potential is defined as the proportion of total company sales that should come from each territory. Assuming *unequal* potentials, then some territories might have 10 per cent and others as little as 1 per cent of total company potential. Now, actual sales volume is related to this sales potential and expressed as sales volume per 1 per cent of potential. It might be found that territories with a 1 per cent potential have yielded £100,000 of sales and those with 10 per cent potential £300,000 sales. Thus the 1 per cent potential territories have yielded £100,000 per 1 per cent of potential; the 10 per cent territories have yielded only £30,000 per 1 per cent of potential. A relationship such as depicted in Figure 18.2 may be discovered.

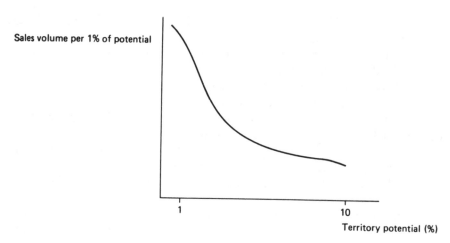

Source: After W.J. Semlow, 'How many salesmen do you need?'
Harvard Business Review, May/June 1959.

Figure 18.2   *Territory potential and sales volume*

If territories were now to be restructured into equal potential areas, the implications for total company sales can be calculated from this relationship. One hundred territories would imply 1 per cent potential each and the expected sales volume for such territories can be read off. Twenty territories of 5 per cent potential will have a different total sales volume. The analysis can then be extended to include cost and profit calculations for each size of salesforce, and the size with the highest profit chosen.

The validity of this approach rests heavily upon the curve shown in Figure 18.2. Its shape and locations are crucial, as is its 'goodness of fit' to the observed data, since a wide scatter would render it inappropriate. The approach would also be limited by the feasibility of restructuring into equal potential territories.

Designing sales territories

Sales representatives work in sales territories. In most cases this is defined as a geographic area, although it could be a segment of customers defined in another way, such as type of industry to which the customer belongs, or type of business such as repeat orders, or type of product or service bought. The discussion here concentrates on the typical case of geographic territories.

Territories give definition to the representative's job. It will be seen later that an important aspect of salesperson motivation is role clarity. Blurred expectations by the manager or the representative are not conducive to high motivation or to effective control. Ill-defined or haphazard territory construction contributes to blurred expectations. Fuzzy territory distinctions can lead to conflict between salespeople, disputes over large accounts located in overlap areas, and insufficient coverage of 'difficult' accounts in contentious locations. Customers may also be aggrieved if they do not know to whom they should relate. Sales managers will be cost-conscious and anxious to minimise travel and accommodation expenses and so put effort into designing territories that contain these costs.

Basic control units

With a geographically defined territory it is common to select local government areas as the basic control unit. This has the advantage that government-produced statistics use this base. Census of population statistics are available regionally, by county and by district and, if needed, by small area within each district. Statistics on industry and distribution are available using the same definitions of geographic areas, and commercially produced data such as Acorn also use these definitions.

Three kinds of adjustment may be necessary. First, physical characteristics and road networks may dictate territory shape. Second, trading areas around cities and towns are insensitive to administrative boundaries. Third, some companies may wish to align their territories to regional definitions employed by television contractors, so that salesforce and advertising efforts can be co-ordinated.

Given four levels – region, county, district and small area – it is useful to take the analysis to the finest level possible. These are the building blocks for territories, and if the blocks are only of regional size then territory construction has great limitations. On the other hand, if the blocks are small areas within district councils then the amount of analysis for a small national salesforce would be excessive. Generally, the larger the salesforce the smaller the block size.

Territory potential

Once the control unit is determined, an estimate of its sales potential is required. There is a strong connection between territory potential and salesforce performance, and Ryans and Weinberg argue that sales managers do not give the estimation of potential sufficient attention [10]. Inadequately assessed potential can lead to unrealistic expectations if it is too high, and missed opportunities if it is too low. Chapter 8 considered some approaches to the measurement of market potential.

Estimating potential can start on the simple assumption that it is a function of population. More complex analyses would bring in more variables in an attempt to explain the geographic variation of sales. At all four levels it is possible to obtain a range of demographic data, income and housing characteristics. Retail sales, in total and by sector, new car registrations and new house building are also available by county or district. These factors could be combined into a 'buying power index' by a regression model. Other factors may be more sensitive for particular applications. Sales of mayonnaise might be expected to vary with mean temperatures or with the price of lettuce. Sales of rainwear would obviously be expected to relate to rainfall. If full figures for all sales by all competitors, down to the country or district level, are accessible then this would be preferred. In some industries, for example new cars, this is routinely collected. In others, detailed consumer panel data may also assist, at least as far as a regional breakdown.

Salesforces in industrial markets are smaller than those in consumer markets, and so the basic control units are usually larger, seldom breaking below regional or county level. Estimates of potential proceed in a similar manner, with the variables differently specified. A first approximation might use employees in place of population. This would be employees in customer industries. The output of customer industries could also be considered. Special surveys may be needed to obtain a better fix on potential. If consumption of the material, component or service was related to a particular kind of input to an industry this might not be readily discernible from published statistics. However, in other situations very full information is obtainable, perhaps with census data developed by a trade association, the trade press or a market research firm.

The aim of the studies mentioned so far is to estimate sales potential for each of the basic building blocks. Output of the analyses would be statements of the proportion of total national potential available in each block. These blocks may be at any of the four levels, and it follows that the complexity will vary from a few tens to many thousands of blocks. In the more complicated cases computer analysis would be obligatory.

Assembling territories

Adjacent blocks can now be combined until the percentage of national potential assigned to one representative is reached. This would not be done uncritically. Territories have to be seen to be sensible and workable. Sales managers would adjust for the situation, bearing in mind the qualifications introduced in the discussion of the basic control units.

In the research into each of the blocks sufficient information may have been uncovered to identify prospects and customers. In the industrial market this may be a listing of plants in each block, and in the consumer market a listing of relevant retail outlets. It could include estimates of the relative size of each of these. With this possibility an alternative approach to assembling territories is feasible. A sales call workload approach would establish the number of calls needed in each block to achieve the company's reach and frequency objectives. Having determined the numbers of prospects and customers, classified them by size or propensity to buy, and decided the differential call frequency by class, then the volume of calls in each block can be deduced. Blocks are aggregated until a reasonable call workload for one sales-person is attained.

Whatever assemblage is arrived at, some checks are worthwhile. Practicalities must constrain the result. For example, calls on some factories with head offices elsewhere may be fruitless; others may only be essentially distribution depots, or just assemblers of components made at other plants in their group. Some retail outlets may not allow visits by sales representatives, or limit them in a fashion at variance with the call rate supposed in the calculations of workload. These types of practicality have limited the full-blooded introduction of computerisation in this problem area. Computer analysis is useful, and sometimes indispensable, in territory planning.

A corollary of call workload determination by blocks has been experimentation with computer-generated route plans. Some large companies have tried and subsequently abandoned such route planning; others take it as a datum with flexible interpretation. More sophisticated applications of computers can be expected, although Anderson and Hair argue that the detailed programming of sales representatives' time will continue to be decided in the field [11].

Assigning the salesforce

Two aspects of the assignment problem are now considered: assigning the sales-force to territories and to customers.

Assigning to territories

Sales representatives differ in their abilities. Recognising this, the sales manager

Table 18.2 *Sales manager's estimates of annual sales of each sales person in each of four territories*

Salesperson	Territory				Average
	1	2	3	4	
A	92,000	95,000	75,000	70,000	83,000
B	90,000	57,000	82,000	45,000	65,500
C	73,000	75,000	40,000	51,000	59,750
D	60,000	30,000	51,000	75,000	54,000
Estimated potential	78,750	64,250	62,000	60,250	

Source: P. Kotler, *Marketing Decision Making: A model-building approach.* New York: Holt, Rinehart & Winston, 1971.

Table 18.3 *Probabilities of moving a prospect between states*

State of customer before sales call	State of customer after call			
	1	2	3	4
1	0	0.5	0.1	0.4
2	0	0.7	0.2	0.1
3	0	0	1.0	0
4	0	0	0	1.0

Note: The states are defined in text.
Source: H.W. Boyd and W.F. Massy, *Marketing Management.* New York: Harcourt Brace Jovanovich, 1972.

could explore the best pattern of assignments by estimating what sales each person would make in each territory [12]. Table 18.2 gives hypothetical data. This means that the sales manager would expect salesperson A to sell 92,000 if in territory 1 and 70,000 if assigned to territory 4. Salesperson A is the best performer and D the worst performer. Territory 1 has the highest potential and 4 the lowest. With only 24 possible combinations, trial and error can produce the optimal solution of assigning: A2, B3, C1 and D4. More complicated problems could employ operational research techniques.

Assigning to customers

An analysis employing a dynamic sales call allocation model is used by Boyd and Massy [13]. This concerns the probabilities of moving prospects from one state to another as a result of sales call. To illustrate, it is assumed that prospects can only be in one of the following four states:

1. New prospect, no sales history.

2. An interested prospect, but no purchase yet made.

3. A current customer.

4. A prospect who has just refused to buy.

Table 18.3 shows the estimated probabilities of the effects of one additional sales call on prospects in these four states. For example, a call on a state 1 prospect will definitely move him out of that state. There is a 50 per cent chance that he will move to state 2, a 10 per cent chance that he will go to state 3, and a 40 per cent chance that he will refuse to buy and go to state 4. States 3 and 4 are said to be 'absorbing', in that it is assumed that once in those states there is no way out.

From these data the following can be deduced:

1. The probability that a prospect in state 2 will eventually buy is $\frac{2}{3}$. That is, the probability distribution in row 2 shows that there will be movement from state 2. When movement occurs from that state, then on $\frac{2}{3}$ of the occasions it will be to state 3 (to buy).

2. The probability that a prospect in state 1 will eventually buy is 0.43. That is, 0.1 for the direct movement from 1 to 3, plus 0.33 for the indirect movement from 1 to 2 to 3: $[0.1 + (0.5 \times \frac{2}{3}) = 0.43]$. Only 0.5 of the $\frac{2}{3}$ is taken because only a half of the prospects take the route from state 1 to 2 to 3.

3. The expected number of calls that will be required before a prospect in state 2 will move is 3.33, i.e. 1/0.3. On 30 per cent of the occasions a call on state 2 will move them; on average it will take just over three calls to move.

4. The expected number of calls to move a prospect in state 1 to states 3 or 4 is 2.66. Movement can be direct or via state 2 therefore:

$$[(0.5 \times 1) + 0.5(1 + 3.33) = 2.66]$$

    0.5 of 1 is for the direct route and 0.5 of 1 + 3.33 is for the indirect route (1 is added to 3.33 because the prospects have to be moved through state 2).

Now assume a typical sale is for £100, and assume that the cost of a call is £12, so the expected profit of a call on prospects in different states can be calculated. Expected profit from calls on state 1 prospects:

$$(0.43 \times £100) - (2.66 \times £12) = £11$$

Expected profit from calls on state 2 prospects:

$$(0.67 \times £100) - (3.3 \times £12) = £27$$

Concentration on state 2 prospects will move all of them to states 3 or 4 and so the pool of state 2s will have to be replenished by calls on state 1. A more radical recommendation would emerge if more than the simple four states were considered. In particular, states 2 and 3 could be graded by degree of interest and size of account. State 4 could be classified into rigid refusals and temporary refusals.

The attraction of this method is that many of the data are objective and could well exist in internal records. Furthermore, once established, the transition probability matrix can be revised periodically in the light of recent experience. Revision to the probabilities will itself be instructive. The approach is also amenable to use in market segmentation by specifying different states for different segments. Some measure of the relative worth of calls on different segments could then be deduced.

This approach determines the problem of reach by calculating the profit contribution from different classes of customer. Frequency is monitored through time, and decisions about optimum frequency by class of customer are derived from analysing the estimated differential response of different customers. It is interesting to speculate how much easier advertising decisions would be if a similar analysis were possible of reach and frequency of media schedules.

Summary

Several important determinants of the role of the salesforce were considered. The need for personal contact with customers is partly to persuade, and partly to accomplish non-selling tasks. But these basic justifications for personal selling are mitigated by other factors. The past role of the salesforce can be a major determinant of its present role, and this inertia could lead to suboptimisation. Customer and channel expectations about salesforce activity can also be important in shaping the role, as can competitors' use of personal selling. The size and location of markets and the alternative communication means available will be fundamental elements in this decision.

Five trends in the employment of salesforces were noted. These are the special attention now paid to account management, the increased use of team selling, the need sometimes to sell to a team and, because of increased costs, the trend to sell to several customers at the same time by organising seminars or 'customer update' sessions. Developments in communications technology have already impacted on the role of the salesforce, and future changes can be expected.

Two practical methods of establishing the size of the salesforce were introduced. The workload approach has more general application than the sales potential method. Attempts to measure the sale response function would be a first step in applying marginal analysis to this problem. More detailed aspects of the allocation problem concern the assignment of sales representatives to territories and to customers. The design of sales territories was introduced, and procedures for the allocation of effort considered.

Questions for review and discussion

1. Why might a company maintain a 400-strong salesforce when if it were to start trading again today it might only employ forty?

2. Draw up a table of salesforce role determinants with two extra columns, one for the industrial market and one for the consumer market. For each role determinant suggest any differences between the two markets.

3. Assume that you have a graph relating salesforce size to sales revenue over a ten-year period, and that only a weak relationship is evident. What questions would you ask about the original data and what explanations would you offer about the relationship?

4. In the dynamic sales call allocation method how might the probabilities of moving prospects between states be estimated?

5. How significant will developments in communications technology be for the role of the salesforce? Will there still be the need for a field salesforce in the next century?

References

1. Lancaster, G. and Jobber, D. 1990. *Sales Technique and Management*. Plymouth: Macdonald & Evans, ch. 9.
2. Shapiro, B.N. 1978. 'Account management and organisation: new developments in practice', in Bagozzi, R.P. (ed.), *Sales Management: New Developments from Behavioral and Decision Model Research*. Cambridge, Mass.: Marketing Science Institute.
3. Kirkby, P. 1981. 'How to tackle major sales', *Marketing*, 21 January.
4. Burnett, K. 1992. *Strategic Customer Alliances*. London: Pitman, p. 54.
5. Buttle, F. 1984. 'Education in merchandising', *Proceedings of the 17th Annual Conference of the Marketing Education Group*.
6. Wotruba, T.R. 1971. *Sales Management*. New York: Holt, Rinehart & Winston, p. 169.
7. Talley, W.J. 1961. 'How to design sales territories', *Journal of Marketing*, vol. 25, January.
8. O'Shaughnessy, J. 1965. *Work Study Applied to the Sales Force*. London: British Institute of Management.
9. Semlow, W.J. 1959. 'How many salesmen do you need?' *Harvard Business Review*, May/June.
10. Ryans, A.B. and Weinberg, C.B. 1978. 'Determinants of salesforce performance: a multiple company study', in Bagozzi, R.P. (ed.), *Sales Management: New Developments from Behavioral and Decision Model Research*, Cambridge, Mass.: Marketing Science Institute.
11. Anderson, R.E. and Hair, J.F. 1983. *Sales Management*. New York: Random House, p. 353.
12. Kotler, P. 1971. *Marketing Decision Making: A Model Building Approach*. New York: Holt, Rinehart & Winston.
13. Boyd, H.W. and Massy, W.F. 1972. *Marketing Management*. New York: Harcourt Brace Jovanovich, pp. 415–19.

Chapter 19

Salesforce motivation and control

What should the sales manager do, apart from issuing exhortations, in the attempt to ensure that the performance of the salesforce meets company goals? This chapter considers modern views on work motivation applied to the salesforce and draws out implications for the design and operation of control systems. The bulk of the chapter is the development of analytical frameworks which give focus to the necessarily subtle and sensitive direction by the manager.

Salesforce motivation

Traditionally, salesforce motivation has been a dominant part of the sales manager's job. Historically, the crude model of motivation employed was one of 'sticks and carrots' and the 'carrots' were usually totally monetary. Today's sales manager employs more sophisticated models, takes a more analytical approach and is far less dogmatic about what enables sales representatives to maximise their contribution.

Theories of motivation

Mullins proposes that the essence of the concept of motivation is 'some driving force within individuals by which they attempt to achieve some goal in order to satisfy some need or expectation' [1]. Two broad approaches have been taken to the study of motivation. Content theories, such as those of Maslow or Herzberg, concentrate on the content of motives and their prescriptions are well known. Latterly, research into salesforce performance has followed a second approach, which attempts to understand more about the process of motivation by studying the relationship between variables that have impact. This second approach is based on what are termed expectancy models.

Expectancy theory

According to Vroom's theory, people are motivated to work towards a goal when they expect their efforts to pay off. The three basic components are [2]:

1. Expectancy – whether the effort involved will produce better performance.

2. Instrumentality – whether the performance will pay off in terms of outcomes, e.g. promotion.

3. Valence – whether the possible outcomes are attractive for the individual concerned.

There are two key relationships: that between effort and performance, and that between performance and outcome, with the outcomes having varying attractiveness. Effort will depend on what the individual expects to result – will more effort lead to better performance, and that in turn to a valued outcome?

Refinement of this model by Porter and Lawler acknowledged that there may not be a direct flow from effort to performance. Two additional elements can mediate the relationship: individual ability and role perceptions. Additionally, it was recognised that both intrinsic and extrinsic rewards affect satisfaction.

Expectancy theory applied to the salesforce

Empirical testing of the theory in the context of the salesforce has been under-

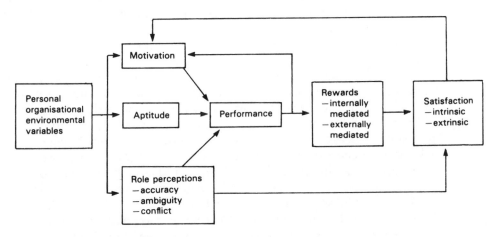

Source: O.C. Walker, G.A. Churchill and N.M. Ford, 'Motivation and performance in industrial selling: existing knowledge and needed research', *Journal of Marketing Research*, vol. 14, p. 158, May 1977.

Figure 19.1   *Salesforce motivation and performance*

taken by Walker, Churchill and Ford and in general the theory has been supported [3], [4]. The model is shown in Figure 19.1.

Performance is a function of motivation, aptitude and perception of how the role should be performed and it follows that if any of these is low, then performance will be low. An important influence on motivation is the expectancy that effort will have an effect on performance. This connection is not as obvious as it first appears because it depends on the salesperson's perceptions of the degree of control he or she can exert on his or her own performance. Several personal and environmental characteristics can mitigate this control, such as self-esteem or perceptions of 'real' territory potential. Much will also depend on the particular task. If the performance is related to some service activity – like an aspect of account management associated with product quality of delivery – then the performance is highly dependent on other people. A more direct connection between effort and performance would be apparent where personal control was perceived to be higher, for example if the task being measured was simply number of sales calls made.

Role perceptions influence performance. In studying role stress of industrial salespeople, Behrman and Perreault [5] determine the two key aspects as being role conflict and role ambiguity. For sales representatives conflict is caused by their 'boundary' function; they are at the boundary between a firm and its customers and need to integrate the conflicting goals these will have. Representatives will have to demonstrate innovativeness in finding solutions, which might prove stressful. As described, such conflict is not necessarily negative. It was found to be negatively related to job satisfaction but positively related to performance. Coping with the kind of conflict defined above is an inherent part of the successful representative's job. A more straightforward situation is found with role ambiguity. Lack of clarity about what the job entails and how it is evaluated by management leads to poorer performance and lower job satisfaction.

Aptitude, experience and hard work overcome many difficulties. But in all these there could be a difference between what is measured and what the individual perceives to be his own position. Management and representative need to share their views and to disentangle discrepancies.

So far this discussion of the application of the theory to the salesforce has dealt with expectancy. Instrumentality and valence are now introduced. Instrumentality is the individual's estimate that performance will be rewarded, and valence his estimate of the attractiveness of that reward. An important distinction is made between internally mediated rewards, including recognition and achievement, and externally mediated rewards bestowed by the organisation, including pay and conditions. If the salesperson believes that there will be a strong correlation between performance and reward, and if the reward is valued, then effort is high. Consequently, job satisfaction should be high, particularly if there is clear role specification, and this will give positive feedback to motivation. There are a number of 'ifs' in that sequence, and at any stage it could break down. A low correlation between performance and reward could hardly be anticipated to stimulate effort. A reward viewed by the individual as being of little value would be similarly unstimulating. But even a good measured performance need not lead to high job satisfaction, with reinforced motivation. If the representative was unclear about the role undertaken, or believed the performance measures to be inappropriate, job satisfaction could none the less be low. This might occur where she or he thought management out of touch with field conditions and they really ought to be monitoring, say, quality of customer contact rather than quantity. Or, where she or he judged that management's preoccupation with orders received did not reflect adverse economic conditions or the impact of competitive activity [6].

Implications of expectancy theory

Perhaps the main implication is that there is no universal motivator. That might appear obvious now, yet managers in the past have implemented naive models of work motivation, anticipating a direct relationship between effort and pay. Other implications include:

1. A highly prized reward for one individual may be of little value to another – the first may value a sense of accomplishment in what he perceives to be a difficult task, or finds the respect and recognition of his colleagues and managers to be important; the second may be attracted to job security and conditions of work or the remuneration package.

2. The manager needs to be sensitive to these variations and to how they might change as the individual's circumstances change.

3. There should be congruence between how the manager defines the salesperson's role and how that individual perceives it to be; this will be greatly influenced by selection and training, by the clarity of the communication between manager and representative, and by the appropriateness of the role assigned by management.

4. Linkages between effort and performance should be as clear as possible; with the salesperson's job this may sometimes be difficult because of lagged effects – today's efforts may not result in improved performance until next year; there are also many small, trivial tasks that only have cumulative effect, but which in total could be crucial – this may be apparent in the nurturing of clients, where the steady attention to their detailed requirements fixes them as loyal customers.

5. Performance indicators need to be clear and mutually understood; it is astonishing what have been taken to be sensitive indicators – for example, relying on car mileage checks (not that this is irrelevant, but it cannot be the dominant measure of anything other than how far the milometer has moved); clear performance indicators require the prior specification of the tasks and this again gives problems – it may be easier to prescribe and monitor minor tasks, or it may be that only a crude indicator can be devised (say number of calls per day).

6. Performance indicators should relate to tasks which the sales representative can control, and, where possible, tasks over which he has exclusive control.

7. Tasks assigned should not conflict; it was mentioned earlier that the representative's boundary position necessarily implies conflict resolution as an important part of the job, but that referred to conflict between his company and his customer; conflicting demands by the company are quite different – for example, where he is expected to develop a prestige image for the company and its services, only to be asked to 'knock out' some old stock at low prices, or where he is asked to develop friendly, favourable customer attitudes and then apologise for poor product quality, or insist on payment with delivery.

Salesforce rewards

Sales managers usually operate complex reward systems. They have a wide range of rewards to offer, both financial and non-financial, and this is needed to stimulate a wide range of people to undertake a wide range of tasks. A prime reason for developing a range of rewards is the general one, consistent with motivation theory, which recognises that individuals vary in their reaction to any one kind of reward. More specific reasons derive from the nature of the sales representative's job.

Salespeople undertake a variety of tasks. Some are continuing and programmed, others are ad hoc. Some have immediate impact, others delayed impact. Some are obligatory, and some to a degree voluntary. Some are needed for the representative to fulfil his job, and others are needed so that other people can do their jobs. This mix of tasks requires a mix of incentives.

The most distinctive feature of the representative's job is its boundary position, and this has two characteristics. The reconciliation of opposing interests, common to many jobs, takes place with the organisation's customers. It therefore has uncommon sensitivity, and involves questions of the firm's external image and reputation. Moreover, this dealing with customers is in the field, without close supervision. To an extent, the reward system becomes a surrogate for detailed supervision.

Characteristics of reward systems

Reward systems attempt to link what is good for the organisation with what is good for the individual, given that the individual offers himself or herself for employment. They should be designed to encourage what the firm considers to be valuable performance and to offer what the individual considers to be worthwhile recompense. In balancing these perspectives a first element is the job market. The firm competes for the kinds of employee that it wishes to attract, and it does this most obviously in the average salary levels it offers. Some deliberately pitch above an industry or regional norm, and make that fact well known. Others assume that non-financial rewards are more important, offer below-average salaries and emphasise job security, personal development and challenging work assignments. Where a company positions itself in this spectrum is a reflection of its basic mission – the kind of organisation it wants to be. At an operational level there are three additional factors: flexibility, equity and simplicity.

Flexibility is required first because of the plethora of tasks. Different tasks demand different treatment. For example, the firm may wish to stimulate sales of one part of its product line and a financial incentive might be appropriate. Alternatively, it may wish to encourage high-level performance in product demonstrations, in which case an appropriate incentive might be a better car, a shopping voucher at an exclusive shop or a family weekend at a good hotel. In the second of these examples the sales manager may also have in mind a more general objective, such as fostering a competitive spirit in the salesforce, and so it may have been arranged as a form of contest or competition.

Flexibility is required second to allow matching of rewards to individuals. How exact this match becomes is framed by the organisation's size. Big firms engender bureaucracy and systematic procedures; exceptions may be difficult to handle. To overcome this problem, large salesforces have several layers of supervision, each manager having a relatively short span of control. The aim is for the manager to have detailed knowledge of his subordinates' performance and to know what rewards each one values.

An equitable reward system gives to each his due, and what is due mirrors performance. This relates perceptions held by the individual to perceptions held by other group members. Managers try to ensure that individual perceptions are realistic, and this includes the development of shared understanding of what are the main indicators of good performance, and how well the individual is doing in those tasks. Confusion is possible because the representative may not believe that the right indicators are employed, or because he questions the validity of the measurement. It could also be that his self-image is at variance with that perceived by others, and he starts with an assumption that his performance is bound to be above, or below, average. With this background, management seeks a reward system which is objectively determined, yet can be tuned by sensitive interpretation.

Meeting the criteria of flexibility and equity might fall foul of the third factor: simplicity. In some firms salesforce compensation plans achieve notoriety because of their complexity, stretching the imagination of systems analysts. Alternative base salaries, varying commission rates on numerous products, individual and group bonuses related to a collection of tasks, regional or district incentives, company profit sharing calculated against 'salary', adjustments due to returns and various allowances for 'drawings' or expenses can result in an unwieldy system that is difficult and costly to administer. Computerisation helps the processing, but the essential input derives from the forms completed by representatives and their managers. The system must be understood and deemed to be workable by these principal parties.

Rewards offered

The range of rewards that can be offered is demonstrated in the following listing:

Financial	*Non-financial*
Salary	Promotion
Commission	Special training expected to lead to promotion
Individual bonus	
Group bonus	Achievement awards with publicity inside and outside the organisation
Contests	
Eligibility for profit-sharing	Advanced or otherwise special work assignments
	Recognition by praise
	Recognition by symbol of status
	Contests with non-financial rewards, e.g. travel prizes

Salespeople are normally paid a straight salary or a salary with an element of commission or bonus [7]. The other financial incentives may or may not apply. Companies using a salary-only system do so in the belief that sales orders received are not sufficiently sensitive indicators of performance. This might be because there are many tasks which will not show up in short-term sales, such as advising customers, product demonstrations or gathering market intelligence. It could also be because demand is highly seasonal or cyclical, or otherwise out of the representative's direct control, for instance where a team effort is involved. Companies using an element of commission stress the incentive that extra money can give, particularly in dynamic and highly competitive markets, where long hours, hard work and frequent rebuffs demand resilience, resourcefulness and creativity – every day.

If a commission system is to be implemented, a number of searching questions need answers. Should it apply to all representatives, or only some, and if the latter, why? Should it apply to all sales of all products, or only to some sales of some products? Commission is frequently paid after some predetermined quota is attained, and in some cases it starts just below quota to encourage at least quota fulfilment. Is the commission to be on sales value, volume, net of returns, paid on order receipt, on delivery to customer or after the customer has paid? Is it to be a continuing system or one that is intermittent, only operating in line with tactical plans? If it applies to only some products, why? If it applies to sales to only some types of customer, why? Should the commission rate be flat, progressive or regressive, and should the rate vary with products and customer types?

These many variations need careful manipulation to ensure that they have the desired impact upon activity while meeting the criteria developed in the previous section. New or refurbished systems should be put through fairly rigorous simulation before introduction if management credibility is to be maintained.

Individual or group bonuses are widely employed and very flexible. They can be used to reward exceptional effort, to mark a significant achievement, to encourage particular non-selling tasks, to foster competitive feelings and to convey management's rating that certain activities have urgency and importance. Group schemes imply regular group meetings if they are to be effective, and they can manifest regional 'league tables' as an activity monitor.

Contests have many of the same utilities but may be more tactical, aimed at more specific targets and within short time periods. The company may operate a number of promotion periods in the year, and contests may be aligned to these. The aim is to maintain the freshness and interest of the salesforce, as well as to direct effort to particular products or to particular customers or prospects.

Control of salesforce activity

Control can be a contentious issue in the salesforce because it might be thought of as betraying a lack of trust, as stifling initiative and representing an overbearing and insecure management. If they are properly selected, salespeople will be high on maturity, confidence, self-reliance and energy. Control may be perceived as interference. On the other hand, 'support' may be viewed in a much more

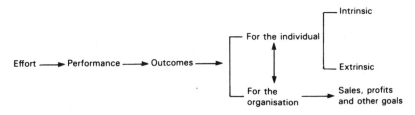

The reward system works on the individual outcomes and the control system on the organisational outcomes

Figure 19.2 *Motivation and control*

positive light. Informed direction, assistance in uncovering market opportunities, relevant training, help in clarifying role expectations and timely feedback of results are possible benefits to the representative from a control system. The manager may be controlling, but for many kinds of salesforce it is probably best seen as supporting and steering.

The variety of salesforce situations means that tighter or looser control may be appropriate. This will be partly a function of the tasks expected of the sales-force, the extent of routine, predictable activity and that of creative problem-solving. In turn this will have influenced the kinds of people employed, their training and their expectations about how their performance is evaluated.

In studying motivation the essential relationships were seen to be the link-ages between effort, performance and outcomes. Consideration of control exam-ines the same effort and the same performance, but concentrates on the outcomes for the organisation rather than those for the individual. Figure 19.2 illustrates.

Performance standards

Reward systems can be interpreted as control mechanisms in so far as they encourage performance consistent with the organisation's goals. Some few firms rely on this as their only control of salesforce activity; most introduce a collec-tion of additional control devices more explicitly related to organisational goals, in the attempt to direct performance to those outcomes desired by the organi-sation. This involves the determination of acceptable standards of performance, measurement of actual performance, comparison of actual against standard and the application of corrective action if that comparison is unsatisfactory.

The critical problem is the specification of the performance standard, and it would be useful to recall the discussion on the implications of expectancy theory, which has relevance here. Taking points from that discussion and adding a few more, the following criteria for effective performance standards can be stated:

1. The performance–outcome link should be clear; that implies that the firm has explicit goals and knows what kind of salesforce activity will contribute to their attainment; it is often assumed that sales goals meet this criterion, but that cannot always be so because of lagged effects, and because representatives may be required to carry out many non-selling activities.

2. The effort–performance link should be clear; this requires knowledge about what kinds of effort are needed for a particular performance; on one level it could be said that increased sales (the outcome) result from the representative taking a sales order (the performance) after making a sales call (the effort); but the order did not result just from the representative making a visit – it flowed from identification of a receptive target customer, perhaps a history of visits, and effective communication and persuasion; also, other kinds of outcome might be desired because they contribute to the ultimate outcome of the sale – this might be as detailed as wanting representatives to be perceived by customers as experts in a

given technology (the outcome) which requires that they have the requisite knowledge (the performance) and that means they must learn (the effort).

3. The performance should be as nearly as possible one which the representative can exclusively control; if the sale is made as a result of several people's efforts then their individual contributions need to be disentangled and this might mean that for each the measured outcome is not the sale itself but, say, effective product demonstration or well communicated technical advice to the customer.

4. Performance indicators should be all of the following:
    (a) Relevant – different performances are more or less amenable to measurement, and so the measures taken may or may not actually reflect the true performance. If the measures are believed to be crude then more detailed breakdown of the outcome, with perhaps a hierarchy of outcomes, could lead to more specified performance and more relevant indicators, as noted in 2 above.
    (b) Unambiguous.
    (c) Understood by both manager and representative.
    (d) As objective as possible, and if subjectively assessed then the representative should have confidence in the procedures.
    (e) Used – redundant indicators waste time and puncture management's credibility.

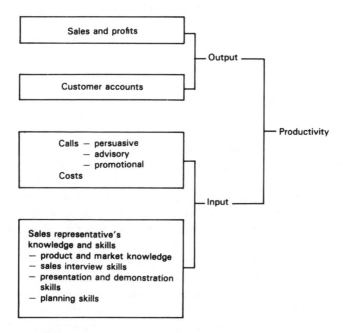

Figure 19.3 *Sources of performance standards*

Performance standards can be of three types: input, output or productivity. From the company's standpoint the input can be seen to be effort or costs, the output viewed as profits resulting from sales to customers, and productivity as the ratio of input to output. Figure 19.3 depicts inputs and outputs in a hierarchy. The salesperson has the desired knowledge and skills with which he undertakes calls on customers. These calls may have a persuasive intent, may have advisory or promotional goals and they impose costs. They result in the development and maintenance of customer accounts, from which the company derives sales and profits.

Input standards

The most widely used input standards concern calls and costs. The desired frequency of calls – the call rate or call norm – usually refers to calls in general, but can be detailed by type of customer or prospect, by product, product line and by purpose of call. There may or may not be standards for the amount of time spent on each call. The control period also varies; it might be daily, weekly or monthly. The kind of activity to be engaged in the call may be more or less prescribed. Firms may specify standards for displays put in, demonstrations conducted or promotional literature distributed.

Setting call frequency standards tests management's understanding of what makes a sale, or otherwise contributes to company objectives. On a gross level it could be assumed that calls make sales, with an ill-defined response function linking the two. Analysis of historical data might afford some refinement and experimentation further insights. But most sales managers utilise their own experience, and industry norms.

Well-conceived call norms can meet most of the criteria for effective performance standards. The only really difficult area is in the performance–outcome link. What is the relevant outcome? If the outcome was a visit to a customer then the performance is the accomplishment of that visit – just that. It is therefore insufficient as a control.

Costs are monitored in all aspects of business, and expense standards established. For the salesforce these may be expressed as various ratios, by call, customer and product.

Knowledge and skills apparent in the salesforce provide another area for the development of input standards. Product and market knowledge may be objectively tested, but measuring sales skills, and sometimes other personal attributes, requires more subjective evaluation, with perhaps rating scales calibrated to the supervisor's 'average in your experience'. Clearly, these standards are much more difficult to implement; they do not meet all the criteria established earlier. They continue to be used by many companies because of the insufficiency of the call standard. Some firms believe the quality of customer contact, and what transpires in the sales interview, to be more crucial than the quantity of customer contact as measured by call frequency.

Output standards

Some managers play down or completely ignore input standards in the belief that what counts is output. That simplifies, but it does forgo the diagnostic help offered by monitoring input, and especially that in discovering deficiencies in work practice and the revelation of training needs. Most sales managers operate a mix of input and output standards.

A difficulty with many performance standards, and in particular with output standards, is that any one outcome may be dependent upon a set of performances. For example, reaching a sales revenue quota would subsume a very wide range of performances and consequently a collection of efforts. For this reason an increasingly common practice is to involve the representative in the process of determining the performance outcomes desired and in tracing back the performance standards judged necessary. This has the advantage of making the standards well understood and means that responsibility for eliciting what activities are required to reach a given performance rests with the representatives themselves. Participation of this nature is inherent in a system of management by objectives [8].

Several performance standards can be based upon customer accounts. They could cover total current accounts, new accounts and new accounts opened, and each of these by customer or product type. But the dominant performance standards relate to sales, with various specifications of the desired value or volume or kinds of sale. These standards are usually referred to as sales quotas, and their derivation may be problematic. One company was not aware that it had problems in this area, because quotas had been fixed in historical times and adjusted ever since by an arbitrary percentage applied across all territories. The West Country representative never reached his quota, while the Midlands representative always exceeded his. The latter took three months off to recover from an operation, and a review of the quota system was set in train when it became apparent that Midland sales were hardly affected by his absence. Later it was revealed he only really worked part-time for the company, because he had other private business interests. A study of relative potentials for all territories uncovered enormous untapped potential in the Midlands, and saturation coverage in the West Country. Judgements about the two salesmen involved were turned on their head.

This example underlines the need to measure relative territory potentials. The sales forecasting chapter, and the section of the previous chapter on designing sales territories, dealt with this issue. But an additional point occurs; territories may be in different states of development with regard to the firm's products. Some will have a full history, others may have only more recently marketed a full product line, and the pattern of competition could be varied across regions. Past actual sales by territory could be used to deflate potential in order to allow for this. A composite index might use percentage of national potential and percentage of actual national sales. The weight attached to each would be debatable.

Constant monitoring of sales performance against quota for each territory can provide a valuable diagnostic tool. It is readily available information that can be used as frequently as the accounting system allows. Its efficiency is dependent on a none too rigid interpretation. Salespersons will be annoyed if they are not allowed to explain variances. Field conditions can never be fully anticipated and so a routine mechanism for explanations of deviations from quota seems essential. Careful attention to these explanations can be of great use in understanding more about the work of the salesperson and can have the added spin-off of demonstrating management interest in the salesperson's problems.

Profit can be considered as another output of the salesforce, and the possibility of adopting some profit standard could be investigated. This might be arrived at by calculating the average profit contribution per order and the average number of orders expected. It does require some reasonable system for the apportionment of costs. Multi-product companies with crude accounting procedures would probably find this difficult. It also has implications for the length of time in the control period. Monthly profit estimates across three product lines with ten items in each line, and each in two sizes, and all for 200 salespersons can consume a considerable amount of computer printout. Smaller salesforces, and especially those in the industrial market, may use a profit standard in a longer time period, perhaps annually. An extreme is where virtually no other control is applied. Very responsible and experienced salespeople, selling high value equipment, may respond better to this 'business manager' approach than to minute, detailed control of their activity. But the company is then very much in the hands of its salesforce. They may even consider that it is their business which they are periodically pleased to pass back to the firm. When they leave employment they could well take their business with them. Some industries are particularly prone to this, and sales managers have to tread a carefully balanced line between allowing initiative on the one hand, and ensuring that the company has adequate information about customers and prospects on the other.

Customer service levels may be viewed as another output of the salesforce. That is the adequacy of salesforce service as perceived by customers. Measures could be taken in customer attitude surveys but, more commonly, some qualitative assessment by a regional sales manager might be made. Salespeople might be evaluated against the 'average in your experience' on a range of elements such as promptness in dealing with enquiries, handling delivery problems and advising customers on product use.

Productivity standards

Ratios of the various output and input standards could provide a final area of control. Sales per call, profit per call, costs per order for each product and each representative can provide interesting analyses. For large salesforces, district, regional and national summaries can offer significant insights, especially if annual comparisons are monitored.

Dual standards

Proper control is founded upon realistic standards which can be achieved by reasonable effort. There may be the temptation to add something extra onto the realistic standard, to give an incentive. This artificially high standard is then used to make comparisons with current performance, and most representatives might fall short of the standard. The sales manager then institutes a system to cajole his salesforce to reach the desired level. The implications for the morale of the salesforce, their readiness to co-operate in exceptional enterprises, their bickering to customers about the company, and staff turnover become apparent immediately. All this argues against dual standards of realistic assignments and artificially inflated ones.

Data requirements

Efficient operation of the control system relies upon the timely collection of measures of performance. In turn this relies upon the salesforce supplying a large part of the data. Call reports, expense claims and sales orders provide the basic information. Great care is needed in designing forms to minimise the time required for completion and to maximise the data available. Support in these activities is sometimes provided by special allowances, and co-operation in supplying information may form part of salesforce appraisals. Thus participation in the operation of the control system becomes a performance standard.

Evaluating salesforce controls

Criteria for the evaluation of performance standards were introduced earlier in this chapter. Each of the areas in which performance standards are derived can now be assessed against those criteria, and this is done in Table 19.1. The overall conclusion from that table is that effective performance standards can be established in most of the critical areas, but that individually they are only of limited utility. This would argue for a battery of performance standards. The selection and mix of standards are among the most important activities of the sales manager, and could itself become a performance standard for the evaluation of the manager. The battery chosen will reflect the manager's understanding of how representatives undertake their work, his or her knowledge of what kinds of effort are needed to achieve a given result, and reveal his or her perceptions of market and competitive conditions. The assembly of standards and the implementation of control will also reflect much about the organisation. It will be a major element in the organisational climate and, by definition or default, heavily condition salesforce effectiveness.

Table 19.1 *Evaluating salesforce controls*

Criterion	Sales representatives' performance standards						Profits
	Knowledge	Skills	Calls	Costs	Accounts	Sales	
Clarity of performance–outcome link	Good	Good, if well chosen	Good, but limited	Good	Good	Often clear	Unclear
Clarity of effort–performance link	Good	Good, if well chosen	Good	Good	Good	Often clear	Unclear
Controllable by the individual	Yes	To an extent	Yes	Not always	Not always	Not always	Rarely
Performance indicators:							
Relevance	High	Depends	High	Depends	High	High	Depends
Ambiguity	Low	Perhaps	Often low	Often low	Low	Often low	Variable
Understood	Yes	Perhaps	Usually	Usually	Usually	Usually	Not always
Objective	Yes	Not	Yes	Yes	Yes	Usually	Perhaps
Used	Sometimes	Sometimes	Often	Often	Often	Often	Not widely
Overall	Effective but limited	Varied depending on implementation	Effective but limited	Effective but limited	Effective but limited	Effective depending on implementation	Much less effective

Organisational citizenship

Sales managers may not just give attention to objective measures in their assessment of sales representatives. They may also pay attention to activities of their staff that are useful for the organisation, but which do not reflect in increased sales by individual representatives. In order to explain this use has been made of the notion of 'organisational citizenship' which constitutes:

> discretionary behaviors on the part of the salesperson that directly promote the effective functioning of an organization, without necessarily influencing a salesperson's objective sales productivity . . . and take a variety of forms including altruism, courtesy, sportsmanship, civic virtue and conscientiousness [9].

It is possible that the overall assessment of individual performance may therefore be a blend of objective measures and a more subjective assessment of how well the individual contributed to the general well-being of the organisation. This also gives the prospect of typing members of the salesforce as 'sales-makers' and as 'good citizens', with a preponderance of either having quite different implications.

Summary

The chapter set the topics of salesforce motivation and control within the context of modern theories of work motivation. Applications to the salesforce have utilised expectancy theory, which stresses the importance of the link between effort and performance, and that between performance and outcome. Role perceptions were seen to be a significant influence on performance, and the boundary role of the sales representative causes particular problems.

Implications of expectancy theory include the need for sensitive and flexible interpretations of the nature of the rewards sought by individual representatives, and the central importance of clear performance indicators.

Control of salesforce activity can be analysed using notions derived from expectancy theory. Criteria for the development of effective control standards were developed, and after reviewing the sources of relevant performance standards, an evaluation was made of the relative worth of alternative approaches to control.

Questions for review and discussion

1.   'Expectancy theory applied to the salesforce confuses more than it clarifies.' Does it?

2. Can one realistically expect the words expectancy, instrumentality and valence to enter the vocabulary of the average sales manager?

3. 'In the sales representative's job, role conflict and ambiguity are par for the course, and so they need no special attention.' Do you agree?

4. Is there any justification for the development of an analytical framework if implementation relies upon sensitive adjustments in individual cases?

5. 'Salesforce rewards should be tailored to individuals.' Is that inconsistent with the need for systems and policies?

6. In the context of expectancy theory it could be said that the reward system works upon the outcomes for the individual and that the control system works upon the outcomes for the organisation. How can it be ensured that these are not opposed, and that the outcomes are mutually satisfying?

References

1. Mullins, L.J. 1993. *Management and Organisational Behaviour*, 3rd edn. London: Pitman.
2. Robertson, I.T. and Cooper, C.L. 1983. *Human Behaviour in Organisations*. Plymouth: Macdonald and Evans, p. 82.
3. Walker, O.C., Churchill, G.A. and Ford, N.M. 1977. 'Motivation and performance in industrial selling: existing knowledge and needed research', *Journal of Marketing Research*, vol. 14, May.
4. Churchill, G.A., Ford, N.M. and Walker, O.C. 1981. *Sales Force Management*. Homewood, Ill.: Irwin.
5. Behrman, D.N. and Perreault, W.D. 1984. 'A role stress model of the performance and satisfaction of industrial salespersons', *Journal of Marketing*, vol. 48, Fall.
6. See also Donaldson, B. 1990. *Sales Management: Theory and Practice*. Basingstoke: Macmillan, ch. 13.
7. Shipley, D. 1988. 'Using salesforce compensation as an effective management tool', *Quarterly Review of Marketing*, vol. 13, no. 3.
8. Futrell, C. 1981. *Sales Management*. Hinsdale, Ill.: Dryden, pp. 134–42.
9. MacKenzie, S. and Podsakoff, P. 1993. 'The impact of organizational citizenship behaviors on evaluations of salesperson performance', *Journal of Marketing*, vol. 57, January, pp. 70–80.

Chapter 20

Channel structure and conduct

Marketing channels are needed so that products can reach buyers and so that buyers can reach service points. They bridge the gap between production and consumption, and in doing so add value to the products or service by making them available when required. The particular channel arrangement adopted by an organisation expresses much about its search for competitive advantage, and is a central aspect of its marketing strategy.

Two chapters are devoted to marketing channels. This chapter considers channel structure and conduct and examines trends in a major sector, that of retailing. The next chapter is concerned with planning channel operations and details of distribution planning.

Channel structure

Channels for both products and services are to be discussed, and so a first influence on channel structure is the location of the exchange and consumption, whether near to the buyer or to the seller. A second influence is the employment of intermediaries. It may be advantageous to all parties to use middlemen, and this raises complications in channel structures. Large-scale and widespread structures can become very complex and difficult to organise and co-ordinate. A systems view may aid understanding of channel performance and demonstrate the varying effects of changes in the ways that channel activities are undertaken. Finally, channel structures will reflect the availability of scale economies and, depending upon where they occur, can lead to the rearrangement of the power structure in the channel.

Channels and exchange transactions

Marketing channels exist to facilitate exchange: they bring together the buyer and the seller. They enable exchange transactions to be completed by affording two

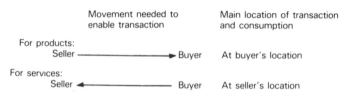

Figure 20.1 *Exchange location affects channel structure*

essential flows between the exchange partners. First, both need information on the exchange possibilities. Sellers need to know what buyers will value, and buyers need to know what sellers have to offer. Second, the transaction is only accomplished when the object of the exchange passes from one to the other. Marketing channels assist this passage.

The fundamental influence on the structure of these channels is the nature of the exchange transaction, which is dependent on the content and location of the exchange. The exchange might take place near to the buyer's location, at the seller's location or quite elsewhere, and it follows that different types of channel have emerged to cater for these differences. Generally, if a product is involved in the exchange then the transaction and subsequent consumption take place near to the consumer's location. If a service is involved, then, usually, the transaction is at the seller's location (Figure 20.1). In neither case is this absolute because there are products bought and consumed at the seller's location, and there are services performed at the buyer's location.

Channel intermediaries

In today's economy most exchanges are initiated by sellers and they need to devise mechanisms to move product to buyer, or buyer to service point. In both cases there will be the need for an information flow about what is on offer. In product channels numerous products have to be collected, sorted and transported to the buyer; in service channels numerous buyers have to be (somehow) collected, sorted and transported to the seller. The processes and institutions in the two situations have been subject to different patterns of evolution. For some product channels powerful middlemen developed and took on many of the activities needed for the transfer. For service channels middlemen have generally been far less powerful, and the service provider frequently works directly with the buyer without middlemen. There are exceptions, such as package tour holidays, where middlemen assemble the package of services and take responsibility for selling and moving the buyer. But there is a similarity in product and service channels: buyers need to be informed and persuaded that the offering meets their requirement.

The emergence of middlemen in a channel arrangement is a frequent characteristic, though not always an essential one. Buyers and sellers have different motives for wishing to engage a middleman (Figure 20.2). Buyers will be

Seller's motives

Buyer's motives

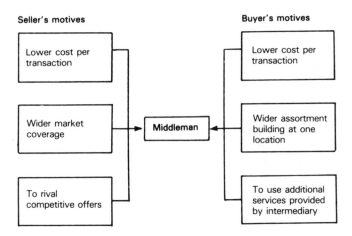

Figure 20.2 *Motives for employing middlemen*

interested in minimising their costs, but their transaction cost for dealing individually with manufacturers could be prohibitive. Middlemen can deal simultaneously with numerous sellers and buyers and so entail lower average transaction costs. Buyers will also wish to purchase a very wide range of goods, referred to as wide assortment building. There are considerable economies if they can consolidate their purchasing at a few places, rather than having to trip around to many sellers. Middlemen can perform the function of consolidating the wide assortment buyers need. From the seller's viewpoint there may be a similar cost advantage in using middlemen. A second advantage could be in market coverage. With the help of an intermediary the seller could reach a greater potential market.

Once established, a system employing intermediaries can afford further advantages. For the seller, the middleman provides a forum in which competitive offers are made, so that the seller can demonstrate the superiority of his offering. For the buyer, the middleman can provide additional services such as repair facilities, the availability of spare parts, advice on product use, breaking bulk and repackaging, fitting services and sometimes product modifications.

However, the possibility of using intermediaries poses problems for the seller. He has to decide whether direct dealing with consumers is feasible and economic. Can he achieve sufficient market coverage with his own resources, at reasonable cost, and will this enable competitive advantage? If not, what kinds of arrangement are offered by middlemen? Should there be just one channel, or are several channels possible? If indirect channels with intermediaries are used, then how is the system to be organised and controlled? And if there are intermediaries between seller and buyer, how is the seller to know, and keep track of, the changes emerging in what buyers require? All sellers need to respond to these problems. The response is central to defining the competitive posture that the firm adopts, and is an integral part of its business plans. The impact of these problems is more fully examined in the next chapter.

Channel systems and activities

Complex channel structures may be studied by taking a systems perspective. This allows consideration of the performance of the total system, as well as its parts, and emphasises the interdependency of the parts. The effects of changes in one area can be traced through to their impact upon other areas in the system. For example, in a product channel changes in the form and style of retailing can substantially shape the entire system. The trend to vast increases in the scale of retail operations does not just affect retailers, it conditions the very survival of other traditional channel members, and has severe implications for the allocation of activities, and costs, within the channel structure. A systems perspective can also account for novel developments in channels, which might be viewed as responses to inadequate performance by established structures, to the incursion of new technologies, or to other environmental influences, including legislative or demographic changes.

The viability of a given channel is a function of how well it accomplishes the flows needed for the exchange. This accomplishment depends on certain activities being effectively undertaken, and Stasch [1] has summarised the activities for a product channel as comprising the following:

An inventory function.
A materials handling function.
A communication and order processing function.
A transportation function.

Service channels require different activities to accomplish the flows. There is a similar need for communication, but the flow of buyers to sellers poses particular problems requiring particular activities. For some services the physical movement of buyers is an integral activity of the channel, such as in package tours, but for other services the movement problem is solved by moving the point of service, such as in fast food operations or car rental. The transportation function in the product channel therefore becomes, in the service channel, either a transportation function or a locational activity.

In the product channel the inventory function serves to adjust production to consumption. In the service channel there is also a need to adjust – but it is the other way around. Consumption needs to be adjusted to production. Because service production is real-time, usually with the buyers present, and because there will be limited productive capacity, the flow of buyers needs to be smoothed. As Lovelock says, 'an important task for service marketers, therefore, is to find ways of smoothing demand levels to match capacity' [2]. This smoothing may be effected by differential pricing, by adding or reducing service facilities at times, by 'qualifying' buyers so that only some can use the service at times, or by developing several distinctive images of the service in the hope of attracting only some buyers at one time. The allocation of the responsibility for this smoothing within the channel is a major decision, since inappropriate performance of this activity can have calamitous effects.

Each of the groups of activities noted in Table 20.1 can be performed several times at several layers in the channel. This complexity encourages a systems perspective because 'what is considered best for the whole system is not necessarily best for each component' [3]. Or, as Christopher [4] points out, it is possible to have efficient parts in the system, yet not achieve an optimum overall result. The complexity also introduces the prospect of trade-offs within and between the activities. Improvements or changes in one activity have ramifications on other activities. Thus better transportation might mean greater inventories, or, in service channels, smoothing demand might mean that different transportation arrangements are required, or stimulate a change in the location of the service. This leads to a further complication: if all the channel activities are not under the control of one organisation, then how are they to be allocated? The dynamic nature of channel environments makes this especially difficult because there will be periodic reshuffling of the activities in response to economic, technical and social change, and as a result of changes in the perceptions of channel members.

Scale economies

Evolution of channel structure will reflect partly the availability of scale economies in the activities. In product channels intermediaries can often reap scale economies. Bucklin [5] has studied many types of merchant wholesaler and finds evidence of these economies. He suggests that they become significant whenever inventory and order processing costs are greater than those of selling and service. Thus large meat wholesalers gain considerable savings. Alternatively he argues that selling costs are relatively invariant to scale, and so wholesalers supplying small retailers, as in beer and laundry supplies, are not likely to achieve much reduction in average costs by adding new customers.

Among retailers generally, evidence of the possibility of scale economies is seen in the ever-increasing size of outlets. Thorpe and Shepherd have examined retailing scale economies and demonstrated a fairly linear decline in wage costs as a percentage of sales with increases in store size [6].

Scale economies have not been so apparent in service channels, which accounts for the smaller size of service outlets. There are exceptions, but services are usually performed by smaller organisations. Where large organisations operate in service markets, the economies are often not associated with channel economies. But there is scope for some economies in the channel, and these are

Table 20.1   *Product and service channel activities*

Product channels	Service channels
1. Communication and order processing	1. Communication and order processing
2. Inventory	2. Adjusting consumption to production
3. Transportation and materials handling	3. Transportation or locational activities

related to the availability of a network of service points. Buyers may be attracted by the possibility of using the service in a distributed fashion: picking up a rental car at one point and leaving it at another, sending flowers, drawing cash from various bank branches, or planning holiday itineraries on an inter-hotel referral system. However, distributed service points need not be owned by the same organisation, and that is why there has been widespread development of franchise arrangements and 'marketing consortia' in service channels. In both these cases there is more or less formal agreement between independent organisations that they should work together, in order to impress an image of controlled quality and to co-ordinate distributed service points.

Channel relationships

Complex channels with intermediaries or numerous service points give rise to the need to organise and co-ordinate activities. If it is not a vertically integrated channel under the control of one organisation, then ways have to be found to obtain the co-operation of independent organisations. Because these organisations will have their own motives for engaging in the channel, Brown [7] suggests:

> The relationships therefore tend to exist in a condition of co-operation or conflict, as one or other attempts to dominate the network of relationships to achieve their own goals. The ability to dominate is attributed to the possession of power . . .

The importance of power in channel relationships is recognised by Sturdivant and Granbois [8] when they say:

> The literature clearly suggests, therefore, that power is a major determinant of channel member behaviour. Through power, firms attempt to influence the behaviour of their co-operating, and yet essentially egocentric, fellow channel members.

Financial standing and market position are important bases of power. Financial strength gives the apparent ability to hold out in bargaining situations, and for any single bargain to be perceived as of little significance. Market position is based ultimately upon consumer loyalty. The relative position of manufacturers' brands *vis-à-vis* retailers' own labels will be a case in point. Where the manufacturer's brand attracts strong consumer preference, then all suitable retailers will wish to stock that brand, giving bargaining strength to the manufacturer. In the face of consumer indifference between brands, the retailer will have more bargaining strength. Where the retailer's own brand is preferred the retailer can totally dominate the channel and every aspect of its operation.

Stern and El-Ansary [9] have commented on other bases of power in the channel, and point particularly to the following:

1. Rewards – reward power is based on the belief by B that A can offer him a reward, e.g. granting wider margins.

2. Coercion – coercive power stems from B's acceptance that A could potentially punish him, e.g. by withdrawal of exclusive distribution rights.

3. Expertness – B may perceive A to be expert, e.g. A may offer B special promotional services or technical advice.

4. Identification – B may wish to be identified with A, e.g. he believes that A is prestigious, and that he will benefit from that association.

5. Legitimacy – although no formal authority relationship exists, some channel members may consider the largest firm to be the channel leader, and effectively may allow him authority over some of their activities.

Channel members' perceptions of their own role and those of other members can also affect the relationships and the potential for conflict. Each will have an expected role in respect of the four kinds of activity noted at the beginning of this chapter. If there is a marked difference between this and the enacted role, then conflict is likely. For instance, the manufacturer may expect wholesalers to carry a given level of stock, to engage in a level of promotional activity, and to offer delivery dates which the wholesaler finds unacceptable.

Another source of conflict could be where a small retailer had different objectives to a growth-conscious manufacturer. There is evidence that small retailers and wholesalers have relatively static expectations [10]. They are interested in reaching and maintaining a given size, and may resist a manufacturer's attempts to persuade them to give maximum point-of-sale promotion to a new product launch. The manufacturer may look for alternatives and may even be forced into forward vertical integration. Conflict is also possible where a manufacturer uses a dual distribution system, and competes with his middlemen by selling directly to customers.

Alternatively, the retailer's perceptions of the manufacturer's role may cause some backward integration, or a degree of control over manufacturer's operations which is tantamount to full integration. This may occur in respect of perceptions of product quality demanded by the market. A fragmented manufacturing industry – such as in clothing – may be markedly reorganised on the insistence of retailers. The influence of Marks & Spencer is often quoted in this context.

Finally, channel relationships can be influenced by the development of some norm of behaviour. It may become accepted that a given channel member will normally be expected to carry out certain activities in a prescribed manner for a prescribed reward. Departures from the norm are possible, but to be effective they need to be based upon a powerful position. Much attention has recently been focused on two aspects of these norms: minimum drop levels by manufacturers to retailers, and discount structures. Companies such as Heinz or Lever Brothers seem sometimes to have the power to adjust these to their advantage; smaller companies have more chance of meeting retailer resistance.

Distribution of portable power tools

An interesting example of channel management is presented in the case of portable power tools. Black & Decker (BD) has dominated this market and has been the undoubted channel manager. Fundamental restructuring of the intermediaries brought that into question, and a focus for channel conflict has been the issue of loss leaders. Some characteristics of this market and BD's strategies are noted below.

In 1988 UK DIY power tool sales were £103m, of which 45 per cent were drills, 12 per cent jigsaws and 10 per cent sanders.

Market share

	1984	1988
BD	79%	66%
Bosch	10%	20%
Hitachi	1%	2%
Makita	2%	3%

The competitive structure can be explained partly as being a result of the operation of significant barriers to entry. These are:

1. High rate of innovation, e.g. BD introduces at least ten new models annually.
2. Strong brand images.
3. Manufacturing scale economies.

Market entry has been easiest for manufacturers already established in another country.

Distribution

	%
National DIY superstores	39
Independents	32
Mail order and catalogue showrooms	22
General retailers	7

After-sales service
BD has 38 service stations and uses 500 independent stores as collection points. The sharp decline in the numbers of independents is a problem because multiples usually refuse to act as a collection point.

BD advertising and in-store promotions strategy

There are four elements:

1. Special added-value packs, containing free products such as accessories.
2. Each year four or five additional products not in the company catalogue are supplied to retailers to use in aggressive price promotions.

3. Financial support to retailers for in-store and local promotions.
4. £1.25m in-store display material supplied each year.

Pricing and discounts
Retailers take Argos as a benchmark because they are perceived as offering keen prices which are published in their catalogue. BD gives retailers 38 per cent off suggested retail price, plus a 2 per cent volume discount.

Loss leaders
This issue became the critical factor in the relationship between BD and a number of important retailers in the late 1980s. BD has had an express policy of not supplying retailers who they believe would use their products as loss leaders. The Resale Prices Act 1976 provides for withholding supplies if there is 'reasonable cause' to suppose a product will be used as a loss leader. In 1987–8 BD says there were nine instances when it withheld supplies. One of these involved Argos and followed complaints by other retailers about Argos retail prices.

BD is against loss leading because it wants to create wide distribution, with good regional coverage and reasonable width and depth of their product range widely available. They believe loss leading reduces the number of retailers. It also causes others to reduce the extent of the BD range that they offer because margins in this market are not large. In 1988 eight multiples, including Woolworth, Tesco, Asda and Halfords, all cut back on their BD ranges.

BD argues that its products are used as loss leaders because of their strong brand image and very high levels of customer awareness. Loss leading damages that image.

In 1988 B&Q asked the Office of Fair Trading (OFT) to investigate the distribution policies of BD. This was a consequence of the refusal by BD to supply B&Q, because BD thought that B&Q would use their products as loss leaders. In 1989 the OFT found that BD used a 'going rate' as a suggested retail price and that this served to fix a floor to retail prices. The OFT believed this to be anti-competitive and therefore there was a case to answer and referred BD to the Monopolies and Mergers Commission.

Source: Report of the Investigation into the Distribution of Portable Power Tools, Office of Fair Trading, 1989.

The balance of power, and how that power is exercised, influence many aspects of channel operations, including the following:

1. The specification and allocation of activities between different levels in the channel – who does what and when – which often centres on the allocation of the inventory function.

2. The type and relative scale of effort devoted to competing product lines – given that most intermediaries in consumer and industrial markets carry ranges from several manufacturers in each product area.

3. The methods used to accomplish the physical and (increasingly) the information flows – developments in information technology stress the need for some harmonisation in systems within the channel, but who chooses the standard?

4. The kinds of conflict that might emerge and the ways in which it could be resolved.

In striking the balance of power in industrial distribution Corey [11] comments:

> The more a distributor can get his customers to standardize, the larger the percentage of his supplier's business he represents, the greater his geographical coverage, clearly the more bargaining power he has. On the other side, the more the manufacturer represents of any one distributor's total gross margin dollars, the more its products are differentiated, have high brand identity, and require highly technical selling, the more active it is in creating user demand, then the greater the power of the manufacturer. Another factor is the use of multiple, competing channels systems as opposed to exclusive representation in each geographic market area. To be completely dependent on one distributor in a market area is to allow that distributor to control the user accounts in the area and the volume of business they represent as a bargaining lever.

Channel lifecycles

In the discussion of product lifecycles a distinction was made between product class and product form lifecycles. A similar distinction is warranted between total retailing and its particular forms. Bucklin [12] offers a fourfold classification of the stages through which retailing has historically developed:

1. Periodic markets – 'participants in these markets were principally local producers with excess supplies of foodstuff or homecrafts to trade' (p. 48).

2. Permanent markets – 'in addition to being open for business on a regular basis, usually boasted a variety of goods beyond local foodstuffs . . . they reflected the presence of an improved wholesale mechanism' (p. 48).

3. Fragmented markets – 'customers . . . turned with greater frequency to stores carrying a more limited range of goods in depth that allowed better display and product information, and more freedom of consumer choice . . . London listed 270 different retail trades by 1791' (p. 52).

4. Vertically integrated markets – 'in the largest cities the increasing density of pedestrian traffic was creating opportunities for enterprising merchants to sell unheard-of quantities of goods . . ... Somewhere between 1800 and 1850, the idea evolved in the United States to allocate responsibility for each group of merchandise to a trusted employee. With this first real delegation of management responsibility in retailing, the era of the department store was accompanied by other innovations in the sale of goods at retail. There was at once a greater perception of demand

Table 20.2 *Retail institution lifecycles*

Institutional form	Time required to saturation	Years
Department store	1865–1965	100
Variety store	1910–1960	50
Supermarket	1935–1965	30
Discount store	1955–1975	20
Fast food outlet	1960–1975	15
Home improvement centre	1965–1980	15
Furniture warehouse showroom	1970–1980	10
Catalogue showroom	1970–1980	10

Source: B.C. McCammon, 'Future shock and the practice of management', in P. Levine, *Attitude Research Bridges the Atlantic*. Chicago: American Marketing Association, 1975.

elasticities . . . and wider circulation of newspapers provided a natural medium for reaching wider markets' (p. 55).

This last stage has spawned many distinctive retailing forms, each with its own lifecycle. These cycles seem to be getting shorter as the pace of change quickens, as indicated in Table 20.2.

Presently, service channel lifecycles are particularly dynamic. New types of service are being demanded as consumers have more disposable income and more free time, and have become interested in undertaking for themselves what was previously provided as a complete product. More and novel kinds of service points are required, and with developing technology, especially in communications, infinitely distributed service points are becoming feasible for some types of service. Channels for entertainment, some kinds of education and hobbies are changing, and those for some financial services and various rental services could alter quite radically.

Brown has investigated cycles in the evolution of retailing and shown some strategic implications. Building upon Porter's generic strategies he typifies four broad retailing approaches: narrow range/cut price, e.g. Superdrug; wide variety/cut price, e.g. Littlewoods; wide variety/image-led, e.g. John Lewis, and narrow range/image-led, e.g. Next. Figure 20.3 shows these four.

Brown emphasises the dynamic nature of retailing and finds evidence of movement between these strategies. For example, Tesco has moved from cost focus to cost leadership and may now be moving to a more image-led strategy. Ratners has been moving in the opposite direction, Marks & Spencer has widened its range and Woolworth drastically reduced its range. This dynamism creates opportunities for others to occupy the vacated position. Environmental and competitive forces drive such changes. Developments in economic, social, legislative and technological conditions unfold new possibilities for alert retailers. Additionally [13]:

Retailing is a very combative and highly imitative industry and any successful innovation or exploitable differential advantage is quickly analysed, avoided and/or

	Price-led	Image-led
Wide variety	Cost leadership	Differentiation
Narrow range	Cost focus	Differentiation focus

Source: S. Brown, 'Retailing change: cycles and strategy', *Quarterly Review of Marketing,* vol. 13, no. 3, 1988.

Figure 20.3   *Retailing changes: cycles and strategy*

adopted (sometimes unwillingly) by rival retailing concerns. The successful move up market by Sainsbury and Tesco, for instance, has been belatedly followed by Asda, the Dee Corporation and Argyll (through the acquisition of Safeway).

Channel types

Channels are structured with varying degrees of centralised control. Consensus or conventional channels are the one extreme with no central control. The other extreme is where one organisation owns the operators at all stages in the channel network. The term vertical marketing systems (VMS) is applied to structures other than consensus channels to indicate that the system is to some extent vertically integrated.

Consensus channels
These channels are composed of sellers and autonomous intermediaries freely and independently associating to perform channel activities. They are typified by the small, independent retailer or wholesaler and by the small industrial distributor.

Administered VMS
If there is some agreement, tacit or overt, on the apportionment and management of activities within the channel then the system can be described as being 'administered'. The administrator can be at any level in the channel and typically would be a powerful manufacturer or retailer. To be effective this leadership needs to be acknowledged as such by other channel members, and this usually involves the offer of incentives. These might entail granting some concessions, such as exclusive distribution rights, the provision of services such as in accounting or stock control, or discounts and other preferential terms. Leadership might also be based on market power, such as a manufacturer of a brand leader which retailers believe they need to stock to be credible in that product field. Channel activities are much more planned and co-ordinated than in consensus channels, with the channel leader determining important facets of operations.

In the industrial market the small size of most distributors means that they often lack effective marketing. This can stimulate the formation of informal partnerships between suppliers and distributors, so that the channel becomes increasingly administered. Many distributors carry products from competing suppliers and to increase the attention given to their products manufacturers may offer inducements such as thorough marketing training and support and information management services. The relationship requires careful nurturing because, as Shipley and Prinja point out, the distributor's prime loyalty is given to customers rather than suppliers [14].

If a strong retailer leads the channel then the incentive to belong to the administered system might simply be the listing of a manufacturer as an approved supplier.

Contractual VMS

More concerted co-ordination is possible if there is a contractual agreement. Several variants have been developed:

1. The Co-operative Movement represents a very particular kind of contractual VMS. Owned by its customers the Co-op has its own supply organisation which even does some manufacturing and farming.

2. Voluntary associations between intermediaries are attempts by independent firms to gain some of the advantages enjoyed by multiple chains in terms of buying power, promotion of store image and increased professionalism in some aspects of management. Examples in groceries include Spar, VG and Wavy Line, and there are similar organisations in many other branches of retailing.

3. Voluntary associations in the service sector include hotel marketing consortia.

4. Franchise systems usually involve a more rigorous contractual arrangement and can cover a complete trading format, sometimes with strictly enforced requirements on operations and sourcing. During the 1980s there was rapid growth in the number of franchise arrangements in the United Kingdom [15].

Corporate VMS

Vertical integration with ownership of organisations at several levels in the channel network constitutes a corporate VMS. Manufacturers may establish their own retail outlets, such as brewers or oil companies. Retailers may own manufacturing, processing or packaging plants. Under common ownership, the entire operations of the channel can be regulated to minimise the possibility of suboptimisation at any particular level in the network.

All the above types are evident in product channels. They are also possible in service channels. But there are often additional considerations which shape service channels. For instance, in hotel marketing channels the intermediary could be a transit operator, a tour operator or a travel agent. The first two may or may not work through a travel agent, and the channel could be consensus or vertically integrated by one of these intermediaries. For other services the channel could be very simple, composed entirely of independents without intermediaries, or with some kind of franchise operation. Therefore, depending on the nature of the service, the channel could be highly complex or very simple, and so the problems in the organisation and control of channel activities are highly variable. With a wide range of channel options this also means that the possibilities for channel innovation offer great scope. Such possibilities are enhanced where the service has communication as an inherent part of its value to the buyer. Developments in communication technology allow quite novel channels to emerge, to co-ordinate previously disparate service points and to inspire the parallel provision of service in one channel when they may have been separately provided in several channels before.

Direct channels

In some industries direct sales to the customer, without intermediaries, have been the tradition, and that remains so in many industrial markets. In other industries, particularly in the consumer market, indirect sales with a profusion of intermediaries have come to dominate distribution systems. Yet, emphasising the dynamic nature of distribution channels, there has been recently considerable growth in the use of direct channels in the distribution of many different kinds of products and services. An example is in the distribution of PCs.

Direct marketing nowadays usually implies database marketing (discussed in Chapter 7). It may involve using telephone, direct mail or advertising to contact and to sell to potential customers. This may, or may not, be accompanied by an agency system and the widespread distribution of catalogues. In the United Kingdom catalogues tend to be associated with the established, general mail order houses, although there are many smaller operations. In the United States there is much greater use of catalogues, and that trend may be followed. Some US manufacturers, for example in sports equipment, employ their own catalogues, which are mailed to perhaps a million people.

One of the advantages of direct marketing is in the ability to control the contact with customers, because the media for the contact are owned or directed by the user. This also means that the direct marketer has a much enhanced ability to measure customer response. Direct marketing allows sophisticated planning of campaigns targeted at particular segments, and experienced companies build considerable knowledge of their target markets. They can undertake more controlled experiments than are usually possible in the marketplace, and may develop detailed insight into the variables affecting customer response.

A distinction is drawn between telesales and telemarketing. Fletcher [16] sees the latter as the more professional, with a planned and measured approach, and not subject to abuse, such as selling under the guise of market research, or 'sugging' as it has come to be known.

Distributing PCs: multi-brand and multi-channel

The market for PCs is very volatile and highly segmented. Business PC users, ranging from the small firm to the multinational, make up almost 60 per cent of the market. Home and hobby PC users represent another 30 per cent, with educational and technical users the remainder. In Europe IBM has about 20 per cent of the market, Compaq about 7 per cent and Olivetti 5 per cent. Ten other manufacturers have 2 per cent or 3 per cent each, and a host of small suppliers make up the balance.

A major trend has been the swift evolution of processor types from 8086 to 80586. Just as dramatic has been the fall in prices, as can be seen in any PC magazine. Along with these changes there has been considerable disturbance in the channels of distribution.

The main channel of distribution has been manufacturer to distributor to dealer to customer, but today there are many variants. Direct sales to customers via mail order now account for about a quarter of the market, through companies such as Dell, Elonex and Opus. There has also been a shift from advertising to direct mail. Sales through mass retailers, specialists and department stores are also increasing, as is the importance of office equipment stores.

Fragmentation of both the market and the distribution system has challenged the major manufacturers, and they have reacted with new strategies. For example, IBM now sells its PS/1 through Dixons and has launched the new low-cost Ambra brand, and introduced its Value-Point range. Compaq now has products at three levels of price and specification. And firms such as ICL, Digital and Olivetti have newly established direct selling operations.

Advertising, sponsorship and direct marketing have all increased along with these changes.

Source: Based partly on 'Survey on personal computers and software', *Financial Times*, 30 September 1992.

Another growth area has been in door-to-door selling, and in direct selling to a party of individuals, often employing part-time staff. This has spawned another term – multi-level selling – which is simply where salespeople not only sell, but also recruit additional salespeople.

Trends in retailing

The discussion now turns to trends in the structure, conduct and performance of major intermediaries – the retailers. Much of the discussion relates to grocery retailing, although the trends first evident in that field are subsequently mirrored amongst other kinds of retailer.

Retail marketing

During the 1970s and 1980s retail marketing became increasingly sophisticated. Walters [17] suggests that a fundamental change was:

the switch from merchandise category dominance to target marketing or the close and detailed identification of the shared needs and responses of a specific group of customers. The needs are translated in terms of merchandise, trading format and customer service. Examples of such an approach can be seen in the strategies of Next, Burton and Laura Ashley.

This shift from an operations orientation to a market orientation was encouraged by the substantial social change in recent decades. In addition to the major demographic changes, Walters refers particularly to the 'structural revolution' embracing much more relaxed attitudes to authority and the change in the role of the family and the use of the family as a reference group. He also notes the 'expressive revolution' whereby aspirations and expectations feature as important buying motives for large groups of consumers who use their purchasing behaviour to express their views of themselves. These changes created opportunities for new approaches to retail marketing, but required the ability both to interpret the changes and to respond appropriately.

Positioning strategies have been taken seriously by retailers, and are one expression of the response. Many large retailers now make explicit statements of their desired market positioning, based on extensive marketing research and with co-ordinated strategies for its implementation.

Over the years there have been additional important changes in the structure and form of competition. In most areas of retailing there has been a dramatic concentration resulting from the development of powerful national chains, together with massive increases in the size of outlets. Apart from anything else, this has stimulated the enhancement of retail marketing simply due to the employment of more professional managers. Furthermore, the form of competition has been becoming more complex. Price competition was once paramount. In the 1970s the quality of the merchandise range became just as important, and in the 1980s the quality of the shopping environment was added as another means of differentiation. Successful retailers now have to compete on price, quality and shopping environment, and a result has been escalation in the cost of competing. The stakes are higher, the issues more complex and hence the pressure for sophisticated marketing strategies.

New technology and retailing

In retailing, as in most industries, developments in information technology have had enormous impact. Computerised stock control has enabled thorough stock and in-store merchandising planning and the monitoring of activities across very large enterprises. EPoS (electronic point of sale) allows the rapid production of sales analyses and offers the possibility of co-ordinated control of both stocks and sales, and consequent efficiency in ordering routines. Increasingly, they might come to affect the relationship between manufacturer and retailer. One aspect of this concerns the added power that access to an invaluable information base bestows upon the retailer. On one level this could relate to more effective vendor appraisals by the retailer. On another level it relates to the wealth of data on prices and sales across the whole merchandise range carried by a large retailer, which might constitute a sizeable fraction of the national market. Potentially, the retailer could enhance the database by adding one or more shopping panels, perhaps in association with a market research firm. The retailer would then have an information service that could be offered to manufacturers and would gain standing from the added expertise derived from its unique market knowledge, and this would strengthen further its negotiating position.

Technological innovation in retailing also affects customers. Experiments are proceeding with new kinds of information displays in stores, ranging from the simple application of VCRs to menu-driven computer displays on prices, availability and location. Non-store applications include various forms of teleshopping. Usually these employ an interactive viewdata system such as Prestel with home deliveries from a normal store and payment in cash, by cheque or credit card. In the future there may be dedicated warehouses and electronic funds transfer. Walters [18] gives details of systems employed in Gateshead and London as well as some alternatives currently being developed. Presently the scope is very restricted because few homes have Prestel. McKay and Fletcher [19] have researched consumers' attitudes to teleshopping and conclude that:

> The positive attitude which prevails towards conventional store-shopping will indubitably act as an impediment to the future development and diffusion of teleshopping services ... The widespread diffusion of teleshopping will not be secured until either the majority of the population demonstrate a dislike for traditional store-shopping, or until teleshopping is improved well beyond its present system to gain a major relative advantage for specialised segments of the population.

Concentration and superstores

Clear trends emerge when the share of total grocery sales taken by the main channel types is investigated. The inexorable rise of the multiples has been the dominant feature, which has been at the expense of the Co-op and the independents. To predict how shares might change by 1996, Killen and Lees consulted a panel of 78 experts with the conclusion that the same trends will continue, and it is thought that the multiples will take over three-quarters of the grocery market (Table 20.3).

There have been two other noteworthy trends: a sharp reduction in the number of shops and a remarkable increase in the size of the average outlet. The multiples now conduct their business through little more than 4,000 stores, compared with the eleven thousand that they operated twenty years ago. The 1980s became the era of the superstore, defined as having over 25,000 square feet of selling space. In 1986 there were 432, and Killen and Lees predict up to 650 by 1996. Perspective can be added to those figures by the 1971 Nielsen survey which found only 73 grocery stores with a sales area over 10,000 square feet.

Table 20.3 *Grocery retailing by channel type*

| | % sales | | | | | |
	1950	1961	1971	1982	1986	1996
Multiples	20	27	44	65	71	77
Co-operatives	23	20	13	13	12	9
Independents	57	53	42	22	17	13

Sources: 1950 to 1982: *Nielsen Researcher.*
1986 and 1996: V. Killen and R. Lees, 'The future of grocery retailing in the UK', *Retail and Distribution Management*, July/Aug. 1988.
More detailed statistics on retailing can be found in *The Retail Pocket Book*. Oxford: NTC Publications.

Consensus channels – the independents

The independents have obviously had problems. They have suffered mostly from their small size of shop. They attract only minimum discounts from manufacturers and so charge relatively high prices. Moreover, they have been disadvantaged by the sheer professionalism of the multiples. All of the advances in retail management and merchandising have originated with multiples or the Co-op. Inefficient stock control, restricted consumer choice and even, sometimes, inadequate attention to hygiene have damaged the independents' competitive position. Additionally, their locations have been aligned more to historical population concentrations, and often they are now left in run-down inner-city areas.

One of their prime advantages also serves periodically as the focus of their demise. As much as a half of their trading can be on a credit basis, and without interest charges. This attracts business, but can cause a chronic cashflow problem. With small, sometimes localised, economic depressions, customers take extended credit. Suppliers become nervous and demand prompt payment, and this added pressure often forces the independent out of business, particularly since it may have been operating for several years on a very marginal basis.

Another problem has been the manufacturers' reactions. They have been faced with greatly increased distribution costs and have sought to increase their minimum case drop at each outlet. It is common for this to have been raised from five to ten cases in recent years. The independents sometimes find this too high a volume of one brand to merit direct delivery from the manufacturer. As Walters says [20]:

> Servicing the independents had become a problem. Not only was his future bleak but so too was that of the conventional wholesaler . . . However it was accepted both that the independent was unlikely to completely vanish and that the wholesaler continued to have a function in servicing the independents. Cash and carry permitted total systems costs to be reduced.

The move away from direct contact between manufacturer and small independent does itself raise new issues for the manufacturer. Cash-and-carry depots are operated on a self-service basis. This causes problems for manufacturers wishing to interest retailers in special promotional plans and in passing promotional materials through the channel. Product range is also restricted in these depots, and new product launches can be particularly difficult without intensive salesforce activity aimed at the cash-and-carry operators.

Competition, saturation and internationalisation

In the 1990s competition on a European scale poses particular problems for the multiples. Knox and Thompson argue that until now they have built market share at the expense of smaller competitors and that,

> This has cushioned them from the full forces of having to compete with each other whilst adapting to changing market conditions. In an industry that is characterised by openness, enforced by shareholders' requirements, and with very little protection from patents or technological edge, it has been all too easy to imitate successful strategies of peer organizations. Therefore, UK multiples have become increasingly similar since the real focus of differentiation has been between them and the smaller shops [21].

They go on to suggest that with the arrival of major continental competitors, such as Aldi from Germany and Netto from Denmark, the multiple grocery retailers should develop more distinctive identities, and perhaps focus on particular customer groups. But it is not only the continental food discounters that have been making an impact. There are also domestic operations in the United Kingdom: Food Giant (associated with Gateway), Kwik Save, Dales (Asda) and Lo-Cost (in the Safeway Group). And Costco, a large American food discounter, is now also in the United Kingdom. In 1993 food discounters took only 4 per cent of the British market, but in Germany they took 20 per cent.

Another problem in the 1990s is the impending saturation of superstores. Alexander and Morlock [22] surveyed retailers, manufacturers and analysts and found that most thought the saturation level for superstores was less than 900 in Great Britain, against the less than 700 in 1993. That saturation level was generally anticipated by the turn of the century. The most popular response strategy expected from the 'big five' superstore operators was to move increasingly to international operations in North America and Europe.

The multiples

Above all else, the multiples have size on their side. They can negotiate discounts of more than 10 per cent greater than the independents, and this has led many manufacturers to publish separate price lists for bulk delivery, and to grant additional promotional allowances. The power that the multiples have gained has been a great source of controversy, so much so that in 1981 the Monopolies Commission investigated discounts to retailers. At that time they ruled that the scale of discounts was not against the public interest. But manufacturers continue to worry about their relationship with the multiples. They point especially at the power derived by retailers from the threat to 'delist', that is not to stock, if sufficiently favourable terms are not forthcoming. An example of where this has occurred is in beer: both Bass and Whitbread have accepted delisting rather than agree the discounts demanded by multiples [23].

Growth in the share of total grocery trading taken by the multiples has been paralleled by concentration in the largest firms. In the early 1970s Sainsbury, Tesco and Asda took about 20 per cent of the grocery market between them. By the early 1990s the 'big five' (Sainsbury, Tesco, Safeway, Gateway and Asda) held well over a half of total grocery sales.

One of the characteristics of the multiples has been the development of their own labels which now account for about a third of their sales. Originally they were conceived as low-cost items and formed a major component in the multiples' strategies in price competition. They still perform that function but with quality improvements they increasingly feature as attractive merchandise in their own right. They represent one aspect of the broadening scope of retail marketing and, as Walters notes [24], have led the retailer:

> to extend either investment or its influence beyond the business itself. It is interesting to note how this has been achieved. Large retailers, e.g. Marks & Spencer and Sainsbury, have achieved all the benefits of backward vertical integration without the need for investment in the production facilities. By creating large sales volumes they have been able to achieve the product specification, production volumes and distribution service and coverage required.

Own labels, or retailer brands, present a problem for manufacturers: should they engage in this business? Mintel, a research firm, reported the reactions of fifteen major manufacturers, and four were adamant that they only made their own manufacturer's brands. Three of eleven supplying retailer own-labels said they were of lower quality, and three said they took this business so seriously that they employed special salesforces to ensure its continuity [25].

A trend in the early 1980s was for the introduction of generics – products with basic packaging and without emphasis upon brand names. All these had been withdrawn by the late 1980s. According to de Chernatony and McWilliam this was because consumers perceived them as simply an extension of own labels, but there was something of a metamorphosis with some classes of products that were not only unbranded but also unpackaged [26].

The Co-operative movement

Founded in Rochdale in 1844, the Co-op has developed into both a political movement and a fully integrated channel system. Its activities span banking, insurance, farming and over 100 factories, as well as wholesaling and retailing. The retail societies are owned by its members, who are any of its shoppers. In turn, the retail societies own the Co-operative Wholesale Society, which controls the manufacturing and farming activities.

In southern England the Co-op accounts for less than 10 per cent of grocery sales; in the North for 20 per cent or more. In many towns the retail societies offer services across the whole spectrum of retailing: bakeries, butchers, coal merchants, dairies, garages, undertakers, hairdressers, hardware stores, clothing stores, department stores, superstores, banks, hotels and insurance. It is possible to shop co-operatively for every consumer requirement. However, the movement has encountered considerable difficulties in the past twenty years.

The Co-op has an image problem. Most of its retail outlets were built before the Second World War, and many are small and dated in appearance. The quality of its products, especially in non-food lines, has not attracted above-average income groups, and the average age of its shoppers has been high. Moreover, the political nature of the movement has had some effect on management. Each retail society has a non-professional management committee, and career progression for professional managers in the past was partly conditioned by the political opinions they held. Aggressive attitudes to competition were not the hallmark of the movement.

Until 1960 there were almost 1,000 retail societies. Since then there have been amalgamations reducing this to below 100, with the largest twenty-five accounting for 85 per cent of the turnover. Along with this there has been considerable rationalisation involving the closure of 7,000 of the smaller grocery stores and the movement into superstores by some societies. The national organisations – the Co-operative Wholesale Society (CWS) and the Co-operative Retail Society (CRS) – have influenced these changes. But it may be indicative of some of the Co-op's difficulties that for more than ten years there has been talk of a merger between the CWS and the CRS, so far without a conclusion.

The voluntary chains

A defence mechanism employed by many independent grocers has been to collaborate both with other retailers and with wholesalers in a voluntary association. The three largest voluntary chains are Spar/Vivo, VG and Mace. The first two of these are as significant in most EU countries as in the United Kingdom. There are numerous smaller groupings, sometimes based on just one wholesaler.

Essentially the attraction for the retailer is the benefit from the bulk purchasing power of the chain. With the larger groups national television advertising campaigns also serve to announce promotions and establish a competitive image. In some cases a thorough retail management advisory service encourages modernisation in facilities and operations. Not every retailer is eligible for membership; there are often restrictions against the smallest outlets. One of the most successful areas for the voluntary chains has been in modern residential developments. New, small supermarkets in such situations are more likely to be part of a voluntary association than any other form of retailing.

Vertical integration is proceeding in this channel. Spar's wholesalers now own the majority of the largest retailers in the chain. Mergers between the chains may also continue to concentrate buying power.

Many chains discourage direct sales activity by manufacturers at the retail outlet. Furthermore, they restrict the numbers of brands held at their distribution depots. New product launches by other than the most firmly established manufacturers are therefore difficult in this channel. A further complication is that about a quarter of the stock held by retailers comes from cash-and-carry depots. Manufacturers are rightly concerned with attempting to understand and monitor trends in their distribution in this channel which is responsible for about a fifth of total grocery sales.

Implications of trends in retailing

Common factors in the developments in all four of the main channel types considered are a rationalisation in numbers of outlets, an increasing shop size, and mergers of operating units. The most apparent consequence of this has been a concentration of 'buying power' within the channels into a relatively small number of 'buying points': in 1975 344 retail organisations controlled 75 per cent of grocery turnover, and in 1980 275 organisations controlled 82 per cent. Trading practices adopted by the head offices of these few organisations are the most crucial influence upon the prospects of an individual brand and a critical force on manufacturers' profitability. The decision not to 'list' a new product by just the major multiples can destroy its future outlook. Many smaller multiples and the voluntary chains are impressed by the reactions of the big chains to new brands, and so a rejection by these is sometimes irreversible. The impact of this concentration, by reducing the initiative that some manufacturers have in promotional and distribution planning, has also already been noted.

This has led to the development of special salesforces for these 'key accounts'. The operation of these salesforces is quite different from that of the traditional grocery representative. They are selling to big organisations and are in effect 'industrial' sales representatives. They meet the same kinds of problem as seen in the earlier chapter on organisational buying behaviour. Defining DMU membership, understanding buying motives, analysing organisational structure and purchasing procedures are of paramount importance. Furthermore, these salesforces need contain only a relatively small number of people, naturally of high quality. A corollary is that the role of grocery salespersons calling at retail outlets is much more routine. The concern is with reordering and sales promotion.

The manufacturer–multiple relationship needs careful and consistent nurturing. But it can be overdone. Davidson [27] points out the case of one grocery company which, after a careful audit of its distribution costs, discovered that all its profits were earned from independents: they had given excessive over-riding discounts to the multiples and had devoted an unreasonably high proportion of salesforce time to them.

Another implication is the possibility that special research may be required to 'prove' to key buyers the value of a new product launch or a new promotional scheme. Professional presentation of research findings can strengthen credibility, although it can work in reverse. As the managements at multiple head offices are becoming more sophisticated in interpreting research, they can probe research methodology. An untutored salesperson can find such probing embarrassing and even damaging to a company's reputation. This might serve as another illustration of what White has called 'the skirmishing and sniping currently in vogue between the two groups' [28].

Retailers – indeed manufacturers – are essentially self-serving in their policies. Neither is interested in the survival of a particular channel form for its own sake. Both continually assess their commitment to a given arrangement, and both evolve new policies in new circumstances. Both take on or drop elements of the distribution activities, and sometimes such changes have drastic side-effects for other channel members and supporting agencies. Entire businesses can collapse after channel realignments. Companies that aim to survive need to be very alert to developments in retailing and possibly to be in the vanguard. 'New approaches to distribution are often easier to develop than superior products' [29].

Despite the trend to increase concentration in retailing, Porter [30] contends that in convenience goods the large manufacturers still hold the bulk of the power. He ascribes this to retail structure. For retailers to win higher margins, competition between them would have to be moderated. Yet it is very evident that concentration has led to more intensive retailer competition. The major multiple chains and the Co-operative societies are now very large advertisers – exceeding most individual brand advertising. Interestingly, Porter sees retailer advertising as leaving manufacturers as the net beneficiaries. However, in product categories with less differentiation the situation may be the reverse. In the absence of strong brand images the retailers would probably hold the bargaining strength.

Trade marketing

Concentration is particularly marked in groceries and pubs, and is becoming an issue in DIY and some consumer durable retailing. One response of manufacturers was noted above with the development of 'key accounts' salesforces. Another kind of response in the 1980s was the introduction of trade marketing managers in some manufacturing companies. Parts of the Allied-

Lyons Group have adopted this response to develop and maintain relationships because [31]:

> we depend to a great degree upon our strong links with our immediate customers – the supermarkets and the retail outlets – for we are manufacturers and processors with no direct interface with the ultimate consumer. Conversely, with growing demand, supermarkets have more shelf-space to fill and we intend that they should increasingly rely upon us to provide the goods to fill them. We grow together – our policy is interdependence.

Practice varies. Some trade marketing managers are sales managers with a new title; some are effectively trade sales promotion managers, co-ordinating various incentive schemes for the trade; and some have much fuller responsibilities for developing a trade marketing mix, covering all aspects of marketing activity directed at trade channels. This might include sales calls, advertising to other channel members as well as co-operative advertising with them, pricing and discount structures, merchandising plans, various advisory services for distributors and sales promotions to the trade. The planning role of such trade marketing managers has some similarities, and some possible duplication, with that of product managers. The implementation role of these managers raises other kinds of issues for the marketing organisation because it might cut across the responsibilities of sales, advertising and sales promotion managers. Resolution of these issues hinges upon the development of clear role definitions.

Changes in channel structure have led some manufacturers to change their organisational structure to match new circumstances. A main theme in this chapter has been the dynamic nature of channels and it can be expected that the dynamism will remain a key feature. The implication is that manufacturers' marketing organisation will continue to evolve to meet future changes in channel arrangements.

Summary

Marketing channels bridge the gap between production and consumption by moving products to buyers or by moving buyers to service points. Frequently they employ middlemen, which can be beneficial both to buyers and sellers. Different kinds of activity are required on product and service channels. Communication activities may be similar but different problems are encountered in adjusting supply and demand and in transportation.

In complex channels the need to organise and to co-ordinate the activities leads to special problems in channel member relationships. Conflict and power were seen to be aspects of channel conduct which have significant impact.

Channel types were reviewed and particular note taken of developments in retailing, including the trend to increased concentration in the largest multiple chains.

Questions for review and discussion

1. Contrast the adjustments between supply and demand in product and service channels. 'Inventories don't talk back' and so does that make the product channel adjustment easier to accomplish?

2. The activities listed in Table 20.1 may be needed at several stages in the channel and could be undertaken by several intermediaries. What will influence the allocation of these activities to channel members?

3. If channel members are all self-serving, then how can their activities be co-ordinated?

4. It has been suggested that channel innovation may sometimes be easier than product innovation. What kinds of channel innovation might a financial services company consider?

5. Both Bass and Whitbread have accepted de-listing rather than agree to the discounts demanded by retailers. What factors would they have evaluated before reaching this decision?

6. What innovations in channel design might allow Black & Decker to maintain its channel leadership?

References

1. Stasch, S. 1972. *Systems Analysis for Marketing Planning.* Glenview, Ill.: Scott Foresman.
2. Lovelock, C.H. 1984. *Services Marketing,* Englewood Cliffs, NJ: Prentice Hall Inc., p. 4.
3. Christopher, M., Walters, D. and Gattorna, J. 1979. *Distribution Planning and Control.* Farnborough: Gower, p. 37.
4. Christopher, M. 1972, see Chapter 4 in Christopher, M. and Wills, G. (eds), *Marketing Logistics and Distribution Planning.* London: Allen & Unwin.
5. Bucklin, L.P. 1972. *Competition and Evolution in the Distributive Trades.* Englewood Cliffs, NJ: Prentice Hall Inc., p. 254.
6. Thorpe, D. and Shepherd, P. M. 1977. 'Some aspects of economies of scale in food retailing', Research Report No. 26, Manchester Business School.
7. Brown, A.J. 1983. 'Channel management', in Baker, M.J., *Marketing: Theory and Practice.* London: Macmillan, p. 251.
8. Sturdivant, F.D. and Granbois, D.L. 1973. 'Channel interaction: an institutional behavioral view', in Walker, B.J. and Haynes, J.B. (eds), *Marketing Channels and Institutions.* New York: Grid Inc., p. 165.
9. Stern, L.W. and El-Ansary, A.I. 1988. *Marketing Channels,* 3rd edn. Englewood Cliffs, NJ: Prentice Hall Inc., ch. 6.

10. McCammon, B.C. 1973. 'Alternative explanations of institutional change and channel evolution', in Walker, B.J. and Haynes, J.B. (eds), *Marketing Channels and Institutions*. New York: Grid Inc., p. 83.

11. Corey, E.R. 1985. 'The role of information and communication technology in industrial distribution', in Buzzell, R.D., *Marketing in an Electronic Age*. Boston, Mass.: Harvard Business School Press, ch. 2.

12. Bucklin, L.P. 1972. *Competition and Evolution in the Distributive Trades*. Englewood Cliffs, NJ: Prentice Hall Inc., ch. 2.

13. Brown, S. 1988. 'Retailing change: cycles and strategy', *Quarterly Review of Marketing*, vol. 13, no. 3.

14. Shipley, D. and Prinja, S. 1988. 'The services and supplier choice influences of industrial distributors', *Service Industries Journal*, vol. 8, no. 2.

15. Ayling, D. 1988. 'Franchising in the UK', *Quarterly Review of Marketing*, vol. 13, no. 4.

16. Fletcher, K. 1990. *Marketing Management and Information Technology*. Hemel Hempstead: Prentice Hall International, p. 305.

17. Walters, D. 1988. *Strategic Retailing Management*. Hemel Hempstead: Prentice Hall International, p. 10.

18. Ibid., p. 268.

19. McKay, J. and Fletcher, K. 1988. 'Consumer attitudes towards teleshopping', *Quarterly Review of Marketing*, vol. 13, no. 3.

20. Walters, D. 1976. *Futures for Physical Distribution in the Food Industry*. Farnborough: Saxon House.

21. Knox, S. and Thompson, K. 1990. 'The UK grocery retail market and 1992: a structural analysis', *Proceedings of the 1990 Annual Conference of Marketing Education Group*, Oxford, pp. 648–83.

22. Alexander, N. and Morlock, S. 1992. 'Saturation and internationalization', *International Journal of Retail & Distribution Management*, vol. 20, no. 3.

23. Gibbs, S. 1984. 'Bass hits at supermarket muscle', *Guardian*, 7 December.

24. Walters. 1988. op. cit., p. 18.

25. *Financial Times*, 29 January 1976, p. 15.

26. de Chernatony, L. and McWilliam, G. 1988. 'Clarifying the difference between manufacturers' brands and distributors' brands', *Quarterly Review of Marketing*, vol. 13, no. 4.

27. Davidson, J.H. 1975. *Offensive Marketing*. Harmondsworth: Penguin Books, pp. 236 and 135.

28. White, R. 1976. *Consumer Product Development*. Harmondsworth: Penguin Books, p. 94.

29. Davidson, op. cit.

30. Porter, M.E. 1976. *Interbrand Choice, Strategy and Bilateral Market Power*. Cambridge, Mass.: Harvard University Press.

31. Allied-Lyons, *Report and Accounts* 1988.

Chapter 21

Channel and distribution planning

Two British marketing professors put the distribution function into perspective when they say:

> It is sometimes suggested that the role of customer service is to provide 'time and place utility' in the transfer of goods and services between buyer and seller. Put another way, there is no value in a product or service until it is in the hands of the customer or consumer. [1]

> while availability is a necessary condition for consumption, it is by no means a sufficient one and we are not seeking to re-establish the now largely discredited Say's Law, which holds that supply creates its own demand. [2]

In making the product or service available, plans are made in two main areas. First, the channel has to be designed to match the firm's understanding of the buyer's requirement, bearing in mind what is possible and profitable. Second, plans are needed to accomplish the inherent physical movement of product to buyer or buyer to service point. This chapter addresses the main issues in assembling these plans.

Channel design

Three sets of factors have to be evaluated simultaneously in designing channels. They are shown in Figure 21.1. All three sets interact, and so the design process is necessarily iterative. For example, product factors influence product positioning decisions, and the positioning decision is tested against the product factors. Perhaps a desired positioning requires that some product characteristic is changed, and the feasibility of that change feeds back to the positioning decision, which itself might be adjusted in the light of that feasibility. Similarly, environmental factors can affect the other two. For example, aspects of buyer behaviour inevitably influence product and service characteristics, and so shape the viability of given product positioning strategies.

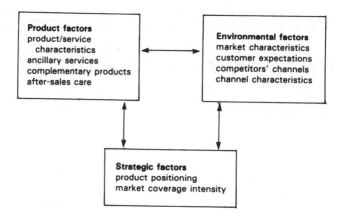

Figure 21.1   *Influences on channel design*

Strategic factors

Product positioning is so fundamental to marketing strategy that it naturally occurs as a basic element in channel design. Its influence is related to how the positioning is defined. If the positioning emphasised a product or service feature then the channel chosen would have to support and perhaps enhance that position. Claims such as 'instant access', 'guaranteed freshness', 'the full service company', 'the one with the widest product line', 'top technical back-up' or 'buy with confidence – lifetime care warranty', all impose strictures on channel options if they are to be credible. If the positioning relates to particular users or use occasions then again the channel choice needs to be consonant. If the position taken relies on competitive positioning, head-on or side-step, it must be influenced by the channel choices of competitors. With head-on competitive positioning it would follow that channel design mirrors that of the competitors. With side-step competitive positioning a deliberate decision to employ distinctive channels might be more supportive.

Intensity of market coverage intended by the firm will be one of the outcomes of the product positioning strategy. This intensity is dependent upon the decision made about product or service availability to buyers. Intensive coverage implies numerous outlets or service points. Selective coverage implies far fewer, and this might be taken as far as implying an exclusive franchise for one outlet or service point in an area or region. To reinforce a high quality image the firm may decide to restrict availability. Rolls-Royce or BMW cars cannot be bought at just any car showroom. Ercol, G-Plan or Nathan furniture is only available at restricted outlets, though frequently together. Many expensive kinds of clothing or jewellery are similarly restricted. The opposite approach is apparent for goods and services with a high purchase frequency which people wish to buy with minimum effort, such as groceries or petrol or fast food. An important consideration in this decision is the trade-off between market exposure and control over the channel. Wide availability in numerous outlets reduces the seller's control, but restricted availability limits potential sales.

Environmental factors

Market characteristics will inform and constrain channel design. Numbers and dispersion of potential buyers provide the backcloth to decisions on availability. Large, widely dispersed markets present quite different possibilities to those in small, concentrated markets. The former may point to the need for complex, indirect channels and the latter to more direct means. But market characteristics do not include only numbers of buyers; purchase behaviour can also influence channel choice. Customers may expect to be able to buy certain products in certain channels, and they plan their shopping trips on those expectations. Further, they may restrict their search activity to those channels. Their shopping behaviour for a particular product category may also be conditioned by their shopping for other products. Consumers may wish to minimise the number of retail outlets visited and to cluster several product purchases at one place. If there were some regularity in this clustering, then analysis of the typical outlets for those associated product classes could affect the channel decision.

Purchase size and frequency should also be considered. This will be related to consumer willingness to hold stocks, and to their consumption levels. Products with a weekly repurchase cycle provide enormous distribution problems and require vast channel arrangements. These would be eased if customers were willing to take a six months' supply of (say) breakfast cereal at a time. They would be simpler still if customers were willing to travel fifty miles to collect their breakfast cereal. But naturally, customers value convenience in the availability of such products.

Customers' expectations about product availability can vary from one country to another and even regionally within the same country. In the United Kingdom many people expect a daily home delivery of milk and newspapers, and some expect a similar service for bread. This is not the case elsewhere. The high cost of such a system is apparently acceptable to British consumers, although it seems a matter of historical accident that it has endured in this country. Departures from established custom are possible, but they can encounter considerable consumer resistance. This has been demonstrated in recent years with the experiments with one-trip, non-returnable milk containers, which had to be withdrawn from the experimental areas after consumer action groups collected all the containers and deposited them at the Town Hall.

Competitors' channel arrangements will also have to be investigated. It may be necessary to ensure similar market coverage by employing the same channels. But as mentioned earlier, strategic advantage may be gained by being different. Both product positioning and market coverage decisions embody the impact of competitors' channel strategies.

Channel characteristics refer to actual and latent channels. Performance of existing channels needs to be evaluated. They may give insufficient or inappropriate market coverage and, if so, the firm would have to investigate the possibility of its own channel innovation. This could entail making the product or service available through its own outlets, some franchising agreement or introducing novel mechanisms for transferring product to buyer or buyer to service point.

Product factors

Product or service characteristics condition channel design. For instance, perishable products require particular treatment, and the channel necessarily needs the facilities to handle the product in an acceptable manner. This may mean adequate equipment in transit and at the final outlet, but just who owns and operates this equipment can be contentious. Some firms insist on manufacturer control, but that can be expensive.

Some products require special services at the point of sale. Shoe manufacturers may make a point of stressing fitting services; optical products firms may emphasise the need for qualified advice; fast food companies or various rental firms may underline the need for consistent quality. In all these cases, mechanisms have to be devised to ensure that the service is available and appropriate. Sometimes existing channels may not be able to cope, and new channels might be considered or the possibility of changing current channel behaviour investigated. This could imply training schemes for personnel in the channel, or special financial inducements for participation in a revitalised channel. How this is accomplished will be very dependent upon the existing power structure.

The availability of complementary products or services can offer added values to buyers, or be part of their established expectations. In either case this could become another important influence upon channel design.

Cost factors

Channel design options will have varying cost implications and so some analysis will be necessary. Estimates will be required for the cost imposed by each alternative. This might proceed by estimating the costs in a given channel for various sales volumes. In a direct channel this could relate to the number of sales representatives needed for several levels of sales volume. With indirect channels the middlemen costs would have to be estimated. The firm would assess the costs implied by discounts allowed, any special incentives to be given and any allowances made for equipment or sales promotion. The analysis in a single channel, single market segment network would be fairly straightforward, assuming the treatment of items such as inventory charges pose no problem. However, multiple channel, multiple market segments networks can induce complex analyses, and would probably be dependent on a host of judgements. These would include the likelihood of 'cannibalisation' between channels; in a three-channel system the analysis of the costs imposed by any two rests on assumptions about the market coverage of those two, and how much of the third channel's coverage they would take.

In assessing channel acceptability it may also be necessary to include a number of additional factors, many derived from consideration of the factors considered earlier in this chapter. They could be combined into a listing of criteria, and subjective evaluations made about the actual or likely performance of alternative channels. This might be with each criterion being given a differential weight to reflect its importance to the firm at that time [3]. Or, as discussed in new product screening, some kind of series of hurdles may be operated, where each channel alternative is assessed against one criterion and those that pass move on to be assessed against a further criterion, and so it continues until all criteria have been employed.

Distribution planning

This discussion will concentrate on some of the major issues in product/service availability, adjustments between production and consumption, warehouse and service point location, and transportation planning. Throughout, the concern will be the potential impact that decisions in these areas might have on costs and revenues.

Planning product/service availability

Channel output is in making the product or service available for exchange. There are two aspects to this availability: time and place. Demand will be more or less responsive to availability, and a form of customer response function can be envisaged. More correctly, there may be many kinds of response function according to the nature of the sensitivity. A durable product may be in a circumstance where time was the dominant issue in availability. A reasonably simple response function may apply, such as that in Figure 21.2(a). An S-shaped curve is plotted to indicate a responsive market with quicker availability. Of course, the curve might be differently specified and sales might respond to a greater or lesser extent to variations in availability time. For some non-durable products, and for services, place could be much more significant than time availability. Take fast food as an example. It is either in the place that the buyer demands, or no sale is made. In this case the response function might be drawn as in Figure 21.2(b) with the independent variable being number of service points. More complexity is introduced if demand is both time and place dependent. Figure 21.2(c) supposes that the product/service can be made available at a few or many locations, and that it can be made available at a frequent, moderate or infrequent number of times in a period. Expected sales levels can be deduced by specifying the time/place availability.

Estimating the nature of these response functions will be a trying exercise.

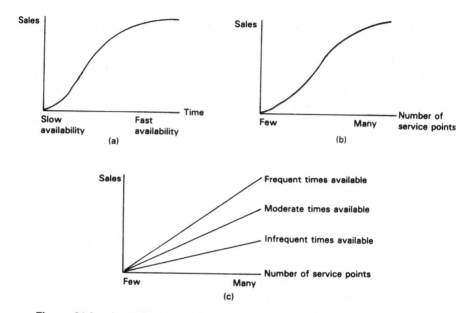

Figure 21.2 *Availability response functions. (a) Time availability. (b) Place availability. (c) Time and place availability*

Service operations have a major advantage in this respect. Due to their widespread distribution of small units, experimentation is a viable option. Learning from competitors' experience could also be considered, and customer feelings captured from survey or more qualitative data.

Buyer reactions to non-availability at the required time will influence the decision on number of service points and speed of delivery. Some buyers may be prepared to wait, some will go elsewhere and some may never return to the market. With fast-moving consumer goods continuous availability in outlets is essential. Nielsen [4] surveyed buyers and found that if a brand was out of stock

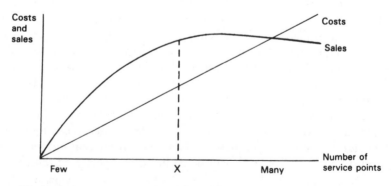

Figure 21.3 *Cost and sales with varied number of service points*

then 25 per cent would buy an alternative, 26 per cent would return to the same store and try again, and 39 per cent would look for the same brand at another outlet.

Increasing availability carries the implication of increasing costs. Same-day delivery of a product anywhere in the country may involve large numbers of depots, each with large stocks and each transporting small loads to outlets. Numerous service points nationwide obviously dictate high costs. The costs associated with each level of availability should be estimated and compared with the expected sales given a specified availability. This is depicted in Figure 21.3 where it is assumed that the market is most sensitive to number of service points. The same procedure could be followed for the other situations shown in Figure 21.2.

Marginal analysis reveals that the optimum number of service points is not necessarily where they are at a maximum. In Figure 21.3 the number at level X is the optimum, since higher levels impose more costs than increases in revenue. But that assumes a maximum profit objective; if sales revenue or market share objectives were being pursued then higher levels might be offered.

Total distribution costs

Decisions about any single element in the distribution system cannot be taken in isolation. The lowest cost transportation option may not be the best choice because of its effects on other elements such as inventory levels required, number of warehouses needed or the order processing involved. The same applies to all elements. It is the lowest cost mix that needs to be evaluated. The total systems cost is the relevant unit of study, and not simply individual cost elements. In addressing this point Davis [5] has said:

> Analysis of the total system requires assumptions to be made about subsystems. For example, the use of advanced warehouse technology is to some extent dependent upon the size of unit. Fewer, larger units may enable more efficient methods to be used in operating the warehouse. Delivery fleet size is dependent upon order processing policy. If orders are accepted for delivery within a short lead time and on an ad hoc basis, a larger delivery fleet will be required and it will be poorly utilised. Customer service is dependent upon the number of units. More units may enable a shorter customer service time simply because of proximity. This may increase sales and thus lead to greater profits.

Arriving at total system cost must then give due regard to the huge number of possible trade-offs within and between the distribution activities. Some further examples of the kinds of trade-off are the following:

1. Transportation–inventory trade-off – fast, expensive transport may increase transport cost but reduce inventory holding costs.

2. Distribution centre–transportation trade-off – more distribution centres will increase warehousing costs but reduce transportation costs, although lower local transport costs may be partly offset by higher trunk transport costs because smaller loads were being sent long distance.

3. Order processing–inventory trade-off – a more sophisticated, expensive order processing system may mean a lower stock requirement.

4. Distribution centre–materials handling trade-off – more distribution centres may lower many costs but smaller warehouses may mean higher handling costs because only simple technologies can be employed.

Thus the nature and scale of the interactions between the activities need to be fully appreciated in the context of total cost analysis of the system. These interactions may lead to unexpected consequences. Ballou [6] has reported a simulation exercise on the reduction of time delays. He found that a reduction in order transmission time could result in higher inventory levels and increased out-of-stock incidence. Tinkering with subsystems, without recognition of total system effects, might then lead to poorer overall performance.

Distribution centres

Decisions on the number and location of warehouses have effects upon the total costs of distribution and upon customer service levels. Figure 21.4 illustrates the possible behaviour of costs with different numbers of distribution depots. Increasing the number of distribution centres considerably reduces transport costs, but increases the cost of the other main activities. The lowest cost number of centres is therefore where these opposing trends are balanced. But the lowest cost number of centres is not necessarily the most desirable number; the effect of increasing the number of distribution points on sales needs also to be considered.

It is likely that availability to customers will be improved by adding more warehouses. Nearness to the customer will speed delivery. However, service levels may not move in proportion to numbers in depots. If availability was to be measured by proportion of orders despatched within 24 hours of receipt, then the following may have been estimated:

Number of depots	2	4	6	8
% orders filled within 24 hours	30	50	80	90

Earlier it was seen how availability level might affect sales, and so there is now some indication of how numbers of depots will affect both costs and sales. The number of distribution centres chosen will reflect the company's concern with sales revenues and profits.

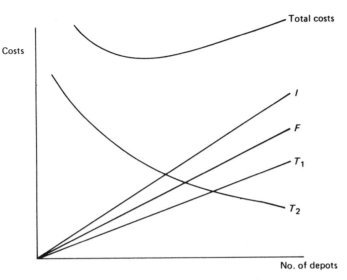

I = inventory costs; F = fixed warehousing costs; T_1 = local transport costs; T_2 = trunk transport costs

Source: C. Watson-Gandy, 'Warehouse-depot location', in M. Christopher and G. Wills, (eds), *Marketing Logistics and Distribution Planning,* London: Allen & Unwin, 1972, p. 214.

Figure 21.4   *Costs and distribution depots*

Inventory decisions

High stock levels assure good customer service but imply high costs to finance the stock. Low stock levels require less financing, but lose sales through period-ically being out of stock. Once again a balance needs to be struck between two opposing considerations.

Two variables cause most concern: customer order quantity and order frequency. To examine the problem let us first assume a controlled, predictable environment where these two are constant. Say all 100 customers place an order for ten units every 100 days, and that they each place their orders in strict rota-tion so that the total demand is for ten units every day. If production can be planned to deliver ten units each day to the warehouse, there is obviously no inventory problem at all. No stocks are needed, no sales are lost from being out of stock, and the only cost is order processing.

By varying just one element we can see how complications creep in. Assume that order quantity is not fixed; customers still order in a strict time sequence, but can ask for anywhere between 1 and 50 units. In any ten-day period demands can therefore total between 10 and 500 units. The company now needs a policy to handle that variability. It could hold a minimum of 50 units in stock at all times; or it could hold some arbitrary level below that, and ignore the lost sales owing to stockout, or it could seek to analyse the nature of the costs imposed by differing order quantities.

Economic order quantity models [7] treat the two principal cost components: that of order processing and stock holding. These are likely to vary with order size (Figure 21.5). Order size O_1 is optimum from the supplier's viewpoint. It would be in his interests to induce customers to place orders of that size. This may be accomplished by simply asking customers to conform, although it may be necessary to offer some discounts for conformity. The basic model can again be used to assess the impact of different discount structures on total costs.

Manufacturers would also be interested in determining a safety stock level that would limit the effects of stockout situations. Statistical analysis of past demand patterns would, hopefully, confirm a normal distribution, in which case confidence limits consistent with the desired customer service level can be set and the safety stock deduced. But which confidence level should one choose? Marginal analysis may assist the choice. Extra safety stocks impose cost increments, yet they save the cost of lost sales (Figure 21.6). Higher levels of safety stock reduce the probability of losing sales from stockout. An approximation of this curve might be derived from our earlier analysis of customer service response functions. It is not likely to be very accurate but it could serve to focus discussion on the relevant variables and assess the broad effect of changes in safety stock levels.

In Figure 21.6 stock level S_1 is optimum because up to that point additions to safety stock add more savings than costs; that is, with higher stock levels fewer customer orders are lost – or put another way, revenue increases because orders are filled. Beyond S_1 very few extra orders are filled because most will have been served from stock levels already on hand. Marginal revenue is therefore below marginal cost, and safety stocks can be reduced.

Because of the impressionistic nature of the marginal savings curve the resultant safety stock figure should be interpreted as indicating a range of stock levels. This range could then be used to select the statistical confidence level. Alternatively, a more detailed study of costs

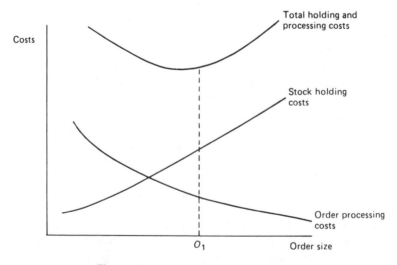

Figure 21.5 *Economic order quantity*

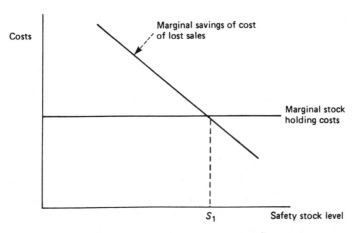

Figure 21.6 *Marginal analysis of safety stock*

of lost sales owing to stockout may be made [8]. This would specify the probabilities and costs of the customer (1) waiting, (2) placing this order elsewhere, and (3) placing all his future business elsewhere. With the possibility of stockouts another consideration is the feasibility of expediting. Herron [9] suggests that using faster transport, working overtime, or product substitution might be an alternative to high stock levels.

The manufacturer is also likely to be affected by stock levels held in the total channel system. Intermediaries at several levels in the channel will probably adopt different policies regarding stocking. Retailers will hold less stock than wholesalers and manufacturers. The effects of this are demonstrated in Table 21.1. Each channel member will react to changes in demand level by stocking enough of both to cover the demand variation and to bring up the average inventory level.

Table 21.1 *Channel stock variations*

	Period 1	Period 2
Consumer demand	+10%	−9.09%
Retailers' 6 weeks' stock	+10 + (6/52 × 10)% = +11.15%	−9.09 + (6/52 × 9.09)% = −10.14%
Wholesalers' 12 weeks' stock	+11.15 + (12/52 × 11.15)% = +13.72%	−10.14 + (12/52 × 10.14)% = −12.48%
Manufacturer 10 weeks' stock	+13.72 + (10/52 × 13.72)% = +16.35%	−12.48 + (10/52 × 12.48)% = −14.88%

Source: M. Guirdham, *Marketing: The management of distribution channels*. Oxford: Pergamon, 1972, p. 190.

Table 21.2 *Multiple shops out of stock of Babycham*

				% out of stock					
Aug.-Sept. '74	Oct.-Nov. '74	Dec.-Jan. '74 '75	Aug.-Sept. '75	Oct.-Nov. '75	Dec.-Jan. '75 '76	Aug.-Sept. '76	Oct.-Nov. '76	Dec.-Jan. '76 '77
16	4	28	11	6	28	8	6	21

Source: Nielsen Researcher.

Thus a 10 per cent increase in demand means that retailers add 10 per cent to their stocks plus another 1.15 per cent (1/52 of the 10 per cent for every week of stock they wish to carry). In this example the manufacturer's warehouse will hold more than a 16 per cent increase in stock level, but by period 2 will hold 15 per cent less. Changes at the consumer level are therefore magnified by stocking policies within the channel. It is evident that the manufacturer would need to understand the dynamics of the channel stocking problem and the stock policies at each level.

To illustrate further, let us consider Babycham. Table 21.2 shows that a high proportion of multiple shops were out of stock of this brand of drink around every Christmas. Special promotional activity directed at the channels did not seem to alter stocking in the stores. Deeper analysis found the problem to lie with the movement of stock through those multiple groups who used their own depots. Greater understanding of stocking policies within these groups could assist Babycham's pre-Christmas sales.

Smoothing demand

Inventory decisions are an attempt to adjust production to consumption. For some products and most services the problem is the other way around. Demand has to be adjusted to the real-time, fixed supply. Gross fluctuations in demand have to be smoothed. Methods for dealing with this problem include the following:

1. Differential pricing – varying prices by time and place, such as railways, theatres, take-away or eat-in, seasonal pricing.

2. Time availability – making the service available only at specified times; for example, drinks only available if food is purchased.

3. Place availability – making the service available only at specified places, such as advisory services being placed away from the point of sale.

4. 'Qualifying' customers – only allowing some buyers to take the service; for example, only those dressed a certain way, or those of a particular age group.

5. Adding/subtracting services – putting on special services when the demand wanes, and taking off services when demand is high, such as extra attention in personal services or 'no frills' when there is pressure.

6. Projecting several images – attempting to distinguish alternative images for the service at different times or places, such as restaurants or hotels.

7. Holding in channel – for some services it may be feasible to hold buyers in the channel; naturally this possibility is limited, but with imagination it could add values for the buyer – by taking the scenic route.

Transportation

Costs and service levels are the essential considerations for decision-making in this expensive part of the distribution system. The several transportation modes have different cost structures for various volumes, and different delivery speeds. A cost comparison must be the starting point in transportation planning, and this is illustrated in Figure 21.7. If costs were the sole concern, then the decision about transportation mode could be made by specifying the volume to be moved. At low volumes, air or road could be employed; with medium volumes, road or rail; and with higher volumes, combinations of warehouses and rail or even branch plants. But other factors may alter the choice. A higher cost mode may be chosen because of speed of delivery, e.g. in perishable products. Road may be preferred to rail for quite high volumes because it may be more reliable, though more costly.

For grocery distribution there appears to be a trend towards the use of contract road carriers [10]. For manufacturers without a back-load availability a

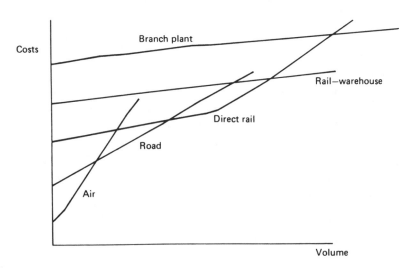

Source: E.W. Smykay, *Physical Distribution Management*, 3rd edn, London: Macmillan, 1973, p. 297.

Figure 21.7 *Transportation costs*

company's own vehicle fleet can be extremely expensive. Contract carriers can therefore be attractive, especially if their performance is continuously assessed and their rates are performance related. A development that is expected to make an increasing impact is the use of consolidation services. These are stockholding and delivery services operated to serve a wide range of manufacturers. They are another demonstration of the dynamics of the distribution system, since they have taken on some of the activities formally undertaken by wholesalers [11].

Distribution cost analysis

Controlled distribution requires periodic cost analyses. All aspects of the distribution system – individually and in total – merit investigation. Studies of comparative channel costs and profitability may be particularly significant. They may reveal unprofitable channels and may be suggestive of ways in which profitability could be improved.

Channel cost analyses may be fairly rudimentary or excessively detailed. The degree of detail necessary is related to the purpose of the analysis: if it is to obtain a broad impression, then little detail will be required; if it is suspected that several costly activities are having a differential effect in several channels, then more detail will be required. But data overload is very possible in this area. Imagine a twenty-brand company selling to twenty markets through five channels. It probably has the data processing system to produce channel cost analyses on a monthly basis, and it probably has a sophisticated enough accounting system to analyse fifty cost categories; in which case it will produce a great volume of printout. Management summaries may be available, but inertia often seems to take over, and endless paper continues to circulate. The simple example in Table 21.3 illustrates the aim of the exercise. From the data it is clear that many questions would be asked about the relative contributions from the four channels. The procedure in this instance is to separate out fixed costs as those that would be incurred irrespective of channel used. The variable costs are calculated in a

Table 21.3 *Transportation costs*

	Total	Channel 1	Channel 2	Channel 3	Channel 4
Sales	1,500	750	250	300	200
Variable cost	1,050	400	100	300	250
Contribution	450	350	150	0	−50
Fixed cost	300				
Net income	150				

Source: R.M.S. Wilson, *Management Controls in Marketing*. London: Heinemann, 1973, p. 161.

simple way by assuming constant unit variable cost across all channels. This may be acceptable in some cases, although a more rigorous treatment may be preferable if it is known that the activities undertaken in each channel differ.

In more complex cases channel costs will need to be computed by first determining functional costs, and then apportioning these to channels. Functional costs are an allocation of costs to type of activity, e.g. advertising, selling, handling and order processing. The apportionment of these costs to channels is on the basis of some reasonable criteria. For example, selling costs may be apportioned according to number of sales visits per channel type. Sevin [12] gives a listing of possible methods of allocating functional costs to products, territories and account-size classes, as well as a wide-ranging treatment of analytical techniques that may be employed in studies of marketing productivity [13].

Summary

Channel design was seen to be influenced by three sets of factors: strategic, environmental and product. Strategic considerations include product positioning decisions and the desired level of market coverage intensity. Environmental factors include market, customer, competitor and channel characteristics. Product factors, such as the need for a particular treatment in the channel, naturally also constrain channel design. Cost must necessarily be an important consideration, although evaluations involving several alternatives, each composed of complex channel arrangements, can be complicated.

In deciding channel structure a key influence will be buyer responsiveness to changes in product or service availability. The difficulties in estimating this response were discussed and response functions for time and place availability investigated.

More detailed problems in deciding the number of distributions points and in transportation were also reviewed, and the adjustment of supply and demand in product and service channels outlined.

Questions for review and discussion

1. 'Product positioning strategy is the overriding influence on channel design.' Do you agree?

2. 'Market coverage intensity is the outcome of the channel design process rather than a constraint on channel options.' Is that so?

3. How might the firm derive some insight into the nature of the response functions in Figure 21.2?

4. Find examples for each of the demand smoothing strategies mentioned in this chapter.

5. Why should total distribution costs be studied in addition to the costs associated with particular activities?

6. Is the decision about the number of depots or warehouses essentially concerned with cost minimisation?

7. Assume that several segments each had a different order quantity pattern and that a manufacturer determined optimum order sizes for each, and then fixed a separate discount structure for each of these segments. Examine the problems.

8. Is the 'cost of the lost sales' an impossible concept to employ realistically?

References

1. Christopher, M. 1987. 'Distribution and customer service', in Baker, M.J., *The Marketing Book*. London: Heinemann, ch. 17.
2. Baker, M.J. 1985. *Marketing Strategy and Management*. Basingstoke: Macmillan, p. 294.
3. Stern, L.W. and El-Ansary, A.I. 1988. *Marketing Channels*, 3rd edn. Englewood Cliffs, NJ: Prentice Hall Inc., p. 214.
4. *Consumer Reactions to Out-of-stock*. Oxford: A.C. Nielsen Co. Ltd.
5. Davis, J. 1977. 'Distribution systems analysis', *International Journal of Physical Distribution*, vol. 8, no. 2.
6. Ballou, R.H. 1976. 'Time delay effects in computerized physical distribution systems', *International Journal of Physical Distribution*, vol. 6, no. 4.
7. Smykay, E.W. 1973. *Physical Distribution Management*, 3rd edn. London: Macmillan, p. 220. Howard, K. 1972. 'Inventory control', in Christopher, M. and Wills, G. (eds), *Marketing Logistics and Distribution Planning*. London: Allen & Unwin. Taff, C.A. 1978. *Management of Physical Distribution and Transportation*. Homewood, Ill.: Irwin, p. 165.
8. Smykay, E.W., ibid.
9. Herron, D.P. 1979. 'Managing physical distribution for profit', *Harvard Business Review*. May/June.
10. Walters, C.H. 1976. *Futures for Physical Distribution in the Food Industry*. Farnborough: Saxon House, p. 26.
11. Harvey, J. 1982. 'Trends in distribution', *Campaign*, 11 June.
12. Sevin, C.H. 1965. *Marketing Productivity Analysis*. New York: McGraw-Hill, pp. 13–15.
13. Detailed examples of distribution cost analyses can be found in Stern and El-Ansary, op. cit., p. 506.

Chapter 22

Price planning

More has been written about price than any other other marketing mix variable. Economists have been writing about it for almost two centuries, accountants probably even longer, and it has featured in marketing texts since the 1900s. Given both this weighty attention and its importance, 'the pricing function is performed in a surprisingly haphazard way' [1]. Not that firms' pricing decisions are wrong, but to be right the procedures used in setting them may sometimes involve too much time and energy. As Hague says after his detailed empirical study, 'we have seen that in some cases, because information was not carefully analysed, or even used correctly, more time was taken and more argument caused in pricing decisions than was necessary' [2].

Part of the problem is the nature of the information relevant to pricing problems. Not that there is a sparsity of information or ideas; there is a wealthy legacy of theory and practice. Despite this legacy there are no axioms in pricing.

On the demand side, classic concepts from economics can be explained elegantly and offer rigorous, theoretical generalisations. But making them operational is essentially synthetic – demand curves do not exist until someone draws them. Fixing the co-ordinates requires data, and if they are not to be assumed then that implies data collection. That in turn requires a range of judgements about the respondents, the nature of the entity which has value (the bundle of product attributes), how that entity is to be described, the questions to be asked, the ways that responses can be made and the types of analysis to be performed.

On the supply side, accounting practice can be just as synthetic with a host of judgements about 'relevant' costs, about whether relatively fixed elements should be apportioned and recovered, and about transfer prices within a large corporation. Accountants also make decisions, or hold assumptions, about the points along the value chain at which a cost analysis is to be undertaken. For historical reasons manufacturing costs have received paramount consideration and elaborate procedures have been developed to understand and control such costs. But for many organisations other costs incurred at other points are more significant. For example, some marketing costs may not be adequately treated.

This plethora of judgements may be set within a highly complex decision structure. Multiple objectives, multiple alternative actions and consequences, over long and short terms, plead for simplification. That simplification can result in trite prescriptions and 'formulae' approaches, which could reduce price planning to a clerical operation. The purpose of this chapter is to examine these problems by considering objectives in pricing, strategic and marketing parameters, customer and competitive reactions, and some special situations in pricing.

The complexities in understanding firms' pricing behaviour have been studied by Diamantopoulos, who comments as follows [3]:

> empirical studies . . . show quite conclusively that pricing in the real world is much more complex than any theoretical perspective suggests. Firms operate within a multifaceted and variable pricing environment, have multidimensional objective functions and employ a variety of pricing methods. Their pricing objectives are often imperfectly formulated and rationalized, their pricing methods sometimes crude and their view of the pricing environment reflects decision-makers' perceptions as well as objective characteristics. Of particular significance is the fact that the typical firm usually faces a variety of potentially distinct environments for its various product markets and has a different set of pricing objectives and/or pricing methods for each; none of the established theoretical perspectives on pricing appears to explicitly recognize and incorporate this fact into its conceptual scheme.

Objectives in pricing

Setting objectives for the price plan is complicated by an obvious distinguishing characteristic of prices: they are prominent in any profit calculation. Assumptions about prices feature widely in business planning spreadsheets and the assumed consequences for profitability are readily obtained. This means that price planning is a highly visible, sensitive management concern.

Just as marketing goals are subobjectives of corporate goals, so too are pricing goals subobjectives of marketing goals, along with the other marketing mix elements. Great confusion is possible because of the interdependence of the mix. For example, the company may have a sales volume goal as one of its marketing objectives. Would it then be reasonable for it to have a sales objective for each mix element? Clearly not. It was argued in the chapters on advertising that the total set for a particular marketing function should be one over which that function can exercise influence – exclusive influence, if possible. So advertising is set communication goals, and the salesforce could be similarly treated. Distribution could be given a customer service level goal and product plans might be aimed at developing customer product perceptions. But what should be the objectives of price strategy?

The objectives need to be the price means of achieving the marketing goal. If that goal is sales and price is the dominant mix element, then some specified sales goal would seem appropriate. In other cases, where price is but a subsidiary

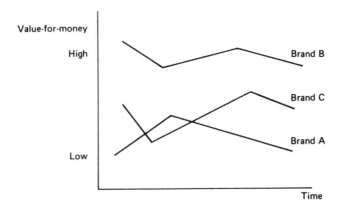

Figure 22.1   *Perceived value*

component, then sales constitute an inappropriate pricing objective. This implies that all goals influenced by sales levels, such as market share, profits and profitability, are also inappropriate. When this problem was met in advertising some intervening variable was sought which could be assumed to influence the higher-order goal – and communication variables were thus focused upon. Price perceptions by channel members and ultimate consumers may supply a useful indicator of the contribution from any given alternative pricing strategy.

Once perceptual factors are accepted as one area of goals for price plans the problem is that of determining the proper variables. A first approach would be to seek customer ratings of 'value', i.e. the brand, and its rivals, might be rated by a sample of consumers on a scale from high to low 'value-for-money'. Repeat monitoring, which would obviously be necessary in times of high inflation, might yield curves as in Figure 22.1.

Such studies could be used in goal-setting in either absolute or relative terms. Brand A's aim could be to achieve and maintain a specified rating on value-for-money, or it could be to match the rating of one or more competitors. It might be done in global terms for a whole market, or for particular segments. Use of this procedure does make the major assumption that such perceptions are closely related to the overall marketing objectives – just as attitudinal variables used as advertising goals make similar assumptions. Validation of this assumption is never likely to be complete, although rough indications of its validity may be derived from regression exercises setting these scale measurements against higher-order variables.

Closer analysis of value-for-money may take note of what Ölander has called 'purchase attractiveness' [4]. Both price and product attractiveness may affect the attractiveness of a purchase, and it would first be necessary to estimate any possible interactions between these. In some cases, high price may be a positive attribute, increasing product attractiveness. Quality judgements by a sample of consumers with and without price information, and with and without brand identifications,

Figure 22.2 *Purchase attractiveness as a function of price*

may be able to discern this interaction. The example illustrated in Figure 22.2 assumes that there is no such interplay. A firm's pricing objective may be fixed in terms of a desired level of consumer evaluation of the attractiveness of the purchase offer. The assumption is made that there is a relationship between this and the higher-order goals. A complication is that the position of the curve relating offer attractiveness to price is likely to be affected by product attractiveness. Changes in product attractiveness due to promotional or product feature changes could push that curve up or down. Specification of a desired level of offer attractiveness is therefore conditional upon a level of product attractiveness.

Such a procedure is contentious. Making it operational as a matter of routine requires a significant amount of data collection and sophisticated analysis. For our current purposes it does, however, serve one invaluable role: it demonstrates just how complex pricing can be, and it illustrates the kinds of variables to which researchers are giving attention.

Perceived value analysis might also be performed by obtaining customer ratings of product attributes for competitive products. This could be similar to the studies reported on attitude research in the chapter on consumer psychology. That is to list key attributes, find the relative importance attached to each by buyers and how they evaluate each product on each attribute. Summing the scores on each attribute for each product gives an overall score, and the differences between products is an indication of the scope for price adjustments. Those with high evaluations might be supposed to offer possibilities for increasing prices, and the opposite would be the case for those with lower evaluations.

More immediately operational pricing objectives identified by Winkler [5] distinguish between short-term tactical objectives and those in the longer run. For the short term he suggests that objectives could be set against the following:

Meeting existing competition
Discouraging new competition
Securing key accounts
Recovering cash rapidly

Attracting new customers, distributors, agents
Using spare capacity
Trimming off overfull demand

In the longer run he suggests objectives could be set against:

Return on sales; return on assets
Stabilising price and margin relationships
Realising target market share
Strategic pricing in different markets
Keeping competition out of key markets

Shipley [6] has surveyed company practice and found that a target profit or return on capital employed was the main objective set. Some notion of equity between the firm and its customers was important to many, and pricing to meet the competition and to achieve a target sales revenue were also widely used objectives.

Strategic and marketing parameters

Price plans are made within the context of strategic choices declared by the organisation. They are constrained by other marketing mix plans and are influenced heavily by the set of internal and external environments. Germane features of these environments are costs, customers and competitors.

Strategic issues

As with all marketing mix variables broad corporate and marketing strategy frames pricing decisions. This will have explicit impact by outlining how competitive superiority is to be achieved, which itself follows critical evaluations of corporate resources and competence. In so doing, this places limits on the way that price plans will contribute. Decisions on relative quality to be offered and on the desired competitive positioning will be important limiting factors. For example, the decision to offer relative high quality, and to stress the quality of product features and services in the positioning, does not result in a price plan, but it would be one pointer to a range of possible prices.

Interwoven with these issues will be assessments and decisions on competitive strategy. Depending upon whether the firm was a leader in the industry, was playing a niche strategy, attacking, defending or entering a new industry, then price plans might be expected to play a different role. A leading firm might be preoccupied with its direct rivals. Their price plans could be a dominant influence and so would be monitored closely. Broad bands of acceptable competitive prices might be derived and added to the insights offered by consideration of positioning strategy. A niche strategist would always be emphasising the basics of the niche position, which might or might not have price as a major weapon. Some attack and defence strategies could rely upon keen pricing and so elevate the significance of price plans. New entry strategies could offer a range of pricing possibilities following an appraisal of lifecycles, competitors and customer responsiveness.

Marketing mix considerations

Channels and pricing

A complication in pricing is that it is not just the ultimate customer who needs to be considered. As Oxenfeldt [7] says:

> a price-setter must develop a price that is acceptable to several different parties that are affected by the price decision. Chief among these parties are colleagues, rivals, resellers, government and ultimate customers, all of whom have conflicting goals.

Reactions to the manufacturer's price plan by channel members will be of particular importance. They will have their own views about the margins that should be allowed within the manufacturer's recommended retail price. Moreover, they will have their own views about ultimate consumer price perceptions. Their willingness to stock and the level of promotional support they will offer will depend upon these two factors (Figure 22.3). Retailers will obviously be most willing to stock and give support to brands in cell 1, and least willing for brands in cell 4. Cells 2 and 3 provide interesting situations. The retailer may still wish to stock, but give little support to, such brands. Cell 2 has implications for the longer-term survival of the channel arrangement: all members need a reasonable return on capital. Cell 3 may have implications for the manufacturer's own profitability.

Manufacturers are not just pricing to, they are also pricing through, their marketing channels. The extent of the discipline or control they might exercise over final prices to end users is highly variable. In the personal computer market both Apple and Commodore attempted to maintain resale prices and withheld supplies from discount stores. The Office of Fair Trading persuaded them that

	Retailers' evaluation of their margins	
	Good	Bad
Good	1	2
Bad	3	4

Retailers' evaluations of consumer price perception of the brand

Figure 22.3   *Retailers' evaluations of margins and of consumer price perception*

this was not in the public interest. In another case, Ford for a long time maintained prices on their replacement body parts by restricting provision to authorised dealers. They argued that independents could not guarantee quality, and that the massive costs in the original designs needed to be recouped [8]. Some licensing agreement has been encouraged by the Office of Fair Trading.

Advertising and pricing

Price planning may take an active or more passive role in the marketing mix. If it is passive then there will be little promotion, but with an active posture prices may be a key element of advertising. The main platform for advertising copy may be price announcements, or direct price comparisons. A more subtle approach uses value for money as its basis, and justifies premium prices by reference to superior quality. But this again reintroduces the perceptual factors mentioned earlier, and emphasises the importance of understanding the price–quality relationship.

Pricing and the salesforce

The salesforce will be eager to obtain maximum latitude in its negotiations with buyers. Representatives will argue that the ability to offer 'better' prices will make all the difference in their performance. This will run counter to the widely held view that price policy should be established at the highest levels in the firm. Key influences on the balance between these perspectives will be the nature of the market and the relative seniority and experience of the salesforce, as well as how informed and knowledgeable the representatives are about financial matters.

Approaches to pricing

Surveys have shown repeatedly that most firms use some form of cost-based pricing, albeit with some flexibility to adjust for particular market circumstances [9]. The simplest approach is cost-plus which, given an assumption about overhead allocation, is straightforward and can lead to convenient price administration. An alternative cost-based approach employs break-even analysis to explore the profit implications of various price levels. These approaches are criticised because they hardly take note of the strategic significance of pricing and largely ignore the fundamental influence of both customers and competitors. In some limited circumstances, marginal cost pricing may be more appropriate, bearing in mind that at some time all costs need to be recovered.

A cost-based approach that could involve strategic issues is based upon an analysis of the experience effect. This posits that unit costs fall systematically with increased volumes, so that with a doubling of production volumes unit costs are some fraction of their previous level. Pricing with an experience curve (which relates unit costs to accumulated volume) anticipates the future unit costs with higher volumes, and prices down relative to that level. There have been some cases reported of firms following rigorously such an approach, but its applicability is limited by the assumption that unit cost should be the overwhelming influence on pricing, as well as by problems in the estimation and projection of the experience curve.

If a demand schedule could be estimated then the volumes sold at different prices could be added to a break-even model. The cost and revenue implications of several alternative prices could be depicted and a profit-maximising price determined. Such a demand-oriented approach is theoretically appealing but does require the estimation of a demand curve as well as assuming that the goal is profit-maximisation. Some impression of price elasticity of demand may be derived from the techniques discussed in the next section. Whether or not assumptions about the demand schedule are made explicit, the basic notion that sales levels will be more or less sensitive to price must be quite crucial, and it will inform the pricing decision.

Customers and pricing plans

The ultimate success or failure of a pricing plan depends upon how the customer perceives and reacts to it. Measures of both attitudinal and behavioural variables may yield useful guides to the ways in which customers have responded in the past and may respond to price changes in the future. Research in this area attempts to gauge consumer cognitions, affections, intentions and actions in relation to price. Methodology includes surveys, analyses of historical data, laboratory and field experiments. Surveys may try to define cognition, affection and intention. Historical data may furnish insight into actions, and experiments may be addressed to any, or all, of the attitudinal and behavioural responses.

Surveys

Recall studies may be employed to determine customer knowledge of prices. One exercise [10] found a generally high price consciousness for grocery products. For over 80 per cent of 5,300 purchases, respondents were able to give a price, and in 75 per cent of these cases it was the correct one. But there was a wide variance between product groups: 79 per cent of tea prices but only 36 per cent of the flour prices were correct.

Consumers' cognition of price can of course be distorted or confused. There may be a difference between perceived and actual prices, but the action required by the manufacturer in this case is not always obvious. Surveys would first have to determine the consequences of the discrepancy. If perceived prices were higher than actual, one would generally expect benefits from a realignment – except where a reduction in perceived price was taken by consumers as a reduction in perceived quality. The quality/price interaction would first have to be established.

Plotting consumer-perceived price differentials between competing brands, and between substitute product categories, may be supposed to be dynamic. In practice it will not be continuously so; it is unrealistic to expect consumers to have either perfect information or the inclination to make continuous reassessments. But that may be too dogmatic: some housewives may very well make weekly evaluations of key product categories. The manufacturer would be well served by knowing if his brand was in one of those key product categories, and knowing something of the frequency with which various segments revise their perception of price differentials.

Surveys may also assist in the search for understanding of consumer affection towards price, that is, the relative attractiveness of the purchase offer. Such a variable was used in the discussion of pricing objectives. Ölander's work quoted there was based upon laboratory experiment. In survey form, the aim may be to explore the connection between price differential and attractiveness of purchase offer, and the probability of switching between brands and product categories at different levels of price differential.

Finally, surveys could be used to measure purchase intentions. Stout [11] reports a procedure where respondents selected a 'purchase' from a collection of price-marked photographs of brands in a product class. Prices of test brands were varied between groups of respondents. The realism of such 'choices' is, of course, highly dubious. After all, if such research were reliable, there would be little need to do other price studies.

Analyses of historical data

Careful assessments of past consumer behaviour are useful because they might give some general feel for market responsiveness to price, and because they may

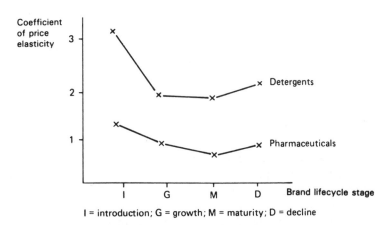

Source: H. Simon, 'Dynamics of price elasticity and brand life cycles: an empirical study', *Journal of Marketing Research*, vol. 26, no. 4, 1979.

Figure 22.4 *Price elasticity and brand lifecycles*

Table 22.1   *Price differentials for butter and margarine*

| | Average retail price per lb (pence) | | | | |
| | Oct.-Mar. | Apr.-Sept. | Oct.-Mar. | Apr.-Sept. | Oct.-Mar. |
	'74 '75	'75	'75 '76	'76	'76 '77
Butter	26	29	33	42	52
Margarine	26	25	25	25	28
Sales shares:					
Butter	70%	69%	67%	63%	57%
Margarine	30%	31%	33%	37%	43%

Source: 'Research in action', *Nielsen Researcher*, 1977.

show something of recent trends in reactions to relative price changes. The data should also be easily available. Regression analysis may provide estimates of the relative importance of price in explaining changes in past sales levels. Coefficients of price elasticity may also be estimated, albeit rather crudely.

But some rigorous attempts to estimate coefficients of price elasticity have been reported. A recent example is by Simon, who studied several brands of detergents and pharmaceuticals and was especially interested in price responsiveness through the brand lifecycle. He found detergents to be more responsive to price changes at all phases of the lifecycle, but as can be seen in Figure 22.4, the coefficient was lower in the growth phase and maturity, and began to increase again in the decline phase.

Monitoring price differentials through time can also be valuable. For example, from 1973 to 1975 the price of butter relative to margarine declined, and butter sales increased in those years by 5, 11 and 10 per cent respectively while sales of margarine fell by 14, 11 and 13 per cent. However, from 1975 to 1977 the position reversed, as can be seen in Table 22.1.

Studies of historic price differentials could lead to investigations of cross-elasticity. Estimates may be made of the extent to which price increases for a substitute result in demand changes. This may be within or between product classes.

Laboratory experiments

On the face of it, simulated shopping trips may appear to be so artificial as to be meaningless. A healthy scepticism about the exact methodology employed is a prerequisite to any interpretation of the results of such experiments. Simple acceptance of data generated, without probing how they were derived, is dangerous.

A method of undertaking such experiments is reported by Pessemier [12]. Respondents were asked to indicate which, if any, was their favourite brand of toothpaste, and were then given lists of brands with their preferred brand offered at several higher and lower prices, while other brands' prices remained constant.

They were then told that they 'needed' to buy toothpaste, and were given a budget constraint (they were told they had $1.75). 'Choices' made were recorded and simulated demand curves derived. Sawyer *et al.* offer a more recent investigation of laboratory experiments in pricing [13].

Marbeau [14] suggests that tests can be monadic (singular) or competitive (with other brands) and can be direct, asking open questions on respondents' attitude to price thresholds or through exposure to a sequence of rising prices, or indirect with respondents exposed to price levels in a randomised order. He illustrates the competitive/direct approach in a simulated shop exercise. Respondents were questioned about a new brand and were shown a shelf of all main competitive brands. All were priced at the same level and the 'consumers' were asked to make 'purchases'. The chosen product was increased in price and a further round of purchases made. The sequence continued until all respondents had stopped buying any of the products.

Field experiments

Adding more realism to an experiment is expensive. Rather than make forced, artificial choices, subjects make voluntary, real choices. This may be in a test market, or in a more controlled shopping environment. Examples of the latter are specially run stores, which may even be owned by the research contractor, or the 'mini-test' shopping panels discussed in Chapter 14.

Experimental control over the marketing mix variables, and over the groups of subjects being studied, is a major problem. Field experiments always give rise to suspicion over the degree to which the results from changes in one variable (say, price) are caused by that change and by no other. Managers are often more willing to accept 'loose' experimental discipline in this respect than researchers, and uneasy compromises between the two perspectives obviously pollute the purity of the experiment. Managers may also be more willing to make bold, almost rash, inferences. This is understandable in that decisions have to be made, but it can lead as easily to disastrous consequences as it can to inspired initiatives. Companies appear to be inordinately variable in their approach to balancing these perspectives. It may well be rooted in the management style and the personalities of the executives.

Customer response to price changes is sometimes obscure because the changes may communicate ambiguous messages to consumers. Any of the following perceptions may be consequent on a price change [15]:

1. The quality of the product has been changed.

2. The product is about to be superseded by another.

3. This price change is a precursor to another change in the same direction.

4. The price change indicates a change in customer responses to the product.

5. The manufacturer of the product is in financial difficulty.

It would be costly and tiresome to sample customer feelings on these points every time a price change was noted. They should at least be borne in mind though, and for crucial price decisions some assessment may be merited. Unstructured depth interviews or more formal scaling procedures could be used to explore perceptions of price changes.

Competitors and pricing plans

Firms worry about competitive reaction to their pricing plans, and about their own reaction to changes in competitors' pricing plans. Implicit in such worries is the proper identification of rivals. Oxenfeldt points out that in oligopolistic markets the degree of rivalry between major suppliers is best viewed with a dyadic model, that is, studying the rivalry between each pair (dyad) in the total set of rivals. In a four-brand market, the six dyads could present entirely different situations, with lesser and greater rivalry. Table 22.2 represents some hypothetical possibilities of customers' assessments of price differentials between four brands. Customer 1 will consider only brand A, B or D. He is prepared to pay $2.00 more for A than B, $1.00 more for A than D and $1.00 more for D than B. If it were assumed that all these brands had identical prices, then those bought by these customers would be:

Customer	1	2	3	4	5	6	7
Brand	A	any	C	B	D	C	D

Table 22.2   *Customers' assessments of price differentials*

Brands	Reactions of 7 customers (or segments)						
	1	2	3	4	5	6	7
A vs B	+2	0	0	*	−2	−1	+1
A vs C	*	0	−1	*	−2	−2	0
A vs D	+1	0	*	*	0	0	−1
B vs C	*	0	−1	0	0	−1	+1
B vs D	−1	0	*	+1	−2	−1	0
C vs D	*	0	*	−1	−2	+2	+2

Notes:
An asterisk indicates that the customer would not purchase from one member of the pair.
A plus or minus sign indicates preference for the first or second member of a pair, respectively.
A number is the dollar amount of price differential that the customer will pay.
Source: A.R. Oxenfeldt, *Pricing Strategies*. Chicago: American Management Association, 1975, p. 109. Copyright © 1975 by AMACOM, a division of American Management Associations, New York. Reprinted by permission of the publisher. All rights reserved.

A $1.00 increase in the price of brand A would have a 50–50 chance of switching customer 1 to D. A $1.00 increase in the price of C could cause switching to A or B and a $1.00 increase in D's price might cause switching to A or B – all this *ceteris paribus*.

Data sources for such a study would have to be surveys or experiments, and the exercise would be improved if probability statements were incorporated regarding the likelihood of switching as a result of various levels of price changes. These data are likely to be somewhat impressionistic, but at least would yield some interesting comparisons between customers' and management's perceptions of rivalry, and would be rich in hypotheses about the form of that rivalry.

Competitive price plans have been divided into initiatory or response strategies [16]. Kelly suggests that initiatory strategies include precedence (being the first to take the action) and pre-emption (taking action that excludes rivals). In oligopoly, firms use precedence to catch rivals off-guard, and hope to establish benefits before retaliation. Pre-emption is the attempt to make it difficult for rivals to follow, e.g. by dropping price to such an extent as to make competitors feel incapable of meeting it. Response strategies include imitation and exploitation. Imitation can be the identical matching of the move, or the attempt to dominate by even bigger price cuts. Exploitation aims at developing a contrasting strategy, implying the imitator was wrong, e.g. a price reduction responding to a price increase.

A crucial factor in competitive reactions to price changes is how the signals are read. Millman warns that the signals may be misinterpreted and, for instance, a short-term tactical price cut may be seen by competitors as the opening of a long-term price war. He comments that [17]:

> In the heat of the moment, it is the marketing manager's job to assess the rationality of the situation. A useful starting point is to ascertain who is the instigator of price cutting and its nature. Is it the market leader, a new entrant, or an existing supplier with aspirations of increasing market share? Can a pattern of price reductions be discerned – perhaps related to a specific product, product line or across the full range of products? This is the stage when clear thinking is needed. Distorted information is received from many sources and the true scale of price cutting can be blown out of proportion.

Accurate market intelligence and perceptive interpretation are essential, but to what extent will the 'fog of war' take over?

Given the wide range of variables and competitive stances possible in decisions about pricing plans it is useful to picture the essential elements in the form of a decision tree. Figure 22.5 gives an illustration of an analysis using this technique.

The aim of the exercise in this figure is to examine potential consequences of alternative price strategies followed by a company and its competitor. Simplifications include the assumption of only one competitor, and the assumption that only two alternative prices can be considered by each firm. Our company can choose to sell at a price of 89 or 79. If we choose 89, then our competitor can respond with either price. Probability estimates are made and show a 70 per cent

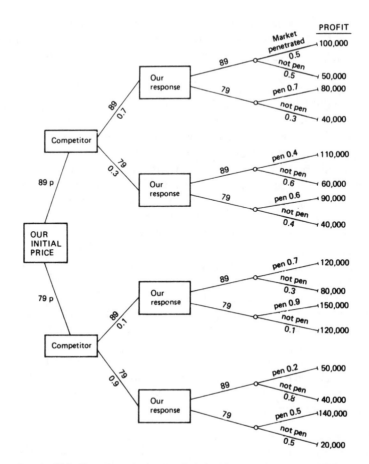

Source: W. R. King, Quantitative Analysis for Marketing, New York, McGraw-Hill, 1967. Copyright © McGraw-Hill, 1967.

Strategy alternatives

Strategy	Initial price	Response price if competitor 89	Response price if competitor 79	Expected payout
1	89	89	89	76,500
2	89	89	79	73,500
3	89	79	89	60,600
4	89	79	79	66,600
5	79	89	89	48,000
6	79	89	79	82,800
7	79	79	89	52,500
8	79	79	79	86,700

Example of calculation of expected payout

Strategy 8: our price always 79

(1)	(0.9 × 0.5 of 20,000)	=	9,000
(2)	(0.9 × 0.5 of 140,000)	=	63,000
(3)	(0.1 × 0.9 of 150,000)	=	13,500
(4)	(0.1 × 0.1 of 120,000)	=	1,200
			86,700

Figure 22.5   Pricing decision tree

chance that he will charge 89. Once more, we can respond with a price of 79 or 89. If we choose 89, that can lead to the market being either 'penetrated' or 'not penetrated'. A 50–50 chance is thought likely in this illustration. If the market is penetrated, then that has an implication for sales levels, and some rough profit calculations can be made. It will be seen that £100,000 profit would be expected in this case. All other possible paths through the tree are worked, probability statements assigned, and profit estimates made.

Eight strategy alternatives are offered and the expected payment calculated. ⌐ tegy 8 yields the highest payout and would be the one chosen. The payout ⌐alculations show that in adopting this strategy our price is always 79. If our competitor charges 79 and we respond with 79, there are two possible consequences. Similarly there are two possible consequences if our competitor's price is 89 and our response 79.

Competitive bidding

Competitive bidding is a characteristic of some markets. Models applied in this area take explicit note of competitors' possible positions. They attempt to estimate the expected profits from alternative bid prices. This amount is determined from the probability of a given bid price being successful multiplied by the profit to be derived in that instance. The major variable is the bid prices of competitors. This may be estimated from past bidding behaviour, but in the following example it is arrived at subjectively.

Palda gives the illustration of firm A bidding to supply an item, and the best estimates that it can make of the competitors' likely bids are given in the first two columns of Table 22.3. A's marginal costs are £4.3 million and so we can derive the unit profits in the fourth column. The probability of A winning the contract ⌐alculated from the second column. That is, at a bid price below £4.4 million A has a better than 90 per cent chance of winning; with a bid of £4.45 million A has a 61 per cent chance of winning (there is a 39 per cent chance that another bid will be below that level). Expected profit is profit times probability of winning. Assuming that A wishes to maximise expected profit, then he would bid £4.45 million.

Table 22.3 *Competitive bidding*

Bids by competition £m	Probability of lowest bid in this range	A's bid £m	A's profit £m	Probability of winning award	Expected profit £m
Over 5.0	0.07	5.1	0.8	Below 0.07	Below 0.06
4.7–5.0	0.18	4.8	0.5	0.07	0.04
4.5–4.7	0.36	4.6	0.3	0.25	0.08
4.4–4.5	0.29	4.45	0.15	0.61	0.09
Below 4.4	0.10	4.35	0.05	Over 0.90	Over 0.05

Source: K.S. Palda, *Pricing Decisions and Marketing Policy*. Englewood Cliffs, NJ: Prentice Hall Inc., 1971.

Pricing new products

In discussing new product pricing it should be remembered that there are three levels of analysis in lifecycle theory: product class, product form and brand. We shall first consider new product pricing at the product class level, i.e. for the first brand into the market.

Dean [18] sees the policy choice on a continuum, with the extremes of what he has called a 'skimming' price and a 'penetration' price. The former would lead to a relatively high price being set, and the latter to a relatively low price.

Circumstances in which skimming would be attractive are typified by fairly inelastic demand responsiveness to price changes – at least in the early launch phase. With more elastic demand at later stages, prices can be lowered, so that the market is being effectively segmented through time according to price sensitivity. Dean also feels that if little is known about cost and demand elasticity then higher prices are safer.

Penetration prices are more appropriate from the outset if there is a high price elasticity of demand, and if substantial scale economies can be readily realised. If competitive entrants are soon anticipated in the market, a penetration price might also be beneficial. But a major variable in the success of a product launch will be sufficient production to the desired quality. In high technology industries this can prove troublesome because of the very nature of the innovation. According to a report in the *Sunday Times* [19], IBM experienced difficulties in 1979 when they launched their very advanced 4300 series of machines with a penetration price – which was a policy contrary to their normal practice. The problem was that the revolutionary silicon chips around which the series was conceived could not initially be produced in the requisite volume, added to which the first machines were small, although larger versions were planned for subsequent introduction. Many customers reacted by leasing rather than buying the new products, lest they become quickly obsolete. This aggravated IBM's cash flow to such an extent that in late 1979 it arranged external funding of well over $1,000 million.

Many new product decisions are made with new brands that may be entering growing or mature markets where competitive brands are already established. This concerns the introductory phase of the brand lifecycle, which may be at later stages of the form and class lifecycles. Gabor and Granger [20] have devised a technique to help in such decisions.

Their buy-response curve is determined by seeking upper and lower price limits that respondents would be prepared to pay for, say, 'a tin of soup sufficient for two helpings'. The cumulative distributions of proportions giving each price, within a range, as either their upper limit (H) or lower limit (L) are then computed. Their buy-response is determined by subtracting from the (L) cumulative distribution the (H) cumulative distribution of the price below it. For example, at a price of, say, 20p the (L) cumulative figure was 93 per cent of the sample that considered 20p *not* to be too low. At a price of 19p the (H) figure was 2 per cent, i.e. 2 per cent felt 19p to be already too high a price. Therefore the buy-response is $(93 - 2)\% = 91\%$. This means that 91 per cent of the sample would be prepared to buy at a price of 20p.

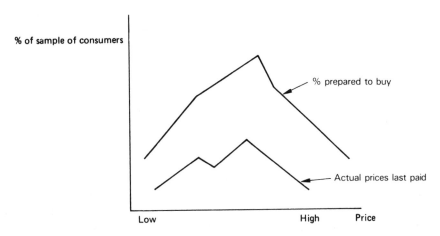

Sources: A. Gabor and C. Granger, 'The pricing of new products', in B. Taylor and G. Wills (eds). *Pricing Strategy*, St Albans: Staples Press, 1969.

Figure 22.6 *Buy response curve*

Figure 22.6 adds one other set of data – the actual prices last paid by the sample members. Comparisons between actual prices paid and those that the sample would be prepared to pay could lead to interesting results. If the distribution of actual prices were well to the left of those they were prepared to pay, then the brands on the market are underpriced. They will be overpriced if the actual price distribution is well to the right.

Managements making a decision about a new brand entering an established market would find such analyses of relevance in indicating price ranges that could meet favourable consumer response [21].

Usually price is but a part of an intricate set of product attributes, and customers will be attracted or not by the full set. They may be willing to pay different prices for alternative collections of attributes. Techniques have been developed to study the kinds of trade-off they would make between several levels of several attributes, with price as one of the attributes. Joint (or conjoint) measurement is explained by Watkins [22] as follows:

> Data are collected from the respondents in the form of ranking judgements about a range of possible attribute levels of products or services. For example, suppose a pricing decision has to be made for a new chocolate confectionery brand which could have one of two fillings (nut or caramel), one of two chocolate types (milk or dark) and one of three prices. This gives rise to $2 \times 2 \times 3 = 12$ possibilities. The consumers are asked to rank these twelve possible products in order of preference.

Great care is needed in ensuring that the different levels of the several attributes are explained sufficiently to respondents and this may require pictorial representations. Marbeau [23] gives examples.

Promotional pricing

Short-term tactical considerations may warrant departures from the established price level. This may be due to competitive factors, stock levels in the channel, an impending price increase or some change in product or package. Promotional pricing may even have a more fundamental purpose, such as inducing non-users to try the brand.

A potential problem area is in the reaction of retailers. In one case reported there was agreement between a manufacturer and retailer that a '5p off' promotion would be undertaken during January. The recommended selling price until then was 37p. Table 22.4 shows what happened. Prior agreement with the head office of the chain did not prevent a quarter of the shops from not following the promotion, although most increased the price to 42p in February, according to the manufacturer's recommendation. Assessments of the effectiveness of a price promotion therefore require careful interpretation and knowledge of the extent to which channel members co-operated.

The effectiveness of promotional pricing must also be rooted in consumer reactions. Miller has reported a series of market research studies on shopper attitudes and behaviour [24]. He finds that:

> The evidence overwhelmingly suggests that shoppers do not know the prices of many (any) products; do not understand many of the mechanics by which price cut offers are presented in-store; and are largely unconvinced that price cuts are genuine.

On the point about not knowing how price cut offers are presented, it was found that 38 per cent believed a '3p off normal price' meant it had already been taken off, 37 per cent thought it would be deducted at the checkout, and the others did not know or were confused. Consumer confusion and cynicism obviously inhibit the effects of a price promotion, giving an additional limitation to the price planner's work.

An increasingly popular way for manufacturers to attempt to cut through some of this confusion is in tying the price offer to coupon redemption. This not only shows the reduction, irrespective of the price in the shop, but it also shows that

Table 22.4 *Variations in selling price between shops in same retail chain*

Price	% of shops selling at each price			
	Sept.	Nov.	Jan.	Feb.
42	0	0	0	91
37	92	88	24	5
33	8	12	0	0
32	0	0	76	5

Source: Audit, Autumn 1975 (AGB Prices Audit), p. 8.

it is the manufacturer who is making the cut. Moss and others show the growth in this activity from 55 million coupons being redeemed in 1965 to 350 million being redeemed in 1983 [25]. The system does rely on retailer co-operation, and assumes that they only redeem coupons against the specified brand.

Marketing with smart cards

Price discounts for frequent product usage are common. They have also been applied to services as diverse as airlines and dry cleaners. An extension has been developed utilising smart cards [26]. In this case a small plastic card is presented by the shopper at the checkout for electronic scanning. The cards contain personal demographic information and a record of previous purchases. General or product-specific discounts might then be administered real-time, depending on the volume of previous purchases recorded. This does raise issues about privacy, though consumer response to airline promotions, where a record of their flying times is kept, has been generally favourable.

Pricing services

Many of the points already made in this chapter are relevant to the pricing of services, but there are further considerations. These may be summarised as consumer factors, location factors and those connected with the nature of the service.

Quality judgements by consumers may be particularly difficult with some services. Given the importance of the price/quality relationship this makes prediction of demand levels at alternative prices problematical. Research into buyer perceptions of quality may be of some assistance, and this might also point the need to 'educate' them in how to make quality assessments in the particular market. For many professional, technical and financial services this may prove to be a challenging task. Another customer-related problem is that for many services time availability is critical. Capacity is limited but demand variable, and so price plans need to take into account the peak and off-peak problem. Lovelock [27] comments on this problem,

> Many service businesses explicitly recognise the existence of different demand curves for different segments during the same time period by establishing distinct classes of service, each priced at levels appropriate to the demand curve of a particular segment. In essence each segment receives a variation in the basic product, with value being added to the core service in order to appeal to the higher paying segments. The objective, of course, is to maximize the revenues received from each segment.

There is a further function of pricing for the consumer of some services. High prices may be welcomed because they constitute an 'entry ticket'. Because some services are consumed by the buyers all together and in a public place, some may wish for the service to discriminate among buyers.

Location: ' factors may serve to establish what may be tantamount to a local monopoly. The extent and durability of the monopoly must be specific to the situation, but it would be anticipated that, in the absence of competition, prices would rise. Entry barriers for most services are, however, usually not as high as in manufacturing and so monopoly profits would be expected to induce the entry of rivals. Despite this, the monopolist would attempt to increase the entry barriers by, for example, ensuring that the latest and most expensive equipment was employed.

The nature of the service must also affect pricing. Most pertinently this refers to the perishable nature of services – they cannot be stocked. This means that the firm nee 's a policy for the handling of prices at the end of each time period. For accommodation sales in hotels, should empty rooms be sold off in the evening at bargain r es? Man hotels do this, but will that condition future customer behaviour, ar d s it consistent with the image being projected? This problem becomes especially difficult in advertising media sales. If a magazine or newspaper has not reached its minimum sales requirement shortly before it closes, should bargain offers be made? How will buyers react in the future?

Summary

Price planning is problematical because of the nature of the information available, in terms of both demand and costs. In practice many firms adhere to sales and profit objectives, and use cost-plus or target rate of return methods for price setting.

Recent work suggests the need to consider some kind of intervening variable as the price goal – if price is not the dominant part of the marketing mix. The problem with this is the proper identification of the variable. 'Value-for-money' and purchase attractiveness have been studied, but there may be considerable difficulty with their routine use.

Ultimately, the success of a price plan depends upon customer perception and action. Surveys, analyses of historical data, and experiments are used to determine customer knowledge, intention and behaviour in connection with price plans.

It will also be important to understand competitive reaction. The correct identification of the rivals is fundamental. Decision trees may be useful in tracing the complex sets of possibilities in deciding about price changes relative to competitors. In some markets competitive bidding is the mode of competitive conduct, and models have been constructed for use in such situations.

Problems associated with pricing new brands differ according to the stage in the product class lifecycle. In the introductory phase, penetration or skimming pricing plans may be adopted. In later phases, the buy-response curve may be employed.

Promotional pricing serves many purposes. Often it is a tactical response to a short-term competitive situation. One difficulty is the need for co-ordination and discipline among channel members, and this may sometimes be impossible to achieve.

Questions for review and discussion

1. What methods might be employed in estimating the shape and position of the conventional demand curve?

2. 'Surely the impact of price changes can easily be seen in terms of their effect on sales. Sales goals are therefore perfectly appropriate for price plans.' Do you agree?

3. Is 'value-for-money' too vague to be used as a routine pricing goal?

4. From the section in this chapter on 'customers and pricing plans' devise a table with cognitions, affections, intentions and actions as the columns, and the various research methods as the rows. Discuss what should go into each cell.

5. Price differentials may exist both across and within product categories. The proper identification of the rivals is essential in both cases. How might this be decided?

6. Is there a difference between a demand curve and a buy-response curve?

References

1. Oxenfeldt, A.R. 1975. *Pricing Strategies*. New York: American Management Association, p. 1.
2. Hague, D.C. 1971. *Pricing in Business*. London: Allen & Unwin, p. 257.
3. Diamantopoulos, A. 1991. 'Pricing: theory and evidence – a literature review', in Baker, M. *Perspectives on Marketing Management*, vol. 1. Chichester: John Wiley, p. 166.
4. Ölander, F. 1969. 'The influence of price on the consumer's evaluations of products and purchases', in Taylor, B. and Wills, G. (eds), *Pricing Strategy*. St Albans: Staples Press, p. 50.
5. Winkler, J. 1984. *Pricing for Results*. London: Pan, p. 248.
6. Shipley, D.D. 1986. 'Dimensions of flexible price management', *Quarterly Review of Marketing*, vol. 11, no. 3.
7. Oxenfeldt, op. cit., p. 37.
8. Office of Fair Trading. 1984. Report of an Investigation into Licensing for the Manufacture or Sale of Replacement Body Parts by Ford Motor Co. Ltd.

9. Atkin, B. and Skinner, R. 1975. *How British Industry Prices*. London: Industrial Marketing Research Ltd. See also reference 6.

10. Gabor, A. and Granger, C. 1969. 'Price consciousness of consumers', in Taylor, B. and Wills, G. (eds), *Pricing Strategy*. St Albans: Staples Press, p. 5.

11. Stout, R.G. 1969. 'Developing data to estimate price–quantity relationships', *Journal of Marketing*, April.

12. Pessemier, E. 1960. 'An experimental method for estimating demand', *Journal of Business*, October.

13. Sawyer, A.G., Worthing, R.M.W. and Sendak, P.T. 1979. 'The role of laboratory experiments to test marketing strategies', *Journal of Marketing*, vol. 43, no. 3.

14. Marbeau, Y. 1987. 'What value pricing research today?', *Journal of the Market Research Society*, vol. 29, no. 2.

15. Oxenfeldt, op. cit., pp. 101 *et seq.*

16. Kelly, A.O., quoted in Oxenfeldt, op. cit.

17. Millman, A.F 1983. 'Price wars', *Quarterly Review of Marketing*, vol. 8, no. 2.

18. Dean, J. 1951. *Managerial Economics*. Englewood Cliffs, NJ: Prentice Hall Inc., p. 174.

19. Hilton, A. 1980. 'How IBM outwitted itself', *Sunday Times*, 20 January.

20. Gabor, A. and Granger, C.W. 1969. 'The pricing of new products', in Taylor, B. and Wills, G. (eds), *Pricing Strategy*. St Albans: Staples Press, p. 541.

21. Eassie, R.W.F. 1979. 'Buy-response analysis: a practical tool of market research', *European Journal of Marketing*, vol. 13, no. 4, pp. 172–82.

22. Watkins, T. 1986. *The Economics of the Brand*. Maidenhead: McGraw-Hill, p. 53.

23. Marbeau, op. cit.

24. Miller, B. 1981. 'Do price cuts really work?', *Marketing*, 14 January, p. 28.

25. Moss, C.D., Thorne, P. and Fasey, P. 1983. 'The distribution of coupons', *Quarterly Review of Marketing*, vol. 8, no. 2.

26. Shaw, R. 1991. 'How the smart card is changing retailing', *Long Range Planning*, vol. 24, no. 1, pp. 111–14.

27. Lovelock, C.H. 1984. *Services Marketing*. Englewood Cliffs, NJ: Prentice Hall Inc., p. 287.

Chapter 23

International marketing

Joe Penn

The discussion thus far has concentrated upon marketing in a national market. The perspective is now changed to take into account the international context. A first problem is in defining the nature of marketing in this widened view.

When an organisation is involved in selling products or services in one or a number of foreign countries, it may describe its activities variously as exporting, international marketing or multinational marketing, and these terms are often used interchangeably. For the purposes of this chapter the definition offered by Cateora and Hess [1] is the one deemed to be the most acceptable: 'International marketing is the performance of business activities that direct the flow of a company's goods and services to consumers and users in more than one nation.'

However, other writers would argue that there is a distinction between the terms. Cannon [2], for example, defines export marketing as the 'emphasis on the successful marketing of goods produced in one or more countries in other overseas markets', and it is true that the term 'exporting' is often associated with the transfer of physical goods across national boundaries. But the distinction goes further than that, and the term 'international marketing' is taken to embrace both exporting and the activities of subsidiaries in other countries which may be influenced to some extent from outside the country.

An attempt to distinguish between international and multinational marketing was made by Keegan [3]: 'An international company usually means a "national" firm operating in foreign markets. The basic orientation of an international firm is towards the home country. A multinational company is world oriented. It pursues global opportunities.'

Although these terms will be used synonymously in this chapter, the reader will need to remain alert to the implied distinctions between them when they are used in other contexts. As far as we are concerned, 'international marketing involves the management not only to but also in foreign countries' [4].

It might be argued that the way in which international markets are managed differs little, in terms of general approaches and principles, from marketing management in a national context. The way in which a company competes and thrives in the international market will be determined by the approach taken to strategy formulation in the home country. Clearly, account must be taken of the various

465

factors affecting international marketing decisions (see below) but the process of formulating strategy at corporate and functional level and translating such strategy into marketing plans is likely to follow a fairly standard pattern.

Having said that, it must be acknowledged that strategies will be adjusted to take account of the dynamic environment in which the company operates, the decision to 'go international' adds just another factor to a list which might include:

1. Industry environment.

2. Stage in product lifecycle.

3. Choice of generic competitive strategy:
    (a) overall cost leadership,
    (b) differentiation,
    (c) focus.

4. Derived market positioning.

5. Decision to be market leader, market challenger or market follower.

The larger the organisation and the more diverse its operations, the more complicated the planning process becomes. It is impossible to generalise about how companies might compete strongly in international markets or how they should develop and sustain international marketing strategies. This chapter attempts to give certain guidelines and provides one example of international marketing success (see below). One way in which organisations might be able to formulate and adjust strategies more effectively is through the study of other firms which have competed successfully in international markets. Common factors which are often found in these seem obvious, operating efficiencies leading to low cost levels, high quality products commanding premium prices with good distribution channels and service support. It is likely that organisations deciding to engage in international marketing will need to adopt an incremental approach notwithstanding the style adopted by the parent company.

International marketing at Benetton

The Benetton company was formed in 1965, initially manufacturing for other retailers. In 1968 it opened its first three stores. A year later it took its initial global step and opened its first retail shop outside Italy. Growth has been relentless with a five-year period in the 1960s during which one store a day was opening somewhere in the world. It now has over 6,000 retail stores in more than 83 countries on every continent. These outlets sell the 60 million garments manufactured each year (one head office, main plant and distribution centre are located on the outskirts of Treviso, 20 km north of Venice). In 1977, 2 per cent of sales were outside Italy. By 1986, this figure had swelled to 61 per cent, of which 40 per cent went to other European countries and 15 per cent to North America; the proportions are similar today.

Benetton's strategy is a truly global one. The same garments are sold throughout the world through the same boutique-style shops, merchandised within strict corporate guidelines and supported heavily with print media using identical advertisements worldwide. The strategy is to brand a 'total look' – from the colour-co-ordinated garments to the ambience of the small stores – rather than individual products.

Early print advertising concentrated on displaying the colourful Benetton garments being worn by its youthful target market – the models always multiracial and multinational. They underlined Benetton's message of world peace and racial and national harmony. The United Colors of Benetton, the company's current corporate banner, is as much a political statement as it is a fashion statement.

The social agenda of the Benetton family now extends to such issues as AIDS, environmental problems and overpopulation. All are addressed through their company's advertising campaigns.

Their advertisements do not now feature clothes, in common with many other fashion houses such as Esprit and Anne Klein but, instead, the models have been replaced by startling images which have created vocal public outcry. Some years ago double-page advertisements, which featured only multicoloured condoms, were banned by some US magazines. More recently, advertisements which showed a black woman breastfeeding a white baby caused a furore among American blacks. The banned advertisements were replaced by the far more innocuous images of a parrot sitting on the back of a zebra or multiracial Pinocchio puppets. The most recent campaign included an advertisement featuring a photograph of a newborn baby still attached to the umbilical cord. The advertisement was displayed as a poster in London. An outburst of 800 complaints from the public in less than a week caused the Advertising Standards Authority to ban the poster, but not before it had raced to the top of the *UK Marketing* magazine's top ten list of spontaneous recall advertisements.

Although Benetton claims the provocative advertisements are not designed simply to attract free publicity, it does not deny that the attention is welcome. The advertisements are designed to be noticed and provoke reflection on the social issues of concern to the Benettons. The baby advertisement was described as 'a documentary-style bit of social reality' symbolising 'the beginning of life – how all human beings come into the world in the same way'. The advertisements also seem to be effective in selling clothes.

Benetton operates in a highly competitive, mature industry characterised by a fickle consumer base demanding an increasing variety of products. The market is volatile and risky. Competitive activity can render one's product lines unfashionable overnight. Product lifecycles are planned to be short to maintain consumer interest. In fact, Benetton plans for eight fashion collections on top of the two basic fashion seasons – that is, a complete change of product lines ten times a year.

The strategic responses in such an environment are complex. The successful marketer needs the vision and the skills to manage diversity. On the one hand, there is the need to meet the demands of fashion – the rapidly changing needs of the customer. Hence, the need to develop flexibility and speed. On the other hand, to compete in the 'industrial fashion' stakes, there is the need to maintain high levels of efficiency. Benetton has learned how to adapt rapidly and constantly to changing consumer tastes while gaining efficiency through economies of scale.

Benetton operates using a blend of in-house expertise and outsourced resources throughout the value chain. Benetton was involved in partnership arrangements (nothing more than a version of the Italian extended family) long before the term strategic alliance became fashionable. Manufacturing, for example, is carried out with the help of 450 subcontractors. The third-party manufacturers receive production planning support, technical assistance and quality control support. It is not unusual for Benetton to provide financial assistance to encourage contractors to equip themselves with specialised machinery for special effects and to have Benetton help financially when the equipment is no longer required. Without this encouragement, the contractors would not have the motivation to change their technology. It is also not unusual for Benetton to encourage employees to convert internal processes to externally contracted ones and so assist employees to become self-employed entrepreneurs. In return, Benetton demands exclusivity. This is essential to ensure that Benetton always has capacity available to handle peaks and to be able to co-ordinate effectively these external production units.

The purchasing function is centralised in-house given the economies inherent in large-scale buying. Benetton is one of the largest wool buyers in the world and at one stage was contemplating establishing a wool scouring plant in Australia.

Benetton works through a network of 85 agents around the world. Agents in each country are responsible for recruiting the retailers, showing the fashion collections, processing retailer orders, selecting retail sites, carrying out training and, importantly, feeding market intelligence to Benetton. For this they receive commission, usually around 4 per cent, based on sales in their territory.

Although often called franchises, the retail outlets are more accurately described as licensees. The licensees, unlike a franchised arrangement, pay no fees or royalties. This neatly allows Benetton to sidestep the often restrictive franchise legislation in many countries. Licensees must agree to stock and sell only Benetton products, merchandise and display the garments according to Benetton guidelines and also follow price guidelines.

For Benetton the stores are not simply outlets for their garments but information probes measuring the level of customer acceptance of the Benetton 'look'.

In true partnership mind set, the key desirable qualities of the licensees are their commitment to Benetton and their ability to expand the market.

Benetton has created for itself a borderless world. It has linked 180 raw material suppliers, 450 manufacturers and 6,000 retailers to deliver 60 million garments a year to satisfied customers in 83 countries.

Source: Based on Dapiran [5].

Motives for international marketing

An organisation might decide to enter into international markets for a number of reasons. Economists have traditionally emphasised the principles of comparative and absolute advantage to explain why international trade takes place, i.e. where products can, by virtue of raw material availability, low unit labour costs, etc. be produced much more cheaply in one country than in another. While this analysis is valid, indeed it may explain a great deal of multinational activity, it remains rather narrow. Apart from any cost advantage, a firm may decide to engage in international marketing because, for example:

1. It might simply have excess production capacity. In order to avoid wasting such capacity the firm might decide to enter overseas markets.

2. It might have problems with the domestic market. For example, the domestic market might have become saturated; more and more competitors may have entered the domestic market and thus restricted growth opportunities; technological change and changes in tastes and

fashions might mean that the product is out of date in the domestic market whereas it might still be appropriate to the consumer's requirements in one or a number of overseas markets.

3. The firm may have a product which is so unusual, unique or superior that it has attracted interest and enquiries from potential buyers overseas.

4. An overseas market might suggest itself by the sheer 'pulling power' of its demand and disposable income. The markets of the Middle East have, in recent years, been classic examples of this.

5. There might be a government-sponsored 'export drive' which provides the incentive for a firm to try its hand at international marketing.

6. In some product lines, competition in foreign markets may be less intense than in the domestic market.

Of course, as Terpstra [6] says, the reverse is sometimes true and, he adds, 'Already many firms are finding that to be competitive nationally, they must be competitive internationally.'

Before entering into overseas markets, managements should analyse not only the products and capabilities of their own organisations but also examine the rationale behind such a decision and look closely at the many criteria which will affect such a decision. An analytical, logical approach is required, as Chisnall [7] makes clear:

> Some companies almost stumble into exporting; much to their surprise, and even alarm, they suddenly find themselves with an unsolicited enquiry from abroad. Others have become involved through merging with a business that already had overseas activities. In some cases, personal links had resulted in business being developed with certain countries. From the accidental to the planned approach there are clearly many events which may trigger off overseas marketing, but even today many companies prefer to adopt a passive attitude or if they go abroad they tend to take up a defensive posture. Positive dynamic marketing often appears to be sadly lacking in many firms which seem to have little real conception of the need to tackle market opportunities in a systematic, planned way.

In Chapter 9 it was seen how, for example, environmental analysis and company resources and competences can be used to formulate strategy. This type of systematic, planned approach is exemplified by Ford Tractor International Operations which used a product portfolio analysis approach to evaluate the potential of overseas markets [8]. Using four basic elements – market size, market growth rate, government regulations, and economic and political stability – the company's executives were able to quantify the 'country attractiveness'; they then evaluated their competitive strengths using the following factors: market share, product fit, contribution margin and market representation and market support. The resulting scales were plotted on the 3×3 matrix shown in Figure 23.1.

This sort of strategic planning tool is a great aid to management decision-

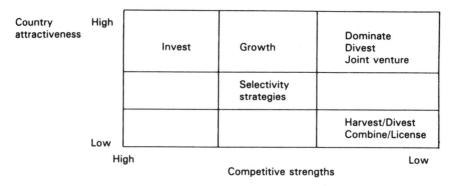

Figure 23.1   *International portfolio planning*

making but will not make decisions for management. No amount of analysis can legislate for the dynamic and unpredictable nature of many international markets. Having said that, the factors identified by Ford require close examination before any decision is taken on whether or not to enter any particular overseas market and it is for that reason that they will be given further consideration here.

Factors affecting international marketing decisions

1. Market size
This may be measured in a number of ways: Ford selected a three-year projected average annual sales in units. The GNP of each country may also be used as an indicator plus, if the statistics are available, patterns of consumption, population, income distribution, disposable income, etc.

2. Market rate of growth
This measure has always been crucial in product portfolio analysis and its inclusion in Ford's list is not, therefore, surprising. They estimated it by using a ten-year annual compound percentage increase in sales but in many instances this calculation may be made difficult by unavailability of precise figures.

3. Government regulation
This factor, often euphemistically referred to as 'legal constraints', is the nettle which many companies fail to grasp and is often the cause of failure in international markets. They are outlined by Hovell and Walters [9] thus:

1. Differences in the legal system, e.g. as to:
   (a) Regulations laying down product performance and safety specifications.

(b) Laws regulating advertising and other forms of promotion and branding.

(c) Legislation governing such conditions of sale as price, guarantees, warranties, etc.

(d) Ordinances controlling various aspects of distribution.

2. Intergovernmental regulations relating to foreign trade and corporate investment, e.g.:

(a) Documentary procedures for exporting, importing and foreign exchange control (many attempts have been made to simplify these – notably SITPRO).

(b) Barriers to international trade, e.g. as to:
   (i) import controls – tariffs, quotas, 'anti-dumping', etc.
   (ii) export controls for specific goods and materials.
   (iii) effects of regional groupings, free trade areas, etc.

(c) Control of foreign exchange rates.

(d) Restrictions on capital movements, including remissions.

(e) Tax treatment of international remissions and foreign direct investment.

A daunting list indeed. Yet it may not be comprehensive and any one of these items can change literally overnight: witness the fluctuations in the value of the pound sterling with relation to most international and even European currencies given the decision to leave the Exchange Rate Mechanism.

4. Economic and political factors

Easy to identify, difficult to define, these may include inflation and the balance of international trade. Ford has used sophisticated measures of political stability developed in conjunction with consulting groups and government agencies.

5. Market share

The experience effect is likely to vary for the same company in different countries, not least because of the presence of domestic competitors in the market. This factor will be not only a most important characteristic in international marketing but also a good discriminator as between alternative potential markets. An organisation needs to take account of the number of competitors and how hard they will fight to retain their share of the market, and the basis on which this might be done. A price war on foreign soil is not desirable and may in any case be precluded by the sort of 'anti-dumping' regulations referred to above.

6. Product fit

This is a key strategic factor. All marketing should be concerned with how well the product fits a particular market need but here we are dealing with different tastes, fashions and many environmental differences. Analysis of social trends and lifestyles as well as attitudes will be important. Later in this chapter we shall investigate the statement made by Ryans [10] that 'despite obvious language and cultural differences, peoples of the world have the same basic needs and wants', but for the moment suffice to say that a product which fits well in a European market cannot be assumed to fit as well the needs of for example, a Middle Eastern market.

7. *Contribution margin*

Some measure of potential profit per unit must be calculated before any decision to enter a foreign market can possibly be taken.

8. *Market support*

There is also the need to take into consideration the general marketing capacity in an overseas country. If the firm has its own staff in that country it must ensure that there are enough of them and that they are of sufficiently high calibre. They must receive technical support and be budgeted for marketing communication activity. Clearly, support from a distance is a difficult matter but no marketing manager seriously believes that a product will sell itself.

This list has been supplemented by Cooke [11], who would add cultural anthropological indicators; these include geographical, climatic and topographical as well as population features:

> Traditional indicators include not only the attitudes of the population but also the mechanics of the market, its credit facilities and structures, the historic demand for goods, historic links with other manufacturing countries and markets and the protection of home markets . . . legal indicators [as covered above but Cooke places particular emphasis on consumer and public safety] . . . marketing mix indicators . . . concerned not with the product itself but with the way in which it is presented and marketed in an attempt to gain total empathy.

This approach is also taken by Meidan [12], who stresses the importance of anthropological and non-controllable variables in international marketing. He in turn is supported by Calof and Lane [13], who state that:

> Understanding culture, our own and others is good business. Understanding cultural differences alone is not a guarantee of success. Product, price, delivery and service are critical. However, not understanding cultural differences, and the inability to resolve misunderstandings and conflict that arise from these differences may be the reason for failure – overcoming even a good product and a competitive price.

Therefore, whereas many of the factors affecting our decision as to whether or not we enter foreign markets may be measured objectively, there are other, subjective and thus less easily measured factors which must be given serious, if not equal, consideration. Reinforcing this need is the growing fragmentation of individual demand, which clearly calls for not only a profound understanding of consumer cultures but also an appreciation of the dynamics of change. In an article which examines the diversity and complexity of Europe, Homma [14] identifies some of these dynamics (see below) and goes on to state:

> Many users of research have become disenchanted with concepts operating at a high level of cross-cultural generality. Quite often, this kind of research lacks the depth required for addressing specific target groups or positioning brands in a highly competitive market.

The dynamics which Homma lists are:

Mature consumer cultures	←——————→	Incipient consumer cultures
High media penetration	←——————→	Low media penetration
Modernity	←——————→	Traditionalism
Political stability	←——————→	Political instability
Decline of ethnic conflicts	←——————→	Increase of ethnic conflicts
Decline of nationalism	←——————→	Revival of nationalism
Pro-European sentiments	←——————→	Anti-European sentiments
Centralism	←——————→	Regionalism

Having outlined the sort of information needed, the discussion now turns to the task of gathering market intelligence in an overseas environment.

Researching foreign markets

From the above it is clear that a great deal of information about overseas markets is required before any decision to enter into such a market can be made. Chisnall [15] identifies three categories of information needs in international markets:

1. Information for strategic decisions (e.g. whether or not to enter a particular overseas market, or to diversify into new markets).

2. Information for tactical decisions (e.g. planning of sales territories).

3. Information to provide a 'data bank'; this will require periodic updating to ensure that it retains its usefulness.

Turning now to the major sources of such information it will be seen that there is certainly no shortage of advice. According to Wilson and Lockhart [16] the United Kingdom is particularly well provided with organisations which are both capable and anxious to give advice and practical support to potential exporters, and it is to some of these organisations that we first turn our attention.

1. The General Export Services Branch of the British Overseas Trade Board (BOTB) which publishes many helpful documents, especially *Hints to Exporters* and will give confidential advice on a whole range of matters. Address: Export House, 50 Ludgate Hill, London EC4M 7HU; there are also nine regional offices.

2. Overseas departments of clearing banks will provide advice not only on financial matters but also a great deal of market intelligence, e.g. size of market, political stability, economic performance and prospects.

3. Export Credits Guarantee Department, Waverley House, 7–12 Noel Street, London W1V 3PB plus two other London offices and seven regional offices. The department will provide help in obtaining bank finance and provide insurance against the insolvency of overseas buyers as well as other risks.

4. Chambers of Commerce.

5. Confederation of British Industry.

6. Institute of Export.

7. Institute of Freight Forwarders.

8. Chartered Institute of Marketing.

9. British Export House Association.

Business Link, a DTI initiative, has created partnerships involving central government, Chambers of Commerce, Training and Enterprise Councils and local authorities. It aims to streamline all business development services into one operation so that organisations can find their way to the precise assistance they need on any business issue. In 1994 twenty-two advisory centres were in operation, and the objective is to establish 200 by the end of 1995, using information technology to link them in a national network.

These organisations can provide reliable, practical information. Other sources of information are fairly obvious: public libraries and the libraries of colleges and universities; overseas organisations such as the EU, UN, OECD, World Bank and ESOMAR (the European Society for Opinion and Market Research) should not be neglected.

Many helpful articles can be found in journals. In one example, Spiers [17] explained the 'secrets of doing business successfully in France' providing a useful checklist of the fundamental practical problems and the administrative hurdles (the legendary French bureaucracy) that a company might have to face. He even outlines some of the aids to manufacturing industry which are available in France and identifies the major institutions concerned.

It is worth noting that most of this information is free or virtually free. Using it will certainly help avoid the sort of comment made by Martin van Mesdag [18] who bemoans the lack of knowledge of people trying to break into overseas markets:

A company may budget £1.5m on advertising and promotion and £500,000 on research and development and it will have an eighty-strong salesforce for its domestic marketing operation, yet it will send one £7,000 a year man abroad for three months and expect him to generate business. Worse still, that one man will have no knowledge of the overseas market, he will have few resources beyond his travelling expenses, he will have a product carefully developed for the UK market he will have f.o.b. UK prices and a discount schedule based on UK practice. He will know one language, which is English and have the title of export manager. He will find that he has no exports to manage.

Paulden [19] has a different view of this unfortunate person:

> Recent research has shown that the average British export salesman produces as much as five times more business than his home sales counterpart. The reason is that they are given such a huge chunk of the world to handle that they can cream business from here and there. It looks good but it proves, surely, that there must be bigger volumes of business that they are missing. It is not unusual for a British firm to have five or six salesmen covering the UK and one or two covering the rest of the world.

All of which goes to demonstrate that organisations must be serious about entering foreign markets and must make a great deal of effort in order to be successful. Even if a company cannot afford to send a representative to the country concerned to gather information, there really is no excuse not to find out as much as possible. This is being made even easier by access to computerised databases like the Export Intelligence Service of the BOTB or one announced by Thorn-EMI's subsidiary Datashare called 'World Exporter'. This latter database provides details of major business opportunities and at the same time gives access to BBC, *The Economist*, Associated Press and the *Guardian* news bulletins and features. A user can search through over 200,000 articles using keywords in a matter of seconds.

Companies may get into overseas markets by accident but if they are to survive they need to research and plan their activities. Brown [20] gives two such examples: Butterly Building Materials (BBM) which export bricks, and Burlington Slate (BS). Brown describes how:

> Rose [of BBM] and his team plunged in, not quite sure where to start: 'We went to Belgium first of all, and literally just arrived and walked round the place. We went to building centres and places like that, to try and get a feel of what was happening. But once having put a toe into Europe it soon became apparent that the best place to start an export drive was not Belgium but next door, in Holland.'

And similarly for BS:

> Burlington first broke into the European market by chance, Wallace explains. It was in the mid-60s. 'We had been importing French slate into the UK, and we suddenly found that there was a surfeit of slate in the UK. So somebody had the breadth of vision to switch the operation, and start exporting British slate back into France. It was fortuitous, really, and totally unplanned.'
>
> Having almost fallen into France, Burlington began to look at Europe in a more considered way. Soon it was selling to Germany, now its largest export market. It also expanded into Holland, Belgium, Denmark and Sweden.

One much neglected source of information, advice and assistance is the diplomatic service, and the Foreign and Commonwealth Office (FCO) produced a video, entitled 'Ambassadors for Export' to tell organisations about their commercial services. Claudette Hall [21] explains that there are currently commercial officers in 200 posts in 130 countries. About 320 London-based commercial officers work abroad, supplemented by around 270 senior locally engaged officers. She quotes Alan White of the Trade Relations and Exports Department of the FCO describing the different levels on which commercial work is carried out: 'Quite apart from information on market conditions, how to do business in the country, the nature of the market place, the local tax structure and what the competition is doing, the diplomatic posts can give the businessman a rundown on the political and economic situation.'

In another article [22] dealing with Hungary as a specific example, Hall describes how Guy Hart, First Secretary Commercial at the embassy in Hungary gathers information through field work and considers knowledge of the market a prime concern. The best way for the commercial section to impart its market information, Hart maintains, is to see a British businessman in person, but the embassy will deal with postal enquiries.

Clearly, therefore, the tasks of strategic analysis and the planning of marketing effort can be greatly facilitated by the generation and analysis of relevant information which is widely available.

Hibbert summarises some research into the sources of information used by UK companies which demonstrates that organisations have not fully developed, or do not make significant use of international marketing intelligence systems (Table 23.1).

One glaring omission from Table 23.1 is any reference to the use of professional marketing research, either ad hoc or continuous. Buckingham and Penford outline the services of their organisation in this respect and state [23]:

Nielsen's global consumer goods databases cover 27 national markets and the concept of strategic tracking has now become a reality. It is now possible to

Table 23.1   *Information sources used by UK companies*

Information source	%
Feedback from export sales staff	61
Trade Associations and Chambers of Commerce	54
General knowledge	44
Press reports	32
Export departments of banks	29
Local press and journals	20
Test marketing	5
Financial Institutions	14
No information base	15

Source: E.P. Hibbert, *Marketing Strategy in International Business.*
Maidenhead: McGraw-Hill, 1989, p. 29.

provide the global president of a business with a clear one-page summary of the strategic position world-wide of a major brand or a key market sector. Moreover as international databases and analytical tools become more powerful, it is becoming easier to assimilate massive quantities of information into readily understandable global information. The key here is not just the creation of internationally compatible database structures . . . but also the availability of powerful global decision support systems.

Clearly, therefore, organisations, both large and small, need to adopt a much more disciplined and sophisticated approach to researching international markets than they seem to have previously done. It could be argued, of course, that market knowledge is a necessary but not sufficient condition for success in any form of marketing and that other elements of the marketing mix are equally, if not more, important. There are as many points of view on this as there are observers so we will conclude this section, without comment, with a brief quote from Higgins *et al.* [24]: 'Marketing information is as much a resource as are the firm's products, because this information helps determine the definition of future products and services.'

The marketing research task will differ from organisation to organisation and from country to country. As with any research the objective is to gather accurate information in order that decisions can be made to ensure, as far as possible, optimum performance in the target market. There are two major problems associated with international marketing research. The first is the availability, validity and comparability of secondary data which may not be of the standard researchers expect in their own country. Second, in attempting to collect primary data, researchers may encounter practical difficulties such as accurate translation of questionnaires and obtaining responses from a representative sample in the target market. However, in many overseas markets there is now a great deal of experience and these problems can now be accounted for. As long as researchers, or those responsible for commissioning research, are aware of potential difficulties and allow for these, there is no reason why research should not be conducted in overseas markets with the expectation that high quality information can be elicited.

But what sort of information? Some requirements will be the same as those for domestic markets: market potential, consumer behaviour, availability and structure of channels of distribution, availability and costs of media, etc. Specific information will clearly be required about the target country. Some of this will be general (the economic, social and political environment) and some will be detailed, e.g. foreign exchange and interest rates, taxation on project, dividends and interest, legal requirements concerning operating in the target country, any incentives or controls affecting foreign trade, existing and potential competitors and availability of resources (human, financial, raw materials, technology, etc.) in the target country.

The practicalities of conducting international marketing research are, therefore, not that different from conducting domestic marketing research. An organisation determines its objectives, identifies information needs, conducts or commissions research and assesses market potential against objectives. Finally, a detailed product-market–company mix should be designed to take advantage of the foreign marketing opportunities.

Distribution

In an international marketing context the emphasis has invariably been on distribution. Porter [25] states that firms can participate in international activities through three basic mechanisms – licensing, export and foreign direct investment.

From research conducted by Kim and Daniels [26] in the United States, it was found that, once companies engage in international marketing, their decisions on distribution channels are determined not by any network they might have established in their domestic market but by the host country's local norms. While not surprising in itself, it seems that the lessons learnt in adapting to local distribution patterns have not always been applied to other elements of the international marketing mix.

Firms entering international markets normally go through an evolutionary process which has different implications for the marketing mix elements at different stages. This process has been described by Keegan [27] as having five stages or phases:

1. *Opportunities (passive)*. This is where organisations enter into foreign markets by chance. That is not to say that this sort of opportunity cannot be developed into a far greater degree of involvement.

2. *Linked commitment (active)*. This is a low-risk degree of involvement where no long-term fixed investment is undertaken and production for overseas markets will be limited to marginal capacity.

3. *Limited fixed investment (recognition of overseas trading)*. Management really start to take overseas markets seriously and make some long-term commitment to international marketing. It is at this stage that mix elements will be consciously tailored to meet the needs of the overseas market.

4. *Major dependence for overseas building (exporting of major importance)*. This is where the decision to set up an overseas division with a local manufacturing capacity will be taken which demonstrates total commitment on the part of the organisation to international marketing.

5. *No distinction between home and export markets (birth of multinational organisations)*. Up to this point (notwithstanding the comments in 4, above) the overseas operation will always have been seen as being 'different' in some way from the other divisions within the company. If and when an organisation reaches this point, strategic business opportunities will be assessed across entire continents and involving diverse cultures using the same criteria and having to perform according to targets set at the centre.

Decisions related to distribution policy are, in domestic as well as international markets, largely strategic in nature. Not just because they are invariably long-term

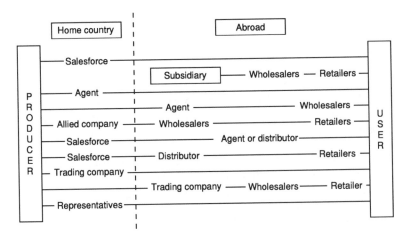

Source: Kahler and Ruel, *International Marketing*, 5th edn, Cincinnati, Ohio: Southwestern Publishing Company, 1983, p. 165.

Figure 23.2 *Selection of international marketing channels*

but also because of the impact such decisions have on the other elements of the marketing mix. In turn, decisions on distribution policy are greatly affected by the entry strategy adopted by the organisation. Similarly, the physical distribution task affects entry strategies. According to Mahon and Vachani [28], 'The distribution and logistics issues will in many ways frame the strategies and tactics of entry for a given organisation.'

The channel options available to organisations engaged in international marketing were summarised by Kahler and Ruel (see Figure 23.2). Research conducted by Jones, Wheeler and Young [29] into the European market for the UK machine tool industry revealed that over half the companies surveyed used a distributor plus an agent or a sales subsidiary only. The same authors, when reviewing the range of strategic options available to companies who are attempting 'to consolidate or improve their competitive positions', came up with the following list:

1. Improved market definition so as to widen the niches served by these mainly specialist producers.

2. Seeking association with other suppliers to extend product and or market coverage.

3. Improving downstream capabilities to match the emerging needs of the industry, namely developing engineering and consultancy services and turnkey skills, for application in their core product areas or more widely.

4. Internationalising through a variety of means including:
   (a) piggy-backing – using other manufacturers' marketing organisations in foreign markets;

(b) selling through complementary manufacturers based in foreign markets or extending this on a reciprocal basis;

(c) establishing joint-venture marketing companies in third country markets; and

(d) closer ties with agents and distributors, with improved marketing materials, training and back-up services. Where manufacturers have the financial resources, the option of buying up distribution companies is also possible.

This approach is extended by Lei and Slocum [30], who looked at the question of forming strategic alliances through licensing arrangements, joint ventures and consortia, in an attempt to establish competitive advantage. As evidence of the potential of such an approach the authors cite the following three examples:

1. In the pharmaceutical industry, Merck, Eli Lilley, Fujisawa and Beyer aggressively cross-license their newest drugs to one another, not only to support industry-wide innovation, but also to amortise the high fixed costs of R&D and distribution.

2. Corning Incorporated aggressively uses its twenty-three joint ventures with such foreign partners as Siemens of West Germany, Samsung of South Korea, Asahi Chemical of Japan and Ciba-Geigy of Switzerland to penetrate and thrive in a growing number of related high-technology markets.

3. Airbus Industrie, the European consortium backed by four governments, to produce commercial aircraft, is slowly but steadily gaining market share in this highly lucrative but risky industry.

Distribution is clearly one of the most important and complex aspects of international marketing. Given the high cost associated with any attempt to penetrate foreign markets, we can only conclude that this element of the marketing mix be given the highest priority in the decision-making process. The ultimate test of consumer satisfaction and, therefore, the level of customer service is our ability to deliver the products where and when they are needed. This is difficult enough to do in domestic markets, and this difficulty is greatly multiplied whenever we try to serve international markets where expectations, in terms of delivery performance and levels of customer service, are invariably higher.

Pricing

Setting a price in international markets is an extremely difficult task, yet this crucial element in the marketing mix is often the one given least attention. The straightforward argument about competitive advantage enabling companies to penetrate markets through their ability to charge lower prices takes no account of factors such as the prestige often associated with certain products, e.g. Jaguar cars from Britain sold in the United States and Scotch whisky sold in France. In addition, currency fluctuations might make a nonsense of even the most carefully planned international pricing strategies. According to Keegan [31] there are three broad positions that a company can take:

1. *Extension/ethnocentric*. This simple approach requires that the price of an item be the same around the world and that the customer absorbs the freight and import duties. However, it takes no account of the competitive and market conditions of each national market and profit-maximisation opportunities may be missed.

2. *Adaption/polytechnic*. This is a policy of permitting subsidiary or affiliated companies to establish whatever price they feel is most desirable. There are several disadvantages associated with this approach, not least that the company loses control and cannot co-ordinate pricing policy effectively across a number of markets.

3. *Invention/geocentric*. Here the company takes into account the unique local factors in each market (e.g. cost structures, income levels, competition and local marketing strategy) that should be recognised in arriving at a pricing decision. This would seem the most sensible method; the company retains control and is able to co-ordinate its overall strategy, but it does require a high level of commitment and involvement from the company. As Keegan states: 'International pricing is complicated by the fact that an international business must conform to different rule-making bodies and to different competitive situations in each country. Both the countries and the competition are constraints on pricing decisions. Each company must examine the market, the competition and its own costs and objectives and local and regional regulations and laws in setting prices that are consistent with the overall marketing strategy.'

The story does not end there: additional complications arise all the time and it is no wonder that many companies take the easiest possible option, setting profit targets and leaving pricing decisions to be taken at local level. Cooke [32] gives an example of the difficulties associated with setting a price.

> Export pricing policy is even more complex than its domestic counterpart, not only because of the additional cost and taxes which may have to be taken into consideration, but also because of the different national attitudes to pricing. For a product to remain competitive it does not necessarily have to be priced in line with similar product offerings – the leather trim offered as an option on one well known European car imported into Britain costs just over three times the price of an equivalent trim on a British competitive product. This pricing differential occurs in markets where both cars are offered, yet both appear to sell.

What companies face, therefore, when considering the pricing decision is the fact that product costs, marketing costs, inflation and interest rates and competitive activity are among the factors which not only need to be taken into account but which will also inevitably vary from country to country. In an attempt to put this complexity into context, Lancioni [33] suggests that price-setting should be done on two levels in international marketing:

1.   The external market level must account for:
     (a)   customer price sensitivity,
     (b)   competitors' pricing strategies,
     (c)   government regulation.

2.   The internal level must account for:
     (a)   cost-reduction goals,
     (b)   return on investment objectives,
     (c)   sales volume requirements,
     (d)   production volume quotas.

We are convinced that any marketing executive with experience in price-setting for international markets could easily add to this list but it does at least serve as a basic framework.

The strategic aspect of pricing should also be taken into consideration. Multi-national companies have consistently used transfer pricing to compete effectively and profitably in the markets which they serve. Al Eryani, Alam and Akhter [34] classify international transfer pricing strategies into two groups: market-based and non-market-based. They state:

> Market-based transfer pricing used the prevailing market price for exchanging products within the corporate family. . . . Non-market-based pricing includes a wide array of transfer pricing methods, including negotiated prices, cost-based prices, mathematically programmed prices and dual prices.

Pricing decisions should be taken at the highest level in the organisation. An input from marketing personnel is clearly vital, but pricing should not be seen as their exclusive province. Lancioni and Gattorna [35] argue that strategic value pricing strategies can be grouped into four types and that the chosen strategy depends very much on the philosophy of the company and its attitude towards quality and innovation:

Type I –   Premium pricing strategies. This approach requires a continual investment in innovation and quality improvement as well as the development of a value-added selling approach.

Type II –   Lookalike pricing strategies where firms charge the current market price and often where all of the products are viewed as commodities by customers.

Type III – Factor cost strategies. Referred to as 'break-even pricing', where little or no margins are made as prices are often equal to costs.

Type IV – Below-cost strategies. To survive in a highly competitive market. It often occurs in international commodity markets where countries will price their exports below costs to maintain market share. The extreme form of Type IV pricing is 'dumping', whereby the intent of the competition is to ruin the market and drive competitors out.

An option which companies might have to consider as an alternative to payment in hard cash is barter. According to Yoffie [36] 'Barter is back'. He quotes estimates of between 8 and 30 per cent of international trade ($160 billion to $600 billion) being conducted in this fashion. There are many reasons for this, the most simple being that many countries are broke. Other reasons include the fact that for some nations countertrade is one way (perhaps the only way) to exert power over multinational corporations which might have turnovers in excess of the GDP of the country. Whatever the reason, companies who are not prepared to barter are likely to lose their share of international competition. For companies wishing to enter an international market, however, the willingness to barter might be a good thing. As Yoffie [37] says:

> Countertrade can enhance a firm's strategic position when it is used to promote marketing, procurement or financial objectives. Sometimes the willingness to be flexible with countertrade can help a firm compensate for uncompetitive products, inadequate financing and other traditional problems in winning overseas markets. By providing a service that others may be unwilling or unable to perform, countertrade can help differentiate one's products from the competition.

However, as indicated above, barter is only one form of countertrade. Imeson [38] lists the forms that this approach to international marketing can take, and states: 'Countertrade is an umbrella term for a whole range of commercial mechanisms for reciprocal trade':

1. Straightforward bartering is where one type of product or service is exchanged for another.

2. Counterpurchase is where an exporter agrees to buy goods from the country it is selling to. There are two parallel but separate contracts – one for the principal order (which is paid for by the importer on normal cash or credit terms) and another for the counterpurchase. The value of the counterpurchase may vary between 10 and 100 per cent or more of the original export order and it is the most common form of countertrade.

3. Buy-back, favoured by the former USSR, is where suppliers of capital plant or equipment agree to be paid in the future by the output of the factory they are supplying. A few years ago a British construction firm sold an irrigation system to Romania and was paid in the crop subsequently grown which was then sold in Brazil for cash.

4. Offset is where an exporter incorporates into its product something that is made in the importing country. This is used particularly in high-tech areas and for defence equipment.

5. Switch trading is when a Western exporter is paid by a third country that has a trade debt with the importer.

6. A multinational firm with a manufacturing subsidiary in a developing country may have to counterpurchase goods to the value of goods and materials imported by the subsidiary. In such cases an 'evidence account' keeps imports and exports in balance.

When a company as important as Pepsi-Cola sells $3 billion worth of equipment and expertise to the Soviet Union in 1990 and receives payment in vodka, tankers and ships, countertrade looks like a serious option for organisations dealing with countries who, for various reasons, cannot engage in 'normal' international marketing.

Marketing communications

The communications (or promotion) mix for international marketing has the same ingredients as for national or domestic marketing, i.e. advertising, personal selling, sales promotion and public relations. The extent to which any or all of these is used, and in what proportions, will usually be dictated not only by the nature of the product and the market but also by other factors unique to the country in which we are marketing. Terpstra [39] identifies and explores some of the constraints on international marketing communications and these are shown in Figure 23.3.

Some of these will be explored in more detail below, but the problems

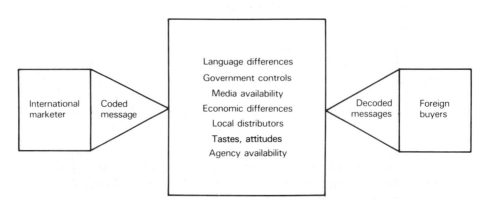

Figure 23.3 *Constraints on international marketing communications*

associated with language, or more usually, translation, are always difficult to overcome. When Japanese products first came to Britain numerous jokes were made about the language used in their instruction booklets, but even large multinationals can have unfortunate experiences. Adrian [40] tells of how Rolls-Royce, when searching for a name for the car which eventually became the Silver Shadow, gave very serious consideration to the name Silver Mist until it was discovered that the German translation was Silver Dung. Similarly, although more unfortunate because this actually went to print, Winnick [41] tells how Procter & Gamble, when translating advertisements for their French Canadian market, wished to communicate how the product should be applied to 'dirty parts'. The literal translation used in the advertisement became 'private parts' in Quebec slang.

Of course, as Cannon [42] stresses, companies using local people can overcome problems such as language, culture and the distance from head office when communicating with 'alien, sometimes hostile, environments' and this could well help the organisation to cope with some of the constraints identified above.

International advertising

Many companies attempt to simplify marketing communications by adopting a standardised approach to a number of different countries, others have adopted policies specific to each market and/or country. This not only varies from company to company but also by type of medium. Hite and Fraser [43] advocate a local approach. They state:

> In contrast to the declining barriers to standardisation of products, barriers to standardisation of international advertising appear to remain significant in many cases. Given the smaller potential for cost savings from centralised advertising functions and the apparent value of localised adaption in advertising, dispersed activities seem to be most profitable.

However, there is still a case for some selective standardisation. As Mueller [44] points out:

> This study revealed that the overall use of standardised messages was more common for products transferred between Western markets than for products transferred between Western and Eastern markets. Product type played a much lesser role than did the market distance. Message standardisation, however, was found to be significantly more common for television advertisements than for print advertisements, regardless of country.

Colvin *et al.* [45] describe how Ford of Europe developed an international product range which at the same time allowed for cross-country differences in product perceptions and product attribute differences. Figure 23.4 is a diagrammatic representation of the process.

The major factors in managing advertising effectively in another country are

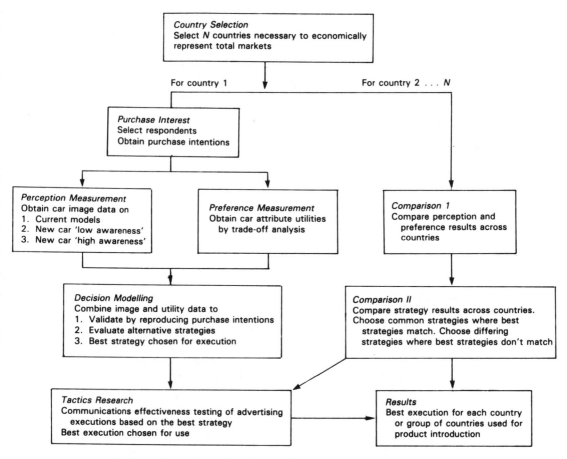

Source: M. Colvin, R. Heeler and H. Thorpe, 'Developing international marketing strategy', *Journal of Marketing*, vol. 44 p. 75, Fall 1980.

Figure 23.4   *Advertising strategy development*

media availability and agency availability. With international expansion of the media and the growth of international advertising agencies, these have become somewhat less of a problem than previously. Rachel Simpson [46] looks at the growth of the 'international media' citing such examples as the *Financial Times* (which has 25 per cent of its circulation outside the United Kingdom) whose coverage of European business topics has created demand for space from international advertisers.

The expansion of European satellite broadcasting (not just the UK-based BSkyB but also other European services in France, West Germany and Luxembourg) has opened up opportunities for international advertisers. And, just as the media are going international so are many advertising agencies giving companies the opportunity to benefit from the local experience of media planners, buyers and researchers while perhaps dealing with the same account executive at home. However, the management of international advertising can still be a fairly complex business. ITT, for example, has to monitor the efforts of over eighty advertising agencies worldwide and manage a budget of over $200 million. Ford markets cars and trucks in 185 countries and territories and works with thirty different agencies. One compensation, however, is that the principles of effective management of advertising are fairly universal (as described in Chapters 16 and 17).

Personal selling

When companies enter overseas markets they often use a local agent to sell on their behalf. After a time, however, the fact that agents are outside the control of the organisation and, by definition, will be working for a number of organisations and, therefore, not concentrating exclusively on the company's products, means that an organisation will have to consider setting up its own sales office. Once this need has been acknowledged, managing the personal selling effort will be similar to that of administering the domestic market, i.e. the same general functions must be covered including recruitment, selection, training, motivation and supervision. According to Terpstra [47] 'personal selling involves personal contact and is more culture bound than impersonal advertising'. This invariably means that we will have to recruit locally for our salesforce and might mean that we have to use local recruitment consultants to help with the task. Of course, if we have successfully used tests or screening techniques at home or in other subsidiaries, they could be used in the selection process in our new market. When it comes to training the salesforce, head office will normally have a high level of involvement determining such things as: content of the training courses, supplying training materials, monitoring the effectiveness of the training, supplying experts to give specialised training in product applications, new products, target markets, etc. Once we have found and trained our sales people we need to keep them (not have them 'poached' by some other company) and control their performance. There is the need to find the appropriate mix of monetary (salary vs. commission) and non-monetary rewards for each location (in some countries there might be a reluctance to accept commission as a form of payment and it might even be illegal to offer cash bonuses as inducements) and this could mean a radical change from existing structures. Control techniques are fairly standard: territory allocation, setting and agreeing objectives, quotas, call rates and reporting arrangements but, once again, these must reflect conditions in the country or area and, to a great extent, will be determined at local level.

Sales promotion

This is a very broad area of activity and includes the usual incentives to buy e.g. money-off, additional product, banded packs, point-of-sale material, coupons, free samples and competitions. One obvious constraint on their use is the legal framework which may restrict the types and frequency of the promotion that the

Table 23.2 *Regulation of promotional tools*

	Premiums	Gifts	Competitions
No restrictions or only minor ones	17	29	9
Authorised, but with important restrictions	10	6	22
General ban, but with important exceptions	7	3	6
Almost total prohibition	4	0	1
Number of countries	38	38	38

Source: J.J. Boddewyn, *Premiums, Gifts and Competitions: An International Survey.* New York: International Advertising Association, September 1978.

company can use. Table 23.2 shows that in many countries some form of restriction is placed on many promotional tools.

While not discounting the importance of such techniques (especially for customer goods) it might be that, in international markets, the company places greater emphasis on other promotional activities such as those listed by Hibbert [48], i.e. trade fairs, trade missions, store promotions, trade symposia, sponsorship and endorsements, and marketing weeks in trade centres. As Terpstra [49] optimistically concludes:

> The international firm should have some advantages over its national competitors in sales promotion. For example, there may be economies of scale in generating ideas and in buying materials. Ideas and materials may be suitable for several markets. One country can be used as a test market for others which are similar. Analysis of company experience in different markets will help in evaluating sales promotion and in determining the budget that should be allocated to it.

Public relations

Public relations (PR) has been defined by the Institute of Public Relations as: 'the deliberate planned and sustained effort to establish and maintain understanding between an organisation and its public'. The steps involved are fairly straightforward and could be standard for any country:

1. Define objectives.
2. Establish current image or level of understanding.
3. Identify the 'public'.
4. Select PR methods.
5. Monitor results.
6. Plan for the future.
7. Check for cost-effectiveness.

However, it would be naive in the extreme to think that we could write PR material or develop a PR programme in one country and then 'expect' it to happen. According to Ovaitt [50]:

> Public relations is arguably even more culture bound than advertising or marketing . . . barriers to global PR programs are still thought to be very high. The people I talked to offered many reasons for this – differences in culture, language, media, and political context, plus wide disparities in the sophistication of PR from country to country. Aware of the stupid mistakes of others (or regretting their own) they see uncommon merit in the common wisdom. Learn the culture and localise everything.

What this means, of course, is that companies need to be at least as, if not more, structured and disciplined in their approach to public relations in someone else's country.

The global debate

Thus far we have considered how management can cope with entry into a different country where people might use a different language and currency and where they have different perceptions and preferences. One way around this is to use the strategy that Keegan [51] calls 'same product, same message worldwide'. His identification of this lowest cost international product strategy has led to many others enthusiastically supporting this approach (notwithstanding the fact that it is only one of five strategies offered for consideration by him), notably Theodore Levitt. In a controversial article [52] he sounds the clarion call for a global approach to international marketing by saying:

> The globalization of markets is at hand. With that, the multinational commercial world nears its end, and so does the multinational corporation. The multinational and the global corporation are not the same thing. The multinational corporation operates in a number of countries, and adjusts its products and practices in each – at high relative costs. The global corporation with resolute constancy – at low relative cost – as if the entire world (or major regions of it) were a single entity; it sells the same things in the same way everywhere. Which strategy is better is not a matter of opinion but of necessity.

The same enthusiastic approach is taken by Draper [53] who states that: 'Time is running out for these multinational companies that do not recognise the powerful challenge posed by global rivals producing global products which are promoted using a powerful global advertising strategy.' As far as Draper is concerned, the global market is typified by the same business traveller and his patterns of consumption. This person is said to be a member of the Global Set (which, according to

Draper, has now replaced the Jet Set of yore). He is aged 30 to 45, wears a Christian Dior shirt and tie, carries a Samsonite suitcase containing a bottle of duty-free Black Label whisky, Dior and Hermes aftershave, Sony radio, Gold Gross pen, *Time* magazine, Amex card and travellers cheques, and a Canon camera. He wears a Seiko or Omega digital watch and drives a Mercedes or BMW. He has first class or business class airline tickets, stays at the best hotels and is a member of various airline travellers' clubs. Prestige and the desire to be recognised as a global trend-setter are key factors in his life.

A more measured approach is taken by Wind and Douglas [54] who, never-theless, consider that international markets are becoming more integrated, and this poses a particular challenge to management. They consider that a firm can no longer view its international operations as a set of independent decisions. Oper-ations across a diverse range of sociocultural, linguistic, economic, geographic and political environments involving a multiplicity of autonomous organisational units require the adoption of a global portfolio perspective to determine the optimal combination of countries, products, market segments and modes of operation to maximise long-term profitability. The short- and long-term financial resources and management time and effort should be optimally allocated on a worldwide rather than a country-by-country basis. Wind and Douglas then outline an approach to the design and implementation of an international business portfolio which is intended to help organisations in their strategic planning.

One company which has tried a new strategy is Schweppes International. Tisdall describes how the company decided that the future lay with international brands and, accordingly aimed for a consistent advertising message which could be used throughout the fifty-four countries in which it had a presence [55]. This led to the 'Schwepping' campaign, based on the idea of a central commercial with a voice-over which could be adapted to any language. After eighteen months Schweppes products, despite their premium price and a recession, were outper-forming the rest of the market. In less than two years Schweppes moved its marketing approach a long way from fairly watertight national compartments to one with an international flavour; they considered that advertising standards had been raised and more effective use was being made of budgets. Most importantly, the improvements had been translated into enhanced brand shares.

Success indeed, but not everyone agrees. Chisnall [56] quoting from an inter-esting article by Sinclair [57] states:

> Superficially, modern cities over the world tend to look alike: 'the modern "super culture" . . . built upon the culture of airports, throughways [urban motorways], skyscrapers and artificial fertilizers, birth control, and universities', but beneath the surface, cultural shackles may not be loosened as easily as old buildings are demolished.

Cannon [58] supports this view, suggesting that linguistic, religious, cultural, tech-nological and legal differences between countries effectively preclude standard-isation except in rare cases, in which a high degree of 'similarity in market conditions, consumer attitudes and product benefits' exists. Even campaigns with superficial similarity such as the Marlboro cowboy can mean different things in different markets. Standardisation is made increasingly difficult to achieve with the sometimes conflicting regulations and regulatory systems operating around the world. Even in industrial markets it is being recognised that the scope for standardisation is quite limited.

Lest this be thought a straight fight between American and British marketing academics, an eminent practitioner, Ray Higgs, marketing director, Middle East, Africa and Indian subcontinents, Rothmans International, weighs in attacking global marketing as 'the newest piece of nonsense, one of the fads and fashions in marketing techniques promulgated by marketing academics'. According to him, the concept that the consumer needs of the population of West Africa are similar to those of India, China and the United States is as naive as assuming that everyone in the world speaks English. Talk to the marketing directors of successful United States companies. They recognise that consumer needs differ across their own continent, let alone across the world. To support his argument Higgs quotes a number of companies which have achieved success by adopting a different approach to the different countries in which they operate. He then attacks the notion of the Global Set (see Draper above), and the relevance of its archetypal member to the sorts of market upon which many companies rely to generate their revenue [59]:

> I am not sure that such a person has any impact on consumers in the north of England, let alone those in Third World countries. This archetype of the familiar business airline traveller – the mainstay of airline profits – is the prime target for advertising in magazines such as BA's 'High Life'. But look carefully at the type and style of this advertising the next time you see a copy of such a magazine, and ask: would this advertising persuade the vast majority of consumers in major domestic markets to buy this product, or service? The answer, in most cases, is no.

Some companies have reached the same conclusion for a variety of reasons. Thackray [60] tells how Cadbury learned a painful lesson in the US confectionery market when, after building a manufacturing base costing $10 million the company also made a fateful marketing decision: to leave unchanged the British formula for its milk chocolate, despite its considerable difference from the dominant US chocolate taste. 'It was as if David, about to take on Goliath, had thrown away his slings in favour of hand-to-hand combat.'

In a very different context, Lace [61] describes how May and Baker simply cannot take a global approach to the international marketing of drugs. This is mainly due to the 'vastly differing rules imposed by various governments around the world. What is more, governments all seem to feel that drug regulation is a sign of political virility.' The author then gives some examples: the UK pharmaceuticals industry has a 'reasonable' relationship with the government, the Australian market is 'very difficult', and 'India has a policy of only supporting locally produced products'.

As with every debate, the truth probably lies somewhere between the two extremes. Hovell and Walters [62] discuss the 'standardised' approach to international marketing and outline the many advantages that can accrue from it. In the end, however, they must concede that complete standardisation is likely to be inimical to the achievement of high levels of market penetration in individual markets. As stated previously, a 'localised' strategy, taking fully into account individual market forces and needs, will invariably be more successful in terms of maximising sales in those foreign markets that the company has decided to enter.

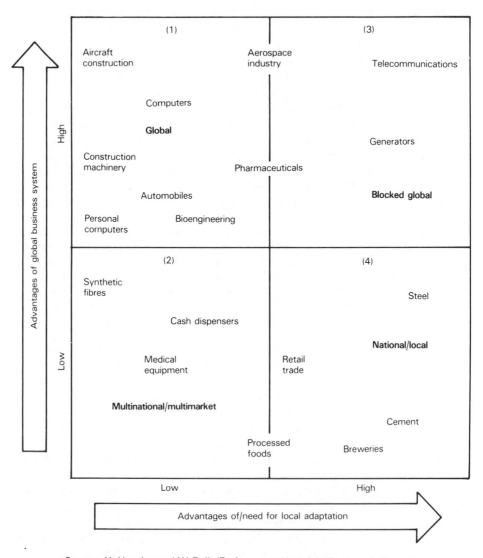

Source: H. Henzler and W. Rall, 'Facing up to the globalization challenge', The McKinsey Quarterly, Winter 1986.

Figure 23.5 *Matrix of 'trade-off': global vs national marketing policies by major industry sectors*

One company which 'sits astride the global fence' is the Volvo Car Corporation. According to Lester [63] this company pursues a strategy of worldwide niche marketing in which each national market is given the autonomy to develop in its own way. In the words of Carleric Haggstrom, senior vice-president marketing:

> It's a blend of the national and the international. The hardware is international –
> we have to make sure that we've got the product right, with enough customers and
> so on. But what the customer is really buying is the use of the product – for three
> years on average. Customer satisfaction in that time is the software, and that's
> local.

A further contribution to this debate comes from Domzal and Unger [64] who attempt to provide an overview of the various means by which global companies are achieving worldwide marketing success, through an investigation of the use of print media. Bolt [65] takes this a step further by trying to identify the 'common denominators' among successful global competitors, identifying ten 'somewhat arbitrary' criteria. Halliburton and Hunerberg [66] review some of the major issues in this debate which has been going on for over twenty years. They feel that, as has been seen above:

> the debate has been polarised, and that a sensible solution must be to avoid a
> universal quest for actionable conclusions based upon hard evidence. The task
> should be to produce practical recommendations for given international firms
> facing given market conditions rather than the construction of elegant theories.

This implies the sort of trade-off shown in Figure 23.5 which supports the notion that, despite the obvious advantages associated with a global approach, this is not a formula which can be followed by all companies engaged in international marketing. Rather they must give serious consideration to many factors.

The European Single Market

It has taken almost forty years, generated mountains of paperwork, split political parties, toppled prime ministers from power and has engaged the interest (or bored to tears) millions of people, but the European Single Market is now, at least in theory, a reality. The European Union accounts for more than a quarter of world economic output, has a total population of over 346 million and, with an estimated 1992 GDP of 5408.2 billion ECU, is claimed to be the world's largest trading entity. Clearly, therefore, this is not a market which can be ignored by any company contemplating international marketing. Those involved in international (and even domestic) marketing quickly become accustomed to analysing and coping with dynamic and turbulent environments but, it could be argued, the pace of change in Europe has defied the best efforts of many. A glance at some of the key dates

and events during the growth and development of the Union gives some indication of the reason why many organisations have encountered difficulties.

1951   Signing of the Treaty of Paris establishing a European Coal and
        Steel Community.
1957   Signing in Rome of Treaties establishing the European Economic
        Community (EEC) and the European Atomic Energy Commission
        (EAEC).
1968   The Community becomes a customs union (abolition of all import
        and export duties between the member states).
1970   Werner Plan for monetary union by 1980.
1973   Accession of Denmark, Ireland and the United Kingdom to the
        European Community.
1979   The European Monetary System (EMS) comes into operation. First
        direct elections to the European Parliament.
1981   Greece accedes to the European Community.
1984   Second direct elections to the European Parliament.
1985   White Paper on Single Market containing nearly 300 legislative
        proposals setting out the framework for the market.
1986   Portugal and Spain accede to the European Community. The Single
        European Act amends basic Treaties.
1989   Third direct elections to the European Parliament. First competitive
        tenders for EC public contracts.
1990   The Federal Republic of Germany embraces the new *Länder* of the
        former GDR after the collapse of the Communist regime there.
1991   Maastricht Treaty agreed.
1994   Fourth direct elections.

Add to this the outstanding applications for membership from Austria, Cyprus,
Malta, Sweden, Turkey, Finland and Norway (total population approximately 80
million) and it can be seen that organisations will need to devote a great deal of
time and effort just to keep up with what is happening in Europe and that forecasting future market trends will be increasingly complex.

One company which has made a great effort in Europe is Unilever. According
to De Jonquières [67] 'the creation of Lever Europe has established for the first time
a body charged with treating the region as one market. The 17 national companies
which previously reported to the detergents co-ordinator now report to Lever Europe
and the heads of the four biggest companies sit on its board.' The author attributes
the success of the reorganisation to the chief executive of Lever Europe, Jon Peterson,
who has shown the sort of dedication necessary to welding all of Unilever's European detergents operation into a more cohesive entity by spending at least half of
the 22 months he has been working on the reorganisation 'on the road'. The potential benefits to the company are claimed to be huge. As well as faster product

development, they include annual savings of several hundreds of millions pounds on manufacturing and a reduction of as much as three years in the time taken to launch new products internationally. Further, it is claimed that the new approach is already showing results. A concentrated dishwasher powder, introduced in Germany as Sun Progress in 1990, was available almost everywhere in Europe a year later.

Other companies have had to rethink their approach to Europe. Among these was ICI which, according to Lorenz [68], did a U-turn over Europe. He states:

> It must rank as one of the most rapid corporate rethinks ever. Amid a fanfare of proclamations by its senior managers about the need to 'reshape for the single market challenge' the world's fourth largest chemicals multinational creates a new regional organisation based in Brussels. Then, barely 16 months later, it decides quietly – although amid internal controversy – to shut it down.

(The complex reasons behind this decision bear further reading.)

Derwent Valley Foods, whose flagship brand is Phileas Fogg, still persevere in their attempts to penetrate the European market despite disappointing results in the early 1990s. Among the reasons for their initial lack of success, Lorenz [69] cites:

> the company had encountered the same problems which beset most medium-sized would-be exporters of consumer products within Europe: fragmented and sometimes impenetrable distribution patterns. In most industries these represent a far greater barrier to the creation of a single market than do national and regional differences in consumer preferences.

Perhaps one common element in successful pan-European marketing has been the move towards standardised (as far as is possible) packaging. In 1991 Galbani harmonised their packaging design at a cost of £100,000. Sales increased by 22 per cent in the United Kingdom, by 33 per cent in Germany and 50 per cent in France without any advertising. The chairman of the design company responsible for the new packaging, Marcella Minale, claimed that 'At least 65–70 per cent of the sales increase can be linked to design' [70]. Similar results have been claimed for Campbell Biscuits Europe, which wanted to position its Belgian Delacre brand as Europe's premium biscuit brand, Sun Progress (see above) and Sara Lee coffee brands.

Clearly, this short consideration of the European Single Market has been written from the parochial perspective of a European. Other countries (and trading blocs) regard 'Fortress Europe' with varying degrees of suspicion and hostility. We would argue, however, that, notwithstanding the claimed advantages for those European companies working within a 'single' Europe, their task remains one of truly international marketing and that any such advantages should not be overestimated. If and when political and monetary union become a fact, and if and when all countries implement EU legislation at the same rate and with the same vigour, the picture may change. However, differences in culture, language and consumer preference, as well as vastly differing distribution networks, will need to be taken into account for a very long time.

Summary ≡≡≡≡≡≡≡≡≡≡≡≡≡≡≡≡≡≡≡≡≡≡≡≡≡≡≡≡≡≡≡

This chapter first defined what is meant by international marketing and then went on to consider the reasons why organisations might decide to enter international markets. Various approaches to strategic planning were considered, notably a product portfolio analysis model, which helped identify the factors affecting international marketing decisions. This led to the recognition that a great deal of information was required about international markets and some sources of information were identified and their potential use and usefulness suggested. Various aspects of the international marketing mix were then considered, notably distribution, customer service, pricing and marketing communications. The current debate about the value or otherwise of a standard or global approach to international markets was reviewed with examples given to support each point of view. Finally, consideration was given to current progress towards a single European market and the implications for marketing management.

Questions for review and discussion ≡≡≡≡≡≡≡≡≡≡≡≡≡≡≡≡≡≡

1. What lessons might organisations contemplating international marketing learn from the Benetton experience?

2. How might an organisation decide which is the best form of overseas representation for it to use?

3. What factors influence the price that will be charged in an overseas market?

4. Researching international markets relies on the existence of up-to-date, reliable data. What would you do if these data were not available in a country that your organisation was considering as a potential market?

5. 'Successful international marketing planning looks for a balance between the local pulls for heterogeneity in marketing and the advantages that can be gained from looking for common elements which have general application in a number of markets' (Doyle and Hart, 1982). How can such a balance be struck?

6. The chairman of your company has just read about global strategies and wants to see the company's global marketing plan. How would you respond?

7. What approaches to planning and control of the international marketing operation of your company would you suggest?

References

1. Cateora, P.R. and Hess, J.M. 1975. *International Marketing*, 3rd edn. Homewood, Ill. Irwin, p. 4.

2. Cannon, T. 1979. 'Managing international and export marketing', *European Journal of Marketing*, vol. 4, no. 1, p. 34.

3. Keegan, W.J. 1980. *Multinational Marketing Management*, 2nd edn. Englewood Cliffs, NJ: Prentice Hall Inc.

4. Miracle, G.E. and Albaum, G.S. 1970. *International Marketing Management*, Homewood, Ill: Irwin.

5. Dapiran, P. 1992. 'Benetton – global logistics in action?, *International Journal of Physical Distribution and Logistics Management*, vol. 22, no. 6.

6. Terpstra, V. 1987. *International Marketing*, 4th edn. Hinsdale, Ill: Dryden, p. 8.

7. Chisnall, P.M. 1977. 'Challenging opportunities of international marketing', *European Research*, vol. 5, p. 15.

8. Harrell, G.D. and Keifer, R.O. 1981. 'Multinational strategic market portfolios', *MSU Business Topics*, Winter, pp. 5–15.

9. Hovell, P.J. and Walters, P.G.P. 1972. 'International marketing presentation: some options', *European Journal of Marketing*, vol. 6, no. 2, pp. 70–1.

10. Ryans, J.K. Jr 1969. 'Is it too soon to put a tiger in every tank?', *Columbia Journal of World Business*. March/April.

11. Cooke, P. 1979. 'Market analysis utilizing cultural anthropological indicators', *European Journal of Marketing*, vol. 6, no. 1.

12. Meidan, A. 1976. 'The importance of anthropological and noncontrollable marketing variables in international marketing', *Quarterly Review of Marketing*, Spring.

13. Calof, J.L. and Lane, H.W. 1987. 'So you want to do business overseas? Or Ready, Fire, Aim', *Business Quarterly*, Winter, pp. 52–7.

14. Homma, N. 1991. 'The continued relevance of cultural diversity', *Marketing and Research Today*, November.

15. Chisnall, op. cit.

16. Wilson, A. and Lockhart, G.W. 1981. *How to Start Exporting. A Guide for Small Firms*. London: Department of Industry and the Central Office of Information, p. 7.

17. Spiers, J. 1984. 'Doing business in France – successfully', *The Accountant's Magazine*, July, pp. 270–1.

18. van Mesdag, M. 1981. 'Why UK exports miss the tide', *Marketing*, 2 December.

19. Paulden, S. 1984. 'UK sells itself short on exports', *Marketing*, 24 June.

20. Brown, M. 1982. 'How to open export doors', *Marketing*. 2 December.

21. Hall, C. 1984. 'The diplomatic sell', *Marketing*. 6 September.

22. Hall, C. 1984. 'Fighting on in foreign fields', *Marketing*, 13 September.

23. Buckingham, C. and Penford. M. 1990. 'Thinking global, acting local – integrated information services for European companies in the 1990's', *ADMAP*, November.

24. Higgins, L., McIntyre, S. and Raine, C. 1991. 'Design of global marketing information systems', *The Journal of Business and Industrial Marketing*, vol. 6, no. 3. 4, Summer/Fall.

25. Porter, M.E. 1980. *Competitive Strategy*. New York: Free Press, p. 277.

26. Kim, J. and Daniels, J.D. 1991/2. 'Marketing channel decisions of foreign manufacturing subsidiaries in the US: the case of the metal and machinery industries', *Management International Review*. vol. 31.

27. Keegan, W.S. 1968. 'Multinational marketing strategy and organization: an overview', in Moyer, R. (ed.). *Changing Marketing Systems*. Chicago: American Marketing Association. pp. 203–9.

28. Mahon, J.F. and Vachani, S. 1992. 'Establishing a beachhead in international markets – a direct or indirect approach', *Long Range Planning*, vol. 25, no. 3.

29. Jones, M., Wheeler, C. and Young, S. 1992. 'European marketing and distribution in the 1990's: the case of the machine tool industry in the UK', *European Journal of Marketing* vol. 26, no. 7.

30. Lei, D. and Slocum, J.W. 1991. 'Global strategic alliances: payoffs and pitfalls', *Organizational Dynamics*, Winter.

31. Keegan, W.J. 1989. *Global Marketing Management*, 4th edn. Englewood Cliffs, NJ: Prentice Hall Inc., p. 421.

32. Cooke, op. cit.

33. Lancioni, R.A. 1991. 'Pricing for international business development', *Management Decision*, vol. 29, no. 1.

34. Al-Eryani, M.F., Alam, P. and Akhter, S.H. 1990. 'Transfer pricing determinants of US multinationals', *Journal of International Business Studies*, third quarter.

35. Lancioni, R. and Gattorna, J.L. 1992. 'Strategic value pricing', *International Journal of Physical Distribution and Logistics Management*, vol. 22, no. 6.

36. Yoffie, D.B. 1984. 'Barter: looking beyond the short-term payoffs and long-term threat', *International Management*, August, p. 36.

37. Ibid., p. 37.

38. Imeson, M. 1993. 'Swap shop', *Marketing Business*, April.

39. Terpstra, op. cit., p. 428.

40. Adrian, W. 1968. 'Baptism of brand X', *Reader's Digest Association*, January, p. 77.

41. Winnick, C. 1961. 'Anthropology's contribution to marketing', *Journal of Marketing*, July, p. 54.

42. Cannon, T. 1980. *Basic Marketing: Principles and Practice*. London: Holt, Rinehart & Winston, p. 141.

43. Hite, R.E. and Fraser, C. 1990. 'Configuration and coordination of global advertising', *Journal of Business Research*, vol. 21.

44. Mueller, B. 1991. 'Multinational advertising: actors influencing the standardised vs specialised approach', *International Marketing Review*, vol. 8. no. 1.

45. Colvin, M., Heeler, R. and Thorpe, H. 1980. 'Developing international advertising strategy', *Journal of Marketing*, vol. 44, Fall, pp. 73–9.

46. Simpson, R. 1987. 'Going global: the power of Babel', *Marketing*, 3 December, pp. 20–2.

47. Terpstra, op. cit., p. 484.

48. Hibbert, E.P. 1989. *Marketing Strategy in International Business*. New York: McGraw-Hill, p. 81.

49. Terpstra, op. cit., p. 494.

50. Ovaitt, F. 1988. 'PR without boundaries: is globalization an option?', *Public Relations Quarterly*, Spring, pp. 5–9.

51. Keegan, W.J. 1973. 'Five strategies for international marketing', in Thorelli, H.B. (ed.), *International Marketing Strategy*. Harmondsworth: Penguin Books, pp. 195–8.

52. Levitt, T. 1983. 'The globalization of markets', *Harvard Business Review*, May/June, pp. 92–102.

53. Draper, G. 1984. 'Time to go global or die', *Marketing*, 9 August.

54. Wind, Y. and Douglas, S. 1981. 'International portfolio analysis and strategy: the challenge of the 80s', *Journal of International Business*, Fall, p. 69.

55. Tisdall, P. 1982. 'Success for Schwepping', *Marketing*, 21 October.
56. Chisnall, op. cit.
57. Sinclair, C. 1973. 'Technological change – social change', *Industrial Marketing Management*, vol. 2.
58. Cannon, op. cit.
59. Higgs, R. 1984. 'Not yet a global village', *Marketing*, 13 September.
60. Thackray, J. 1983. 'Harsh lesson for Cadbury', *Marketing*, 14 July.
61. Lace, G. 1983. 'M & B's new formula', *Marketing*, 12 May.
62. Hovell, and Walters, op. cit.
63. Lester, T. 1984. 'How Volvo has found its world sales', *Marketing*, 11 October.
64. Domzal, T. and Unger, L. 1987. 'Emerging positioning strategies in global marketing', *Journal of Consumer Marketing*, vol. 4, no. 4, pp. 23–7.
65. Bolt, J.F. 1988. 'Global competitors – some criteria for success', *Business Horizons*, vol. 31, no. 1, pp. 34–41.
66. Halliburton, C. and Hunerberg, R. 1987. 'The globalization dispute in marketing', *European Management Journal*, vol. 5, no. 4, pp. 243–9.
67. De Jonquières, G. 1991. 'Unilever adopts clean sheet approach', *Financial Times*, 21 October.
68. Lorenz, C. 1993. 'Second thoughts above moving in', *Financial Times*, 1 February.
69. Lorenz, C. 1993. 'Innocents abroad', *Financial Times*, 4 January.
70. Quoted in Dickenson, N. 1993. 'The shape of things to come', *Financial Times*, 14 January.

Chapter 24

The broader application of marketing

Richard Christy

Scope of chapter

It is now generally accepted that the marketing concept and the range of marketing techniques are useful to a very wide range of organisations, broadening the scope of marketing beyond the commercial companies of its origin. Kotler and Levy, for example, propose that no organisation can avoid marketing. Hospitals, schools, government, trade unions and charities have marketing problems – if marketing is defined in terms of exchange relations between an organisation and its public. Non-profit organisations should, then, also expect to benefit from the more explicit use of modern marketing techniques, since [1]:

> Marketing is that function of an organisation that can keep in touch with the organisation's consumers, read their needs, develop 'products' that meet those needs, and build a programme of communications to express the organisation's purposes.

The broadening of the use of marketing into 'non-business' organisations became significant in the 1970s, when it was recognised that all organisations may have 'marketing' problems, or at least can make use of some marketing techniques in their activities. Lovelock and Weinberg [2] identified four characteristics of the non-business sector at the end of the 1970s:

1. *Multiple publics*; including, for example, clients and funders of an organisation.

2. *Multiple objectives*; non-business organisations may pursue a more complex range of objectives than businesses.

500

3. *Services, rather than physical goods*; marketing concepts developed for services are more likely to be of value to non-business organisations.

4. *Public scrutiny and non-market pressures*; non-business organisations are subject to close public scrutiny because they are subsidised, tax exempt and sometimes mandated into existence. They experience pressures from various publics and are expected to operate in the public interest.

More recently, however, this type of distinction between the use of marketing in business and non-business organisations has started to become less clear: on the one hand, many types of non-business organisation have been undergoing a process of commercialisation in response to new emphases in government policy; on the other hand, business organisations are beginning to take far more notice of their own 'multiple publics' and 'non-market pressures' in developing their commercial strategies. The simple business/non-business distinction is now an unsatisfactory way of describing the ways in which different types of organisation are making use of marketing ideas and techniques.

The point about the commercialisation of non-business organisations is brought out by the comments of Hadley and Young [3], who consider the radical changes that have taken place in the UK public services environment and propose a 'responsive' model of public service, with the following characteristics:

> The responsive model is *businesslike* in its emphasis on clarity in goals, planning, evaluation and the information systems these require. It is *service-oriented* in that goals are strongly influenced by concern to meet the needs of users as effectively as possible . . . it is *entrepreneurial* in a way which few public service organisations have been in the past, and *decentralist*, pushing decisions and responsibility into the front line . . . the responsive organisation would seem to hold the potential for the development of the effective *involvement and influence of its users* . . .

Commenting on user orientation in a responsive public service orientation, the authors suggest that such an organisation should [4]:

> set aside the tendency to define people's needs for them, and will work to establish dialogue with the users, not only through the formal democratic machinery . . . but also through direct contacts with users . . .

This emerging model of a public service organisation illustrates the blurring of the business/non-business distinction described above and begins to suggest how the concepts and techniques of commercial marketing are likely to be of relevance to these non-business organisations. Hannagan [5] elaborates this point:

> hospitals can make patients more welcome, colleges can provide training at firms' premises and orchestras can make their music more accessible by playing at lunch times at places where people congregate.

Over the last decade or so, the adoption of marketing techniques by the public sector in the United Kingdom (covering both profit-targeted and non-profit organisations) has been a pervasive trend: Cousins [6], for example, found that UK public sector organisations were significantly more likely to produce an annual marketing plan than organisations in the private sector and that the plans of the two types of organisation were not radically different in coverage, allowance having been made for their different environments.

Rather than adopt the simple business/non-business typology in looking at the broadened application of marketing, this chapter seeks to review the range of types of organisation – both business and non-business – that have successfully taken the marketing approach or at least the use of marketing techniques into contexts that differ significantly from the original model.

This approach takes as its starting point the idea that the main concepts and techniques of marketing were developed in the context of suppliers (usually organisations) of goods and services acting in more or less free competition with each other: by developing and implementing effective marketing strategies, these organisations were able to compete successfully for the business of their chosen customers. Put another way, marketing techniques were developed to allow commercial organisations to fulfil their profit-related objectives by competing more effectively for customer business. This now applies to consumer and industrial markets and to the marketing of both products and services.

The pressure on business to make a profit in competition with others has provided a powerful stimulus for innovation and refinement in the development of effective marketing techniques, and more broadly to the emergence of a true marketing orientation on the part of successful competitors. Without competitors, it would, of course, be much easier to set prices at a level that would ensure a profit: similarly, it is usually easier to sell a product at a loss than at a profit, whether in competition or not. The marketing approach, with its emphasis on competing through understanding and satisfying customer needs, offers both a successful strategic orientation for firms in competition together with a set of techniques for use in implementing the strategy.

However, marketing ideas are also now routinely applied in a number of contexts that differ significantly from the original model of the competitive market. Organisations with different roles and types of objective have learned to use the techniques of marketing to further their aims. Smith [7] discusses the relevance of marketing to the public sector and suggests that a distinction should be drawn between:

- 'Quasi' public organisations, such as nationalised industries, which face extensive competition and are expected to maximise profit/revenue.
- 'Social' public sector organisations, such as local fire services or social security offices, which do not see themselves as driven by market forces, but may none the less make use of some marketing research and promotional techniques in pursuit of their aims.
- 'Mixed' public sector organisations, such as leisure centres, which may pursue both social and commercial objectives, may be financially

subsidised, but which may also be in direct or indirect competition. Marketing is potentially relevant to these organisations in understanding and meeting the needs of its customers.

The approach adopted for this chapter adapts and extends this typology, in order to be able to include the extension of marketing into both public sector and other types of organisation. With this broader perspective, five main categories of the extended application of marketing principles can be identified:

1. Organisations such as utility service providers (sometimes state-owned), which clearly have commercial objectives and deal directly with end-users of their services, but operate in monopoly or strongly dominant market conditions. In sectors where partial liberalisation has taken place, supply of the service may be subject to independent and specialised regulation.

2. Non-profit commercial organisations, which are involved in the supply of goods or services (usually in direct competition with similar organisations or potential substitutes) and which operate with a subsidy, either from the public or private sector.

3. Organisations operating within artificial and regulated 'internal market' conditions (including parts of the UK National Health Service), often as a result of public sector restructuring by governments.

4. Non-profit organisations whose objectives are related in some way to the promotion of an idea, which may be indirectly related to the provision of goods and services associated with that idea. Such organisations may be mostly public sector funded, as is the case with a tourist board, or privately funded, as would apply to political parties.

5. Non-profit organisations, such as many of the charities, whose principal marketing-related objective is to raise funds to be applied to specific social causes.

The Appendix (p. 527) shows how these various extensions of the marketing concept can be said to differ from the original in terms of degree of competition, the existence of profit goals, whether the organisations are concerned with the supply of goods and services and whether they are involved in fund-raising.

Before looking at these broader applications of marketing, a note of caution should be sounded concerning the extent to which *true* marketing orientation, as opposed to the use of selected marketing techniques, can realistically be aimed at by organisations whose environments lack the key forces found in business. Foxall [8] discusses the application of marketing ideas in non-business contexts, suggesting that the central marketing notion of commercial 'exchange' between parties should be amended to that of 'matching' or the alignment of relationships between organisations and individuals in order to cover both business and non-business organisations. He suggests, however, that a distinction should be drawn between non-business organisations that make use of one or more marketing functions (e.g. advertising, market research) and those that have a true marketing orientation in the traditional sense. In his view [9]:

> For non-business organisations (charities, schools etc.), genuine and lasting marketing orientation is unlikely . . . simply because such organisations rarely encounter the conditions which compel it. Naturally the officers of these undertakings may display consumer orientation . . . but sustained consumer orientation is not at all predictable in these circumstances as it is in the case of competitive business.

The distinction between true marketing orientation and the use of certain marketing functions in the various broader applications of marketing is an important one, which will be examined further in this chapter. Only time will tell whether Foxall's doubts concerning the durability of true marketing orientation in less than fully competitive environments are justified, but remarkable recent changes of style, approach and performance can certainly be observed in many of the organisations considered here.

'Utility' service providers

While the term 'utility' may be broadly understood to cover a group of service-providing industries, the general heading potentially includes a very wide range of commercial activity, ranging from highly dynamic sectors such as telecommunications, broadcasting and the various energy supply industries through to more recently commercialised sectors such as postal services, public transportation and water and sewerage.

Despite the important differences between the various utility sectors in marketing terms, the dominant supply organisations in these sectors share several common characteristics, which tend to influence the way in which marketing ideas are used.

The first common feature of many of these organisations is their public service background. In some countries and sectors, this may be connected to a history of public ownership. In many cases in recent years, such organisations have formed part of the extensive programmes of privatisation around the world, often associated with moves towards partial or complete liberalisation of their markets. This public service history has often been associated with an uncommercial culture and set of management attitudes, together with underdeveloped management information. This lack of information is especially evident in relation to the market and to customer needs, which rightly or wrongly have taken a lower priority in a monopoly supply environment. There are, therefore, significant practical as well as cultural issues to be faced in introducing a more marketing-oriented culture into these organisations.

The public service history is also often associated with particular issues in pricing, which may include a complex set of traditional cross-subsidies between services, as well as special difficulties in estimating the actual cost of individual services resulting from the dominance of shared network costs in most of these industries. Bleek [10], in a review of market dynamics after deregulation in the United States, has described how the introduction of competition into these environments can result in major pricing upheavals as the traditionally profitable parts of the market, whose apparent profitability may in part depend on long-established cross-subsidies, are targeted by new entrants.

In many of the utility service provider industries, 'natural monopoly' arguments are advanced and high market entry barriers may apply. Liberalisation of supply (where introduced) may be only partial, and may anyway result in markets, or at least market segments, dominated by the former monopoly supplier. For these reasons, the process of sector restructuring and commercialisation often includes the establishment of a specialist regulator, whose influence on the dominant provider's main service pricing, service quality, service specification, distribution policy and business conduct may be far-reaching. Complex inter-business pricing systems may be established (as in the case of UK electricity supply) and regulatory policy is often an important determinant of market structure.

At a strategic level, the 'traditional' marketing approaches of identifying and selecting product markets and of segmenting, targeting and then positioning for chosen targets within those markets may also be influenced by the regulatory environment in which these types of organisation operate. Many of these organisations are not allowed an entirely free choice in these vital areas of marketing strategy:

1.   In some cases, they may be formally obliged to remain in certain product markets or to maintain universal availability of a particular service. In most countries, for example, the national postal service is required to provide a universal basic postal service, often at a uniform price, irrespective of distance conveyed or type of origin or destination.

2.   In other cases, the dominant suppliers may be formally excluded from certain markets, usually with the aim of restricting artificially the extent of their dominance. Dominant telephone companies in both the United Kingdom and the United States, for example, have experienced regulatory restrictions on carrying television programming on their networks, despite the increasing availability of technology that would allow this and the apparently natural development of their core business that this would represent.

3.   There may also be restrictions on the extent to which a dominant supplier can target attractive segments of the market and put together special packages for those segments. Regulators have been particularly keen to ensure that prices in the competitive parts of the market are not cross-subsidised by profits from the monopoly or dominated parts of the market.

4. In cases where regulators have adopted a policy of compulsory interconnection as a way of addressing the very high entry barriers that may be associated with these industries, the effect of the policy is to compel the dominant supplier to provide specified services to one particular group of customers: their competitors.

The development of marketing in British Telecom during the 1980s, when its markets were partly liberalised and when the organisation itself was privatised, provides a view of many of the common problems to be overcome in the early stages of the process of commercialisation. At a general level, the organisation needed to establish a stronger corporate identity, not least to distinguish itself from the Post Office from which it had recently separated. Its customer service had been based on supplying a monopoly service to 'subscribers', with frequent problems of delay caused by lack of network capacity, together with a general reputation for unresponsive and indifferent service. Improving the actual service supply performance and the quality of the customer interface became a priority in the new environment, but one that would take many years to tackle satisfactorily, as many telephone companies around the world have found in similar circumstances.

Despite the long-established practice of sending bills to each customer every quarter, the lack of reliable and detailed marketing information was quickly identified as a problem, hindering the process of segmentation, targeting and positioning that was becoming much more important. Major efforts were made in the fledgling marketing department in the 1980s to overcome this difficulty. As the process of market liberalisation started to unfold, the restricted and outdated nature of BT's range of products and services became an urgent problem, exacerbated by the rapid technological advances associated with electronic technology. BT's response was to extend its range very rapidly indeed, taking it into parts of the telecommunications market where previously it had not operated. During the same period, it also pioneered new channels of distribution, opening its own shops and business centres and also supplying its telephone products through third-party retailers for the first time. BT also stepped up its TV-based demand stimulation activity, both to increase network revenue and also in response to growing competitive promotional activity.

In the business user market, it built up the size, expertise and capability of its field and office-based salesforce in order to improve the quality and effectiveness of its interface with business customers. For the very largest users, BT introduced major account management programmes designed to understand and better meet the telecoms needs of these important customers, who naturally became a prime target for the new competitors.

With the partial liberalisation of the UK telecommunications markets came the establishment of Oftel, a new specialist regulator. Oftel's responsibilities included the regulation of BT's prices for its main services, which has been achieved by a price-cap mechanism. The evolution of this regulatory regime has seen the broadening and tightening of price-cap control, together with an extension of regulatory attention towards service quality levels. BT has therefore had to develop its pricing structure for the new environment under significant regulatory constraints, inevitably not without friction from time to time. Oftel has also intervened directly in the determination of pricing for the interconnect service which BT provides to its long-distance competitors over its own local network.

The monopoly-dominated past had also left a legacy in terms of price structures for network services. As the scope of competition was extended, many historical cross-subsidies (for example, from long-distance call prices to local call prices) became potential sources of instability and competitive opportunity for the new entrants. BT therefore embarked on a major programme of tariff 'rebalancing', designed to reduce progressively the key anomalies, which had the effect of changing markedly the real prices of many of its main services over the decade.

During its first decade in the new business environment, BT had to learn to develop and manage a mixed portfolio of regulated and fully competitive services, ensuring that it also complied with a range of regulatory rules designed to offset the effect of its dominant presence in many telecom markets. These regulations had an impact on pricing policy and service development and also influenced the framework within which BT's sales strategy was developed. The evidence from the 1990s suggests that regulation will continue to be an important influence in BT's marketing and that the rapid pace of change in the telecommunications and associated media markets will continue. Similar issues have also been faced for some years in the liberalised US market and a wide range of other countries are currently engaged in restructuring their telecommunications sectors.

Although not yet privatised, British Rail (BR) provides a further example of the way in which marketing ideas and techniques can be taken up and applied in a nationalised industry not previously noted for its responsiveness towards customers. By the mid-1980s, marketing managers in BR faced a serious challenge. As one of the organisation's senior managers put it in 1990: 'People love trains, but hate BR' (in Mitchell [11]).

BR's monopoly of train services leaves it none the less exposed to fierce competition on many routes from other means of transport, such as coaches, air services and the private car. Even where its market position is apparently very strong, such as on commuter routes into London, any widespread customer dissatisfaction with service quality or value for money is likely to translate into difficulties for BR in dealing with its owner. BR therefore has much to gain from understanding and seeking to satisfy the needs of its customers more effectively. Mitchell [12] describes how BR sought in the 1980s to transform itself from the traditional and rather unresponsive regional model inherited from the 1940s. Key initiatives included the selling off of non-core businesses, such as ferries and hotels, and the reorganisation of BR into stronger quasi-autonomous business units such as InterCity and Network South East. InterCity, for example, developed its own identity and applied itself vigorously to marketing [13]: 'customer service, product differentiation, market segmentation and precise targeting – price, product and image – plus an obsessively beady eye on the bottom line are the formulae now being applied'.

Brand management techniques have been applied to service categories such as First Class, Pullman, Railcards and Savers and airline-style seat planning has helped to improve the perception of quality. Matthews [14] reports how InterCity's marketing approach has evolved further: to compete with car travel on the M4, InterCity offers special reception services at key stations for its London to Bristol and Cardiff shuttle service and is considering further added value for its customers in the form of newspapers, coffee and fax services. Even where its business is not directly threatened by competition, the introduction of new service standards for rail users under the Citizen's Charter programme has underlined the importance for BR of reliably providing a service of very high quality.

Clearly, these developments go a long way beyond merely referring to rail passengers as 'customers': the external changes and BR's marketing responses are having the effect of transforming the organisation, with plenty of scope for a continuing flow of innovation in the development of services for customers. The present preparations for the restructuring and eventual privatisation of the rail service are likely to result in even more significant changes, including the introduction of specialised regulation of the market to respond to customer concerns about pricing, service availability and other issues under the new arrangements.

Further examples can be found across the spectrum of utility service providers, both in the United Kingdom and elsewhere. Since its privatisation in 1986, British Gas has been transforming itself from its former role as a monolithic national energy supply utility, partly in response to the introduction of higher levels of competition by Ofgas, the specialist regulator for the industry, but also with the aim of building up its international activity. During this time, the company has been a prominent user of television and other advertising media, seeking to establish a new corporate image with its markets and aiming to reinforce a competitive position in the energy supply business. The company has announced plans to abandon its regional structure and establish new business units, which separate the formerly integrated activities of gas transport/storage from gas supply to users [15]. As the present plans to liberalise the domestic supply of gas unfold [16], pricing issues similar to those faced in other liberalised utility services, such as the approach to be taken to traditional cross-subsidies, seem likely to emerge and it can be expected that regulatory controls will be an important influence on British Gas's pricing policy for some time.

Elsewhere in the utilities sector, UK water companies since privatisation have diversified into related engineering businesses, but also into more general waste management activities, such as solid waste collection and landfill [17]. As part of long-running deliberations by the government on the future of the postal sector, the Post Office is pressing for greater commercial freedom (for example, to diversify into new businesses), in order to allow it to compete more effectively against other European postal services.

Special marketing issues faced by newly commercialised utility service providers can be seen to be relevant to a wide and significant area of economic activity: marketing is of great importance in each case, helping these businesses to reshape their activities in order to serve customers more effectively in a more competitive environment. Experience to date has shown how valuable marketing can be in facing up to the new challenge, but also how the legacy of the monopoly-dominated past and the influence of specialist regulators impose particular restrictions on the application of marketing in some areas. Foxall [18], writing at a time when many of these UK organisations had not been privatised, observed that they operated in a similar structural context to that of private business, but that they were not subject to the same degree of competitive rigour and that their owners did not allow them the same ability to let their buyers determine the business that they were in. Privatisation and partial liberalisation have had the effect of narrowing these differences in most cases, but important 'public service' obligations are still applied to the core businesses of the new companies, by independent regulators, rather than by government departments.

Non-profit commercial organisations

The second category of marketing organisations whose context differs significantly from the 'traditional' model is the wide range of organisations which are engaged in the commercial supply of goods or services. These organisations are often in full competition with other similar organisations or potential substitutes, but are not required to run at a profit in the normal sense. In some cases, these organisations charge a price for their services, while in other cases, the service may be provided for free. Although there is no requirement to operate at a profit – sometimes because the service in question is felt to be desirable, but not viable at a cost-related price – it would normally be expected that these organisations manage separate revenue and cost budgets. In effect, they may be required to contain a loss strictly or to break even at an agreed level of subsidy. Many of the practical disciplines imposed on profit-making organisations by the imperative to sell their goods and services at a profit will also be present in these non-profit commercial organisations, although they may lack some of the pricing flexibility enjoyed by 'traditional' organisations.

Also, as discussed by Hannagan [19], the marketing exchange relationships of the public sector examples of these organisations may be more complex than for private sector profit-making organisations. In some cases, revenue may come from government or similar sources, but continuing flows of this revenue may none the less depend on the effectiveness of the organisation in satisfying the needs of its consumers. In the case of universities and colleges, for example, the government funding bodies are closer in role to shareholders than customers and will wish to be convinced by managers that they are making a sound investment.

Some entertainment organisations fall into the category of non-profit commercial organisations: many theatres, concert halls and art galleries, for example, are formally subsidised, either from public or private sector sources. To a degree, the attraction by an arts organisation of a sponsor may involve elements of a marketing exchange process: in the case of commercial sponsorship of arts organisations, for example, there is sometimes a tension between the desire of the sponsor for publicity and the priorities of the arts organisation.

Arts and leisure organisations are often well experienced in the use of a range of marketing techniques, in order to:

- understand the needs of the various groups into which their customers fall;
- develop the service they provide for these segments;
- communicate the availability and benefits of the services;
- develop more sophisticated pricing systems (where applicable) to appeal to different segments and to increase revenue.

Dibb and Simkin's [20] review of marketing in a range of profit-oriented and not-for-profit leisure service organisations describes the intensive tactical use of marketing techniques in this sector, but they comment that:

> The strategic role of marketing – anticipating and pre-empting the future – seems to be missing, compounded by the often narrow definition of competition, vague understanding of customers and misunderstanding of the potential impact from broader environmental issues. (p. 123)

Gardiner and Collins [21], in an issue of the *Journal of the Market Research Society* dedicated to the use of market research in the arts, look at the use of survey research techniques to understand audience needs and priorities. Blamires [22], in the same issue, looks at the use of pricing research for the arts, drawing an analogy between the components of customer value in a typical fast-moving consumer good (fmcg) product and the equivalent components of a 'product' such as an opera, play or musical. It is also clear (Tomlinson [23]), that computerised box office data offer considerable potential for marketing research for arts organisations.

Educational institutions provide a second example of this category: in the United Kingdom, educational organisations at all levels have become a great deal more commercial in their outlook and have been given increased autonomy in managing their resources. Like sponsored entertainment institutions, at this stage they generally lack the same level of freedom to select their 'products' and 'markets' that a commercial company would exercise, but they have been encouraged to diversify and expand their sources of revenue through marketing their existing 'products' and skills more effectively. Barnes [24] notes that customers of schools may not have the same freedom of choice as in commercial products and services and also points out that the principle of consumer sovereignty in schools may need to be qualified by the predominance of other organisational objectives, such as those which have to do with educational standards.

In a review of the growth of marketing in education at all levels in the United Kingdom, Sargent [25] looks at the way in which schools and colleges are using marketing ideas to understand the markets for educational services, develop the portfolio of products they offer, build new sources of revenue and make student recruitment more effective. These changes result from a deliberate shift in government policy, which places more decision-making authority with the schools and colleges, but also creates a significantly more competitive market in the provision of these services. Institutions that fail to respond to the new challenges will not only fail to develop, but may also ultimately disappear. Although major changes in outlook are under way across the whole sector, the growth of marketing orientation still has some way to go in many educational institutions, which are characterised as 'producer-led' and insufficiently concerned to understand and satisfy student needs. Educational institutions may benefit, for example, from understanding and responding to the choice process exercised by potential students; Davies, Preston and Wilson [26], for example, report on the way in which perceptions by potential students of accommodation quality can influence choice among higher education institutions.

At a general level, UK local government organisations are increasingly conceiving themselves as providing services to users and are turning to marketing to help them to do so more effectively. Hannagan [27] makes the point that many public services are relatively labour-intensive, that there is considerable interaction between service-providing staff and users, which makes the producer/consumer interaction crucial. However, Skelcher [28] points out that there have been important constraints to the growth of customer orientation in local public services, including lack of information about users, difficulties experienced by potential users in finding out about and accessing some services and variable quality of service delivery, together with a traditionally bureaucratic and unresponsive management culture. The feature of democratic accountability further complicates the environment in which these services are delivered, but great efforts are now being made to improve customer orientation in local services. Latham [29] reviews the growth of marketing departments in UK local authorities, highlighting the cultural challenge faced by incoming recruits in persuading their senior managers and political masters of the value of marketing and also in the need to operate under constant public scrutiny.

Some local government services may lend themselves more readily than others to the introduction of the marketing approach. Smith and Saker [30], for example, discuss the application of marketing to public library and leisure services. In a similar area, Yorke [31] provides a practical example of the way in which segmentation techniques can be used to understand and respond to the needs of leisure centre users. It is clear that a wide range of local government services can potentially be treated in a similar way.

In many of the cases discussed above, the awakening of interest in marketing is to some extent due to sector restructuring or changes in government policy. Another more general aspect of the present UK government's reform of public sector organisations is also of relevance to the adoption of marketing techniques, since it concerns the relationship between the service providers and the users of those services. The Citizen's Charter initiative introduced in the early 1990s sought, among other things, to define and develop the relationship between public service providers and users of these services. Inevitably, therefore, the service providers must begin to view those members of the public that they deal with as 'customers', even if in some cases, such as that of the Inland Revenue, many aspects of the normal customer relationship are necessarily absent. It can be expected, therefore, as pointed out by Burns [32], that public service providers will turn increasingly to market research in order to determine public wants and to advise on the setting of standards and targets. Once again, the adoption of these techniques may be an unreliable indicator of the emergence of true marketing orientation: Aldersley-Williams [33], in a review of progress to date in the Citizen's Charter, found that resultant service standards could be either very difficult for customers to understand or could focus on areas of relative unimportance to them.

'Internal market' participants

The third category of 'non-traditional' organisations in which marketing techniques are becoming much more significant is the various types of 'internal market' arrangements that have been established. As can be seen from the Appendix, participants in these internal markets operate within a framework of regulated competition, not necessarily with formal profit objectives (although revenue and cost budgets are likely to apply) and are often primarily concerned with the provision of goods and services to intermediaries, rather than end-users.

Many commercial firms are defining, specifying and monitoring 'customer/supplier' relationships between the various departments or divisions involved in the creation of the main product or service, sometimes in connection with the introduction of Total Quality Management techniques. These internal market relationships may also permit the 'customers' to look outside the group for the goods or services provided by another division, and may also permit 'suppliers' to seek to extend their activities to external customers. In the early stages of these arrangements at least, it is usual for internal trading to represent the great majority of business for buyers and sellers, although some marketing priority may be given to the new, but fast-growing external markets. Under these circumstances, the company or group rules governing external trading (including pricing) are likely to be one of the main determinants of the marketing scope enjoyed by the participants.

Examples of this category of marketing application may also be found in various parts of the UK public sector, where 'internal market' structures are beginning to emerge in:

- the new commercial relationships between the various parts of the National Health Service, based on establishing 'purchaser/provider' relationships between users, or those acting on behalf of users, and the suppliers of the various services;
- the results of compulsory competitive tendering (CCT) of certain activities by local government, in which some units of direct employees have been obliged to bid competitively with third parties for contracts to carry out their former role in the organisation;

- the central government Executive Agencies established as part of the far-reaching reform of the Civil Service under the 'Next Steps' programme, which again is likely to involve substantial amounts of contracting out of services hitherto provided by direct employees of the organisation concerned.

In these cases, the increased use of marketing techniques has been one of a number of radical changes associated with the establishment of quasi-autonomous commercial units. At the simplest level, these units may seek to establish and publicise a new, more independent identity (e.g. with both the service 'purchasers' and the ultimate 'consumers' of the service as target audiences), but there is also scope to apply some of the approaches of strategic marketing in:

- analysing and understanding the needs, priorities and choice criteria of the service 'purchasers' in the new environment and the way in which the competitive supply market is likely to develop under the new regulations;
- carrying out an audit of the new unit's strengths and weaknesses against potential competitors and substitutes in the emerging supply market;
- developing a strategic positioning for the new unit, taking account of the external and internal situation analysis and also of any service obligations or restrictions applied by the relevant regulator or authority.

This type of marketing response by the newly established 'provider' units is relatively easy to describe in general terms: the extent to which and the speed with which public sector organisations are actually able to respond in this way will also depend on a wide range of situational and cultural factors. One example of barriers to be overcome in the development of internal markets is provided in an article by Ellwood [34], which describes the practical difficulties experienced by NHS health care provider organisations in obtaining reliable service cost information to support pricing policy development just after the introduction of the NHS reforms in 1991. As in many of the former monopoly utility organisations described above, information systems development must provide an important support to commercialisation.

Whether or not the principal purchasers of health care services are intermediaries (such as GPs), rather than end-users, modern health care provider units are placing greater emphasis on understanding the needs of their users in more detail. Hayden [35] discusses the application of marketing ideas to the provision of public health services, looking at the ways in which product, production, sales and finally marketing orientation can be interpreted in the health care context. Because of the necessary dominance of professional expertise and experience in the delivery of health care services, product or production orientation is often found in this sector; as she comments, however, marketing orientation in health care means using the consumer view as the basis for professional or managerial judgements, rather than simply giving consumers everything they ask for.

Evans [36], in a paper discussing the traditional approach of the NHS to strategic planning, comments that the inherited emphasis had been on incremental service strategies, a 'forecast and allocate' approach that the corporate sector had found to be inadequate in dealing with increasingly turbulent business environments. For the NHS, the position was compounded by:

> the absence of a flow of information about the consumption of the product and satisfaction with it . . . the absence of a market intelligence leaves public service organisations with a profound gap in their evaluation and control of their activities, and in assessment of their own performance.

Schaeffer [37] looks at the experience of commercialisation of health service provision in the United States in the Minneapolis/St Pauls area of the Midwest and comments:

> we learned that in health care, as in other service industries, the customer is always right. This is a difficult concept for health care providers. Health care professionals typically see their job as diagnosing and treating medical needs, and they do that well. However the old process of unilaterally diagnosing a problem and prescribing treatment is not enough in an increasingly competitive environment. Patients expect service, courtesy, communication and understanding – not just quality medical care. Our market research shows that patients take quality of care for granted . . . the lesson is that we must meet service expectations as well as medical needs.

Similarly, Bennett [38] discusses how the concept of branding might be applied to the health-care environment and concludes:

> when we really develop a strategic approach to marketing, it means getting as close as possible to the customer, and listening. The supplier (or provider) who listens and learns, and gives just that little bit extra to the customer, will find that exchange of values to be real and lasting. This will involve health-care business-units working smarter, not harder, to build the brands of the future.

In each of these quotes, there are strong parallels with the evolution of commercial companies from a production orientation towards customer orientation and the marketing concept. There are, however, many special aspects of the provision of health care services and the application of traditional marketing ideas to this area is a cause of controversy. Scheaff [39] reviews the reservations that have been expressed about the applicability of marketing to health care services and concludes that: 'Marketing can and should be applied to NHS services, but simply imitating commercial marketing is unlikely to be successful or desirable. A hybrid form of marketing is required for the NHS and comparable organisations.' He then proposes a set of special requirements that should be applied to marketing in the NHS in order to increase the chance of success and to avoid adverse effects for users. He also suggests that variants of marketing in the NHS will need to be developed, reflecting, for example, the special priorities of those buying from the new providers and of the providers themselves. It is clear that both types of organisation will need to work together effectively to ensure that the needs of actual consumers of health care services are met effectively.

Hayden [40] proposes and discusses a useful set of guidelines for purchasing and service-providing health care organisations seeking to build up market orientation. Besides underlining the importance in this process of such aspects as market research, segmentation and the development of good communications, she highlights the value of top management commitment and the involvement of those staff most closely involved in service delivery, who may have detailed understanding of the distinguishing features of good and bad service from the consumer's point of view. In transforming a large health care providing organisation, some units may be able to achieve market orientation earlier than others, which may suggest that an increased autonomy on the part of those business units may assist the process. As she concludes, each health care organisation will need to develop its own specific strategy to achieve market orientation, placing emphasis on different aspects of the guidelines as circumstances demand.

It is clear from the comments reviewed in this section that marketing techniques and marketing orientation – at least in a specialised form – are likely to play an increasing role in the provision of health services. In some parts of the sector, major changes are already evident to users: the retail outlets of opticians, for example, have for the most part moved a long way towards customer (i.e. end-user) orientation in the last decade and there are signs that some dentistry practices are moving in a similar direction [41]. Consequent benefits for users of the increasing commercialisation of a wider range of health services can certainly be imagined, but care will be needed to develop an approach to marketing that will take due account of the special aspects of health care services and also the misgivings that have often been voiced about the commercialisation of this sector.

'Idea-promoting' organisations

As can be seen from the Appendix, idea-promoting organisations may be funded from either public or private sources and may in either case be parts of larger organisations: their main characteristic is that they do not trade in goods or services or seek to attract customers, but are rather established in order to create, sustain or change attitudes towards a particular topic. In so doing, they are to some extent in competition, both with promoters of opposing or alternative ideas in the same area and more generally with all other calls on the attention, sympathy and concentration of the target groups. These organisations are therefore likely to find great value in a range of marketing techniques, ranging from market research into attitudes through to the use of advertising and public relations techniques to communicate, inform and persuade. Some types of this activity are known as 'social marketing', defined by Kotler and Zaltman [42] as:

the design, implementation and control of programmes calculated to influence the acceptability of social ideas and involving considerations of product planning, pricing, communication, distribution and market research.

It can be argued, however, that idea-promoting organisations are primarily users of certain marketing techniques, rather than organisations that are truly marketing-oriented in the traditional sense. The ideas to be promoted by one of these organisations, for example, are determined by the sponsors of the organisation, rather than by an appreciation of the needs of any 'marketplace'. For example, while an idea-promoting organisation will need to understand the basis of the current attitudes and beliefs in the area of interest in order to construct and present its argument effectively, there is generally little possibility of changing the 'product', or core idea in response to prevailing market attitudes. As such, the outlook of these organisations can be characterised as production- rather than marketing-oriented (Foxall, [43]).

Several types of idea-promoting organisation can be distinguished:

1. Government-sponsored bodies with a specific idea-related remit, such as the Health Education Authority, which has been a major user of press and poster advertising.

2. Trade associations, whose activities on behalf of their members may include the promotion of a well-informed and favourable public attitude towards the industry in question. In the United Kingdom, examples of this type might be the National Dairy Council (see below) or the Advertising Association.

3. Pressure groups, whose sponsorship may come from both private individuals and corporate organisations, and who operate with different degrees of marketing sophistication to draw attention to their cause and to persuade target groups to change their attitudes towards the subject in question.

4. Political parties, who are obvious and heavy users of marketing and communication techniques during election periods and whose advertising may sometimes be a prominent part of the campaign as a whole.

The Health Education Authority (HEA) is funded by the Department of Health and provides a good example of an organisation making use of marketing techniques to promote ideas, in this case to do with healthy living and the avoidance of illness. It is a major user of advertising and other forms of promotion such as support literature: recent campaigns have covered areas such as HIV/AIDS, smoking, heart disease and immunisation. Advertising expenditure in 1992/3 was more than £6 million [44], from a total expenditure by the organisation of £32 million. A more detailed view of the use by the HEA of marketing communications and research techniques can be seen, for example, in its report on its mass media activity between 1986 and 1993 [45] in the different elements of its campaign in the area of HIV/AIDS and sexual health education. The organisation makes use of research into advertising awareness among its target audience, together with tracking studies of attitude change as the campaign develops. Marketing research has also been extensively used to develop message strategies and evaluate results in other HEA ventures, such as the campaign to discourage teenagers from smoking. In its campaigns to promote healthy living, the HEA usually has to compete with other ideas, either in the form of conflicting commercial messages or in the form of ignorance or mistaken beliefs.

As mentioned above, the National Dairy Council (NDC) could be described as a type of trade association within the fast-changing UK market for milk. The NDC's role is evolving in response to the 1994 restructuring of the market. Prior to these changes, however, it worked on behalf of the Milk Marketing Board, which was then the organisation representing producers, and the Dairy Federation, which represents processors, manufacturers and distributors of dairy produce, aiming to coordinate the dairy industry's generic information and promotion activities in England and Wales [46]. In recent years, the NDC has run a number of advertising campaigns to promote the desirability of milk as a drink, in the face of stiff competition from soft drink manufacturers, whose advertising expenditure in 1992 was more than five times that of the milk industry [47]. Perhaps the organisation's most memorable advertising campaign, however, has had a more specific aim: that of promoting the British concept of doorstep delivery of milk. Between 1985 and 1992, the share of household milk purchases via doorstep delivery fell from 81.9 per cent to 61.4 per cent, reflecting a growth in sales through supermarkets. The much admired 'Dancing Bottles' TV advertising campaign produced for the NDC in 1991 by the agency BMP DDB Needham aimed, in effect, to relaunch this very traditionally British concept, using humour and superb animation. According to Summers [48], the advertising had the effect of arresting the rate of decline of doorstep delivery; the campaign also won the Institute of Practitioners in Advertising's 1992 prize for advertising effectiveness.

A further example of the use of marketing techniques by this type of organisation in furthering an idea is provided by Johnson's [49] review of the marketing activities of the Meat and Livestock Commission (MLC) in the late 1980s on behalf of the diverse interests of farmers, abattoir owners and butchers. Faced with a falling consumption of meat, increasingly sophisticated and effective efforts on the part of vegetarian organisations, the crisis caused by the cattle disease BSE for beef producers and general accusations of insufficient urgency in its response, the MLC sought to fight a rearguard action, developing strategic and tactical advertising campaigns and increasing the funding allocated to information and education.

Pressure groups have often made very professional and effective use of advertising and public relations activities to communicate their concerns to the public. In the field of environmental issues, for example, the use of marketing communications techniques over the years by organisations such as Greenpeace and Friends of the Earth has helped to raise the profile of these ideas amongst a much broader audience. There is a often a substantial overlap between this type of activity and the fund-raising activities of charities: the adverts produced by the RSPCA against long-distance live animal transport, for example, may have an influence on government policy development as well as attracting further public support for the campaign. In the 1980s, the shocking and disturbing images used by the organisation Lynx in its campaign against the fur trade brought home powerfully how modern advertising methods could just as readily be deployed by pressure groups as by commercial organisations.

Political groups represent a final type of idea-promoting organisation: in this case, a clearer exchange relationship may be evident, in that a political party may seek to suggest that it will act in a certain way, in the hope of winning votes from those who approve of the proposals. At election times, messages about policies may also be sent by groups other than the political parties: trades unions, for example, have sometimes sought to communicate to voters their perspectives on particular policy issues through mass media advertising. Not all of this type of idea-promoting activity is carried out by mass media advertising and leaflets: Elsden [50], for example, reports on the use of direct marketing by political parties. By using direct marketing, political organisations can refine and make more relevant the message they send to particular target groups.

Smith and Saunders [51], in a review of the application of marketing to British politics, have suggested that political activity, like commercial activity, can be seen as having moved from an era of unsophisticated selling at the turn of the century through intermediate stages towards an era of strategic marketing. In this phase, political protagonists, making extensive use of private polls, may see themselves as identifying wants amongst the electorate and bidding to satisfy them more effectively than any other political party. Again, care must be taken in applying the commercial marketing analogy to the field of politics: the authors discuss the likely tension between policy principles and short-term, populist issues that might result, suggesting that political parties need to build for themselves an enduring 'brand image' with a distinctive positioning, thus avoiding the flight to the middle ground. Their paper also demonstrates the potential value of psychographic segmentation techniques in understanding voting behaviour.

Fund-raising organisations

Two main types of organisation can be distinguished under this heading: voluntary sector organisations and charities. The distinction between the two is not a firm one, but the different focus of the two types of organisation will tend to determine the use which they make of marketing techniques. For the purposes of this chapter, voluntary sector organisations will be defined as those that carry out defined charitable activities, making extensive use of the skills and experience of volunteers. Their funding may come from a range of sources, including individuals, corporate organisations, charities and government departments: they may thus be involved in fund-raising, but not necessarily to the extent of more publicly prominent charities. While charities as defined here may well be involved directly in performing charitable activities (i.e. acting as voluntary sector organisations), they are distinguished for the purposes of this section by a focus on fund-raising to support a programme of charitable activities, some of which may be carried by other organisations at the behest of the charity. It should also be noted that some of the non-profit commercial organisations discussed earlier may have charitable status and may from time to time engage in fund-raising in support of their own operations [52]. Similarly, political parties and many pressure groups are also active in the use of marketing techniques to raise funds to support their idea-promoting activities.

In each case, while these fund-raising organisations do not directly compete with each other in a commercial sense, they can, like the idea-promoting organisations discussed above, be seen as being in competition with other charitable causes for the attention, sympathy and support of their target groups and also, perhaps more significantly, for a share of funds which these groups may be prepared to donate to charitable causes. This competition seeks to persuade the potential donor that a contribution would be both effective and worthwhile: promotional material, for example, may take the form of demonstrating the urgency and importance of the cause in question and also of explaining how effective the activities of the charity in question have been in the past in responding to these problems.

Charities may also share with idea-promoting organisations the relative lack of flexibility concerning the 'product' or central cause of the organisation, as compared to the core businesses of commercial organisations. From one point of view, a charitable donation can be seen as a form of exchange, in that the charity promises to do something to respond to an issue that causes the donor concern. However, donors or groups of donors can also be seen as analogous to 'investors', rather than 'customers', since they may be persuaded to make repeated (and sometimes covenanted) donations over a period of time to support a particular programme of activity by a charity. From either point of view, however, there is likely to be a short-term limit on the extent to which a charity is prepared to amend its position or priorities in response to 'customer' or 'investor' views, although it may well adjust the presentation of its cause, the direction of its appeals or the details of its approach in order to communicate more effectively. Over the longer term, of course, a charity will use its understanding of its area of specialism to develop more effective ways of addressing the needs of those it serves, the success of which may well render the charity more effective and thus more attractive to its actual and potential donors. This can be seen as analogous to the process of product development in a traditional marketing context.

A number of marketing techniques are clearly of potential value to charities in their fund-raising activities and many of these organisations have built up experience in:

- segmenting and targeting their potential donor markets;
- the use of market research techniques;
- the effective use of mass media advertising;

- understanding the process through which donors decide to give to a particular cause;
- building up and making effective use of donor databases;
- making effective approaches to various types of potential donor;
- using direct marketing and sales promotion techniques and monitoring effectiveness.

Some of the larger charities have been significant users of mass media advertising, although increasingly fund-raisers are seeking to develop campaigns that more tailored to specific audiences and to make use of advertising as part of a properly co-ordinated programme of promotional activities [53].

As part of the move towards more closely targeted appeals, UK fund-raising organisations began to make much greater use of direct marketing in the 1980s, following the earlier lead of the US market. This rapid growth resulted in many successes, particularly while the techniques were relatively new to potential donors, but it also had the effect of raising the competitive stakes for fund-raisers. As charities became more and more effective at presenting their appeals, the phenomenon of 'compassion fatigue' among the public began to be a problem for fund-raisers, exacerbated by the effects of the economic recession on donors' ability and willingness to give. The marketplace is also becoming crowded: Latham [54], for example, describes the PR-based launch of a new cancer charity BreakThrough, which in 1991 joined over thirty-nine other cancer charities competing for funds in the market.

Successful fund-raising via direct marketing in the 1990s demands ever-increasing skill and professionalism. Pidgeon and Saxton [55] suggest that charity databases will need to become much more sophisticated, that the days of mass mailings are numbered, that charities will build up their own in-house marketing skills and that above and below-the-line activities will need to be better integrated. They also point out that success is likely to depend on pushing the right motivational buttons, addressing the right audience and using the right vehicle (e.g. insert, advertisement or mailshot). They suggest that charities should seek to appeal at one of five possible motivational levels:

1. *Identity*: helping the donor to identify with the aims of the charity and to feel part of what they are doing. A number of environmental organisations, for example, have successfully presented themselves in this way.

2. *Belief standards*: appealing to the donor's view of what is right and wrong: that children, for example, have a right to education and health care.

3. *Capability*: assuring the donor that the charity has the expertise and resources to address the problem described, perhaps by describing the organisation's track record.

4. *Behaviour*: promising a specific action, for example by linking, say, a £10 donation to a number of vaccinations.

5. Referring to the donor's *immediate environment*, which may be very effective for locally based appeals, where benefits will be directly evident to donors.

Despite the high level of fund-raising activity, most charities know relatively little about the audience they are addressing in their appeals [56], but effective fund-raising today is increasingly demanding a detailed understanding of who the donors are and what motivates them to give. Mindak and Bybee's [57] review of the potential application of marketing ideas to charitable activities looks at the way in which the presentation of the appeal can be analysed in the same way as commercial marketing communications and also reviews how marketing techniques can be applied to identify and reach heavier donors to charities. In a later study, Drucker [58] discusses the critical importance of fund-raising to many non-profit organisations and discusses the difference between fund raising and fund development:

> Fund raising is going around with a begging bowl, asking for money because the *need* is so great. Fund development is creating a constituency which supports the organisation because it *deserves* it. It means developing what I call a membership that participates through giving.

Success in fund development relies in part on the development of effective positioning in the minds of actual and potential donors. To achieve this, it is just as important for a charity to understand in detail the priorities and needs of its donors as it is for a successful commercial firm to understand its customers. Marketing techniques can be used to identify and understand potential and actual donors: Schlegelmilch [59], for example, showed how segmentation could be used to target fund-raising appeals more effectively and a number of studies have investigated the relative importance of 'heavy' donors to charitable organisations. Success in this area will also depend on the establishment of a successful track record by, say, a charitable institution in dealing with its chosen area of specialism: an organisation of this type will need to measure and communicate that effectiveness to its potential 'customers'.

Many charities have also sought to encourage giving via legacies and have built up experience in the use of marketing techniques to establish and maintain what is usually a long-term relationship with the donor. Morris [60] describes the way in which the RNLI aims to maintain regular contact with its loyal donors and thus has the potential to monitor and develop lifetime relationships with donors. Great skill is needed to design a programme of contact that will be relevant, appropriate and cost-effective.

Fund-raisers have also been successful in partnership with commercial companies, seeking their sponsorship for fund-raising events, for example, or their co-operation in sales promotions in which donations to charity are the principal attraction. Smith and Alcorn [61] provide a thorough review of the development in the United States of so-called 'cause marketing', whose defining characteristic is to link traditional product marketing with creative promotional appeals that encourage charitable giving. The authors suggest that this trend represents a departure from corporate 'cheque book' philanthropy by integrating traditional marketing with corporate social responsibility. Three main forms of cause marketing have emerged so far: (1) corporate sponsorship of media support for the charity, in exchange for product links with a cause; (2) the provision of media support plus conditional donations, which may be tied to product purchase levels; and (3) the provision of media support plus 'dual incentive' donations, in which coupons towards product purchase also trigger donations to the cause. Their survey of consumers segments the market on the basis of likely response to cause marketing and provides practical advice to corporations contemplating this type of activity. They conclude that cause marketing may be the most creative and cost-effective marketing strategy to evolve in years. Dwek [62] looks at the growth of cause-related marketing in the United Kingdom and describes the way in which a wide range of commercial organisations have used links with charities to enrich and broaden their communications with consumers and other stakeholders, suggesting that companies are only just starting to understand the potential of this type of activity.

Charities, like commercial organisations, have to address a range of publics: actual and potential donors, those helped by the charity's activity, actual and potential volunteers, other charitable organisations in similar or related fields, governments, and so on. Their success in fulfilling their objectives will depend to an important extent on how well they understand and deal with the needs of these various publics and the techniques of marketing have proved to be of great value in an increasingly competitive fund-raising environment. The degree of sophistication with which these techniques are applied varies a great deal across the diverse range of charitable organisations and is likely to become even more important in future.

Summary

This chapter has looked at the way marketing has grown from its origins in the competitive commercial world to play an important role in a range of institutions with significantly different operational contexts and roles. At one end of the range reviewed here, the utility service providers are becoming a great deal more commercially and customer-oriented, sometimes as a result of deliberate restructuring of their sectors through privatisation and partial or complete liberalisation of their former monopoly environments. In some cases, such as telecommunications, former monopoly-based national utility service providers are transforming themselves into leading players in highly dynamic and competitive world markets, but are still subject to significant special regulatory influences in their day-to-day marketing activities. In the case of some of the other former utility service providers, the commercial transformation has not so far been as far-reaching, but significant shifts from production orientation towards marketing orientation are evident in the behaviour of these organisations.

This chapter has also reviewed the use made of marketing by a range of 'non-profit' organisations, some involved in the supply of goods and (more often) services, but others involved in the promotion of ideas or fund-raising. Virtually all these organisations can make use of selected marketing techniques, such as market research or advertising, in carrying out their activities, but experience in some of these organisations suggests that there may be further clear benefits in the adoption of a more thorough marketing orientation, pervading all of the organisation's activities and allowing an understanding of customer needs to shape the way the organisation conceives and carries out its work. This distinction between partial and thorough adoption of the marketing approach is brought out in Drucker's [63] interview with Philip Kotler on the use of marketing in non-profit organisations. Discussing the experience of hospitals in the United States, Kotler comments:

> The problem has arisen in hospitals lately that the hospitals have used their budgets for advertising purposes. They have spent big dollars trying to communicate to their communities that they are a friendly hospital, they are a 'caring' hospital, and so on. And they are all wondering now whether those ads have really established in the minds of the community an identity for that hospital and a preference for the hospital. Some CEOs are disturbed by the results; they don't see enough net gain.
>
> My analysis is that these hospitals have often put their budgets to the wrong use. They've gone into advertising before they had a character to their hospital. Before they had a true patient focus to their hospital. And they haven't really gone into marketing in the right order. The order being: first, do some customer research to understand the market you want to serve and its needs. Second, develop segmentation and be aware of different groups that you're going to be interacting with. Third, develop policies, practices and programs that are targeted to satisfy these groups. And then the last step is to communicate these programs. Too many hospitals and other non-profit organisations go right into advertising before they've gone into the other three steps, and that's really doing things backwards.

It has been argued in this chapter that developments in both the commercial and non-profit sectors of modern economies have tended to blur some of the formerly clear distinctions between profit and non-profit organisations and that it may be more useful to consider a range of contexts in which marketing is applied, each significantly different from the profit-oriented fmcg environment in which marketing grew up. This review has demonstrated how the marketing approach can potentially help a wide variety of organisations to carry out their roles more effectively and that current policy trends of liberalisation and commercialisation of public services are likely to increase further the priority given to marketing in these organisations. Marketing, then, can be seen as a set of ideas that allows a wide range of commercial and non-profit organisations to 'harmonise the needs and wants of the outside world with the purposes and the resources and the objectives of the institution' (Kotler, quoted in Drucker [64]). In the coming years, it seems likely that each of the types of organisation considered in this chapter will continue to build up a specialised body of applied marketing expertise, reflecting the various public policy and other special influences that define the environments and functions of these organisations and above all helping the organisations to become more effective in pursuing their objectives.

Questions for review and discussion

1. How important is the existence of competition and the profit motive in encouraging true marketing orientation in an organisation? What tests of true marketing orientation might be applied to a non-profit organisation?

2. Concerns are sometimes expressed about the use of marketing techniques by idea-promoting organisations to 'manipulate' public opinion. Under what circumstances might these concerns be justified? What safeguards could be applied to avoid any unwelcome effects of this type of activity?

3. Specialist regulators of monopoly or strongly-dominant commercial organisations have placed a great deal of emphasis on price in the measures they have developed. To what extent can a price-dominated regulatory framework simulate the effects of competition on the dominant provider?

4. How are the special features of health care provision likely to affect the development of marketing in that sector?

5. What marketing measures might a charity consider to overcome a problem of 'compassion fatigue' in its donors and potential donors?

References

1. Kotler, P. and Levy, S.J. 1969. 'Broadening the concept of marketing', *Journal of Marketing*, January.
2. Lovelock, C.H. and Weinberg, C.B. 1978. 'Public and nonprofit marketing comes of age', in *Review of Marketing*, ed. Zaltman, G. and Bonoma, T.V., quoted in Kotler, P. 1984. *Marketing Management – Analysis, Planning and Control*, 5th edn. London: Prentice Hall International.
3. Hadley, R. and Young, K. 1990. *Creating a Responsive Public Service*. Hemel Hempstead: Harvester-Wheatsheaf, p. 9, emphasis in original.
4. Ibid., p. 64.
5. Hannagan, T. 1992. *Marketing for the Non-profit Sector*. Basingstoke: Macmillan, p. 10.

6. Cousins, L. 1990. 'Marketing planning in the public and non-profit sectors', *European Journal of Marketing*, vol. 24, no. 7, pp. 15–30.

7. Smith, G. 1988. 'Applying marketing to the public sector: the case of local authority leisure centres', *International Journal of Public Sector Management*, vol. 1, no. 3, pp. 36–45.

8. Foxall, G. 1986. 'Marketing and matching', *Management Decision*, vol. 24, no. 1, pp. 26–32.

9. Ibid., p. 29.

10. Bleek, J.A. 1990. 'Strategic choices for newly-opened markets', *Harvard Business Review*, Sept./Oct., pp. 158–65.

11. Mitchell, A. 1990. 'Train of thought', *Marketing*, 8 March, pp. 38–9.

12. Ibid.

13. Ibid., p. 38.

14. Matthews, V. 1993. 'Railway cuttings', *Marketing Week*, 19 November, pp. 40–3.

15. Corzine, R. 1994. 'Paying a high price for being in control', *Financial Times*, 25 February, p. 26.

16. Corzine, R. and Lascelles, D. 1994. 'Gas proposals aim to open up market', *Financial Times*, 10 May, p. 8.

17. Foster, A. 1993. 'Takeover flood as UK water spreads out', *Financial Times*, 23 February, p. 21.

18. Foxall, op. cit.

19. Hannagan, op. cit., p. 22.

20. Dibb, S. and Simkin, L. 1993. 'Strategy and tactics: marketing leisure facilities', *Service Industries Journal*, vol. 13, no. 2, pp. 110–24.

21. Gardiner, C. and Collins, M. 1992. 'A practical guide to better audience surveys', *Journal of the Market Research Society*, vol. 34, no. 4, October.

22. Blamires, C. 1992. 'What price entertainment?', *Journal of the Market Research Society*, vol. 34, no. 4, October.

23. Tomlinson, R. 1992. 'Finding out more from box office data', *Journal of the Market Research Society*, vol. 34, no. 4, October.

24. Barnes, C. 1993. *Practical Marketing for Schools*. Oxford: Blackwell Business.

25. Sargent, V. 1993. 'Back to school', *Marketing Business*, March, pp. 18–21.

26. Davies, M., Preston, D. and Wilson, J. 1992. 'Elements of not-for-profit services: a case of student accommodation', *European Journal of Marketing*, vol. 26, no. 12, pp. 56–71.

27. Hannagan, op. cit., p. 25.

28. Skelcher, C. 1992. 'Improving the quality of public services', *Service Industries Journal*, vol. 12, no. 4, pp. 463–77.

29. Latham, V. 1991. 'The public face of marketing', *Marketing*, 28 November, pp. 22–3.

30. Smith, G. and Saker, J. 1992. 'Developing marketing strategy in the not-for-profit sector', *Library Management*, vol. 13, no. 4, pp. 6–21.

31. Yorke, D.A. 1984. 'The definition of market segments for leisure centre services – theory and practice', *European Journal of Marketing*, vol. 18, no. 2, pp. 101–13.

32. Burns, T. 1992. 'Researching customer service in the public sector', *Journal of the Market Research Society*, vol. 34, no. 1, January.

33. Aldersley-Williams, H. 1993. 'Wooing the customer – the Citizen's Charter', *Financial Times*, 10 May.

34. Ellwod, S. 1991. 'Costing and pricing in healthcare', *Management Accounting*, November, pp. 26–8.

35. Hayden, V. 1992. 'How market-oriented is your service?', *Journal of Management in Medicine*, vol. 6, no. 1, pp. 5–9.

36. Evans, T. 1986. 'Strategic response to environmental turbulence', in *Managers as Strategists:*

Health Service Managers Reflecting on Practice, ed. G. Parston, King Edward's Hospital Fund for London, p. 27.

37. Schaeffer, L.D. 1986. 'Managing change in health care', in ibid.

38. Bennett, A.R. 1993. 'Marketing: can there ever be a real exchange of values in the Health Service?', *International Journal of Health Care Quality Assurance*, vol. 6, no. 3, pp. 17–19.

39. Sheaff, R. 1991. *Marketing for Health Services*. Milton Keynes: Open University Press, p. 39.

40. Hayden, V. 1993. 'How to increase market orientation', *Journal of Management in Medicine*, vol. 7, no. 1, pp. 29–46.

41. Bidlake, S. 1993. 'Dentist finds new roots in the salon', *Marketing*, 22 April, p. 21.

42. Kotler, P. and Zaltman, G. 1971. 'Social marketing: an approach to planned social change', *Journal of Marketing*, vol. 35, July, p. 5.

43. Foxall, op. cit.

44. Health Education Authority, 1993. *Annual Report 1992/3*.

45. Health Education Authority, 1994, 'Mass media activity 1986–1993'.

46. National Dairy Council, 1993. 'Towards 2000: Liquid milk report 1993', p. 16.

47. Ibid, p. 11.

48. Summers, D. 1994. 'Gambling on a gut feeling', *Financial Times*, 24 April, p. 22.

49. Johnson, M. 1991. 'One man's meat, another's poison', *Marketing*, 27 June, pp. 20–1.

50. Elsden, S. 1991. 'On the hustings', *Direct Response*, November, pp. 33–4.

51. Smith, G. and Saunders, J. 1990. 'The application of marketing to British politics', *Journal of Marketing Management*, vol. 5, no. 3, Spring.

52. Dibb and Simkin, op. cit., p. 116.

53. Plant, F. 1993. 'Charity fatigue', *Campaign*, 14 May, pp. 28–9.

54. Latham, V. 1991. 'Breaking the taboo', *Marketing*, 3 October, p. 21.

55. Pidgeon, S. and Saxton, J. 1992. 'How fundraising will change in the 90s', *Direct Response*, September, pp. 37–43.

56. Ibid., p. 42.

57. Mindak, W.A. and Bybee, H.M. 1971. 'Marketing's application to fund raising', *Journal of Marketing*, vol. 35, July, pp. 13–18.

58. Drucker, P.F. 1990. *Managing the Non-Profit Organisation*. New York: HarperCollins, p. 56.

59. Schlegelmilch, B. 1988. 'Targeting of fund-raising appeals – how to identify donors', *European Journal of Marketing*, vol. 22, no. 1, pp. 33–41.

60. Morris, N. 1993. 'The client challenge', *Direct Response*, August, pp. 20–1.

61. Smith, S.M., and Alcorn, D.S. 1991. 'Cause marketing: a new direction in the marketing of corporate responsibility', *Journal of Services Marketing*, vol. 5, no. 4, Fall.

62. Dwek, R. 1992. 'Doing well by giving generously', *Marketing*, 23 July, pp. 16–18.

63. Drucker, op. cit., p. 82.

64. Ibid., p. 84.

Appendix: A typology for the broader application of marketing ideas

Organisation type	Acting in strong competition?	Profit objectives?	Engaged in the supply of goods or services?	Engaged in fund-raising?
Utility service provider	Often monopoly or near monopoly conditions for main services; some competition from substitutes	Yes	Yes	No
Non-profit commercial organisation (e.g. subsidised theatre)	Yes, both direct and substitute	No, but revenue and cost budgets are likely to apply	Yes	Not as part of core business
'Internal market' participant	Strictly regulated competition	Revenue and cost budgets likely to apply	Yes, but often not direct to end-users	No
'Idea-promoting' organisations (private or public sector-funded)	No (except more generally with rival ideas)	No	Not directly, but may act as communication channel to relevant suppliers	Sometimes
Charities	No (except more generally with other fund-raising causes)	No	Not to donors, unless related to fund-raising (e.g. supply of charity greetings cards; gift catalogues)	Yes

Chapter 25

Organising and appraising marketing operations

Companies are purposive; they are in business to achieve some set of aims. They employ numerous people whose activities towards those ends are interdependent and frequently concurrent. It follows quite simply that their activities should be structured into a cohesive set of relationships: they should be organised. It also follows that more efficient and effective achievement of these goals would be possible if the activities were periodically, or continuously, appraised. Thus the topics for this chapter.

Organising marketing operations

Organisational arrangements to accomplish marketing tasks differ widely. Explanations of such differences refer to variations in both the external and internal environments faced by firms, as well as to the pursuit of contrary corporate strategies. High levels of uncertainty in the external environment, due mainly to chronic technological or economic change but sometimes to developments in the social or regulatory environment, encourage more fluid, flexible arrangements characterised by moderate levels of standardisation and relatively little centralisation. The less the uncertainty the more the standardisation and centralisation.

A feature of the internal environment, which, it may be thought, would influence the organisation of marketing, relates to the views held by those with power in the company about its basic orientation to meet its purpose or mission. Surveys by Piercey [1], Hooley *et al.* [2] and Doyle [3] asked firms to self-report on their orientation and, in general, about two-thirds claimed to be marketing-oriented, a quarter sales-oriented and a tenth production-oriented. Doyle also found a significant number to be financially-oriented, which he defined as being about the use of assets and resources to optimise profit and return. A reasonable hypothesis would be that marketing-oriented firms would show stronger marketing departments, controlling and integrating a wide range of marketing activities. That may not be the case because of the nature of marketing activities, and because marketing is not just undertaken by those in a marketing department. In a fully marketing-oriented company everyone contributes, or at least marketing must permeate all operations; Spillard suggests [4]:

> At that point there may be no need, except in strategic, sales and staff functions, for there to be a marketing unit at all. It will have worked itself out of a job.

Irrespective of degree of marketing orientation, marketing activities are by no means left to a marketing department to organise. Piercey [5] found in a sample of companies that:

> On the face of it if they are organised at all, advertising and marketing research would appear normally to be marketing department functions; trade marketing and sales are organised in marketing in two-thirds of the firms, although 25 per cent do not recognise a trade marketing function, and perhaps most importantly nearly 40 per cent organised sales separately from marketing; while the functions of customer service, exporting and distribution were part of marketing only in a minority of companies – most usually being organised separately from marketing, rather than not being organised at all.

Marketing is not just undertaken by marketing people in a marketing department, although much of the following discussion of organisational designs is about marketing departments.

Current organisational designs

Five broad types of design are found. These are based upon function, product, region or customer, or they might be more complex involving a matrix organisation.

Function-based structures

'The functional type of organisation is a line and staff structure with the different marketing activities separated into groups, each under a functional head who has line authority. The usual line staff system differs from this because the specialists would have a staff role as advisers' [6]. An example is shown in Figure 25.1. Such structures are common because they fit so easily into the overall design of the company. The accounting, personnel and production functions are probably

Figure 25.1　*Function-based structure*

similarly organised. The appropriateness of this system is related to how well the marketing manager co-ordinates the work of the specialists and the type of control systems employed.

Product-based structures

Product-based structures emerged in this country in the 1950s. The essential feature is the establishment of the product or brand manager. With several product managers in a firm there may also be a product group manager reporting to the marketing manager. The original impetus for introducing product managers was to ensure that no brand was neglected and to perform a resource allocation function. Medcalf [7] says:

> The brand manager is the advocate for his brand. At all times he is pressing for the maximum single-minded drive behind that one brand, regarding the company's other products not so much with indifference, as with deep rooted hostility.

Product managers compete for resources, and they may also compete for specialists' time. They have no line authority over advertising, market research, sales representatives or research and development, yet the success of their job largely rests upon the work of these specialists. This leads to the apparent anomaly that the product manager is responsible for his brand's profitability, but has no authority over those implementing the plans for the brand. Davidson [8] comments on this as follows:

> Brand profitability is useful to general management as a means for pinpointing product groups which are doing poorly. However, it is not realistic to assess the performance of a brand manager by his profit results alone, without examining why the figures were poor.

Another implication of the imbalance between authority and responsibility is to throw the onus on the brand manager to work through the informal, rather than formal, organisation. He seeks to influence the specialists and gain their support, and time, for his brand. There is some evidence that those that attempt to gain this support by establishing their reputations as experts are more successful than those who attempt coercive tactics [9]. Indeed, it has been argued that product managers should be accorded a greater role in decision-taking because of this expert power [10].

A common element in the product manager's job is the preparation of plans for this brand. He will recommend strategies covering the whole marketing mix for his brand. Once these plans are accepted Davidson [11] argues that the discrepancy between authority and responsibility is diminished because:

> He has more de facto authority than the empty catalogue of his formal powers would indicate. His practical authority derives from his responsibility for the well-being of his brand, and his right to recommend to management how it should be run.

While the product manager system was first applied in consumer markets, it has been successfully employed in industrial markets [12]. Edgar Vaughan, an industrial oils and chemical firm, are reported as deriving the following benefits from switching to such a structure [13]:

1. Technical expertise and consultancy are an intrinsic part of their service; product managers are technically expert and well placed to offer this consultancy as back-up to the salesforce.

2. New product development has been found to be more systematic and controlled.

3. The flow of information to the salesforce about products and trials has been improved.

4. Advertising is better researched and more specific campaigns are designed.

5. Forecasting and planning procedures have been more rigorous.

It does appear that there is a contrast in the product management system in consumer and industrial goods companies. In consumer companies the managers are likely to be younger, and assistant brand managers may be graduates in their first job. In industrial firms they tend to be older, control several products and may have more direct influence over production planning [14].

Two recent trends in product manager organisations have been noted by Buell [15]. First, he sees a major shift in arrangements in grocery companies with the transfer of much increased responsibility for advertising to product managers. This has had the effect of removing a separate advertising department in some companies, or at least of maintaining only a much reduced function concerning media planning. Second, he reports some decline in the 'little general manager' concept. That is, the product manager is viewed less as a profit centre and more as a revenue generator. This has had the effect of emphasising the product manager's planning role. Bureau [16] emphasises this planning role and sees developments in information technology as supporting and reinforcing this function.

This type of structure may be useful to some companies as a training ground. Product managers may receive a breadth of experience across all marketing activities which they might not otherwise obtain. It could also be a fairly adaptable structure because brand managers can be added or dropped in response to the health of current brands and the opportunity of developing new brands.

However, Thomas [17] criticises this form or organisation because it is product-centred, rather than market-oriented, and believes that sales management, and particularly national account managers, may become more powerful than product managers in the future.

Regionally-based structures

Companies operating over a widespread geographical area often employ a regional organisational pattern. Salesforces are usually organised on this basis, although in large organisations several marketing functions may be passed down to the regional level.

Customer-based structures

This might take the form of structuring according to type of marketing channel employed. A grocery manufacturer might then have one salesforce concentrating on small independent shops and cash-and-carry outlets, and another dealing with the multiples. Alternatively, it might be related to the use that the customer has for the product. In the industrial market, sales, market research and customer service engineering may be structured by type of user. Benefits of this approach would be the in-depth appreciation that company personnel would derive of the problems that customers meet in that application of the product. An example may be in computers, where the applications can be so very diverse. Banks clearly have different data processing problems from those encountered by process industries.

Matrix structures

Functionally-based structures give the advantage of specialisation and the development of expertise. Product management structures allow that, with the added insurance that individual brands are not neglected, and that marketing plans for specific products are better co-ordinated. But many large, complex organisations have recognised the need for much greater co-ordination. This might be achieved in a matrix organisation where broad business areas are identified, variously described as projects or missions, and responsibility is assigned to a project manager. He draws personnel from the functional areas, either on a temporary or continuing basis, and concentrates upon fulfilling the project's goals. The personnel have a responsibility to the project manager and at the same time to the head of that functional activity. The skills from many functional areas are therefore utilised and integrated around a given project or business.

Some firms call heads of the business areas market managers, and the matrix is confined to marketing activities, with other parts of the organisation adhering to a functional pattern (Figure 25.2). Some operate a matrix system without physically changing the location of staff. That is quite common in accounting where an accountant may be concerned with a particular project/programme/market/mission, but remains a member of the accounting department. But there has been the development of the role of the marketing accountant in some few companies, with the physical assignment of an accountant to a project.

Organising marketing subsystems

Salesforce organisation

The simplest approach is a geographical one: salespeople are assigned a geographically defined territory and sell all company products to all possible customers in that area. With large salesforces regional and district control levels can be

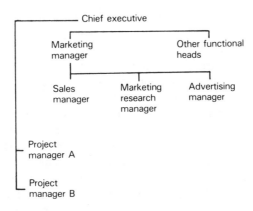

Figure 25.2 *Matrix organisation*

introduced. Advantages of this pattern are that controlled coverage of prospects and customers is facilitated by the clear specification of the salesperson's work-load. Planning can be simpler, regional and territory potentials established, definite sales goals determined and performance continuously monitored. Within this structure, individual salespeople may respond with zeal. They may identify with their territory and feel responsible for company activities in that area. They may perceive themselves to be – and may be accorded the title of – area managers. This close identification could be an important motivating factor. Customers may also favour this structure because they have just one representative to deal with, irrespective of the number of products offered by the company. If they have any problems with any of the product range, and if they wish to know more about any of it, they will know the established channel and arrangements. This organisational structure therefore has a degree of certainty and definition from which companies depart only for powerful reasons.

More complex arrangements may be used on markets (customers) or products. With large organisations, either of these might also employ a geographical split. Structures based on customer segments might arise if these segments displayed a marked difference in requirements. Grocery manufacturers may divide their sales-force by type of channel, e.g. independent and cash-and-carry or multiple groups. They may also have an extra salesforce concentrating on 'key accounts' such as the head offices of the multiples. In the industrial market the structure may be by industry type. In this case the applications of the product may be a more important distinguishing characteristic than the nature of the product itself. For example, a manufacturer of crushing and grinding machinery could have applications in mineral and food processing industries. The problems in each of these cases are entirely different, and by specialising the sales representatives could derive a greater knowledge of solutions, and so provide a more comprehensive advisory service to customers. They may become more credible than competitors' 'all purpose' sales-people. The disadvantage of such an organisational pattern is the greater geographical spread of customers. A company with, say, four industry-based sales-forces and twenty sales representatives would assign each salesperson a fifth of the total area to be covered, rather than a twentieth if it used a straight geographical division. Each region would have four salespeople, and there could well be problems in co-ordination and control, and disputes over customers whose business could not be automatically assigned to one industry group or another.

A more radical departure from the simple structure is where the salesforce is structured around products. Multi-product firms may devise several salesforces, each dealing with only a part of the full product range. A machine tool manufacturer could have one salesforce selling standard machines, one handling advanced machines and one selling cutting tools and parts. The rationale is that it is the nature of the product that is the distinguishing characteristic. It might be unrealistic to expect one representative to have the requisite depth of product knowledge across diverse product groups. Further, the same customer/industry may require products right across the range. This provides an illustration of the benefit, and the difficulty, with product-based sales organisations. Customers may be frustrated if the sales representative has insufficient product knowledge because he or she does not specialise – he or she may even give the wrong advice. On the other hand, the customer may be bemused by having a succession of salespeople calling from the same supplier. He may request a sales visit only to find he has contacted the wrong person.

Trade marketing

In response to developments in distribution channels, some companies in the consumer market have established trade marketing departments or sections. These developments have included the increasing concentration among retailers and the rise of superstores. In addition, the dynamic nature of marketing channel structures has motivated greater attention to emerging trends and changes in the relative importance of established channels. In some firms this has meant the redesignation of key account sales managers as trade marketing managers, while still undertaking essentially a selling function. In others, trade marketing has been equated with trade promotions, running in support of key account managers. An extension is where a trade marketing manager is responsible for a much wider range of marketing activities, and plans and controls a trade marketing mix. This latter role cannot easily be fitted into an existing organisational arrangement without recognising the potential for duplication and conflict. This is particularly the case if a product manager system is being operated, since many of the interests and concerns will be common to trade marketing managers and product managers. Reflections of the clarity of these role definitions will be in the flow of marketing information, responsibility for commissioning special marketing research and in relative contributions to product development.

Organising marketing research

'The precise functions of market research departments vary widely. In some companies they may be low status groups, while elsewhere they are rated highly' [18]. Company attitude to its marketing information system is the central determinant of the structure of the market research function. Primitive information systems may be served by just one or two junior employees who may merely collate sales statistics. More advanced systems may encompass both central departments and divisional market research functions to reflect the different demands for information that may be placed by corporate planning activities on the one hand and divisional control on the other.

It could well be argued that the degree of use and integration of marketing research into company marketing decision making is a crude index of the acceptance of the marketing concept, in which case the following quote from Wills and Hayhurst [19] takes on an ominous ring:

> How can we summarise the MR position at present? Poorly paid; little understood and acted upon; not even present in visible, institutional form in the vast majority of medium/large companies in British industry.

Piercey and Evans [20] have studied the use of marketing research and stress the organisational context as a factor conditioning the employment of research. Information may play a role within the organisation which is not directly a function of the particular task at hand. Information may be used to rationalise decisions already made, it may be seen as an organisational glue or lubricator to delay or speed decisions, it may be part of the power structure and it may reinforce the organisation's view of itself, for example as a modern, sophisticated company or one which is more traditional. The extent to which marketing research is used is thus not just a function of marketing problems. To examine this in more detail Deshpande and Zaltman [21] questioned 1,000 users of research and 300 researchers. Users were found to believe that organisational structure was the most important influence on the employment of research. More decentralised and less formalised companies used more market research because greater interaction between researchers and managers led to better understanding of the possible research contribution and quicker implementation. The second most influential factor was 'surprise'. That is, information is needed to decrease, not increase, uncertainty, and so very surprising research results would be less likely to be attended to. Managers put research to a 'reality test' to assess its credibility.

Organising new product development

Without much thinking, arrangements for new product planning can be grafted on to existing organisational structures. The responsibilities of traditional functional areas can be expanded to encompass new business opportunities. Typically, R&D would have prime responsibility in early phases; manufacturing considerations might then become uppermost, and finally the product would surface to marketing. Criticisms of this approach need hardly be stated.

But let us assume another approach, with marketing playing a fuller role. There is still ample scope for compounding the difficulties through the isolation of the various functional experts. As Midgley notes, new product development 'is very different from day-to-day management tasks, because it requires a wider perspective and knowledge than more routine matters, knowledge which spans all the organisation's activities and functions' [22].

New product development also requires different thrusts through the successive stages, from the more creative and conceptual at the search stage to the more planned and prescribed at the implementation stage. Researchers suggest that different organisational arrangements are suited to these stages, from the more organic to the more mechanistic [23].

One response in some large organisations has been to establish separate new product departments, with several functional specialists. Their brief frequently covers advising top management on the specification of product policy, the coordination of search and screening activities, and the overall progressing of the new product through to launch. In some food companies it even covers test marketing. To digress a moment, it is interesting to see what happens at that point. What are the mechanics of handover from the new product department to the routine business division? In one large company an embarrassing situation arose when none of the marketing divisions wished to take over a new product which had finished in test, and the new product team would not drop it because they had more faith in it than apparently did the operating divisions. In consequence, the product was put into another test market, was much more convincing there, and eventually was accepted by one of the operating divisions.

A more flexible approach is found in venture management. These structures usually bring together functional specialists only for the duration of the project, after which they return to their normal department. Frequently they have more authority than new product departments. They may act almost as separate small companies, building pilot plants and pioneering sales [24].

Organising physical distribution

Bowersox [25] considers that the evolution of the management of physical distribution conforms to four broad stages. From a totally dispersed function within the organisation, the structure becomes cohesive and unitary, and then extends across the whole of the logistics problems from raw materials to finished products. His four stages are:

1. Dispersed authority for logistics functions.
2. Some logistics functions grouped together without any significant change in position within the organisation.
3. Physical distribution isolated and elevated to be equal with other main functional areas in the firm.
4. Integration of physical distribution with materials management to form the integrated logistical function.

It seems that many companies are now at the second or third stage in this evolutionary scheme. Maister [26] has reported that half of the firms in his survey had seen some increase in the status of the distribution department, and that most of the others expect some similar rise in the near future. He anticipates that distribution will develop in two ways. 'Backward' integration would involve the control of raw material storage and control of such inventories; 'forward' integration would involve greater control over finished product inventories and customer order processing routines.

The trend to integrate physical distribution with materials management is logical in that it allows more co-ordination of materials flow and might provide better inventory decisions. It will have profound implications for the organisation of the total marketing activity. Until now marketing has been seen to be responsible for distribution. Does it also, then, encompass materials management, or is distribution pried away from marketing to become part of the logistics function? Some may contend this is a non-issue because adequate co-ordination will overcome any difficulty. Within individual companies it is likely to be a very important issue since old empires will fall and new empires rise.

Appraising marketing operations

We now turn to appraisals of marketing operations. These may involve fairly conventional short- to medium-term controls on activities (referred to here as system controls); they may involve the more unconventional viewpoint of the corporate mission and output budgeting; or they might take less periodic assessments incorporated in the marketing audit, which could review the objectives, strategies, plans and actions in all or any part of the marketing effort. Whatever form the controls take, an important consideration is the utilisation of accounting information, and so the development of marketing accounting systems should also be investigated.

System controls

Viewed as a system, marketing employs a set of inputs in the hope of achieving a desired set of outputs. Control of such a system might concentrate attention on the inputs, the outputs or the overall productivity expressed in the ratio of output per unit of input. Whichever approach is taken, the essence of control must be the determination of the desired standards of performance, the measurement of current activity, the analysis of the variances between these, and the implementation of corrective action if gross variances are uncovered.

Careful study is required properly to identify the inputs and the outputs. Generally, inputs are costs and outputs are sales. More detailed consideration reveals it is not that simple. Throughout the discussion of marketing planning it has been seen that the operational definition of outputs is complex: for example recall Chapter 14 on advertising objectives. There it was seen that a simple sales output was insufficient for operational planning of advertising. Furthermore, with regard to inputs, it would probably be inadequate to restrict analysis to costs. Salesforce controls would not be sensitive enough if confined to costs. Sales managers therefore look to other input measures, e.g. effort, as represented by number of calls, and to an estimation of the quality of input.

Selection of the appropriate measure of input and output will be influenced by the time horizon chosen and the desired level of control sensitivity. Very short-term horizons (weekly/monthly) with high sensitivity pose the major problem. Distribution and salesforce activity may warrant much close attention; whether they effectively receive it will depend on the operational adequacy of the definition of the chosen variable. Costs and sales controls, and their surrogates, may be out of date, or subject to massive revisions, if inappropriately chosen. They may also lack precision and effect, if they are being applied to areas that have only partial authority over the indicator taken as a measure of activity. For example, stock levels could be taken as a control variable of one subsystem, but are necessarily affected by activities in several other subsystems. In fact, an increase in stock levels may be totally attributable to delays and difficulties elsewhere.

Ratio analyses of various kinds usually form important control devices [27]. These would cover ratios within and between the inputs and outputs for each of the marketing subsystems. Inputs may be studied by several types of labour, material and other costs as well as appropriate measures of effort (calls made, orders assembled, quotations offered, miles travelled, and so on). Outputs may employ several types of sales and profitability studies, as well as other appropriate output measures such as orders despatched. All these analyses could be performed by order size, customer type, product type and sales territory, for shorter or longer time periods. Comprehensive controls could then generate a mass of data, only small parts of which might be relevant to any one 'controller'. Clear thinking, and prudent scrutiny of data needs/uses, seem essential ingredients in devising an acceptable control system. Cumbersome controls, often employed long after their useful life, suggest a senescent bureaucracy.

Choice of control variables, and the interpretations put upon movement in them, present an interesting set of comments upon a management's understanding of its marketing system. Deliberate, planned control systems based on thorough understanding of system dynamics and data collection mechanisms must be the aim. As such it will be intimately related to organisational structure, and the design factors were considered under marketing information systems.

Marketing and accounting

The quality of the control system is dependent on the capture of pertinent and timely information. New information and communication technology provides the potential for an effective system, but only if appropriate kinds of analyses are undertaken. An essential is the proper utilisation of accounting information. Barrett's studies have led him to comment [28]:

However, while practices in this area have shown some development, at least among the more concerned companies, the surveys which have been carried out of such practices are uniform in criticising both the accounting processes and the analytical techniques utilised.

He suggests that accounting for the functional marketing areas has been progressing but analysis by segments has lagged considerably. So that:

> heavy reliance continues to be placed on arbitrary allocation routines, promotional expenses are not usually lagged, market performance indices are not incorporated into the reports, costs which may be viewed as investments in the market are expensed as incurred, and the segment analysis is often confined to revenue or gross margin with no attempt to match costs with the revenues to which they contribute.

An important inhibitor of the development of better marketing accounting systems is the uncertain environment within which marketing operates. And there is another twist: the lack of better accounting information adds to the uncertainty. One example of this might be in variance analysis where price and cost variances may be analysed in detail, but volume variances are treated in aggregate without attempting to disentangle market size and market share variances [29]. Furthermore, there may be no attempt to break this down by product or by market segment. The problem with market data is that it might be perceived to be 'softer' than, say, production data. But it is only as 'soft' as the methodology employed in its capture.

With regard to mode of analysis, Thomas [30] has reported that marketing productivity analysis is being improved in some firms by the refinement of contribution accounting. He suggests that a key ratio is that between gross marketing earnings and marketing expenditure, and analysis by segments should allow attention to focus on those with opportunity for profit improvement, especially if the analysis is incremental comparing one period to the next.

Output budgeting

If a matrix form of organisation is being employed, it follows that the planning and control systems should mirror the organisational structure. Output budgeting could be appropriate in these circumstances. Its purpose has been defined by Christopher [31] as:

> Essentially this concept suggests that whereas traditional organisational and accounting structures are designed along functional lines, it is more appropriate to organise and control along 'mission' lines. That is, an acknowledgement is made that business is not about using up inputs but about creating outputs . . .

'Missions' are deduced from the nature of the business and lead to statements of corporate objectives. Wills *et al.* [32] give the example of a brewery defining four 'missions': thirst satisfaction, entertainment, catering and the use of by-products.

Table 25.1 *Output budgets*

	Activity centre 1	Activity centre 2	Activity centre 3	Activity centre 4	Total cost
Mission A	100	80	20	80	280
Mission B	50	70	200	20	340
Mission C	70	30	50	70	220
Required activity centre inputs	220	180	270	170	840

Source: M. Christopher. 'Marketing logistics', in G. Wills (ed.), *Strategic Issues in Marketing*. Leighton Buzzard: International Textbook, 1974, p. 66.

In calculating budgets the requirement of each functional activity in contributing to each 'mission' is stated, and a matrix of functions (activity centre) and missions derived (Table 25.1). The activity centres could be whole functional divisions of the organisation or smaller parts of one division. The functional budgets are derived from the study of that function's contribution to the 'mission' and the mission budget from summing across the functional budget. Given a mission budget, then continuing appraisals can be made, comparing actual performance to that budgeted. Another example would be the grocery manufacturer who determined his missions as: (1) serving the consumer market, (2) serving the institutional market (e.g. hospitals), (3) serving the hospitality market, and (4) supplying own-label. The functional activities could be production, finance and marketing [33].

Doyle [34] sees part of the reason for the development of such thought as aiming to integrate ever more complex businesses, and the need to plan resource allocation and control around the individual businesses (or missions or programmes) within the total organisation. One possible implication of this is that some managers may be reporting to several heads within the missions and the functions. This may be even more complex if a third dimension, that of geographical centre, is added. While this might fall foul of classical thought about organisational design, it does offer one important advantage: that is, a shift in the focus of attention away from inputs and towards the organisation's outputs.

A further implication is that many non-marketing managers will be very influential in marketing planning, because the missions stretch across functions. It therefore emphasises the need for these managers to be familiar with the problems in marketing planning. Equally well, it highlights the need for marketing personnel to be familiar with the problems in the other functional areas.

Summary

Current organisational designs were reviewed, with most attention given to product-based structures. Some of the main subsystems were then investigated. Organisational patterns for salesforces, marketing research, new product development and physical distribution were studied. Finally, on organisations some thought-provoking ideas from Wills were considered concerning possible future developments.

Appraisals of marketing operations are normally concentrated on system controls, that is, control and appraisal of the inputs and outputs of each marketing subsystem, and of the total system. Output budgeting deliberately moves the focus of the appraisal on to the outputs, or missions of the organisation. It is a response to the increasing complexity of business operations.

Questions for review and discussion

1. Why might the product or brand manager be thought of as an organisational anomaly? Review the strengths and weaknesses of this form of organisation.

2. List the factors that ought to be assessed in choosing between alternative types of salesforce organisation.

3. In what ways is the problem of organising for new product development different from that in organising other marketing activities?

4. 'Responsibility for physical distribution should pass from marketing to materials management.' Do you agree?

5. 'Marketing operations should be separated from marketing development and the latter merged with technical development.' Do you agree?

6. Discuss the difficulties in the selection of appropriate measures of input and output in marketing systems controls.

7. Does output budgeting supplement or supplant more conventional marketing system controls?

References

1. Piercey, N. 1986. *Marketing Budgeting*. Beckenham: Croom Helm.
2. Hooley, G.J., West, C.J. and Lynch, J.E. 1984. *Marketing in the UK – A Survey of Current Practice and Performance*. Cookham: Institute of Marketing.
3. Doyle, P. 1987. 'Marketing and the British chief executive', *Journal of Marketing Management*, vol. 3, no. 2.
4. Spillard, P. 1987. 'Organization for marketing', in Baker, M.J. (ed.), *The Marketing Book*. London: Heinemann, p. 67.

5. Piercey, op. cit.

6. Hayhurst, R. and Wills, G. 1972. *Organisational Design for Marketing Futures*. London: Allen & Unwin, p. 57.

7. Medcalf, G. 1967. *Marketing and the Brand Manager*. Oxford: Pergamon, p. 1.

8. Davidson, J.H. 1975. *Offensive Marketing*. Harmondsworth: Penguin Books, p. 100.

9. Gemill, G.R. and Wilemon, D.C. 1972. 'The product manager as an influence agent', *Journal of Marketing*, vol. 36, no. 1.

10. Cunningham, M.T. and Clark, E.J. 1975. 'The product manager's functions in marketing', *European Journal of Marketing*, vol. 9, no. 2.

11. Davidson, op. cit., p. 101.

12. Kelly, J.P. and Hise, R.T. 1979. 'Industrial and consumer goods product managers are different', *Industrial Marketing Management*, vol. 8, no. 4.

13. 'Edgar Vaughan's switch to product management', *Industrial Marketing Digest*, vol. 4, no. 2, 1979.

14. Eckles, R.W. and Novotny, T.J. 1984. 'Industrial product managers: authority and responsibility', *Industrial Marketing Management*, vol. 13, no. 2.

15. Buell, V. 1975. 'The changing role of the product manager in consumer goods companies', *Journal of Marketing*, vol. 39, July.

16. Bureau, J.R. 1981. *Brand Management*. London: Macmillan.

17. Thomas, M.J. 1987. 'Product development and management', in Baker, M.J. (ed.), *The Marketing Book*. London: Heinemann, p. 250.

18. Hayhurst, R. and Wills, G. 1972. *Organisational Design for Marketing Futures*. London: Allen & Unwin, p. 70.

19. Wills, G. and Hayhurst, R. 1974. 'Future structure of marketing information systems', in Wills, G. (ed.), *Strategic Issues in Marketing*. Leighton Buzzard: International Textbook, p. 53.

20. Piercey, N. and Evans, M. 1983. *Managing Marketing Information*. Beckenham: Croom Helm, p. 11.

21. Deshpande, R. and Zaltman, G. 1984. 'A comparison of factors affecting researcher and manager perceptions of marketing research use', *Journal of Marketing Research*, vol. 21, February.

22. Midgley, D.F. 1976. *Innovation and New Product Marketing*. Beckenham: Croom Helm, p. 194.

23. Neale, C.W., Johnson, P.D. and Reid, M.J. 1988. 'New product development, capital allocation systems and organisational structure', *Proceedings of the 21st Annual Conference Marketing Education Group, Huddersfield*, vol. 1, p. 259.

24. Peterson, R.N. 1967. 'New venture management in a large company', *Harvard Business Review*, vol. 45, May/June.

25. Bowersox, D.J. 1974. *Logistical Management*. London: Macmillan, p. 427.

26. Maister, D.H. 1977. 'Organising for physical distribution', *International Journal of Physical Distribution*, vol. 8, no. 3.

27. McNamee, P. 1988. *Management Accounting*. London: Heinemann, part 8.

28. Barrett, T.F. 1984. 'The design of marketing accounting systems', *Proceedings of the 17th Annual Conference of the Marketing Education Group*. Cookham: Institute of Marketing.

29. Hulbert, M. and Toy, E. 1977. 'A strategic framework for marketing control', *Journal of Marketing*, April.

30. Thomas, M.J. 1984. 'The meaning of marketing productivity analysis', *Proceedings of the 17th Annual Conference of the Marketing Education Group*. Cookham: Institute of Marketing.

31. Christopher, M. 1974. 'Marketing logistics', in Wills, G. (ed.), *Strategic Issues in Marketing*. Leighton Buzzard: International Textbook.

32. Wills, G., Christopher, M. and Walters, J. 1974. 'Output budgeting in marketing', in Wills, G. (ed.), *Strategic Issues in Marketing*. Leighton Buzzard: International Textbook.
33. Christopher, M., Walters, D. and Gattorna, J. 1979. *Distribution Planning and Control*. Farnborough: Gower, pp. 28–33.
34. Doyle, P. 1979. 'Management structures and marketing strategies in UK industry', *European Journal of Marketing*, vol. 13, no. 5, pp. 319–31.

Chapter 26

Challenges to marketing

The norms to be expected in the performance of the marketing system have been changing. Two principal pressures for change in these norms derive from consumerism and environmentalism.

Consumerism

One of the chronic challenges to marketing since the 1960s has been the development of consumerism. Broadly, this can be defined as those attempts that aim at strengthening the consumer's power in the marketplace.

It is only quite recently that the consumer interest has been accorded sufficient weight to become a topic of everyday conversation and media comment, but that should not be construed as meaning that until now business has been free of critics. In 1820 Frederick Accum exposed the following deceits practised by some industries [1]:

> alum in flour to whiten it; copperas in beer to give it a 'head'; capsicum in mustard; dried leaves disguised as tea; sand in sugar; dust in salt; tallow in butter; chocolate enriched with brick dust; arsenical colorants in confectionery.

Such abuses have been eradicated yet many claim there is still cause for concern in other areas. There has been long-standing attention given to misleading advertising and sales promotion, wasteful packaging and faulty products. The scale of the debate has escalated in recent years to question the very credibility of profit-seeking institutions.

There has now been so much written and talked about the new responsibilities of business and the rise of consumerism that it cannot be said to be a passing fashion. It is an established phenomenon which has been at least partly assimilated into the public conscience. This is reflected in the following comment [2]:

> It would be a great mistake to think that consumerism will, if left to itself, quietly

go away. For better or worse, conditions have changed for keeps. The cause of consumerism is merely one manifestation of the social unrest that has burst upon us in the last half decade. It is no coincidence that consumerism has emerged at the same time as separatism, racial unrest, women's liberation and a host of other revolutionary movements.

Evolution of these demands on business cannot be ascribed simply to the organised consumer movements. The demands are no longer just about consumption; they include assessments of changes in affluence, technology, the media, education levels, lifestyles and public attitudes. Six groups of issues have been given particular attention [3]:

1. Health and safety.
2. Information.
3. Redress of grievances.
4. Representation in policy-making, especially at government level.
5. Misrepresentation in advertising, packaging and selling.
6. Waste, pollution and the quality of life.

In pursuit of betterment on all or some of these issues there is a great diversity of approaches. They have been grouped into three broad categories [4]:

1. The adaptationists, who seek to educate the consumer.
2. The protectionists, whose primary concern is with health and safety.
3. The reformers, who wish to do both the above plus gain a greater voice for consumers in government.

Each of these groups would subscribe to a greater or lesser degree to the following prescriptions [5]:

1. *Protection against clear-cut abuses.* This encompasses outright fraud and deceit and dangers to health and safety from the voluntary use of a product. Business and consumerists would agree that abuses need to be checked, although these two parties apparently have different perceptions of the extent of the problem. A recent survey found that consumerists perceive a deterioration in business ethics, whereas no business executive agreed to that [6]. It is also interesting to note that a majority of business executives taking part in that survey saw consumerism as being essentially 'political' in nature.

   With regard to services Cowell believes that much remains to be done and he says, 'the situation in the service sector of the economy in respect of consumer protection is complex and inadequate' [7].

2. *Provision of adequate information.* Do consumers have a right to be

informed, as distinct from a right not to be deceived? Most people would agree that consumers have a right not to be deceived, but their right to be informed is far more problematical. Western economies support freedom of choice and in doing so implicitly assume perfect information in the marketplace. Perfect information that would facilitate rational choices. The difficulty is in determining what would be an adequate quality and quantity of relevant information once the perfect market assumption is relaxed. Marketing managers would not accept that impartial data on performance characteristics, price and availability constituted the totality of information that consumers both need and want. Product differentiation, the creation of favourable associations for the brand, and the establishment of secure and credible brand names are precursors to an enormous amount of the marketing manager's activities. They would see these as enhancing product value and providing the consumer with added benefits.

Consumer rights advocates would argue that, whether or not impartial performance data were all the information the consumer required, they are nonetheless necessary. A notable area in this context concerns the consumer's use of information on nutrition. Rudell's empirical study [8] found that:

> greater use of nutrition information by higher income respondents . . . offered evidence for the argument that consumerism will benefit most those who need it least . . . It may be that nutrition information is actually of less use to lower income consumers because nutritional concerns are over-shadowed by price considerations. Special campaigns might be designed to promote use of nutrition information on economic grounds, for example, more nutritional value for the dollar.

Another dimension of this problem is in technical information. Should the consumer be given massive information which may be redundant to his choice behaviour? Would the consumer interest be better served if consumer durables were sold with technical data sheets and no brand advertising? Probably so, if technical and performance factors were the sole evaluative criteria employed by consumers. It requires little thought to see that many, if not most, consumers probably consider styling, reputation and the security of the brand name. The problem is compounded when it is realised that many of the performance characteristics are not obvious and perhaps are understood only by experts. The consumerist view would be that all this speaks for independent comparative testing – which is irrespective of branding and other considerations. However, Porter argues that 'social measures to provide . . . more information about convenience goods . . . [will be ineffective because consumers] place little value on informed choice' [9].

The presentation of the information is also the subject of debate. There is a growing movement for the sale of competing products in standardised sizes so that price comparisons are made easier. Unit pricing is spreading, although the requirements differ in each of the EU members. France and Germany require it for all foods not pre-packed in standard quantities; Belgium, Denmark and the United Kingdom require it for some food. There is pressure to standardise across the EU up to the practice in those countries with the more stringent requirements.

3. *The protection of consumers against themselves.* Some consumers want to use potentially harmful products, such as tobacco, alcohol and cars; other consumers may be vulnerable because of lack of experience or education and make decisions harmful to their own best interests. This has led to 'growing acceptance of the position that paternalism is a legitimate policy' [10]. It finds expression in government activity on regulating advertising, the wearing of seat belts, drinking and driving, and the protection of children as consumers, as well as in the longer established concern with weights and measures and product quality.

Environmentalism

The concern expressed by consumerists for 'quality of life' is shared by environmentalist groups. Underlying the environmentalist viewpoint is a dissatisfaction with the way in which the community evaluates business performance. Currently stress is placed on economic criteria in any assessment of that performance. Environmentalists would argue that comprises an insufficient set of criteria, and that explicit note should be taken of societal criteria. The development of this line of argument has followed from the recognition that marketing is part of the economic system, and that the economic system is just one component of the wider social and ecological systems. Marketing has economic inputs and outputs; it also has inputs and outputs to and from the higher-order systems. Traditionally marketing performance has been evaluated simply in terms of its role in the economic system, and profits provided the measure of its effectiveness. Increasingly we are asked to see the wider context and to judge the social and ecological impact of marketing decisions.

This widened perspective has been initiated partly by the fact that 'society has a greater willingness to respond to questions about credibility', and partly because 'institutions have done nothing . . . they have refused to move along the same continuum on which society is moving' [11]. The marketing concept impelled firms to serve consumers; to be responsive and adaptive to customer requirements. However [12]:

> Business has historically defined the area in which legitimacy is conferred too narrowly. Profitability does not ensure legitimacy. The marketplace is but one of the many sectors in the firm's environment from which legitimacy must be won if the firm is to survive.

> Legitimacy for any social organisation is thus conferred and confirmed by other organizations or systems within the social system which demand its outputs.

A similar point was made earlier by Wills when he said that the efficiency and worth of marketing must be judged by what it does for society as a whole, and that what it does for shareholders is only one part of the debate [13]. To achieve reasonable profitability marketing has stressed individual consumer brand choices and in doing so, it has been argued, it has sacrificed the wider public interest and deepened 'the predicament of the powerless, disadvantaged and poor consumers' [14].

In this view the mutual satisfaction of companies and customers may not be enough. If, in reaching for profit and consumer satisfaction, there are adverse effects on other parts of the social and ecological systems, then that activity is illegitimate. If, for example, the process polluted the environment, exploited children or other vulnerable groups or threatened the long-term health of the nation, then marketing is illegitimate and attempts will be made to check its activities. Not that the marketing concept will inevitably lead to transgressions, but there is no built-in mechanism to allow for evaluations of the wider impact of marketing activity. And not that consumer orientation is redundant: it is necessary but insufficient. The marketing concept implies that firms adapt and respond to consumers. The newer view is that it should also adapt and respond to environmental forces.

Two reasons make the burden of this argument uncomfortable, and they both concern the standards used in evaluations of enterprise performance. First, business managers are well used to the conventional measures of performance: sales, cost, profits and profitability. These are quantitative and more (or less) objective. They can be readily and regularly gauged. Unfortunately, measures of the social and environmental impact of business are much more qualitative and subjective, and they cannot easily be incorporated into routine performance evaluations. Audits employing economic criteria abound; audits employing social criteria are, as yet, sketchy, and the relevant criteria are unsettled. Firms carry out their profit reporting according to government and professional body guidelines, but there are not yet any such clear guidelines for social reporting – although there are plenty of demands for the development of appropriate accounting standards [15].

This leads to the second problem: environmental standards change. In the last century there was consensus among those with power in society that business activity should be only very lightly circumscribed. Just twenty or so years ago there was some tolerance of coal tips, gravel quarries, smog and river pollution. Today's standards make such tolerance unacceptable, and tomorrow's standards could equally well change. Thus firms are increasingly expected to count the environmental cost of their activities against a shifting standard of acceptability.

Responses to criticism

Business, government and consumers have all been urged to change their attitudes and behaviour. Before considering their responses we need first to address the problem of consumer sovereignty.

As originally conceived consumer sovereignty was used in two senses: first, that market performance is responsive to consumer demands; and second, that the performance of an economy can be evaluated in terms of the degree to which consumer wants are fulfilled [16]. This has led to the conception that the consumer dictates what merchandise is produced. If this notion is accepted, then it follows that the rise of consumerism is a response to the erosion of consumer sovereignty – or a new recognition that the consumer has always lacked sovereignty.

Implied in this line of argument is the value judgement that this lack of sovereignty is not in the consumers' interest because they will not be getting the products they want. The difficulty is that it is assumed that they, or perhaps someone else, will know what they really want, and that they are fully and impartially informed. Yet if asked, consumers would probably say more about what they did not want than about what they ideally required. Their judgements would be fixed to what was currently available and about which they knew something. For some product categories this might cover several brands; in others very few. They would have little appreciation of the full range of current options and of those not presently available. Furthermore, our study of consumer choice behaviour showed that consumer information processing precludes the possibility of consumers using standardised, full information. Selective exposure, selective perception and perceptual distortion are just some of the factors that work against it. Thus, while the use of the concept of consumer sovereignty is superficially appealing, it lacks precision and clearly shows that it was conceived well before recent developments in buyer behaviour theory.

Business responses

A first response from business is that followed by some companies: to ignore social questions in the belief that they are in business purely and simply to make profits. Other responses can be seen on three levels: the manager's personal self-regulation; the company's self-regulation; and co-operative, industry-wide self-regulation.

On the personal level there is the belief that the support for ethical standards comes from professional expertise and in market acceptance [17]. Food technologists and company experts on nutrition know more than consumers do about what is good or bad food. Generally consumers acknowledge this by trusting the packaged foods that they buy, thus giving market acceptance – or refusing it. The exercise of such personal integrity is obviously highly variable and is heavily influenced by the organisation, and by the extent to which the individual accepts a professional rather than managerial status and responsibility.

Companies' self-regulation spans a considerable range of activities and inactivities.

On the one hand, this could mean merely the dropping of a particularly flamboyant advertising claim, and on the other, it could entail a much more concerted attempt to interpret the consumer interest. This latter approach has led some firms to establish consumer affairs departments. Cynics see these as just housing the company's conscience, and having little impact on policy since they are established by top management as a PR exercise and are ignored by middle management.

This appears different from the concept of the Consumer Ombudsman advocated by Wills. This executive would do more than handle complaints: 'In association with conventional marketing researchers, [he] must search out the unvoiced dissatisfactions of customers if [his] full contribution, both to society and to the enterprise, is to accrue' [18]. It is apparent that this approach involves a much greater recognition of the discontented consumer than many firms would currently accept.

Self-regulation at the industry level may be through a trade association. Without adequate sanctions and monitoring, such self-regulation may be impotent, and so the Consumer Affairs Division of the Office of Fair Trading has encouraged the establishment of more rigorous self-regulation. It has overseen the formation of Codes of Practice in twenty-one industries [19]. One example is that of the Association of Manufacturers of Domestic Electric Appliances (AMDEA). A quarterly report by AMDEA's own conciliation service shows a decline in numbers of complaints. Complaints to local authorities about poor service for appliances are also down. To monitor this code further, the Office of Fair Trading commissioned a survey which indicated that speed of service is, for the most part, reasonable. Another example of such codes of practice is that of the Footwear Distributors' Federation; they now have the Footwear Testing Centre, to which dissatisfied customers can send their shoes. If this centre's report finds in favour of the customer, then the fee it charges is returned. Other examples of industry codes of practice are in motor dealing and launderers and cleaners [20].

More widely known than the above are the codes in advertising and sales promotion. The three most important are the British Code of Advertising Practice, the British Code of Sales Promotion Practice and the IBA Code of Advertising Standards and Practice. The first two are based on self-discipline, and are supervised by the Advertising Standards Authority. This body receives complaints about advertising and sales promotion, and attempts to obtain compliance with the Codes largely through persuasion and publicity. To this end it began an advertising campaign in 1975 to encourage consumers to complain about potentially misleading advertisements. This had the effect of increasing the number of complaints from 516 in 1974 to 2,869 in 1975. The IBA has less problem in gaining compliance with its code since its drafting and enforcement is a statutory requirement.

A directive on misleading and unfair advertising has been introduced by the EU Commission. This gives the director general of fair trading new powers as a back-up to reinforce existing arrangements.

Environmental reporting

Most companies do not mention environmental issues in their annual reports.

BT and the environment

Comprehensive environmental performance reporting is far from standard practice for most companies. BT sets an example with its annual reporting which its deputy chairman says,

> provides a focus for the whole BT environment programme. It highlights shortcomings, it records achievements and acts as a stimulant for future action. . . . Published targets have motivated BT people to deliver and, realising that BT is looking for continuous improvement at all stages in a product's life cycle, BT's suppliers are also contributing to the process. They are also beginning to recognise the competitive advantage this brings.

In 1993 thirty-six specific targets were set and twenty-six of those were met successfully. Areas covered included the recycling of cables, telephones, directories, batteries and paper. For example in 1993 3.7 million phone books were printed on recycled paper. Water consumption is being monitored and controlled. BT aims to stabilise its carbon dioxide emissions by 1995 and to reduce to the 1990 level by 2000. An illustration of supplier relationships is that BT will not accept any goods incorporating hardwoods unless the supplier provides written evidence that the wood is from sustainably managed forests.

Annual quantitative data is published on twenty-four main categories of consumptions and emissions.

Source: *BT and the Environment – annual environmental performance reports*.

Ethical business

Grand Metropolitan regularly tracks issues of consumer concern. The most pertinent issues that are likely to arise in the next 3–5 years are sent to operating companies to assess their likely impact. Managers then decide whether to change policy, to lobby government or direct efforts into re-educating the public. Thus Green Giant phased out CFCs in freezing vegetables before very high levels of public concern were reached.

Levi-Strauss has issued global sourcing policies, excluding those operating in countries with 'oppressive' regimes.

Premier Brands has launched its 'fair trade' initiative of selecting tea plantations on social and environmental criteria.

Timberland, the shoe manufacturer, has run an advertising campaign in Germany against racism.

Source: N. Dickenson, 'Catering for the ethical shopper', *Financial Times*, 15 April 1993, p. 19.

According to research by Company Reporting in 1992 the proportions of companies making environmental statements in annual reports were:

	%
No disclosure	77.0
General statement only	12.0
Environmental policies	5.0
Environmental audit	3.0
Costs incurred	0.5

A study by the Institute of Chartered Accountants found that if any information on environmental matters was given at all by companies, then it was likely to be partial and to stress good news. More organisations are employing environmental consultants, but few publish any independent verification of the full environmental impact of their operations.

Government responses

The most crucial and far-reaching response to consumerism has come from government. There is now a considerable legal requirement on companies in their relation with consumers [21]. The Sale of Goods Act (1893), as amended by the Supply of Goods (Implied Terms) Act (1973), is of quite basic importance in its implications that goods correspond to their description, are of merchantable quality and are fit for their purpose. The various Weights and Measures Acts, Consumer Protection Acts and the Food and Drugs Act (1955) also place considerable obligations upon companies. The Trade Descriptions Acts of 1968 and 1972, apart from other things, prohibit false and misleading statements, and the Fair Trading Act (1973) brought into existence the Office of Fair Trading.

The Office of Fair Trading has four main divisions [22]. Its Consumer Affairs Division was referred to earlier in connection with codes of practice. Other activities of this division include the mail order protection scheme adopted in 1975, whereby major publishing trade associations reimburse customers who lose money because of the failure of mail order traders. It has also been active in petrol price displays, party plan selling and pyramid selling. The Consumer Credit Division administers the licensing system established by the Consumer Credit Act (1974). The Monopolies and Mergers Division obtains and monitors undertakings from monopolists identified in its reports, e.g. petrol, cross-channel car ferries, plasterboard, condoms, primary batteries, household detergents, metal containers and colour film. There is also the Restrictive Practices Division.

In addition to these statutory bodies there are three other kinds of government-sponsored activity. The British Standards Institution was incorporated in 1929 as an independent, non-profit organisation [23]. There are now 7,000 British standards with the familiar kite-mark, and twenty-six European standards. The National Consumer Council, financed by government grant, represents the

Table 26.1 *Consumer complaints received by local enforcement and advice agencies*

	1985 total	1987 total	1987 complaints per £m spent
Food and drink	36,011	33,207	0.7
Footwear	24,286	18,937	6.0
Clothing and textiles	54,611	48,734	3.1
Furniture and floorings	67,468	60,853	12.7
Household appliances	92,104	88,469	11.4
Toys, games, sports goods	10,715	10,626	4.7

Source: Annual reports of the Office of Fair Trading.

consumer viewpoint to government, and there are consumer councils associated with the nationalised industries.

At the local level the Trading Standards Officers (formerly the Weights and Measures Inspectors) receive consumer complaints and enforce the relevant legislation. Something of the scale of this is indicated in Table 26.1.

The activities of the Commission of the EU are increasingly becoming part of the governmental response in general directives, such as on product safety, and in the regulation of competition. An example of the latter is in the milk packaging market where Tetra Pak held a 90 per cent market share in the EU, developed from its exclusive licence to the technology for a new method of sterilising cartons suitable for long-life milk. The licence holder, British Technology Group, agreed to negotiate licences with other firms [24].

Prothero and McDonagh point out the significance of trends in policy-making in the EU on environmental issues when they say:

> In order to operate successfully within the EC, marketing departments will need to keep abreast of its environmental policies, especially if their company wishes to operate on a pan-European platform. [25]

They suggest that there are three major areas of environmental policy development within the EU that will have great importance. These are:

1. The introduction of Eco-labels.

2. The introduction of Eco-audits.

3. Proposals for packaging and packaging waste.

Eco-labels will be granted to those that demonstrate the environmental impact of all stages in marketing a product from raw materials through production, distribution and disposal. Proposals for Eco-audits are that they should be voluntary and at first confined to mining, general manufacturing and utilities. Considering both Eco-labels and Eco-audits, Prothero and McDonagh argue that:

It would appear that marketers who wish to adopt the EC Eco-label for their companies' products to gain a European competitive advantage will be best equipped to do so if the organisation also establishes an Eco-audit. This provides a framework within organisations to allow environmental impact assessments to be made, upon which companies can adopt a Corporate Environmental Policy. [26]

The EU Directive on packaging aims to reduce the amount of waste and to ensure that any waste that is produced becomes more environmentally acceptable.

Organised consumer response

With seven million members the Consumers' Association (CA) is the largest and most significant organised consumer movement in the United Kingdom. Established in the mid-1950s, its comparative product tests contained in *Which?* magazine are its most evident activity. One judgement on its role came from Fulop [27]:

> In view of its deficiencies – in particular the problem of keeping pace with innovations and growing product differentiation, the volatile market situation created by more widespread price competition, lack of consultation with manufacturers, and its monopoly which prevents comparison of testing techniques with a competing consumer service – CA by itself will never provide a complete solution to the consumer's shopping problems, but will remain a valuable supplement to other sources of information and advice.

Eleven years later she maintained that same general assessment, but appears to have detected some increase in the impact of CA. This is due to the enhanced value of *Which?* stemming from better appreciation by the CA of marketing practice and consumer behaviour, and to a broadening of its publications [28].

Most European countries have organisations similar to CA, but a common limitation is that their membership tends to be heavily middle class. All these national movements are affiliated to BEUC (Bureau Européen des Unions de Consommateurs) which seeks to influence the Economic and Social Committee of the Consumer Affairs Division of the EU.

More local issues are the concern of the National Federation of Consumer Groups. Each of these groups concentrates upon surveys of local shops, restaurants and public services, and makes representations to local and central government. It is interest at the local level that has frequently led the media to take up the consumerist viewpoint. The national media also campaign spasmodically, sometimes with considerable effect.

The individual consumer

Some argue that individual consumers themselves can take a more responsible approach to consumption. Their purchase decisions should shun products with unfortunate environmental effects, and [29]:

> the individual consumer choices [should] reflect his awareness of the critical social problems of resources (scarcity) and environment (pollution) . . . . Intelligent consumption patterns would result in self-selection of four rather than eight cylinder cars, generic rather than branded drugs, returnable (recyclable) rather than disposable containers . . .

In this view government and the organised consumer movement would play supporting roles in encouraging and stimulating the change in consumer values. Antil [30] gives a profile of the kinds of US consumer who are most likely to act in a socially responsible manner.

Others contend that there is no incentive to buy voluntarily a car with pollution control equipment. Government should therefore shape and guide business behaviour. This view is more traditional in that it relates to conceptions of the mixed economy. Government intervention in a market economy is also well understood by business, and it builds on considerable precedent.

Responses by individual consumers to 'green' products have been mixed [31]. There have been some notable changes in buying behaviour: a majority of car drivers now use lead-free petrol, and recycled tissues and bin liners are here to stay. But many consumers have been confused by the welter of product claims to be 'environmentally friendly' or 'ozone friendly'. Some of these claims were in error, or were partial, being based on a single aspect or product attribute, and without assessment of the full impact back through the supply chain. Some consumers also believed that 'green' claims were an excuse to increase prices, and there was a consequent resistance to the 'green premium'.

In the late 1980s and early 1990s many retailers expanded their 'green' product line considerably, sometimes with very active promotion. Now retailers are pruning these product lines, because sales are down and because they believe consumers' environmental concern is flagging. Organic vegetables, 'green' detergents and grey, recycled nappies are less evident in shops than a few years ago.

Consumerism and the marketing concept

The marketing concept is about consumer orientation. It suggests that firms should define and then deliver customer satisfaction. Contented consumers will then become loyal consumers and the business will survive in the long term. The opposing interests of production and consumption will be resolved in mutual satisfaction from marketplace transactions. Any dissatisfaction from either side will be transitory, and such friction in the system will be eased as consumers learn what products not to buy, and as firms learn what products not to make. The resultant harmony is to everyone's benefit. How then can consumerism be accounted for? Drucker's view is as follows [32]:

> We have asked ourselves where in the marketing concept consumerism fits or belongs. I have come to the conclusion that, so far, the only way one can really define it within the total marketing concept is as the shame of the total marketing concept. It is essentially a mark of the failure of the concept.

He implies that consumerism is the result of the failure fully to implement the marketing concept. Kotler [33] goes a step further:

> But even if the marketing concept as currently understood were widely implemented, there would be a consumerist movement. Consumerism is a clarion call for a revised marketing concept.

He goes on to draw Edmund Burke's distinction, 'I serve your interests, not your desires.' According to Kotler, most business executives interpret customer satisfaction in terms of consumer desires, not consumer interests. This leads companies to produce products that pander to desires that may be harmful to the long-term consumer interest. The problem is how to reconcile consumer desires, consumers' long-run interests and company profit. Kotler's view is that there is a need for a wider marketing concept with a societal marketing concept: 'The societal marketing concept calls for customer orientation backed by integrated marketing, aimed at generating customer satisfaction and long-run consumer welfare as the key to attaining long-run profitable volume.'

A first reaction to this definition might be to dismiss it as impractical and to assert that competition would ensure adherence to consumer desires rather than to their long-run interests. This assertion rests on the assumption that profits can be made only by attempting to fulfil consumers' desires, and that a single competitor cannot take the initiative in supplying what is to consumers' long-term advantage. If the consumer does not, and never will, buy what is palpably in his long-run interest, then this is realistic, in which case government action may sooner or later be expected. But the whole thrust of consumerism, media comment and perhaps even home economics classes in schools is to create a more aware consumer. Increasingly, if given the opportunity, some are incorporating long-run welfare considerations into their choice criteria: in which case competition would assist, rather than hinder, the adoption of the reformulated marketing concept.

More radical views are expressed by Anderson et al. [34] when they say:

> The process of marketing management is essentially a balancing act, and requires the most delicate sensitivity to the inherent conflict in legitimacy and powerseeking, short- and long-term social priorities, and individual and social priorities. The management of the marketing process requires a refined sense of awareness and perspective concerning the likely impact of an infinite variety of environmental forces upon the firm's operations, as well as the impact of the firm upon its environment. Marketing is both formative and adaptive. It shapes as well as responds to its environment.

Marketing has been responding to the new perspectives and pressures; it does not consider the wider systems perspective. For example, a survey of business executives and consumer advocates has found that 90 per cent of the former and 75 per cent of the latter agreed that the objectives of marketing and consumerism are not in conflict [35]. Other recent surveys have indicated an increasing acceptance of an 'environmental' view by many companies [36]. Marketing is no longer tied to micro-profit applications, and it has started to respond to new norms in the expectations of the behaviour of the marketing system. These changes demonstrate the dynamic nature of the marketing environment and the necessity for marketing executives to be both alert and informed.

Summary

The main issues in consumerism concern health and safety, information, redress of grievances, representation in policy-making, misrepresentation and waste, pollution and the quality of life. Prescriptions include, first, attempts to protect consumers from clear-cut abuses such as fraud, deceit and dangers to health and safety. Second, it is suggested that consumers need adequate information. This is more difficult and involves judgements about consumer information processing and a definition of adequacy. Third, it is prescribed that some consumers need protection against themselves, and so a paternalistic attitude is seen as legitimate in some situations.

Environmentalists have become increasingly vocal. Underlying their viewpoint is a dissatisfaction with the way in which the community evaluates business performance. The emphasis on economic criteria has been seriously questioned, and a wider perspective advocated to reflect the interrelationship of the economic system with the social and ecological systems. Critics have been exercised by the fact that profit criteria could lead business to stress individual consumer brand choice, without considering the possible cost of any environmental pollution, or adverse effects upon the social system.

Responses from business to these criticisms have been mainly in terms of company self-regulation and industry self-regulation. The former has led some firms to establish consumer affairs departments, dealing with more than just complaints. The latter has seen the formation of some industry codes of practice.

The most far-reaching response has been from government, in the weighty legislation now enacted, and in government encouragement of bodies such as the British Standards Institution.

Organised consumer response is very largely in the hands of the Consumers' Association, and its most visible activity is the comparative product tests published in *Which?* magazine.

The rise of these consumerist and environmentalist pressures has had impact upon basic values and orientations taken in marketing, including a growing recognition and acceptance of the wider responsibilities of business.

Questions for review and discussion

1. Do the issues in consumerism apply equally strongly in developed and developing countries?

2. How do modern ideas about consumer information processing complicate the problem of the provision of adequate information?

3. Should companies appoint their own consumer ombudsman?

4. Can industry self-regulation work effectively without government intervention?

5. Should market and opinion research be used to determine residents' attitudes on issues being decided by local councillors?

6. Can societal evaluations of business ever be made routine?

7. Should companies' annual reports just be made for shareholders? If they were for 'society' what indicators should be included?

8. Should firms consider consumer interests as well as consumer wants? Can consumer interests be as easily determined as consumer wants?

References

1. Accum, F. 1974. 'Treatise on the adulteration of food and culinary poisons', in Robertson, A. (ed.), *The Lessons of Failure*. London: Macdonald, p. 99.
2. Leighton, D.S.R. 1973. 'Responding to consumerism', in Lazer, W. and Kelly, E.J. (eds), *Social Marketing*. Homewood, Ill.: Irwin, p. 124.
3. See also Barksdale, H.C. and French, W.A. 1976. 'The response of US business to consumerism', *European Journal of Marketing*, vol. 10, no. 1. Roberts, E. 1975. 'Consumers in the Common Market', *European Studies*, vol. 22.
4. Herrmann, R.O. 1970. 'Consumerism: its goals, organization and future', *Journal of Marketing*, vol. 54, October.
5. Aaker, D.A. and Day, G.S. 1971. 'Introduction: a guide to consumerism', *Consumerism*. New York: Free Press.
6. Gaedeke, R.M. 1972. 'What business, government and consumer spokesmen think about consumerism', in Gaedeke, R.M. and Etcheson, W.E. (eds), *Consumerism*. San Francisco: Canfield, p. 90.
7. Cowell, D. 1984. 'Service markets: the effects of competition policy and consumer protection', *Service Industries Journal*, vol. 4, no. 3.
8. Rudell, F. 1979. *Consumer Food Selection and Nutrition Information*. New York: Praegar, p. 55.

9. Porter, M.E. 1976. *Interbrand Choice, Strategy and Bilateral Market Power*. Cambridge, Mass.: Harvard University Press, p. 237.

10. Aaker, D.A. and Day, G.S. 1971. *Consumerism*. New York: Free Press.

11. Zoffer, H.J. 1977. 'Restoring institutional credibility', *MSU Business Topics*, vol. 25, no. 4.

12. Anderson, W.T., Bentley, C.C. and Sharpe, L.K. 1976. *Multi-dimensional Marketing: Managerial, Societal and Philosophical*. Austin, Texas: Austin Press.

13. Wills, G. 1976. 'Marketing's social dilemmas', *European Journal of Marketing*, vol. 8, no. 1.

14. Fuat Firat, A. 1977. 'Consumption patterns and alacromarketing: a radical perspective', *European Journal of Marketing*, vol. 11, no. 4.

15. Cooper, S.K. and Reiborn, M.H. 1974, 'Accounting for social responsibility', *MSU Business Topics*, vol. 12, no. 2. See also the *Journal of Accounting Organizations and Society*.

16. Rothenburg, J. 1962. 'Consumer's sovereignty resisted and the hospitality of freedom of choice', *American Economic Review*, vol. 52, no. 2. Reprinted in Murray, B.B. 1975. *Consumerism*. Santa Monica, Calif: Goodyear.

17. Clasen, E.A. 1967. 'Marketing ethics and the consumer', *Harvard Business Review*, vol. 45, Jan./Feb. Reprinted in Lazer, W. and Kelley, E.J. (eds) 1973. *Social Marketing*. Homewood, Ill.: Irwin.

18. Wills, G. 1974. *Strategic Issues in Marketing*. Leighton Buzzard: International Textbook, p. 223.

19. Moss, C.D. and Richardson, W. 1984. 'Consumerist self-regulation', *Quarterly Review of Marketing*, vol. 9, no. 4.

20. Mitchell, J. 1978. *Marketing and the Consumer Movement*. Maidenhead: McGraw-Hill, chs 14 and 15.

21. Smith, P. and Swann, P. 1979. *Protecting the Consumer*. Oxford: Martin Robertson.

22. *Annual Report of the Director General of Fair Trading, 1976*. London: HMSO, 1977.

23. Ashworth, G. 1978. 'Standards and marketing', in Mitchell, J. (ed.), *Marketing and the Consumer Movement*. Maidenhead: McGraw-Hill, ch. 11.

24. *Bulletin of the European Communities*, vol. 21, nos 7/8, 1988.

25. Prothero, A. and McDonagh, P. 1993. 'The European Community and environmentalism – the impact of EC environmental policies upon the marketing function', in Baker, M. *Perspectives on Marketing Management*. Chichester: John Wiley, p. 104.

26. Ibid., p. 105.

27. Fulop, C. 1967. *Consumers in the Market*. London: Institute of Economic Affairs Research Monograph 13.

28. Fulop, C. 1978. *The Consumer Movement and the Consumer*, Research Studies in Advertising, no. 10, pp. 27–37. London: Advertising Association.

29. Rothe, T. and Benson, L. 1974. 'Intelligent consumption: an attractive alternative to the marketing concept', *MSU Business Topics*, vol. 22, no. 1.

30. Antil, J.H. 1984. 'Socially responsible consumers: profile and implications for public policy', *Journal of Macromarketing*, vol. 4, no. 2.

31. Ryan, S. and Skipworth, M. 1993. 'Shoppers guillotine the "green" revolution', *Sunday Times*, 4 April, p. 17.

32. Drucker, P. 1972, see Chapter 6 in Gaedeke, R.M. and Etcheson, W.E. (eds), *Consumerism*. San Francisco: Canfield.

33. Kotler, P. 1972. 'What consumerism means for marketers', *Harvard Business Review*, vol. 50, May/June.

34. Anderson, W.T., Bentley, C.C. and Sharpe, L.K. 1976. *Multi-dimensional Marketing: Managerial, Societal and Philosophical*. Austin, Texas: Austin Press.

35. Gaedeke, R.M. 1972. 'What business, government and consumer spokesmen think about consumerism', in Gaedeke, R.M. and Etcheson, W.E., *Consumerism*. San Francisco: Canfield, p. 90.
36. Gidengil, B.Z. 1977. 'Social responsibilities of business: what marketing executives think', *European Journal of Marketing*, vol. 11, no. 1.

Glossary

Adoption process – the acceptance of new products by consumers.

AIO inventories – the results of research into consumers' activities, interests and opinions to determine 'lifestyle segments'.

Attention – the process of selecting which stimuli the individual will consider.

Attitude – predisposition towards an object or concept; in marketing it is also used as predisposition towards the act of buying.

Augmented product – features and services which go beyond the normal customer expectation.

Beliefs – an individual's view about the existence of something, e.g. the belief that a brand is associated with another concept; so a particular car may be thought of as being associated with 'low petrol consumption'.

Benefit segmentation – a form of market segmentation which divides the market according to differences in the benefits sought by the buyer.

Brand extension – the use of an established brand name to move into a related or unrelated product field.

Brand launch analysis – studies of the performance of a new brand.

Brand mapping – a diagram or 'map' of consumers' perceptions of a brand; sometimes called 'perceptual mapping'.

Buying rate index – a comparison of the volume of purchases by different buyers.

Call rate/call norm – sales representatives' visits to customers and prospects; 'call rate' often denotes actual and 'call norm' desired levels.

Channels of distribution – the system of agencies needed to provide the flow of information, goods and legal title from producer to consumer.

Choice criteria – criteria employed in making choice decisions; sometimes termed 'evaluative criteria'.

Cognitive dissonance – a state of some psychological discomfort caused by inconsistency between a new piece of information and the individual's established understanding (of a product); it is usually thought of as a post-purchase phenomenon.

Competitive parity – a method of setting the advertising budget to match the competition.

Comprehension – part of the 'perceptual system'; new information is compared with the established store of meanings held by the individual, in order to understand and classify the new information.

Concept tests – research undertaken early in new product development; potential customers' views are sought about the product idea prior to the development of prototypes.

Consumerism – organised attempts to improve the position of consumers in the marketplace.

Copy tests – research to assess and improve advertising copy ('copy' is often taken to include both text and illustration).

Cost-per-thousand – used in media planning: calculated by dividing the cost of advertising by the numbers in the audience; it is normally based upon circulation or readership.

Cross-elasticity of demand – a measure of the proportional change in sales (demand) of one product divided by the proportional change in the price of another product; it therefore determines the sensitivity of demand to competitive price changes.

Cumulative penetration – in this context 'penetration' is the proportion of consumers buying a brand at least once; cumulative penetration is therefore a measure of the build-up in successive time periods.

Decision-making unit (DMU) – the group of people that may influence purchase decisions; the concept can apply in all market circumstances, but has been most associated with industrial marketing.

Decision trees – a mode of analysis of complex decision situations; the impact upon profitability of alternative marketing plans is determined and the probabilities of the several outcomes occurring are estimated.

Demographics – population characteristics; those studied in marketing include age, sex, family size and education; some writers now use the term to include social class.

Derived demand – where demand for a product is dependent on the demand for another product; industrial goods are in derived demand, since they are useful only in so far as they (ultimately) provide consumer goods.

Derived forecast – a sales forecast obtained by first forecasting total market demand and then applying the expected company market share.

Desk research – research using extant material, i.e. that already available.

Diffusion – often referred to as the diffusion of innovations; it is the process associated with the market acceptance of a new product.

Distribution cost analysis – the study of the costs, sales and profits of alternative distribution systems.

DRTV – direct response television commercials.

Eco-labels – granted to companies that show the full environmental impact of their operations.

Evaluative criteria – the set of factors used in making choice judgements.

Evoked set – a small group of brands which is considered by the buyer as possible purchases.

Exposure weights – one kind of 'media weight'; measures of the value of the exposure of an advertisement in several different media.

Extended problem-solving – a type of buying situation in which the buyer has no knowledge or experience of the product category; in industrial marketing it is termed a 'new task'.

External stimuli – information reaching the individual from his environment.

Family brands – the use of the same brand name across several product categories.

Frequency – the number of times an individual is exposed to a given advertisement.

Generic product analysis – one part of market opportunity analysis; it is at the level of broad product categories.

Geodemographics – consumer classifications based on residential neighbourhood.

Group discussion – an informal meeting convened by a company or agency with eight or ten consumers to elicit their views about a product or advertisement.

Hierarchy-of-effects – a model of the buying process which suggests that buyers move through set sequences from awareness to purchase; has received most comment as a model of the advertising process.

Ideal point – consumers' perceptions of the ideal product attributes; used in attitude models and perceptual mapping.

Innovators – the first buyers to be attracted to a new product; it is they who begin the adoption process.

Input standards – benchmarks used to control costs and effort.

Intentions model – a model of consumer attitudes which attempts to predict intentions to buy by considering attitude-to-the-act; brings in the notion of subjective norm.

Laboratory techniques – often taken to mean techniques in advertising research which use apparatus from psychological laboratories; the term is now becoming more widely employed in other marketing studies such as simulated shopping in pricing research.

Lifestyle segmentation – the subdivision of a market based upon lifestyles, as measured by activities, interests, opinions and values.

Limited problem-solving – a buying situation in which the buyer has some knowledge and experience of the product category, although some change prompts new search activity; in industrial marketing it is termed a 'modified rebuy'.

Loyalty schemes – inducements offered to customers to retain their patronage.

Macromarketing – investigates aggregate marketing behaviour, i.e. for the whole of a marketing system.

Market aggregation – a strategy that assumes that all consumers in the market are very similar in their requirements and that they can be reached and persuaded in identical ways; also termed 'undifferentiated marketing'.

Market development – a strategy for obtaining growth by attracting new market segments.

Market opportunity analysis – the definition of prospective markets and competitors in order to establish possible target markets.

Market penetration – a strategy for obtaining growth by increasing market share with the same product and no change in target market.

Market potential – the maximum amount of a product that could be bought in a period from all suppliers, given a level of industry promotional effort.

Market research – the collection and analysis of data to provide a description of market characteristics; a part of 'marketing research'.

Market segmentation – the subdivision of a market into parts that are relatively homogeneous, so that separate and distinctive marketing plans can be prepared for each segment; it is one way of clearly identifying target markets.

Market testing – one of the purposes in test marketing; it tests the effects of alternative marketing mixes, or of alternative plans for any single element in the mix.

Marketing – a set of processes which stimulate and facilitate market exchanges for the mutual benefit of an organisation and its consumers.

Marketing concept – the view of marketing's role in an organisation which emphasises the need to understand and to anticipate consumer requirements as a basis for all decisions that may affect the market.

Marketing information system – the orderly gathering, storage, retrieval and analysis of information relevant to marketing decision-making.

Marketing mix – the composite of plans made by an organisation dealing with products, prices, promotion and distribution.

Marketing research – research undertaken into any area of marketing planning and operations.

Media vehicle – a particular example of a communication medium, e.g. a specific newspaper or magazine.

Media weight – a term with two separate meanings: (1) measures of several qualitative factors in advertising media planning; (2) also used in the context of 'media weight tests', which concern the volume or 'weight' of advertising.

Micromarketing – the marketing behaviour of an individual firm or consumer.

Modified rebuy – 'limited problem-solving' in industrial markets.

Multi-brand strategy – the strategy that operates if the manufacturer has several brands within the same product category.

Multi-product brand – the use of the same brand name in several product categories.

Opportunity to see (o.t.s.) – exposure of an advertisement: total exposure is given by 'reach' multiplied by average 'frequency'.

Output standards – benchmarks used to control sales and profits.

Own brands/own-label brands – retailers' private brands.

Page traffic – estimates of the numbers reading each page in a publication.

Penetration pricing – the setting of a low price to encourage widespread consumption.

Penetration rate – the proportion of a market buying a brand at least once; used in test marketing and brand launch analysis.

Perceptual distortion – an individual's understanding of an object or concept which is confused, inaccurate or distorted.

Perceptual mapping – a diagram or 'map' of consumers' perceptions of a brand; sometimes called 'brand mapping'.

Perceptual system – processes by which an individual draws information from his environment, compares it with information he already has, and attaches meaning to it.

Pilot launch – one of the purposes in test marketing; a trial run to investigate problems prior to a national launch.

Positioning – customer perceptions of a product or organisation relative to competitors.

Primary data – information especially collected in a marketing research study, not previously available and not normally published.

Product attributes – specific elements of the product's overall appeal to consumers.

Product development – a strategy for obtaining growth by changing (developing) the product to be offered.

Product lifecycle – stages in the market acceptance of a product; it can be analysed at the level of the product class, the product form or at the level of the individual brand.

Product manager – an individual given responsibility for the overall planning of a product's success.

Product portfolio analysis – a method of plotting all of a company's brands against their market growth rates and market shares.

Projectable test launch – one of the purposes in test marketing; it attempts to estimate national sales levels.

Promotion mix – the composite promotional plan, i.e. the personal and non-personal (e.g. advertising) means of communication to be employed.

Psychographics – personality and lifestyle studies.

Rate card – the schedule of prices for an advertising medium.

Reach – the proportion of a target audience that is exposed at least once to an advertisement; sometimes termed 'coverage'.

Recall tests – memory tests; used in advertising research to gauge how many of a sample of respondents remember having seen an advertisement.

Reference group – people to whom an individual either compares his behaviour or ascribes a set of standards, and then models his behaviour accordingly.

Relationship marketing – emphasising the development of long-term relationships with customers, and not just a concern with a single transection.

Repeat (purchase) rate – the proportion of purchases made by those buying for the second (or more) time; used with penetration rate in test marketing.

Response function – relates changes in a dependent variable (e.g. sales) to change in an independent variable (e.g. advertising).

Role behaviour – individual behaviour influenced by a person's distinctive position in a group.

Routine response behaviour – buyer behaviour in routine situations; choice criteria are well established and alternative brands well known; in industrial marketing it is referred to as a 'straight rebuy'.

Salient attributes – product attributes that the buyer finds most significant.

Search activity – buyers' search for information about products; could also include search for information to determine choice criteria.

Secondary data – published data used in marketing research – government statistics are a major source.

Segment base/segment variable – the base or variable chosen for a market segmentation study, e.g. a demographic variable such as age.

Skimming price – the establishment of a high price in a product launch; the aim is to appeal to a small number of buyers before the subsequent development of the mass market.

Societal marketing concept – a view of marketing's role in the organisation which stresses consumer long-run welfare and not just short-run desires.

Source credibility – the degree of trust placed on a source of communications.

Strategic group – competitors following similar strategies.

Test marketing – limited marketing operations on an experimental basis; three purposes have been identified: (1) pilot launch; (2) projectable test launch; (3) market testing.

Thematic apperception tests – literally 'test of the perceived themes'; they use ambiguous material (e.g. cartoons) aimed at discovering a respondent's feelings about an object or situation.

TVR – television rating; the proportion of an audience exposed to a commercial.

Undifferentiated marketing – a strategy which treats all consumers as being homogeneous; sometimes termed 'market aggregation'.

Vertical integration – a process by which an enterprise takes over suppliers or distributors.

Index